MARIOLOGY

Contributors

JOHN F. MURPHY, S.T.D
RENÉ H. CHABOT, M.S.
FRANCIS D. COSTA, S.S.S.
GERARD S. SLOYAN, PH.D.
GEORGE W. SHEA, S.T.D.
CHRISTIAN P. CEROKE, O.CARM.
PATRICK J. GAFFNEY, S.M.M.
PETER A RESCH, S.M.
LEONARD PEROTTI, O.F.M.
MARION A. HABIG, O.F.M.
CHARLES J. CORCORAN, C.S.C.
WILLIAM F. KEEGAN, C.S.C.
RICHARD L. ROONEY, S.J.
ROGER M. CHAREST, S.M.M.
ERIC MAY, O.F.M. CAP.
WILLIAM G. MOST, PH.D.
EAMON R. CARROLL, O.CARM.
SLAVATORE J. BONANO, C.M.F.
EDWARD A. RYAN, S.J.
HAROLD C. GARDINER, S.J.
JOHN C. SELNER, S.S.
LAWRENCE A. BURKE, O.F.M.
KENNETH F. DOUGHERTY, S.A.

Mariology

VOLUME 3

Edited by
Juniper B. Carol, OFM

MEDIATRIX PRESS
MMXIX

NIHIL OBSTAT:
Bede Babo, O.S.B. Censor librorum

IMPRIMATUR:
✠ James . MCNULTY BISHOP OF PATERSON
DECEMBER 30, 1960

The nihil obstat and imprimatur are official declarations that a book or pamphlet is free of doctrinal or moral error. No implication is contained therein that those who have granted the nihil obstat and imprimatur agree with the contents, opinions or statements expressed.

Mariology, volume 3.

ISBN: 978-1-953746-77-1

©Mediatrix Press, 2018
Mariology, volume 3 is in the public domain. The typesetting and editorial changes made in this volume ©Mediatrix Press. No part of this work may be reproduced in print or electronically except for quotation in articles, blogs, and educational works.

607 E. 6th Ave.
Post Falls, ID 83854
www.mediatrixpress.com

Cover art:
Our Lady of Loreto
by Michelangelo Merisi da Caravaggio
San Agostino, Roma, 1609.
Design: ©Ryan Grant, 2019

TABLE OF CONTENTS

PREFATORY NOTE... xiii

ORIGIN AND NATURE OF MARIAN CULT
    by REV. JOHN F. MURPHY, S.T.D. 1

    I. Origin of Marian Cult 2
    II. The Nature of Marian Cult 9
    III. The Usefulness of Marian Cult 16
    IV. The Necessity of Marian Cult 20

FEASTS IN HONOR OF OUR LADY
    by REV. RENÉ H. CHABOT, M.S. 23

    I. Universal Feasts 24
    II. Feasts Celebrated in Some Dioceses or Religious Orders .. 51

MARY'S DAY AND MARY'S MONTHS
    By FRANCIS D. COSTA, S.S.S. 55

    I. Saturday, Mary's Day 55
    II. The First Saturdays Devotion 58
    III. The Month of May 59
    IV. October, Month of the Rosary 63

MARIAN PRAYERS
    By REV. GERARD S. SLOYAN, PH.D. 66

THE DOMINICAN ROSARY
    by VERY REV. MSGR. GEORGE W. SHEA, S.T.D. 90

    I. Nature of the Dominican Rosary 93
    II. Origin of the Rosary 112
    III. Excellence of the Rosary 120
    IV. Indulgences for Reciting the Rosary 127

THE SCAPULAR DEVOTION
    By CHRISTIAN P. CEROKE, O.Carm. 131

    I. The Origin of the Scapular Devotion.................. 132
    II. The Sabbatine Privilege: Origin and Historical Critique.. 137
    III. The Decision of the Holy Office on the Sabbatine Privilege 139
    IV. The Interpretation of the Scapular Promise............ 140
    V. The Scapular Devotion in Modern Life................ 143
    VI. Other Marian Scapulars 143
    VII. Recent Popes and the Scapular...................... 144

THE HOLY SLAVERY OF LOVE
    By PATRICK J. GAFFNEY, S.M.M........................ 147

    I. The History of "Holy Slavery" Prior to St. Louis 147
    II. Total Consecration According to St. Louis............. 154
    III. Approvals of St. Louis' Doctrine 163

FILIAL PIETY
    by VERY REV. PETER A. RESCH, S.M. 167

THE IMMACULATE HEART
    by REV. JOHN F. MURPHY, S.T.D. 172

    I. History of the Devotion............................. 172
    II. The Object of the Devotion 175
    III. The Purpose of the Devotion 179

THE PIOUS PRACTICE OF EXPIATION TO MARY
    by LEONARD PEROTTI, O.F.M........................... 183

MARIAN ORDERS AND CONGREGATIONS
    by MARION A. HABIG, O.F.M. 186

    I. Orders and Congregations of Men with a Marian Name . 187
    II. Notable Marian Orders and Congregations of Men Without a Marian Name................................. 206
    III. Marian Sisterhoods in the United States............... 218

MARIAN CONFRATERNITIES
    by CHARLES J. CORCORAN, C.S.C....................... 227

MARIAN ASSOCIATIONS
  by WILLIAM F. KEEGAN, C.S.C. 239

  I. The Children of Mary 239
  II. The Pious Union of Our Lady of Good Counsel 241
  III. The Court of Mary 241
  IV. The Militia of the Immaculate Conception 241
  V. The Reparation Society of the Immaculate Heart of Mary 242
  VI. The Blue Army 243

THE SODALITIES OF OUR LADY
  by RICHARD L. ROONEY, S.J. 245

  I. Birth and Cradle Days............................... 246
  II. The Sodalities Grow 249
  III. The Prima Primaria................................. 249
  IV. Death and Resurrection 252
  V. The Sodalities in Modern Times 253
  VI. Signs of Decadence................................. 254
  VII. Sodalities in the United States 255
  VIII. A Look at the Sodalities' Future 258

THE LEGION OF MARY
  by ROGER M. CHAREST, S.M.M. 260

  I. Marian Origin....................................... 260
  II. Organizational Framework.......................... 262
  III. Methods and Techniques 264
  IV. Spiritual Outlook.................................. 266
  V. Growth and Conquests.............................. 271

MARIOLOGICAL SOCIETIES
  by ERIC MAY, O.F.M.Cap............................... 275

  I. Belgium (Flemish Society) 275
  II. France 276
  III. Spain 278
  IV. Portugal 279
  V. Canada 279
  VI. United States 280
  VII. Belgium (French Society) 282

VIII.	Germany	283
IX.	Italy	284
X.	Mexico	284
XI.	Poland	285

MARIAN CENTERS, LIBRARIES, AND PUBLICATIONS
    by REV. WILLIAM G. MOST, Ph.D. 286

    I. Marian Libraries and Marian Centers 286
    II. Marian Publications 293

MARIAN CONGRESSES
    by EAMON R. CARROLL, O.Carm. 298

    I. International Congresses 300
    II. National and Particular Congresses 309

MARIAN SHRINES AND APPARITIONS
    by SALVATORE J. BONANO, C.M.F. 329

    I. The Holy Land 329
    II. European Shrines 331
    III. Africa 345
    IV. North American Shrines 345
    V. Central American Shrines 349
    VI. South American Shrines 350
    VII. Asiatic Shrines 353

DEVOTION TO OUR LADY IN THE UNITED STATES
    by EDWARD A. RYAN, S.J. 355

    I. Mary's Privileges 356
    II. Mediatrix of All Graces 360
    III. Mariology in America 361
    IV. Official Devotion 363
    V. Marian Churches and Institutions 366
    VI. Marian Shrines 371
    VI. Novel Forms of Devotion 373

THE BLESSED VIRGIN IN LITERATURE
    by HAROLD C. GARDINER, S.J. 383

OUR LADY IN MUSIC
    by JOHN C. SELNER, S.S. 399

    I. Our Lady in Early Liturgy 399
    II. Dogmatic Themes 400
    III. First Compositions and Feasts 401
    IV. Gregorian Music 403
    V. The Major Antiphons 404
    VI. Polyphonic Era 407
    VII. The Change in Musical Art 408
    VIII. Modern Times 409
    IX. Contemporary Compositions 412

OUR LADY IN ART
    by LAWRENCE A. BURKE, O.F.M. 413

    I. Catacombs 413
    II. Byzantine 414
    III. Gothic 415
    IV. The Renaissance 418
    V. Baroque 419
    VI. Modern Period 420

OUR LADY AND THE PROTESTANTS
    by KENNETH F. DOUGHERTY, S.A. 423

    I. Our Lady and the Reformation 424
    II. Contemporary Protestants and Our Lady 428
    III. The Contemporary Protestant Marian Revival 431

To His Excellency
The Most Reverend John J. Wright, D.D.
Bishop of Worcester
Episcopal Chairman of
The Mariological Society of America
Outstanding Promoter of Marian Studies
This Mariology Set Is Dedicated
With Sentiments of Profound Gratitude

PREFATORY NOTE

CHRISTIANITY without Mary has been trenchantly appraised by a contemporary Protestant divine as a veritable monstrosity. Phrased somewhat differently: Christianity with Mary in her rightful place is the only Christianity that makes sense. If this is true in the speculative domain of doctrine, it must be true also, *a fortiori*, in the province of cult and devotion. The laws of interrelationship between the sphere of the mind and that of the heart obtain here as inexorably as in any other human discipline.

Thus the publication of the present volume brings to its logical completion the rather ambitious project of our Marian trilogy launched nearly a decade ago. Having patiently culled and judiciously assembled the Mariological data scattered in the sources of revelation (Vol. I), and having further expounded the various prerogatives of Our Lady in the systematic manner proper to theology (Vol. II), there remained only to focus our attention on that vast field generically known as Marian cult. The prime object, then, of the present work is simply to explore, in their origin and development, the multiple manifestations of devotion to Mary which enrich every facet of Catholic life. Since an adequate appraisal of Our Lady's position in the scheme of salvation could not but prompt her children to express outwardly their inner sentiments of gratitude and dependence, the chapters we are now introducing may be rightly regarded as a logical sequel to the topics discussed in the previous volumes of this set.

Originally scheduled to follow shortly after the second volume, the publication of the present symposium was somewhat delayed by factors beyond the control of the editor and the publishers. It is felt, nevertheless, that its timeliness, far from having diminished, is considerably enhanced by the happy circumstance of the forthcoming General Council. We are now at a juncture in the history of the Church in which the preponderant concern of theologians seems to center on ecumenism. Essential to this movement is the noble endeavor of our Catholic people to familiarize themselves with the origin, gradual development, and *raison d'être* of the Church's devotional practices, particularly in what concerns Our Blessed Lady. For it is precisely in this area that we encounter some of the stumbling blocks which allegedly retard the much-hoped-for return of our separated brethren to the source and center of doctrinal unity. Paradoxically, it is also in this very area that the hope of reunion lies. If Our Blessed Lady is properly styled the "Destroyer of All Heresies" and the "Channel of All Graces," then it stands to reason that the cult of which she is the object cannot but exert a profoundly beneficial influence on the complex and delicate process of reuniting all God's children into the one fold of salvation.

As a matter of fact, the increasing interest in devotion to Mary noticeable within certain Protestant groups already constitutes a very promising index of tangible progress toward reunion. In this respect, the pages contributed to this symposium by the Rev. Dr. Kenneth F. Dougherty, S.A., are both revealing and encouraging indeed. To be sure, we still have with us a Paul Tillich in Harvard, a John Mackay in Princeton, and the ubiquitous tracts of the Swiss Karl Barth monotonously lamenting our "heretical" aberrations in matters Mariological. But in our Christian optimism we like to feel that their voices are becoming more isolated and less representative of their own denominations. At any rate, the contents of the present symposium, particularly the masterful chapter by the Rev. Dr. John F. Murphy, should do much toward dispelling the last vestiges of misunderstanding in the minds of our sincere brethren outside the fold. It is with this cherished hope in our hearts that we now submit these essays to the thoughtful consideration of our readers in the English-speaking world.

On the completion of this volume — perhaps our last tribute to Mary in this form — it is our pleasant duty to congratulate the publishers on the competence and skill evidenced in the technical presentation of this work, and to express our sincere appreciation to the various collaborators for their stimulating and well-documented contributions. We make a particularly grateful and prayerful memento for that zealous apostle of Mary, the Very Rev. Peter A. Resch, S.M., who has in the meantime answered the summons to his eternal reward.

Rev. Dr. J. B. Carol, O.F.M.
Editor
February 11, 1961

Mariology

ORIGIN AND NATURE OF MARIAN CULT

by REV. JOHN F. MURPHY, S.T.D.

DEVOTION to Our Lady is a thing of grandeur. It has brought warmth and richness to man's service of God; it has added depth and beauty to man's cultural achievements.

As in her mortal life or in the development of Sacred Theology, so too in the history of Marian veneration the Mother of God is associated always with Christ. With Him she forms both cornerstone and capstone in the structure and economy of salvation. Not only did she bring the Incarnate Word into the world; she shared intimately also in the work He came to accomplish, the redemption of men. Therefore, because of the full implications of her relationship with God and man, she occupies a unique and exalted place in Christian life, and in the dogma, liturgy, and general veneration of the Church.

It seems natural that down through the centuries the best minds of Christianity should have sung the praises of Mary ... "all generations shall call her blessed, the Mother of God, the Mistress of the world, the Queen of heaven ... who has given life and glory to all generations. For in her the angels find joy, the just grace, and sinners forgiveness. Deservedly the eyes of all creatures are turned toward her, because in her, by her, and from her the benign hand of the Almighty re-created that which He had already made."[1]

Without question, after the example of Christ, Mary is the greatest external grace the human soul encounters during life. To us Mary is Our Mother and Our Queen. Christ has given her to us as among His greatest gifts, and it is His wish that we honor her as He honors her and love her even as He loves her.

As Mary among all creatures held and will hold forever the first place in the Heart of Christ, so also Christ wishes that, next to our love for Him and our worship of the Triune God, His Blessed Mother should be the principal object of our devotion. To honor Mary is not simply to do Christ's will, for because of the union of Mother and Son, to honor Mary is to honor Our Lord Himself. To know, love, and serve Mary is to know, love, and serve Christ.

---

[1] St. Bernard, *In festo Pentec.*, sermo 2; *PL*, 183, 430.

2 Mariology

We are concerned here with the origin, necessity, and usefulness of Marian veneration, and for the present, therefore, with the earliest beginnings of devotion to the Mother of God in the history of the Church.[2]

I. ORIGIN OF MARIAN CULT

A realization of the significance of the Mother of God was part of Christian consciousness from the earliest times, for from its very inception Mary was always associated with the redemptive work of her Divine Son. In fact, her *Fiat* gave it reality.

Certainly the Mother of God, like all great mysteries in the Christian dispensation, had been anticipated in the literature of the Old Testament.[3] Quite plainly in the Protoevangelium, in the prophecies of Isaias concerning the virgin birth, and in the prophecy of Micheas concerning Bethlehem, as well as in the references to created Wisdom and to the types of the Virgin, there is revealed a portion of dogmatic truth which in later centuries naturally helped form the basis of orthodox Marian veneration.

Even today, the Liturgies of the East and the West, capturing much of their richness from Old Testament types and prophecies, give testimony to the ancient sources of Marian cult.

It is, of course, in what we call Our Lady's Gospel, the first two chapters of St. Luke, and in other pertinent New Testament passages

that we find the concrete portraits of the Blessed Mother which were to influence the course and development of devotion to Mary in

---

[2] The bibliography on Marian cult, in general, is vast. Some of the standard references are: E. Campana, *Maria nel culto cattolico*, 2nd ed., 2 vols. (Torino, 1944); E. Dublanchy, S.M., art. *Marie*, in *D.T.C.*, Vol. 9, coll. 2439-2474; A. Haine, *De hyperdulia ejusque fundamento* (Lovanii, 1864); F. A. von Lehner, *Die Marienverehrung in den ersten Jahrhunderten* (Stuttgart, 1881); A. Noyon, S.J., art. *Mariolatrie*, in *D.A.F.C.*, Vol. 3, coll. 326-331; G. M. Roschini, O.S.M., *Mariologia*, 2nd ed., Vol. 2, part 3 (Romae, 1948); H. Thurston, S.J., art. *Virgin Mary*, in *The Catholic Encyclopedia*, Vol. 15 (New York, 1912), pp. 459-464.

[3] Cf. E. May, O.F.M.Cap., *Mary in the Old Testament*, in *Mariology*, ed. J. B. Carol, O.F.M., Vol. I (Mediatrix Press, 2018), p. 57 ff.; A. Robert, *La Sainte Vierge dans l'Ancien Testament*, in *Maria. Études sur la Sainte Vierge*, ed. H. du Manoir, Vol. 1 (Paris, 1949), p. 23 ff.; F. Ceuppens, O.P., *De Mariologia Biblica* (Torino, 1948), pp. 1-61; J. Arendzen, *Our Lady in the Old Testament*, in *Our Blessed Lady*, Cambridge Summer School Lectures, 1933 (London, 1934), pp. 1-17; M. Burbach, O.S.B., *Mary in the Old Testament*, in *Mary in the Liturgy* (Elsberry, Mo., 1955), pp. 17-41.

subsequent centuries.[4]

If the Apostles themselves and their contemporaries seem not to celebrate Mary's glory in any external and obvious way, it is adequately explained by the fact that the attention of the faithful was at first directed entirely to Christ Himself, whose glory and preeminence had first to be firmly established before it could reflect upon anyone associated with Him.

At the same time, in the historical narrative of the New Testament Mary habitually appears in the Gospel scene in circumstances which reveal her unique association with Christ and His work, and significantly indicate her position of singular importance. Especially St. Luke pondered over the association of Christ and His Mother and the sublimity of her vocation. The simple and seemingly incidental references to Mary in the New Testament in general are of such nature as to indicate that the contemporary eyewitnesses of Gospel times would necessarily have felt a personal love and veneration for Our Lady long before any liturgical cult could have been born.

Consequently, the point must be made that the historical and theological foundations upon which the framework of Marian devotion rests were actually laid in the first century.[5] To deny this is to discount the fact of Mary's presence in the early Church. "All these with one mind continued steadfastly in prayer with the women and Mary, the mother of Jesus, and with his brethren" (Acts 1:14).

Rather than positing a hypothesis, then, as to the specific where and when of the earliest manifestations of Marian cult, it would seem better to describe it as a gradual realization and growing practice from the earliest times.

Cultus, as we understand it in reference to creatures and implying direct invocation, appears in its earliest unmistakable manifestations in the honor and respect shown the early martyrs. The martyrs of the early

---

[4] Cf. M. Gruenthaner, S.J., *Mary in the New Testament*, in MARIOLOGY, ed. J. B. Carol, O.F.M., Vol. 1 (Mediatrix Press, 2018), p. 89 ff.; G. Hilion, *La Sainte Vierge dans le Nouveau Testament*, in *Maria. Études sur la Sainte Vierge*, ed. H. du Manoir, Vol. 1 (Paris, 1949), p. 43 ff.; R. Knox, *Our Lady in the New Testament*, in *Our Blessed Lady*, Cambridge Summer School Lectures, 1933 (London, 1934), pp. 48-67.

[5] A. Agius, *The Beginnings of Devotion to the Blessed Virgin*, in *The Downside Review*, Vol. 58, 1940, p. 41 ff.; H. St. John, O.P., *The Authority of Doctrinal Development*, in *Blackfriars*, Vol. 36, 1955, p. 483 ff.; E. Campana, *Maria nel culto cattolico*, Vol. 1 (Torino, 1933), pp. 41-42.

Church were considered the most perfect imitators of Christ and able to intercede for men left behind in the warfare of life.[6]

Perhaps largely as an outgrowth of such devotion the early Christians saw clearly the logic of seeking Mary's intercession. On the other hand, it is most reasonable to expect that Marian veneration developed also in the wake of Christological clarifications in a parallel and complementary, if somewhat belated fashion, through the customary channels of the teaching Church.

Certainly, when personal devotion to Our Lady first appeared in actual literary expression, it broke forth in a richness and energy that indicated an earlier widespread appreciation.[7] The literature which we consider the authoritative expression of Christian tradition is preceded by testimony of Marian cult both in the catacombs and in apocryphal writings.[8]

If we are to measure only direct concrete evidences of Marian cult which remain today and bear up under historical scrutiny, however, we might say that devotion to Mary was born in the catacombs.[9]

In the catacombs Mary is depicted in both historical and symbolical representation. In the latter, where she is more than simply part of a scriptural scene, she is portrayed both with and without the Divine Child.[10]

---

[6] Cf. P. Pourrat, *Christian Spirituality*, Vol. 1 (Westminster, Md., 1953), p. 57.

[7] G. Jouassard, *Marie à travers la Patristique*, in *Maria. Études sur la Sainte Vierge*, ed. H. du Manoir, Vol. 1 (Paris, 1949), p. 69 ff.; Agius, art. cit., p. 48.

[8] Cf. A. Rush, C.Ss.R., *Mary in the Apocrypha*, in *Mariology*, ed. J. B. Carol, O.F.M., Vol. 1 (Mediatrix Press, 2018), p. 249 ff.

[9] M. Armellini, *Antichità del culto di Maria Vergine* (Roma, 1888), p. 9 ff.; J. Garvin, *Devotion and Devotions to Our Lady*, in *Our Blessed Lady*, Cambridge Summer School Lectures, 1933 (London, 1934), p. 229: "This lack of [earlier] documentary evidence in an age when documents were uniformly rare, and when there was no peculiar necessity to defend such a practice either from the attacks of pagans or the abuses of such sects as the fourth century Collyridians, does not necessarily point to the non-existence of the cultus ... this was an age when Christians felt it their first duty to commemorate the God-Man. ... It is also reasonable to suppose that the same reasons of prudence which prohibited any open worship of the Cross and resorted to the symbols of the Anchor and the Ixthus, also counselled certain strictures on the free cultus to Our Lady in a people not yet weaned from the myths and genealogies of the pagan goddesses." See also O. Marucchi, *The Evidence of the Catacombs* (London, 1929), pp. 69-70.

[10] Cf. *Dictionary of Christian Antiquities*, ed. Smith & Cheetham (London, 1880), pp. 1148-1149.

The oldest and one of the most beautiful frescoes of the Blessed Virgin is that found in a very early part of the catacomb of St. Priscilla. This is the famous fresco of Mary, Infant, Isaias presumably, and the star of Divinity. It dates from the first half of the second century.[11]

Of the best known images from the second and third centuries, three more are found in this same apostolic cemetery of Priscilla. One shows Mary and child as a model of virginity, a second presents a scene of the adoration of the Wise Men, and a third is an Annunciation scene.[12]

Most commonly in the catacombs Mary is represented with the Christ Child and the Magi. In the catacomb of St. Domitilla she is portrayed with the Child and four approaching Eastern Kings, and elsewhere in the same catacomb with three Magi.

In the cemetery of St. Callixtus on the Appian Way there is a scene of similar make-up. In the catacomb of SS. Peter and Marcellinus she appears with but two Wise Men.

Finally, of the more famous Mother and Child frescoes, there is the striking monogramed representation in the catacomb of St. Agnes on the Via Nomentana.[13] In this cemetery, too, is found the sketch of Mary with arms outstretched between SS. Peter and Paul.[14]

Without the Christ Child Mary appears in other paintings as an *Orans*. These are not always easily identified, but the appearance of the name *Maria* on some gilded glass pieces of the third and fourth centuries removes any possible doubt in many cases.

The number of representations of Mary and especially the locations where they are found indicate that she was not considered a mere historical personage. Her image on the tombs was a sign of protection and defense, indicating reverence. Here she is not merely an ornament or part of an historical scene as she may be when her image appears over the large center vaults in the catacombs. Consequently, the testimony of

---

[11] Cf. H. Liell, *Marien-Darstellungen in den Katakomben* (Freiburg, 1887), p. 199 ff.; J. Ferretto, *Vestiges du culte de la Sainte Vierge dans certaines fresques des Catacombes*, in *Marie*, Jan.-Feb., 1950, p. 10 ff.; A. Weber, *Die Römischen Katakomben* (Regensburg, 1906), p. 137; Northcotoe and Brownlow, *Roma Sotterranea*, Vol. 2 (London, 1879), pp. 138-141; Marucchi, *op. cit.*, p. 72, in comparing this figure of Mary with the frescoes in the house of Livia on the Palatine and those in the houses of Pompei, indicates it may date even from the end of the first century!

[12] Liell, *op. cit.*, p. 225; Marucchi, *op. cit.*, p. 73.

[13] Cf. G. Kirsch, *The Catacombs of Rome* (Rome, 1946), p. 82; Weber, *op. cit.*, p. 138.

[14] Weber, *op. cit.*, p. 139; Northcote and Brownlow, *op. cit.*, p. 312.

prayer is here added to that of simple ornamental portrayal, for she is recognized as a mediator before her Divine Son.[15]

The testimony of our literary heritage confirms what these artistic endeavors established. The Patristic concept of Mary as the Second Eve goes back to our earliest writers, Justin,[16] Irenaeus,[17] Tertullian,[18] and Origen.[19] The Apocrypha, too, though of little historical value, indicate the customs and beliefs of early Christian times.[20]

In reference to Marian cult our chief concern is with the earliest testimony of direct invocation of the Mother of Jesus. In Irenaeus Mary appears as the Advocate of Eve. In St. Gregory Thaumaturgus Mary is depicted in heaven as helping those on earth. For cases of simple address our earliest chief examples are perhaps the many in St. Ephraem's sermons. The first recorded example of direct supplication seems to be that found in a sermon of St. Gregory Nazianzen (330-389).[21] Further examples undeniably explicit in testifying to a devotion to Mary are prominent in St. Ambrose and St. Epiphanius.[22]

Liturgically, it is difficult to assign a specific date for the prevalence of Marian cult. There is obvious proof of its widespread practice by the fourth century, but again its appearance is gradual. The establishment of feasts in honor of Our Lady was retarded by the uncertainty of dates, absence of relics, and the custom of not separating Our Lady's feasts from

---

[15] M. Armellini, *Antichi cimiteri cristiani* (Roma, 1884), p. 149; Marucchi, *op. cit.,* p. 74; Garvin, *art. cit.,* p. 231; C. Hergenroether, *Primitive Christianity and the Catholic Church* (New York, 1885), p. 140 ff.; F. Kraus, *Real-Encyklopädie der Christlichen Alterthümer* (Freiburg, 1886), p. 361 ff.

[16] Justin, *Dialogus cum Tryphone,* cap. 100; *PG* 6, 709 ff.

[17] Irenaeus, *Adversus haereses,* lib. 3. cap. 32; *PG* 7, 958-959.

[18] Tertullian, *De carne Christi,* cap. 17; *PL* 2, 823-824.

[19] Origen alludes to it. Cf. *In Lucam hom.* 6; 7: *G.C.S.* 35, 40 & 48. For a complete survey of the Mary-Eve concept see W. J. Burghardt, S.J., *Mary in Western Patristic Thought,* in *Mariology,* ed. J. B. Carol, O.F.M., Vol. 1 (Mediatrix Press, 2018), p. 121 ff.; and *Mary in Eastern Patristic Thought, op. cit.,* Vol. 1, p.175 ff.; T. Livius, *The Blessed Virgin in the Fathers of the First Six Centuries* (London, 1893), pp. 35-59; Agius, *art. cit.,* p. 45; G. Montague, *Mary and the Church in the Fathers,* in *The American Ecclesiastical Review,* Vol. 123, 1950, p. **331** ff.

[20] A. Rush, C.SS.R., *art. cit.,* p. 156.

[21] *PG* 35, 1181.

[22] Cf. Ambrose, *De virginibus,* lib. 2, cap. 2; *PL* 16, 221 ff.; *De instit. virginis,* nn. 86-88; *PL* 16, 339-340; Epiphanius, *Adv. haer.,* 3, t. 2; *PG* 42, 735, 742; Cf. E. Neubert, *Marie dans l'Église anténicéenne* (Paris, 1908), p. 275.

Our Lord's.[23]

Again, our historical testimony carries us back at least to the fourth century when the Offering in the Temple, called the *Hypapante* in the East, or in the West the Purification, was celebrated. Even of earlier origin are perhaps the Feasts of the Conception of Christ, March 25, and the Nativity. Earliest of all is perhaps the Feast of the Epiphany. Only after the Council of Ephesus (431) did separate feasts of Our Lady find their way into the liturgical calendar beginning probably with the Feast of her Nativity, or the Commemoration of Mary honoring her Divine Maternity and the Virginal Conception of Christ.[24]

Proof of liturgical prayer honoring Mary can be established in the East as early as *c.* 600 from fragments bearing variations of the *Hail Mary*. However, the *Sub tuum praesidium* has been discovered to date from the fourth or even perhaps the third century, and is therefore considered the most ancient prayer in honor of the Mother of God.[25]

Several other Marian prayers and antiphons are attributed by some authors to apostolic times; however, extant manuscripts do not antedate the seventh century.[26]

The earliest churches dedicated to Mary appear to be those founded by the Empress Pulcheria in Constantinople in the fifth century. However, the Council of Ephesus (431) which proclaimed Mary the Mother of God,

---

[23] Cf. Cabrol-Leclercq, *Dictionnaire d'Archeologie et de Liturgie*, Vol. 10 (Paris, 1932), col. 2035; Agius, *art. cit.*, p. 50.

[24] Cf. F. Holweck, *Calendarium Liturgicum festorum Dei et Dei Matris Mariae* (Philadelphia, 1925), p. 88; C. Gumbinger, O.F.M.Cap., *Mary in the Eastern Liturgies*, in *Mariology*, ed. J. B. Carol, O.F.M., Vol. 1, p. 281. M. Doumith, *Marie dans la liturgie syro-maronite*, in *Maria. Études sur la Sainte Vierge*, ed. H. du Manoir, Vol. 1 (Paris, 1949), p. 329, holds that this feast antedates the Council of Ephesus.

[25] The Greek papyrus containing fragments of this prayer was discovered by C. H. Roberts. Cf. the *Catalogue of Greek and Latin Papyri in the John Rylands Library*, edited by Roberts, Vol. 3 (Cambridge, 1939), n. 470. The date of the prayer is disputed. Roberts himself believes that it was not composed before the second half of the fourth century. G. Vannucci, in his *La più antica preghiera alla Madre di Dio*, in *Marianum*, Vol. 3, 1941, pp. 97-101, dates the document not later than the third century. O. Stegmüller thinks that it should not be dated before the end of the fourth century. Cf. his article *Sub tuum praesidium: Bemerkungen zur ältesten Überlieferung*, in *Zeitschrift für katholische Theologie*, Vol. 74, 1952, pp. 76-82. For further literature cf. W. J. Burghardt, S.J., *Mary in Western Patristic Thought*, in *Mariology*, ed. by J. B. Carol, O.F.M., Vol. 1 (Mediatrix Press, 2018), pp. 147, n. 108.

[26] Cf. G. Roschini, O.S.M., *Mariologia*, Vol. 2, part 3 (Romae, 1947), p. 175 ff.; E. Campana, *op. cit.*, Vol. 1, p. 768 ff.

and consequently with ecclesiastical sanction offered her to the faithful for veneration, was held in a church dedicated to her name. Some kind of church under her protection existed in Jerusalem before the death of Bishop Juvenal, c. 458. And in Rome, both the Liberian Basilica and Sta. Maria in Trastevere gave public acclaim to the Mother of God before the sixth century.[27]

Once the Council of Ephesus offered ecclesiastical approbation, and the liturgy as such saw enrichment through the enhancement of Marian cult, both throughout the East and the West the veneration of the Mother of God increased with magnificent splendor. Soon her image and her name were everywhere to be found. To write of Mary in subsequent centuries is to write the entire history of the age.

It is established, then, as Catholic theology teaches, that the cult of the Blessed Virgin Mary finds its source in the Gospels and in Apostolic times. In Sacred Scripture are offered the objective elements for cult which spontaneously evoked the subjective element of submission and veneration in ensuing decades.

The glory due the Son necessarily overflows upon His Mother. Her dignity, sanctity, and power are indicated in the Gospels (Lk. 1:28; 1:44; Jn. 2:1-11). "Blessed is the womb that bore thee and the breasts that nursed thee" (Lk. 11:27). "Behold, all generations shall call me blessed" (Lk. 1:48).

The universal tradition of the cultus of Our Lady appears as no unique exception in doctrinal or devotional development. It rather follows the traditional course of theological and religious processes even as in the case of Christ, from whose person Mary is never separated.

There remains to be mentioned the two ordinary objections proffered against the traditional Catholic position. First, that devotion to Mary had its source in early pagan rites, and again that it arose in response to some vague mystic impulse.

In answer to the first objection it is quite obvious that true Marian cult always differed both in nature and in its effects from any pagan rite. Pagan worship attributed divinity to its goddesses, and strangely enough at the same time, often turpitude. In the Christian tradition any such

---

[27] Cf. F. Grossi Gondi, *I monumenti cristiani* (Roma, 1923), pp. 406-409. According to tradition Pope Liberius founded the Basilica in 366. It was dedicated to Our Lady by Sixtus III (d. 490).

leanings or corruption were quickly condemned by the teaching Church.[28]

In the conversion of the pagans, the veneration of Mary may have succeeded an earlier idolatry, but as a vastly superior, appealing, and more dignified pattern of honor and respect, it could have found nothing to draw from pagan rites.

To indicate that the cult of the Blessed Virgin grew out of some vague mystic urge is to forget the sound historical and theological basis for Catholic traditions in Marian devotion. From the beginning a concrete image of Mary and her association with Christ existed in the minds of the faithful to be further delineated by the teaching Magisterium. Moreover, the fullness of the Christian dispensation supplies completely for any human psychic need long before it arises as some vague mystic impulse.[29]

From the above it is clear, then, that devotion to Our Lady is scripturally and historically the heritage of an ancient Christian faith. It remains for us to see that it is also theologically legitimate and religiously fruitful.

II. THE NATURE OF MARIAN CULT

To honor Mary is to glorify God. The grace of divine Motherhood makes Our Lady pre-eminent among all creatures; her extraordinary privileges and her singular offices imply a unique dignity. Moreover, her role as Mother of men implies on the part of all mankind a relationship of dependence upon her. As her subjects and spiritual children we need her mediation and intercession, and we owe her our gratitude and love. It is our privilege to render her cult, to be devoted to her, and in honoring her to honor God.[30]

In the framework of the virtues whereby we perform acts honoring God, there is annexed to the cardinal virtue of justice as one of its potential parts, that noble moral virtue which inclines man to show due

---

[28] As an early example, note St. Epiphanius' rebuke of the Collyridians. *PG* 42, 739-755; cf. J. Danielou, S.J., *Le culte marial et le paganisme,* in *Maria,* ed. H. du Manoir, Vol. 1 (Paris, 1949), p. 161 ff.; H. Johnson, *The Cultus of Our Lady and the Graeco-Roman World,* in *The Clergy Review,* Vol. 25, 1945, p. 199 ff.; J. Garvin, *art. cit.,* p. 232; G. Roschini, O.S.M., *op. cit.,* Vol. 2, part 3, p. 234.

[29] G. Roschini, O.S.M., *op. cit.,* Vol. 2, part 3, p. 235; Danielou, S.J., *art. cit.,* p. **174**.

[30] Cf. Pius XII, *Mediator Dei,* Official Vatican English translation, 1948, p. 54; Pius IX, *Ineffabilis Deus,* in *Acta et Decreta Sacrorum Conciliorum recentiorum,* Collectio Lacensis, Vol. 6 (Friburgi, 1882), p. 836 ff.

cult to God as the first principle of all things — the virtue of religion.[31] The virtue of religion has as its material object divine cult or worship, and as its chief interior act, that of devotion.[32]

In general, we define cult as the manifestation of submission and acknowledgment of dependence shown toward the excellence of another;[33] or, according to St. John Damascene's classical definition, "the evidence of subjection ... that is to say, the sign of submission and abasement, of deference and reverence."[34]

In the concept of cult we must distinguish two elements, the material and the formal. Considered materially, cult means any deferential act, external or internal, which we perform in recognition of another person's excellence to excite in ourselves or others the esteem we ought to have for this excellence; considered formally, it means the esteem itself due such excellence.

Ordinarily understood, cult implies three acts: intellectual recognition of another's excellence, voluntary submission, and an act expressing this recognition and submission. If this cult is offered to a person whose excellence is uncreated, it is called *latria;* if to a person whose excellence is created, it is called *dulia.*[35] If, however, this created excellence is altogether and entirely singular, as in the case of the Blessed Mother, the cult offered is called *hyperdulia.*[36]

Cult is absolute, if rendered to an object because of that object's own excellence; relative, if offered because of the excellence of another object morally connected with the former object. Cult may be internal or external, private or public.

Devotion, in its specific meaning, is the first act of the virtue of

---

[31] II-II, q. 81, a. 1; cf. B. Merkelbach, O.P., *Summa Theologiae Moralis,* Vol. 2 (Parisiis, 1947), p. 681.

[32] II-II, q. 82.

[33] II-II, q. 81, a. 1, a 4um et 5um; a. 3, ad 2um; a. 5.

[34] St. John Damascene, *Orat. de imaginibus; PG,* 94, 1347.

[35] More properly, *dulia communiter sumpta.* Cf. II-II, q. 103, a. 4.

[36] Cf. II-II, q. 103, a. 4; III, q. 25, a. 5.

religion,[37] and ought to be considered in a wider sense than divine cult,[38] for it includes something beyond such cult, namely, the will to recognize *promptly*, with alacrity and eagerness, the excellence of the Supreme Being.

Participating in the virtue of religion, moreover, is the virtue of supernatural dulia and consequently that of hyperdulia. Accordingly, the devotion we manifest toward Our Lady, though immediately elicited by hyperdulia, does not for that reason fail to participate in the nature of that devotion which is the act of the virtue of religion. The devotion one has to God's saints does not terminate in them, but reaches even to God in the servants of God.[39]

Moreover, since the formal object of every act of religious cult is the supernatural dignity, excellence, or perfection of the persons venerated or worshiped, we distinguish different kinds and degrees of cult according to the various species or degrees of perfection inherent in the persons themselves.

Now the privileges of the Blessed Mother upon which hyperdulia is founded differ in degree and *nature* from those of the saints which cause us to venerate them. Mary shares more than the ordinary grace of adoptive filiation. To her is attributed the plenitude of grace, and over and above this great gift is added the specifically distinct privilege of special affinity to God, the grace of Divine Motherhood. Mary, as the Mother of God, enjoys an altogether unique excellence and a dignity by far transcending that of any other creature. In bringing forth Jesus, she brought forth God and enjoys therefore a special relationship not only with the Second Person of the Blessed Trinity, but mediately, through

---

[37] II-II, q. 83, a. 3, 1um; cf. J. Curran, O.P., *The Thomistic Concept of Devotion* (River Forest, 1941), p. 35; D. Prümmer, *Manuale Theologiae Moralis*, Vol. 2 (Barcelona, 1945), p. 278.

[38] In ordinary parlance these terms are employed in a wider meaning than theological writers often attribute to them. They are in common language frequently used interchangeably. Even by theologians, cult is sometimes identified with honor (cf. J. Keuppens, *Mariologiae Compendium* [Antverpiae, 1947], p. 146), or a species of honor (cf. A. Lépicier, O.S.M., *Tractatus de B.V.M. Mater Dei* [Romae, 1926], p. 547; P. Parente, *De Verbo Incarnato* [Romae, 1939], p. 93). Though cult and honor are often used as synonyms, it must be noted that St. Thomas indicates cult to imply not only honor and reverence, but further, a certain subjection or servitude (cf. II-II, q. 81, a. 3, ad 2um; q. 102, a. 2; q. 103, a. 3, ad 4um), and devotion to add the note of promptitude in realizing this excellence of another (II-II, q. 82, a. 1).

[39] Cf. Difficulty 3 and its answer in II-II, q. 82. a. 2.

Him, with the other Persons of the Godhead. All other creatures, even St. Joseph, no matter how closely associated with Christ, pertain to the Hypostatic Union only extrinsically; the Blessed Mother, however, intrinsically.[40] The inherent dignity of this calling of Mary as the Mother of God required a corresponding worthiness on the part of the recipient and gave her a position entirely unique among all creatures. Abstracting from the divine Maternity, however, the cult due the Blessed Virgin would be simply that of dulia; but in that she is really and truly the Mother of God, this foundation and root of all other graces and privileges proper to her gives her the right to the specifically distinct and superior type of veneration called hyperdulia.[41]

Veneration is due the Blessed Virgin, then, because of her extraordinary sanctity, for the higher the dignity and holiness of a person, the greater is his or her claim to veneration and respect. Our Blessed Mother possessed holiness in a far more eminent degree than any of the angels or saints. She possessed a singular excellence. Pope Pius XII says: "... her life is most closely linked with the mysteries of Jesus Christ, and there is no one who has followed in the footsteps of the Incarnate Word more closely and with more merit than she: and no one has more grace and power over the Sacred Heart of the Son of God and through Him with the Heavenly Father."[42] Further, her office of Coredemptrix, whereby she co-operated with Christ in our Redemption, her role as Mediatrix of all graces, and her position as Spiritual Mother of all men and Queen of the Universe give her a title to cult due in no way to any other saint. Especially, however, it is her divine Maternity that constitutes the ultimate basis and measure of veneration due her, and remains the privilege which entitles her to the special cult of hyperdulia.

Mary co-operated physically and morally in the Incarnation. She was the means and the instrument of the Holy Spirit in bringing about the Hypostatic Union of the Divine Word and human nature. The objective

---

[40] Cf. Suárez, III, q. 27, disp. 1, sect. 2; M. Nicolas, *L'appartenence de la Mère de Dieu à l'Ordre Hypostatique*, in *Bulletin de la Société Française d'Études Mariales*, 1937, p. 163 ff.; G. Rozo, C.M.F., *Sancta Maria Mater Dei* (Mediolani, 1943), p. 75 ff.; B. Merkelbach, *Mariologia* (Paris, 1939), p. 59.

[41] St. Thomas and practically all contemporary theologians regard hyperdulia as differing from the dulia we offer the angels and saints not simply in degree, but in kind. Cf. II-II, q. 103, a. 4; Lépicier, *op. cit.*, p. 564; P. Lumbreras, O.P. *De justitia* (Romae, 1938), p. 352.

[42] Pius XII, *Mediator Dei, ed. cit.*, p. 54.

dignity of Mary's Motherhood places her in a position entirely unique among all created beings. It elevates her to a position next to her Incarnate Son in the hierarchy of rational creatures and places her as an intermediary between God and the universe.[43]

Moreover, this sublime dignity and excellence of divine Motherhood is not a quality, but a relation, and as such may be considered to have a certain infinity. It is infinite not in an absolute sense, yet in a very real sense in that the term of this relation is a Divine Person. It is a reflection of the essentially infinite dignity of God. Apart from the Godhead, no higher dignity is conceivable. Thus the entirely unique dignity of Mother of God cannot be equaled, and is, in fact, beyond comparison with that of any other created person.[44]

This ineffable dignity proper to the Blessed Virgin is seen as the root and reason for all her extraordinary privileges and gifts. Mary's maternal relationship with her Divine Son appears as the distinguishing mark of her person, and might well be defined, not simply as a physiological relation of mother to offspring, nor simply as an office given her by God endowed with special graces, but further, as a supernatural spiritual union of the person of Mary with that of her divine Son, a union which implies a most intimate affinity and relationship with the Blessed Trinity. The dignity of the Blessed Mother, arising not simply from her physical

---

[43] Several authors have tried to attribute to the Blessed Virgin, in virtue of her divine Maternity, the *relative* cult of latria, reasoning that inasmuch as we attribute the cult of relative latria to the Holy Cross as having supported the body of Christ, so, *a fortiori*, we ought to attribute this type of honor to the Blessed Mother, who not only supported but actually formed His body. They further posit the argument that, because of Mary's pre-eminence of sanctifying grace she bore a most perfect image of the Trinity in her soul. Although perhaps possible in the abstract and speculative order, this type of cult is not extended to the Blessed Mother, for relative cult is not ordinarily rendered to rational creatures. If a creature has excellence proper to himself there is ordinarily rendered *absolute* cult. Disregard for this common appropriation can easily lead to error. Cf. III, q. 25, a. 3, ad 3um; a. 5; Keuppens, *op. cit.*, p. 147; Lépicier, *op. cit.*, pp. 572-573; Merkelbach, *Mariologia*, p. 395; Roschini, *op. cit.*, Vol. 2, part 3, p. 18.

[44] Pius XI, *Lux veritatis*, in *A.A.S.*, Vol. 23, 1931, p. 513: "From this dogma of the divine maternity ... flows the singular grace of Mary and, after God, her great dignity. Indeed, as Aquinas writes, 'The Blessed Virgin, by the fact that she is the Mother of God, has a certain infinite dignity from the Infinite Goodness that is God.' " I, q. 25, a. 6, ad 4um. The English translation, and the ensuing, when indicated, are taken with some adaptations from *Papal Documents on Mary*, compiled by Doheny and Kelly (Milwaukee, 1954). Cf. p. 175; Leo XIII, *Quamquam pluries*, in *A.S.S.*, Vol. 22, 1889, p. 66; St. Thomas, *IV Sent.*, lib. 1, dist. 44, q. 1, a. 3; II-II, q. 103, a. 4.

maternity but also from her affinity to God consequent upon it, is seen as belonging to the hypostatic order, for the Blessed Virgin, in becoming the Mother of God, proximately and efficaciously co-operated with the Holy Spirit in bringing about the Hypostatic Union. Without question, there does not exist a more perfect association between a created personality and God.

The Divine Maternity is, then, the basic motive for the cult of hyperdulia, which special veneration is due Mary not because of her fullness of grace alone, or her pre-eminence among men, but because she is really and truly the Mother of God.

Consequently, the Divine Maternity remains the foundation for every type or aspect of Marian veneration. When we honor Mary through any special cult, e.g., in recognizing a mystery of her life, as the Immaculate Conception, or a special virtue, as her purity, or something pertaining to her person, as her heart, we ultimately honor her entire person and implicitly recognize her as God's Mother. In every case the type of veneration offered possesses the rank of hyperdulia.[45]

From the point of view of our recognizing the various privileges and the offices of the Blessed Mother, Marian cult in general consists of a number of constitutive elements or acts. We speak of the cult of honor and respect to Mary, recognizing her especially as God's Mother, and the cult of filial and reciprocated love, acknowledging her as our spiritual Mother. We offer also the cult of gratitude, based on Mary's title and function as Coredemptrix; the cult of invocation or supplication, based on Mary's role as Dispensatrix of all graces; and the cult of imitation, recognizing Mary, after Christ, as the perfect model of all the virtues. Finally, we offer Mary the cult of loyalty and obedience as Queen of heaven and earth.[46]

These elements in Marian veneration are naturally interrelated just as are the offices and privileges of Mary which evoke them. They formulate the pattern of a complete appreciation on the part of the Church and her members of Mary's position of grandeur in the Christian dispensation.[47]

---

[45] In any particular devotion or special veneration there is in common the same "obiectum materiale adaequatum seu mediatum." Cf. III, q. 25, a. 1.

[46] Cf. Pius X, *Ad diem illum,* in *A.S.S.,* Vol. 36, 1904, p. 449; G. Roschini, *op. cit.,* Vol. 2, part 3, pp. 21-41; G. Alastruey, *Mariologia* (Vallisoleti, 1934), p. 441 ff.; J. Trombelli, *Liturgia Mariana,* in *Summa Aurea,* ed. J. Bourassé, Vol. 4 (Paris, 1866), p. 23 ff.

[47] Cf. Leo XIII, *Octobri mense,* in *A.S.S.,* Vol. 24, 1891, p. 193 ff.

The legitimacy of Marian cult is easily defended; her excellence is of incomparably greater degree than that of any other creature, and it is both proper and beneficial to honor even these lesser creatures.[48] Pope Pius XII has with brevity and precision given expression to the logic and propriety of such cult. "The Christian people should honor the Saints in heaven to implore their help that we be aided by the pleadings of those whose praise is our delight."[49]

In venerating the saints or the Blessed Mother, whenever we honor some virtue or some great work in their lives, in reality our honor refers to their entire person, for all cult terminates in the person, and any object or quality of an individual looks in its final analysis toward the whole subsistent being.[50] All cult rendered to the Blessed Mother, then, all types of devotion shown here, are directed ultimately to her person as such. Hence the legitimacy of offering cult to her Heart, her relics, and her images.

The multiple objections against the legitimacy of Marian veneration down through the ages of Christianity can be reduced more or less to the following difficulties: that it is derogatory to divine cult, usurping or competing with the place of Christ in man's redemption; that it is not in keeping with the place and position accorded Mary in the New Testament; and that it contains an element of overemphasis or even superstition, at least in the minds of a vast number of unlettered Catholics.[51]

In the teaching of the Church the cult of *latria* is offered to God alone, and the cult offered Mary, that of hyperdulia, by its very nature does not detract from but rather redounds to the glory of her Son. To know and appreciate the wonder of God's creation is to know and appreciate better God Himself. Further, history gives testimony to the fact that faith in the divinity of Christ and orthodoxy of doctrine in reference to the nature of the Incarnation are best preserved in those areas where devotion to Mary has flourished. New Testament references to Mary are not abundant, but their significance and their implications far outweigh any evidence

---

[48] *D.B.*, 302, 984; III, q. 25, a. 6; G. Roschini, O.S.M., *op. cit.*, Vol. 2, part 3, pp. 54-56.

[49] Pius XII, *Mediator Dei, ed. cit., p. 54.*

[50] II-II, q. 82, a. 2, ad 3um; III, q. 25, a. 1.

[51] W. Orchard, *The Cult of Our Lady* (London, 1937), pp. 9-10; J. H. Newman, *Difficulties of Anglicans,* Vol. 2 (London, 1882), pp. 89-118; B. Grimley, *Protestantism and Our Lady,* in *Our Blessed Lady,* Cambridge Summer School Lectures of 1933 (London, 1934), p. 251 ff.

formulated through arguments from the silence of the Gospels.

Finally, since acts of cult honoring Mary are normally appealing and highly perceptible to the senses, it is possible for some to perform acts of veneration with exceptional intensity. But even such honor is displayed with the realization that the cult of the Godhead is of superior nature.

To ignore the mediators whom God in His providence has given us for our salvation is a costly imprudence. In practice, devotion to Mary will increase one's devotion to Almighty God.[52]

"Among the Saints in heaven the Virgin Mary Mother of God is venerated in a special way. Holier than the Cherubim and Seraphim, she enjoys unquestionably greater glory than all the other saints for she is 'full of grace,' she is the Mother of God, who happily gave birth to the Redeemer for us... Let us all confidently place ourselves and all we have under her patronage... She gives us her Son and with Him all the help we need, for God 'wished us to have everything through Mary.' "[53]

III. THE USEFULNESS OF MARIAN CULT

"What graces may we not promise ourselves from Mary, sinners though we are, in life and in the agonies of death!"[54] These words of Pope Leo XIII indicate the power and will of Our Blessed Lady to help her spiritual children, a reality which the Sacred Liturgy never ceases to echo and re-echo throughout the Church year.

The benefits of Marian cult, both individual and social, are, of course, a matter of historical record as well as theological fact. Everywhere, and in every age, devotion to the Mother of God has been the source of countless blessings and the inspiration for the greatest human

---

[52] Orchard, *ibid.*, pp. 16-31; cf. Pius XII, *Fulgens corona*, in *A.A.S.*, Vol. 45, 1935, p. 581

[53] Pius XII, *Mediator Dei*, ed. cit., p. 54.

[54] Leo XIII, *Jucunda semper*, in *A.S.S.*, Vol. 27, 1894, p. 180. Cf. Leo XIII, *Magnae Dei Matris*, in *A.S.S.*, Vol. 25, 1892, p. 142: "Nobody knows and comprehends so well as she everything that concerns us: what helps we need in life; what dangers, public or private, threaten our welfare; what difficulties and evils surround us; above all, how fierce is the fight we wage with the ruthless enemies of our salvation. In these and in all other troubles of life her power is most far-reaching. Her desire to use it is most ardent to bring consolation, strength, and help of every kind" (Doheny-Kelly, pp. 70-71).

achievements.⁵⁵

From the point of view of the individual, the honoring of Mary is salutary not only during life, but in a special way at the end of life, and in the life to come.

During one's lifetime devotion to Mary is beneficial in three ways: as the source of special graces, as the basis for a strong motivation to virtue in the imitation of Mary, and as a sign of predestination to eternal life.

In reference to the first benefit, Mary, constituted in the providence of God as Mediatrix of all graces, is prompted to shower with abundant blessings those who seek her intercession and show a recognition and appreciation for her sublime office.

As a source of motivation, even apart from the consideration of Mary's special relationship with her spiritual children, very humanly we benefit objectively from the example of Mary's life and character, and this to a much greater degree than we can benefit from the example of any lesser saint. Mary exemplifies *all* the virtues and each of them in a more perfect way.⁵⁶

It is the final benefit, however, that attaches a special efficacy to Marian cult. Devotion to Mary as an indication of our firm hope for salvation rests primarily on Our Lady's great power of intercession and her special love for all who invoke her. Although the teaching of the Church, apart from a special revelation, precludes the possibility of certainty concerning salvation,⁵⁷ nonetheless there are obviously signs and indications pointing to a special providence on the part of God for the souls of the elect.

St. Thomas indicates two special signs of predilection, the prayers of the saints and the performance of other good works.⁵⁸ *A fortiori*, therefore, devotion to Mary, the greatest of the saints, is a sign of predestination. Pope Pius XII lamented the neglect of Marian cult precisely because, among other benefits, it is a "sign of predestination according to the

---

⁵⁵ Pius XII, *Superiore anno*, in A.A.S., Vol. 32, r940, p. 145: "Let everyone hasten to have recourse to Mary ... and ... confidently following the example of our forefathers, let us not fail to do that which, as history testifies, they did with such gratifying results" (Doheny-Kelly, p. 193).

⁵⁶ Pius XII, *Mediator Dei, ed. cit.*, p. 54; Leo XIII, *Magnae Dei Matris*, in A.S.S., Vol. 25, 1892, p. 145.

⁵⁷ D.B., 805.

⁵⁸ I, q. 23, a. 8.

opinion of holy men."[59]

Since the Apostolic age such has been the teaching of the Fathers, Doctors, and Ecclesiastical writers.

St. Ephraem, St. Germain of Constantinople, and St. John Damascene indicate how Mary is the Mediatrix of graces;[60] that, in fact, we are not saved except through her intercession,[61] through whom we receive the efficacious gift of grace.[62]

After the eleventh century this conviction is voiced more and more explicitly. St. Anselm indicates that anyone who turns to Mary cannot possibly perish for she is the mother of salvation and the saved.[63]

Since the seventeenth century writers have presumed the fact, and tend rather to elucidate the conditions required to make the assertion in effect valid. Obviously, a lukewarm or nonbenevolent love and devotion could never be an indication of a firm hope or promise of salvation.[64]

In considering the benefits of Marian cult at the time of death, those devoted to Mary are obviously the beneficiaries of her intercession to obtain the grace of contrition and the desire to conform their wills to that of Almighty God. Further, she offers the dying her protection against the final onslaughts of the enemy.[65] The *Hail Mary* itself calls special attention to Mary's importance at the hour of death, as do many of the Church's liturgical prayers in reference to the dying.

The benefits which Marian cult offers after death refer to the

---

[59] Pius XII, *Mediator Dei, ed. cit.*, p. 56: Leo XIII, *ibid.*, p. 141: "Whatever the necessity that presses upon us, especially in attaining eternal life, she is instantly at our side. ... She dispenses grace with a generous hand. ... It is a great thing in any saint to have grace sufficient for the salvation of many souls; but to have enough to suffice for the salvation of everybody in the world, is the greatest of all; and this is found in Christ and in the Blessed Virgin!" (St. Thomas' *Super Salut. Ang.*) (Doheny-Kelly, p. 69.)

[60] St. Ephraem, *Hymni et sermones*, ed. Th. J. Lamy, Vol. 2, pp. 526 and 528; also *opera omnia*, ed. Assemani, Vol. 3, p. 607. For further references cf. J. M. Bover, S.J., *S. Ephraem, Doctoris Syri, testimonia de universali B.M.V. mediatione*, in *Ephemerides Theologicae Lovanienses*, Vol. 4, 1927, pp. 161-179.

[61] St. Germain of Constantinople, *Oratio 2 in dormitionem Deiparae; PG*, 98, 350; cf. also *PG*, 98, 377.

[62] St. John Damascene, *Hom. 2 in dormitionem Deiparae; PG*, 96, 746. Further references in V. A. Mitchel, S.M., *The Mariology of St. John Damascene* (Kirkwood, Mo., 1930), pp. 154-215.

[63] St. Anselm, *Or. 52; PL*, 158, 957.

[64] Alastruey, *op. cit.*, p. 476; Roschini, *op. cit.*, Vol. 2, part 3, p. 60 ff.

[65] Benedict XV, *Inter sodalicia*, in *A.A.S.*, Vol. 10, 1918, p. 182.

particular judgment, to heaven, purgatory, and hell.

Those devoted to Mary have a powerful advocate with Christ at the time of their judgment.[66]

In heaven the Blessed Virgin contributes to the joy and *accidental* glory of those devoted to her in three ways — by her presence, by her special revelations, inasmuch as she possesses an eminent share in the treasury of divine knowledge, and because of the realization on the part of the *beati* of what she does for souls.[67] The full realization of the fact that the essential glory of the blessed depends on the merits of Christ and of Mary, gives rise to a love and gratitude in the saved which accidentally augments their beatitude.

In Purgatory, souls are benefited in that Mary applies to them the fruits of her merits and those of Christ. Further, she prompts the faithful on earth to pray for souls detained in Purgatory while she herself offers these prayers to God thereby augmenting their value.

Even in hell, according to a number of theologians, souls devoted to Mary during their lifetime will find their punishments in some ways mitigated.[68]

Beyond these individual benefits, the usefulness of Marian cult is apparent on the social level as well, for devotion to Mary brings advantages to the family, civil society, and the Church.[69]

In reference to domestic society, since the time of Cana, Mary's presence in the family circle assures both material and spiritual blessings, and especially the presence of Christ. Women have done most for their families and the realization of their motherly vocation where, being devoted to Mary, they have understood the dignity and gravity of their calling before God.[70] Conversely, to women themselves have come innumerable and invaluable social benefits under Christianity, colored and formed as they are by the realization of Mary's singular dignity as the ideal of all womankind.

---

[66] Cf. St. Jerome, *Ep. 22, PL*, 22, 424. V. Sedlmayr, O.S.B., *Theologia Mariana*, in *Summa Aurea*, ed. Bourassé, Vol. 8, cols. 253-255, refers to Mary as personally present at the time of judgment to intercede for those devoted to her.

[67] Cf. R. Garrigou-Lagrange, O.P., *The Mother of the Saviour and Our Interior Life* (St. Louis, 1948), p. 274; Roschini, *op. cit.*, Vol. 2, part 3, p. 66.

[68] Cf. I, q. 21, a. 4 ad 1um; Garrigou-Lagrange, *ibid.*, p. 275.

[69] Cf. Lépicier, *op. cit.*, p. 431; Roschini, *ibid..*, p. 70 ff.

[70] Cf. Pius XII, *On Women's Duties in Social and Political Life* (Ad mulieres a societatibus christianis Italiae delegatas), Oct. 21, 1945, in *A.A.S.*, Vol. 37, p. 248.

Likewise, of obvious import are the benefits of Marian cult toward civil society and its objectives, namely, the pursuit of learning, the conservation of morals, and the fostering of the arts. As history testifies, the influence of Mary in all three of these categories has been exceptional. To Mary, indeed, men have turned for their greatest inspiration. It is she who has given womankind the example and inspiration to succeed as custodians of morals and preservers of Christian culture.[71]

Perhaps of even greater significance is the influence of Marian cult on religious society. In both the realm of faith and of morals devotion to Mary has brought a richness and beauty that have benefited mankind.

Pope Leo XIII reminds us that "from her, the Seat of Wisdom, as they themselves [the Fathers and Doctors of the Church] gratefully tell us, a strong current of the most sublime wisdom has coursed through their writings."[72] Traditionally, Mary is hailed as "alone destroying all the heresies of the world." True devotion to Mary has been the touchstone of Christological orthodoxy. She through whom Truth came leads men back to the source of truth.

In the realm of morals, Mary's example of virginity, dedication to vocation, and loyalty to Christ has been the inspiration of religious groups down through the centuries.[73]

The entire Liturgy is itself a living testimony to the usefulness and value of Marian cult within the life of the Church. Devotion to Mary is so vast in the ramifications of its benefits that a simple outline precludes the possibility of a complete appreciation. Yet a mere sketch of the breadth of its influence is sufficient to indicate that Marian cult is not only useful but in some way necessary.

IV. THE NECESSITY OF MARIAN CULT

Since God could have brought men to eternal salvation apart from the pattern in Divine Providence which He has chosen, we do not, in speaking of the necessity of Marian cult, refer here to an absolute and antecedent

---

[71] Pius XII, *ibid.*; Address to the 14th Congress of the World Union of Catholic Women's Organizations, Sept. 29, 1927. Cf. *L'Osservatore Romano*, 30-9-57. Leo XIII, *Laetitiae sanctae*, in *A.S.S.*, Vol. 26, 1893, p. 194 ff., indicates that three evil influences in society can be remedied by devotion to Mary, especially through the recitation of the Rosary.

[72] Leo XIII, *Adiutricem populi*, in *A.S.S.*, Vol. 28, 1895, p. 152.

[73] Cf. Pius XI, *Lux veritatis*, in *A.A.S.*, Vol. 23, 1931, p. 514.

necessity, but to a necessity that is hypothetical and consequent.

It seems theologically certain that at least some devotion to God's Mother is necessary in the ordinary framework of salvation. In the present order, if anyone with sufficient knowledge positively rejects or neglects to offer at least some cult to Mary, such an individual is thereby rejecting and neglecting the ordinary means to salvation.[74] Hence the words of Pope Pius XII, who says, "So powerful, indeed, is the Blessed Virgin with God and His only-begotten Son that, as Dante observes, anyone who desires His help and fails to have recourse to Mary is like one attempting to fly without wings."[75] The necessity of Marian cult is implicit in the Doctors of the Church, especially in their writings and sermons on Mary as the Almoner of God's graces. Since the seventeenth century theologians have been more outspoken in voicing what today appears presumed in the liturgy of the Church and has been included in her law.[76]

Beyond the theological arguments logically derived from Mary's being the Mother of God and the Mother of men, and obviously meriting through these offices our filial respect and love, the necessity of Marian cult is implied also in Mary's role as Mediatrix between God and man.[77] Mary has co-operated in the acquisition of all graces as our Coredemptrix, and she co-operates in the distribution of all graces as our Dispensatrix. As Coredemptrix she has a right to men's gratitude. As Dispensatrix she is the channel through whom grace comes to us. Therefore, she most properly should be saluted through prayer, the ordinary means whereby grace is obtained, and the universal practice of the faithful in recognizing her offices gives expression to their realization of the necessity of Marian cult.

Hence, in the words of St. Pius X, "God could have given us the Redeemer of the human race, and the Founder of the Faith, in another way than through the Virgin, but since Divine Providence has been pleased that we should have the Man-God through Mary, who conceived Him by the Holy Ghost and bore Him in her womb, it remains for us to receive

---

[74] Cf. E. Campana, *op. cit.*, Vol. 1, p. 133; J. B. Terrien, S.J., *Le Mère de Dieu et la Mère des hommes,* 2nd part: *Le Mère des hommes,* 5th ed., Vol. 2 (Paris, 1902), pp. 253-268.

[75] Pius XII, *Superiore anno,* in *A.A.S.,* Vol. 32, 1940, p. 145 (Doheny-Kelly, p. **193).** These same words were employed by Leo XIII, *Augustissimae Virginis,* in *A.S.S.,* Vol. 30, 1897, p. 133.

[76] Canon 1276: "... all the faithful shall especially cultivate a filial devotion for the Blessed Virgin Mary."

[77] Cf. J. Bittremieux, *Doctrina Mariana Leonis XIII* (Brugis, 1928), p. 78.

Christ only from the hands of Mary."[78]

---

[78] Pius X, *Ad diem illum,* in *A.S.S.,* Vol. 36, 1904, p. 451.

FEASTS IN HONOR OF OUR LADY[1]

by REV. RENÉ H. CHABOT, M.S.

T. THOMAS teaches that due honor is rendered to God when, in the light of His transcending and awe-inspiring superiority, we bow our wills in humble submission, signifying thus our total and unlimited dependence on Him, as Creator and First Principle.[2] The virtue of religion — the first and principal act of which is devotion — has as its specifying object this honor or debt due to God. The interior submission of the will, however, may be extended and exteriorized by means of signs, words, or even bodily positions. In this way only is it possible for us, social beings by nature and composed of matter and spirit, to render to God an integral honor, where both the spirit and the body participate, the one as the manifestation of the other, in this humble submission to God.

Though God alone may possess the supreme dignity of First Principle and, consequently, to Him exclusively is restricted the honor of total

---

[1] General bibliography: J. Alvarez, C.M.F., *Conspectus festorum B. Mariae Virginis in Missali Romano*, in *Marianum*, Vol. 4, 1942, pp. 128-130; A. Arrighini, *Le feste cristiane nella teologia, storia, liturgia, arte, folklore*, 2 vols. (Torino-Roma, 1936); Benedictus XIV, *De festis Beatae Mariae Virginis*, in *Summa Aurea*, ed. J. Bourassé, Vol. 3, coll. 1399-1526; B. Botte, O.S.B., *La première fête mariale de la liturgie romaine*, in *Ephemerides Liturgicae*, Vol. 47, 1933, pp. 425-430; B. Capelle, O.S.B., *La liturgie mariale en Occident*, in *Maria. Études sur la Sainte Vierge*, ed. H. du Manoir, S.J., Vol. 1 (Paris, 1949), pp. 217-245; G. Cavalleri, *Le feste mariane nella liturgia di rito romano*, in *Enciclopedia Mariana*, ed. R. Spiazzi, O.P. (Milano, 1954), pp. 427-432; C. Feckes, *So feiert dich die Kirche. Maria im kranz ihrer Feste* (Steyl, 1954); J. Hennig, *Feasts of the Blessed Virgin in the Ancient Irish Church*, in *The Irish Ecclesiastical Record*, Vol. 81, 1954, pp. 161-171; F. G. Holweck, *Calendarium liturgicum festorum Dei et Dei Matris Mariae* (Philadelphia, 1925); B. Manuel, O.S.B., *Fiestas de la Sma. Virgen en la iglesia griega y eslava*, in *Liturgia*, Vol. 12, 1957, pp. 201-211; *Mary in the Liturgy. National Liturgical Week, Milwaukee, Wis.*, 1954 (Elsberry, Mo., 1955); H. R. Philippeau, *Le cycle liturgique des fêtes mariales*, in *Marie, salut du monde* (Paris, 1954), pp. 53-62; F. Sarandrea, *Le feste di una grande Regina* (Rovigo, 1954); A. Tonne, O.F.M., *Feasts of Our Lady* (Emporia, Kansas, 1951); J. C. Trombelli, *De cultu publico B. Mariae ab Ecclesia exhibito*, in *Summa Aurea*, ed. J. Bourassé, Vol. 4, coll. 9-425; S.J.P. Van Dijk, O.F.M., *Feasts of the Blessed Virgin Mary in the Thirteenth-Century Roman Liturgy*, in *Archivum Franciscanum Historicum*, Vol. 48, 1956, pp. 450-456; E. Campana, *Maria nel culto cattolico*, 2 vols. (Torino, 1933); G. M. Roschini, O.S.M., *Mariologia*, 2nd ed., Vol. 4 (Romae, 1948), pp. 128-173.

[2] *Summa theol.*, 2-2, 81, 7.

submission and dependence, nevertheless there are many other persons in whom we find superior dignity, and to whom we are deeply indebted for our salvation. Among these the great Mother of God stands out. Hers is a dignity surpassed by God alone, and her activity and role in the work of Redemption has had, next to God, unparalleled importance and effect. She not only freely consented to give mankind its Redeemer; she not only consented to her part in the glorious but painful Redemption at the foot of the Cross, but even at this hour, as Heavenly Queen and Universal Dispensatrix, hers is the task of distributing the innumerable supernatural favors that flood the universe. It behooves us, therefore, to pay a debt of recognition and honor to Our Lady, not exclusively through interior acts of love and thanksgiving, but publicly, so that everything in us, body and soul, may join in this loving task.

Catholics have always endeavored to manifest adequately their recognition of Our Lady's unparalleled dignity, just as they have always been deeply conscious of the important role she played in the process of their salvation. It is precisely in order to express these sentiments of veneration and thanksgiving that so many Marian feasts have been instituted down through the centuries.[3]

The purpose of this chapter is not, of course, to evaluate the doctrinal contents of these feasts, but rather to trace their origin and to indicate their historical development as briefly as possible. For the sake of order and clarity, we shall divide this chapter into two sections: the first, dealing with Marian feasts celebrated in the universal Church; the second, with those observed only in certain dioceses and religious orders.

I. UNIVERSAL FEASTS

The calendar of the universal Church contains not less than eighteen feasts honoring Our Blessed Lady. We shall discuss them in chronological order, as they appear in the ecclesiastical cycle.

1. The Immaculate Conception
(December 8)

In the Orient:
St. Andrew of Crete (660-740), in his canon *In conceptionem Sanctae ac*

---

[3] F. G. Holweck, *op. cit.*, enumerates some six hundred Marian feasts. A few more could now be added to the already impressive list.

Dei aviae Annae, provides us with the first historical document bearing testimony to the existence of the present feast. John of Euboea (fl. *c.* 750), on the other hand, is the first to hand down a homily especially composed for this solemnity. He states that, chronologically speaking, the feast of the Conception is first, but readily admits that it was not then a universal feast. It is highly probable that it did receive universal recognition within the entire Byzantine Empire at the time of Photius of Constantinople (897?). Its observance as a holyday of obligation may also date back to this period, if we are to judge from the numerous homilies composed for this solemnity. George of Nicomedia († after 880) writes that the feast of the Conception ranks among the important feasts.[4] It is also found, celebrated on December 9, in the Byzantine Calendar drawn up at the request of the Emperor Basil II in 984.

One must clearly understand, however, the true object of this feast as found in the Orient. Some authors, indeed, intent on finding proofs from Tradition for the dogma of the Immaculate Conception, have given undue importance to the Oriental feast of the Conception. It must be remembered always that the origin of this Oriental feast, contrary to what happened in the West, was not dependent on dogmatic issues.

As found in the early Byzantine documents, this feast has a threefold object: (1) The miraculous visitation of an angel announcing to Anna that she would conceive; (2) The miraculous conception of Anna (active conception), who, until then, had been sterile; (3) The passive conception of Mary. The Protoevangelium of James had furnished the necessary historical background for this feast when its author wrote that Anna was sterile and that an angel appeared to her announcing that she would conceive. Luke's narration of similar events in the case of John the Baptist undoubtedly inspired the author of the Protoevangelium. The primary object, therefore, obviously was to commemorate the Annunciation of the angel to Anna of the future conception, to which object was immediately linked that of Anna's miraculous active conception and Mary's passive conception, with no necessary reference to the dogma of the Immaculate Conception. This explains the variety of names attributed to this feast, e.g., Feast of the Conception of Anna; Feast of the Conception of the Mother of God; Feast of the Annunciation of the Conception of the Mother of God. But in daily preaching and throughout the many homilies

---

[4] Cf. M. Jugie, A.A., *L'Immaculée Conception dans l'Ecriture sainte et dans la tradition orientale* (Rome, 1952), pp. 135-136.

composed for this solemnity, it was but natural to put more emphasis, if not all, on the Conception of Mary, the great Mother of God, rather than on the legendary narrative of the Protoevangelium. Again, it was natural that the annual observance of this feast gave a propitious opportunity for the faithful to express publicly their deeply rooted admiration and respect for Mary's unique purity and saintliness. The truth remains, nonetheless, that it was not originally instituted on a dogmatic basis with the purpose of celebrating Mary's Immaculate Conception.[5]

In the West:

As in many other instances, credit must be given to the Oriental Church for having been the first to institute the feast of Mary's Conception. It was only many years later that the West accepted it, and not without strong opposition. The very first testimony to the existence of the feast in the West is had from a celebrated marble kalendarium found in Naples dating as far back as the ninth century. Indications are that the feast was celebrated on December 9. But, because Naples and Sardinia were then under the rule of the Byzantine Empire, one cannot truly say that, as such, the feast had been introduced in the West. We must also reject as false testimony those documents according to which Ireland might have observed the feast during that same century.[6]

It is England, in fact, that first introduced this Marian feast into the Latin liturgy. In a precious document, Leofric's kalendarium (eleventh century), in which is found the present feast, the collect states: "Deus qui beatae Mariae Virginis conceptionem angelico vaticinio parentibus praedixisti." We note from this that in England, as in the Orient, traces remained of the Protoevangelium narrative establishing a parallel between Mary's Conception and that of St. John the Baptist. Judging also from other kalendaria of that same period wherein no mention is made of this feast, it would seem that at the outset this feast was limited to Winchester,

---

[5] Jugie, *op. cit.*, p. 141. Cf. also E. Vacandard, *Les origines de la fête et du dogme de l'Immaculée Conception*, in *Revue du Clergé Français*, Vol. 42, 1910, pp. 5-41; 257-278; 681-701.

[6] Cf. Capelle, *art. cit.*, p. 226; H. Thurston, S.J., *The Irish Origins of Our Lady's Conception Feast*, in *The Month*, Vol. 103, 1904, pp. 449-465; Fr. Grosjean, *Le prétendue fête de la Conception de la Sainte Vierge dans les eglises celtiques*, in *Analecta Bollandiana*, Vol. 61, 1943, pp. 91-95.

Worcester, Exeter, Canterbury, and the surrounding localities.[7] The conquest of England by William I of Normandy, however, resulted in the disappearance of this feast from the English liturgy. It was re-established shortly thereafter by young Anselm (cousin of the Saint and Bishop of Canterbury) about the year 1127. Through his efforts and influence the feast quickly spread throughout England. As a result of the strong opposition which ensued, we have the first treatise written in defense of Mary's prerogative, the *Tractatus de conceptione S. Mariae,* by Eadmer of Canterbury († 1121). The opposition was probably broken by a council of London in 1129. In 1329 the Council of Canterbury prescribed that the feast of Mary's Conception be observed within the entire Province.

Shortly thereafter it passed into Normandy and the northern part of France. But, "in general, the introduction of this feast and the enthusiasm for its purport seem to have been lacking in theological guidance. Childlike piety, incited by accounts of miracles and revelations, had the upper hand. In favor of the doctrine and the feast these miracles were advanced together with the appreciation of its eminent appropriateness, but positive theological reasons were not stressed. Further, a clear exposition of the idea of the feast was also lacking. For that reason it was quite proper for St. Bernard, in his famous letter about 1140, to urge the prebendaries of Lyons to a careful research. He pointed out the danger of error and confusion which could and must ensue from a demand, none too clearly defined, for the celebration of Mary's conception as well as her birth, since the latter supposes the former."[8] The appeal of St. Bernard did not, however, result in checking the propagation of the feast, because already in 1154, fourteen years later, Atto, prior of a Benedictine monastery in the Gascogne, claimed that it was observed throughout the whole of France.

In the closing years of the twelfth century it had penetrated into many regions of Germany and Belgium, and also into Navarre, in Spain. In summing it up, Roschini states that, notwithstanding strong opposition on the part of such great men as St. Bernard and St. Thomas, it may be safely said that in the middle of the fourteenth century the feast of Mary's Conception, in the sense of a preservation from original sin, had found its way into every single diocese of the world and in every monastery of

---

[7] Roschini, *op. cit.,* p. 131. Cf. M. Cecchin, O.S.M., *L'Immacolata nella liturgia occidentale anteriore al secolo XIII* (Roma, 1943).

[8] M. J. Sheeben, *Mariology,* Vol. 2, (St. Louis, Mo., 1953), p. 87.

some importance, with the exception of Cistercian and Dominican monasteries.⁹

The attitude adopted by the Roman Pontiffs during the many years of controversy about the doctrine of the Immaculate Conception, to which was intimately linked, in the West, the very existence of the feast itself, may best be described as that of tolerance first, of assent next, and finally of approbation, when, in 1477, Sixtus IV approved the Mass and Office drawn up by the Franciscan Leonardo of Nogarole, in which the present collect appears. Four years later the same Pontiff gave his approval to another office for Mary's feast. Faced with such obvious Papal approbation, the opposition party became more resolute in its attacks against Mary's Immaculate Conception; to such an extent that Sixtus IV deemed it necessary to intervene with the bull *Grave nimis* wherein he forbade all censure of those who believed in the Immaculate Conception, while at the same time he forbade calling the denial of it a heresy. He also denounced as false the assertion that, on the feast of the Conception, the Roman Church celebrated only in a general way the spiritual conception and sanctification of the Blessed Virgin.¹⁰ Years later, Alexander VII declared in his famous bull *Sollicitudo omnium ecclesiarum* (1661): "The devotion to the Blessed Virgin Mary is of long standing among the faithful followers of Christ who feel that her soul, from the very first instant of its creation and infusion into her body, was preserved immune from the stain of original sin by a special grace and privilege of God, through the merits of her Son Jesus Christ, the Redeemer of the human race, and *who in this sense esteem and solemnly celebrate the festivity of her conception.*"¹¹

In 1693, Innocent XII proclaimed that the octave of the feast of Mary's Conception be universally celebrated, elevating it at the same time to the rank of double of second class. Pius IX in 1863 (having defined the dogma of the Immaculate Conception in 1854) promulgated a new Mass and Office. It was Leo XIII, lastly, who in 1879 elevated its rank to that of

---

⁹ Roschini, *op. cit.*, p. 133.

¹⁰ D.B. No. 735.

¹¹ D.B. No. 1100. On the attitude of the Holy See toward the feast of the Immaculate Conception, cf. R. Laurentin's interesting and well-documented article, *Role du Saint-Siège dans le développement du dogme de l'Immaculée Conception*, in *Virgo Immaculata*, Vol. 2 (Romae, 1956), esp. pp. 14-56.

double of first class.[12]

2. The Purification of the Blessed Virgin
(February 2)

The threefold object of this feast is found in St. Luke's narrative of chapter II, verses 22-39: the presentation of Jesus in the Temple, the purification of the Blessed Mother, and the consequent encounter of Mary with Simeon and Anne. Down through its long and ancient history, this feast has acquired — due especially to its multiple object — a variety of names: e.g. *Hypapante* (from the Greek meaning "the encounter" with Simeon and Anne); *Feast of Saint Simeon the Patriarch; The Advent of the Son of God in the Temple; The Purification of the Blessed Virgin* (especially used throughout the Latin Church); *The Feast of the Candles* (suggested from the accompanying ceremony of the Blessing of the Candles).

In the Orient:

The Oriental Church, once again, may lay claim to having originated this Marian feast. Signs of its early existence in Jerusalem are found in the *Peregrinatio ad loca sancta* (between 383 and 384) of Sylvia (or Etheria), most probably a nun from the southern part of France. She refers to the feast of the Purification as the *Quadragesima Epiphaniae* for the obvious reasons that, first, the prescribed purification and presentation were to take place forty days after childbirth; and second, the feast of the Nativity having not yet been set for December 25, the forty days were counted from the Epiphany. And so it was that the feast of the Purification was originally celebrated, in the Oriental Church, on February 14. The *Peregrinatio* describes the feast as one of great solemnity, with solemn procession from the Basilica of the Holy Sepulcher to the Basilica of the Resurrection, at which point a homily commenting on the above-mentioned passage of St. Luke's Gospel was addressed to the faithful. A noteworthy fact, however, is that, as yet, this feast does not appear as a Marian feast, but rather as one of Our Lord.

When Juvenal, Patriarch of Jerusalem (425-458), decreed that the Feast of the Nativity be celebrated on December 25, common sense required that

---

[12] For further details on the history of the feast, cf. Capelle, *Le fête de la Conception de Marie en Occident*, in *L'Immaculée Conception; VIIe Congrès Marial National* (Lyon, 1954), pp. 147-161.

the feast of the Purification be brought back to February 2, thus keeping the prescribed forty days. There is no doubt that at least in the middle of the sixth century this feast was being celebrated on February 2. We gather this from a homily written by Abraham, Bishop of Ephesus (fl. *c.* 550).

The candlelight procession dates back to the fifth century, probably by reason of Simeon's prophetic words: "Lumen gentium."

The solemnity of this Jerusalem feast was contagious and quickly spread to the monks of Syria and Palestine; at the very outset of the sixth century, Constantinople had received it and made it its own. But here at Constantinople we behold a Marian feast, celebrated in a Marian church and opening with an exhortation to Mary begging her assistance and protection.

In the year 542 Emperor Justinian decreed that the feast be celebrated throughout the Greek Empire.

In the West:

There can be no doubt that the feast of the Purification had found its way into the Western Church by the end of the seventh century, during the reign of Pope Sergius.[13] St. Bede the Venerable (675-735), in his *De ratione temporum,* is first to speak of the Candle Procession. Many ancient calendars also refer to this feast as the *Hypapante Domini,* thus clearly indicating its Oriental origin. From here on, this feast has taken on a definite Marian aspect.

Some authors, however, have suggested and endeavored to prove that the Purification owes its origin to the Latin Church, as a Christian substitute for pagan vestiges. Innocent III, for example, firmly believed that the Purification was a substitute, brought about by Pope Gelasius, for the pagan feast *Lupercalia.* Benedict XIV, nevertheless, argued against this hypothesis, since the pagan feast *Lupercalia* was not celebrated on February 2, but rather on February 15, and because it was not customary in the pagan festivity to carry lighted candles. No one doubts the fact that Pope Gelasius did put an end to the pagan *Lupercalia,* but it is not as evident that he instituted the Purification as its substitute.

During the eighth century, the feast of the Purification spread to many parts of France, Spain, and Germany and thus gradually became a universal feast.

---

[13] Cf. *Liber Pontificalis,* ed. Duchesne, Vol. 1, p. 376.

3. Feast of the Blessed Immaculate Virgin
(February 11)

Every Catholic is undoubtedly familiar with the object of this feast. Who, in truth, has not heard or read of Bernadette Soubirous or of the famed Grotto of Masabielle? The ever increasing popularity of these apparitions at Lourdes have had the happy effect of producing numerous literary works recounting in every detail the many historical developments that surround this memorable event. Suffice it, therefore, to note that the feast itself was first approved by Leo XIII and granted to the diocese of Tarbes in the year 1890. Less than twenty years later, on November 13, 1907, his successor, St. Pius X, proclaimed that it be observed the world over.

4. The Feast of the Annunciation
(March 25)

It is not to be marveled at that popular piety and devotion, ever conscious of the deep signification of St. Luke's passage of chap. I, 26-38, instituted at an early date a special feast whose object was to commemorate both Mary's initial consent to the work of Redemption and Christ's first moment of temporal existence among men.

In the Orient:

Benedict XIV, along with the Bollandists, convinced of the antiquity of this time-honored feast, ventured the opinion that the Apostles themselves might have originated it. This opinion, however, does not satisfy and appears rather improbable and utterly lacking of historical proof, for the very obvious reason that up to the fourth century, with the exception of Easter and Pentecost, there were no specifically Christian feasts. There did exist in this century a basilica of the Annunciation erected by St. Helena, a fact which might indicate that perhaps a commemoration of the Annunciation was initiated at the time. But nonetheless, no historical document certifying without a shadow of a doubt to the existence of this feast can be found until the middle of the sixth century. A certain Abraham, Bishop of Ephesus, in a homily on *The Annunciation of the Mother of God* speaks of the "magnificent feast" of March. So it is that Jugie asserts that the origin of the feast of the Annunciation dates back to the reign of Justinian between the years 530 and 550.[14]

The *Chronicon Paschale* (from the beginning of the seventh century to the year 624) places the feast on March 25.

When the Annunciation is compared with the Nativity, the question as to which feast determined the date of the other naturally arises. The following seems to be the more probable explanation. According to an ancient tradition (whose historical proof is uncertain and rather doubtful) Our Lord would have suffered and died on March 25.[15] For reason of symbolism (so dear to the Fathers) it seemed incongruous that Christ's life would have extended for a fraction of a year. It was, therefore, concluded that He had first become man on March 25. The Annunciation thus established, it was logical to place the feast of the Nativity on December 25.[16]

It was customary, at the time, that no feast be celebrated during the Lenten Season. What would become of the Annunciation? The Council of Trullanum, held at Constantinople in 692, having cautiously examined the problem, moved that an exception be made for the feast of the Annunciation, and thus it remained on March 25.

Already during the eighth century the Annunciation was a universally recognized feast, both in the Orient and in the West. From that century also dates (in the Orient) the vigil attached to it.

In the West:

To judge from the testimony of the *Liber Pontificalis*,[17] there is no doubt whatsoever that the Annunciation, along with the Nativity and the feast of the *Dormition*, was celebrated in Rome during the reign of Pope Sergius I (687-701). Its diffusion within the Latin Church was rapid indeed. The one obstacle that did retard somewhat its universal acceptance lay in its date (March 25 occurring during the Lenten Season). In Spain, at one time, the Annunciation was observed on many different days. The Council of Toledo (656), however, remedied this awkward situation by a decree

---

[14] Cf. Jugie, *La mort et l'Assomption de la Sainte Vierge. Etude historico-doctrinale* (Città del Vaticano, 1944), p. 82.

[15] Cf. St. Augustine, *De Trinitate*, lib. 4, cap. 5; *PL* 42, 894.

[16] Cf. Duchesne, *Origines du culte chrétien. Etude sur la liturgie latine avant Charlemagne*, 5th ed. (Paris, 1909), pp. 265-269. Cf. also S. Vailhè, *Origines de la fête de l'Annonciation*, in *Echos d'Orient*, Vol. 9, 1906, pp. 138-145.

[17] *Ed. cit.*, Vol. 1, pp. 371, 376, 381.

prescribing that it be kept throughout the entire nation on December 18. In later years, though, influenced, no doubt, by the Roman observance, Spain also chose to observe it on March 25, retaining the solemnity of December 18 under the title of *The Expectation of the Blessed Virgin Mary* or also *The Feast of the Blessed Virgin Mary.*

The Milanese, like the Spaniards, and for the same reason, chose to observe this feast in December (Sunday preceding the Nativity). But they also, in later years, returned to the original March 25.

5. Our Lady of the Seven Dolors[18]
(Friday following Passion Sunday)

In recent years, due especially to a stimulus given by many Pontiffs, theological developments in Marian studies have taken on gigantic proportions. More and more evident has become Mary's unique role as Coredemptrix in the acquisition of grace, or in the objective Redemption. Mariologists the world over have fathomed the deep significance and full richness of Mary's intense interior sufferings throughout her life and principally at the foot of the Cross on Calvary Hill. Of course, one cannot expect Catholic theologians of the past centuries to possess so explicit an understanding and knowledge as modern theologians do of the unique efficacy of the Virgin Mary's sorrows in God's redemptive plan; nevertheless, traces of this devotion may be found already in the fourth century. St. Ambrose, for example, along with St. Augustine and St. Ephraem, have left us memorable pages concerning Mary's sorrows. The Greek liturgy, after the seventh century, also shows evidence of some interest in Mary's Transfixion. During the thirteenth century, however, this growing devotion received a new impetus, as an immediate result of a newly founded order, the Servites of Mary, whose aim was to propagate Marian devotion in general but above all to foster and spread that one specific devotion to the Sorrowful Mother.

Small wonder, therefore, that during the fourteenth century, as a result of the ever growing devotion to Mary's sufferings, came to life a feast commemorating her Compassion. In the year 1423 we find the pious Archbishop of Cologne, Theodoric, prescribing that this feast be kept by his people in public reparation for the scandalous and sacrilegious attacks

---

[18] Cf. Aug. M. Lépicier, O.S.M., *Mater Dolorosa. Notes d'histoire, de liturgie et d'iconographie sur le culte de Notre-Dame des Douleurs* (Spa, 1948), esp. pp. 44-47.

of the Hussites against the images of Christ and Mary. He assigned to this newly instituted feast the title of *The Commemoration of the Anguish and Sorrow of the Blessed Virgin Mary*. Already at the end of the sixteenth century it had found its way throughout the entire Latin Church, under various titles, however, and celebrated on many different days of the year.

It was known, for example, as the *Feast of Sorrows, Feast of the Seven Dolors, Feast of the Compassion, Our Lady of Pity*, and *Feast of the Transfixion*. The Cistercians observed its annual solemnity on April 16; the Carthusians, on the Saturday following Passion Sunday; the Canons Regular, on the Friday after Easter Sunday. Others preferred, as in Cologne, the Friday after the fourth Sunday of Lent. The Friars Preachers had selected the Friday following Passion Sunday. Benedict XIII, a Dominican himself, by a decree of the Congregation of Sacred Rites, April 22, 1727, extended this feast to the universal Church and prescribed it to be kept on the Friday of Passion Sunday under the title of *Our Lady of the Seven Dolors*, or *Feast of the Transfixion*, thus establishing uniformity of date and title.

The specific title of Seven Dolors (most probably from the Seven Joys of Mary) dates back to the thirteenth century, during which was founded the order of the Servites of Mary. But only in the fifteenth century was uniformity established concerning which specific seven sorrows should be represented by this feast.

6. The Queenship of Mary
(May 31)

As the title clearly indicates, the object of this feast is to honor Mary as the sovereign of heaven and earth, who stands indissolubly united with her Divine Son, Christ the King. Together, indeed, they have an indisputable claim to our submission and homage. Hers is a queenship by affinity and by conquest. Pope Pius XII, a truly devoted and loving subject of Mary, in his encyclical letter *Ad coeli Reginam*, explained in clear and concise terms the basic principles of Mary's royal dignity: "The basic principle ... is without doubt her divine Maternity ... It is easily deduced that she, too, is Queen since she brought forth a Son who, at the very moment that He was conceived, was, by reason of the Hypostatic Union of the human nature with the Word, even as man, King and Lord of all things." But Mary is also Queen by right of conquest. "The most Blessed Mother," continues the holy Pontiff, "is to be called Queen not only by reason of her divine Maternity, but also because by the will of God she has had an outstanding part in the work of our eternal salvation. ... Hence we may certainly conclude that just as Christ, the new Adam, must be called King, not only because He is the Son of God, but also because He is our Redeemer; so, by a certain kind of analogy, the most Blessed Virgin is Queen, not only because she is the Mother of God, but also because, as the new Eve, she was associated with the new Adam. And so it is that Jesus Christ alone, God and man, is King in the full, proper, and absolute sense of the term. Yet Mary also, although in a restricted way and only by analogy, shares in the royal dignity as the Mother of Christ who is God, as His associate in the labors of the Divine Redemption, and in His struggle against His enemies and in the victory He won over them all."[19]

It came not as a surprise, therefore, that the Holy Father, in this same encyclical, dated October 11, 1954, in the closing days of the ever memorable Marian Year, instituted the feast of the Queenship of Mary to be universally celebrated on May 31. "Since, after long and careful consideration," writes the Pontiff, "we have come to the conclusion that great benefits will accrue to the Church if that solidly established truth were to shine forth even more clearly to all, like a bright light placed on its pedestal, We by Our Apostolic power, decree and institute the feast of Mary as Queen to be celebrated throughout the entire world every year on May 31. And likewise We command that on that same day there be renewed the consecration of the human race to the Immaculate Heart of the Blessed Virgin Mary. Upon this there is founded a great hope that there may arise an era of happiness that will rejoice in the triumph of religion and in Christian Peace."[20]

7. The Visitation of the Blessed Mother
(July 2)

Shortly after Mary's generous and loving reply "Behold the handmaid of the Lord," reported by St. Luke (1:38), it is written that she "rose and went with haste into the hill country ... and saluted Elizabeth." Momentous events occurred at this meeting: the pre-sanctification of John the Baptist, the proclamation of Mary as Mother of God, and, not least in importance, Mary's triumph of humility in her "Magnificat anima mea."

---

[19] Pius XII, *Ad caeli Reginam*, N.C.W.C. trans., pp. 8-10. Cf. A. Rivera, C.M.F., *De liturgia festi B.M.V. Reginae*, in *Ephemerides Mariologicae*, Vol. 6, 1956, pp. 193-196.

[20] *Ad caeli Reginam*, ed. cit., p. 12.

It was not surprising, therefore, that, due no doubt to ever increasing public devotion, a special feast was instituted, the object of which was to commemorate the Visitation of the Blessed Mother to her cousin Elizabeth.

First records of this feast are to be found, according to Roschini, in the decrees of the Provincial Council of Le Mans (1247).[21] We find it also in the Mozarabic Missal, whereby we conclude that Spain observed this solemnity. Einstein, Archbishop of Prague (1388-1396), had already prescribed that the feast be kept on April 18. Many religious orders, in turn, had accepted it at a very early date: e.g. the Cistercians, Franciscans, Carmelites, Dominicans, and the Servites of Mary. By a decree dated April 6, 1389, Pope Urban VI extended this feast to the universal Church, adding to it a vigil and an octave. But it was only in November of the same year that Boniface IX, his successor, promulgated this document. Practically speaking, however, it was not until the Council of Basel (1441) that the Visitation did become a universal feast.

One might ask why the present feast was set for July 2. Due to the fact that Mary most probably undertook the journey shortly after the Annunciation (March 25), and that she remained with Elizabeth for a period of three months (Lk. 1:56), it seemed quite natural to select the latter part of her stay, eliminating in this way all possible concurrence with Lenten and Holy Week ceremonies.

Pius V, with a view to uniformity no doubt, abolished all the then existing Offices for the Visitation and decreed that the Office of the Nativity be used also, *mutatis mutandis,* for the present feast. Clement VIII, in turn, entrusted to a Father Ruiz of the Order of Minims the task of rewriting a new Office, the text of which may be found in the present Roman Breviary.

8. Our Lady of Mount Carmel
(July 16)

When, in the closing years of the thirteenth century, the recently approved Order of Carmelites began to spread beyond the sea to establish itself in Europe, a remarkable and outstanding love and devotion to Mary permeated the entire religious atmosphere of the community. Proof of this is had in the many devotions found within their convents, and in the rich solemnity given to the then five universal Marian feasts: Purification,

---

[21] Cf. Roschini, *op. cit.,* p. 144.

Annunciation, Assumption, Nativity, and the Immaculate Conception.[22] It seems that out of this deep love and reverence for Mary, and in thanksgiving for numerous favors obtained through her intercession, the *Solemn Commemoration of the Blessed Virgin Mary of Mount Carmel* originated. Its date was set on July 16. Zimmerman[23] maintains that its origin goes back no later than 1387 or thereabouts, but Forcadell refutes his arguments as false and inconclusive.[24] He believes, on the contrary, that it originated at a much earlier date (under the title of a *Solemn Commemoration*), possibly even during the first half of the thirteenth century. Sixtus V gave it official approbation in 1587, and shortly thereafter (1600) it was declared the patronal feast of the entire Carmelite Order. Its solemnity spread rapidly through Europe. Already in 1628 it was observed in the Kingdom of Naples, in parts of Sicily and Spain. In the year 1674 it was granted to the whole of Spain and its territories, and one year later, to Austria and Portugal. The Pontifical States made it their own in 1726, in which year, by decree dated September 24, Benedict XIII proclaimed it a universal feast.

9. Our Lady of the Snow
(August 5)

The object of the present feast is the annual solemnity of the dedication of Mary's greatest monumental tribute, that of the Roman Basilica *Santa Maria Maggiore,* erected on the Esquiline in the early centuries of Christianity. According to the *Liber Pontificalis,*[25] it was Sixtus III (432-440) who ordered its construction as a lasting memory of Mary's ever glorious victory at the Council of Ephesus (431). Its name has varied rather often during its many years of existence: e.g. *The Liberian Basilica* (named after the Pope Liberius who might have first erected it, to be later reconstructed by Sixtus III), *St. Mary of the Crib, St. Mary Mother, St. Mary Major,* which last title is amply justified by the pre-eminence always given to it by the Sovereign Pontiffs. At the close of the ninth century, however, it received, along with the feast of its dedication, a new title: *Our Lady of*

---

[22] Cf. A. Forcadell, O.Carm., *Le scapulaire du Carmel et sa fête liturgique,* in *Marie,* Vol. 6, Nov.-Dec., 1952, p. 22.

[23] B. Zimmerman, *Monumenta historica carmelitana,* Vol. 1 (Lirinae, 1907), pp. 323-363. Cf. Roschini, *La Madonna secondo la fede e la teologia,* Vol. 4 (Roma, 1954), p. 374.

[24] Forcadell, *art. cit.,* p. 24.

[25] *Ed. cit.,* pp. 232, 235.

the Snow, as the result of a fast-spreading story (void of any solid documentary evidence and, therefore, the authenticity of which may be rightfully doubted) concerning the alleged miraculous origin of this Basilica. An account of this story may be found in the Roman Breviary for August 5, of which the following is the general tenor: Under the pontificate of Liberius, John, a Roman patrician, and his wife, having no children to whom they might leave their riches, vowed their whole fortune to the Blessed Virgin Mother of God, asking her most earnestly to indicate to them in what way she desired them to spend the money. The Blessed Virgin answered their prayer by a miracle. On the Nones of August, generally the hottest month in Rome, a portion of the Esquiline hill was covered with snow. That same night Mary appeared to both of them, and told them to build a church on the exact spot covered with snow, and to dedicate this church to the Virgin Mary. John, in turn, told this to the Pope Liberius, who said he had dreamt the same thing. On account, therefore, of the miraculous fall of snow the anniversary of the dedication is celebrated by the feast of Our Lady of the Snow.

It is certain that the annual feast of the dedication was celebrated at a very early date; even as early as 435, according to Nilles.[26] But it was not yet a universal feast during the thirteenth century, since Gregory IX, in the bull of canonization of St. Dominic, whose death occurred on the 6th of August (1221), anticipated his feast on the 5th of the month, as being at that time vacant, whereas the 6th was already taken. During the fourteenth century, the solemnity of the dedication was extended to all of Rome and to some other dioceses. In the middle of the sixteenth century it became a universal feast, the Office of which Pius V promulgated to the entire world. Clement VIII raised it to the rank of double major.[27]

10. The Assumption of Mary
(August 15)

Much has been written on the subject of the feast of Mary's Assumption. There are still some aspects of the problem not totally solved. The following pages aim to present the actual status of the problem along

---

[26] Referred to by Roschini, *op. cit.*, p. 375.

[27] Cf. Holweck, *op. cit.*, p. 258.

with the result of the latest studies on the subject.[28]

In the Orient:
A. *Palestine — especially Jerusalem:*

Up to the closing years of the fourth century, no testimony is available concerning Mary's last days, much less her Assumption. Positive proof is had, on the contrary, in a letter written by St. Epiphanius (377), that no one was aware at the time of what had happened to Mary. In his earlier years, Epiphanius had traveled far and wide throughout the whole of Palestine in search of local traditions concerning the first Christians. His love for Mary was deep and sincere, and he had put himself seriously to work on the study of her death. Yet after his many journeys and studies, he clearly testifies, in the above-mentioned letter, that no one knew exactly how Mary ended her life here below. Did she die? Was she buried? he asks himself; it is impossible to say. A few apocryphal writings, it is true, have been said to date as far back as the second century, but Father Jugie is convinced that none have been found to extend beyond the end of the fifth century or the beginning of the sixth, the oldest of which are not of Palestinian but of Syrian origin.[29] It was alleged also that a certain priest of Jerusalem called Timothy, in a homily composed between 400-450 for the feast of the *Hypapante* (Epiphany), had alluded, *en passant* and as to an audience well aware of what he was saying, to Mary's Assumption. This might have been a priceless document, had it not been established in later years that Timothy was, in truth, a Byzantine of the seventh century. One may even doubt, judging from his four other homilies, whether the passage in question has been correctly interpreted.[30]

---

[28] Cf. A. Amore, O.F.M., *La festa della morte e dell'Assunzione della B. Vergine nella liturgia orientale*, in Atti del Congresso Nazionale Mariano dei Frati Minori d'Italia (Roma, 1948), pp. 197-222; F. Antonelli, O.F.M., *La festa dell'Assunzione nella liturgia romana*, ibid., pp. 225-239; P. Gassó, O.S.B., *La Asunción en la liturgia. Sobre los orígenes de la fiesta*, in Estudios Marianos, Vol. 6, 1947, pp. 137-146; M. Gavriloff, *The Assumption in the Liturgy of the Eastern Church*, in Life of the Spirit, Vol. 5, 1950, pp. 231-238; A. King, *The Assumption of Our Lady in the Oriental Liturgies*, in The Eastern Churches Quarterly, Vol. 8, 1949, pp. 198-205, 225-231; W. O'Shea, S.S., *The History of the Feast of the Assumption*, in The Thomist, Vol. 14, 1951, pp. 118-132; A. Raes, S.J., *Aux origines de la fête de l'Assomption en Orient*, in Orientalia Christiana Periodica, Vol. 12, 1946, pp. 262-274.

[29] Cf. Jugie, *op. cit.*, pp. 103-171.

[30] Cf. Capelle, *Le témoignage de la liturgie [sur l'Assomption]*, in Bulletin de la Société Française d'Études Mariales [1949] (Paris, 1950), p. 36.

As Capelle remarks, this total mystery concerning the miraculous happenings at the end of Mary's life continued till the beginning of the sixth century.[31] It is true that, in the early years of the fifth century, there did exist a feast in honor of the Blessed Mother, celebrated on August 15 in the church named *Kathisma* (meaning "rest") in Jerusalem. But it seems rather evident that this is not the feast of the Assumption or the *Dormition*. First of all, no references to Mary's death or Assumption are found in the liturgical texts of the feast. And more important yet, a sermon delivered on this occasion by a priest named Chrysippus, wherein he presents an exegetical account of these same texts, contains no allusion whatsoever to Mary's death or to her glorious Assumption. Every text, on the contrary, even that of "Surge Domine, in requiem tuam," is interpreted in favor of Mary's divine Maternity.[32] The general pattern takes on a new light if one recalls that it was but a few years earlier (431) that Mary had solemnly been declared, at the Council of Ephesus, the *Theotokos,* or Mother of God. Undoubtedly this feast of August 15 had been instituted, just as the church of *Kathisma* had been constructed, to commemorate this memorable event and to honor Mary as the Mother of God. It may, therefore, be stated safely, with Dom Capelle, that nowhere in Palestine did there exist, prior to the opening years of the sixth century, any indications of a belief in Mary's bodily Assumption into heaven, much less of a feast whose object would have been to commemorate this Assumption.

From then on (500), however, due undoubtedly to the influence of the apocryphal writings, there is an awakened interest in the problem of the end of Mary's life. We are told of a basilica at Gethsemane in Jerusalem dedicated to Mary and wherein, according to the *Breviarium de Ierosolyma,* her tomb is found: "Ibi est basilica sanctae Mariae, et ibi est sepulchrum ejus." Not too many years later (570), another source states that Mary's body had been taken away, although there is no reference made concerning the Assumption: "In ipsa valle est basilica sanctae Mariae, quam dicunt domum ejus fuisse, in qua et de corpore sublatam fuisse."[33] It must be noted that, notwithstanding the fact that much was now being said about Mary's death and the consequent disappearance of her body, not until the first years of the eighth century do we find it

---

[31] *Art. cit.*, p. 42.

[32] Capelle, *art. cit.*, pp. 38-39.

[33] Cf. Capelle, *art. cit.*, p. 39.

explicitly and forcefully stated that she had been assumed into heaven, body and soul. St. Andrew of Crete (660-740), well versed in Jerusalem lore, is credited with this testimony.

But how can we explain that the feast of Mary's *Dormition* is now celebrated on August 15? Capelle, along with Roschini, argues in this fashion: As previously stated, there already existed, in the first half of the fifth century, a feast in honor of Our Lady which was kept on the 15th of August. The object of this solemnity was of a rather general aspect, that of the great Mother of God. In later years, when Mary's tomb supposedly had been found and located in Gethsemane, it was but natural that on this day (August 15) the liturgy in this given church put more, if not all, emphasis on Mary's *Dormition* or Assumption, and thereby give a more specific object to the already existing feast of Mary the Mother of God.[34]

Emperor Maurice (582-602), who had restored the church of Gethsemane, prescribed that the above feast of the *Dormition* of Mary be celebrated throughout the entire Byzantine Empire on August 15.

B. *In Syria:*

Of the many apocryphal works on the *Transitus Mariae* or Mary's *Dormition,* it has been established and recognized, as previously stated, that the oldest of them all (end of the fifth or beginning of the sixth century) originated in Syria. For a complete study of these works, we recommend Father Jugie's excellent treatment as given in his *La mort et l'Assomption de la Sainte Vierge.*[35] Suffice it to note here that, historically speaking, these works have little or no value at all, the greater part of them bearing the marks of a fertile imagination. Nevertheless, to the historian of any given dogma they take on considerable importance, because through them he may acquire some knowledge of the actual belief of the faithful, and of the festivities then observed. It must be remembered, second, that although all apocryphal writers are in unison in asserting that Mary died, opinions differ greatly as to what might have happened to her body. It is false to claim that all took sides for Mary's Assumption as we understand it now.

We find in one of these Syrian apocryphal writings, dating back possibly to the later part of the fifth century, the following: Immediately after Mary's death, the Apostles prescribed that Mary be honored and

---

[34] Roschini, *Mariologia,* Vol. 4, p. 151; Capelle, *art. cit.,* p. 40.
[35] Pp. 103-173.

remembered by three special commemorations to be kept on the following days: (*a*) January 5, under the title of *Our Lady of the Seed;* (*b*) May 15, as *Our Lady of the Sowing;* (*c*) August 13, as *Our Lady of the Ripening*. One may easily conclude from this testimony that, in the closing years of the fifth century, Syria observed a first commemoration or feast of Mary on January 6. It is important to note here, that prior to the setting of Christ's Nativity on December 25, this solemnity was celebrated in Syria on January 6 along with the Epiphany. When, therefore, in later years, the feast of Christ's Nativity was transferred to December 25, along with it came the commemoration of the Mother of Christ. It must be stated further that this first Marian solemnity included a commemoration of her *Dormition*. The *Transitus Mariae,* indeed, explicitly states that Mary died on the very same day on which she had given birth to Christ, but in view of the fact that it was highly incongruous that the faithful celebrate Mary's Dormition on the same day as that of Christ's Nativity, the Apostles had deemed it wise that the solemnity of Mary's death be put off until the following day, namely, December 26. Thus, in Syria, a commemoration or feast of Mary's *Dormition* did exist at an early date (end of the fifth or beginning of the sixth century). It was celebrated, however, not on August 15, but on December 26. Authors do not quite agree on the specific object of this feast. Was it Mary's Assumption in body and soul as we now understand it, or was it the more general object of her *Dormition* with no explicit reference to the subsequent lot of her body? Basing themselves on a poem written by James of Sarug (451-521), Roschini and Faller are of the first opinion, while Jugie and Raes have serious doubts on the matter.[36] The latter fail to see any allusion to Mary's Assumption.

In the West:

The feast of Mary's *Dormition* was not destined to remain exclusively an Oriental solemnity. As in a number of similar cases, the West integrated this feast into its own liturgies. Rome was first to accept it along with the date of August 15. It appears certain that at the time of Saint Gregory's death (609), Rome was without a single feast in honor of the Blessed Mother. A few years later, however, as stated in the *Liber*

---

[36] Cf. Roschini, *Op. cit.,* p. 152; O. Faller, S.J., *De priorum saeculorum silentio circa Assumptionem B. Mariae Virginis* (Romae, 1946), p. 26; Jugie, *op. cit.,* pp. 172-184; Raes, *art. cit.,* p. 272.

Pontificalis,[37] Pope Sergius I (687-701) instituted a solemn procession or Litany, leaving from St. Andrew's and arriving at St. Mary Major's, for the following four feasts of Mary: the Annunciation, the *Dormition,* the Nativity, and the Purification. And since the *Liber Pontificalis* indicates that these four festivities were celebrated in Rome before the election of Sergius I, the present feast was, therefore, introduced in the Holy City between the years 609 and 687. Dom Capelle[38] strikingly brings out that a close and attentive examination of the *Oremus* or Collect of the above mentioned procession, especially if one bears in mind that Sergius I was of a Greek-Syrian origin, will reveal an important fact, namely, that the Pontiff very definitely intended to commemorate Mary's Assumption as we now understand it. Toward the end of the eighth century, the title of the *Dormition* was changed to the more familiar one of the *Assumption* of the Blessed Virgin. Leo IV (847-855) decreed that a vigil and an octave enhance the already widely spreading solemnity.

It was not too many years later that Our Lady's Assumption found its way into England and France under a variety of names, as the *Dormition,* the *Nativity,* the *Depositio,* and also the *Requies.* Until that time, indeed, England had been totally without any strictly Marian feast. But in 747, at a synod of Cloveshoe, it was decreed that the entire Anglo-Saxon Church should adopt and follow the Roman liturgy, and thus was introduced the feast of Mary's Assumption. In France, the newly adopted feast of the *Dormition* replaced the already existing feast of the Blessed Mother, celebrated on January 18. When, shortly after, its name was changed to that of Mary's Assumption, strong opposition was felt. Without explicitly denying the bodily Assumption of Mary, the opponents of this change were emphatic in maintaining that no scriptural text could be found, nor any traces be had in Tradition, substantiating the belief of Our Lady's Assumption in body and soul. The new name remained, however, and in time completely replaced the older but not so specific one of *Dormition.*

11. The Immaculate Heart of Mary
(August 22)

The object of the present feast, as clearly indicated in the title, is to honor Mary's most admirable Heart.

This wholesome devotion, though widely spread at the beginning of

---

[37] *Ed. cit.,* p. 376.
[38] Capelle, *art. cit.,* pp. 49-51.

the seventeenth century, had not as yet taken on the definite aspect of a public veneration. St. John Eudes (1601-1680) effected the transition by his ever memorable book *The Admirable Heart of Mary*. Pius X confirmed this when, in 1909, he referred to St. Eudes as the first Apostle of the liturgical devotion to the Hearts of Jesus and Mary: "Primum apostolum cultus liturgici Cordium Jesu et Mariae."

The liturgical feast of Mary's Immaculate Heart, the Office and Mass of which had been composed by St. John Eudes himself, was celebrated for the first time in 1648. Fourteen years later, twelve bishops had already approved this newly instituted feast. Shortly thereafter, due especially to the approval of the above mentioned Office and Mass by the Cardinal Legate of Clement IX (1668), virtually the whole of France had accepted this solemnity. In 1765, after some years of hesitation concerning the usefulness of the devotion to the Hearts of Jesus and Mary, the Congregation of Sacred Rites granted permission to the Polish hierarchy to celebrate the feast of the Most Sacred Heart of Jesus. This cleared the path for an eventual final approbation of the corresponding feast of the Heart of Mary. Pius VI, on the other hand, refused permission to the Carmelite Sisters of France to observe the feast of the Heart of Mary on the basis that, as yet, it had never received any formal and direct approbation from the Holy See.[39] However, on July 21, 1855, Pius IX gave formal approbation to the feast of the Most Pure Heart of Mary, along with its special Office and Mass. The Pontiff added that permission to celebrate this feast would be granted to all who petitioned it. In 1914, innumerable requests were submitted to the Holy See entreating the Sovereign Pontiff to extend the feast to the universal Church. It was Pius XII, however, who gave it its crowning perfection, when, on May 4, 1944, as a lasting memory of his previous consecration of the Church and the entire world to the Immaculate Heart of Mary (October 31, 1942), he proclaimed that it be universally observed on August 22, that is, the Octave of Mary's Assumption. Its rank is that of double of second class.[40]

---

[39] For a more detailed account of the development of, and opposition to, the feast, cf. G. Geenen, O.P., *Les antécédents doctrinaux et historiques de la consécration du monde au Coeur Immaculé de Marie*, in *Maria. Études sur la Sainte Vierge*, ed. H. du Manoir, Vol. 1 (Paris, 1949), pp. 824-873.

[40] Cf. *A.A.S.*, Vol. 37, 1945, pp. 50-51. For further details, cf. E. Pujolrás, C.M.F., *La festa liturgica del Cuore Immacolato di Maria*, in *Il Cuore Immacolato di Maria* (Roma, 1946), pp. 107-141.

12. The Nativity of Mary
(September 8)

One need not scrutinize the liturgical calendar very closely to note that the determining factor in setting the date of a feast of any given saint is his birth into everlasting life. It is not customary to institute a feast to commemorate the temporal birth of a saint. Three exceptions only are found, and the obvious reason for these exceptions is that all three were born presanctified: Jesus, by reason of the Hypostatic Union; Mary, who by special privilege was preserved from all stain of sin at the very instant of her conception; and St. John the Baptist who was presanctified in the womb of his mother.

The Sacred Scriptures are silent concerning the birth of Mary. In many apocryphal writings, however, dating as far back as the second century (*Protoevangelium of James*) we do find explicit reference to it.

In the Orient:

It seems probable that the feast of the Nativity of Mary stemmed from the long existing feast of the Nativity of Saint John the Baptist, of which St. Augustine writes.[41] However, there is no explicit document testifying to the existence of this feast until the time of Andrew of Crete (660-740). Among his many homilies we find four which undoubtedly were written for the feast of Mary's Nativity. St. John Damascene (who died no later than 754) also composed a homily for this feast. We may, therefore, safely infer that the Nativity of Mary originated no later than the first half of the seventh century. Jugie traces its origin to an even earlier date, i.e., the middle of the sixth century.[42]

In the West:

Few years had elapsed before Rome already had made this feast its own. The *Liber Pontificalis*[43] clearly states that Pope Sergius I (687-701) prescribed a solemn procession, leading to the Basilica of St. Mary Major, to be held on the following feasts of Mary: the Nativity, Annunciation, Dormition, and Purification.

From Rome it gradually found its way into England, France, Germany, and Spain. In his *De partu Virginis,* Paschasius Radbertus († 860) writes

---

[41] St. Augustine, epp. 196, 287; *PL* 38, 1021 and 1301.

[42] *Op. cit.,* p. 174.

[43] *Ed. cit.,* p. 376.

that the Nativity of Mary was being preached throughout the universal Church. It became a holyday of obligation for the West at the time of St. Fulbert, Bishop of Chartres (1007-1020), and no doubt through his strong influence.

In 1241, Innocent IV, in fulfillment of a promise made by him and the other cardinals united in conclave with the purpose of finding a successor to Gregory IX, established that the feast (which at that time was already universally accepted) should have an octave in the whole Church. Gregory XI († 1378) added to it a vigil with fast.

Actually, the feast of the Nativity of Mary is observed, both in the East and in the West, on September 8. But it was not always thus. Its date varied with different countries and dioceses.

To the query as to why and how it was finally set for September 8, Roschini answers thus: The feast of the Nativity preceded that of the Immaculate Conception, but at the time, its date varied greatly. When, however, the feast of the Immaculate Conception became universally accepted, it was but natural to set the Nativity on September 8, that is, nine months later.[44]

13. The Most Holy Name of Mary (September 12)

"The Angel Gabriel was sent from God to a town of Galilee called Nazareth, to a virgin ... and the Virgin's name was Mary" (Lk. 1:27). Next to "Jesus," no other name has won, down through the centuries, such universal recognition and respect. Small wonder, then, that a feast was instituted whose object would be to render public honor to so great a name. Just as the feast of the Holy Name of Jesus immediately follows His Circumcision, so too the feast of the Holy Name of Mary closely follows her Nativity.

Spain was the first country to which permission was granted to celebrate this feast. It was given by Julius II, in 1513, to one particular diocese of that country and celebrated on the octave of the Nativity. Pius V, however, in his reformation of the Divine Office, abolished it. But it was re-established by his immediate successor Sixtus V. In the year 1671 it was extended to the whole of Spain and to the Neapolitan Kingdom. In memory of the world's gratitude to Mary for Sobieski's defeat of the Turkish army at Vienna (September 12, 1683) Innocent XI decreed that the

---

[44] Roschini, *op. cit.*, p. 162.

feast of the Most Holy Name of Mary be extended to the universal Church. Innocent XII prescribed that it be observed on the Sunday within the octave of the Nativity, but Pius X, in his reformation, and in memory of the above mentioned victory, ordered that it be celebrated on September 12.[45]

14. Feast of the Seven Dolors
(September 15)

Throughout the entire liturgical year only two exceptions are found wherein two distinct feasts commemorate the same object: the Compassion, or Seven Dolors (Friday of Passion Week and September 15), and the Chair of St. Peter (January 18 and February 22); although a distinction could be made between the Chair of Peter at Rome and that at Antioch.

It is solely to the Order of the Servites of Mary that we are indebted for this second feast of Mary's Compassion. Its origin can be traced to the fifteenth century. It was customary at the time (within the Order of the Servites itself) for the enrolled members of the Association of the Seven Dolors of Mary to assemble on a Sunday of each month. In later years, greater solemnity was given to one particular gathering held on the third Sunday of September, from which has come the actual feast of the Seven Dolors, whose original date was not, therefore, the 15th, but the third Sunday of the month.

On January 9, 1668, the Holy See authorized the Servites to observe this second commemoration of Mary's Transfixion. In 1734 this privilege was extended to Austria and, the following year, to Spain and her territories. Pius VII, by a decree of September 18, 1814, proclaimed it a universal feast. Its observance was kept on the third Sunday of September until Pius X, in his liturgical reformation, determined that it be celebrated on September 15. By a special indult, however, the Servites have maintained their traditional third Sunday of the month.[46]

15. Our Lady of Mercy
(September 24)

---

[45] Cf. *A.A.S.*, Vol. 3, 1911, p. 644.
[46] Cf. Campana, *op. cit.*, Vol. 1, pp. 319-336.

The Saracens, in the fifth century, became indiscriminate pirates scouring the seas to obtain slaves for the African markets. To offset this threat, a new order came into existence under the title of *The Religious Order of Our Lady of Mercy*, whose primary goal was to guard the coasts and ransom the captives. In order that due thanks be rendered to God and to His Virgin Mother for the many favors and benefits showered upon this newly formed order, its members instituted the present feast of Our Lady of Mercy. In the year 1680 Innocent XI extended it to the whole of Spain, and a few years later, Pope Alexander VIII to all of France. It became a universal feast by a decree of Innocent XII, dated February 22, 1696. It must be noted, however, that not until the seventeenth century was its date set as September 24. Prior to this time its solemnity was observed on the 8th of that month.[47]

16. Our Lady of the Rosary
(October 7)

In its present form the Rosary was made known to the world by the sons of St. Dominic at the outset of the thirteenth century, during the period of struggle with the Albigensians. But even prior to this date, popular devotion was familiar with what was called the *Psalter of the Faithful*, that is, the Angelical salutation repeated one hundred and fifty times. Also of ancient tradition are the Confraternities of the Holy Rosary, dating as far back as the latter part of the fifteenth century, the members of which had set aside the first Sunday of October as their principal feast. The Mass *Salve, radix sancta* and solemn processions, enriched with special indulgences, lent great solemnity to this day.

The historic and memorable happenings of October 7, 1571, the first Sunday of the month, gave rise to the feast of Our Lady of the Rosary. The Western world faced total disaster and ruin from the Turks whose powerful fleet had already mastered the greater part of the Mediterranean and was actually threatening Italy. St. Pius V and other Christian leaders, convinced that only supernatural help could now ward off the oncoming invasion, turned their eyes heavenwards and begged their heavenly Mother to intercede on their behalf. The saintly Pontiff also asked that the Confraternities of the Holy Rosary intensify their devotion on this October 7 and celebrate it with an even greater solemnity. It was on this day, indeed, that the allied Christian naval power encountered the

---

[47] Cf. Benedict XIV, *op. cit.*, ed. Bourassé, Vol. 3, col. 1487.

confident Turkish fleet in the Gulf of Lepanto. It is said that while the all-important battle raged, Pius V, favored with a heavenly vision, exclaimed: "Victoria, Victoria!" The enemy fleet, in truth, suffered a deadly blow which broke the backbone of the Turkish power. It was not the Pope's privilege to celebrate the anniversary of this momentous grace of God. His days had come to an end, but not before his proclamation of March 17, 1572, to the effect that in public thanksgiving to Mary and in deep appreciation for her protection, a special commemoration be given to her on October 7 under the title of *Our Lady of Victory*.

Gregory XIII, his successor, altered this title to *Our Lady of the Rosary*, and on April 1, 1573, decreed that the new feast be kept on the first Sunday of October, authorizing its celebration in those churches which possessed an altar under that invocation. One hundred years later, at the request of Mary Anne, Queen of Spain, this feast was extended to all of Spain, and shortly after, to numerous dioceses of Italy and other countries. On October 3, 1716, as a public acknowledgment for the victory gained by Prince Eugene of Savoy over the Turks in Hungary on August 5 under the protection of Our Lady of the Snow, Clement XI promulgated a document, prepared by his predecessor Innocent XI, extending the feast of Our Lady of the Rosary to the universal Church. Leo XIII elevated the feast to the rank of double of the second class. Finally, Pius X, in his *Motu proprio* of October 23, 1913, assigned the feast to October 7.[48]

17. Mary's Divine Maternity (October 11)

Convened at Ephesus for the third Ecumenical Council (431), the Fathers solemnly defined Mary to be the *Theotokos*, that is, Mother of God. Even today, this is still her greatest title and one which proclaims that she, more than all other creatures put together, was the recipient of a unique dignity and the object of a very special predilection of God. The object of this feast, therefore, ranks first in importance among the many other Marian prerogatives. Moreover, the liturgical feast itself comes first in the order of time.[49] Its solemnity dates back to the end of the fourth century, or the beginning of the fifth. Later on (end of the fifth century) its object evolved considerably and it finally became the commemoration of Mary's

---

[48] Cf. Campana, *op. cit.*, Vol. 1, pp. 407-413.

[49] Cf. Jugie, La *première fête mariale en Orient*, in *Echos d'Orient*, Vol. 21, 1923, pp. 129-152.

Dormition. Thus, for many centuries to come, the Church was left without a feast whose explicit object was Mary's Divine Maternity. We say "explicit" because it can be safely stated that all feasts of Mary at least implicitly refer to her as the great Mother of God.

In 1751, Benedict XIV, in answer to the prayers of King Joseph Emmanuel of Portugal and of his people, granted permission to commemorate Mary's Divine Maternity by a special feast (composed by the Pontiff himself), to be kept on the first Sunday of May. From that time on, it gradually penetrated into other countries until in 1931, Pius XI, wishing to perpetuate the memory of the fifteenth centenary of the Council of Ephesus, decreed that the feast be celebrated the world over. Its rank was elevated to that of double of the second class.[50]

18. The Presentation of the Blessed Virgin (November 21)

The object of this feast is not to be found in any of the Biblical writings. On the other hand, the apocryphal *Protoevangelium of James* (second century) is the first to mention Mary's presentation in the Temple. Though at that early date there is yet no indication of a liturgical feast, it is evident from the *Protoevangelium* that already in the early years of Christianity the faithful were conscious of the deep mystery that surrounded Mary's self-offering and dedication to the service of her God.

In the East:

According to Dom Capelle,[51] the present feast of the Presentation of the Blessed Virgin was celebrated in Jerusalem in the sixth century. Its origin most probably coincides with the Dedication of the Church of the Blessed Mary (543), built, by order of Emperor Justinian, upon the ruins of the Temple. Frequently, indeed, did the dedication of a church give rise to a new feast commemorating a given mystery. In 1143, Emperor Emmanuel determined that this feast should rank among the holydays of obligation. It should be added also that in the East the feast of the Presentation of Mary has constantly been celebrated with much greater

---

[50] Cf. Pius XI, enc. *Lux veritatis,* in *A.A.S.,* Vol. 23, 1931, esp. p. 517. Cf. also N. Pérez, S.J., *Historia de la fiesta liturgica de la divina Maternidad,* in *Estudios Marianos,* Vol. 8, 1949, pp. 392-395.

[51] Capelle, *La liturgie mariale en Occident,* in *Maria. Études sur la Sainte Vierge,* ed. H. du Manior, Vol. 1 (Paris, 1949), p. 233.

solemnity than in the West. As just stated, it became a holyday at an early date, and even now it is considered one of the twelve major feasts of the year.[52]

In the West:
It was only centuries later that the feast of the Presentation at long last found its way into the Western liturgy. Roschini claims that already in the ninth century it was observed in a certain Greek monastery of Southern Italy, whence it passed into England.[53] In 1372 Gregory XI, through the intercession of Philip of Mazières just returned from the East, permitted that it be celebrated for the first time by the Roman court at Avignon. Shortly thereafter (1373), Charles V of France introduced it into the chapel of his palace, and in the following year, in a letter to the masters and students of the college of Navarre, dated November 10, he expressed the desire that it be kept throughout his kingdom. The new feast gradually became general. But Pius V, in the hope of reducing the number of universal feasts, later abolished it. In 1585, however, Sixtus V re-established it in the Roman Breviary. Clement VIII elevated its rank to that of double major.[54]

II. FEASTS CELEBRATED IN SOME DIOCESES OR RELIGIOUS ORDERS

1. Our Lady of Loreto

The object of this feast is to commemorate the miraculous transfer of the Holy House at Loreto. It was first celebrated, by special indult of the Sacred Congregation of Rites dated November 29, 1632, in the Province of Piceno. Already in 1729, the entire Venetian Republic and all its territories observed this solemnity. It is kept on December 10.

2. The Expectation of the Blessed Virgin Mother

---

[52] Cf. S. Salaville, A.A., *Marie dans la liturgie byzantine ou gréco-slave*, in *Maria. Études sur la Sainte Vierge*, ed. H. du Manoir, Vol. 1 (Paris, 1949), p. 252.

[53] Roschini, *op. cit.*, p. 167.

[54] Cf. E. Bouvy, *Les origines de la fête de la Présentation*, in *Revue Augustinienne*, Vol. 1, 1902, pp. 581-594; Sr. M. J. Kishpaugh, O.P., *The Feast of the Presentation of the Virgin Mary in the Temple. An Historical and Literary Study* (Washington, D. C., 1941); G. S. Sloyan, *The Presentation of Our Lady*, in *The American Ecclesiastical Review*, Vol. 129, Nov., 1953, pp. 314-316.

Concerning the origin of the present feast, we refer the reader to what has been written on the feast of the Annunciation, in its development in Spain. Though not a universal feast, its observance had already spread far and wide by the end of the eighteenth century. It is celebrated on December 18.

3. The Espousals of Our Lady

The historical development of this feast has been a rather turbulent one. It was originally instituted in France in the early fourteenth century, but, surprisingly, as a feast of St. Joseph. Shortly after, however, through strong influence exerted by the Friars Minor, it evolved into a specific Marian feast. Paul III, in 1537, granted permission to the entire Order to observe this feast on March 7. In the following years, a middle note was struck, wherein both Mary and Joseph were honored. After the death of Paul IV, who had had the thought of suppressing it entirely, it quickly spread throughout France, Holland, and Moravia. It was extended to the whole of Austria in 1678, and two years later, to Spain and the Holy Roman Empire. Even far off Palestine received it in 1689. This solemnity is kept on January 23.

4. Our Lady of Good Counsel

Benedict XIII first instituted this feast in 1727. A few years later (1789), Pius VI authorized the Augustinian Fathers to celebrate it on April 26. As of now, practically speaking, it is a universal feast within the Latin Church.

5. Mary, Help of Christians

It was Pius VII who instituted the present feast in 1815, in thanksgiving to God for his liberation from captivity under Napoleon. It is kept on May 24, and was first observed within the Pontifical States.[55]

6. Mary, Queen of Apostles

This solemnity, a special Office of which was granted to the Fathers of the Society of the Catholic Apostolate and to the Pious Society of St.

---

[55] Cf. L. Càstano, S.D.B., *Il culto liturgico del titolo Auxilium Christianorum*, in *L'Ausiliatrice nel domma e nel culto* (Torino, 1950), pp. 91-107.

Feasts in Honor of Our Lady

Paul, is observed on the Saturday within the octave of the Ascension. Pius XI enriched the invocation *Regina Apostolorum, ora pro nobis* with an indulgence of 300 days.

7. The Humility of the Blessed Virgin Mary

This feast was first celebrated in the diocese of Salford, England. It is kept on July 17.

8. Mary Mediatrix of All Graces[56]

Benedict XV, due mostly to the influence of Cardinal Mercier, Archbishop of Malines, instituted this solemnity on January 12, 1921. It was granted at the same time to all the dioceses of Belgium and was to be celebrated on May 31. It is now observed by several religious orders and by numerous dioceses throughout the world.[57]

9. Mary, Mother of Grace

The present solemnity was first celebrated in Faenza, Italy, in the hope of checking an oncoming epidemic. It is kept on June 9.

10. Our Lady of Perpetual Help

Pius IX instituted this feast in 1876. It is generally kept on June 27, with the exception of Rome where it is observed on April 26.

11. Mary, Mother of Mercy

The present feast (kept on the Saturday prior to the second Sunday of July) is observed with much solemnity at the Shrine of Mother of Mercy in Savona. It was first celebrated in the diocese of Cremona in 1516.

12. Mary, the Refuge of Sinners

---

[56] Cf. J. Lebon, *A propos des textes liturgiques de la fête de Marie Médiatrice*, in *Marianum*, Vol. 14, 1952, pp. 122-128. See also additional and interesting observations on the same subject in G. Geenen's article *Monseigneur J. Lebon (1879-1957)*, in *Marianum*, Vol. 20, 1958, pp. 120-126.

[57] When Pius XII ordered the new feast of Mary's Queenship to be celebrated on May 31, some religious orders dropped the feast of Mary's Mediation; others have transferred it to a different day. The Franciscans now observe it on May 23.

This feast has been celebrated in Speyer ever since the year 1884. It is kept on August 13.

13. Our Lady of Consolation

Gregory XVI instituted this solemnity in 1838. It was granted, along with a new Mass and Office, to the Augustinian Fathers.

14. Our Lady of the Miraculous Medal

Pope Leo XIII instituted this feast in 1894. It is celebrated on the anniversary of the second apparition of the Blessed Virgin to St. Catherine Labouré, that is, on November 27.

15. Our Lady of Purity

Instituted in the year 1751, this feast is celebrated on October 16 by the Theatine Fathers, and also in Brazil, Portugal, and Algeria.

MARY'S DAY AND MARY'S MONTHS

By FRANCIS D. COSTA, S.S.S.

HILE Catholics everywhere faithfully follow the traditional custom of dedicating certain days and months of the year to Our Blessed Lady, relatively few are familiar with the centuries-old process of development which culminated in the well-established forms of devotion which we practice today in this connection. The purpose of this chapter is to supply this information in a condensed fashion by briefly tracing the origin and gradual evolution of these devout practices according to available data. We shall treat separately the following subjects: (I) Saturday, Mary's day; (II) the devotion of the First Saturdays; (III) the month of May; and (IV) the month of October.

I. SATURDAY, MARY'S DAY[1]

The practice of setting aside the last day of the week for special liturgical observance is almost as ancient as the human race. We gather from the pages of the Old Testament that the Jews and the Babylonians were wont to keep Saturday as the happy anniversary of the day on which God completed the creation of the world. During the early centuries of the

---

[1] On the dedication of Saturday to Our Blessed Lady, see the following: Abbé Baudhuin, *Les fêtes de la Sainte Vierge, les jours et les mois qui lui sont consacrés*, in *Les Fêtes Mariales et le Congrès Marial de Namur, 1904* (Namur, 1905), pp. 92-105; J. J. Bourassé, *Conciliorum decreta mariana*, in *Summa Aurea de laudibus B. V. Mariae*, ed. J. J. Bourassé, Vol. 7 (Parisiis, 1862), col. 740; E. Campana, *Maria nel culto cattolico*, Vol. 1 (Torino-Roma, 1933), pp. 439-464; G. Colvenerius, *Kalendarium Marianum*, in *Summa Aurea de laudibus B. V. Mariae*, ed. cit., Vol. 3, coll. 638-651; [J. M. Keane, O.S.M.], *Saturday Is Our Lady's Day*, in *The Age of Mary*, Vol. 3, June-July, 1956, pp. 37-41; H. J. M. Polman, S.M.M., *Zaterdag-Mariadag*, in *De Standaard van Maria*, Vol. 25, 1949, pp. 48-51, 95-102, 184-187, 240-247; G. M. Roschini, O.S.M., *La Madonna secondo la fede e la teologia*, Vol. 4 (Roma, 1954), pp. 337-341; J. C. Trombelli, *De cultu publico ab Ecclesia Beatae Mariae exhibito ...* , in *Summa Aurea de laudibus B. V. Mariae*, ed. cit., Vol. 4, coll. 367-402; A. Wichmans, O.Praem., *Sabbatismus Marianus ...* , [Antverpiae, 1628], in *Bibliotheca Virginalis ...* , ed. P. Alva et Astorga, O.F.M., Vol. 3 (Matriti, 1648), pp. 381-445; G. M. Zinkl, O.S.M., *Die goldenen Samstage*, in *Theologisch-praktische Quartalschrift*, Vol. 63, 1910, pp. 754-770; L. Gougaud, O.S.B., *Pourquoi le samedi a-t-il eté consacré à la Sainte Vierge?* in *Dévotions et pratiques ascétiques du Moyen Age* (Paris, 1925), pp. 64-73.

Christian era, the followers of the Gnostic Marcion observed a strict fast on Saturday in order to manifest their sadness over the creation of matter, which they held intrinsically evil. The vigorous reaction of Eastern Christians to this blasphemous practice went so far as to consider it a sin to fast on Saturday.[2] In the West, however, where the Gnostic heresy exerted but little influence, the early Christians did not react in the same way; they continued to observe Saturday (along with Friday) as a day of weekly abstinence and prayer in commemoration of Our Lord's stay in the sepulcher, and to imitate the fast of the Apostles sorrowing after the death of their Master. That this was the principal reason for the practice, especially in Rome, is evident from a letter of Pope Innocent I (409-417) to Decentius, Bishop of Gubbio,[3] notwithstanding the contrary testimony of St. Augustine and St. Cassian.[4] At any rate, this practice, which did not become universal until several centuries after Innocent I, retained its original purpose up to the tenth century, when it was transformed into a Marian observance.

Many reasons have been advanced to explain this transition, such as, for example, extraordinary favors received through Mary's intercession on Saturday.[5] But they are mere conjectures. It seems more likely that the choice of Saturday as a day of special veneration to Our Lady was made at this time (tenth century) in order to commemorate her extreme desolation on the day following her Son's burial. If, as Innocent I claimed, the Saturday observance in his time was meant to commemorate the sorrow of the Apostles on that day, is it not natural to suppose that Christian piety would gradually lay more and more stress on the incomparable sorrows of the Queen of Martyrs until finally this latter aspect replaced the former?

Be that as it may, the fact is that as early as the beginning of the eleventh century St. Peter Damian († 1072) mentions the custom of celebrating a Mass in honor of the Blessed Virgin every Saturday, except on feast days and during Lent.[6] His contemporary, Bernold of Constance, testifies to the same thing, noting that the practice was introduced, not at

---

[2] Cf. Campana, *op. cit.*, Vol. 1, p. 440.

[3] Innocent I, *Ep. ad Decentium*, in PL 20, 555.

[4] St. Augustine, *Ep. ad Casulanum*, in PL 33, 136; Cassian, De institutis coenobiorum et de octo principalium vitiorum remediis, lib. 3, cap. 10, in PL 49, 147-149.

[5] Cf. Wichmans, *op. cit.*, pp. 394-396; also Keane, *art. cit.*, 37-41.

[6] St. Peter Damian, *Opusc.* 33, *de bono suffragiorum*, in PL 145, 566.

the command of ecclesiastical authority, but rather to satisfy the devotion of the faithful.[7] Similarly, in a Sacramentary of the same period, preserved in the library of the metropolitan church of Cologne, we find two Masses in honor of Our Lady to be celebrated on Saturday.

At about this time, too, the Little Office of the Blessed Virgin came to be recited on Saturday. It seems that the Benedictine monks of Monte Cassino and Cluny were among the first to adopt this method of sanctifying Our Lady's day.[8] In 1095, at the Council of Clermont, Pope Urban II (1088-1099) ordered, or at least recommended, this Marian devotion to insure the success of the First Crusade.[9]

From the Benedictines the practice soon spread to other religious orders whose members were also eager to signify their tender devotion to Mary by means of a special observance on the day dedicated to her. And so we find, for example, that as early as 1269, at the fourth general chapter of the Franciscans held in Assisi, St. Bonaventure himself, the general of the Order, directed that a special Mass in honor of the Blessed Virgin be sung in each convent every Saturday.[10]

It is interesting to note in this connection that the old English custom of stopping all servile work at noon on Saturdays was introduced by order of King William I of Scotland in order to show his love for the Church and for the Blessed Virgin.[11] Belief in the "sabbatine privilege" of the brown scapular preached by the Carmelites from the fifteenth century also helped to make more general the custom of consecrating Saturday to the praise and veneration of Our Lady.

By the middle of the sixteenth century the Saturday Mass and Office in Mary's honor were so widely accepted and fervently kept that St. Pius V (1566-1572), while radically reforming the Roman liturgy, left this usage intact. Something similar was done on behalf of the Ambrosian rite by St.

---

[7] Bernold of Constance, *Micrologus*, in *PL* **151, 1029**. Cf. Trombelli, *op. cit.*, coll. 367-368; Colvenerius, *op. cit.*, col. 646.

[8] Cf. S. Beissel, S.J., *Geschichte der Verehrung Marias in Deutschland während des Mittelalters* (Freiburg i.B., 1909), p. 310.

[9] Cf. Campana, *op. cit.*, Vol. 1, p. 454. Roschini, *op. cit.*, Vol. 4, p. 339, notes that the decree is not found in the acts of the council probably because it was not a command but a suggestion.

[10] Cf. *Definitiones generalis capituli 1269*, in *Archivum Franciscanum Historicum*, Vol. 5, 1912, p. 708.

[11] Cf. C. R. Montalembert, *Histoire de Sainte Elisabeth de Hongrie* (Paris, 1861), p. 43; Roschini, *op. cit.*, Vol. 4, p. 339.

Charles Borromeo as Cardinal Archbishop of Milan.[12]

At this juncture mention should also be made of the *Fifteen Saturdays*, a devout practice introduced by the Dominicans in the course of the seventeenth century which became quite popular especially in France, Italy, and Belgium. It consisted primarily in offering various acts of devotion and mortification to Our Lady on the fifteen consecutive Saturdays preceding the feast of the Holy Rosary. The practice was enriched with many indulgences by Pope Alexander VIII (1689-1691), Pius IX (1846-1878), and particularly by Leo XIII (1878-1903) in his decree of September 21, 1889.[13] The required conditions for gaining the indulgences are as follows: confession within the week; Holy Communion on each Saturday (or, if impossible, on the following Sunday); the recitation of five decades of the rosary.

II. THE FIRST SATURDAYS DEVOTION

Another devout practice which deserves mention in this context is the one relative to the *First Saturday* of each month. Its first seeds were sown, it would seem, by St. John Eudes († 1680), apostle of the devotion to the Sacred Hearts of Jesus and Mary, and by Ven. John J. Olier († 1657), founder of the Sulpician Fathers. The specific purpose of this devotion, at least from the eighteenth century on, was to set aside the first Saturday of each month as a day of reparation to Our Blessed Lady for all the blasphemies of which she is the object. The act of reparation so widely used in this connection was composed by the great Marian apostle, Joseph de Galiffet, S.J. († 1749).

In more recent times the chief organizer and promoter of this devotion was undoubtedly the Servant of God, Sister Dolores Inglese († 1928), of the Congregation of Servants of Mary Reparatrix, founded in Adria, Italy. It was she who, in February of 1889, having obtained ecclesiastical approval, inaugurated the beautiful practice known as the Saturday "Communion of Reparation." This devotion, which was soon taken up by over seven hundred groups of Children of Mary, thus spreading through Italy and other countries, has been lavishly indulgenced by the popes. On June 13, 1912, St. Pius X (1903-1914) decreed that all the faithful could gain a plenary indulgence, applicable to the souls in Purgatory, on the first

---

[12] Cf. *Acta Ecclesiae Mediolanensis*, Vol. 1 (1599), pp. 9 and 422; Campana, *op. cit.*, Vol. 1, pp. 458-459.

[13] Cf. F. Beringer, *Die Ablässe. Ihr Wesen und Gebrauch*, Vol. 1 (Paderborn, 1915), p. 272.

Saturday of each month, provided they went to confession, received Holy Communion, and performed some act of reparation in honor of Our Blessed Lady. Again, on November 9, 1920, Pope Benedict XV (1914-1922) granted a plenary indulgence, obtainable at the moment of death, to those making these acts of reparation on eight successive first Saturdays.[14]

Among the events which may be credited for giving the greatest impetus to the growth and popularity of the practice, the apparitions of Fatima in 1917 are second to none. In answer to Our Lady's explicit plea, addressed to the world through the three Portuguese children, countless Catholics are observing the first Saturday of every month as a day of reparation for the many insults hurled at the Mother of God. Moreover, Our Lady has promised to show herself a true mother at the hour of death, and to obtain all the graces needed for salvation, on behalf of those who keep the *five consecutive first Saturdays* in reparation to her Immaculate Heart. This devotion consists of the following: reception of Holy Communion (with confession made sometime during the eight days before or after the first Saturday); recitation of five decades of the rosary; and a fifteen minute meditation on one or more of the mysteries of the rosary.

III. THE MONTH OF MAY

Not content with consecrating one day of the week to Our Lady, Catholics dedicate a whole month to her honor.[15] The thirty-one days of May are looked upon popularly as one long Marian feast. In the temperate zone of the northern hemisphere May is a month especially fit to be set aside in Our Lady's praise. The flowers of Maytime are reminders of the spiritual beauty of the Mother of God.

As in other manifestations of devotion, the East preceded the Western Church in the choice of a month of Mary. The Copts, for example, set aside December, a mild month in the Nile climate, as the month of Our Lady. And they observe this month liturgically. Each evening the faithful

---

[14] Cf. Roschini, *op. cit.,* Vol. *4,* pp. 342-343; Canon Bourchat, *Les premiers samedis du mois* (Namur, 1943); J. Henry, *La dévotion du premier samedi du mois,* in *Le Messager de la Très-Sainte Vierge,* Vol. 41, 1947, pp. 13-15, 25-27.

[15] On the month of May, see Roschini, *op. cit.,* Vol. 4 (Roma, 1954), pp. 345-352; Campana, *op. cit.,* 2nd ed., Vol. 1 (Torino-Roma, 1946), pp. 404-446; F. G. Holweck, *Months, Special Devotions for,* in *Catholic Encyclopedia,* Vol. 10, pp. 542-543; D. Attwater, *Month of Mary,* in *A Dictionary of Mary* (New York, 1955), pp. 191-192.

gather to chant the office, and on Saturday the celebration is still more solemn. Some authorities claim the custom goes back to the time of St. Cyril of Alexandria, defender of the divine maternity against Nestorius. The Byzantine Greeks also keep a Marian month, in August, with a fifteen-day preparation for the feast of the Assumption and a fifteen-day celebration after it.[16]

In the West the choice of May as Mary's month seems to have been a counter measure to the vices that flared up particularly at this time of year. Certain pagan festivals for May encouraged immorality. Lactantius reports that public acts of indecency were the order of the day during the Roman rites, the *ludi florales,* in honor of the goddess Flora at the end of April and the beginning of May. This annual observance was hundreds of years old when Christianity appeared, and although it was officially abolished, the habits of human beings changed more slowly. During the Middle Ages the problem became so acute that religious authorities felt obliged to take action. St. Charles Borromeo as late as 1579 ordered devotions to Mary during May in his cathedral city of Milan as an antidote to the orgies of May 1. Thus the natural exuberance of man was wisely directed toward the Blessed Virgin, to the singing of her praises and the contemplation of her spiritual beauty.

The first to associate Mary and May appears to have been King Alphonsus X of Spain († 1284). In one of his poems he sings of May, the month of Mary, describing how the people gather round her altar to sing her glories and pray for protection from all harm. This would point to some public celebration of May as Mary's month.

In the fourteenth century, Blessed Henry Suso, O.P., of Germany adopted the practice of honoring Mary in a special way during springtime. He would gather flowers, weave them into a crown, and then place it on the statue at Our Lady's altar. On one occasion he was privileged to hear angel choirs joining him in singing Mary's praises, and another time he heard them singing the Magnificat.

In 1549 Wolfgang Seidl, O.S.B., published at Munich a small book, *The Spiritual May,* in order to counteract the profanations so common in that month. St. Philip Neri († 1595), sometimes credited with founding May devotions in Italy, used to urge the youth of Rome to pay special homage

---

[16] Cf. Roschini, *op. cit.,* pp. 351-352; S. Salaville, *Marie dans la liturgie Byzantine ou Gréco-Slave,* in *Maria, Études sur la Sainte Vierge,* ed. H. du Manoir, S.J., Vol. 1 (Paris, 1949), pp. 285-288.

MARY'S DAY AND MARY'S MONTHS

to Mary in this month. Another instance was the devotion of a monastery of Dominican novices at Fiesole. In 1676, under the guidance of Father Angelo Giunigi, they formed an association to honor Mary during May. In 1692 the German Capuchin Lawrence von Schnueffis published a book of Marian hymns that may owe their origin to May devotions.

The stage of "codification" was reached when the first handbooks were published. In 1725, A. Dionisi, S.J., published at Verona a small book, *The Month of Mary, or the Month of May*. It was an immediate success, reaching eighteen editions in a hundred years. The tone of the book was moral; there were chapters on decorating Mary's altar or statue, the practice of the daily rosary or the singing of her litany, the suggestion of a special virtue to be practiced daily, and subjects of meditation on Our Blessed Mother for each day.

In 1758, F. Lalomia, S.J., published *The Month of Mary*, in which he narrated the life of Our Lady and explained her virtues and privileges. It was translated into French and German and quickly went through sixty printings, setting the standard for many other such manuals.

In the early eighteenth century the month of May began to pass from private celebrations in the family or religious houses to public churches. In 1739 it was celebrated in the parish church at Grezzana near Verona, in 1774 at St. Andrew's in Verona, and soon spread to almost every parish church in the area so that the Jansenists forced the bishop to interpose and put a stop to the movement. But it had caught on at nearby Ferrara and thence spread through all Italy. The great apostle of the period was Alphonsus Muzzarelli, S.J., a native of Ferrara, who published an extremely popular *The Month of May* in 1785. The 1787 reprinting was prefaced by an open letter to all the bishops of Italy, urging the adoption of May devotions. In the nineteenth century the book was reprinted over a hundred times in Italy, and there were editions in other languages as well. Muzzarelli was called to Rome by Pope Pius VI, and under Pius VII established the devotion at the Gesù and in many other Roman churches.

By the middle of the nineteenth century the month of May was celebrated all through Europe, the United States, and even the missions of China. Great leaders in the Church were strong advocates of it — Cardinal V. Deschamps, C.Ss.R., of Belgium, Bishop Gasser of Austria, and Cardinal Reisach of Germany. St. Anthony Claret preached it in Spain and Cuba. The Irish-born American bishops, the brothers Kenrick, and many others spread it. Popes Pius VII and Pius IX indulgenced the May devotion. It spread through Ireland from Waterford where it was introduced about 1818. Father Aloysius Gentili, I.C., brought the custom to England about 1840. Cardinal Newman and G. M. Hopkins are among English Catholic literary figures who take up the May devotions in their writings.[17]

Recent popes have favored May devotions and spoken of this form of Marian piety with praise. During each year of World War II, 1939 through 1945, the late Pope Pius XII addressed a whole series of documents urging prayers for peace during Our Lady's month of May.[18] Full of doctrinal content as well as of deep devotion to Mary, these appeals are directed particularly to children and Christian families. The encyclical, *Auspicia quaedam*, of May 1, 1948, urged consecration to the Immaculate Heart of Mary. And in one of the last Marian acts of his pontificate Pius XII instituted the new feast of the Queenship of Our Lady for May 31.

A discourse of Pope Pius XII to the international convention of rose growers delicately plays on the theme of dedicating the natural beauty of May to Mary's honor: "Gentlemen, We like to think that you find encouragement in your work from the mere thought that the month of roses is and will always be the month of Mary. Thus, while cultivating the flowers that are the adornment of the soil, so often unprofitable and difficult for men, you are naturally led to honor the Creator, to lift your hearts toward her who bears the beautiful title of Mystical Rose, the honor and the joy of the human family."[19] The strongest of all papal references to the month of May is in Pius XII's encyclical on the Christian liturgy, *Mediator Dei:* "There are certain other pious practices which, though not belonging strictly to the liturgy, nevertheless enjoy a special importance and dignity, such that they are regarded as raised to liturgical rank, and have received repeated approval from this Apostolic See and the Episcopate. Among these are special devotions to the Virgin Mother of God during the month of May, and to the Sacred Heart of Jesus during the

---

[17] J. H. Newman, *Meditations and Devotions. Part I. The Month of May* (London and New York, 1920). Gerald Manley Hopkins wrote a poem, The May Magnificat.

[18] The first four of these letters are to be found in English in the compilation, *Papal Documents on Mary*, by W. J. Doheny, C.S.C., and J. P. Kelly (Milwaukee, 1954), pp. 188-201: *Quandoquidem in gubernanda*, April 20, 1939; *Superiore anno*, April 15, 1940; *Quamvis plane*, April 20, 1941; *Dum saeculum*, April 15, 1942.

[19] *Le concours international*, May, 10, 1955, in *A.A.S.*, Vol. 47, 1955, pp. 495-496; English in *The Pope Speaks*, Vol. 2, 1955, pp. 134-135.

month of June. ..."[20]

IV. OCTOBER, MONTH OF THE ROSARY

Leo XIII, pope of the rosary, regarded himself as particularly responsible for dedicating October to Our Lady. In one of many mentions of this fact, he wrote: "To this heavenly mother we have offered the flowers of the month of May; to her we would also have fruit-bearing October dedicated with a particularly tender devotion. It is fitting that both parts of the year should be consecrated to her who said of herself: 'My flowers are the fruit of honor and riches.' "[21]

The remote antecedents of the dedication of October to Our Lady were the Dominican October rosary devotions in commemoration of the victory of Lepanto, October, 1572, and the institution of the feast of the holy rosary by Gregory XIII in 1573. This was a centuries-old usage when Joseph Morán, a Spanish Dominican, obtained from Pope Pius IX in 1868 indulgences for all who would attend such October observances.[22]

In 1883 by his encyclical *Supremi apostolatus* Pope Leo XIII extended the month of October to all parish churches, confirming this obligation the following year in *Superiore anno*.[23] Decrees of the Sacred Congregations, of Indulgences and of Rites, in 1885 fixed precise norms for gaining indulgences by attending October devotions.[24] With the signing of the Lateran Pact in 1929 the strict obligation of such parochial observance of October ceased, notes Adazzi, because peace between the Vatican and the Italian State was the particular reason why Pope Leo had commanded the October devotions. Nonetheless, the custom of the October prayers remains, warmly recommended of course by Rome, and the indulgences

---

[20] *Mediator Dei*, November 20, 1947, in *A.A.S.*, Vol. 39, 1947, pp. 521-595. See J. Hofinger, S.J., *Mary in Popular Devotions*, in *Mary in the Liturgy. National Liturgical Week*, 1954 (Elsberry, Missouri, 1955), pp. 142-143, for a discussion on conducting May devotions in the spirit of Eastertide, as Hofinger suggests has been done by J. A. Jungmann in Die Frohbotschaft unseres Verkündigung.

[21] *Augustissimae Virginis*, September 12, 1897, in *Leonis XIII Pontificis Maximi Acta* (abbreviated: AL), Vol. 17, pp. 285-295.

[22] Reginaldo G. M. Adazzi, O.P., *Il Rosario nei documenti ufficiali della chiesa*, in *Alma Socia Christi*, Vol. 9 (Romae, 1953), pp. 198-201.

[23] *Supremi apostolatus*, September 1, 1883, in *AL*, Vol. 3, pp. 280-289; *Superiore anno*, August 30, 1884, in *AL*, Vol. 4, pp. 123-127.

[24] Cf. Adazzi, *art. cit.*, p. 201; also Campana, *op. cit.*, pp. 450-451.

are fully valid.[25]

Evidence of Pope Leo XIII's pastoral anxiety that all say the rosary is provided by his permission to farm workers, so often busy through the harvest month of October, to have these indulgenced devotions in November or December at the discretion of the local bishop.[26] *Iucunda semper,* September 8, 1894, one of the more important of Pope Leo's many rosary messages, refers in its opening words to the pope's joy at seeing the month of the rosary approaching once again: "It is always with joyful expectation and renewed hope that we look forward to the return of the month of October. At Our exhortation and by Our express order, this month has been consecrated to the Blessed Virgin. ..."[27] Pope Pius XII spoke of October in almost identical language in his *Ingruentium malorum,* September 15, 1951.[28] Pius XI's rosary encyclical, *Ingravescentibus malis* (The ever worsening evils), September 29, 1937, whose title so well describes the gathering storm of World War II, was also issued in preparation for October.[29]

Pope John XXIII's first Marian encyclical in its opening words, *Grata recordatio* (Grateful memory), refers explicitly to the series of rosary letters of Leo XIII. Pope John also recalls Pius XII's encyclical urging the keeping of the month of the holy rosary.[30] And again like his predecessors, Pope John sees in the rosary not merely a great help to individuals and to families, but a social remedy. Among the intentions of the October prayers the pope includes: "that the men responsible for the destinies of communities great and small, whose rights and whose immense spiritual wealth must be preserved intact, may be aware of the grave task that awaits them in this hour."

With the emphasis on the rosary since Lourdes and Pope Leo XIII the month of October has had a greater development than the month of May. Yet in May as well as in October recent pontiffs have turned to the contemporary needs of the Church and of society in suggesting intentions for the prayers to Our Lady in these months. Pope Pius XII used the occasion of May devotions to Mary to urge prayers to the Queen of peace,

---

[25] Adazzi, loc. cit.

[26] *This permission is found in Superiore anno.*

[27] Cf. *AL,* Vol. 14, pp. 305-316.

[28] In *A.A.S.,* Vol. 43, 1951, pp. 577-582.

[29] In *A.A.S.,* Vol. 29, 1937, pp. 373-380.

[30] *Grata recordatio,* September 26, 1959, in *L'Osservatore Romano,* September 30, 1959.

Mary's Day and Mary's Months

particularly through the war years. Pope Leo XIII's rosary documents are an extended commentary on the spiritual needs of those years, and Popes Pius XI, Pius XII, and John XXIII have advocated the October rosary in the same sense.

Marian Prayers

By REV. GERARD S. SLOYAN, PH.D.

GYPTIAN *ostraka* of uncertain date (later than A.D. 325 and probably sixth century) contain liturgical prayers which refer to the mystery of Christ's birth from the Virgin Mother Mary. Thus a Christmas hymn speaks of Christ, begotten by an "unfathomable" Father before the ages, as one whom we now adore, "become incarnate in a Virgin's womb ... O holy God, you have deigned to be born a tiny child of a virgin. O holy, strong God, you have willed to rest in Mary's arms."[1] The third member of the invocation refers to Christ as "holy and deathless" (*hagios athanatos*), a phrase familiar to the Western ear because of its usage in the Roman liturgy of Good Friday. The prayer continues to address Mary as "immaculate Virgin, Mother of God and filled with every grace ... whose maternal breast has nourished all men. She is the joy of angels; she has outrun the predictions of all the prophets in her fullness of grace. The Lord is with her and she has given birth [this] day to the Savior of the world."

An Egyptian eucharistic liturgy similarly addresses the God who spoke to Moses on Sinai as the recipient now of a sinless nature from an immaculate virgin; he who nourished Israel is nourished by the milk of a mother who knew not man; the chastiser of kings has himself fled to Egypt to escape a king; he who is enthroned in majesty on high is laid in a crib.[2] For all these marvels, "in a spirit of faith we praise the Mother and sing to the child."

A prayer which had had a long history of popular usage before the discovery in Egypt in 1917 of a Greek papyrus containing it, was the *Sub tuum praesidium,* which is none other than the trope *Hypò tēn sēn eusplagchnían* of Byzantine Lenten vespers. In the Roman Little Office of the Blessed Virgin it is the antiphon for the canticle *Nunc dimittis* at Compline. It is translated: "We fly to your patronage, O holy Mother of

---

[1] Cf. *Monumenta Ecclesiae Liturgica*, ed. Cabrol-Leclercq, Vol. 1, sectio altera (Parisiis, 1913), p. ccxxxii, *ostrakon* No. 10952 in the National Museum of Brussels; cited by A. Hamman, O.F.M., *Prières des premiers chrétiens* (Paris, 1952), pp. 120-121.

[2] Cf. *Monumenta Ecclesiae Liturgica*, p. ccxxxi, *ostrakon* No. 8156, Cairo Museum; cited by Hamman, *op. cit.,* p. 124.

Marian Prayers

God; despise not our petitions in our necessities, but deliver us always from all dangers, O glorious and blessed Virgin." The publication of the text in 1938 by C. H. Roberts laid the groundwork for the claim that it was the oldest known prayer to Mary. An article by Dom Mercenier of Chevetogne (Belgium) a year later first made this identification, since the editor had not given any indication of familiarity with it. The Papyrus is about 7 by 3⅔ inches in size; the sheet was not bound to any other. A Latin translation of the text as reconstructed by Mercenier follows.[3] It is of ten lines in good uncials, so ornamented that some have thought this papyrus a model for scribes.

(1) Sub praesidium (2) misericordiae tuae (3) confugimus o (4) Deigenetrix: nostras (5) deprecationes ne despicias (6) in necessitate (*or* in necessitatibus) (7) sed a periculo (8) erue nos, Tu quae (9) sola es pura (*or* gloriosa) et (10) benedicta.[4]

Roberts was inclined to date the papyrus as of the latter fourth century, even going so far as to say, "it is almost incredible that a prayer addressed directly to the Virgin in these terms could be written in the third century," but his colleague Lobel thinks there are no good reasons for putting it later than the third.[5]

Mercenier based his reconstruction on those Coptic and Byzantine liturgies still in use which employ the prayer. The version on papyrus uses numerous phrases from the Septuagint, e.g. *sképē* (*praesidium,* protection, shelter), found in Isa. 49:2; 51:16, also Ps. 16(17):8. Interestingly, the Coptic version leaves the sacred term *sképē* untranslated, while the Syriac, Syro-Chaldean, and Armenian versions fill out the biblical phrase "under the shadow of your wings." Taken altogether, this invocation to Mary has something of the flavor of those Psalms which beg protection from the Lord who is the psalmist's refuge (*kataphygḗ*) and deliverer (*hrýstēs*). The

---

[3] C. H. Roberts, *Catalogue of the Greek and Latin Papyri in the John Rylands Library,* Vol. 3 (Manchester, 1938), pp. 46-47. Cf. F. Mercenier, O.S.B., *L'Antienne mariale grecque la plus ancienne,* in *Le Muséon,* Vol. 52, 1939, pp. 229-233; J. Delamare, P.S.S., *La plus ancienne prière à la Sainte Vierge: Sub tuum praesidium,* in *La Vie Spirituelle,* Vol. 95, 1956, pp. 149-159.

[4] The constructed Greek text (as done by Mercenier; Roberts' reconstruction is quite different) reads: (1) [hy]pò [ten sképēn tēs] (2) euspl[agchías sou] (3) kat aphe[ýgomen, ō] (4) theotóke t[às hēmōn] (5) hikesías mē pa[r-] (6) eídēs em peristás[ei] *or* peristás[esi] (7) all' ek kindýnou (8) hrýsai hēmâs [sú hē] (9) mónē [hagnē kaí] *or* [semnē kaí] (10) hē eulog[ēménē].

[5] Roberts, *op. cit.,* p. 46.

plea for deliverance from dangers in the *Sub tuum praesidium* is an echo of near-identical phrases in the Septuagint versions of Pss. 17:3; 60:5; 70:4; 90:1 ff.; 114:2-5; 142:9 (all Vulgate enumeration), while the phrase "but deliver us from danger" (*all' ek kindýnou hrŷsai hēmâs*) is found substantially in a prayer of a papyrus of Dêr-Balyzeh.[6] Mary's intercession was evidently thought to be such that she could be counted on, as Mother of God, to insure the protective care of God Himself.

Cechetti makes the point that the normal verb of the Greek liturgies to implore deliverance, theologically understood, is *lýtrōsai*. The use of *hrŷsai* in this prayer (in Latin, *erue*) is taken by him as probably describing the cry for deliverance uttered by Christians in the persecutions of Valerian and Decius. Similarly, the *perístasis* of line six, generally translated "necessity" or "extreme," is a calamitous situation that could easily be persecution for the faith. Whatever the cause, Mary is called on to show *eusphlagchnía*, "mercy," under the shadow of which virtue of hers (not the *éleos* which is most commonly the divine mercy of the Septuagint) the petitioners seek refuge. Yet her "merciful heart" is not entirely unlike the *splágchna eléous* or "bowels of mercy" familiar to the English Bible reader (Lk. 1:78).

The prayer addresses her as *theotókos*, "God-bearer," an indication that thus early in Egypt the term had liturgical significance and was not confined to the debates of theologians. The fifth century historian Socrates refers to Origen's explanation of the term in his no longer extant first volume of commentary on *Romans*.[7] Support is likewise found in the use of *theotókos* for the contention that Cyril sought a term consecrated by Alexandrian liturgical usage, in the pre-Ephesine struggle over the divine maternity. There had been, in fact, before the discovery of Papyrus Rylands 470 no documentary evidence of devotion to Mary before Nicea. The development of a feast jointly honoring Christ and Mary, which culminated in the Eastern observance of her divine motherhood, is assumed for the period of the early fourth century.[8] If paleography's earlier date for the *Sub tuum praesidium* is accepted, the uncertainty of

---

[6] Cf. *An Early Euchologium*, ed. Roberts-Capelle (Louvain, 1949), p. 14; cited by I. Cecchetti, art. *Sub tuum praesidium*, in *Enciclopedia Cattolica*, Vol. 11 (Città del Vaticano, 1953), col. 1470. An abridgment of this article is contained in *The American Ecclesiastical Review*, Vol. 140, January, 1959, pp. 1-5.

[7] Socrates, *Historia Ecclesiastica*, 7, 32; *PG* 67, 812B.

[8] Cf. E. Dublanchy, S.M., art. *Marie*, in *Dictionnaire de Théologie Catholique*, Vol. 9, col. 2443.

any formal euchology to Our Lady by the third century is removed.

Mary alone is "pure" (*hagnē*) in the Byzantine liturgical reading of the prayer;[9] the adjective is lacking from the mutilated papyrus. She becomes "gloriosa" in the Roman version, which Mercenier admits might have existed originally as *semnē,* in the Ambrosian version.[10] She is also "blessed" (*eulogemenē, benedicta*). The Roman version asks Mary: "libera nos semper, Virgo gloriosa et benedicta," in a phrase which joins the newcomer "semper" to the preceding phrase both musically and in punctuation, but which undoubtedly started its career as "ever virgin" (*aeipárthenos, semper virgo*).[11]

The Coptic version remains closest to the Rylands papyrus. In English it would read, "We fly to the protection of your mercies, O Mother of God, despise not our petitions in [our] necessities, but deliver us from perdition, oh [you] who alone [are] blessed."[12]

The *Sub tuum praesidium* serves also as an *Antiphona post Evangelium* in Masses of the Virgin in the Ambrosian rite.[13] The version there and in the Roman Office is as follows:

Sub tuum praesidium confugimus, sancta Dei Genitrix; nostras deprecationes ne despicias in necessitatibus [nostris][14] sed a periculis cunctis libera nos semper, Virgo gloriosa et benedicta.

The words *sancta, cunctis* and *semper* (explained above) were either introduced for rhythmic reasons, or else originated in some entirely different fashion as in the case of the adverbial prefix *"aei-."* The *similarities of the Roman version with the Egyptian (of the papyrus) are marked*, according to Mercenier, a fact as well known as the relation of Byzantine and Gallican liturgies.[15]

---

[9] Cf. Mercenier, *art. cit.,* p. 231 (*Hōrologion tò mega* [ed. Roma, 1938], p. 232).

[10] Mercenier, *loc. cit.,* citing the *Missale ambrosianum* (Mediolani, 1831).

[11] Mercenier, loc. cit.

[12] The prayer occurs in Vespers, at least in Catholic editions. Mercenier points out that since the fifth-century separation of the Monophysites, the latter follow the custom of the Byzantine *Hōrologion* of putting other tropes in this place. Cf. John, Marquis of Bute (tr.), *The Coptic Morning Service of the Lord's Day* (London, 1908), p. 155; *Hōrologion* [in Slav: *Ciasoslov*] (Roma, 1879), p. 105.

[13] Mercenier, p. 229. Cecchetti observes that it is the only prayer recited in common each day by the Jesuits; it is also of daily obligation for the Salesians of Don Bosco.

[14] This additional word is given in *The Raccolta,* ed. Christopher-Spence-Rowan (New York, 1952), p. 235, No. 333, where the indulgences attached are also listed.

[15] Cf. *ibid.,* p. 233.

Although the prayer seems to have been used as the *Nunc dimittis* antiphon starting only in the twelfth century, it is found as a responsory at the gospel in a manuscript of Compiègne (from which the word *gloriosa* is missing), dating to the late ninth century.[16] The whole *Liber Responsalis* is attributed to Gregory the Great.

* * *

The Latin text of the *Hail Mary* as we know it was fixed by its insertion into the Roman breviary of Pius V in 1568. The first half had appeared in Greek on an Egyptian potsherd, dated around A.D. 600. It reads:

> Hail Mary, full of grace, the Lord is with thee, blessed art thou amongst women, and blessed is the fruit of thy womb, because thou didst conceive Christ, the Son of God, the Redeemer of our souls.[17]

The naturalness with which Gabriel's greeting to Mary (Lk. 1:28) was joined to Elizabeth's (1:42), and her name "Mary" inserted into the account, is evident.[18] He greets her with the word *Chaîre* ("Rejoice!"), a term not without Messianic significance in the Septuagint passages Joel 2:23, Zach. 9:9, and Soph. 3:14. As early as the Greek liturgy of St. James the "join" is to be found at the prayer of intercession or "diptychs." It passes into the Egyptian liturgy known as that of St. Mark,[19] and presumably from there into the Latin liturgy, where it appears as the offertory of the Mass of the fourth Sunday of Advent in the antiphonary ascribed to St. Gregory the Great. It occurs there by way of transfer from Ember Wednesday, and goes back farther still to the feast of the Annunciation, introduced into Rome toward the end of the seventh

---

[16] *PL* 78, 799; cf. Capelle, *La liturgie mariale en Occident*, in *Maria. Études sur la Sainte Vierge*, ed. H. du Manoir, S.J., Vol. 1 (Paris, 1949), p. 239; S. Salaville, A.A., *Marie dans la liturgie byzantine ou gréco-slave, ibid.*, p. 295.

[17] H. Thurston, S.J., *Familiar Prayers* (Westminster, Md., 1953), p. 92, following W. L. Crum, *Coptic Ostraca* (London, 1902), p. 3; cf. H. Leclercq, art. *Marie (Je vous salue)*, in *Dictionnaire d'Archéologie Chrétienne et Liturgie*, Vol. 10, coll. 2043-2062; J. Jungmann, art. *Ave Maria*, in *Lexikon für Theologie und Kirche*, Vol. 1 (Freiburg, 1957), p. 1141.

[18] So natural was it, in fact, that the phrase "Blessed art thou among women" worked its way into v. 28 in many mss. from v. 42.

[19] Cf. Leclercq, *art. cit.*, col. 2044; F. E. Brightman, *Liturgies Eastern and Western* (Oxford, 1896), pp. 56, 128, 328. At Vespers the prayer is recited even today in the form given above, prefixed by "O Virgin *Theotokos* ..."

century.[20]

Mabillon's theory was that the popular usage of the first half of the *Hail Mary* resulted not from its once or twice-yearly liturgical employment, but from its incorporation into the hours of the Little Office of Our Lady in the eleventh century. In this prayer, which was added for piety's sake to the Divine Office by numerous religious orders and then adopted by the secular clergy and laity, phrases from the *Hail Mary* are used throughout (invitatory, responsories, antiphon at tierce). Often a genuflection accompanied the utterance, "Ave Maria."[21] Miracle stories proliferated in the twelfth century in which clients who called on Mary in terms of the *Ave* knew no limitations of nature. St. Peter Damian, who died in Italy in 1072, was a strong propagator of Our Lady's Office. He has left us a Mary-story of a tepid cleric who was saved through calling on her in the familiar formula of the first half of the prayer.[22]

Documentation from the twelfth century leaves us to conclude that the fairly common recitation of the Day-Hours to Mary resulted in making the phrases of the Angel's greeting an integral part of popular piety.[23] Statues to her were commonly greeted in Gabriel's words. There was no uniform practice concerning the length of the prayer. Sometimes the speaker stopped at *tecum,* sometimes at the *in mulieribus* of the Vulgate (which critical texts of the Greek do not contain), and sometimes at the *fructus ventris tui* of Elizabeth's greeting. The name of Jesus in apposition with "fruit of thy womb," had not yet been supplied. Mary was

---

[20] Capelle, *op. cit.,* p. 238. P. Wiertz (H. Dünninger) cites the study of W. de Grüneisen (Rome, 1911) on the church of Santa Maria Antiqua, which carries the two Lucan phrases joined in Greek in a seventh-century fresco of the Annunciation; cf. *Das A. M. in der Frömmigkeitsgeschichte,* in *Lexikon der Marienkunde,* fasc. 3/4 (Regensburg, 1959), p. 482. W. Lipphardt, *Das Ave Maria in der Liturgie (ibid..,* p. 487), asks whether the Syrian Pope Sergius (687-701) may not have brought it from East to West.

[21] Cf. the biographer of the Norbertine canon, Blessed Herman Joseph, in *Acta Sanctorum,* April, Vol. 1 (Parisiis, 1866), p. 690B; also Hildebert of Tours (c. 1130), in *PL* 171, 631.

[22] *Opusculum* 33, *PL* 145, 564. The three foregoing references are provided by Thurston (*op. cit.,* pp. 98 f.), who also gives full documentation on the 19th century studies of A. Mussafi on the Mary-legends, published by the Vienna Academy.

[23] E.g., Franco, Abbot of Afflighem, *De gratia Dei,* in *PL* 166, 745; *Meditationes* (ascribed to St. Anselm), in *PL* 158, 785; *Monumenta Germaniae Historica,* Scriptores, Vol. 14, pp. 298 f., which contains the story of Countess Ada of Avennes who prayed the *Ave Maria* sixty times daily. Thurston identifies her (c. 1090) and the Tournai region with the "longer form."

everywhere hailed as *gratia plena*. The evangelist's *kecharitōménē* ("Most highly favored") with its distinctive Old Testament significance, strengthened by "the Lord is with thee" and the assurance "thou hast found grace with God" (v. 30), had come to be taken by the Church to mean the fullness of holiness in terms of the new dispensation.[24]

It is Baldwin, Archbishop of Canterbury, who recorded while still a monk, before 1180, that it was the custom in England to add "and blessed is the fruit of thy womb" to the angel's salutation.[25] A twelfth-century manuscript (Additional 21, 927) has, as the responsory of Compline, Gabriel's greeting and the versicle, Elizabeth's. There is all sorts of evidence that the recitation of one hundred and fifty *Aves*, in the form known to the twelfth century, was a common devotion in imitation of the Psalter.[26]

As to the second half of the Hail Mary, it became evident in time that mere greeting and praise to Mary required some sort of completion in the form of impetratory prayer. A hymn to Mary from the late eleventh century, attributed universally to Gottschalk of Aachen, has as its first stanza Gabriel's words only (the same form as that known to Gottschalk's Italian contemporary Peter Damian). There are six remaining stanzas, the last of which reads:

> Hic nobis et mortis in
> hora succurre
> ac in orbis examine
> nos tuos recognosce.[27]

This plea for succor at the present moment (hic) and at the hour of death, and recognition at the world's judgment, clearly foreshadows the

---

[24] Cf. R. Laurentin, *Structure et théologie de Luc I-II* (Paris, 1957), pp. 64-68, for a careful exegesis of the verses in question, complete with *OT* parallels; cf. especially S. Lyonnet, *Chaîre kekaritōménē*, in *Biblica*, Vol. 20, 1939, pp. 131-141.

[25] *PL* 204, 477. The synod held under Odo, Bishop of Paris (1198) requires knowledge of the *Salutatio Beatae Virginis* (Mansi, 22, 681); that under Alexander, Bishop of Coventry (*ca.* 1237), requires the *Ave Maria* to be prayed seven times daily (Mansi, 23, 432).

[26] Cf. S. Beissel, S.J., *Geschichte der Verehrung Marias in Deutschland während des Mittelalters* (Freiburg, 1909), pp. 228 f.; *Acta Sanctorum*, April, Vol. 1 (Paris, 1866), p. 674E (life of St. Aybert, before 1140); Dreves-Blume, *Analecta hymnica medii aevi*, Vol. 30 (Leipzig, 1886-1922), p. 278; Vol. 35, pp. 254-262.

[27] Dreves-Blume, *op. cit.*, Vol. 1, p. 363; Vol. 40, p. 115.

Marian Prayers

petition in the form in which we know it. No other completion of the prayer precedes the fourteenth century, when the following verse occurs, erroneously attributed to Dante:

> O Vergin benedetta, sempre tu
> Ora pro noi a Dio, che ci perdoni
> E diaci grazia a viver sì guaggiù
> Che'l paradiso al nostro fin ci doni.[28]

By "no other completion" a full petition is meant. Numerous instances are recorded of concluding the twofold greeting of Scripture with "Jesus" or "Jesus Christ. Amen." The latter addition is attributed to Pope Urban IV (1261-64), who, according to Michael ab Insulis in 1497 in a treatise on the rosary from Cologne, gave an indulgence of thirty days to all who prayed it.[29] Pope John XXII (1316-34) reportedly increased this to sixty days. Georg Witzel is found defending this gloss on Scripture in his *Catechismus Ecclesiae* (1559) on the basis of the power of the Holy Name. The Council of Narbonne (1551) sanctioned the shorter ending "Jesus," and Ulrich Zwingli is discovered attributing it to the Holy Spirit.[30]

As to "Sancta Maria, Mater Dei, ora pro nobis peccatoribus," it appears in sermons of St. Bernardine of Siena (d. 1444)[31]; in a variety of Carthusian breviaries (Paris 1521, 1551); and in the synodal decrees of Augsburg and Constance from 1567. Inscriptions on late fifteenth-century bells contain the substance of the full petition,[32] and a decree from the Archbishop of Mainz sent on to Pope Alexander VI in 1493 contains all but the word *sinners*, adding the title "Virgin" to "Holy Mary." "O Du Helge Jungfraw Marie, Mutter Gottes, bidt Gott vor uns itzunde und in der Stundt des Dodes. Amen."[33] Savonarola died in 1498, and he gave us the entire *Ave*

---

[28] "O blessed Virgin, pray for us always to God that He may pardon us and give us grace so to live here below that He will give us heaven at the end."

[29] Manuscript documentation given by Dünninger, *op. cit.*, p. 480, includes *Quodlibetum de veritate fraternitatis rosarii* (Coloniae, 1497), c. 5; Henry of Langenstein, ms. 35 of the Dominican Monastery in Vienna.

[30] *Werke*, Vol. 1, p. 407; in Dünninger, loc. cit.

[31] Cf. *Opera omnia*, Vol. 4 (ed. Venetiis, 1845), pp. 94 and 226 f.: "Holy Mary, pray for us sinners."

[32] K. Walter, *Glockenkunde* (Regensburg, 1913), p. 282.

[33] Similar versions are given in Pelbart of Temervar, *Stellarium Beatae Mariae Virginis* (Hagenau, 1515), lib. 1, pars 4, art. 3, c. 4; lib. 12, pars ult., c. 12, mirac. 2.

Maria as we have it now, the final word *nostrae* alone excepted.[34]

A Mercedarian breviary produced in Paris in 1514 had the final petition; so did one of the Camaldolese (Venice, 1525) and of the Franciscans (Paris, 1525). The *Breviary of the Cross* of the Franciscan Cardinal Quiñones (1536) contained the formula, "Sancta Maria, Mater Dei, ora pro nobis peccatoribus, nunc et in hora mortis."[35] The great folio of the Sarum Breviary (1531) has the same, having added "Christus" to "Jesus." Strangely, the *Catechismus Romanus* (1566) proceeds only as far as "amongst women," although it mentions in the immediate context the Church's practice of adding "prayers ... and supplications to the most holy Mother of God" to the thanks expressed for her singular privileges.[36]

It was the Roman Breviary of Pope Pius V (1568) that made the modern text of the "Hail Mary" secure, though truncated versions continued to be used widely. A Belgian calendar of Our Lady, for example (Douai, 1638), gives only the first half of the prayer. The latter portion is also missing from the day hours of the Dominican breviary from 1629 until now. France still knew the ending "peccatoribus. Amen," in 1613;[37] sixteenth and seventeenth century German songbooks end the prayer with: "Jesus Christus. Amen." Peter Canisius, on the other hand, in his Dillingen *Catechismus Minor* of 1560, gives the ending: "Jesus Christus. Heylige Maria, muter Gottes, bitt für uns arme (*poor*) sünder. Amen."[38] Certain manuscripts of his Ingolstadt catechism of 1584 have all this, plus "jetzt und in der Stund unsers Absterbens. Amen."[39]

To complete the catalogue of endings employed at various times we may mention the Swedish religious of Wadstena, who in 1447 concluded the prayer, "Jesus Christus in aeternum"; while the German *Chronicle of Windesheim* gives "Jesus Christus Amen, qui est gloriosus Deus benedictus

---

[34] H. Thurston, *The Angelus. I. The Hail Mary*, in *The Month*, Vol. 98 (Nov., 1901), pp. 496 f. *The Kalender of Shepardys* of about the same time regularly adds: "Holy Mary, mother of God, praye for us synners, amen." Cf. *ibid.*, p. 499. The edition was that of R. Pynson of London, "MCCCCC and VI," though the French original had been published in 1493.

[35] Cf. Dünninger, *op. cit.*, p. 481.

[36] *Catechismus Romanus* Venetiis, 1566), 4, c. 5, q. 8.

[37] Peter de Bollo, *Le rosaire de la Mère de Dieu* (Lyon, 1613); cited by Dünninger, *op. cit.*, p. 482.

[38] *S. Petri Canisii ... Catechismi*, ed. F. Streicher, S.J., Vol. 1 (Romae, 1936), p. 42.

[39] *Ibid.*, p. 130.

in saecula."[40]

Numerous religious congregations and canons had recited the *Ave Maria* before each canonical hour, from the thirteenth century onward (e.g., Dominicans, Benedictines, Canons Regular of Nicosia). It was the action of Pope Pius V with regard to the breviary, however, which standardized the formula with its prescription that each canonical hour of the Roman Office should be preceded by the *Pater* and *Ave*. By the time Pope Pius XII came to suppress the practice in his modified breviary reform of March 23, 1955,[41] the prayer had become the treasured possession of the entire Christian West.

*   *   *

The antiphon *Salve Regina misericordiae*, to give it its original title, is attributed to a variety of persons by medieval chroniclers: Peter, Bishop of Compostella (who reportedly translated it from the Greek), St. Athanasius, St. John Damascene, and Pope Gregory IX among them.[42] A manuscript of the monastery at Reichenau takes the prayer back to the early eleventh century at the latest, with its quotation of the phrases, "*Salve Regina misericordiae ... In hac lacrymarum valle ... Eia ergo.*"[43] The Cistercian monk Amedeus of Lausanne is found employing certain phrases of the prayer in the mid-twelfth century: *illos misericordissimos oculos ... ad nos convertens*, and *o clemens, o pia, o dulcis Maria!*[44]; but they are so casually interwoven into his two homilies, which are filled with snippets of Marian invocation, that it is hard to attribute them unequivocally to a metrical prayer in common use. Certain manuscripts from the twelfth century contain the antiphon without musical notation.[45] A few words were added over the centuries, e.g. *Mother* of mercy, in

---

[40] *Scriptores rerum suevicorum medii aevi* (Uppsala, 1818), and Busch, *Chronic. Windesheim*, Vol. 1, p. 70 [ed. Grube, p. 215]; both cited by U. Berlière, art. *Angélique (Salutation)*, in *D.T.C.*, Vol. 1, col. 1276.

[41] *A.A.S.*, Vol. 47 (1955), p. 222.

[42] Cf. Leclercq, art. *Salve Regina*, in *Dictionnaire d'Archéologie Chrétienne et Liturgie*, Vol. 15, col. 714; A. Manser, *Salve Regina*, in *Lexikon für Theologie und Kirche*, Vol. 9, p. 137 f.

[43] *Cod. Augiensis LV*, fol. 42 v°, according to Leclercq.

[44] *Sermones* 7 et 8; *PL* 188, 1342 and 1346.

[45] British Museum (Additional 18 302, fol. 130), where it is given as the antiphon at tierce on the feast of the Assumption; ms. 230 of Einsiedeln is also referred to as containing it without notation (*ca.* 1200).

apposition to the opening term of address "Queen" — (just as "holy" is added to "Queen" in English for euphonic reasons); *"virgin* (Mary)" after the triple invocation "o clement, o loving, o sweet"; and "(show unto us the blessed fruit ...) *benign."* While "Queen of mercy" is the primitive form, the medieval title "Mother of mercy" was so widely used that it is no problem why it should have dislodged it. Despite the incomplete state of the prayer in certain thirteenth century readings — where it ends in *"in hac lacrymarum valle," for* example — there is no reason to think that it was not in use in the form familiar to us by the twelfth century.

The antiphon has no history of usage apart from its familiar musical setting, a fact which doubtless prompted its attribution to the monastic writer on music Herman the Cripple, monk of Reichenau (d. 1054).[46] This authorship is first claimed in the late fifteenth century, however, in the *Chronicle* of James of Bergamo, where it is entered under the year 1049.[47] A catalogue of Herman's works made by John of Tritenheim in the early sixteenth century included the *Salve* and the *Alma Redemptoris Mater;* the double authorship was copied many times over thereafter.

Hermann's disciple, Berthold of Constance, seemed to know nothing of these works of genius. If he did, it is doubtful he would have named the musical sagas (*"cantus historiales"*) on SS. George, Afra, and Magnus, and hidden the great Mary-prayers under the anonymity of the phrase, "and very many other such works besides."[48]

St. Bernard seems to have no better title to authorship of the *Salve*, despite the late twelfth-century report of Jean l'Hermite of a dream in which the saint of Clairvaux hears the hymn sung by the heavenly court from first word to last, and relays the words to Pope Eugene III.[49] Another legend, less fanciful, has the saint adding the triple invocation at the end while on a visit to the cathedral of Speyer in 1146. He genuflected three times before Our Lady's statue, chanting with each reverence: "O thou

---

[46] Cf. *PL* 143 for the works of Hermannus Contractus, especially his *Opuscula musica*, coll. 413-458.

[47] Jacobus Bergamensis, *Supplementum chronicarum orbis ab initio mundi usque ad annum 1482*, 2nd ed. (Brescia, 1485), lib. 15.

[48] "... quo musicus peritior non erat ... De S. Georgio ... mira suavitate et elegantia euphonicos, praeter alia hujusmodi perplura, neumatizavit et composuit." Cf. *PL* 143, 28. Berthold did not know of his master's familiarity with Hebrew and Arabic, as a chronicler of four centuries later seemed to, but then neither did he know that his Reichenau colleague was a monk of St. Gall.

[49] *PL* 185, 544.

deboner, o thou meke, o thou swete maide Marie" (to quote the translation of a fifteenth century Cambridge primer). The only trouble with the attribution to Bernard, as Thurston remarks, is that the Swabian manuscript from the early twelfth century, referred to above (note 45), contained the hymn complete. Thurston incidentally remarks, in support of Dom de Valois, that he knows of no manuscript which terminates with *nobis post hoc exsilium ostende,* except where it is a case of erasure.[50]

There is certain good ground to connect the origins of the *Salve* with France, and specifically the city of Le Puy. In the text of a *Chronicle* by Albert of Three Fountains which recounts a visit of St. Bernard to Dijon in 1130, the *Salve* is called *antiphonam de Podio* because authorship of it is attributed to Naymerus (Adhémar, d. 1098), Bishop of that city.[51] It is almost needless to add that Bernard heard the antiphon miraculously sung by angel choirs *there* too, and specified its adoption by his whole Cistercian order. The hymn is connected with Le Puy in other medieval writings. In any case, it gained considerable vogue on French soil as a liturgical piece, even though twelfth-century German manuscripts contain it.[52] Peter, Abbot of Cluny, decreed its use as a processional hymn on the feast of the Assumption and other feasts which had no canticle proper to a saint, as the community made its way to Mary's chapel.[53]

Persistent reference to the piece as an "antiphon" indicated its origins as a musical setting for the *Benedictus* or *Magnificat,* as for example in its use at first vespers on the feast of Mary's Nativity in a thirteenth century Cistercian antiphonal.[54] In no legend, however, is it described in any setting but a processional one. The Cistercians began to recite it daily in 1218 and were largely instrumental in popularizing it, despite the fact that its first statutory appearance was in a Cluniac source. Blessed Jordan of Saxony specified it daily after compline for the Dominicans, whose second general he was (1230). A Council of Peñafiel in Spain (1302) specified that

---

[50] Cf. Thurston, *Familiar Prayers,* p. 119. The work referred to is Jean de Valois, *En marge d'une antienne: le Salve Regina* (Paris, 1912).

[51] Valois, *op. cit.,* p. 23. P. Wagner, *Ursprung und Entwicklung der liturgischen Gesangsformen,* cited in Pius Parsch, *The Breviary Explained* (St. Louis, 1952), p. 182, is of this opinion.

[52] Cf. Dreves-Blume, *Analecta hymnica medii aevi,* Vol. 1, p. 319. Four mss. of Seckau or Graz are cited.

[53] *PL* 189, 1048. The document is dated around 1135.

[54] Parsch, *loc. cit.* Valois states that it was used as an antiphon at lauds or vespers on the four great feasts of Our Lady from the mid-twelfth century.

it be sung in a loud voice daily after compline, to be followed by the versicle and response, "Pray for us, O holy Mother of God," and the prayer, "Grant unto thy servants, we beseech thee, O Lord, perpetual wellbeing in mind and body. ..."[55]

Mercati's edition of the *Rubricae novae* of the fourteenth century indicated that Pope Clement VI in 1350 was the first to adopt the four seasonal anthems to Mary for recitation after Lauds and Compline (*Salve, Alma, Ave Regina,* and *Regina Caeli*).[56] The Franciscans, however, had specified them in 1249, according to the *Chronica XXIV generalium O.M.*[57] This followed the act of Pope Gregory IV in 1239, which enjoined the *Salve* every Friday after compline. With the Breviary of 1568 came the obligation to pray it after compline in the form *"Salve, Regina, Mater misericordiae."* The anthem in question is the fourth in seasonal succession, being prescribed for the period from first vespers of Trinity Sunday until the Saturday before the first Sunday of Advent. Its occurrence after compline is probably traceable to the monastic practice of intoning it in the chapel and chanting it on the way to sleeping quarters. There is considerable evidence that the hymn was popular as a song of exultant joy, a tribute more to its lilting melody than to its references to "mourning," "weeping," and "exile." Seafaring men doubtless came to favor it because it was so eminently "singable." It came to be used as part of the ritual for the blessing of a ship, and the core of evening service on shipboard. The mention of it in Columbus' journal is well-known.[58] It is there also described, along with the *Ave* and the Sign of the Cross, as the earliest prayer formula taught to the docile Indians of the Caribbean isles.

Thurston reports at length on the prayer's great popularity in late medieval and Renaissance times, when "chantries" were erected with funded moneys to assure its solemnization with music and candles each

---

[55] Hardouin, *Concilia*, Vol. 7, col. 1156; cited by Thurston, *Familiar Prayers*, p. 129.

[56] G. Mercati, *Appunti per la storia del Breviario romano nei secoli XIV-XV, tratti dalle 'Rubricae Novae'* (Roma, 1903). Peter Amelius († 1401) is the probable author.

[57] C. Batiffol, *Histoire du Bréviaire*, 3rd ed. (Paris, 1911), pp. 244 and 261.

[58] "Thursday, 11 October. ... When they said the *Salve*, which all the sailors were accustomed to sing in their way, the Admiral asked and admonished the men to keep a good lookout on the forecastle and to watch well for land." Quoted in H. S. Commager and Allen Nevins, *The Heritage of America*, a book of documents and selections (Boston, 1951), p. 6. Mention is also made of it in Columbus' logbook, under 16 February, 1493, on the return journey.

evening, but on Saturday especially.[59] It was the popular evening hymn of medieval university colleges;[60] it served as the setting for Benediction of the Blessed Sacrament (still called "the Salve" in parts of Europe and often *salut* in France). Erasmus and Luther attacked it at various times because in it prayer to Christ was replaced by Mary-worship. John Hollybush of London printed a little book in 1538 which was a "Confutation" of the song. In it he revamped the ancient text to read, "Hayle Jesu Christ, Kynge of mercy," ending "O gracious, o swete Christe and sonne of the virgine Mary." While this altered version never dislodged the popular hymn, Thurston observes that the evening reverence to Christ's eucharistic body, which the *Salve* led to, accomplished the positive part of the unhappy man's wish in roundabout fashion.

Our final attention to the *Hail, Holy Queen* will look into the terms of its designation by Pope Leo XIII as a prayer to be said after low Mass. In accord with the teaching of liturgiologists at that time (when it was forbidden even to translate the ordinary of the Mass; a revision of the *Index of Forbidden Books* in 1897, by omitting the prohibition, terminated it), any intercessory prayer spoken by the people had to come before or after the Mass. Pope Pius IX had asked prayers in 1859 for the cause of retaining the Papal States. Even after they fell the prayers continued and on January 6, 1884, Leo extended these prayers to the whole Church as part of his final effort to win back the Church's liberty against the laws of the *Kulturkampf*.[61]

The *Pater* had been said kneeling at the end of Mass by the Carthusians before 1259; the *Ave* among the prayers at the foot of the altar toward the close of the medieval period.[62] Jungmann lists all those

---

[59] Thurston, *op. cit.*, pp. 133-145. Cf. also his article *Benediction of the Blessed Sacrament*, in *The Month*, Vol. 98 (Sept., 1901), pp. 268 f. and 275.

[60] St. Thomas More in describing the wretchedness of Oxford fare during his student days says that the only step conceivably lower in the economic scale is, "with bags and wallets, [to] go a begging together, and hoping that for pity some good folk will give us their charity, at every man's door to sing *Salve Regina*. ..." Cf. W. Roper, *The Life of Sir Thomas More*, ed. E. V. Hitchcock (London, 1935), p. 54.

[61] The text is given in *A.S.S.*, Vol. 16, 1883, p. 239 f. The revision of the prayers to their modern form was achieved in 1886, but Jungmann points out that A.S.S. does not record this. Cf. *The Mass of the Roman Rite*, Vol. 2 (New York, 1955), P- 456, n. 7; R. Brennan, *The Leonine Prayers*, in *The American Ecclesiastical Review*, Vol. 125, 1951, pp. 85-94. In an allocution of June 30, 1930, Pope Pius XI specified that the Leonine prayers should be said for the conversion of Russia. Cf. A.A.S., Vol. 22, 1930, p. 301.

[62] Jungmann, op. *cit.*, p. 457.

liturgical books where the *Salve* came either after St. John's gospel or between the last blessing and the gospel, among them a French monastic missal (1524), the Cologne rite (sixteenth century), and the Carmelite missal (1935). It had also been the practice in the fourteenth and fifteenth centuries in Germany to pray the *Salve* at the altar before beginning Mass.[63] In any case, it is noteworthy that the "breakthrough" of the people's participation in the prayers of the Mass in the West, and in their own tongue at that, should have been accomplished through these two most beloved of prayers to the Mother of God. A decree of June 20, 1913, permitted omission of these prayers when the Mass is celebrated "with some solemnity." This was interpreted to mean all dialogue Masses on Sundays and feast days, and Masses at which a homily is preached, in a response dated March 9, 1960 (Cf. *Decreta authentica S.R.C.*, Appendix II (Romae, 1927), pp. 8-9; *A.A.S.*, Vol. 52, 1960, p. 360.).

* * *

The foregoing treatment of the *Salve* requires at least brief mention of the other Marian anthems. Of the three, the *Regina caeli* of Paschaltide is the most recent in authorship. This hymn is specified in the breviary after compline from Holy Saturday until the Saturday after Pentecost. It first appears in an antiphonary found in the Vatican Library which may have been composed as early as 1171 but is more likely a thirteenth-century product.[64] The text is almost as we know it today; a Franciscan codex of 1235 differs very little in wording. Blume's conviction is that it is an adaptation of a Christmas hymn which first appears in French and German manuscripts from the twelfth century: "Ever rejoice, o Virgin Mary, /Who hast been found worthy to bear Christ, the Creator of heaven and earth, /For thou hast brought forth from thy womb the Savior of the world."

There can be no doubt whatever that Franciscan influence was strongest in spreading this prayer. The Latin text reads:

> Regina caeli laetare, Alleluia,
> Quia quem meruisti portare, Alleluia,
> Resurrexit sicut dixit, Alleluia,
> Ora pro nobis Deum, Alleluia.

The versicle and response are as follows: "Gaude et laetare, Virgo

---

[63] *Ibid.*, Vol. 1, p. 267 f.

[64] C. Blume, art. *Regina caeli*, in *Kirchliches Handlexikon*, Vol. 2, p. 1706.

MARIAN PRAYERS

Maria, Alleluia. /Quia surrexit Dominus vere, Alleluia."[65]

While there is as yet no mention of the *Regina caeli* in the *Ancren Riwle* (about 1200), the *Alma Redemptoris* and *Ave Regina caelorum* are both referred to there. The *Alma*, almost a paraphrase of the ninth-century *Ave Maris Stella,* is composed of six hexameters; it is, according to the historical note which prefixes the works of Hermannus Contractus in Migne, the composition of the monk of Reichenau.[66] Its text is as follows: "Alma Redemptoris Mater, quae pervia caeli/ Porta manes, et stella maris, succurre cadenti,/ Surgere qui curat, populo: tu quae genuisti,/ Natura mirante, tuum sanctum Genitorem,/ Virgo prius ac posterius, Gabrielis ab ore. Sumens illud Ave, peccatorum miserere." The following is an English version circulated by the Liturgical Press, Collegeville, Minnesota, the quantities of which are identical with the Latin for purposes of song (the same is true for the *Regina caeli* in footnote 65):

> O loving Mother of our Savior, forever abiding heaven's
>   gateway and star of the sea,
> Oh hasten to aid us, who oft falling strive to rise again.
> Maiden, thou who borest, while nature stood in awe, thine
>   own Maker, thine all-holy Lord:
> Virgin ever, after, as before through the mouth of Gabriel
> Heaven spoke its Ave, have compassion on us sinners.

The anthem figures in that unfortunate piece of medieval anti-Jewish writing, Chaucer's *Prioress's Tale,* in which the little lad in an "Asian town, murdered at Satan's behest by those Jewish hearts which are his waspish nest," continues to sing Mary's praises from the grave:

> ... But Christ, whose glory you may find In books, wills it also be kept in mind.
> So for the honor of his mother dear
> I still may sing *O Alma* loud and clear.[67]

---

[65] "O Queen of heaven, rejoice now, / Rejoice, for He whom meetly thou bearest, / He is risen as He foretold. / Pray for us to the Father. . Rejoice and be glad, O Virgin Mary, / . For the Lord is truly risen."

[66] PL 143, 9, ex Joanne Egone, *Liber de viris illustribus Augiae Divitis* (1630); cf. H. Lausberg, s.v., in *Lexikon für Theologie und Kirche,* Vol. 1, 1957, p. 358 f.; *Analecta hymnica medii aevi,* Vol. 50, p. 317.

[67] Geoffrey Chaucer, *The Canterbury Tales,* tr. Nevill Coghill (Harmondsworth, Essex, 1951), pp. 199 f. For a view on the position of Jews in Chaucerian England, cf. R. J. Schoeck, *Chaucer's Prioress: Mercy and Tender Heart,* in *The Bridge,* Vol. 2 (New York,

82 MARIOLOGY

The tale does honor to Mary, if little to the mentality of that period on her people Israel. "Merciful God, reach mercy down to us," prayed the abbot who finally stilled the boy's tongue, "Though we be so unstable, though we vary,/ In love and reverence of His mother Mary." The antiphon had a history of being prayed at sext on the feast of the Assumption before it became the hymn at compline from the first Sunday of Advent until Candlemas Day, a stipulation connected with the pontificate of Clement VI (1350).[68]

*   *   *

The *Memorare* is frequently attributed to St. Bernard, but the closest any writing of his comes to the prayer as we have it (a fifteenth-century product, in its present form) is the following phrase from a sermon of his, *De quatriduo Lazari, et praeconio Virginis:* "O blessed Virgin, let there be silence concerning your mercy if there is anyone who recalls that you failed him when called on in the hour of need."[69] The English translation of the form given in the *Preces et Pia Opera* is as follows:

> Remember, O most gracious Virgin Mary, that never was it known that any one who fled to thy protection, implored thy help or sought thy intercession, was left unaided. Inspired with this confidence, I fly unto thee, O Virgin of virgins and Mother; to thee do I come, before thee I stand, sinful and sorrowful; O Mother of the Word Incarnate, despise not my petitions, but in thy mercy hear and answer me. Amen.[70]

Actually, the *Memorare* seems to be part of a longer prayer which is first recorded in the *Anthidotarius animae* of Nicholas Salicetus (1489), a Cistercian of Strasbourg. J. Wellinger included it in a collection entitled *Little Garden of the Soul* published in that same city in 1503.[71] This

---

1956), pp. 239-255.

[68] Cf. P. Wagner, *Einführung in die gregorianischen Melodien*, Vol. 1 (Leipzig, 1911), p. 157.

[69] St. Bernard, *Sermo 4 in Assumptione B. V. Mariae; PL* 183, 428.

[70] Translated as *The Raccolta* (New York, 1952), No. 339, p. 247.

[71] A. Lanz, art. *Memorare*, in *Enciclopedia Cattolica*, Vol. 8, p. 661. The Latin text of the modern version is: "Memorare, o piissima Virgo Maria, non esse auditum a saeculo, quemquam ad tua currentem praesidia, tua implorantem auxilia, tua petentem suffragia esse derelictum. Ego tali animatus confidentia ad te, Virgo virginum, Mater curro; ad te venio; coram te gemens peccator assisto. Noli, Mater Verbi, verba mea despicere, sed audi propitia et exaudi. Amen." Pope Pius IX first attached an indulgence to it for the whole Church in 1846.

Hortulus animae prayer begins, "Unto the feet of thy holiness, O dearest virgin Mary," and contains the phrase, "remember that never was it known." Its sole omission is, "implored thy help." We read "run," for "come"; "sinful and sorrowful" is *"gemens et tremens."*

Claude Bernard, known as the "Poor Priest" (1588-1641), was so active in spreading devotion to the *Memorare* that some assume that his surname accounts for the attribution of the prayer to the Saint of Clairvaux. His work was with prisoners and criminals, and he appears to have employed the prayer to Mary as an instrument of conversion.[72] During his lifetime he had some 200,000 copies of it circulated.

An edition of the *Precationum piarum Enchiridion* of 1572 (Dillingen) adds the phrase, "Despise not my petition, O Mother of God, but in thy mercy hear and answer *the words of my mouth.*"[73] At various times the prayer has been ascribed to SS. John Chrysostom and Augustine, but history cannot trace it back farther than the late fifteenth century.

*   *   *

The *Angelus* is a prayer comprised of four versicles and responses interspersed with Hail Marys, concluding with a petition for God's grace through the Incarnation of which the angel's message gave us first knowledge.[74] The concluding couplet and *oratio* were added to the medieval prayer sometime around the year 1600. By a decree of Pope Benedict XIV of April 20, 1742, recitation of the *Angelus* is replaced by that of the *Regina Coeli* throughout Eastertide.

So closely is the *Angelus* associated with the *Ave Maria* that in some places such as Italy it is known simply by that name. Its connection with the ringing of bells is a matter of some importance. Thurston collected a good amount of information on the curfew bell (from *couvre-feu,* in Latin

---

[72] Cf. Le Commandeur de Broqua, *Claude Bernard,* 2nd. ed. (Paris, 1913), the frontispiece of which is one of the many engraved portraits of the man beneath which is inscribed the *Memorare* and "Oraison du R. P. Bernard."

[73] N. Paulus, *Das Alter des Gebetes Memorare,* in *Zeitschrift für Katholische Theologie,* Vol. 26, 1902, p. 605.

[74] The text reads: ℣. Angelus Domini nuntiavit Mariae. ℟. Et concepit de Spiritu Sancto. Ave, etc. ℣. Ecce ancilla Domini. ℟. Fiat mihi secundum verbum tuum. Ave, etc. ℣. Et Verbum caro factum est. ℟. Et habitavit in nobis. Ave, etc. ℣. Ora pro nobis sancta Dei Genitrix. ℟. Ut digni efficiamur promissionibus Christi. Oremus: Gratiam tuam, quaesumus, Domine, mentibus nostris infunde: ut qui Angelo nuntiante, Christi Filii tui Incarnationem cognovimus, per passionem ejus et crucem ad resurrectionis gloriam perducamur. Per eundem Christum Dominum nostrum. ℟. Amen.

commonly *ignitegium*) sixty years ago, including the idea of the importance of bells hung in watchtowers in the highly organized town-life of the mid-thirteenth century.[75] The medieval study of Luchaire, *Les Communes Françaises,* cited by Thurston, provides a complete explanation of the mentality of the townsfolk of John Hersey's *Adano.* The town-bell is rooted not in superstitious folk-identity but in the concept of human and municipal rights. Civil in its origins and early dissociated from the covering of fires (a morning "curfew" becomes a commonplace; often it is a "peace bell" or "police bell" — in southern France, *"salva terra"*), this signal is identified in the tractate *De laudibus Papiae* (1330) with the closing of taverns in Pavia. It is distinguished carefully from a bell rung just previously known as "the signal for the Virgin Mary's salutation." The town of St. Omer had a similar tavern curfew. Important is the fact that whereas in England the bells were hung in church towers, on the continent they were indiscriminately found either there or in public buildings. Since their function was practical, the time for ringing at evening varied — six, nine, and even ten o'clock, depending on the possibilities of artificial light.

Though it would seem that the *Angelus* took its rise from the curfew-bell, there is nonetheless manuscript testimony from Germany around the year 1000 that in certain monasteries it was customary after compline to have three prayers said, led by the abbot and accompanied by a bell.[76] A Franciscan ordinance dated 1269 (1263?), probably in conjunction with a General Chapter at Pisa, requires three *Aves* to the sound of a bell "after compline."[77] The Carthusians are reported doing the same in 1342 for the sake of an indulgence, seemingly the one granted by Pope John XXII.[78] In England the monastic practice of well before 1000 was to have a *trina oratio,* with bell but not devoted to Mary; rather, "Sanctae Trinitatis et individuae Unitatis reverentia legitime a servulis exhibeatur Catholicis ..."[79] Every indication is that this trinitarian invocation served as both

---

[75] Thurston, *The Angelus. II. The Curfew Bell,* in *The Month,* Vol. 98, December, 1901, pp. 609-616.

[76] Martène, *De antiquis Ecclesiae ritibus,* Vol. 4 (Rotomagi, 1738), p. 39.

[77] *Analecta Franciscana,* Vol. 3, p. 329; cited by Thurston, *The Angelus. III. Compline or Curfew Bell — Which?* in *The Month,* Vol. 99, January, 1902, p. 61.

[78] Le Couteulx, *Annales Ordinis Carthusiensis;* cited by Thurston, *art. cit.,* p. 62.

[79] *Regularis Concordia,* in *Anglia,* Vol. 16, p. 394; cited by Thurston, *art. cit.,* p. 63.

morning and night prayer — an addendum to the divine office. The Canons Regular of Windesheim in their constitutions (fifteenth century) specify the triple bell and triple *Ave,* morning and evening.

Whatever the definitive answer concerning its relation to both curfew and *orationes tres,* the threefold *Ave* with bell — recited on one's knees at evening — had attached to it by John XXII an indulgence of ten days (1318; reiterated from Avignon in 1327).[80] The practice is recorded in documents of the period from Winchester and Wells; a canonist of that time, Calderini, judges that the bells "pro Ave Maria" should not be silenced in time of interdict because they were introduced "primarily for layfolk" and are not a function of any hierarchical rank.[81]

The Council of Sens (1346) follows the papal teaching on the *Ave,* "tempore seu hora ignitegii," and at Nantes (*ca.* 1370) we find the same. The absolutely earliest synodal decree comes from Esztergom (Strigoniensis) in Hungary, 1307; in it the practice is described as already well established.[82] A Spanish document from the hand of the Bishop of Lérida says substantially the same. Thurston's final view on all this is that the curfew grew out of the monastic bell at evening; witness the synod of Caen in 1061 with its legislation summoning people to prayer at the evening bell in emulation of the monastic practice.

With a boldness that not all students of the question presume to show, Schnitzler dates the first testimony to the morning Angelus 1317/18 at Parma, the noonday 1386 at Prague, and the evening 1307 at Esztergom and 1327 at Rome.[83]

The Franciscan Benedetto Sinigardi d'Arezzo (d. 1281) records that an antiphon was sung after compline: "Angelus locutus est Mariae: Ave Maria, etc." Other evidence from Franciscan convents of this period, including a note of St. Bonaventure, describes one Hail Mary prayed while a bell was being rung three times. Some persons added three Hail Marys to a noonday prayer in honor of Christ's passion: "Tenebrae factae sunt ..." "Christus factus est ..." The three versicles of the modern *Angelus* are of sixteenth-century origin. A synod of Strasbourg (1546) does not yet

---

[80] Raynaldi, ad annum 1318, 58; ad annum 1327, 54.

[81] Thurston again provides the citation: *Tractatus tractatuum,* XIV (Venetiis, 1584), fol. 330, v°. St. Antoninus follows Calderini in this view.

[82] C. A. Kneller, *Zur Geschichte des Angelus-Läutens,* in *Zeitschrift für Katholische Theologie,* Vol. 25, 1901, p. 353.

[83] Th. Schnitzler, *Angelusläuten,* in *Lexikon für Theologie und Kirche,* Vol. 1, 1957, p. 542.

seem aware of the wording, while that of Prague (1605) presumes it as already known together with the prayer, "Pour forth, we beseech thee, O Lord ..." but without the versicle, "Pray for us, O holy mother of God ..." Fifteenth-century England knew the custom of a single versicle of different wording from today's, and three Hail Marys. A catechism printed in Venice in 1560 proposes the present wording by way of a prayer at an evening bell; Pope Pius V's edition of the little office of the Blessed Virgin also contains it, as does a catechism of Canisius dated 1577.

The extension of the prayer to morning and mid-day recitation seems to be a seventeenth-century development. The morning prayer was interpreted (e.g., at the Prague synod of 1605) as commemorating Christ's resurrection and that at noon His passion, while the evening bell recalled the Incarnation — according to Bonaventure because the angel's visit was at evening. Other interpretations transpose the significance of the morning and evening recitations. In any case, the prayer following, "Gratiam tuam quaesumus, Domine," commemorates all three mysteries; it is found incorporated into a Cracow prayer book as early as 1609. The specification of the prayer by Pope Benedict XIII as one bearing an indulgence (Sept. 14, 1724) crystallized it in its modern form. Various relaxations concerning standing and kneeling in order to gain the indulgences attached have been made over the years. On February 20, 1933, the Sacred Penitentiary removed all such conditions for gaining the indulgence.[84]

*   *   *

For the sake of completeness, we must include the fourth and final anthem to Mary prescribed for recitation after Compline in the Breviary. It is entitled *Ave Regina Caelorum,* and an English translation reads:

> Queen of the heavens, we hail thee,
> Queen of angel hosts, we salute thee,
> Thou the root and thou the portal,
> Thou the font of light immortal.
> Hail thou Virgin robed in glory,
> Crown of all creation's story!
> Beauty excelling, we greet thee,
> Oh, beseech thy Son for us, we pray thee.

This hymn is prescribed from the Feast of the Purification (Feb. 2) to

---

[84] Much of the foregoing material is found in H. Schauerte, art. *Angelus,* in *Lexikon der Marienkunde,* fasc. 2, p. 218.

Wednesday of Holy Week.[85]

A twelfth century manuscript from Paris contains it as the antiphon for none on the feast of the Assumption.[86] The various addresses to our Lady as queen, mistress, rood, and gateway are reminiscent of the titles in the Eastern *Akathistos* hymn. Authorship of this hymn is unknown.[87]

*   *   *

The Litany of Loreto which is in modern use contains forty-nine invocations to Our Lady taken from Scripture and the Fathers of the Church. This ancient prayer in dialogue form (Gr., *litaneúō* = *rogo,* I beseech, supplicate) was recited either during the Mass liturgy or in procession on the way to it. At first the invocations were in praise of God only but later of the saints (eighth-ninth centuries) and then of Mary in particular. Her title in the early litany of the saints had been threefold: "Holy Mary; Holy Mother of God (*Genitrix*); Holiest of Virgins." It was the titles devised for Our Lady by the Eastern Fathers that led to the expansion of these three into an entire series. The occasion in the West was probably the singing of the Little Office of Our Lady. Early forms before the standardization imposed by Pope St. Pius V contain litanies like that of Loreto.[88] The earliest manuscript containing a litany to Mary is a twelfth century one from Magonza. It bears the title "Letania de Domina nostra Dei genitrice virgine Maria. Oratio valde bona cotidie pro quacumque tribulatione dicenda est." The invocations are lengthy and each begins with *Sancta Maria* as in the latter half of the *Hail Mary.* There is a fourteenth century litany of seventy-five titles which gained much in popular favor, especially in the Venice area where it was used until 1820 in processions honoring Mary through the miraculous image of

---

[85] The Latin text reads: Ave, Regina caelorum, / Ave, Domina angelorum: / Salve, radix, salve, porta / Ex qua mundo lux est orta: / Gaude, Virgo gloriosa, / super omnes speciosa, / Vale, o valde decora, / Et pro nobis Christum exora.

[86] Hence the *Vale.* Cf. M. Steinheimer, art. *Ave Regina caelorum,* in *Lexikon der Marienkunde,* fasc. 3/4, p. 502 f.

[87] Cf. *Uffizio dell'Inno Akathistos in onore della SS. Madre di Dio* [text in Greek and Italian] (Grottaferrata, 1949). Cf. also Carlo del Grande, *L'Inno Acatisto in onore della Madre di Dio* (Firenze, 1948); G. G. Meerseman, O.P., *Der Hymnus Akathistos im Abendland*(Freiburg [Schweiz], 1958); H. Barré, C.S.Sp., *L'Hymne Acathiste en Occident,* in *Marianum,* Vol. 21, 1959, pp. 291-297.

[88] Cf. T. Jacuboski, O.S.M., *Le 'Laudes Virginis',* in *Studi Storici sull'Ordine dei Servi di Maria,* Vol. 1 (Roma, 1933), pp. 66-77.

Nicopeia.[89]

The fifteenth and sixteenth centuries saw a proliferation of litanies to Mary. From the early 1500's one in particular, of unknown authorship, became customary at the shrine of Loreto. Pope Sixtus V in 1587 gave approbation to a certain set of responses sung at Loreto, but this did not curtail the composition of as many as one for every day of the year in some places; in Loreto itself a different one for each day of the week. Finally Pope Clement VIII stabilized matters with the decree *Quoniam multi* (6 Sept., 1601) which suppressed all present and future litanies "except that one customarily sung at the holy House of Loreto." A decree of the Sacred Congregation of Rites (1631) required special permission for the addition of any invocation to it. The title "Queen conceived without original sin" was allowed to the bishops of Forlì, Ghent, Algiers, Saint-Fleur, and any others who petitioned it, by Pope Gregory XVI in 1839. Leo XIII added "Queen of the most holy rosary" in 1883, and in 1903, "Mother of good counsel." The contribution of Benedict XV (16 November, 1915) was "Queen of peace," while Pius XII added "Queen assumed into heaven" shortly after that dogma was defined in 1950.

The ideas around which the titles are grouped are chiefly Mary's motherhood of God, her perpetual virginity, intercessory office, and universal queenship. Roschini has indicated which of these four privileges of Mary are celebrated by which titles.[90] Gerald Vann requested not so long ago that some thought be given to a more suitable English rendition of some of the titles of the Latin prayer. He claimed that certain of the invocations were either poor translations or downright mistranslations, "or at any rate show a lamentable lack of any sense of language, any

---

[89] G. M. Roschini, O.S.M., *La Madonna secondo la fede e la teologia*, Vol. 4 (Roma, 1954), p. 310.

[90] *Ibid.*, p. 312. For various pre-Loretan litanies taken from German manuscript sources, cf. W. Schleussner, *Zur Entstehung der lauretanischen Litanei*, in *Theologische Quartalschrift*, Vol. 107, 1926, pp. 254-267; N. Paulus, *Die Einführung der lauretanischen Litanei in Deutschland durch den seligen Canisius*, in *Zeitschrift für Katholische Theologie*, Vol. 26, 1902, pp. 574-583. On the general subject, cf. M. Boval, O.S.B., *Les Litanies de Lorette, histoire, symbolisme, richesses doctrinales* (Paris, 1946); R. Klaver, O.S.C., *The Litany of Loreto* (St. Louis, Mo., 1954); and G. G. Meersseman, O.P., *"Virgo a doctoribus praetitulata." Die marianischen Litaneien als dogmengeschichtliche Quellen*, in *Freiburger Zeitschrift für Philosophie und Theologie*, Vol. 1, 1954, pp. 129-178.

feeling for the beauty of words."[91] Among his tentative suggestions were the following: *Mater purissima:* Mother of perfect love (or, of undivided heart); *Mater castissima:* Mother of flawless chastity; *Mater inviolata:* Mother ever a maiden; *Mater intemerata:* Mother unsullied by evil; *Virgo prudentissima:* Virgin most wise; *Virgo veneranda:* Virgin whom we revere; *Virgo praedicanda:* Virgin whose praises we sing; *Virgo potens:* Virgin so powerful; *Virgo clemens:* Virgin so gentle; *Virgo fidelis:* Virgin so true; *Speculum justitiae:* Mirror of holiness; then "Fountain" for "Seat of wisdom"; "Source" for "Cause of our joy." Lastly, *Vas spirituale:* Chalice of spiritual life; *Vas honorabile:* Chalice of honor; *Vas insigne devotionis:* Splendid chalice of dedication.

---

[91] G. Vann, O.P., *Notes on Our Lady's Litany,* in *Worship,* Vol. 30, July-August, 1956, pp. 437-441. — Additional literature on some of the prayers discussed in this chapter: C. Boyer, S.J., *Le "Salve Regina,"* in *Marianum,* Vol. 14, 1952, pp. 270-275; J. M. Canal, C.M.F., *En torno a Ademaro, obispo de Le-Puy-en-Velay* [on the authorship of the *Salve Regina*], in *Ephemerides Mariologicae,* Vol. 8, 1958, pp. 488-493; J. P. de Castro, O.F.M., *Salve Regina,* in *Revista Eclesiástica Brasileira,* Vol. 1, 1941, pp. 796-802; E. Flicoteaux, O.S.B., *Le Salve Regina,* in *Marie,* Vol. 3, No. 4, 1949, pp. 104-107; P. Hermenegildo, O.F.M., *Estudio sobre el Ave María,* in Actas del Quarto Congreso Mariano Internacional celebrado en Zaragoza, 1908 (Madrid, 1909), pp. 943-945; G. Lefebvre, O.S.B., *L'Ave Marie; son origine historique, son interprétation,* in *Marie,* Vol. 8, No. 3, 1954, pp. 168-175; D. G. Maeso, *Exégesis lingüística del Avemaría,* in *Cultura Bíblica,* Vol. 11, 1954, pp. 302-319; J. E. Martins Terra, S.J., *Ave Maria,* in *Revista Eclesiástica Brasileira,* Vol. 17, 1957, pp. 624-649; F. Mercenier, O.S.B., *La plus ancienne prière à la Sainte Vierge: le Sub tuum praesidium,* in *Questions Liturgiques et Paroissiales,* Vol. 25, 1940, pp. 33-36; S. Navarro, C.M.F., *El autor de la Salve,* in *Estudios Marianos,* Vol. 7, 1948, pp. 425-442; I. Rodríguez, O.F.M., *Consideración literario-musical sobre la "Salve Regina,"* ibid., Vol. 18, 1957, pp. 381-401; O. Stegmüller, *Sub tuum praesidium. Bemerkungen zur ältesten Überlieferung,* in *Zeitschrift für Katholische Theologie,* Vol. 74, 1952, pp. 76-82; D. J. Unger, O.F.M.Cap., *The Angelus* (Chicago, 1956); G. Vannucci, O.S.M., *La più antica preghiera alla Madre di Dio,* in *Marianum,* Vol. 3, 1941, pp. 97-101; M. Vidal Rodríguez, *La Salve explicada,* 2nd ed. (Santiago, 1923); A. M. Vincentini, O.S.M., *Le quattro antifone finali del Breviario Romano* (Treviglio, 1915).

THE DOMINICAN ROSARY

by VERY REV. MSGR. GEORGE W. SHEA, S.T.D.

N CURRENT popular usage, the word *rosary* has come to be applied to any series of prayers, especially those recited with the aid of a string of beads or other device for keeping count, and also to the beads themselves. According to this very generic use of the term, there are non-Christian[1] as well as Christian rosaries, and among the latter there are non-Marian[2] as well as several Marian rosaries.[3]

But such is not the language of the Church. The Church has long known only one 'rosary." Over the centuries her official vocabulary came, after some initial vacillation,[4] to reserve that name exclusively for one particular method and form of prayer in honor of Mary, that which our

---

[1] Buddhist, Mohammedan, Hindu, etc.; cf. H. Thurston, S.J., *The Rosary*, in *The Month*, Vol. 96, 1900/II, pp. 405-406; Vol. 97, 1901/I, pp. 383, 395, note **2**; *idem*, art. *Rosary* in *The Catholic Encyclopedia*, Vol. 13 (New York, **1912**), p. **185**; *idem*, art. *Chapelet* in *D.A.C.L.* (*Dictionnaire d'Archéologie Chrétienne et de Liturgie*), Vol. 3 (Paris, reprinted 1946), col. 400-401; J. Volz, art. *Beads* in *The Catholic Encyclopedia*, Vol. 2 (New York, 1907), p. 362; J. Shaw, *The Story of the Rosary* (Milwaukee, 1954), pp. 4-6, 143 158.

[2] Cf. D. Attwater, *A Dictionary of Mary* (New York, 1956), articles *Rosary; Rosary, Bridgettine; Rosary of Our Lady of Consolation; Rosary of the Immaculate Conception; Rosary of the Immaculate Heart; Rosary of the Seven Joys; Rosary of the Seven Sorrows*. Cf. also E. Campana, *Maria nel culto cattolico*, ed. 2, edited by G. Roschini, Vol. 1 (Torino, 1946), pp. 524-527; Beringer-Steinen, *op. cit.*, Vol. 1, pp. 433-451. On the *"Rosary of Tears,"* cf. T. Henry, The Rosary, *in* The Homiletic and Pastoral Review, *Vol. 39, Oct.,* 1938, p. 7.

[3] On "rosaries" in honor of Christ, cf. F. Willam, *The Rosary: Its History and Meaning* (New York, 1953), pp. 31-32, 41, 42; J. Shaw, *op. cit.*, p. 60; F. Beringer, S.J., *Die Ablässe, ihr Wesen und Gebrauch*, ed. **15**, edited by P. Steinen, S.J. (two volumes, Paderborn, 1921-1922), Vol. **1**, nn. 396, 865-867; T. Henry, *The October Devotions*, in *The Homiletic and Pastoral Review*, Vol. 38, Oct., 1937, p. 15: "The Rosary of the Five Wounds of Our Lord, and the Rosary of the Precious Blood." On the "Angelic Rosary," in honor of the angels, cf. Beringer-Steinen, *op. cit.*, Vol. 1, n. 833.

[4] For example, the bull of Clement VIII, *Cum sicut,* Feb. 2, 1598, speaks of the *"Rosarium SS. Nominis Dei"*; cf. J. Larroca, O.P., *Acta Sanctae Sedis necnon Magistrorum et Capitulorum generalium sacri Ordinis Praedicatorum pro Societate SS. Rosarii, Confraternitatibus SS. Rosarii*, etc. (two volumes, Lugduni, 1890-1891), Vol. 2, Part 3, p. 703, note 2. We shall cite this work as Larroca, after the Dominican Master General who ordered its compilation (by P. Nothon, O.P.) and publication.

title calls "The Dominican Rosary."[5] As to other Catholic devotions using prayer-beads, the Church refers to them, and to their beads, as *"coronae,"* that is, crowns, chaplets.[6] The so-called Apostolic Rosary, and the so-called Crosier Rosary, are none other than the usual rosary beads which have received special indulgences. One should speak of the Apostolic indulgences rather than of the Apostolic Rosary. Apostolic indulgences are those gained by one who carries on his person or keeps in a suitable place at home an object of devotion (rosary-beads or other prayer-beads, cross, crucifix, small religious statue, religious medal) which has been specially blessed by the Holy Father or by a priest having the necessary faculty, and who performs any of the works enjoined for these indulgences by the Pope at the beginning of his reign.[7] Similarly, one should speak, not of the Crosier Rosary, but of the Crosier indulgence (a

---

[5] See the decrees of the Sacred Congregation of Rites, Nov. 24, 1663, and Dec. 3, 1663 (both in Larroca, *op. cit.,* Vol. 2, Part 3, nn. 273, 274), also Mar. 15, 1664, and Nov. 22, 1664, in *Decreta authentica Congregationis Sacrorum Rituum, ab anno 1588 ad. a. 1946* (Romae), Vol. 1, nn. 1289, 1306; see also Alexander VII, Brief *In supremo,* May 28, 1664, in *Bullarium Romanum,* Vol. 17 (Augustae Taurinorum, 1869), pp. 274-275; Clement XI, Brief *In supremo,* Mar. 8, 1712 (in Larroca, *op. cit.,* Vol. 2, Part 1, p. 338); Benedict XIII, Apost. Const. *Pretiosus,* May 26, 1727, in *Bullarium Romanum,* Vol. 22 (Augustae Taurinorum, 1871), p. 525. Pope Leo XIII, Apost. Const. *Ubi primum,* Oct. 2, 1898, decreed that beads (*coronae*) not composed of either five, ten, or fifteen decades should not be given the name "rosary"; A.S.S. (= *Acta Sanctae Sedis*), Vol. 31 (Romae, 1898-1899), p. 261; W. Lawler, O.P., ed., *The Rosary of Mary: Translations of the Encyclical and Apostolic Letters of Pope Leo XIII* (Paterson, 1944), p. 186. Cf. J. Proctor, O.P., *The Rosary Guide* (New York, 1901), pp. 2-3.

[6] *"Coronae"* is a general term for all longer prayers, or repetitions of prayers, whether accompanied by meditations or not, and be they recited with the aid of prayer-beads or not; the beads sometimes used in such devotions are likewise called *corona,* chaplet, crown (on occasion, "material crown," to distinguish the beads from the devotion they serve); cf. Beringer-Steinen, *op. cit.,* Vol. 1, pp. 611-612, index, s.v. "Korone," and p. 397, note 3. Official publications of the Holy See use this generic term also for the rosary, both the recitation thereof (as *Corona in honorem B.V.M. a SS. Rosario,* in the *Enchiridion Indulgentiarum: Preces et Pia Opera,* ed. 2 [Typis Polyglottis Vaticanis, 1952], index), and its beads (cf. *Benedictio Coronarum Sacratissimi Rosarii B.V.M.,* in the *Rituale Romanum,* editio typica [Typis Polyglottis Vaticanis, 1952]; also, *Codex Iuris Canonici,* can. 239, 1., 5°: "benedicendi . . . rosaria, aliasque coronas precatorias"). These and other official publications of the Holy See know several *coronae,* but only one that is a "rosary" — the *Corona SS. Rosarii B. V. M.*

[7] Cf. W. Kent, art. *Indulgences, Apostolic,* in *The Catholic Encyclopedia,* Vol. 7 (New York, 1910), pp. 78-79; T. Bouscaren, S.J., A. Ellis, S.J., *Canon Law,* ed. 2 (Milwaukee, 1951), pp. 401-405; S. De Angelis, *De Indulgentiis,* ed. 2 (Città del Vaticano, 1950), nn. 229-242. Some Apostolic indulgences will he listed later.

partial indulgence of 500 days which may be gained for each Our Father and each Hail Mary recited on rosary-beads blessed by a Crosier Father or other priest having the necessary faculty).[8]

It turns out, then, that this chapter could have been entitled simply "The Rosary." However, in view of the broad usage of "rosary" mentioned above, a more specific designation seemed preferable. Besides, the inclusion of "Dominican" in our title makes possible a prompt and express acknowledgment of the magnificent part played by the sons of St. Dominic, the great Order of Preachers, in enriching the Church with so beautiful and so efficacious a form of prayer as the Rosary of Our Lady.[9] To say "Dominican Rosary" is to recognize the provenance of a devotion which, far from being confined to the Dominican Order, has become — largely through that Order's initiative and efforts — the treasured possession of the entire Church, a devotion dear to every Catholic, a devotion so esteemed by Mother Church that she wishes her clerics and religious to practice it daily,[10] a devotion which Pope Julius III could hail as "the glory of the Roman Church" and of which Pope Leo XIII was able to say: "Among the various methods and forms of prayer which are devoutly and profitably used in the Catholic Church, that which is called the Rosary of Mary is for many reasons to be especially recommended."[11] Briefly, the rosary is a devotion Dominican in its provenance, Catholic in its practice, "a choice jewel in the common treasure of the Church."[12]

So far as the allotted space allows, this chapter will set forth the

---

[8] Cf. De Angelis, *op. cit.,* nn. 269-272.

[9] "The Dominican Order, which from its very beginning has been most devoted in honoring the Blessed Virgin, and by which the institution and propagation of the Confraternity of the Rosary was accomplished, holds as its inheritance all that belongs to this devotion" — Pope Leo XIII, Apost. Const. *Ubi primum,* Oct. 2, 1898; *A.S.S.,* Vol. 31, p. 258; Lawler, *op. cit.,* p. 179. Whence the Dominicans have a special right (*praecipuo quodam iure*) in stimulating and maintaining the Rosary devotion; *idem,* Apost. Letter *Salutaris ille,* Dec. 24, 1883; E. Tondini, ed., *Le Encicliche Mariane,* ed. 2 (Roma, 1954), p. 82; Lawler, *op. cit.,* p. 16.

[10] Cf. *Codex Iuris Canonici,* can. 125, 2° and 592; M. Castellano, O.P., *Riflessi legislativi del culto mariano,* in *Enciclopedia Mariana,* ed. R. Spiazzi, O.P. (Genova, 1954), pp. 445-446.

[11] *Salutaris ille;* Tondini, *op. cit.,* p. 82; Lawler, *op. cit.,* pp. 15-16.

[12] A. Duval, O.P., *La dévotion marial dans l'Ordre des Frères Prêcheurs,* in *Maria. Études sur la Sainte Vierge,* ed. H. du Manoir S.J., Vol. 2 (Paris, 1952), p. 781; cf. W. Bonniwell, O.P., *A History of the Dominican Liturgy* (New York, 1944), pp. 252-253, and H. Thurston, S.J., art. *Rosary,* in *The Catholic Encyclopedia,* Vol. 13, p. 187.

nature (composition and manner of recitation), origins, and excellence of the Dominican rosary, and a résumé of the main indulgences granted to all the faithful for its recitation. In the pages on the manner of reciting the rosary it will be necessary to distinguish the various requirements, on the score of recitation, for gaining the Apostolic indulgences, the Crosier indulgence, the Bridgettine indulgences,[13] and the diverse Rosary indulgences properly so-called. The latter, one gathers from the list published, with the approval of Pope Leo XIII, by the Sacred Congregation of Indulgences on Aug. 29, 1899, are all those granted by the Popes: (1) to the Confraternity of the Most Holy Rosary (the majority of these are indulgences for Confraternity members only, but some can be gained by nonmembers as well, upon participation in certain devout exercises closely associated with the Confraternity); (2) to all the faithful "for the devotion of the Most Holy Rosary," notably for the recitation of the rosary, but also for certain other forms of devotion in honor of Our Lady of the Rosary.[14] For all practical purposes, one may refer to the first group as the "special Rosary indulgences," and to the second as the "general Rosary indulgences."

I. NATURE OF THE DOMINICAN ROSARY

According to the Roman Breviary, the complete rosary consists in the recitation of fifteen decades or tens of Hail Marys with an Our Father preceding each decade, while at each of these decades we recall in pious meditation one of the principal mysteries of our Redemption.[15] Similar is

---

[13] A priest with the requisite faculties can give the specially indulgenced Bridgettine blessing not only to the six-decade Bridgettine prayer beads hut also to the five-decade rosary beads. To gain the Bridgettine indulgences in reciting the five decades of the rosary, one must add the Apostles' Creed after each decade, but does not have to conclude the five decades with the extra Our Father and three Hail Marys that come at the end of the Bridgettine chaplet. All the Bridgettine indulgences can be gained by this shorter form of recitation, save one (cf. Beringer-Steinen, *op. cit.*, Vol. 1, p. 437, note 5).

[14] Cf. *A.S.S.*, Vol. 32 (Romae, 1900), pp. 228-241.

[15] Cf. *Breviarum Romanum*, Feast of the Most Holy Rosary of the Bl. Virgin Mary (Oct. 7), Matins, fourth lesson; the latter was authorized on Mar. 26, 1725, on Sept. 1, 1756, and again on Aug. 5, 1888; cf. Larroca, *op. cit.*, Vol. 2, Part 3, pp. 793-795, 828-834, 995-997, 1000; Bonniwel, *op. cit.*, pp. 333-334. The formula for the Dominican blessing of rosary beads, in the *Rituale Romanum*, makes reference to meditation as part of the rosary ("divina contemplando mysteria devote oraverit"). So too the Collect in the Mass of the Feast of the Most Holy Rosary (Oct. 7), which begs God to grant "that, meditating on these mysteries . . . , we may both imitate what they contain, and obtain what they promise."

the much earlier description in the Apostolic Constitution of Pope St. Pius V, *Consueverunt Romani Pontifices*, Sept. 17, 1569.[16] The latter is the first papal document to speak expressly of meditation as part of the rosary devotion. However, many earlier ecclesiastical documents refer implicitly to the practice of meditating on mysteries (to be sure, not yet our fifteen, but as many as fifty and even 150). Thus Bishop Alexander Nanni Malatesta, papal legate to Germany, in granting an indulgence to the Rosary Confraternity at Cologne, Mar. 10, 1476, spoke of "reading" the rosary — an indication that then there were rosary mysteries too numerous to be memorized, which therefore had to be read from a book.[17]

Because its 150 Hail Marys correspond to the 150 Psalms of the Psalter, the complete rosary is sometimes called Our Lady's Psalter. In fact, the latter was its common designation down to the end of the fifteenth century, while "rosary" was reserved for a part, e.g., a third, of Our Lady's Psalter.[18] English-speaking Catholics now employ the term "rosary" both for the complete rosary and for a third thereof (whereas the French tend to use "rosaire" for the complete rosary, "chapelet" for a third of the "rosaire"). To be sure, where clarity is needed, one uses, e.g., "the small rosary," "the lesser rosary," "a third of the rosary" for five decades, and "the full rosary," "the complete rosary" for fifteen decades, and even "the double rosary" for ten decades. Similarly, when clarity calls for it, the

---

[16] *Bullarium Romanum*, Vol. 7 (Augustae Taurinorum, 1862), p. 775: "modum ... orandi et precandi Deum, Rosarium seu Psalterium eiusdem B. Mariae Virginis nuncupatum, quo eadem beatissima Virgo, Salutatione Angelica centies et quinquagies ad numerum Davidici Psalterii repetita, et Oratione Dominica ad quamlibet decimam, cum certis meditationibus, totam eiusdem Domini N. Iesu Christi vitam demonstrantibus, interposita, veneratur."

[17] Cf. Larroca, *op. cit.*, Vol. 2, Part 3, pp. 588-589; J. Schütz, *Die Geschichte des Rosenkranzes* (Paderborn, 1909), p. 33, with note 1. The above grant of an indulgence for "reading the rosary" was referred to and confirmed by Pope Leo X, Apost. Const. *Pastoris Aeterni*, Oct. 6, 1520; *Bullarium Romanum*, Vol. 5 (Augustae Taurinorum, 1860), p. 758. "To read the rosary" occurs frequently in the 15th century monuments on the rosary; cf. Larroca, *op. cit.*, Vol. 2, Part 3, p. 588, note 3; and p. 591, for a document of Francis de Claromonte, Cardinal Legate, Apr. 9, 1514.

[18] Cf. Y. Gourdel, O.Cart., *Le culte de la Très Sainte Vierge dans l'Ordre des Chartreux*, in *Maria. Études sur la Sainte Vierge*, ed. H. du Manoir, S.J., Vol. 2 (Paris, 1952), p. 653; A. Duval, *art. cit.*, p. 773, note 186; J. Schütz, *op. cit.*, pp. 39-41; Larroca, *op. cit.*, Vol. 2, Part 4, p. 1219. The Apostolic Constitution of Pope Leo X, *Pastoris Aeterni*, Oct. 6, 1520, gives the first certain indication from a Pope that the Psalter of Mary is commonly called "rosary": "et modum orandi huiusmodi Psalterium sive Rosarium eiusdem Beatae Virginis vulgariter appellatum;" *Bullarium Romanum*, Vol. 5, p. 758.

THE DOMINICAN ROSARY

official vocabulary of the Church speaks of "a third of the rosary," that is, five decades.

The authentic rosary is a happy combination of vocal and mental prayer, each of which is essential to the devotion. It is incorrect to say, with H. Thurston, that meditation is "the very essence of the Rosary devotion," for vocal recitation of the prayers is also of the essence. Meditation is, of course, the nobler element, the "soul," while vocal prayer is the "body" of the devotion; in the felicitous formula of Maisie Ward, "the beads are there for the sake of the prayers, and the prayers are there for the sake of the Mysteries."[19] The rosary, Pope Leo XIII declared, "is composed of two parts, distinct but inseparable — the meditation on the mysteries and the recitation of the prayers. It is thus a kind of prayer that requires not only some raising of the soul to God, but also a particular and explicit attention, so that by reflection upon the things to be contemplated, impulses and resolutions may follow for the reformation and sanctification of life."[20]

Hence, as Pope Pius XI stated, they err "who consider this devotion merely a boresome formula repeated with monotonous and singsong intonation."[21] This is certainly true when the rosary is prayed in the ideal way, with meditation during, rather than only before or after, each decade. But since the latter ways of meditating are also permissible, in which case one would have the repetition of Our Fathers and Hail Marys unaccompanied by meditation, it seems appropriate to note that such repetition of vocal prayers cannot fairly be viewed as sterile, as superstitious mechanism. For one thing, vocal prayer always implies,

---

[19] Cf. Thurston, art. *Rosary*, in *The Catholic Encyclopedia*, Vol. 13, p. 188; M. Ward, *The Splendor of the Rosary* (New York, 1945), p. 7. On the way in which the vocal prayers facilitate meditation, cf. Ward, *op. cit.*, pp. 11-12; A. Herring, *The Rosary*, in *The Month*, Vol. 146, 1925/II, pp. 289-302; F. Willam, *The Rosary: Its History and Meaning* (New York, 1953), pp. 182-184, 212; G. Vann, O.P., *Our Lady and her Rosary*, in *The Life of the Spirit*, Vol. 12, 1958, pp. 491-494.

[20] Ency. *Iucunda semper*, Sept. 8, 1894; Tondini, *op. cit.*, p. **210**; Lawler, *op. cit.*, p. 120. According to Leo XIII, Ency. *Diuturni temporis*, Sept. **5, 1898,** the rosary is "an admirable garland woven from the Angelic Salutation, together with the Lord's Prayer, conjoined with the obligation (*officio*) of meditation"; Tondini, *op. cit.*, p. 274; Lawler, *op. cit.*, p. **173**. This passage was repeated by Pius XI, Ency. *Ingravescentibus malis*, Sept. 29, 1937; Tondini, *op. cit.*, p. 416; W. Doheny, J. Kelly, editors, *Papal Documents on Mary* (Milwaukee, 1954), p. 192. Also by Pius XII, Epistle *Novimus libenter* (to the Master General of the Dominicans), July 11, 1957; *A.A.S.*, Vol. 49, 1957, p. 726.

[21] Ency. *Ingravescentibus malis;* Tondini, *op. cit.*, p. 418; Doheny-Kelly, *op. cit.*, p. 183.

under penalty of losing its religious value, some attention and consideration. Moreover, as Pius XI put it, "both piety and love, although always breathing forth the same words, do not, however, repeat the same thing, but they fervently express something ever new which the loving heart always sends forth." And finally, in the words of Pius XII, "the recitation of identical formulas, repeated so many times, rather than rendering the prayer sterile and boring, has on the contrary the admirable quality of infusing confidence in him who prays, and brings to bear a gentle compulsion on the motherly heart of Mary."[22]

Through the meditations of the complete rosary one recalls and has impressed on his mind, the Popes tell us, "the chief mysteries of the Christian religion," "the mysteries of our Redemption," "the great mysteries of Jesus and His Mother united in joys, sorrows, and triumphs."[23] The fifteen mysteries are divided into three equal groups, known as "The Joyful," "The Sorrowful," and "The Glorious Mysteries."

The five Joyful Mysteries are: the Annunciation (to Our Lady by the Angel Gabriel), the Visitation (of Our Lady to St. Elizabeth), the Nativity of Christ, the Presentation of the Christ Child in the Temple, the Finding of the Christ Child in the Temple. The five Sorrowful Mysteries are: the Agony in the Garden, the Scourging at the Pillar, the Crowning with Thorns, the Carrying of the Cross, the Crucifixion. The five Glorious Mysteries are: the Resurrection, the Ascension, the Descent of the Holy Spirit upon the Apostles, the Assumption, the Coronation of Mary as Queen of Heaven.[24]

These fifteen themes have been definitively fixed as "the Mysteries of the Rosary." Others are not to be substituted in their stead. Meditation on

---

[22] Cf. Pius XI, *Ingravescentibus malis, ubi supra;* Pius XII, Ency. *Ingruentium malorum,* Sept. 15, 1951; Tondini, *op. cit.,* p. 664; Doheny-Kelly, *op. cit.,* p. 245. See B. Thierry D'Argenlieu, O.P., *La théologie du Rosaire,* in *Maria. Études sur la Sainte Vierge,* ed. H. du Manoir, Vol. 5 (Paris, 1958), pp. 748-751. The above reflections will have further application when it is learned that meditation is not absolutely required of everyone for gaining the Rosary indulgences, and is not required at all for the Apostolic, Bridgettine, or Crosier indulgences.

[23] See the Encyclicals of Leo XIII, *Magnae Dei Matris* (Sept. 8, 1892), *Adiutricem populi* (Sept. 5, 1895), *Octobri mense* (Sept. 22, 1891); Tondini, *op. cit.,* pp. 138, 160, 162, 230; Doheny-Kelly, *op. cit.,* pp. 58, 71, 72, 109. Also Pius XI, Ency. *Ingravescentibus malis,* Sept. 29, 1937; Tondini, *op. cit.,* p. 418; Doheny-Kelly, *op. cit.,* p. 183.

[24] On the fifteen mysteries of the rosary, see the Rosary Encyclicals of Pope Leo XIII, *passim,* e.g., *Iucunda semper,* Sept. 8, 1894; Tondini, *op. cit.,* pp. 204-206; Doheny-Kelly, *op. cit.,* pp. 91-93.

them, according to one's ability, is requisite both for practicing the authentic Rosary devotion (the Popes, we have heard, declare such meditation to be of the devotion's essence), and for gaining those of the Rosary indulgences which have been granted for the recitation of the rosary.[25]

In support of the foregoing assertions we may note the following. Although the Apostolic Constitution of Pope St. Pius V, *Consueverunt Romani Pontifices,* in declaring meditation to be of the essence of the Rosary devotion, did not expressly state it to be a condition for gaining indulgences,[26] such a requirement seems to have been already in force at an earlier date. A pamphlet published in Rome around 1560 records the then existing Rosary indulgences, describes the manner in which the rosary is to be recited, and lists our 15 mysteries in such a way as to suggest that the indulgences could be gained only if one retained this series of mysteries, and — by the same token — meditated upon them.[27] In any case, with the approval of Pope Benedict XIII, the Sacred Congregation of Indulgences decreed, Aug. 13, 1726, that the indulgences granted by the Popes for the recitation of the rosary are not gained by those who omit the customary meditation on the mysteries of our Redemption and substitute other topics of meditation.[28] In setting forth the general rosary indulgences for recitation of the rosary, the *Enchiridion*

---

[25] Meditation is not a condition for the Apostolic, Bridgettine, or Crosier indulgences. On the Apostolic indulgences, see S. C. Indul. (= Sacred Congregation of Indulgences), July 1, 1839, in *Decr. auth.* (= *Decreta authentica Sacrae Congregationis Indulgentiis Sacrisque Reliquiis praepositae ab anno 1668 ad annum 1882 edita iussu et auctoritate SS^i D. N. Leonis PP. XIII,* Ratisbonae, 1883), n. 273, ad 2^m; Beringer-Steinen, *op. cit.,* Vol. 1, p. 414, note 4; De Angelis, *op. cit.,* n. 227, b. As to the Bridgettine indulgences, see S. C. Indulg., July 1, 1839, in *Decr. auth.,* n. 273, ad 1^m; De Angelis, *op. cit.,* n. 246; Beringer-Steinen, *op. cit.,* Vol. 1, n. 882. Regarding the Crosier indulgence, see A.S.S., Vol. 40, 1907, p. 442, note 1; De Angelis, *op. cit.,* n. 227, c. and n. 272, a; Beringer-Steinen, *op. cit.,* Vol. 1, n. 885.

[26] Cf. R. Addazi, O.P., *Il Rosario nei documenti ufficiali della Chiesa,* in *Alma Socia Christi,* Vol. 9 (Romae, 1953), p. 196.

[27] Cf. Beringer-Steinen, *op. cit.,* Vol. 1, pp. 444-445; Willam, *op. cit.,* pp. 78, 200.

[28] *Decr. auth.,* n. 92. Benedict XIII confirmed this anew in the Apost. Const. *Pretiosus,* May 26, 1727; *Bullarium Romanum,* Vol. 22 (Augustae Taurinorum, 1871), p. 525. Leo XIII reconfirmed it in his Apost. Const. *Ubi primum,* Oct. 2, 1898; A.S.S., Vol. 31, p. 261; Lawler, *op. cit.,* pp. 186-187. Relevant also are the decrees of the S. C. Indulg., July 1, 1839 (*Decr. auth.,* n. 273, ad 2m, ad *4m*), and Jan. 28, 1842 (in A. Prinzivalli, *Resolutiones seu decreta authentica Sacrae Congregationis Indulgentiis . . .* praepositae ab anno 1668 ad annum 1861, Romae, 1862, n. 528, ad 3m, ad 4m).

Indulgentiarum does not expressly mention meditation as a requisite. However, this requirement is clear not only from the foregoing legislation but also from what the *Enchiridion* itself says elsewhere: "if they devoutly recite at least a third part of the rosary or meditate on its mysteries in some other manner."[29] Pope Benedict XIII granted that for persons lacking the capacity to meditate on the usual mysteries, it is enough that they recite the rosary devoutly.[30]

Recitation of the complete rosary all in a day is not necessary either for practicing the authentic Rosary devotion or, with one exception, for gaining indulgences.[31] Among those who daily recite a third of the rosary, there has long been the custom of rotating each series of mysteries throughout the week, namely, the joyful mysteries on Mondays and Thursdays, the sorrowful on Tuesdays and Fridays, the glorious on Sundays, Wednesdays, and Saturdays. Although, as far as indulgences are concerned, one is not held to this rotation by any hard and fast rule,[32] nevertheless the Church has approved the custom for the faithful generally, and Pope Leo XIII wished it retained by members of the Rosary Confraternity, at least when reciting the rosary publicly at the Rosary Altar.[33] Insistence on holding to the glorious mysteries for all Sundays of the year,[34] if warranted at all, should in our opinion be limited to the

---

[29] Cf. *Enchiridion Indulgentiarum,* ed. 2 (Typis Polyglottis Vaticanis, 1952), nn. 395, 397; De Angelis, *op. cit.,* nn. 263-264.

[30] Benedict XIII, Apost. Const. *Pretiosus,* May 26, 1727; *Bullarium Romanum,* Vol. 22, p. 525. See also S. C. Indulg., Jan. 28, 1842, in Prinzivalli, *op. cit.,* n. 528; and the official *Raccolta di orazioni e pie opere per le quali sono state concesse dai Sommi Pontefici le SS. Indulgenze* (Roma, Tipografia Poliglotta della S. C. de Propaganda Fide, 1898), pp. 350-351. This concession is still in force; cf. Beringer-Steinen, *op. cit.,* Vol. 1, p. 449, note 3; De Angelis, *op. cit.,* n. 263.

[31] Cf. the Bull of Clement VII, *Etsi temporalium,* May 8, 1534; *Bullarium Romanum,* Vol. 6 (Augustae Taurinorum, 1860), pp. 168-169; Addazi, *art. cit.,* pp. 510-511. Pope St. Pius X (S. C. Indulg., June 12, 1907) granted a plenary indulgence, once a day, to Rosary Confraternity members for reciting the entire rosary within a day, dividing the decades at will, for the triumph of Holy Mother Church, on condition of Confession, Communion, and a visit to a church or public oratory; *A.S.S.,* Vol. 40, pp. 510-511.

[32] Cf. F. Leather, O.P., *The Rosary: Its Power and Its Use* (London, 1932), p. **32**.

[33] See S. C. Indulg., July 1, 1839, in *Decr. auth.,* n. 273, *ad 5m;* Leo XIII, *Ubi primum,* in *A.S.S.,* Vol. 31, p. 262. Cf. De Angelis, *op. cit.,* n. 267, b; Beringer-Steinen, *op. cit.,* Vol. 1, n. 905.

[34] Cf. *The Rosary: The Crown of Mary,* new and revised edition, by A Dominican Father (New York, 1947), pp. 24, 37.

THE DOMINICAN ROSARY 99

above-mentioned public recitation. In other public recitation, and certainly in private recitation,[35] the glorious mysteries may be replaced by the sorrowful on the Sundays in Lent, and by the joyful on the Sundays of Advent and those from Epiphany until Lent.[36]

For Rosary indulgences it is no longer necessary to say the five decades without interruption; one may now separate the decades, provided that all five are said the same day.[37] Whether the Apostolic and the Bridgettine indulgences can be gained despite such separation of the decades is not altogether clear.[38] For Crosier indulgences the question does not arise, since these are given for every bead recited, even if one does not intend to complete a decade.[39]

As will be emphasized later, the Our Fathers and the Hail Marys are the only vocal prayers prescribed for the authentic rosary, and for gaining the indulgences granted for its recitation. Therefore it is not necessary, though it is highly recommended, to announce (in public recitation) or to enunciate (in private recitation) the appropriate mystery at each decade; it suffices that one recall the mystery mentally.[40] The meditation itself

---

[35] Cf. *ibid.*, p. 23. Public religious exercises are those held in common in churches or in public or semi-public oratories (in the case of those who may lawfully use the latter); in all other cases they are private; *Enchiridion Indulgentiarum, praenotanda*, n. 7.

[36] Cf. *A Manual of Prayers for the Use of the Catholic Laity*, prepared and enjoined by order of the Third Plenary Council of Baltimore, new ed. (New York, 1930), pp. 397-403.

[37] Cf. S. C. Indulg., July 8, 1908 (*Acta Pontificia et decreta SS. Romanorum Congregationum*, Vol. 7 [Romae, 1909], p. 57); *Enchiridion Indulgentiarum*, n. 395, note 1; De Angelis, *op. cit.*, n. 267, c; Beringer-Steinen, *op. cit.*, Vol. 1, n. 905. However, in fulfilling their obligation of a weekly recitation of the entire rosary, Rosary Confraternity members may spread the fifteen decades throughout the week; they are not held to complete five decades within a day; S. C. Indulg., Jan. 22, 1858 (*Decr. auth.*, n. 385, *ad 2^m*); cf. Beringer-Steinen, *op. cit.*, Vol. 2, p. 163.

[38] Cf. Bouscaren-Ellis, *Canon Law*, ed. 2, pp. 401-402. De Angelis does not discuss the matter. F. Cappello, S.J., *De Sacramentis*, Vol. 2; *De Poenitentia*, ed. 4 (Taurini, 1944), n. 685, considers it more probable that neither the Apostolic nor the Bridgettine indulgences are lost by separation of the decades. Silent as to the Bridgettine indulgences, Beringer-Steinen, *op. cit.*, Vol. 1, p. 414, note 4, says separation of the decades does not affect the Apostolic indulgences.

[39] Cf. S. C. Indulg., Mar. 15, 1884, *ad 3^m*; A.S.S., Vol. 16, 1906, p. 405; cf. De Angelis, *op. cit.*, n. 272, b; Beringer-Steinen, *op. cit.*, Vol. 1, n. 885.

[40] S. C. Indulg., July 1, 1839; *Decr. auth.*, n. 273, *ad 4^m*: "(Non requiritur mentio specialis mysterii in recitatione Salutationis Angelicae, dicendo, v. gr., post haec verba: ventris tui Jesus haec alia: quem concepisti, vel quem visitando Elisabeth portasti, etc. vel quem peperisti, etc.) quia quando requiritur meditatio mysteriorum pro acquirendis

should be made at least immediately before or after the vocal prayers of the decade,[41] but preferably while the latter are being recited,[42] in which case one's thoughts should dwell on the mystery rather than on the words of the vocal prayers.[43] Among the various ways of meditating on the Rosary mysteries, a centuries-old one still in vogue is that of considering at each Hail Mary a distinct point connected with the mystery.[44] Devotion is sometimes intensified if each decade is said for some particular intention, of one's own choosing.[45]

No less than meditation, vocal prayer — formation of the words with tongue and lips (not necessarily audible unless circumstances, such as public recitation or alternate recitation with a companion, call for this) — is of the essence of the authentic rosary, and is a condition for gaining any indulgences.[46] Note, however, that, according to the general law of the

---

indulgentiis, sufficit meditatio mentalis eodem tempore, quo recitantur Oratio Dominicalis et Angelicae Salutationes. ..."

[41] Cf. Beringer-Steinen, *op. cit.,* Vol. 1, n. 904; Larroca, *op. cit.,* Vol. 1, n. 135. In some devotional works, such as *The Reign of Jesus Through Mary,* rev. ed., by G. Denis, S.M.M. (Bay Shore, 1944), pp. 153-164, and manuals of prayer, such as that prepared and enjoined for the Catholic laity by the Third Plenary Council of Baltimore, one finds a short meditation to be read immediately before each decade. One may, of course, combine this with free meditation on the relevant mystery during the recitation of the decade.

[42] Cf. S. C. Indulg., July 1, 1839; *supra,* footnote 40.

[43] Cf. W. Most, *Mary in Our Life* (New York, 1954), pp. 231-233; *L'Ami du Clergé,* Vol. 26, 1904, pp. 583-584.

[44] Cf. *The Rosary: The Crown of Mary,* new and rev. ed., by A Dominican Father (New York, 1947), p. 41, and, for suggestions as to these 150 "sub-mysteries," pp. 49-78. The antecedents of this method reach back to the fifteenth century; cf. *supra,* footnote 17, on "reading" the rosary.

[45] For some suggestions by Père Monsabré, O.P., cf. Leather, *op. cit.,* pp. 32-33; cf. also St. Louis Mary de Montfort, *The Secret of the Rosary,* transl. by M. Barbour (Bay Shore, 1954), pp. 173-178.

[46] Cf. *Codex Iuris Canonici,* can. 934, 2, understood in the light of can. 934, 1, and confirmed (as the exception confirms the rule) by can. 936 on mutes, and by the decree of the Sacred Apostolic Penitentiary, Dec. 7, 1933, (*A.A.S.,* Vol. 26, 1934, p. 35), which conceded that indulgences attached to invocations and so-called ejaculations can be gained even by reciting them merely mentally; cf. De Angelis, *op. cit.,* n. 89. a. Even apart from this general legislation, the very fact that indulgences are granted for "recitation" of the rosary (cf. *Enchiridion Indulgentiarum,* nn. 395-398) supposes vocal praying of the Our Fathers and Hail Marys which are of the rosary's essence — "recitation," unless qualified by "mental" (as in the Dec. 7, 1933 decree of the S. Ap. Penitentiary, and in *Enchiridion Indulgentiarum,* p. xvi, note 2), means vocal prayer.

The Dominican Rosary

Church, mutes can gain indulgences attached to public prayers if, in company with others praying in the same place, they piously raise their minds and hearts to God, or if, in the case of indulgenced private prayers, they repeat these in their minds, or express them by signs, or even merely run over them with their eyes.[47] In applying this general concession to the praying of the rosary, doubtless some provision should be made for meditation on the mysteries, e.g., by meditating before or after reading, or mentally recalling the vocal prayers, or (if this be possible) while "signing" them.

Strictly speaking, the fifteen Our Fathers and the hundred and fifty Hail Marys are the only vocal prayers that belong to the rosary; no others are mentioned when the Popes undertake to tell what the authentic rosary is. Over the centuries, however, other vocal prayers, varying in different regions, have come to be added. Thus in the U.S.A. and many other countries, the rosary proper is preceded by the Sign of the Cross, the Apostles' Creed, an Our Father, three Hail Marys, and a Glory be to the Father.[48] But in Spain and in other Spanish-speaking countries these prayers come at the end of the rosary.[49] In Italy they are not said at all.[50] The Dominicans, too, omit them, preferring to commence the rosary like the Office of the Bl. Virgin Mary.[51]

Whatever the origin of these three introductory Hail Marys (a question to be touched upon later), they have come to be prayed for an increase of faith, hope, and charity, as was suggested in 1658 by Fr. Henry

---

[47] *Codex Iuris Canonici*, can. 936, which is often given the restrictive but erroneous translation "deaf-mutes." Cf. Beringer-Steinen, *op. cit.*, Vol. 1, nn. 136-137.

[48] Commencement of the rosary with the Creed, the Our Father, and the three Hail Marys became the custom in many parts of Germany near the end of the 16th century; cf. S. Beissel, *Geschichte der Verehrung Marias im 16. und 17. Jahrhundert* (Freiburg im Br., 1910), p. 78. St. Louis de Montfort (d. 1716) popularized this practice in France. On the history of the association of the Creed with recitation of the rosary, cf. Thurston, *The Rosary*, in *The Month*, Vol. 96, 1900/II, p. 522, with note 2, and pp. 632-633; S. Beissel, *Geschichte der Verehrung Marias in Deutschland während des Mittelalters* (Freiburg im Br., 1909), p. 518.

[49] Cf. A. Ellis, S.J., *Our Lady's Rosary*, in *Review for Religious*, Vol. 5, 1946, p. 328.

[50] Cf. Beissel, *Gesch. d. Verehrung Marias im 16. und 17. Jhdt.*, p. 78; E. Campana, *Maria nel culto cattolico*, ed. 2, edited by G. Roschini, Vol. 1 (Torino, 1946), p. 518; L. Andrianopoli, *Il Rosario*, in *Enciclopedia Mariana*, ed. R. Spiazzi, p. 408.

[51] Cf. *The Rosary: The Crown of Mary*, pp. 36-37; Proctor, *op. cit.*, pp. 240-241; Shaw, *op. cit.*, pp. 107-108. *A Manual of Prayers for the Use of the Catholic Laity*, p. 397, begins the rosary in this manner, but then goes on to the usual prelude of Apostles' Creed, etc.

Boedeker.⁵² Germans insert an express petition to that effect after the name "Jesus": "der den Glauben in uns vermehre," "der die Hoffnung in uns stärke," "der die Liebe in uns entzünde." An old and widely used Jesuit manual for the Sodalists of Mary directed that the three Hail Marys honor Our Lady's prerogatives as Daughter of God the Father, Mother of God the Son, Spouse of God the Holy Spirit.⁵³ Sometimes the Trinitarian interpretation of the three Hail Marys is combined with that of Boedeker.⁵⁴

Following a practice which was recommended in 1589 by Thomas Sailly, S.J., and whose fifteenth-century antecedents will be noted later, Catholics in many countries, especially in German-speaking regions of Europe, interpolate in the middle of each Hail Mary of a decade, after the name "Jesus," an express reference to the pertinent mystery; for example, the fifth sorrowful mystery is mentioned, in every Hail Mary of the decade, as follows: "... Jesus, who was crucified for us."⁵⁵ Quite the same

---

⁵² Cf. Beissel, *Gesch. d. Verehrung Marias im 16. und 17. Jhdt.,* p. 79. For the puzzlement often caused by these three Hail Marys, and for various views and practices in their regard, cf. T. Henry, in *The Homiletic and Pastoral Review,* Vol. 36, Sept., 1936, pp. 1244-1247; Vol. 38, Oct., 1937, pp. 10-14; Vol. 39, Oct. 1938, pp. 3-7.

⁵³ Cf. Thurston, *art. cit.,* pp. 633, 635. Perhaps this practice of contemplating Mary in relation to the three Divine Persons has its roots in the "Three Hail Marys Devotion" inaugurated by St. Mechthilde, around 1270. On this devotion, cf. P. Régamey, O.P., *Les plus beaux textes sur la Vierge Marie,* nouvelle éd. (Paris, 1946), pp. 164-165; C. Chamberlain, *Three Hail Mary Devotion,* in *Marian Helpers Bulletin,* Oct.-Dec., 1959, p. 8.

⁵⁴ See, e.g., *A Manual of Prayers for the Use of the Catholic Laity,* p. 397; G. Denis, *The Reign of Jesus through Mary,* pp. 151-153. St. Louis de Montfort recited the one Our Father in honor of the unity of the Divine Essence, the three Hail Marys to honor the Trinity of Persons, and to ask a lively faith, a firm hope, and an ardent charity; cf. his *The Secret of the Rosary,* p. 172, together with Denis, *op. cit.,* p. 266.

⁵⁵ See, e.g., the new *Katholischer Katechismus der Bistümer Deutschlands* (Freiburg im Br., 1956), pp. 280-281. Gourdel, *art. cit.,* pp. 674-675; Beissel, *Gesch. d. Verehrung Marias im 16. und 17. Jhdt.,* p. 15; Beringer-Steinen, *op. cit.,* Vol. 1, nn. 899, 904. France, too, has known this practice; J. Bouvier, *Traité dogmatique et pratique des Indulgences,* ed. 10 (Paris, 1855), p. 145, taught it as a matter of course, and issues of *L'Ami du Clergé* early in this century still refer to it. The insertions were recommended to American Catholics by J. Heaney, O.P., *A Short Treatise on the Rosary* (New York, 1863), pp. 23-24, were incorporated in the *Holy Trinity Manual* (Boston, 1923), p. 17, and have found advocates in F. Weiser, S.J., *Hail Mary and Mystery in the Rosary Prayer,* in *Worship,* Vol. 32, Jan., 1959, pp. 101-104, and C. Callan, O.P., J. McConnell, M.M., *Spiritual Riches of the Rosary* (New York, 1958), according to the review by T. Sparks, O.P., *Cross and Crown,* Vol. 10, 1958, p. 367, who frowns on the proposed innovation.

is St. Louis de Montfort's method of adding after "Jesus" a word or two appropriate to the respective mystery, such as "Jesus incarnate" (1st decade), "Jesus carrying His Cross" (9th decade), "Jesus crowning thee" (fifteenth decade).[56] Some Eastern Catholics, notably those of the Ruthenian and Byzantine-Slavic rites, add a brief mention of the corresponding mystery at the end of their own shorter form of the Hail Mary.[57]

Widespread, but not universal, is the practice of adding at the end of each decade a Glory be to the Father,[58] or, when the rosary is recited for the dead, "Eternal rest," etc.[59] In some places, however, the doxology is said immediately after the Our Father, before the decade of Hail Marys.[60] In Italy it seems to have been omitted, at least in public recitation, until quite recently.[61] At the end of each decade (after the Glory be to the Father, when this is added to the decade), many recite various

---

[56] Cf. *The Secret of the Rosary*, p. 179. The method was featured in an English Rosary booklet, published around 1750, which added after "Jesus" in, for example, the sorrowful mysteries: "agonizing in the garden," "whipped at a post," "crowned with thorns," "portering the Cross," "crucified to death"; cf. Thurston, in *The Month*, Vol. 97, 1901/I, p. 217.

[57] Cf. D. Attwater, *A Dictionary of Mary*, s.v. Hail Mary, and s.v. Rosary. For some other types of insertions and additions to the Hail Marys of the rosary, among Latin rite Catholics, cf. Schütz, *op. cit.*, pp. 19, 239, 240-241; Beissel, *Gesch. d. Verehrung Marias in Deutschland während des Mittelalters*, p. 524.

[58] The custom of adding a Glory be to the Father to each decade — inspired perhaps by a desire to assimilate the recitation of the rosary to that of the Divine Office, whose psalms each end with the doxology — first appears in the 17th century, was still somewhat unusual in the France of St. Louis de Montfort, who helped popularize it, and is not even mentioned in several 18th and early 19th century books on the rosary; cf. Thurston, The Rosary, in *The Month*, Vol. 96, 1900/II, pp. 636-637; Beissel, *Gesch. d. Verehrung Marias im 16. und 17. Jhdt.*, p. 78; Shaw, *op. cit.*, pp. 103-108, 114.

[59] Cf. Larroca, *op. cit.*, Vol. 1, n. 116; Leather, *op. cit.*, p. 30.

[60] Cf. Campana, *op. cit.*, Vol. 1, p. 518. According to W. Barry, *The Sacramentals* (Cincinnati, 1858), p. 155, in this country a century ago the Glory be to the Father was said before each decade. Doubtless this is a survival of the ancient and once widespread custom of concluding the Our Father with a doxology. In contrast with Barry, another work published around the same time, that of J. Heaney, pp. 21, 26, puts the doxology at the end of the decade.

[61] Cf. Campana, *op. cit.*, Vol. 1, p. 518; Beissel, *Gesch. d. Verehrung Marias im 16. und 17. Jhdt.*, p. 78. As to private recitation, we may note that Pope Pius IX used to say the Glory be to the Father, or, when praying the rosary for the dead, "Eternal rest," etc.; cf. *The Homiletic and Pastoral Review*, Vol. 39, Feb., 1939, pp. 512-513.

ejaculations, such as that requested by Our Lady in the third of her apparitions at Fatima: "O my Jesus, forgive us our sins, save us from the fires of hell, and lead all souls to heaven, especially those that most need Thy mercy."[62]

After the five (or ten or fifteen) decades it is usual with us to say the *Salve Regina* ("Hail, Holy Queen ...") and the oration "O God, whose only begotten Son ...", with versicles and responses after each of these. But in some countries the *Salve Regina*, etc., precede the rosary proper, which then concludes with the Litany of the Blessed Virgin and certain versicles and prayers.[63] This is also Dominican practice.[64] Almost everywhere the recitation of the rosary ends, as it had begun, with the Sign of the Cross.

None of the foregoing additions to the fifteen Our Fathers and the hundred and fifty Hail Marys is necessary either for the integrity of the authentic rosary or for gaining indulgences, whether Apostolic, Bridgettine, Crosier, or Rosary indulgences.[65] On the other hand, there is

---

[62] Cf. C. Barthas and G. Da Fonseca. S.J., *Our Lady of Light* (Milwaukee, 1947), p. 32, with note 2; W. Walsh, *Our Lady of Fatima* (New York, 1948), p. 225; there are other versions of Mary's words — some inaccurate, as that in *The Rosarian's Handbook* (New York, 1953), pp. 75, 132. For other ejaculations, see F. Mutch, *Indulgence Aid* (pamphlet, Our Sunday Visitor Press, 1947), p. 22, and Campana, *op. cit.*, Vol. 1, p. 518. Sometimes the Glory be to the Father at the end of the decade is followed by prayers to the Blessed Mother, such as those in *A Manual of Prayers for the Use of the Catholic Laity*, pp. 398-406.

[63] Cf. Leather, *op. cit.*, pp. 31-32. The *Salve Regina*, dear to the Order of Preachers from the beginning (cf. Duval, *art. cit.*, p. 745; Bonniwell, *op. cit.*, pp. 148-154, 356-357), came to be linked with recitation of the rosary through the Dominican-directed Rosary confraternities, whose custom it was to sing the anthem on Saturdays and feasts of Our Lady. We find Lamsheim declaring, in 1495, that it is an optional conclusion of the rosary; cf. Thurston, *The Rosary*, in *The Month*, Vol. 96, 1900/II, pp. 636-637. On the singing of the litany of the Blessed Virgin by early Rosary confraternities, cf. Bonniwell, *op. cit.*, p. 312, note 9.

[64] Cf. Proctor, *op. cit.*, pp. 240-248. The *Salve Regina*, etc., follow the introductory versicles and responses referred to *supra*, footnote 51, and the choral recitation of the rosary is modeled after that of the Little Office of the Blessed Virgin. For descriptions of this attractive service (which has come to compensate for dwindling opportunities to recite the Little Office — cf. Duval, *art. cit.*, p. 744, note 22), see Thurston, *art. cit.*, p. 637; Shaw, *op. cit.*, pp. 107-108.

[65] Cf. Beringer-Steinen, *op. cit.*, Vol. 1, n. 901; Larroca, *op. cit.*, Vol. 1, n. 416; and, with regard to mention of the mystery in the course of the Hail Mary, cf. *Decr. auth.*, n. 273, *ad 4m*, quoted above in footnote 40. Recall from footnote 13 that those wishing to gain Bridgettine indulgences must add the Apostles' Creed after each decade. J. Heaney, *op. cit.*, p. 25, erred in making the doxology a prescribed part of the decades of the rosary.

no reason to fear that any of these additions would imperil the acquisition of indulgences. For none of them alters the substance of the indulgenced prayers of the rosary, and the Sacred Apostolic Penitentiary, in an authoritative interpretation of canon 934, 2 of the Code of Canon Law, has ruled that the indulgences attached to prayers are lost only by those additions, omissions, or interpolations which alter the substance of such prayers.[66] Further, to dispose of another conceivable difficulty, the additions at the end of the decades are not a notable interruption of the rosary,[67] and in any case even a notable interruption of the decades is now permitted without detriment to the Rosary indulgences, and probably without detriment to the Apostolic and Bridgettine indulgences.[68] Although the additions we have been speaking of do not endanger indulgences, and while one may use them in private recitation of the rosary, where they are not yet approved custom for public recitation they should not be introduced into such recitation without permission of the Ordinary.[69]

From what has been said about canon 934, 2, as interpreted by the Sacred Apostolic Penitentiary, it is clear that, to gain indulgences, the prescribed Our Fathers and Hail Marys of the rosary must be said without any omission which would alter the substance of these prayers. Nevertheless, when two or more recite the rosary in common, they may alternate the parts of these prayers, one saying, for example, the first half

---

[66] S. Ap. Penit., Nov. 26, 1934, in *A.A.S.*, Vol. 26, 1934, p. 643; cf. T. Bouscaren, S.J., *Canon Law Digest*, Vol. 2 (Milwaukee, 1943), p. 236. This applies also to the "Fátima ejaculation"; cf. C. Parres, C.M., in *The Homiletic and Pastoral Review*, Vol. 58, May, 1958, p. 809; G. Montague, in *The Irish Ecclesiastical Record*, Vol. 85, 1956, pp. 284-285. The aforesaid decree also removed any uncertainty which, despite a series of earlier responses from the Holy See, may have remained as to the legitimacy of mentioning the mystery in the course of the Hail Mary; cf. De Angelis, *op. cit.*, nn. 91, 268; T. Sparks, O.P., in *Cross and Crown*, Vol. 10, 1958, p. 367. The practice of the Ruthenian, Byzantine-Slavic, and other Eastern rites was endorsed by decrees of the S. Ap. Penit., Apr. 29, 1930, and Jan. 31, 1931, and of the S. Congregation for the Oriental Church, Apr. 22, 1944; *A.A.S.*, Vol. 22, 1930, p. 292; Vol. 23, 1931, p. 88; Vol. 36, 1944, p. 245; cf. Bouscaren, *Canon Law Digest*, Vol. 1 (1934), pp. 456, 457, and Vol. 3 (1954), pp. 386-387.

[67] Cf. J. Donovan, C.M., in *The Homiletic and Pastoral Review*, Vol. 51, June, 1951, pp. 852-853.

[68] Cf. *supra*, footnotes 37 and 38.

[69] Cf. *Codex Iuris Canonici*, can. 1259, 1; G. Montague, in *The Irish Ecclesiastical Record*, Vol. 85, 1956, pp. 285-286.

of the Hail Mary, the other, or others, saying the second half;[70] this now holds good also for recitation of the rosary in conjunction with a radio broadcast, provided that the radio portion of the recitation is "live," that is, not produced by sound tapes, records, or other mechanical means.[71] Also to be noted is the fact that the indulgences attached to the recitation of the rosary can be gained by all, even the faithful of the Latin rite, who recite the Hail Mary according to the shorter form used in the Ruthenian, Byzantine-Slavic, and other Eastern rites.[72]

Beads grouped upon a string or chain facilitate recitation of the rosary.[73] By fingering them successively as prayer follows upon prayer, one can keep count automatically without being distracted from the

---

[70] Cf. S. C. Indulg., Feb. 29, 1820, in *Decr. auth.*, n. 249, *ad 4^m*; *Codex Iuris Canonici*, can. 934, 3.: "To gain the indulgences it is sufficient to recite the prayer alternately with a companion." The canon adds: "or to follow it in one's mind while it is being recited by another," but this general legislation, permitting a mental following of vocal prayers recited by others, would seem applicable to the rosary only if some provision be made for meditation on the mysteries, e.g., by meditating before or after the vocal prayers. Note that, according to a decree of the S. C. Indulg., Nov. 13, 1893 (*A.S.S.*, Vol. 26, 1893-1894, pp. 310-311), those who are engaged in exterior occupations which do not prevent interior recollection, e.g., arranging the altar, folding vestments, etc., can validly take part in the recitation of the rosary in common; cf. De Angelis, *op. cit.*, n. 266, c; Beringer-Steinen, *op. cit.*, Vol. 1, n. 903; G. Montague, in *The Irish Ecclesiastical Record*, Vol. 71, 1949, p. 78.

[71] Cf. S. Ap. Penit., Oct. 8, 1958, in *A.A.S.*, Vol. 50, 1958, p. 973.

[72] See the three decrees for these rites cited in footnote 66; the Holy See warns however, against change in the public recitation of the rosary (S. C. for the Oriental Church, Apr. 22, 1944, *ad 3^m*).

[73] On the archaeology of the rosary beads, see H. Thurston, *The Rosary*, in *The Month*, Vol. 96, 1900/II, pp. 403-418; 513-527; 620-637; Vol. 97, 1901/I, pp. *383-404;* idem, *The so-called Bridgettine Rosary*, in *The Month*, Vol. 100, 1902/II, pp. 189-203; idem, *The Rosary in the Western Church*, in *The Catholic Encyclopedia*, Vol. 13, pp. 184-187; idem, *Chapelet*, in *D.A.C.L.*, Vol. 3, Part 1 (Paris, reprint 1948), col. 399-406; T. Esser, O.P., *Zur Archäologie der Pater-noster-Schnur*, in *Compte rendu du quatrième congrès scientifique international des Catholiques tenu à Fribourg (Suisse) du 16 au 20 août 1897, première section: Sciences religieuses* (Fribourg, 1898), pp. 329-381; L. Gougaud, O.S.B., *Chapelet*, in *Dictionnaire de spiritualité, ascetique et mystique*, ed. M. Viller, S.J., etc., fasc. 8 (Paris, 1938) col. 478-479; J. Volz, *Beads, Use of, at Prayers*, in *The Catholic Encyclopedia*, Vol. 2, pp. 361-362; J. Beissel, *Gesch. d. Verehrung Marias im Deutschland während d. Mittelalters*, pp. 238-241, 426, 549-552; idem, *Gesch. d. Verehrung Marias im 16. u. 17. Jhdt.*, pp. 36, 39, 42, 44, 45, 72, 73, 91, 95, 98; T. Bridgett, *Our Lady's Dowry* (London, 1875), pp. 201-215.

prayers and meditations.[74] Since beads for fifteen or even ten decades are rather cumbersome, and because it is more common to pray only a third of the full rosary each day, the usual rosary beads have but five groups, each consisting of ten small beads (for the Hail Marys) and one larger bead (for the Our Father preceding each decade). For the doxology after each decade one generally fingers the links of chain between the last small bead and the following large bead. To this set of beads there is attached, for the prayers prior to the rosary proper, a pendant consisting of a crucifix or medal stamped with the cross, upon which one recites the Creed; a large bead, for the Our Father, then three small beads for the three Hail Marys.[75] The short length of chain on which these are mounted also bears a large bead for the Our Father preceding the first decade, and is joined with the five decades by a medallion of the Blessed Virgin, on which it is customary to say the concluding *Salve Regina*.

Contrary to a widespread belief, the use of rosary beads is not required either for praying the authentic rosary or, with two exceptions, for gaining the Rosary indulgences.[76] The exceptions are two indulgences granted by Pope Benedict XIII, which demand the use of rosary beads especially blessed by a Dominican Father or other priest having the necessary special faculty.[77] To obtain the indulgences in question,

---

[74] On the psychological advantages of using rosary-beads, cf. M. Ward, *The Splendor of the Rosary*, pp. 8-9, 12-13; G. Vann, *art. cit.*, p. 493; F. Willam, *op. cit.*, pp. 182-183.

[75] Thurston, *The Rosary*, in *The Month*, Vol. 96, 1900/II, pp. 633-635, believes these three Hail Mary beads of the pendant are a remnant from the Bridgettine chaplet which added three beads after the six decades in order to bring the number up to 63, the supposed number of years of Our Lady's life. At one time, the theory runs, people used this six decade chaplet with added pendant for both the Bridgettine crown and the rosary. When the latter's beads came to be fixed at five decades, the pendant was retained and the prayers of the pendant came to be said at the beginning, for the intentions spoken of in our earlier discussion of these three Hail Marys.

[76] Cf. De Angelis, *op. cit.*, nn. 263-266; Beringer-Steinen, *op. cit.*, Vol. 1, nn. 902-903 and Vol. 2, p. 162; R. Addazi, *art. cit.*, pp. 194-195; Larroca, *op. cit.*, Vol. 1, n. 77, and Vol. 2, Part 3, pp. 592-604. The official *Enchiridion Indulgentiarum, praenotanda, 1,* and n. 395, note 2, makes it perfectly clear that, the two exceptions aside, the use of rosary beads is not required for gaining the general Rosary indulgences granted for recitation of the rosary.

[77] Cf. S. C. Indulg., Apr. 13, 1726, in J. Schneider, S.J., *Rescripta authentica Sacrae Congregationis Indulgentiis Sacrisque Reliquiis praepositae* (Ratisbonae, 1885), n. 51; De Angelis, *ubi supra*; Beringer-Steinen, *op. cit.*, Vol. 1, nn. 902- 903. The first known mention of a blessing of rosaries occurs in 1519; cf. Larroca, *op. cit.*, Vol. 2, Part 3, pp. 592-604. One exception aside (cf. Beringer-Steinen, *op. cit.*, Vol. 1, p. 448, note 3), the

normally one must hold the Dominican-blessed beads and even finger them successively.[78] But if several recite the rosary in common, it is sufficient that one of their number have and use the beads;[79] the rest, of course, should unite themselves in prayer with the person holding the rosary, and should refrain from exterior occupations which would prevent interior recollection.[80] Further, in the case of a person reciting the rosary alone, if manual labor or any other reasonable cause prevents him from using the beads, he can gain the indulgences if he has the beads on his person, e.g., in his pocket,[81] and provided, of course, that his occupation does not prevent the requisite meditation. Excused also from holding and fingering the beads are the physically handicapped who are unable to do so[82]; they should, however, one assumes, have the blessed beads on their person.

One and the same set of rosary-beads can receive, from priests having the respective faculties, the indulgenced Apostolic, Bridgettine, Crosier,

---

Dominican blessing can be given only to beads of five, ten, or fifteen decades; cf. Pope Leo XIII, Apost. Const. *Ubi primum,* Oct. 2, 1898, in *A.S.S.,* Vol. 31, p. 261. Moreover, according to various decisions of the Holy See, to be eligible for this indulgenced blessing the beads must be made of durable material; excluded are rosary rings, rosary bracelets, and similar innovations; cf. De Angelis, *op. cit.,* n. 266, b.

[78] That normally the beads should be held and even passed through the fingers is implicit in the decree of the S. C. Indulg., Apr. 13, 1726 (in Schneider, *op. cit.,* n. 51), is presupposed by concessions of the Holy See to be mentioned in footnotes 79, 80, 81, and is expressly stated in the 1898 *Raccolta* (cf. *supra,* footnote 30), p. 350, which is still in force so far as the present matter is concerned; cf. Beringer-Steinen, *op. cit.,* Vol. 1, n. 903; De Angelis, *op. cit.,* n. 266, c; F. Cappello, S.J., *Tractatus Canonico-Moralis De Sacramentis,* Vol. 2: *De Poenitentia,* ed. 2 (Taurini-Romae, 1944), n. 671.

[79] S. C. Indulg., Jan. 22, 1858, in *Decr. auth.,* n. 384. The same decree makes it clear that the person having the rosary does not have to be the leader of the recitation.

[80] S. C. Indulg., Nov. 13, 1893, in *A.S.S.,* Vol. 26, 1893-1894, pp. 310-311; cf. *supra,* footnote 70.

[81] Sacred Apostolic Penitentiary, Nov. 9, 1933, in *A.A.S.,* Vol. 25, 1933, p. 502; cf. De Angelis, op. *cit.,* n. 266, c; G. Montague, in *The Irish Ecclesiastical Record,* Vol. 67, 1946, p. 268. Obviously, religious who wear rosaries on their cinctures satisfy this condition of having the beads on their person.

[82] Since the concession of Pope Benedict XV (S. Apost. Penitentiary, Oct. 22, 1917), mutilated persons unable to perform some bodily act that is prescribed, along with the recital of prayers, for gaining an indulgence, can gain the latter without the act, provided they recite the prayers; *A.A.S.,* Vol. 9, 1917, p. 539.

THE DOMINICAN ROSARY 109

and Dominican blessings.[83] As with the Dominican indulgences, to gain the Bridgettine or the Crosier indulgences one must tell the beads, it seems, or at least hold them.[84] Excepted are the physically handicapped who cannot do so.[85] The further exceptions noted above for the Dominican indulgences also apply here: when several recite the rosary in common, it suffices that one of them have and use the blessed rosary beads;[86] in reciting the rosary alone, if any reasonable cause prevents one from holding the blessed rosary beads, it suffices that these be on his person (and that he be able to give internal attention to the vocal prayers).[87] To gain Apostolic indulgences through recitation of the rosary one does not have to hold the blessed rosary beads or even have them on

---

[83] An object can be enriched with more than one indulgence on various titles; cf. *Codex Iuris Canonici*, can. 933. Contrary to the assertion in Larroca, *op. cit.*, Vol. 1, n. 95, which has misled many (e.g., F. Mutch, *The Dominican and Brigittine Indulgences*, in *The Homiletic and Pastoral Review*, Vol. 43, May, 1943, pp. 741-742, who later retracted, *ibid.*, July, 1943, p. 938), the indulgenced Dominican blessing does not impart at the same time the Bridgettine indulgences. For light on this point, cf. Beringer-Steinen, *op. cit.*, Vol. 1, p. 447, note 3; see also, in Larroca himself, Vol. 2, Part 3, p. 798, note 1, a consultor's *votum* regarding the April 13, 1726, decree of the Sacred Congregation of Indulgences.

[84] De Angelis, *op. cit.*, n. 227, b, and L. Fanfani, O.P., *Manuale theorico-practicum theologiae moralis*, Vol. 4 (Romae, 1951), p. 989, assert that one must tell the beads; Cappello, *op. cit.*, Vol. 2: *De Poenitentia*, n. 685, is content to say the beads must be held. That for the Crosier indulgences normally the beads must at least be held is certain, e.g., from the formula giving the faculty of imparting these indulgences (De Angelis, *op. cit.*, p. 473; cf. n. 269). As to the Brigettine indulgences, Pope Leo X, *Ex Clementis*, July 10, 1515, granted them to those "qui *per* et *super* Rosaria seu Coronas S. Birgittae devote oraverint" (cf. Beringer-Steinen, *op. cit.*, Vol. 1, n. 846); that normally the beads must be held and even passed through the fingers seems implicit in the decree of the S. C. Indulg., May 29, 1841 (*Decr. auth.*, n. 291, ad 8^m).

[85] Cf. *supra*, footnote 82.

[86] This seems to be Cappello's view, *op. cit.*, Vol. 2, n. 685, 2, coll. n. 671, 2. De Angelis, *op. cit.*, n. 248, and Beringer-Steinen, *op. cit.*, Vol. 1, pp. 585-586 ("Nachtrag" to n. 884), invoke the *Codex Iuris Canonici*, can. 934, 3, for the Bridgettine indulgences, while G. Montague, in *The Irish Ecclesiastical Record*, Vol. 71, 1949, p. 78, invokes the same canon also for the Crosier indulgences. See also Montague, *ibid.*, Vol. 67, 1946, pp. 267-268.

[87] Although the S. Apost. Penitentiary's decree of Nov. 9, 1933 (*A.A.S.*, Vol. 25, 1933, p. 502) spoke expressly only of the "indulgences of the Rosary" (and of the Way of the Cross), G. Montague, *ibid.*, Vol. 67, p. 268, and Vol. 71, pp. 78-79, judges it to apply also to the Bridgettine and the Crosier indulgences. Similarly, Cappello, *op. cit.*, Vol. 2, n. 671, 2; also F. Hecht, P.S.M., in *Periodica*, Vol. 27, 1938, p. 251, explicitly as to the Crosier, implicitly as to the Bridgettine indulgences.

his person; in fact, one does not have to have rosary beads at all, if he possesses some other devotional object which has been given the indulgenced Apostolic blessing.[88]

Thanks to express derogations from the general law that several indulgences cannot be gained by one and the same work to which various indulgences are attached by different titles,[89] it is possible to obtain by one recitation of the rosary several indulgences on different titles. Thus the Dominican indulgences can be gained cumulatively with the other Rosary indulgences granted for recitation of the rosary, if the rosary beads have the Dominican blessing.[90] Further, since the Popes declare that their concession of Apostolic indulgences does not derogate from other indulgences which may have been granted by the Supreme Pontiffs for the prayers, pious works, or exercises which are mentioned, a single recitation of the rosary can gain both the Apostolic and the Rosary indulgences — the Dominican indulgences included, if the rosary beads have the Apostolic and the Dominican blessings.[91] Again, if the rosary beads have the Crosier as well as the Dominican blessing, a single recitation of the rosary can obtain the Crosier cumulatively with the Dominican and the other Rosary indulgences.[92] To sum up, the Apostolic, Crosier, Dominican, and the other Rosary indulgences can be gained cumulatively by one recitation of the rosary, if the rosary beads have the three blessings, provided that the other conditions (e.g., the meditation on the mysteries, required for the Rosary indulgences) are fulfilled.[93] It is sometimes, but mistakenly, asserted that the Bridgettine indulgences, too, can be gained

---

[88] Cf. *A.A.S.*, Vol. 51, 1959, pp. 48-50; Beringer-Steinen, *op. cit.*, Vol. 1, n. 851; De Angelis, *op. cit.*, nn. 227, 230, 233.

[89] *Codex Iuris Canonici*, can. 933.

[90] Cf. *Enchiridion Indulgentiarum*, n. 395, note 2.

[91] Similarly, the same recitation can gain the Apostolic and the Bridgettine indulgences, if the beads have the Apostolic and the Bridgettine blessings; or the Apostolic and the Crosier indulgences, if the beads have the Apostolic and the Crosier blessings. Indeed, for cumulation of Apostolic indulgences with the Dominican and the other Rosary indulgences, or with the Bridgettine, or with the Crosier indulgences, the beads themselves do not have to have the Apostolic blessing if the person possesses some other religious object with the latter blessing; cf. *A.A.S.*, Vol. 51, 1959, pp. 48-50; De Angelis, *op. cit.*, nn. 67, e; 227, a; 232; 267, d; 272, d.

[92] S. C. Indulg., June 12, 1907, in *A.S.S.*, Vol. 40, 1907, pp. 442-443. For the correct understanding of this concession, cf. F. Hecht, P.S.M., in *Periodica*, Vol. 27, 1938, p. 251.

[93] Cf. De Angelis, *ubi supra*; Bouscaren-Ellis, *op. cit.*, p. 402.

THE DOMINICAN ROSARY

cumulatively with the Dominican and the other Rosary indulgences, and the Crosier indulgences as well, if the beads have the respective blessings.[94] So far as the Bridgettine indulgences are concerned, the only derogation from the general law about cumulation of indulgences (*C.I.C.*, can. 933) is that with reference to Apostolic indulgences.[95]

Although it is desirable that, when possible, the rosary be said while kneeling, this is not necessary.[96] In fact, one may recite the rosary and gain its indulgences anywhere[97] (for example, while sitting, walking, riding, working, before rising from bed, after retiring) provided one is able to meditate on the mysteries.[98] The rosary may be prayed during Mass: privately by the individual who finds this the best way for him to assist at the Holy Sacrifice;[99] and even publicly, not only during October devotions,[100] but also — if the Bishop consents — at other times of the year.[101] Revival of the ancient custom of our forefathers, daily recitation of the rosary in a family group, has been repeatedly urged by the Sovereign Pontiffs and encouraged by the granting of further indulgences.[102]

---

[94] For authors (Larroca, Mutch, and others cited by him) holding the contrary view, and for the erroneous supposition on which it is based, see *supra*, footnote 83.

[95] See *supra*, footnote 91.

[96] Cf. De Angelis, *op. cit.*, n. 94; Beringer-Steinen, *op. cit.*, Vol. 1, n. 134, and Vol. 2, p. 163.

[97] Except, of course, the indulgence granted by Pope Pius XI for reciting the rosary before the Blessed Sacrament; cf. *Enchiridion Indulgentiarum*, n. 395, c.

[98] Can one drive a car safely and truly meditate at the same time? It does not seem possible.

[99] This is clear from Pope Pius XII, Ency. *Mediator Dei*, Nov. 20, 1947; *A.A.S.*, Vol. 39, 1947, p. 560; N.C.W.C., Encyclical Letter of Pope Pius XII on *the Sacred Liturgy* (Vatican Library Translation), n. 108. Cf. W. Most, *Mary in Our Life* (New York, 1954), pp. 169-170.

[100] Since the foregoing was written, the Sacred Congregation of Rites, in a private reply to the Archbishop of Liverpool, Feb. 6, 1960, has indicated that henceforth, in conformity with paragraph 12 of the Congregation's Decree on Sacred Music and Sacred Liturgy (Sept. 3, 1958), public recitation of the rosary during Mass is forbidden, even in October; cf. *The Clergy Review*, Vol. 45, 1960, p. 306.

[101] This, too, must now be revised, in accordance with the preceding footnote.

[102] See, e.g., Pope Leo XIII, Ency. *Fidentem piumque*, Sept. 20, 1896; Pope Pius XI, Ency. *Ingravescentibus malis*, Sept. 29, 1937; Pope Pius XII, Ency. *Ingruentium malorum*, Sept. 15, 1951; A. Tondini, ed., *Le Encicliche Mariane*, ed. 2 (Roma, 1954), pp. 246-248, 424, 666; W. Doheny, J. Kelly, editors, *Papal Documents on Mary* (Milwaukee, 1954), pp. 116, 186-

II. ORIGIN OF THE ROSARY

The history of the optional features which eventually came to be added to the rosary's essence has been sufficiently treated in our earlier pages. We are concerned here only with the rosary proper, the devotion described by Pope St. Pius V.[103] The first certain evidence of what is substantially our rosary devotion — the recitation of 150 Hail Marys divided into fifties and tens, the fifteen Our Fathers, with some kind of meditation on what are approximately our fifteen mysteries of the Redemption (along with a "sub-mystery" for each of the 150 Hail Marys) — belongs to the latter half of the 15th century, when Alan of Rupe, O.P. (Alan de Rupe, de la Roche, van der Clip, d. 1475), aided by Jacob Sprenger, Michael Francisci, and other fellow Dominicans, propagated throughout northern France, Flanders, the Netherlands, and northern Germany his "Psalter of Christ and of Mary." The foundation by Alan and his colleagues of the first Rosary confraternities, with rich spiritual advantages for their members, the rapid multiplication of such confraternities, the effective use made by the Dominicans of the new art of printing (they quickly produced edition after edition of Rosary picture books, with woodcuts representing the mysteries, and explaining various methods of practicing the devotion) and the hearty support of other Religious Orders and of the secular clergy, spread the rosary (as Alan's "Psalter" came to be called, though he himself disliked and avoided the term) far and wide, and gradually brought about that uniformity which enabled it to become a devotion of the universal Church.[104]

187, 245-246. Initiated in Belgium in 1939, the Family Rosary Crusade has spread throughout the world; Father Patrick Peyton, C.S.C., has been its indefatigable director in the U.S.A. Cf. P. Peyton, *The Family Rosary Crusade*, in *The Homiletic and Pastoral Review*, Vol. 43, May, 1943, pp. 713-717. The indulgences for family recitation of the rosary will be indicated later. For various ways of reciting the family rosary, see *The Rosarian's Handbook* (New York, 1953), pp. 94-96.

[103] Cf. *supra*, footnote 16.

[104] On Alan, and the movement launched by him, cf. A. Walz, O.P., *Compendium Historiae Ordinis Praedicatorum*, ed. 2 (Romae, 1948), pp. 196-199; H. Thurston, S.J., in *The Month*, Vol. 96, 1900/II, pp. 620-632; Vol. 97, 1901/I, pp. 286-304; Vol. 100, 1902/II, pp. 281-299; S. Beissel, S.J., *Geschichte der Verehrung Marias in Deutschland während des Mittelalters* (Freiburg im Br., 1909), pp. 535-549; A. Duval, O.P., *La dévotion mariale dans l'Ordre des Frères Prêcheurs*, in *Maria*, ed. H. du Manoir, S.J., Vol. 2 (Paris, 1952), pp. 768-781. For the later history of the Rosary devotion, cf. Walz, *op. cit.*, pp. 417-420, 586-593; Beissel, *op. cit.*, pp. 511-567; *idem, Geschichte der Verehrung Marias im 16. und 17. Jhdt.* (Freiburg im Br., 1910), pp. 35-99; J. Shaw, *op. cit.*, pp. 69-129. J. Schütz, *Die Geschichte*

THE DOMINICAN ROSARY 113

The origin of Alan's Psalter or rosary is a complex problem, not yet definitively and completely resolved; we have space for little more than a résumé of the major opinions on the subject.[105] To begin with Alan's, according to his posthumously published works,[106] the devotion had been practiced long before the times of St. Dominic Guzmán (d. 1221) but, after dying out, was restored by the founder of the Order of Preachers, in obedience to revelations from the Blessed Virgin, notably in a vision granted to the saint near Toulouse at the height of the conflict with the Albigensians. Later the rosary again fell into disuse, until it was revived by Alan after he, too, had been favored with revelations from Our Lady. Alan's account of the history of the rosary was based, he said, on these revelations, on the writings of a certain John de Monte and a certain Thomas de Templo (described as companions of St. Dominic), and on a tradition of the Dominican Order.[107]

Whereas Alan maintained that St. Dominic was only the restorer of the rosary, in the sixteenth century and thereafter many Dominican and other writers came to present the saint as, under God, the first author of the devotion, whose essentials he devised, if not in response to a formal

---

des Rosenkranzes (Paderborn, 1909), reproduces many valuable documents bearing on the history of the devotion in the fifteenth and sixteenth centuries.

[105] For an excellent, if not altogether perfect and complete, presentation of the problems and opinions regarding the origin of the rosary, cf. J. Shaw, *op. cit.;* see the appreciation of this work by R.-M. Masson, O.P., *L'Histoire du Rosaire,* in *Marie,* Vol. 11, March-April, 1958, pp. 463-465. Also useful, more for its information than for its judgments, is F. Willam's work, *The Rosary: Its History and Meaning* (New York, 1953).

[106] The trustworthiness of these editions has been questioned by many, e.g., A. Duval, *art. cit.,* p. 768, note 166; on the other hand, H. Thurston, in *The Month,* Vol. 97, 1901/I, pp. 288-292, considers them substantially reliable. None of Alan's writings and discourses seems to have been printed during his lifetime, and little of his has survived in manuscript.

[107] For Alan's version of rosary origins, see Thurston and Duval, cited above in footnote 104. Of Alan's claim to rely on a tradition of the Dominican Order we shall speak later. His appeals to special revelations and visions do not deserve to be taken seriously; cf., e.g., A. Duval, O.P., art. *Alain de la Roche* (Bienheureux), in *Catholicisme, hier, aujourd'hui, demain,* ed. G. Jacquemet, fasc. 1 (Paris, 1947), col. 259-260. Dominican historians deny that St. Dominic's companions numbered a John de Monte or a Thomas de Templo; for speculations on the identity of these "authorities" of Alan, cf. Y. Gourdel, O.Cart., *Le culte de la Très Sainte Vierge dans l'Ordre des Chartreux,* in *Maria,* ed. H. du Manoir, Vol. 2, pp. 667-669, and Duval's article in the same volume, p. 771, note 181. The Dominican Breviary accords Alan the title of "Blessed," but he has never been beatified by the Church.

revelation by Our Lady, then at least under the influence of a divine inspiration.[108] This version became and for a long time remained the commonly received view. A great number of official papal statements over the course of four hundred years and the Roman Breviary (second nocturn of Matins for the Feast of the Most Holy Rosary, Oct. 7) endorse this view, but do not impose it.[109] These documents of the Holy See tend to speak of St. Dominic's alleged institution of our rosary as having been prompted by an inspiration from on high, rather than by a formal apparition and revelation of the Blessed Mother.[110]

In 1733, his research on the life of St. Dominic led the Bollandist, William Cuyper, S.J., to regard Alan of Rupe as the real author of the rosary devotion.[111] In the first quarter of the present century, Herbert Thurston, S.J., while rejecting the thesis of Alan's authorship, continued Cuyper's attack on the claims making St. Dominic either the restorer or the institutor of the rosary.[112] According to the English Jesuit, some elements entering into the composition of the rosary antedated St. Dominic, others did not come into existence until long after his death, and there is no evidence connecting any single feature of the devotion with the person of the founder of the Friars Preachers. In Thurston's opinion, repetition of the Hail Mary (the first half of our present prayer — the

---

[108] Cf. H. Thurston in *The Month,* Vol. 97, 1901/I, pp. 67-69, 302-303; Vol. 144, 1924/II, pp. 331-335.

[109] Cf. *ibid.,* Vol. 96, 1900/II, p. 404.

[110] For example, the fourth lesson of Matins for the Feast of the Most Holy Rosary (Oct. 7), after mentioning St. Dominic's prayer to the Blessed Mother for assistance, states that he was "advised" (*cum monitus esset*) to preach the rosary. According to Pope Pius XI, Ency. *Ingravescentibus malis,* Sept. 29, 1937, the practice of the rosary was "admirably diffused by St. Dominic, not without the heavenly suggestion and inspiration of the Virgin Mother of God" (*quem S. Dominicus mirabiliter provexit, non sine Deiparae Virginis instinctu supernoque admonitu*); Doheny-Kelly, *Papal Documents on Mary* (Milwaukee, 1954), p. 183; *A.A.S.,* Vol. 29, 1937, p. 376.

[111] Cf. Cuyper's discussion of the origins of the rosary in *Acta Sanctorum,* Aug., Vol. 1, pp. 422-437.

[112] Most of Thurston's many articles bearing on the origin of the rosary were published in *The Month,* as follows: Vol. 96, 1900/II, pp. 403-418, 513-527, 620-637; Vol. 97, 1901/I, pp. 67-79, 172-188, 217-218, 286-304, 383-404; Vol. 98, 1901/II, pp. 482-499; Vol. 100, 1902/II, pp. 189-203, 281-299; Vol. 102, 1903/II, pp. 95-97; Vol. 111, 1908/I, pp. 518-529, 610-623; Vol. 121, 1913/I, pp. 162-176, 379-388; Vol. 127, 1916/I, pp. 276-278, 441-452, 546-559; Vol. 139, 1922/I, pp. 65-68, 346-356; Vol. 144, 1924/II, pp. 330-342. For a summary of Thurston's views, see his articles *Rosary, The,* in *The Catholic Encyclopedia,* Vol. 13, pp. 184-187; *Chapelet,* in *D.A.C.L.,* Vol. 3, col. 399-406.

second half became common only toward the close of the Middle Ages), generally according to the number 50 or its multiples, and often limited to 150 in imitation of the 150 psalms of the Davidic Psalter, was already widespread early in the 12th century. Further, the introduction of Our Fathers to divide the Hail Marys into tens cannot reliably be traced farther back than the middle of the 14th century, and may have been the contribution of a German Carthusian, Henry Egher (Henry of Kalkar), around 1365.[113] As to the very soul of the rosary devotion, the practice of meditating in conjunction with recitation of the Hail Marys, this seems to derive from another German Carthusian, Dominic of Treves (Dominic Helion, Dominic the Prussian), who, around 1409, composed and popularized 50 short appendages to as many Hail Marys (which in those days still concluded with "Jesus"); these *clausulae*, as they were called, referred to various events in the life of Jesus and Mary.[114] So arose the idea of dwelling on the life of Our Lord and His Blessed Mother while saying the Hail Mary, and, to adapt this idea to the recitation of 150 Hail Marys, Alan and his colleagues amplified the 50 topics of the Carthusian Dominic (whom Alan may have confused with St. Dominic) to 150 which later, if not from the start, were subordinated, as "sub-mysteries," to 15 main mysteries, approximately our present ones.[115] Finally, to render the illustrated Rosary books less costly, and also to make the practice of the devotion independent of printed lists and hence easier, the many sub-

---

[113] Y. Gourdel, *art. cit.*, in *Maria*, Vol. 2, pp. 652-657, provides valuable information on Henry Egher and his insertion of the fifteen Our Fathers into the Psalter of Mary, which insertion is said to have been prompted by a vision of the Blessed Mother between 1365 and 1367.

[114] On Dominic of Treves one must again consult Y. Gourdel, *art. cit.*, pp. 657-667. The first Hail Mary with its *clausula* or addition read: "Hail, Mary, full of grace, the Lord is with thee, blessed art thou among women, and blessed is the fruit of thy womb, Jesus Christ, whom thou didst conceive by the Holy Spirit, through the message of the angel. Amen." Other examples of Dominic's *clausulae* may be seen in Shaw, *op. cit.*, p. 43, and Willam, *op. cit.*, p. 37.

[115] Alan spoke of "articles" (*articuli*) rather than of "mysteries." Thurston, in *The Month*, Vol. 96, 1900/II, pp. 629-630, says that the first to use the latter term in connection with the rosary may have been Alberto da Castello, O.P., in his *Rosario della gloriosa Vergine* of 1521 or 1522. But T. Esser, O.P., in an article published in 1905 and quoted at length by Schütz, noted that in 1481 the famous printing press at the Dominican monastery of St. Jacopo di Ripoli, in Florence, printed a "Carta dei Misteri" which seems to have been a pictorial representation of various rosary-mysteries (cf. Schütz, *op. cit.*, pp. 95-97). Indeed, the term may have been used much earlier, in the Constitutions of the Beguines of Ghent which will be discussed below.

mysteries were dropped, leaving only the readily memorized 15 mysteries.

Briefly, our rosary grew slowly and gradually, did not spring into being ready-made, was not the creation of any one person; of its several elements, some existed before St. Dominic, the others arose long after him, and the final form into which they all crystallized was due, under God's Providence, to accidental circumstances. Thus the late Father Thurston, whose views have found wide favor.[116]

As to our own opinion, leaving aside the question of the merits of his reconstruction,[117] we may say that, in the light of the criticisms leveled by him, Cuyper, and others against the earlier views of Alan, etc., it does not seem likely that our rosary, as such, was either restored or originated by St. Dominic. But one may still doubt that the latter contributed nothing at all to the genesis of our devotion. At the very least, some indirect influence should be conceded to St. Dominic, in that he impressed upon his sons that spirit which made the rosary what it is today.[118] Indeed, perhaps he exercised even a direct influence of one kind or another. Proponents of this view appeal to data not yet known in Thurston's day or overlooked by him. They contend, moreover, that the data he did exploit leave room for interpretations and conclusions quite different from his own.

For instance, it escaped Thurston's notice that Alan of Rupe invoked not only special revelations to himself and the writings of supposed companions of St. Dominic (John de Monte, Thomas de Templo), but also

---

[116] Thurston's findings, and the similar but independent conclusions of H. Holzapfel, O.F.M., *St. Dominikus und der Rosenkranz* (München, 1903), were heartily endorsed, for example, by L. Gougaud, O.S.B., *Les dernières investigations sur les origines du Rosaire,* in *La vie et les arts liturgiques,* Vol. 8, 1921-1922, pp. 538-548; cf. *idem, La question des origines du Rosaire mise au point, ibid.,* Vol. 10, 1923-1924, pp. 402-411.

[117] Among the historians of the rosary who differ from Thurston either substantially, or on important points of detail, we may mention: F. Willam, *op. cit.,* reviewed approvingly by H. Lechner, C.PP.S., *The Rosary: Rooted in the Liturgy,* in *Worship,* Vol. 27, May, 1953, pp. 307-311; M. Gorce, *Le Rosaire et ses antécédents historiques* (Paris, 1931); *idem,* art. *Rosaire,* in *DTC,* Vol. 13, col. 2902-2911; M. Mahé, S.M., *Aux sources de notre Rosaire,* in *Supplément de la Vie spirituelle,* Vol. 4, Feb., 1951, pp. 100-120; *idem, Aux sources de notre Rosaire,* in *Cahiers Marials,* Vol. 1, Sept.-Oct., 1957, pp. 303-314 and Nov.-Dec., 1957, pp. 369-378; C. Cecchelli, *Mater Christi,* Vol. 4 (Roma, 1954), pp. 391-401; Y. Gourdel, *art. cit.,* in *Maria,* Vol. 2, pp. 652-675, and, in the same volume, A. Duval, *art. cit.,* pp. 768-781.

[118] Cf. Duval, *art. cit.,* in *Maria,* Vol. 2, p. 781; R. Masson, O.P., *art. cit.,* in *Marie,* Vol. 11, Mar.-Apr., 1958, p. 464.

"tradition."[119] This gives rise to the possibility that there really was an internal tradition of the Dominican Order connecting its founder with some feature of the rosary, a tradition which Alan so misinterpreted and embellished as to make St. Dominic an apostle of the fully formed devotion. Indeed, some evidence can be offered for the actual existence of such a tradition.

There is, for example, the fact that, in his *De vita regulari,* Humbert De Romanis, O.P., the fifth General of the Dominicans, who died only forty years after St. Dominic (1263), impressed upon the novices the superiority of mental prayer over vocal, and urged that, after Matins of the Blessed Virgin, they should meditate with ardor on the benefits of God, that is, on the Incarnation, the Nativity, the Passion, and similar themes, and then recite the Our Father and the Hail Mary.[120] Further, the Constitutions of the Beguines of Ghent (who had Dominicans as their spiritual directors), believed to have been drawn up around 1236, enjoined daily recitation of the Psalter of the Virgin, at which the presiding Beguine was "to read aloud before each Our Father and each Hail Mary some mystery from the life of Christ or of the Blessed Virgin." To be sure, Thurston holds this passage to be a later interpolation or revision.[121] How much later? He does not say. But M. Mahé assigns the passage to the revised Constitutions of 1354, still long before Alan's time.[122]

Also cited in evidence is a manuscript of 1328, the work of a Dominican of Soissons. Entitled *Rosarius,* the document contains a poem addressed to Mary which seems to suggest that St. Dominic had a mission from on high to save the world by preaching devotion to the Hail Mary, a devotion conjoined with meditation on some mysteries of the

---

[119] Thurston, in *The Month,* Vol. 97, 1901/I, p. 298: "Never once, so far as I am aware, in Alan's numerous references to St. Dominic and the Rosary, does he profess to have acquired his knowledge from any tradition of the Order." In reply, D. Mézard, O.P., *Étude sur les origines du Rosaire* (Rhône, 1912), p. 296, quoted this passage from Alan's *Apology:* "Idem tum ex traditione accepimus, tum ex relictis scriptorum monumentis, ut legi." Cf. W. Most, *Mary in Our Life* (New York, 1954), p. 282.

[120] Cf. Cecchelli, *op. cit.,* Vol. 4, p. 396.

[121] Cf. Thurston, in *The Month,* Vol. 96, 1900/II, pp. 514-515; Vol. 97, 1901/I, pp. 183-185, 188.

[122] Cf. M. Mahé, S.M., *Aux sources de notre Rosaire,* in *Cahiers Marials,* Vol. 1, 1957, p. 304; see also M. Quinlan, S.J., *The Rosary in the Middle Ages — II,* in *The Irish Ecclesiastical Record,* Vol. 72, Aug., 1949, pp. 129-130.

Redemption.[123] Then, too, there is a woodcut produced in 1488 by Francis Domenech, O.P., of the monastery of St. Catherine in Barcelona, depicting distinctly our 15 mysteries, which, moreover, are clearly designated as the Joyful, the Sorrowful, the Glorious.[124] If, as is possible, Domenech was not influenced by Alan's movement in distant northwestern Europe, his woodcut, whose further details relate the rosary to St. Dominic, may be additional evidence attesting, independently of Alan's, to the existence of a tradition within the Order of Preachers.[125]

In their efforts to link the Dominicans' founder to one or more features of the rosary, some, rejecting Thurston's assertions of the prevalence of Hail Marys before St. Dominic, insist that the latter was the real propagator of the prayer.[126] Others, recognizing that the true genius of the rosary is in its combination of vocal prayers to Mary with meditation on the Redemption, say that it does not really matter whether St. Dominic was the first to spread the Hail Mary, or whether the recitation of precisely 150 Hail Marys divided into fifties and tens antedated him, or was inaugurated by him, or arose only later. It is enough, they contend, if he had (whether from a divine inspiration or from a formal revelation is again immaterial) the basic idea of uniting or alternating the saying of Hail Marys with meditation on mysteries of our Redemption — enough even if an exact number and the specification of those mysteries, our fifteen, came to be determined only after St. Dominic's time.

It has been suggested, not implausibly, that the great foe of the Albigensians did in fact have what amounts to that idea: the saint's

---

[123] Cf. M. Gorce, *Le Rosaire et ses antécédents historiques* (Paris, 1931), pp. 51, 53, 61, 63-65; idem, art. *Rosaire*, in *D.T.C.*, Vol. 13, col. 2903, 2904, 2906, 2907; P. Régamey, O.P., *Les plus beaux textes sur la Vierge Marie*, nouvelle édition (Paris, 1946), pp. 157-158; Most, *op. cit.*, p. 283. Duval, *art. cit.*, in *Maria*, Vol. 2, p. 772, note 183, and p. 782, questions Gorce's interpretation of the *Rosarius*. So far as the present writer recalls, Thurston did not discuss the document.

[124] Thurston did not, if memory serves, mention this woodcut. Esser's description of it, published in 1905, is reproduced in Schütz, *op. cit.*, pp. 104-107; see also the detailed description in the unsigned article *Rosario*, in *Enciclopedia Universal Ilustrada Europeo-Americana*, ed. Espasa, Vol. 52 (Bilbao, 1926), p. 357.

[125] See the art. *Rosario, in* Enciclopedia Universal Ilustrada, Vol. 52, p. 352.

[126] Cf., e.g., the art. *Rosario, ibid.*, p. 350. Shaw, *op. cit.*, pp. 38-39, is in sympathy with this view. N. Pérez, S.J., *Piété mariale du peuple espagnol*, in *Maria*, Vol. 4 (Paris, 1956), p. 608, holds that the rosary, at least in substance, and also the diffusion of the Hail Mary are due to St. Dominic.

celebrated sermons on the chief mysteries of our salvation, sermons not abstract but concrete in character, were for his hearers so many meditations on those mysteries, before and in between which he was wont, it is surmised, to invite the congregation to recite Hail Marys in order to obtain the divine blessing.[127] If so, was not the most fundamental aspect of the future rosary already at hand, and should not St. Dominic be credited with authorship of the substance of our devotion?

In support of this hypothesis, it is to be recalled that meditation on the mysteries of our salvation figured largely in the early "Dominican tradition" (Humbert De Romanis, the Beguine Constitutions?, the *Rosarius*), and that in the traditional Dominican understanding of the rosary, as in the Church's estimate of the devotion, meditation is in fact the very soul of the rosary, and indeed, meditation on the mysteries of the Redemption, meditation on the life, death, and glory of Jesus Christ.[128] Despite his seeming preoccupation with Hail Marys and the number of them to be recited, Alan of Rupe himself appears to have regarded meditation as the quintessence of the devotion, and indeed, meditation first and foremost on Christ, secondarily on Mary. Did he not call the devotion the "Psalter of Christ and of Mary"? Moreover, Alan quoted the Blessed Mother as saying to him in a vision: "It is a very beautiful, profitable prayer ... to recite the Angelic Salutation 150 times. But more pleasing to me, and much more profitable, is the Angelic Salutation when it is combined with meditation on the life, passion, and glory of Jesus Christ, for meditation is the soul of this prayer."[129] Hence the celebrated poem of the Danish author, Master Michael, printed in 1496, may have reflected Alan's mind accurately when it said that, although it would be best if one could penetrate the mysteries of the life of the Savior and of His Blessed Mother without any oral prayer, and tarry there, man's

---

[127] Thus A. Mortier, O.P., *Histoire des Maîtres généraux de l'Ordre des Frères Prêcheurs*, Vol. 1 (Paris, 1903), pp. 15-16; Thurston quotes the main passage, in *The Month*, Vol. 144, 1924/II, p. 336. Similarly, Schütz, *op. cit.*, p. xix; R. Garrigou-Lagrange, O.P., *La teologia del Rosario*, in *Alma Socia Christi*, Vol. 9 (Romae, 1953), pp. 179-184; *idem*, *The Mother of the Saviour* (Dublin, 1948), pp. 296-297; cf. Shaw, *op. cit.*, pp. 137-138. To recognize the affinity of this alleged practice of St. Dominic with our rosary devotion, it is enough to recall that essentially the same thing is often done today, when in group recitation a leader reads a meditation aloud to the rest before or after the common praying of the decade.

[128] See the documents cited *supra*, footnotes 15 and 16.

[129] Cf. Willam, *op. cit.*, p. 39.

unstable spirit needs vocal prayer to help him remain recollected, and so Alan wisely added vocal prayer to the meditations.[130]

The hypothesis outlined above would largely vindicate the many papal attributions of the rosary to St. Dominic.[131] Future research may yet verify its one problematic point, the intercalation of Hail Marys between the saint's preaching of the different mysteries.[132] We must await the verdict of history.[133]

III. EXCELLENCE OF THE ROSARY

As Pope Pius XII emphasized, among the special prayers and supplications by which, in addition to the honors of the Sacred Liturgy, Catholics are wont to venerate the Blessed Mother of God above all the other saints reigning with Christ in Heaven, "the Rosary, as all know, has pride of place."[134]

No form of extra-liturgical devotion to Mary is more widely practiced among the faithful or found by them to be more satisfyingly complete than the rosary, which has come to be regarded as the verybadge of Catholic piety. No form of extra-liturgical devotion to Mary has been recommended more warmly or frequently by the Popes. With perhaps two exceptions, all the Sovereign Pontiffs from Sixtus IV in 1478 down to John XXIII, especially Leo XIII (in 23 documents, ten of them encyclicals entirely on the rosary) and his successors, have extolled this form of prayer, which has been the favorite, moreover, of such saints as Teresa of Avila, Francis de Sales, Louis de Montfort, Alphonsus Liguori, Don Bosco, Bernadette, and many more.

Our Lady herself has approved the rosary in the course of numerous apparitions, as at Lourdes in 1858 and at Fatima in 1917. Indeed, God

---

[130] Cf. *ibid..*, pp. 46-48.

[131] On the version of rosary origins given in the Fourth Lesson of Matins for the Feast of the Most Holy Rosary, see Beissel, *Gesch. d. Verehrung Marias in Deutschland während des Mittelalters*, p. 237.

[132] Thurston hesitated to admit even that the Hail Mary had any part at all in St. Dominic's devotional life. This reluctance is hard to reconcile with the scholar's thesis that the prayer was already widely popular by Dominic's time.

[133] These pages have been able to notice but a small fraction of the vast literature on the history of the rosary. For other important books and articles, see the bibliographies in Shaw, *op. cit.*, pp. 167-170; the art. *Rosario* in the *Enciclopedia Universal Ilustrada*, Vol. 52, pp. 358-359; G. Roschini, O.S.M., *Mariologia*, Vol. 2, Part 3 (Romae, 1948), p. 105; idem, *La Madonna secondo la fede e la teologia*, Vol. 4 (Roma, 1954), pp. 313-314.

[134] Ency. *Mediator Dei*, Nov. 20, 1947; N.C.W.C. (Vatican Library Translation), n. 174.

THE DOMINICAN ROSARY

Himself has signaled His approbation by coming to the Church's rescue when, sore beset, she has had special recourse to the rosary and Mary's powerful intercession. Outstanding instances of divine deliverance of the Church through the intercessory power of Our Lady of the Rosary are the crucial victories of the Christian forces over the Turks, at Lepanto in 1517, at Vienna in 1683, and at Temesvar and Corfu in 1716, and the settlement of the "Roman Question" in 1929.[135]

Why is the rosary so excellent and so efficacious a form of prayer? We have room only for some of the reasons advanced by the many, above all the Popes, who have explored this profound subject.[136] To begin with the vocal prayers of the rosary, the flowers out of which this mystic crown or garland is woven for Our Lady, what prayers can be found more suitable or sublime than the Lord's Prayer and the Hail Mary?[137] The first is the noblest and holiest of prayers, that which was taught us by our divine Redeemer Himself. It permits us, as far as in our power lies, to render to God the glory which is His due, and at the same time it takes into account all our spiritual and bodily necessities. How can the Eternal Father, when addressed with the very words of His Son, fail to be pleased, how can He refuse to come to our aid? As to the Hail Mary, it is composed of the divinely inspired salutations of the Archangel Gabriel and of St. Elizabeth, along with the pious entreaty — added by the Church — that God's Mother help us now and at death. How can Heaven's Queen fail to be pleased and moved by this tribute to her dignity, power, and glory, and to

---

[135] On the rosary and the "Roman Question," cf. *Orate Fratres,* Vol. 4, May 18, 1930, pp. 327-329.

[136] Of the voluminous literature on the excellence of the rosary it must suffice to mention the following: W. Lawler, O.P., ed., *The Rosary of Mary: Translation of the Encyclical and Apostolic Letters of Pope Leo XIII* (Paterson, 1944); the Encyclicals *Ingravescentibus malis,* of Pius XI (Sept. 29, 1937), and *Ingruentium malorum,* of Pius XII (Sept. 15, 1951), in W. Doheny, J. Kelly, edd., *Papal Documents on Mary* (Milwaukee, 1954), pp. 180-187, 242-248; St. Louis Mary de Montfort, *The Secret of the Rosary* (Bay Shore, N. Y., 1954); C. Callan, O.P., J. McConnell, M.M., *Spiritual Riches of the Rosary* (New York, 1958); M. Ward, *The Splendor of the Rosary* (New York, 1945); F. Willam, *op. cit.*; R. Guardini, *The Rosary of Our Lady* (New York, 1955); M. Tremeau, O.P., *Le Rosaire. Sa richesse doctrinale et spirituelle,* in *L'Ami du Clergé,* Vol. 67, Sept. 26, 1957, pp. 561-573.

[137] Cf. Leo XIII, Encyclicals *Octobri mense* (Sept. 22, 1891), *Magnae Dei Matris* (Sept. 8, 1892), *Iucunda semper* (Sept. 8, 1894), and Apostolic Letter *Parta humano generi* (Sept. 8, 1901), in Lawler, *op. cit.*, pp. 62, 79-80, 116, 119, 193-194; Pius XI, *Ingravescentibus malis,* in Doheny-Kelly, *op. cit.,* pp. 182-183.

their source, the divinity of her Son?

First, as is meet and just, comes the Lord's Prayer, addressed to the heavenly Father. Only thereafter do we turn to Our Lady. Thus the rosary heeds the proper hierarchy of prayer.[138] If our tongues linger longer with the Hail Mary, repeating it ten times to the Our Father's one, it is precisely that our poor petitions may be supported, commended, enhanced by the much more acceptable ones of her who is full of grace, the most blessed of mere creatures, the very Mother of God — in the Hail Mary we beseech the Blessed Virgin to speak for us, to pray in our name and behalf. Finally, by its repetition of Hail Marys and Our Fathers the rosary is seen to excel in a quality which Christ Himself said prayer must have if it is to be efficacious — perseverance.[139]

Hence, even if it were simply a fervent recitation of so many Our Fathers and Hail Marys, the rosary would still be an admirable form of devotion. But its supreme and unique excellence derives from its wedding of those vocal prayers to meditation, and indeed, meditation on the mysteries of our Redemption. Far from being just an ingenious device for relieving the repeated vocal prayers of "monotony," this meditation is the very soul of the rosary; the mysteries are not there for the sake of the prayers, "the prayers are there for the sake of the mysteries." And, as to these mysteries upon which we should dwell, it would be a mistake to think of them as chiefly the joys, sorrows, and triumphs of the Blessed Virgin. Much rather does the Church describe them as "the mysteries of our Redemption," "setting forth the entire life of Jesus Christ"; "the mysteries of his life, passion, death, resurrection and glory."[140] Thus the rosary is explicitly Christocentric, and one may say of it what Pius XII said of the Liturgical Year: "Our Saviour dominates the scene in the mysteries of His humiliation, of His redemption and triumph."[141] Of course, the rosary honors and contemplates Mary too, and rightly so, for

---

[138] Cf. Leo XIII, Encyclicals *Iucunda semper* and *Augustissimae Virginis Mariae* (Sept. 12, 1897), in Lawler, *op. cit.*, pp. 116-117, 165-166.

[139] Cf. Leo XIII, Ency. *Fidentem piumque* (Sept. 20, 1896), in Lawler, *op. cit.*, pp. 147-148.

[140] Cf. the fourth lesson of Matins, Feast of the Most Holy Rosary, Oct. 7, and the documents cited *supra*, footnote 28; Pius V, *Consueverunt Romani Pontifices,* quoted *supra*, footnote 16; also, the short form of the Dominican blessing of rosary-heads (*Rituale Romanum*), and the Collect and Secret of the Mass for the Feast of the Most Holy Rosary. See R. Garrigou-Lagrange, O.P., *The Mother of the Saviour* (Dublin, 1948), pp. 292-293.

[141] *Mediator Dei;* N.C.W.C. (Vatican Library Translation), n. 151.

the same reason that the Liturgical Year does likewise: "Because of the mission she received from God, her life is most closely linked with the mysteries of Jesus Christ, and there is no one who has followed in the footsteps of the Incarnate Word more closely and with more merit than she."[142] Hence our rosary is truly what Alan of Rupe chose to call it, "the Psalter of Christ and of Mary," wherein we dwell, according to the happy formula of Leo XIII, "on the great mysteries of Jesus and Mary united in joys, sorrows, and triumphs."[143]

Meditation on this cycle of Joyful, Sorrowful, and Glorious Mysteries makes the rosary not only "a breviary or summary of the Gospel and of Christian life,"[144] but also a compendium of the Liturgical Year. Therewith the rosary stands revealed as a dynamic teacher and nurturer of Christian faith, morality, and spiritual perfection, fostering in various ways faith, hope, charity, and the other virtues, and mediating special graces, all to the end that we may become more and more like unto Christ.

To descend to some details, in presenting the chief mysteries of our religion unto an increase of faith, the rosary — like the Gospel, and like the Liturgical Year[145] — proposes them not abstractly but graphically, "less as truths or doctrines to be speculated upon, than as present facts to be seen and perceived,"[146] "almost as though they were unfolding before our eyes."[147] It "presents to the mind, like many pictures, the drama of the Incarnation of Our Lord and the Redemption."[148] "Thus presented with the circumstances of place, time and persons, these mysteries produce the most living effect,"[149] steeping the soul in these salutary truths, enlarging

---

[142] *Ibid.*, n. 169.

[143] *Octobri mense,* in Lawler, *op. cit.*, p. 61.

[144] Pius XI, *Ingravescentibus malis,* in Doheny-Kelly, *op. cit.*, p. 182.

[145] Cf. *Mediator Dei,* N.C.W.C. (Vatican Library Translation) nn. 163, 165.

[146] Leo XIII, *Iucunda semper,* in Lawler, *op. cit.*, p. 120.

[147] Leo XIII, *Magnae Dei Matris,* in Lawler, *op. cit.*, pp. 83-84. The rosary, then, is easy for all, even the untutored; Leo XIII, *Iucunda semper,* in Lawler, *op. cit.*, p. 120. And hence it is well adapted to prayer in common, a circumstance heightening its efficacy, since prayer derives its chief efficacy from perseverance (as we noted earlier), and from the union of many for one end; Leo XIII, *Fidentem piumque* and *Augustissimae Virginis Mariae,* in Lawler, *op. cit.*, pp. 147-148, 163-164.

[148] Pope John XXIII, Ency. *Grata recordatio,* Sept. 26, 1959.

[149] Leo XIII, *Iucunda semper,* in Lawler, *op. cit.*, pp. 120-121.

the soul's hope, intensifying its charity toward God and man.[150]

Other virtues, too, are stimulated, encouraged, and cultivated in the soul of him who meditates on the mysteries of the rosary, so that this devotion effectively leads to the practice of the truly Christian life and to Christian perfection.[151] For, in proposing to our meditation the mysteries of Jesus and His Mother, the rosary, like the Gospel and like the Liturgical Year,[152] offers us inspiring examples of all virtue. Above all, there are the lessons taught by the conduct of our Savior Himself. "What an example we have set before us and shining everywhere in Our Lord Christ's work of salvation ... ," moving us to "straightway set out in the footsteps of Christ and follow them through every obstacle."[153] For a deeper appreciation of this aspect of the rosary's excellence, it should be recalled that, as did Our Lord Himself, the Church, her Fathers and Doctors, notably St. Thomas Aquinas, extoll the efficacy of Christ's example.[154]

As to the power of Mary's example, "lest we be dismayed by the consciousness of our native weakness and grow faint when confronted with the unattainable example which Christ, who is Man and at the same time God, has given, along with the mysteries which portray Him, we have before our eyes for contemplation the mysteries of His Most Holy Mother. ... In Mary we see how a truly good and provident God has

---

[150] Cf. Leo XIII, *Octobri mense* and *Magnae Dei Matris*, in Lawler, *op. cit.*, pp. 62, 81-84, 85. On this exercise and increase of the theological virtues through the rosary, see also Leo XIII, *Fidentem piumque*, in Lawler, *op. cit.*, pp. 152-153; Pius XI, *Ingravescentibus malis*, in Doheny-Kelly, *op. cit.*, pp. 185-186; and confer M. Tremeau, *art. cit.*, pp. 565-566, and B. T. d'Argenlieu, O.P., *La théologie du Rosaire*, in *Maria*, ed. H. du Manoir, Vol. 5 (Paris, 1958), pp. 729-732. Not without reason, then, do we recite the three preliminary Hail Marys for an increase of faith, hope, and charity.

[151] Cf. Leo XIII, *Magnae Dei Matris, Diuturni temporis* (Sept. 5, 1898), in Lawler, *op. cit.*, pp. 77-78, 90, 173; Pius XI, *Ingravescentibus malis*, and Pius XII, *Ingruentium malorum*, in Doheny-Kelly, *op. cit.*, pp. 185, 244-245.

[152] On the way the Liturgical Year, in proposing the life of Christ for our meditation, "gives us examples to imitate, points out treasures of sanctity to make our own," cf. *Mediator Dei*, N.C.W.C. (Vatican Library Translation), nn. 153-165; on the way it proposes the examples of Mary, cf. *ibid.*, nn. 166-170.

[153] Leo XIII, *Magnae Dei Matris*, in Lawler, *op. cit.*, pp. 85-87.

[154] Cf. L. Lercher, S.J., *Institutiones Theologiae Dogmaticae*, ed. 3, Vol. 3 (Oeniponte, 1942), nn. 231-234, on "Christus Exemplar." In particular, as to St. Thomas, who attached transcendent importance to the ethical and moral worth of Christ as our Model, cf. G. Ermecke, *Vorbildnachfolge und Beispielbefolgung in der christlichen Sittlichkeit*, in *Theologie und Glaube*, 1948, Heft 4, pp. 313-323.

established for us a most suitable example of every virtue."[155] The more perfectly we imitate Our Lady, the more like do we become to her Model, Christ. For "there is no one who has followed in the footsteps of the Incarnate Word more closely and with more merit than she."[156] "Nobody ever knew Christ so profoundly as she did, and nobody can ever be more competent as a guide and teacher of the knowledge of Christ."[157] Thus through Mary we learn to clothe ourselves with Christ, we put on Christ; "Christ is formed" in us (Gal. 4:19).[158] Hence, if we imitate Our Lady, it is in order to become like to Christ. She is not our ultimate exemplar, not the center and fundamental principle of our spiritual life — there is only one Christian spirituality, that in which Christ is the Way, the Truth, and the Life, and one may speak of a "Marian spirituality" only in the sense that we are to tend to Jesus through Mary.[159]

So, then, "following these most holy examples (of Jesus Christ and of His Mother), we ascend to the happiness of the heavenly fatherland by steps of ever higher virtue."[160] The Popes also stress that this contemplation, in the rosary, of the inspiring examples of Jesus and Mary is salutary not only for the individual but also for society; for society in miniature, the family,[161] and for civil society.[162]

But it is not just by the power of example that the rosary tends to form Christ in us. For, one may apply to this devotion what Pope Pius XII, invoking the Doctors of the Church, said of the mysteries of Jesus as proposed in the Liturgy: Far from being merely events of the past, "these mysteries are ever present and active ... ; they still influence us because

---

[155] Leo XIII, *Magnae Dei Matris*, in Lawler, *op. cit.,* pp. 87-88; cf. pp. 88-89.

[156] *Mediator Dei*, N.C.W.C. (Vatican Library Translation), n. 169.

[157] Pope St. Pius X, Ency. *Ad diem illum*, Feb. 2, 1904, in Doheny-Kelly, *op. cit.,* p. 138.

[158] Cf. B. d'Argenlieu, *art. cit.,* in *Maria*, Vol. 5, pp. 732-735.

[159] Cf. Lercher, *op. cit.,* Vol. 3, n. 355. Relevant here is Ermecke's distinction, in the above-mentioned article, between "Vorbild" or archetypal model and "Beispiel," patterned after the "Vorbild," and his insistence that there is but one "Vorbild" – Christ.

[160] Pius XI, *Ingravescentibus malis*, in Doheny-Kelly, *op. cit.,* p. 183.

[161] Cf. Leo XIII, *Magnae Dei Matris*, and *Diuturni temporis*, in Lawler, *op. cit.,* pp. 90, 173; Pius XII, *Ingruentium malorum*, in Doheny-Kelly, *op. cit.,* pp. 245-246.

[162] Cf. Leo XIII, Ency. *Laetitiae sanctae* (Sept. 8, 1893), in Lawler, *op. cit.,* pp. 97-108; T. Schwertner, O.P., *The Rosary: A Social Remedy* (Milwaukee, 1934); A. Fuerst, *This Rosary* (Milwaukee, 1954), pp. 101-106.

each mystery brings its own special grace."[163]

Doubtless the Holy Father had in mind the profound teaching of the Angelic Doctor on the efficient causality of the mysteries of Christ with respect to our sanctification.[164] According to St. Thomas Aquinas, the "mysteries of Christ" are not simply speculative truths, they are the events in His life, each of which determined His sacred humanity in such wise as to make it an instrument peculiarly adapted to produce in us the grace corresponding to each mystery.[165] The "mysteries of Christ" are "mysteries" in the sense of "sacrament," that is, sign and instrumental cause of our spiritual progress; they are not totally of the past, they remain as a stable disposition in the glorified humanity of the Savior, to produce in us the effects of grace corresponding to each of them.[166] For us actually to receive such special benefit from this or that mystery, we must come into spiritual contact with the mystery, by faith, hope, and charity.[167] Thus St. Thomas Aquinas. When, therefore, the rosary, stimulating faith, hope, and charity, puts us into spiritual contact with a particular mystery of Christ, it mediates to us a special grace or virtue, making us that much more like unto our Divine Savior.[168]

Truly, then, devout meditation on the mysteries of the rosary enables us to "both imitate what they contain, and obtain what they promise,"[169] and the rosary leads us indeed "to Jesus through Mary."[170] In the light of all that has been said, we can now better appreciate why the Blessed Mother is so pleased by the rosary, why it so effectively enlists her intercession. She would agree with the words Alan of Rupe placed on her lips: "more pleasing to me, and much more profitable, is the Angelic Salutation when it is combined with meditation on the life, passion, and

---

[163] *Mediator Dei*, N.C.W.C. (Vatican Library Translation), n. 165; on some of the special graces brought by the various mysteries of Christ, cf. *ibid.*, nn. 154-159.

[164] For this teaching, cf. J. Lécuyer, C.S.Sp., *La causalité efficiente des mystères du Christ selon Saint Thomas*, in Doctor Communis, Vol. 6, 1953, pp. 91-120.

[165] Cf. *ibid.*, pp. 108-109.

[166] Cf. *ibid.*, p. 109.

[167] Cf. *ibid.*, pp. 112-113.

[168] Compare B. d'Argenlieu, *art. cit.*, in *Maria*, Vol. 5, pp. 728-729.

[169] Collect of the Mass for Feast of the Most Holy Rosary.

[170] Pius XII, Apost. Exhortation *Menti nostrae*, Sept. 23, 1950; N.C.W.C. translation, n. 49.

THE DOMINICAN ROSARY

glory of Jesus Christ, for meditation is the soul of this prayer."[171] She cannot but treasure this devotion whose meditations make us so like to her Divine Son; she cannot resist the pleas of those who so resemble Him. The rosary is the perfect Marian devotion not merely because, synthesis and crown of all devotions to Our Lady, it "sums up in itself the honor due to her,"[172] but also and especially because it is the most explicitly Christocentric Marian devotion.

IV. INDULGENCES FOR RECITING THE ROSARY

Last, but not least, the rosary also excels in that it can greatly expedite our entry into Heaven, speed our union there with Christ. For this devotion has been munificently endowed by the Popes with indulgences — those pardons in whole or in part of the debt of temporal punishment which may still remain even after the guilt of sin has been forgiven, a debt which, unless pardoned, would have to be paid either in this life or in Purgatory.

As to the Rosary indulgences properly so-called, we confine ourselves to the general Rosary indulgences granted for recitation of the rosary.[173] In the present context "rosary" means a third part of the full rosary — five decades, and "recitation" is to be understood as devout recitation. These indulgences, all of which are applicable to the souls in Purgatory, are as follows.[174]

The faithful may gain an indulgence of five years every time they recite the rosary. Farther, if one recites it daily for a whole month, he may

---

[171] As quoted in Willam, *op. cit.*, p. 39. Was Alan, a doctor and professor of theology — and therefore presumably familiar with his fellow Dominican, the great St. Thomas, led to this esteem for meditation on the life, passion, and glory of Christ by the Angelic Doctor's teaching, sketched above, on the ethical and moral value of Christ as our Model, and on His mysteries as instrumental causes of our sanctification? And was St. Thomas himself perhaps influenced by St. Dominic's well-known devotion to and concrete preaching of the mysteries of Christ?

[172] Leo XIII, *Octobri mense,* in Lawler, *op. cit.*, p. 64.

[173] For the special Rosary indulgences, see *The Rosary: The Crown of Mary,* new and rev. ed., by A Dominican Father (New York, 1947), pp. 128-142. Except for a few changes or additions made by the successors of Pope Leo XIII, they are those contained in the list published by the Sacred Congregation of Indulgences on Aug. 29, 1899; cf. *A.S.S.*, Vol. 32, pp. 228-241.

[174] Unless otherwise indicated, our source for these indulgences is the official *Enchiridion Indulgentiarum*, ed. 2 (Typis Polyglottis Vaticanis, 1952), nn. 395, 397, 398.

gain a plenary indulgence, under the usual conditions.[175]

Those who recite the rosary in company with others, whether in public or in private, may gain an indulgence of ten years, once a day; also, a plenary indulgence on the last Sunday of each month, if they perform such a recitation at least three times in any of the preceding weeks, and provided they go to confession, receive Holy Communion, and visit some church or public oratory. If, however, they recite the rosary together in a family group, they may gain, besides the indulgence of ten years: a plenary indulgence twice a month, provided they perform this recitation daily for a month, go to confession, receive Holy Communion, and visit some church or public oratory; further, on condition of daily recitation of the rosary for a week, and of confession and Communion, a plenary indulgence, to be gained on each Saturday, and on two other days of the week, and furthermore on each of the feasts of the Blessed Virgin in the universal calendar.[176]

Those who recite the rosary in the presence of the Blessed Sacrament publicly exposed or even reserved in the tabernacle may gain, as often as they do this, a plenary indulgence, on condition of confession and Communion.

Those who resolve to perform a pious exercise in honor of Our Lady of the Rosary for fifteen uninterrupted Saturdays (or if hindered on Saturday, for as many respective Sundays immediately following) may gain, if they recite the rosary or meditate on its mysteries in some other way, a plenary indulgence, under the usual conditions, on any of these

---

[175] "Under the usual conditions" means: confession, Communion, a visit to a church or public oratory (or even a semi-public oratory in certain cases), and prayer for the intentions of the Pope. The confession which may be required for gaining an indulgence can be made within the eight days which precede the day to which the indulgence is appointed; and the Communion may be received on the day before; or both conditions may be satisfied on the day itself or within the following eight days.

[176] The last-mentioned plenary indulgence was granted by Pius XII in the decree of the Sacred Apostolic Penitentiary, Oct. 11, 1954; cf. *A.A.S.*, Vol. 46, 1954, p. 522. The Feasts of the Blessed Virgin Mary in the revised universal calendar are: the Immaculate Conception, the Purification, the Apparition of Our Bl. Lady at Lourdes, the Annunciation, the Queenship of Mary, the Visitation, Our Lady of the Snows, the Assumption, the Immaculate Heart of the Bl. Virgin Mary, the Nativity of the Bl. Virgin Mary, the Most Holy Name of Mary, the Seven Dolors (Sept. 15), the Bl. Virgin Mary of the Rosary, the Maternity of the Bl. Virgin Mary, and the Presentation of the B. Virgin Mary; see the decree of the Sacred Congregation of Rites on the rubrics of the Roman Breviary and Missal, July 26, 1960, in *A.A.S.*, Vol. 52, 1960, pp. 593-740.

fifteen Saturdays or corresponding Sundays.

Those who, in October, recite the rosary either publicly or privately may gain an indulgence of seven years each day; also, a plenary indulgence, if they recite the rosary on the Feast of the Rosary and throughout the octave, and moreover, go to confession, receive Holy Communion, and visit a church or public oratory; further, a plenary indulgence if they recite the rosary for at least ten days after the octave of that Feast, and go to confession, receive Holy Communion, and visit a church or public oratory.

None of the above indulgences requires the use of rosary beads, much less of blessed rosary beads. If, however, one uses rosary beads specially blessed by a Dominican, or by another priest having the requisite faculties, he may gain, for daily recitation of the rosary throughout the year, one plenary indulgence, to be obtained on any day of the year, under condition of confession, Holy Communion, and prayer for the intentions of the Pope; also, an indulgence of 100 days for every Our Father and Hail Mary, provided one intends to recite and does recite five decades within one day.[177] These two Rosary indulgences were granted by Pope Benedict XIII, and are the only "Dominican indulgences" properly so-called.[178]

So much for the Rosary indulgences. Of Crosier indulgences we have spoken elsewhere. As to Apostolic indulgences, among those decreed by Pope John XXIII for weekly recitation of five decades of the rosary (or certain other religious works) is a plenary indulgence obtainable on certain feasts, on condition of timely reception of the Sacraments of Penance and Holy Communion, and of prayer for the Pope's intentions; an indulgence of seven years on each of the same feasts, for persons not receiving the Sacraments on those occasions but who are contrite and pray for the Pope's intentions; an indulgence of three years for every

---

[177] See the *Enchiridion Indulgentiarum*, n. 395, note 2.

[178] See the *petitio ad obtinendam facultatem* together with the *formula concessionis* of the faculty to impart the Dominican blessing, in De Angelis, *op. cit.*, pp. 471-472. Hence, strictly speaking, the Dominican indulgences should not be equated with the Rosary indulgences. One may, perhaps, with E. Long, in *The Irish Ecclesiastical Record*, Vol. 57, 1941/I, p. 86, also call "Dominican" the special Rosary indulgences, but only in a wide sense. And only in a very wide sense may one so label all the indulgences for reciting the rosary — insofar as their acquisition depends on recitation in the manner evolved under Dominican auspices.

performance of any of the religious works listed in the papal decree.[179]

For good measure, and by way of conclusion, we may mention some of the Bridgettine indulgences: a plenary indulgence, on condition of confession, Communion, visit to a church or public oratory, and prayer for the Pope's intentions: (*a*) once a month for those who daily recite at least the five-decade chaplet for a month; (*b*) once a year for those who daily recite the five-decade or six-decade chaplet for a whole year. Also, for those who are in the habit of reciting at least the five-decade chaplet weekly, a plenary indulgence at the hour of death, provided that the dying person receives the Sacraments of Penance and Communion (or, if unable to receive the Sacraments, has perfect contrition), and devoutly invokes the name of Jesus, with his lips, if possible, otherwise in his heart. Finally, a partial indulgence of 100 days for each Our Father, Hail Mary, and Creed, provided the five-decade chaplet is completed the same day.[180]

---

[179] For the full *elenchus* of Apostolic indulgences granted by Pope John XXIII, Nov. 22, 1958, see *A.A.S.*, Vol. 51, 1959, pp. 48-50.

[180] See De Angelis, *op. cit.*, nn. 242-248; Beringer-Steinen, *op. cit.*, Vol. 1, nn. 880-884 (and "Nachtrag," pp. 585-586); cf. *supra*, footnote 13.

THE SCAPULAR DEVOTION

By CHRISTIAN P. CEROKE, O.Carm.

HE most highly developed of Marian Scapular devotions is that of the Brown Scapular of Our Lady of Mount Carmel. Since the seventeenth century, the Brown Scapular has been a universal Catholic devotion, considered to be, together with the rosary, a customary form of Marian devotional practice. The popularity of the Scapular devotion was due to the sixteenth and seventeenth century popes, who promulgated the so-called Sabbatine Privilege and who approved the Confraternity of the Scapular for every diocese throughout the Catholic world. The growth and development of the Scapular devotion reached its culmination in 1726 in the extension to the universal Church of the feast of Our Lady of Mount Carmel for July 16.[1]

The wearing of the Scapular fosters a true devotion to Mary that is based on her supernatural mission in the redemption of mankind. Two Marian doctrines are proposed in the devotion of the Brown Scapular: Mary's Spiritual Maternity and her Mediation of Grace. The Scapular teaches a practical confidence in the intercession of the Blessed Virgin to obtain for its wearer the grace of final perseverance, or a happy death. The two general conditions to obtain this benefit are that one must honor Mary by wearing the Scapular faithfully until death and endeavor sincerely to lead a Christian life. This reliance on Mary's intercession for the gift of final perseverance derives historically from the belief that the Blessed Virgin promised in an apparition to St. Simon Stock, Prior General

---

[1] The feast spread rapidly in the seventeenth century. For its liturgical history, cf. Augustine M. Forcadell, O.Carm., *Commemoratio Solemnis Beatae Mariae Virginis de Monte Carmelo* (Romae, 1951). The rank of the feast has been reduced to a Commemoration by the decree of the Sacred Congregation of Rites concerning the new calendar for the breviary and the Mass. Cf. *A.A.S.*, Vol. 52, 1960, p. 706. The retention of the feast as a Commemoration in the new calendar preserves the memory of the liturgical intent of thanksgiving for which the feast was originally instituted, as Benedict XIV observed: "Since through the intercession of the Blessed Virgin God worked numerous miracles in favor of those who practised this devotion, it must be conceded that the feast of Our Lady of Mount Carmel was not instituted without serious judgment, and celebrated in the universal Church with proper Office and Mass." *De festis D. N. Jesu Christi et B. Mariae Virginis* (Patavii, 1745), p. 479.

of the Carmelites (1247?-1265), that all who die wearing the Scapular will not suffer the eternal flames of hell. This tradition has become known as the "Scapular promise."

The devotion also teaches that the aid of Mary may be confidently expected in purgatory by all those who have faithfully worn the Scapular and have fulfilled two other conditions: the practice of chastity according to one's state of life and the daily recitation of the Little Office of the Blessed Virgin.[2] This privilege of the Scapular devotion has been thought to stem from an apparition of Mary to Pope John XXII, who then promulgated this spiritual benefit to the faithful in 1322. According to the copies of the Bull of promulgation attributed to John XXII, the devotee of the Scapular would be released from purgatory on the Saturday after death. Because of the allusion to Saturday, the document of John XXII has been called the "Sabbatine Bull" and its Marian privilege the "Sabbatine Privilege."

THE ORIGIN OF THE SCAPULAR DEVOTION

Historically, the devotion of the Scapular among the Catholic laity originated from the tradition of the Marian apparition and promise of the Scapular to St. Simon Stock.[3] From about 1400, Carmelite authors allude to the wearing of the Scapular by the laity in reliance on the Virgin's promise of eternal salvation. Carmelite authors of the fifteenth century begin to record a devotional view of the Scapular, insinuating its heavenly origin. According to Grossi (*ca.* 1411), Mary *gave* the Scapular to St. Simon Stock. According to Bradley (*ca.* 1450), in bestowing the Scapular Mary *changed* the Carmelite habit.[4] Still later authors added new motives for the wearing of the Scapular by the laity. Calciuri (1461) alluded to miracles that had been worked through the Scapular; and Leersius (1483) added

---

[2] As will be noted below, the third condition may be commuted.

[3] The historical documentation pertaining to the apparition of Our Lady to St. Simon Stock has been collected and evaluated by Bartholomew F. M. Xiberta, O.Carm., *De Visione Sancti Simonis Stock* (Romae, 1950).

[4] The implication of fifteenth-century authors that the Scapular came directly from Mary as a new piece of the Carmelite habit is an elaboration of the fourteenth-century narrative of the apparition. The fourteenth-century account, which simply states that Mary appeared holding the Scapular, will be provided below. As the Scapular devotion developed, it was natural that the details of the apparition would be magnified.

that the Scapular had been worn by saints.[5] This tradition of the fifteenth century, which began to develop the devotional value of the Scapular and of its promise, culminated in 1479 in a work by Arnold Bostius, a Belgian Carmelite of Ghent. His manuscript work, *De patronatu et patrocinio B. V. M.*, formulated the solid basis of Marian doctrine on which the Scapular devotion was founded. Bostius explained how the Scapular promise of eternal salvation was a concrete illustration of the doctrine of Mary as Mediatrix of all Graces. The reception of the Scapular as the pledge of Mary's promise of eternal salvation placed the obligation upon the members of the Confraternity to imitate Mary in her practice of virtue. Bostius' work was popularized by John Paleonydor, a Flemish Carmelite, in a book entitled *Fasciculus Tripartitus*. Published in 1495, the book was frequently reprinted in the sixteenth and seventeenth centuries. By the end of the fifteenth century, the theological structure of the Scapular devotion had been essentially outlined: its doctrinal foundation was the cult of Mary as Mediatrix of all Graces; its motive was the tradition of the apparition of Our Lady to St. Simon Stock with the promise of the Scapular.[6]

THE SCAPULAR PROMISE AND HISTORICAL CRITICISM

The question of the historical authenticity of the Scapular promise was raised in the seventeenth century when the modern concept of scientific history was first developed.[7] It cannot be said that the historical value of the tradition has been decided with finality. Recent historical investigations into Carmelite medieval history have provided information on the tradition of the Scapular promise that was not in the possession of scholars of past decades.[8]

---

[5] For these details in fifteenth century Carmelite authors, cf. Xiberta, *De Visione*, pp. 91-93; 107-111.

[6] An analysis of Bostius' thought, based on his manuscript work, has been made by Eamon R. Carroll, O.Carm., *Arnold Bostius and the Scapular*, in *The Sword*, Vol. 14, 1950, pp. 342-355.

[7] John Launoy wrote against the historicity of the Scapular tradition in *Dissertatio Duplex* (Paris [?], 1642) and *De Simonis Stockii Viso, De Sabbatinae Bullae Privilegio* (Paris, 1653). For a discussion of his position, cf. Xiberta, *De Visione*, pp. 31-48.

[8] Our knowledge of medieval Carmelite literature has improved since the studies of Benedict Zimmerman, O.C.D., *The Origin of the Scapular*, in *The Irish Ecclesiastical Record*, Series 4, Vol. 9; 1901, pp. 385-408; Vol. 15, 1904, 142-153; 206-234; 331-351; and Herbert Thurston, S.J., The Origin of the *Scapular: A Criticism*, in the same periodical,

The Carmelites of the fourteenth century preserved the tradition of the Scapular promise as part of the cult within the Order to St. Simon Stock. The narrative of the apparition and of the promise of the Scapular was incorporated in the Carmelite Catalogue of Saints, or Sanctoral, composed for the Order.[9] The account in its earliest known form reads as follows:

> The ninth (saint) was St. Simon of England, the sixth General of the Order. He continually besought the most glorious Mother of God to defend with a privilege the Order of Carmelites, which enjoys the special title of the Virgin. He prayed devoutly:
>
> > Flower of Carmel
> > Vine Blossom-laden.
> > Splendor of heaven,
> > Child-bearing maiden,
> > None equals thee!
> > O Mother benign,
> > Who no man didst know,
> > On all Carmel's children
> > Thy favors bestow
> > Star of the Sea.[10]
>
> The Blessed Virgin appeared to him with a multitude of angels, holding in her blessed hands the Scapular of the Order. She said, "This will be for you and for all Carmelites the privilege, that he who dies in this will not suffer eternal fire," that is, he who dies in this will be saved.[11]

There is no doubt that the origin of the Scapular devotion among the laity is traceable to this fourteenth century narrative.[12] Its composition has

---

Vol. 16, 1904, pp. 59-75; id., *Scapulars*, in *The Month*, Vol. 150, 1927. Xiberta, *De Visione*, has collected and analyzed the documents of the medieval Scapular tradition.

[9] For a discussion of the Sanctoral and its origin, cf. Xiberta, *De Visione*, pp. 198-211.

[10] The Latin text of the *Flos Carmeli* is as follows: Flos Carmeli, vitis florigera, splendor caeli, Virgo puerpera singularis, Mater mitis sed viri nescia, Carmelitis da privilegia, stella maris. The English translation is that of Joachim Smet, O.Carm. The poem incorporates traditional medieval allusions from the Bible that were applied to Mary.

[11] We have omitted the concluding paragraph of the hagiographical notice, which simply states the death of St. Simon Stock at the Bordeaux Carmel. For the complete text, cf. Xiberta, *De Visione*, p. 283.

[12] In an appendix, Xiberta, *De Visione*, pp. 281-313, has published the principal manuscript texts of the Sanctoral. There are noticeable in them gradual additions and changes, the most evident being a notice on the wearing of the Scapular by the laity in the later manuscript copies of the fifteenth century.

THE SCAPULAR DEVOTION 135

been dated about the mid-fourteenth century.[13] Of greater significance, however, than the date of the narrative, is its location in the Carmelite Sanctoral, where it forms the complete hagiographical notice on St. Simon Stock. If this story of the Marian apparition and promise were *not* found in the earliest hagiographical notice on St. Simon Stock, but only in documents of later origin, this fact would cast grave suspicion on the authentic origin of the tradition. The appearance in the fourteenth century narrative of the poem, the *Flos Carmeli*, reveals the existence of a cult of the apparition at this time within the Order.[14] A Marian devotion induced by the Scapular promise existed within the Carmelite Order before it arose among the laity.[15] The story of the apparition of Mary and the promise of the Scapular was a fully formed tradition within the Order by the mid-fourteenth century, one hundred years after the death of St. Simon Stock. The tradition was not originally motivated by the spread of the Scapular devotion among the laity. Nor was the tradition utilized by the medieval Carmelites to claim a unique Marian privilege.[16] The absence

---

[13] Benedict Zimmerman, O.C.D., *The Carmelite Scapular*, in *The Month*, Vol. 150, 1927, pp. 323-327, dated the earliest written account soon after 1361. Xiberta, *De Visione*, p. 205, dates it about the middle of the fourteenth century, perhaps in the early decades of the fourteenth century.

[14] Evidence has been discovered that the apparition to St. Simon Stock was alluded to in the principal Marian feast of the English Province of Carmelites, the Solemn Commemoration of Holy Mary. Margaret Rickert, reconstructing a Carmelite Missal of 1390, found fragments of the Mass for the feast on which were the words of the *Flos Carmeli*. Cf. *Vinculum Ordinis Carmelitarum*, Vol. 3 (1952-1953), pp. 205-206.

[15] The earliest account of the apparition to St. Simon Stock contains no allusion to the Scapular devotion among the laity. The fact that the devotion did not arise until sometime after the acceptance of the apparition within the Carmelite Order is one of the more important discoveries of recent research into the tradition of the Scapular. Scholars in the past have sought historical evidence in the thirteenth and early fourteenth centuries in the belief that the devotion among the laity would have been in vogue. Thus Thurston was inclined to reject the historicity of the apparition because of the absence of evidence in the thirteenth and fourteenth centuries revealing the existence of the Scapular devotion. Cf. *Scapulars*, in *The Month*, Vol. 150, 1927, p. 45. The belief that the devotion was practiced by the laity in the thirteenth century came from the Swanyngton fragments, published by John Cheron, O.Carm., in 1642. The fragments are now recognized as unauthentic.

[16] A clear illustration is the failure of the medieval Carmelites to use the Scapular promise in connection with their title, "Order of the Brothers of the Blessed Virgin Mary of Mount Carmel." John Homeby, who defended the title at the University of Cambridge in 1374, made no appeal to the apparition to St. Simon Stock, although by his time it was long in writing in the Carmelite Sanctoral. Cf. Xiberta, *De Visione*, p.

of these motives behind the tradition tells in favor of its authenticity.

In the past, scholars have urged three difficulties against the historicity of the Scapular promise: (1) absence of documentary evidence for the tradition from the thirteenth century;[17] (2) silence of Carmelite authors of the fourteenth century concerning the promise;[18] (3) confusion in the tradition between the Carmelite habit and the Carmelite Scapular as the garment supposedly designated by Mary.[19] These objections no longer constitute serious difficulties against the authenticity of the Scapular tradition. Documentary evidence cannot be expected from the thirteenth century since the Carmelite Order did not begin to produce an extensive literature until the middle of the fourteenth century.[20] The appearance of the written tradition of the Scapular promise coincides with the blossoming of literary activity within the Order.[21] In the face of modern research into the history of Carmelite literary activity in the fourteenth century, the argument from silence against the tradition of the scapular promise loses point. The account of the Marian apparition to St. Simon Stock is a constant written tradition as far hack as literary activity reveals itself to be an important factor in the life of the Order. Finally, the conclusion of some historians that the apparition was originally associated by the Carmelites with their habit in general rather than with the Scapular

---

150.

[17] This point was pressed in the works of John Launoy. Cf. note 7.

[18] This objection was urged by Benedict Zimmerman, O.C.D., *Monumenta Historica Carmelitana* (Lirinae, 1907), pp. 343-344.

[19] *Ibid.*, p. 343.

[20] P. Rudolf Hendriks, O.Carm., *Le succession héréditaire*, in *Elie le prophète*, Vol. 2 (Bruges, 1956), pp. 34-75.

[21] The fourteenth century account of the Scapular vision appears to be a literary production. It is a stylized, partly poetic, narrative. The story is not told as St. Simon Stock might have told it. It is related with a greater insight, born only with the passage of time, into the Order's mendicant difficulties in the thirteenth century. The *Flos Carmeli* was more probably not composed by St. Simon Stock, but was induced by the tradition of the Marian apparition. The narrative would have passed through an oral stage, and perhaps an initial written stage, before being incorporated into the Sanctoral in its fourteenth century form. Some indication of the initial written form may exist in a fifteenth century Brussels manuscript, which describes the apparition in these simple lines: "St Simon ... always besought the Virgin in his prayers that she would endow her Order with a special privilege. The glorious Virgin appeared to him, holding the Scapular and saying, 'This will be for you and yours a privilege: he who dies in this will be saved.'" For the Latin text, cf. Xiberta, *De Visione*, p. 311.

in particular is certainly mistaken. There is an unbroken line of evidence, beginning with the Chapter of Montpellier in 1287 that the terms *habit* and *Scapular* were used interchangeably by the medieval Carmelites.[22] When the word *habit* is employed in Carmelite authors in connection with the Marian promise to St. Simon Stock, the term means simply "Scapular."

The sole reason for rejecting the historical authenticity of the Scapular promise is the absence of thirteenth century documentation revealing Carmelite knowledge and acceptance of the story of the apparition. The absence of such evidence leaves open the possibility that the Scapular tradition developed as a legend in the thirteenth or early fourteenth century. While the possibility of a legendary origin for the tradition of the Scapular promise must be admitted, its legendary origin cannot be affirmed.[23] Beginning with the documentary evidence in the fourteenth century, the essential details of the tradition remain invariable: (1) the apparition of Mary, (2) to St. Simon Stock, (3) with the Scapular, (4) stating the words of eternal life for all who die clothed in this garment.

THE SABBATINE PRIVILEGE: ORIGIN AND HISTORICAL CRITIQUE

The Sabbatine Bull occupied a place of key importance in the spread of the Scapular devotion in the sixteenth and seventeenth centuries. Throughout this period the popes repeatedly promulgated the Sabbatine Privilege in allusion to the Bull of 1322 attributed to Pope John XXII: Clement VII (1530); Paul III (1534; 1549); Pius IV (1561); Pius V (1566); Gregory XIII (1577); Urban VIII (1628); Clement X (1673; 1674; 1675);

---

[22] The Constitutions of 1294, 1324, and 1357 call the Scapular the habit. For the Acts of the Chapter of Montpellier, which made an explicit identification between "habit" and "scapular," cf. Antoine Marie de la Présentation, O.C.D., *Constitutions des Frères de Notre Dame du Mont-Carmel faites l'année 1357* (Marche, 1915), pp. 158-160. Xiberta, *De Visione*, p. 236, who interprets "habit" to mean "tunic" in the Acts of the Chapter of Montpellier, should be corrected. For the Constitutions of 1294 cf. Ludovicus Saggi, O.Carm., *Constitutiones Capituli Burdigalensis anni 1294*, in *Analecta Ord. Carm.*, Vol. 18, 1953, 152-153. For the Constitutions of 1324 cf. Zimmerman, *Monumenta*, pp. 49-52.

[23] The explanation of Lancelot C. Sheppard, *The English Carmelites* (London, 1943), pp. 13 ff., suggesting a legendary origin for the Scapular tradition, is an oversimplification. The author's statement that the early lessons of the breviary for the feast of St. Simon Stock are silent on the Scapular vision is unfounded. Cf. Xiberta, *De Visione*, pp. 127-130.

Innocent XI (1678; 1679; 1682; 1684).[24] Since according to the Sabbatine Privilege the souls of the faithful departed would benefit in purgatory from the intercession of the Blessed Virgin, the Church found it useful to stress the privilege in order to teach the legitimacy of the doctrine of indulgences and of Marian devotion.[25]

The tradition of the Sabbatine Bull seems to have been first spread in the fifteenth century. The Bull was known to the Carmelites Calciuri in 1461 and Leersius in 1483. It was referred to by the Carmelite General Chapter of 1517. Historically, however, the tradition of the Sabbatine Bull is clearly vulnerable. No evidence of the Bull appears in the registers of John XXII. Although it is recognized that the absence of a papal document from the medieval registers is not a conclusive argument against its authenticity, no positive historical evidence from other sources supports the papal origin of the Bull. Its literary character is entirely too odd to recommend it as the work of John XXII. For these reasons, historians have rejected the authenticity of the Sabbatine Bull.[26] The apparent spuriousness of the Bull naturally casts serious doubt on its tradition that the Sabbatine Privilege originated in a Marian apparition to Pope John XXII. Three theories have been proposed to explain the origin of the tradition of the apparition and the Bull. According to one view the tradition would have originated in an oral declaration by John XXII.[27] This theory accounts for the spurious character of the Bull and for its peculiar style. The explanation is too conjectural to win credence. A second theory would derive the Sabbatine Bull from an original authentic document from John XXII which became corrupt in the course of time.[28] But no evidence has been produced from existing copies of the Bull to show a gradual corruption of its text. A third theory considers the Bull to be an interpretation, based on theological grounds, of the Marian promise to St.

---

[24] Henry M. Esteve, O.Carm., De *valore spirituali devotionis S. Scapularis* (Romae, 1953), p. 61.

[25] *Ibid., pp. 59 ff.*

[26] Papenbroeck, S.J., wrote a firm case against the authenticity of the Bull in his *Responsio ... ad Exhibitionem Errorum* (Antwerpiae, 1696), p. 124 ff. The question was reviewed by Benedict Zimmerman, O.C.D., in *The Irish Ecclesiastical Record*, Series 4, Vol. 15, 1904, pp. 331-351.

[27] Elias Magennis, O.Carm., *The Sabbatine Privilege of the Scapular* (New York, 1923), p. 47.

[28] Zimmerman, The Origin of the Scapular, *in the* Irish Ecclesiastical Record, Series 4, Vol. 15, 1904, p. 347.

THE SCAPULAR DEVOTION

Simon Stock.[29] Since Mary's Mediation of Grace, of which her promise of eternal salvation is a reflection, embraces the final goal of the Christian life, which is union with God, it is logical to conclude that her maternal assistance makes itself felt in purgatory.[30] This third theory, that the Sabbatine Privilege is a more developed understanding of the significance of the Marian promise to St. Simon Stock, is the most plausible explanation of the origin of the Sabbatine Bull. The copies of the Bull indicate a close relationship between the promise to St. Simon Stock and the Sabbatine Privilege. The Bull states, "One who perseveres in holy obedience, poverty and chastity — or who will enter the Holy Order — will be saved." Then follows the declaration of the Sabbatine Privilege concerning release from purgatory for "others" who wear the holy "habit" of the Order. It would seem, then, that the Sabbatine Privilege arose historically in a fuller understanding of the Marian promise to St. Simon Stock.

THE DECISION OF THE HOLY OFFICE ON THE SABBATINE PRIVILEGE

Since the early seventeenth century, Carmelite preaching of the Sabbatine Privilege has been theologically independent of the historical authenticity of the Sabbatine Bull. In 1613 the Holy Office under Pope Paul V issued a decree on the Sabbatine Privilege which took account of the papal bulls of the sixteenth century. These Bulls had promulgated the privilege according to the tradition of the Sabbatine Bull. The decree of the Holy Office made no reference to the Bull of John XXII or to the tradition of the Marian apparition to him. It simply affirmed the privilege itself. The decree follows:

> The Carmelite Fathers may preach that the Christian people can piously believe in the aid of the souls of the brethren and *confratres* of the Sodality of the Most Blessed Virgin of Mount Carmel. Through her continuous intercessions, pious suffrages, merits, and special protection the Most Blessed Virgin, especially on Saturday, the day dedicated to her by the Church, will help after their death the brethren and members of the Sodality who die in charity. In life they must have worn the habit, observed chastity according to

---

[29] Esteve, *op. cit.*, p. 309.

[30] Cf. C. X. J. M. Friethoff, O.P., *A Complete Mariology* (London, 1958), pp. 277-278. The author derives Mary's power to intercede for the souls in purgatory from her Queenship.

their state, and have recited the Little Office. If they do not know how to recite it, they are to observe the fasts of the Church and to abstain from meat on Wednesdays and Saturdays, except for the feast of Christmas.[31]

This decree of Paul V stated in effect that the spiritual authority of the popes of the sixteenth century had sanctioned the Marian teaching of the Sabbatine Privilege. This aspect of the devotion of the Brown Scapular was thus declared spiritually fruitful for the laity.

THE INTERPRETATION OF THE SCAPULAR PROMISE

The first affirmation of theologians concerning the Scapular promise of eternal salvation deals with the necessity of ruling out formalism in the practice of the devotion. Formalism is the physical wearing of the Scapular without sincere intent to serve God. The theological reason for ruling out formalism is that exterior acts of religion must be a reflection of one's interior mind and will if they are not to be hypocritical. The Scapular is merely a symbol having in itself no intrinsic power of grace. As a symbol it possesses a twofold import, one in relation to the Blessed Virgin, one in relation to its wearer. As a sign of consecration to Mary, the Scapular is a reminder of the spiritual prerogatives enjoyed by her in the economy of the redemption, and it is a pledge that her role be activated in favor of the wearer of the Scapular. In relation to its wearer, the Scapular is a sign that one has resolved to dedicate himself to the service of Christ and Mary according to his station in life. The Scapular symbolizes both the recognition of the spiritual maternity of Mary and an acceptance of the spiritual duties that Christians, as children of Mary, are obligated to undertake in the service of God. For the layman who becomes a member of the Scapular Confraternity the spiritual duties are summed up in the observance of the Ten Commandments, daily prayer, attendance at Mass on days of obligation, the reception of the Sacraments of Penance and the Holy Eucharist, and the faithful performance of the duties of one's state. The Scapular devotion does not provide an escape from the ordinary duties of Christianity, but is rather an incentive to undertake them with fervor and exactitude in the knowledge that one thus prepares himself to arrive at the final goal of the Christian life, union with God in eternity. In order to insist that the Scapular is meaningless without interior devotion,

---

[31] The Latin text may be found in Esteve, *op. cit.*, p. 72. The word "piously" in the opening statement of the decree does not mean "with a fond hope," but out of proper interior dispositions. Cf. Esteve, *op. cit.*, p. 74.

the Church has inserted the word *pie,* "piously," into the words of the promise concerning those who die in the Scapular.[32]

The interpretation of the promise to St. Simon Stock, "He who dies in this will not suffer eternal fire," must be based on sound principles of theology. The words themselves simply express the object of Mary's promise, eternal salvation, and the pledge of her assistance, the material sign of the Scapular to be worn continually. To ascertain the meaning of the promise, one must have recourse to two principles for the interpretation of private revelation. (1) All private revelation must be understood in the light of the truths of salvation divinely revealed by Jesus Christ and His Apostles. These truths are proposed by the Church, the divinely appointed teacher. (2) Private revelations concerning the Blessed Virgin must be understood in the light of the spiritual values inherent in true devotion to Mary. These values have been revealed by God and are taught by the Church. Only when these two principles are utilized do we arrive at a correct estimate of the promise of the Scapular.

The practice of the Christian life, however perfectly it may be accomplished, cannot merit in justice the grace of final perseverance. The grace of final perseverance is a gift of God by which we die united to Him in supernatural friendship. All theologians teach it as certain that a good life does not entitle us, in justice, to obtain this grace from God. To live in the supernatural friendship of God is His gift, and so it is His gift also to die in this friendship. The moment of the death of all men, whether in the pursuit of good or of evil, lies in the hands of God. Those who are faithful to the divine commands, truly repentant for their sins, and who avail themselves of the means of grace established by Christ may remain, not absolutely certain,[33] but confident of their salvation. This confidence derives from the virtue of Christian hope, by which we rely on the promises of God that He wills the salvation of all men and gives them the means to attain it. It is precisely in connection with the grace of final perseverance that the Church recommends the devotion of the Scapular. Mary has promised that the grace of final perseverance will be granted through her intercession to all those who, by means of the Scapular,

---

[32] For a more extended discussion of the necessity of interior devotion, see Esteve, *op. cit.,* pp. 80-99, 276-315.

[33] According to the well-known definition of the Council of Trent (*D.B.* 805), absolute and infallible certainty of one's eternal salvation is not possible without a personal divine revelation. Theologians, however, admit certain "signs" that one will be saved, among which is special devotion to the Blessed Virgin.

dedicate themselves to her and wear it until death out of devotion to her and to the teachings of Christ. The particular value of the Scapular devotion consists in the special help of Mary, so that the grace of final perseverance, or of a "happy death," may be obtained through her intercession.

This interpretation of the Scapular promise is but an affirmation of the spiritual value of Marian devotion: one who practices true devotion to Mary cannot lose his soul for eternity. This proposition of the power of Mary's intercession has been expressed in papal teaching.[34] It is the consciousness of the Church on the value of true Marian devotion. The same awareness is expressed in the *Ave Maria,* wherein the gift of final perseverance is requested: "Holy Mary ... pray for us now and at the hour of our death." Reliance on Mary's intercession, put into these words of momentary prayer, becomes in the symbol of the Scapular a continual prayer that spans the moments of a lifetime, to the supreme moment of death.

The necessity of interior devotion does not prevent the sinner from benefiting from the Scapular promise,[35] since all men are sinners. Only the degree, not the fact, of sin in man is debatable. To affirm that the Scapular devotion is not of value to sinners, including those humanly judged to be the worst of them, would be to say that God fails to hear their prayers. The teaching of Christ is that God hears the prayers of the sinner (Lk. 18:9-14). The question of the Scapular and sinners is falsely posed when it is asked how the Scapular promise can save the worst of them. The question can only be whether or not the sinner who wears the Scapular out of devotion makes those interior acts in response to divine grace that are necessary to his salvation. The answer to this question is known only

---

[34] Cf. Benedict XV, *Inter sodalicia,* in *A.A.S.,* Vol. 10, 1918, p. 120; Pius XI, *Explorata res est* in *A.A.S.,* Vol. 15, 1923, p. 104.

[35] This point was forcefully stated by Pius XII: "... How many souls even in circumstances which, humanly speaking, were beyond hope, have owed their final conversion and their eternal salvation to the scapular which they were wearing! How many more, thanks to it, have experienced the motherly protection of Mary in dangers to body and soul..." *Discorsi e radiomessaggi di Sua Santità Pio XII,* Vol. **12 (1950-1951),** p. **165.** The pope's allusion to the miraculous tradition of the Scapular is based on fact, admitted by all authorities on the devotion. Numerous books were written on this subject alone from the seventeenth to the nineteenth centuries, e.g., Guardius, O.Carm., *Thesaurus coelestis* (Brixiae, **1611**); Michael de la Fuente, O.Carm., *Compendium historiale ... gratiarum B. V. Mariae de Monte Carmelo* (Toleti, **1619**); Hugust, S.M., *Vertu miraculeuse du Scapulaire* (Paris, 1879).

to God, who alone may scan the secrets of the heart of man.

THE SCAPULAR DEVOTION IN MODERN LIFE

The popes in modern times have been solicitous in their encouragement of the Scapular devotion. St. Pius X permitted the substitution of a Scapular Medal for the cloth Scapular in recognition of the changed circumstances of life, precisely to encourage the dedication to Mary signified by the Scapular. For any reason, even simple convenience, the faithful invested in any Scapular except that of the Third Orders, may substitute a Scapular Medal which need only be carried on the person. The Medal was not intended as a new form of the Scapular devotion, but only as an aid to its continual practice. Catholics should be instructed to make free and wise use of both Scapular and Medal according to their judgment and circumstances. The permission for the Medal reflects the mind of the Church that the Scapular itself is only the exterior sign of an interior devotion.[36]

In 1890 Leo XIII had begun to grant the faculty to confessors to commute the condition of abstinence into other good works for the gaining of the Sabbatine Privilege. In order to gain the privilege one must (1) wear the Scapular or the Scapular Medal; (2) observe chastity according to one's state in life; (3) recite daily the Little Office of Our Lady, or if one does not know how to recite it, abstain from meat on Wednesdays and Saturdays. The commutation of the third condition, due to practical difficulties in the circumstances of modern life, has become a common practice. The confessor is free to choose any suitable good work as the daily substitute. The commutation of Carmelite confessors is usually to seven *Paters, Aves,* and *Glorias.*

OTHER MARIAN SCAPULARS

From time to time in the history of the Church Scapular devotions have arisen to foster love of Mary and to encourage the practice of

---

[36] The Scapular Medal entitles the wearer to all the benefits of the Scapular devotion, including the promise of eternal salvation and the Sabbatine Privilege. Objection on theological grounds that the Scapular Medal does not entitle the wearer to the benefit of the promise of eternal salvation is unfounded. Cf. *The Decree on the Scapular Medal* in *The Sword,* Vol. **16, 1953,** pp. **343-360;** and in popular form, *The Great Debate: Scapular or Medal,* in *The Scapular,* Vol. 16, July-August, **1957,** pp. **15-20;** reprinted in Vol. 17, July-August, 1958, pp. 15-20.

particular virtues. The Black Scapular of the Seven Dolors originated from the habit of the Servite Fathers. The inspiration for the habit of the Order and for its devotion to Our Lady of Sorrows is attributed to an apparition of Mary to its founders. Pope Martin V approved a rule for the Third Order secular in 1424. The Blue Scapular of the Immaculate Conception, which the Church has favored with an extraordinary number of indulgences, originated in an apparition of Mary to the Ven. Ursula Benincasa in 1617. Great graces were promised by Mary to those who would honor her Immaculate Conception by wearing the Blue Scapular. The condition was expressed that they live chastely according to their state in life. Other Marian Scapulars are of more recent origin: the white Scapular of the Immaculate Heart of Mary, approved by Pius IX in 1877; the white Scapular of the Sacred Hearts of Jesus and Mary, approved by the Congregation of Rites in 1900; the white Scapular of Our Lady of Good Counsel, approved in 1893 by Leo XIII for the purpose of invoking Mary's guidance upon its wearer; the white Scapular of Our Lady of Ransom bearing the cross of Aragon, which originated in the thirteenth century in connection with the Fathers of the Blessed Virgin Mary of the Redemption of Captives; the black Scapular of Our Lady Help of the Sick, the badge of the Confraternity founded by St. Camillus de Lellis for the aid of the sick, approved in 1860 by Pius IX.[37]

RECENT POPES AND THE SCAPULAR

Pius XI and Pius XII have urged those wearing the Brown Scapular of Our Lady of Mount Carmel to be especially attentive in their personal lives to the requirements of true Marian devotion. Pius XI wrote, "... although it is very true that the Blessed Virgin loves all who love her, nevertheless those who wish to have the Blessed Mother as a helper in [the hour of] death, must in life merit such signal favor by abstaining from sin and laboring in her honor."[38] Pius XII stressed the spiritual importance of the Scapular devotion:

> We are not here concerned with a light or passing matter, but with the obtaining of eternal life itself which is the substance of the promise of the most Blessed Virgin which has been handed down to us. We are concerned, namely,

---

[37] For more detailed information, cf. Magennis, *The Scapular Devotion* (Dublin, 1923), pp. 99-160. The Green "Scapular" of the Immaculate Conception, approved by Pius IX in 1870, is a cloth badge rather than a Scapular, since it consists of a single panel.

[38] Apostolic Letter, *Petis tu quidem*, in *A.A.S.*, Vol. 14, 1922, p. 274.

with that which is of supreme importance to all and with the manner of achieving it safely... But not for this reason may they who wear the Scapular think that they can gain eternal salvation while remaining slothful and negligent of spirit, for the Apostle warns us: "In fear and trembling shall you work out your salvation" (Phil. 2:12).[39]

Pius XII likewise emphasized the value of the Scapular devotion for society itself:

> There is no one who is not aware how greatly a love for the Blessed Virgin Mother of God contributes to the enlivening of the Catholic faith and to the raising of the moral standard. These effects are especially secured by means of those devotions which more than others are seen to enlighten the mind with celestial doctrine and to excite souls to the practice of the Christian life. In the first rank of the most favored of these devotions, that of the holy Carmelite Scapular must be placed — a devotion which, adapted to the minds of all by its very simplicity, has become so universally widespread among the faithful and has produced so many and such salutary fruits.[40]

---

[39] Apostolic Letter *Neminem profecto latet*, in *A.A.S.*, Vol. 42, 1950, pp. 390-391. This letter marks a change in the manner of explaining the Sabbatine Privilege. It does not refer to the release from purgatory in the older terminology, "especially on Saturday," but in the words "as soon as possible." The traditional description in terms of "Saturday" alluded to the liturgical practice of dedicating this day to Mary.

[40] *Ibid.* For a detailed discussion of the papal encouragement of the Scapular devotion, cf. Eamon R. Carroll, O.Carm., *The Pope Speaks on the Scapular*, in *Our Lady's Digest*, Vol. 11, 1956, pp. 63-71. Recent writings in English on the Scapular include: *Take This Scapular*, by Carmelite Fathers and Tertiaries (Chicago, 1949); Kilian Lynch, O.Carm., *Your Brown Scapular* (Westminster, Md., 1950); William G. Most, *Mary in Our Life* (New York, 1954), pp. 233-240; Henry M. Esteve, O.Carm., *The Brown Scapular of Carmel* (Marian reprint No. 32. University of Dayton, 1955).

THE HOLY SLAVERY OF LOVE

By PATRICK J. GAFFNEY, S.M.M.

T. LOUIS MARY DE MONTFORT'S present influence on the Christian world, primarily because of his doctrine on total consecration to Our Lady, can only be termed immeasurable. It is this teaching of the French missionary on total consecration — or "Holy Slavery,"[1] as it is also called — which will be briefly studied here. In order to understand the doctrine of St. Louis de Montfort on this subject, we will first trace the history of "Holy Slavery" up to the time of St. Louis (1673-1716), briefly explain his teachings concerning consecration to Mary, and finally cite some of the numerous encomiums which popes and theologians alike have showered upon his works.

I. THE HISTORY OF "HOLY SLAVERY" PRIOR TO ST. LOUIS[2]

---

[1] It may be well to point out from the start that the word *slave* or "slavery" is not to be taken in any servile, pejorative sense. Basing themselves upon the frequent appellation "slave of Jesus Christ" in the New Testament (cf. Rom. 1, 1; Phil. 1, 1; *Tit.* 1, 1 etc.), authors have transcribed the term to devotion to Our Lady in order to express total dependence. Although explained in somewhat different manners throughout the centuries, the expression is, in general, synonymous with "total consecration," "total surrender," "total abandonment" to the Mother of God. The precise meaning Saint Louis de Montfort gives to this term will be seen in the second part of the text.

[2] For a study of the history of "Holy Slavery," the following authors may be consulted: Salvador Gutiérrez Alonso, O.E.S.A., *La Esclavitud Mariana en sus fundamentos teológicos y forma ascético-místico e histórica según el Beato Montfort y según el P. Rios* (Madrid, 1945), pp. 325-436; L. Aquatias, O. de M., *Piedad Mariana en la Orden de Nuestra Señora de la Merced,* in *Alma Socia Christi,* Vol. 7 (Roma, 1952), pp. 509-582; J. Dayet, S.M.M., *Notre Consécration; Le mot de la tradition,* in *La Revue des Prêtres de Marie Reine des Coeurs,* Vol. 26, 1939, pp. 33-44, 65-72, 97-105, 162-169, 193-198, 226-230, 257-263, 290-296, 321-329; Vol. 27, 1940, pp. 2-6, 33-38, 65-71; Vol. 28, 1941, pp. 2-8, 33-37, 65-72, 97-104, 132-142; Vol. 29, 1942, pp. 40-52; Tomas de Echevarría, C.M.F., *La Esclavitud Mariana en los autores místicos y clásicos españoles,* in *Crónica del Congreso Mariano-Montfortano celebrado en Barcelona el Año 1918* (Totana, 1919), pp. 148-188; J. B. Gomis, O.F.M., *Esclavitud Mariana, Fr. Juan de los Angeles y su Cofradía de Esclavas y Esclavos,* in *Verdad y Vida,* Vol. 4, 1946, pp. 259-286; cf. also his *Introducción to Juan de los Angeles, Cofradía y devoción de las esclavas y esclavos de Nuestra Señora la Virgen Santísima,* in *Místicos Franciscanos Españoles,* Vol. 3 (Madrid, 1949), pp. 685-689, and in the same volume, his *Introducción* to Melchor de Cetina, *Exhortación a la devoción de la*

St. Louis de Montfort himself declares that "this devotion [Holy Slavery] is not new,"[3] and adopts H. Boudon's statement: "it is so ancient that we cannot fix precisely the date of its beginnings. It is certain, however, that for more than seven hundred years we find traces of it in the Church."[4]

A. The Term "Slave of Mary"

Although the title "slave of Mary" may be said to be implicit in those Fathers of the Church who recognize the Mother of God as "Queen" or "Lady,"[5] the expression is explicitly used by a number of the Fathers. Several authors cite St. Ephraem († 373) as the first to call himself a "slave of the Mother of God,"[6] yet the text cited is of doubtful authenticity.[7] However St. Ildephonsus of Toledo († 669) did make use of the title,[8] as

---

Virgen Madre de Dios, pp. 711-720; Leo Gommenginger, *Theologische und geschichtliche Anmerkungen*, appended to *Grignion von Montfort, Abhandlung über die volkommene Andacht zu Maria* (Freiburg, Schweiz, 1925), pp. 269-290; B. Hughes, O.F.M., *The Queen's Own*, in *Priestly Studies*, Vol. 20, 1952, pp. 53-58; N. Pérez, S.J., *La Esclavitud de Nuestra Señora según los antiguos ascetas españoles* (Madrid, 1929); *La Esclavitud de amor, perfectísima devoción a la Santísima Virgen*, in *Estudios Marianos*, Vol. 8, 1949, pp. 397-400; G. Roschini, O.S.M., *Mariologia*, Tom. 2, Pars 3, *De Singulari Cultu B.V.M.* (Romae, 1948), pp. 34-39; *La Servitude Mariale* (Nicolet, 1952); *La Madonna secondo la fede e la teologia*, Vol. 4, *Il Singolare Culto di Maria* (Roma, 1954), pp. 95-113.

[3] *True Devotion to the Blessed Virgin Mary* (Bay Shore, 1958), No. 163.

[4] *Ibid.*, No. 159. Cf. Henri Boudon, *Dieu seul; Le Saint Esclavage de l'admirable Mère de Dieu* (Paris, 1769), p. 14.

[5] Cf. e.g., Origen, *Fragmenta in Lucam*, in *PG* 13, 1901.

[6] Cf. N. Pérez, S.J., La Esclavitud de amor, perfectísima devoción a la Santísima Virgen, p. 398; J. Dayet, S.M.M., art. cit., in *Revue des Prêtres de Marie*, Vol. 26, 1939, p. 69; G. Roschini, O.S.M., *La Madonna secondo la fede e la teologia*, p. 96.

[7] Cf. S.P.N. *Ephraem Syri opera omnia quae extant, graece, syriace, latine*, edita a Mobarek-Assemani, 6 vols. (Romae, 1742-1746). The texts cited are from the *Opera graeca*, Vol. 3, pp. 532-533, 536. Of the Greek collection of St. Ephraem's writings in Assemani, J. Bover declares: "graeca plura aut non genuina aut liberius retractata" (*S. Ephraem Doctoris Syri testimonia de universali B.V.M. Mediatione*, in *Ephemerides Theologicae Lovanienses*, Vol. 4, 1927, p. 161). Roschini himself declares: "authentiam horum locorum extra omnem dubitationem non esse" (*Mariologia*, Tom. 2, Pars 3, p. 35, note 2).

[8] Cf. *De virginitate perpetua S. Mariae*, in *PL* 96, 107: "quam prompte servus hujus dominae effici concupisco"; *ibid.*, *PL* 96, 108: "servus fieri appeto Genetricis."

did St. John Damascene († 749),[9] Euthymius of Constantinople († 917),[10] the brother of St. Peter Damian, Blessed Marinus († 1016),[11] the Abbot Odilon († 1049),[12] St. Anselm of Canterbury († 1109),[13] St. Bernard († 1153),[14] and Adam of St. Victor († 1192).[15]

The expression "slave of the Mother of God" is also found on official seals used in the fifth and sixth centuries in Africa[16]; Pope John VII († 707) prided himself on the title,[17] as did Pope Nicholas IV († 1292) and Pope Paul V († 1621).[18] The fact of calling oneself "slave of the Mother of God"

---

[9] Cf. *Homilia prima in nativitate B.V. Mariae*, in *PG* 96, 679: "O Joachim et Annae filia et domina, orationem suscipe servi peccatoris."

[10] Cf. *Sermo de zona SS. Deiparae*, in *PG* 131, 1249: "... ut qui simus servi et debitores, o optima, respice servos tuos, respice." This work was attributed to Euthymius Zigabenus (beginning of the twelfth century), but it is now recognized as the work of Euthymius of Constantinople. Cf. R. Laurentin, *Table rectificative des pièces mariales inauthentiques ou discutées contenues dans les deux Patrologies de Migne*, appended to *Court Traité de théologie mariale* (Paris, **1953**), p. 173.

[11] Cf. Peter Damian, *Opusculum 33, de bono suffragiorum et variis miraculis, praesertim B. Virginis*, cap. 4, in *PL* 145, 566, where the saint relates that his brother, Marinus, "altari se beatae Dei Genetricis, velut servile mancipium, traddit: mox se quasi servum malum coram domina sua fecit verberibus effici. ..."

[12] Cf. Jotsaldus Monachus, *Vita S. Odilonis*, in *PL* 142, 916, where these words are put on the lips of St. Odilo: "Post Deum enim a modo nihil tibi [i.e. B.M. Virgini] praepono et ultroneus in aeternum meipsum tamquam proprium servum, tuo mancipatui trado."

[13] Cf. *Oratio 52 (51)*, in *PL* 158, 954: "usque in finem servus tuus sub tua protectione custodiatur"; *Oratio 51 (50)*, in *PL* 158, 951: "Pie Domine, parce servo matris tuae."

[14] Cf. *In Assumptione B.V.M., Sermo IV*, in *PL* 183, 428: "nos quidem servuli tui."

[15] Cf. *In Assumptione B.V.*, in *PL* 196, 1504: "Jesu Verbum Summi Patris: Serva Servos Tuae Matris." There are some who claim that this text is of an even more ancient author; cf. R. Laurentin, *op. cit.*, p. 155. For a more detailed listing of the Fathers of the Church who use the expression "slave of the Mother of God," cf. Roschini, *La Madonna* ..., Vol. 4, pp. 95 ff.

[16] Cf. A. L. Delattre, *Le culte de la Sainte Vierge en Afrique* (Paris-Lille, 1907), pp. 109 ff.; Découvertes mariales à Carthage *1907-1908, in* Actas del Cuarto Congreso Mariano Internacional celebrado en Zaragoza 1908 (Madrid, 1909), pp. 502-508.

[17] Four ancient inscriptions attest to this fact: one in the ancient Vatican Basilica, another in Pope John's private oratory and two in the church of Santa Maria Antica. Cf. H. Leclercq, art. *Forum chrétien*, in *Dictionnaire d'Archéologie Chrétienne et Liturgie*, col. 2016-2017; Dayet, *art. cit.*, Vol. 26, 1939, pp. 161-169; Roschini, *Mariologia*, Tom. 2, Pars 3, pp. 36-37.

[18] Nicholas IV inscribed this title in the church of Saint John Lateran, and Paul V in the church of Saint Mary Major. Cf. Roschini, *La Madonna* ..., Vol. 4, p. 100, note 1.

was declared customary as early as the seventh century;[19] it existed in Ireland at least by the ninth century,[20] and was given official sanction in the approbation of the community of the "Servites" of Mary in the thirteenth century. Thomas à Kempis († 1471) also made extensive use of the term.[21]

B. Confraternities of the Holy Slavery

Although the expression "slave of Mary" dates from the early ages of the Church, the first Confraternity of the Holy Slavery appears to have originated in Spain on the second of August, 1595, under the leadership of Sister Agnes of St. Paul, of the Franciscan Conceptionists at the convent of St. Ursula in Alcalá de Henares.[22] In 1608 the Franciscan, John of the Angels, not only joined the confraternity but rewrote and enlarged the statutes of the organization, adding a short introduction on the notion of Holy Slavery.[23] At the request of the Conceptionist Community of Alcalá, another Franciscan, Melchor de Cetina, composed in 1618 what may be called the first "Handbook of Spirituality" for the members of the confraternity.[24] The association was approved by Pope Clement XII in 1730.[25]

In 1612 the Benedictine, Anthony de Alvarado, founded at Valladolid, Spain, a distinct confraternity of the Holy Slavery under the title "The Slaves of the Exiled Holy Virgin," which was approved almost

---

[19] Cf. Dayet, *art. cit.*, Vol. 26, 1939, p. 101; I. Kronenburg, C.Ss.R., Maria's *Heerlijkheid in Nederland*, Vol. 1 (Amsterdam, 1904), p. 96 ff.; J. Carbó, *Orientación del Congreso*, in *Actas del Congreso Mariano-Montfortano de Barcelona* (1918) (Totana, 1919), p. 98.

[20] Cf. E. Watertown, *Pietas mariana britannica* (London, 1879), p. 20 ff.

[21] Cf. *Sermones ad novicios; Sermo 23*, in *Thomae Hermerken a Kempis opera omnia*, Vol. 6 (Friburgi Br., 1910), pp. 218-223. This chapter is found in *De imitatione Mariae* (Romae, 1955), pp. 47-57.

[22] Cf. Gutiérrez Alonso, *op. cit.*, p. 339; Gomis, *art. cit.*, in *Verdad y Vida*, p. 271; Dayet, *art. cit.*, Vol. 26, 1939, p. 328. Sister Agnes entered the convent in 1575 at about the age of ten; sometime after her entrance and the official organization of the association in 1595 the devotion of "Holy Slavery" is said to have been divinely revealed to her.

[23] Cf. Juan de los Angeles, *Cofradía y devoción de las esclavas y esclavos de Nuestra Señora la Virgen Santísima*, in *Místicos Franciscanos Españoles*, ed. J. B. Gomis, O.F.M., Vol. 3 (Madrid, 1949), pp. 691-701.

[24] Cf. Melchor de Cetina, *Exhortación a la devoción de la Virgen Madre de Dios*, also found in Místicos Franciscanos Españoles, Vol. 3, pp. 721-817.

[25] The text of the Papal Bull is found in Gomis, *art. cit.*, pp. 285-286.

THE HOLY SLAVERY OF LOVE 151

immediately by Pope Paul V.[26] Father Peter de la Serna, Mercedarian, who was acquainted with the "Slaves of the Exiled Virgin," published at Seville in 1617, *Statutes and Constitutions of the Slaves of Our Lady of Mercy*.[27] The confraternity soon spread throughout the Mercedarian Order.

In 1619 another confraternity was formed at Alcalá de Henares, under the mysteries of the Sorrows, Assumption, Nativity, Conception, and Annunciation of Our Lady; this confraternity received the approval of the Holy See in 1685.[28]

Especially through the work of the Franciscan, John of the Angels, the confraternity of Alcalá numbered among its members even King Philip III of Spain and his wife, Queen Margaret, and many other notables of both Church and State. The devotion of "Holy Slavery" became known therefore to the confessor of Queen Margaret, Simon de Rojas, a Trinitarian († 1624).[29] Asked by the King what reward he wanted for having aided the Queen on her deathbed († 1611), de Rojas requested the King's help in founding a confraternity of slaves of the glorious name of Mary under the invocation "Ave Maria." The Confraternity of the Slaves of the "Ave Maria" soon spread throughout the monasteries of the Trinitarians and was approved by Rome as early as 1616.[30]

Since Belgium was at this period under Spanish rule, it was but natural that Simon de Rojas thought of extending his confraternity to the Low Countries. However, his community possessed no monasteries in Belgium, and de Rojas therefore asked his friend, the Augustinian, Bartholomew de los Rios († 1652), to accomplish this task for him. In 1622 de los Rios left for Belgium as the preacher of Isabella, wife of Archduke Albert, governor of the Low Countries. The first confraternity of the Holy

---

[26] Cf. Gutiérrez Alonso, *op. cit.*, pp. 340-341; Echevarría, *art. cit.*, p. 162.

[27] Cf. Aquatias, *art. cit.*, p. 509 ff.; Gutiérrez Alonso, *op. cit.*, p. 341, note 4.

[28] Cf. Gomis, *art. cit.*, p. 276 ff.; also in his *Introducción* to Juan de los Angeles, *Cofradía y devoción ...* , ed. cit. p. 688. The Spanish translation of the Papal Bull is found in the same volume, pp. 700-701.

[29] Cf. Gutiérrez Alonso, *op. cit.*, pp. 341-344; Echevarría, *art. cit.*, pp. 159-162; Dayet, *art. cit.*, Vol. 27, 1940, p. 4. It is interesting to note that Simon de Rojas was one of the censors of de la Serna's work on the statutes of the Seville confraternity (1614). Cf. Aquatias, *art. cit.*, p. 517.

[30] Cf. Gutiérrez Alonso, *op. cit.*, pp. 343-344. The ultimate source for these facts is the *Hierarchia Mariana* of Bartholomew de los Rios (Antverpiae, 1641). A résumé of the constitutions composed by Simon de Rojas for his confraternity can be found in *Revue des Prêtres de Marie*, Vol. 27, 1940, p. 6, and in Echevarría, *art. cit.*, pp. 180-181.

Slavery was founded in Belgium in 1626, recognized and indulgenced by Urban VIII in 1631.[31] Through the work and writings of de los Rios — and also with the help of his fellow Augustinians — the confraternity of the Holy Slavery spread rapidly throughout the Low Countries.[32]

The devotion was brought to Poland through Prince Wladislaus IV who heard a sermon of de los Rios on the Holy Slavery while on a visit to Belgium.[33] The Theatines especially preached it throughout Italy.[34]

Up to this date, however, "the devotion of 'Holy Slavery' had not as yet reached the clarity and plenitude which it achieved under Saint Louis de Montfort. Moreover, [the consecration] is not addressed to Jesus, the Incarnate Wisdom, in dependence on Mary; it does not present to us the imitation of this filial dependence as its principal motive. Likewise, it leaves the spiritual Maternity of Mary only in the shade."[35]

Thanks to Cardinal de Bérulle († 1629), the devotion of "Holy Slavery" was made part of the French School of Spirituality. Having become acquainted with the confraternities in Spain, he became its great propagator in France.[36] Even as developed by this founder of the French School, however, the devotion of "Holy Slavery" differed greatly from the system which would be explained by St. Louis. "On the part of Jesus, Bérulle assigns as foundation of his Donation, the state of servitude of the Holy Humanity of the Incarnate Word; Montfort, the state of dependence

---

[31] The Papal Bull is found in Gutiérrez Alonso, *op. cit.*, pp. 427-428.

[32] The most famous of the writings of Bartholomew de los Rios is his *Hierarchia Mariana;* he is very probably also the author of *Mancipium Virginis* (Coloniae, 1634), which is a translation of an earlier work, *El Esclavo de María.* Cf. A. Musters, O.E.S.A., *La souveraineté de la Vierge d'après les écrits mariologiques de Barthélemy de los Rios*, O.E.S.A. (Bruges, 1946), p. 30. Saint Louis de Montfort explicitly refers to the *Hierarchia Mariana* (cf. *True Devotion*, No. 160), and alludes to the *Mancipium Virginis* (*ibid.*, No. 161). Cf. Florentino Agudelo, S.M.M., *Naturaleza de la Esclavitud Mariana según el Padre Bartolomé de los Rios y San Luis María de Montfort* (Bogotá, 1958). The Constitutions and Act of Consecration composed by Bartholomew de los Rios can be found in Gutiérrez Alonso, *op. cit.*, pp. 437-445, and in Dayet, *art. cit.*, Vol. 28, 1941, pp. 35-37, 65-71. They are taken from the *Hierarchia Mariana*, Book IV, pp. 290-294.

[33] Cf. Dayet, *art. cit.*, Vol. 28, 1941, pp. 4-6. When he became King, Wladislaus asked the Jesuits to preach this devotion throughout Poland. Father Stanislaus Phalacius, S.J., appears to have been its principal promoter.

[34] Cf. Roschini, *La Madonna* ... , Vol. 4, p. 110; St. Louis de Montfort, *True Devotion*, No. 161.

[35] Dayet, *art. cit.*, Vol. 28, 1941, p. 37.

[36] Cf. A. Molien, *art. Bérulle*, in *Dictionnaire de Spiritualité*, col. 1547.

of the Incarnate Word Himself in relation to Mary in the entire redemptive work. On the part of Our Lady, Bérulle bases his Donation on the Divine Maternity and the Universal Sovereignty which flows from it; Montfort, on the spiritual Maternity and the special dominion of Mary over the members of the Mystical Body."[37] Cardinal de Bérulle did insist, however, on the consecration being the equivalent of the renewal of the Baptismal Promises,[38] also emphasized by Montfort.[39] Following and developing the doctrine of de Bérulle, John Olier († 1657), St. John Eudes († 1680), and Henry Boudon († 1702) also adopted the practice of "Holy Slavery."[40] It was especially from this source, the French School of Spirituality, that St. Louis de Montfort received his knowledge of total abandonment, total consecration to the Mother of God.

Even before St. Louis de Montfort composed his *True Devotion to the Blessed Virgin*, therefore, the devotion of the "Holy Slavery" had spread throughout Catholic Europe, as C. Dillenschneider, C.Ss.R., remarks.[41] It had been approved and indulgenced by numerous popes and was being spread by many religious communities including the Jesuits, Benedictines, Mercedarians, Trinitarians, Franciscans, Augustinians, Oratorians, Sulpicians, Theatines, and Dominicans. At times, some of the members of the various confraternities did go to an excess, insisting solely upon external signs of this devotion, and these abuses were condemned by Rome.[42] Never, however, was the devotion itself condemned; in fact, its many approbations from various popes and the many indulgences

---

[37] Dayet, *art. cit.*, Vol. 29, 1942, p. 40.

[38] Cf. Cardinal de Bérulle, *Voeux à Jesus et à Marie*, in *Oeuvres complètes* (Paris, 1856), col. 614-617.

[39] *True Devotion*, Nos. 126-130.

[40] For a study of the development of the devotion of "Holy Slavery" in the French School of Spirituality, and for the differences on this point between St. Louis de Montfort and his immediate predecessors, cf. M. T. Poupon, O.P., *Le poème de la parfaite consécration à Marie* (Lyon, 1947), pp. 336-374.

[41] Cf. *Mariologie de S. Alphonse de Liguori*, Vol. 1 (Fribourg, Suisse, 1931), p. 229.

[42] By a decree of the Holy Office of July 5, 1673, and by the Apostolic Brief, *Pastoralis Officii*, of December 15, 1675, Clement X abolished certain confraternities of the Blessed Sacrament, of the Blessed Mother, of St. Joseph, and of the Flock of the Good Shepherd, in which "little chains" were used. Benedict XIV confirmed the condemnation in 1758. The condemnations concerned the *abuses* which had crept in, and *not* the devotion itself. Cf. A. Plessis, S.M.M., *Commentaire du Traité de la vraie dévotion à la Sainte Vierge* (Pontchateau, 1942), p. 376; P. Pourrat, *La Spiritualité chrétienne*, Vol. 4 (Paris, 1928), p. 152; Roschini, *La Madonna* ... , p. 112, note 1.

showered upon its confraternities are proof enough of the truth of St. Louis' words: "We cannot see how it could be condemned without overturning the foundations of Christianity."[43]

II. TOTAL CONSECRATION ACCORDING TO ST. LOUIS

St. Louis de Montfort is by no means the founder of the devotion of "Holy Slavery." Yet, because of his particular theological and ascetical explanations of this act of total consecration, he himself boldly declares: "But after all, I loudly protest, that having read nearly all the books which profess to treat of devotion to Our Lady and having conversed familiarly with the best and wisest men in these latter times, I have never known nor heard of any practise of devotion toward her at all equal to the one which I now wish to unfold."[44] Montfort's doctrine on "Holy Slavery" will be best understood by considering first the dogmatic foundations of his consecration and then the consecration itself.

A. THEOLOGICAL FOUNDATIONS OF TOTAL CONSECRATION

During most of his sixteen years of priesthood, St. Louis traveled throughout the countryside of Western France, preaching missions and retreats. He was not a professional theologian. The pulpit was his rostrum, the crowded church his class. Although his writings are relatively numerous,[45] we cannot expect to find a section devoted to a scholastic

---

[43] *True Devotion*, No. 163.

[44] *True Devotion*, No. 118.

[45] The best known of St. Louis' writings are *The True Devotion to the Blessed Virgin* (Bay Shore, 1958), and *The Secret of Mary* (Bay Shore, 1947). It should he noted that when the manuscript of the *True Devotion* was found in 1842, it bore no title. The actual one, an obvious misnomer, since there are many forms of "true" devotion to Our Lady, was coined by the first publishers.
Montfort's other works which have been published in English are: *The Love of the Eternal Wisdom* (Philadelphia, 1949), which summarizes St. Louis' spirituality, insisting that devotion to Mary is but a means to union with the Incarnate Wisdom, Jesus Christ; *The Secret of the Rosary* (Bay Shore, 1954); *A Circular Letter to the Friends of the Cross* (Bay Shore, **1950**); *An Urgent Plea for Marian Apostles* [De Montfort's Prayer asking God to send him missionaries for his Company of Mary] (Bay Shore, 1958). Some of his works have not yet been published in English: his book of Hymns, comprising 23,418 verses (*Les Oeuvres du Bx. de Montfort; Ses Cantiques avec étude critique et notes*, ed. F. Fradet, S.M.M., Pontchateau, **1929**); his Letters (*Lettres du Bienheureux de Montfort*, St. Laurent-sur-Sèvre, **1928**); a pamphlet on preparation for death (*Dispositions pour bien mourir*, St. Laurent-sur-Sèvre, **1927**); the rule of the Daughters of Wisdom (*Règle des*

THE HOLY SLAVERY OF LOVE 155

explanation of total consecration to Our Lady. However, even though he wrote particularly "for the poor and the simple," his books and pamphlets are founded on solid theological principles which a serious study of his works clearly brings to light.[46]

In a very general sense, it may be said that St. Louis de Montfort bases his "Holy Slavery" upon the role which Mary plays in the entire work of salvation. "That grand Lord, always independent and sufficient unto Himself, never had nor has now any absolute need of the Blessed Virgin. ... Nevertheless ... having willed to commence and to complete His greatest works by the most Blessed Virgin ever since He created her, we may well think He will not change His conduct in the eternal ages."[47] Our Lady is, therefore, "the inseparable companion of His life, of His death, of

---

Filles de la Sagesse, Poitiers, **1818)**; the Rule of the Company of Mary and his allocution to the members of the Company of Mary (*Règle de la Compagnie de Marie et Allocution aux associés de la Compagnie de Marie,* found in *Vade Mecum du Montfortain,* Tours, **1932,** pp. **23-64).** Two of his personal writings have never been published: a notebook of texts from the Fathers of the Church and theologians, especially concerning Mariology; a book of Sermon Outlines. Both these manuscripts are in the Archives of the Generalate of the Montfort Fathers, Rome.

[46] he following is only a partial list of the works that may be consulted concerning the doctrine of St. Louis de Montfort: J. Dayet, S.M.M., *Total Consecration to Mary* (Bay Shore, 1956); *La Maternité Spirituelle, fondement de la parfaite dévotion,* in *Revue des Prêtres de Marie, Reine des Coeurs,* Vol. 21, 1934, pp. 129-151; V. Devy, S.M.M., *La Royauté Universelle de Marie, Reine des Coeurs,* in *Nouvelle Revue Mariale,* Vol. 8, 1956, pp. 18-36; H. M. Gebhard, S.M.M., *Commentaire du Traité de la vraie dévotion à la Sainte Vierge,* in *Revue des Prêtres de Marie, Reine des Coeurs,* Vol. 9, 1922-Vol. 28, 1941; J. M. Hermans, S.M.M., *Maria's Middelaarschap volgens de leer van de Heilige Louis-Marie Grignion de Montfort* (Eindhoven, 1947); J. M. Hupperts, S.M.M., *Saint Louis-Marie de Montfort et sa spiritualité mariale,* in *Marie, Études sur la Sainte Vierge,* ed. Hubert du Manoir, S.J., Vol. 3 (Paris, 1954), pp. 251-274; A. Lhoumeau, S.M.M., *La vie spirituelle à l'école de Saint Louis-Marie Grignion de Montfort* (Bruges, 1954): this work will soon be published in English; A. Plessis, S.M.M., *Commentaire du Traité de la vraie dévotion à la Sainte Vierge du Bienheureux Grignion de Montfort* (Pontchateau, 1943); M. Poupon, O.P., *Le Poème de la parfaite consécration à Marie suivant Saint Louis-Marie Grignion de Montfort et les spirituels de son temps; Sources et doctrine* (Lyon, 1947); *À Jesus par Marie; La parfaite consécration à Marie selon Saint Louis-Marie Grignion de Montfort* (Lyon, 1948); F. Setzer, S.M.M., *The Spiritual Maternity and Saint Louis Mary de Montfort,* in *Marian Studies,* Vol. 3, 1952, pp. 197-207; *De singulari missione B.V. Mariae cultuque ei debito juxta doctrinam S. Ludovici-M. de Montfort,* in *Alma Socia Christi,* Vol. 8 (Romae, 1953). The entire September-October 1952 number of the review *Marie* (Nicolet, Canada) is dedicated to the doctrine of St. Louis, as is the Spanish review *Miriam* of September-October, 1958 (Seville, Spain).

[47] *True Devotion,* Nos. 14-15.

His glory, and of His power in heaven and upon earth."[48]

However, what is the precise privilege, that aspect of her redemptive role upon which St. Louis builds his consecration? It appears to be her "complete spiritual maternity," i.e., her motherhood of men considered with its implicit consequence, her authority and dominion over the hearts of men. Since Mary's spiritual maternity is, according to Montfort, deduced from her Motherhood of the Redeemer and her Coredemption, we will first consider these two privileges as the radical foundations of "Holy Slavery"; we can then consider the proximate foundation of total consecration, the "complete spiritual maternity."

1. The Radical Foundations of Total Consecration: Mother of the Redeemer and Coredemptrix

Not only is the Divine Maternity the fundamental mystery of Mary in St. Louis' teaching, but it is also the principal foundation of her spiritual maternity of men. "If Jesus Christ the Head of men is born in her, ... the members of this Head must also be born in her by a necessary consequence ... the Head and Members are born of the same Mother."[49] Basing himself on the unity of Head and Members through Christ's capital grace which existed at the very first moment of the Incarnation, St. Louis — and St. Pius X after him[50] — declares that by conceiving Christ the Redeemer, Mary by that very fact spiritually conceives all those who with Him form but one Mystical Body.

However, Mary's spiritual maternity is also based upon her co-redemptive action, which, therefore, forms a part of the foundation of St. Louis' total consecration. Our Lady's role in the redemption may be considered both at the Incarnation and at Calvary; St. Louis insists on the Blessed Mother's co-operation in both these phases of the one act of redemption.

Our Lady's part in the redemptive Incarnation is considered

---

[48] *Ibid.*, No. 74; cf. *ibid.*, No. 247: "They are so intimately united that one is altogether in the other, Jesus is altogether in Mary and Mary is altogether in Jesus; or rather, she exists no more, but Jesus alone is in her, and it were easier to separate the light from the sun than Mary from Jesus; so that we might call Our Lord, Jesus of Mary, and Our Blessed Lady, Mary of Jesus."

[49] *Ibid.*, No. 32; cf. *Secret of Mary*, No. 12; *Love of Eternal Wisdom*, No. 213.

[50] Cf. S. Pius X, *Ad diem illum*, in *A.S.S.*, Vol. 36 (1904-1905), p. 452. St. Pius X himself declared his dependence on St. Louis in composing this encyclical. Cf. L. Locatelli, S.M.M., *Pie X et Montfort*, in *Marie*, Vol. 6, Sept.-Oct., 1952, p. 94.

principally under two aspects by St. Louis: her merit of the Incarnation, and her consent to become the Mother of God. Montfort explicitly teaches that the patriarchs were unable to merit the Incarnation, for "their cries, their prayers and their sacrifices had not enough force to attract the Eternal Wisdom,"[51] yet Our Lady did merit this "grace of graces": "there was found only Mary who by the sublimity of her virtues attained to the very throne of the Divinity and who has merited this infinite treasure."[52] Our Lady has therefore merited not only the acceleration of the coming of the God-Man — which the Patriarchs of the Old Testament could also do — but the Incarnation itself. Although not explained by St. Louis, we can well presume that he is referring to a "de congruo" merit, "in ordine executionis."

However, Mary is "Coredemptrix" in an even greater sense because her consent was necessary in God's plan for the Incarnation to take place: "The Eternal Wisdom desired to become man in her, provided that she give her consent."[53] St. Louis therefore calls Our Lady a victim with Christ at the very moment of the Incarnation: "Their hearts, united by strong and close ties, are offered both together to be two victims to hold back the chastisement which our crimes merit."[54] Montfort can therefore conclude: "In this mystery [the Incarnation] the elect have received their birth. Mary, united with Jesus, chose them in advance, to have part in their riches, their glory, and their power."[55] Already at this first phase of the Redemption, Mary, the New Eve, "has turned God's maledictions into a blessing" for us.[56]

St. Louis de Montfort also insists on Mary's co-operation in the very formal act of redemption, Christ's death upon Calvary. We may distinguish in this final act of the redemption a double aspect: the suffering and death of Christ on the Cross which forms the material element, and the willing acceptance of His Passion and Death, His obedience to His Father even to the death of the Cross, which make up the formal and principal element. According to Montfort, Our Lady co-

---

[51] *Love of the Eternal Wisdom*, No. 104.
[52] *True Devotion*, No. 16. Cf. J. Hermans, S.M.M., *La corédemption de Marie selon la doctrine du Père de Montfort*, in *Nouvelle Revue Mariale*, Vol. 6, 1955, pp. 181-182.
[53] *Love of the Eternal Wisdom*, No. 107.
[54] *Cantiques*, p. 154, stanza 6.
[55] *True Devotion*, No. 248.
[56] *Secret of the Rosary*, p. 73.

operated in both these aspects. Our Blessed Mother's participation in the material element of the Redemption is clearly explained by the saint when speaking of the intense sufferings of Our Lady caused by the Passion of her Son and offered for the human race.[57] Her role in the formal element is stated in the *True Devotion:* "He [Jesus] glorified His independence and His Majesty in depending on this admirable Virgin, in His conception, in His Birth and His presentation in the temple, in His hidden life of thirty years, up to His Death, where she had to assist, in order that He make with her but one and the same sacrifice and in order to be immolated by her consent to the Eternal Father, as Isaac of old was offered by Abraham's consent to the will of God. It is she who has nursed Him, nourished Him, supported Him, raised and sacrificed Him for us."[58] So strong are these words that they appear to affirm the proximate and immediate co-operation of Our Lady in the objective redemption.[59]

We, therefore, belong to Christ and to Mary as a result of the redemption. She has redeemed us with Christ and hence she, too, has acquired rights over the entire human race.[60]

2. The Proximate Foundation of Total Consecration:
The Complete Spiritual Maternity

Because Our Lady is the Mother of Christ the Redeemer, because she is the companion of Jesus in the work of redemption, she can be called,

---

[57] Cf. *Cantiques*, p. 152, stanzas 4-5.

[58] Cf. *True Devotion*, No. 18; *Letter to the Friends of the Cross*, No. 4, where Montfort calls us "the glorious conquest of Jesus Christ crucified on Calvary in union with His Blessed Mother"; *Cantiques*, p. 40, stanza 2: "You give us life, because you break our chains."

[59] Many authors have declared the immediate proximate co-operation of Our Lady in the objective redemption to be the teaching of St. Louis. Cf. G. Roschini, O.S.M., *La correndentrice degli uomini secondo il beato di Montfort*, in *Regina dei Cuori*, Vol. 28, 1940, p. 24; *Mariologia*, Tom. 2, Pars 1 (Romae, 1947), p. 333; J. Hermans, S.M.M., *La corédemption de Marie*, p. 250; L. Giuliani, *La cooperazione di Maria SS. alla nostra Redenzione e S. Luigi Maria Grignion de Montfort*, in *Marianum*, Vol. 10, 1948, pp. 31-64. J. B. Carol, O.F.M., is a little more cautious. In his opinion, the doctrine of Mary's immediate co-operation in the objective Redemption is *probably* taught by Montfort. Cf. J. B. Carol, O.F.M., *De Corredemptione Beatae Virginis Mariae* (Civitas Vaticana, 1950), pp. 348-349.

[60] Cf. *True Devotion*, No. 74; Benedict XV, *Inter sodalicia*, in *A.A.S.*, Vol. 10, 1918, p. 182; J. McMillan, S.M.M., *We Belong to Jesus and Mary*, in *Queen of All Hearts*, Vol. 3, Nov.-Dec., 1952, pp. 3-4.

and truly is, the Mother of Men. St. Louis clearly deduces this privilege from Mary's Maternity of the Head of the Mystical Body and also from her share in the redemption.[61] It is upon this privilege of the spiritual maternity that St. Louis de Montfort has formally built his edifice of total consecration. Basing himself upon the role which Our Lady plays in the sanctification of men, Montfort often considers Mary's maternity of men as that of a woman with child: "all the predestinate ... are in this world, hidden in the womb of the Blessed Virgin, where they are guarded, nourished, brought up, and made to grow by that good Mother until she has brought them forth to glory after their death, which is properly the day of their birth."[62]

Yet in this prerogative of Our Lady's actual spiritual maternity is contained implicitly her dominion over the souls of men. For since she is the "true Mother"[63] of men and the members of the Mystical Body are in this life "hidden in Mary's womb," she has received a great authority over the souls of the elect in order to accomplish her task as spiritual mother: "For she cannot make her residence in them as God the Father ordered her to do, and as their mother, form, nourish, and bring them forth into eternal life ... she cannot, I say, do all these things unless she has a right and a domination over their souls by a singular grace of the Most High."[64] Mary is therefore the Mother of Men; yet, as Montfort insists, a tender Mother with great authority, a Mother who is the Queen of the hearts of her children whom she is nourishing with grace. This "complete" Maternity appears to be the very foundation of St. Louis' "Holy Slavery of Love." The consecration will be the formal recognition that we have a Mother, a Mother who has true authority over us in order to form us into Christ: "Mother and Mistress"; it will be the formal recognition that we

---

[61] It would appear that St. Louis' principal proof for the spiritual maternity is Mary's Motherhood of the Head of the Mystical Body; however, he also deduces it from her consent to the Incarnation, and implicitly from her co-operation on Calvary.

[62] *True Devotion*, No. 33. Cf. *Love of the Eternal Wisdom*, No. 213; *Secret of Mary*, No. 14. St. Louis attributes this statement to St. Augustine. However, it appears that it cannot be said to be the statement of the Bishop of Hippo, for it is found nowhere in his writings. St. Louis has apparently based himself upon F. Poiré, who declared this text to be of Augustine (cf. *La Triple Couronne de la Bienheureuse Vierge Mère de Dieu*, Vol. 3 [Tournai, 1849], p. 385). In reality, the text appears to be an adaptation of *De Sancta Virginitate* (*PL* 40, 399), and the apocryphal, *De Symbolo ad catechumenos sermo alius* (*PL* 40, 659).

[63] *True Devotion*, No. 201.

[64] *Ibid.*, No. 37. Cf. V. Devy, S.M.M., *art. cit.*, p. 23.

are her children, yet so much her children that we depend completely upon her as a child yet unborn: "children and slaves."

That this is truly the foundation of "Holy Slavery" can be seen from the first 37 numbers of the *True Devotion* where St. Louis summarizes Mary's role in the subjective redemption as a Mother with child, a Mother with authority. Moreover, he sees in the story of Rebecca and Jacob the Biblical figure of this devotion, for Mary, as Rebecca, is a Mother who loves her children, nurtures, protects, and defends them.[65] Although the example used is no longer a woman with child, nonetheless, her spiritual maternity with authority is clearly brought out. St. Louis' Hymn, *The Devout Slave of Jesus in Mary*, constantly extolls the "devout slave" as a "child at the breast" in total dependence on his mother, "in whom and through whom it does all things."[66] And in the very Act of Consecration, Montfort declares: "I choose thee today for my Mother and Mistress," and he calls the consecrated souls: "children and slaves," again expressing Our Lady's spiritual Maternity with the explicit reference to her authority over the hearts of her children in order to carry out her task as Mother.[67]

The solid theological foundation for St. Louis de Montfort's "Holy Slavery of Love" is therefore, radically, the Divine Maternity and the Coredemption. He has, however, "formally based his Holy Slavery of Love ... on the spiritual maternity of the Blessed Mother."[68]

B. THE CONSECRATION OF ST. LOUIS

St. Louis de Montfort's total consecration is the adequate recognition of the "complete" maternity of Mary over the souls of men. The essential part of his formula of consecration clearly brings this out: "In the presence of all the heavenly court, I choose thee this day for my Mother and Mistress, I deliver and consecrate to thee, as thy slave, my body and soul, my goods, both interior and exterior and even the value of all my good actions, past, present and future, leaving to thee the entire and full right of disposing of me and all that belongs to me, without exception, according to thy good pleasure, for the greater glory of God in time and

---

[65] Cf *True Devotion*, Nos. 183-212.

[66] Cf. *Cantiques*, p. 167, stanza 14; p. 168, stanza 19.

[67] Cf. *Act of Consecration*, in *True Devotion*, pp. 227-229.

[68] Devy, art. cit., p. 23; cf. J. Ghidotti, S.M.M., *Fundamentos dogmáticos de la verdadera devoción*, in *Miriam*, Vol. 10, Sept.-Oct. 1958, p. 191.

THE HOLY SLAVERY OF LOVE

in eternity."[69] St. Louis' consecration embraces, therefore, "(1) our body, with all its senses and its members, (2) our soul, with all its powers, (3) our exterior goods of fortune, whether present or to come, (4) our interior and spiritual goods, which are our merits and our virtues and good works, past, present, and future ... we give her all that we have in the order of nature and in the order of grace and all that may become ours in the future in the orders of nature, grace and glory; and this we do without reserve of so much as one farthing, one hair or one least good action; we do it also for all eternity."[70]

As H. Boudon before him, St. Louis explains the meaning of consecrating our interior and spiritual goods: "In this consecration ... we give her all the satisfactory, impetratory, and meritorious value of our good actions; in other words, the satisfactions and the merits of all our good works. We give her all our merits, graces, and virtues — not to communicate them to others, for our merits, graces, and virtues are, properly speaking, incommunicable ... but we give them to her to keep them, augment them, and embellish them for us. ... Our satisfactions, however, we give her, to communicate to whom she likes, for the greatest glory of God."[71] St. Louis de Montfort himself concludes: "By this devotion, we give to Jesus Christ in the most perfect manner — inasmuch as it is by Mary's hands — all that we can give Him."[72]

Following Cardinal de Bérulle, St. Louis insists that this consecration is "a perfect renewal of the vows and promises of Holy Baptism,"[73] because in this consecration we reaffirm what was promised in Baptism: to renounce Satan, his pomps and works, and to take Christ for our sovereign Master in all things. The consecration is, St. Louis points out, a perfect renewal, for it adds three modalities to the promises of Baptism: "... in Baptism we ordinarily speak through another ... but in this devotion we do it ourselves, voluntarily, knowing what we are doing; ... in holy Baptism, we do not give ourselves to Jesus through the hands of Mary, at

---

[69] Cf. *Act of Consecration*, in *True Devotion*, pp. 227-229.

[70] *True Devotion*, No. 121.

[71] *Ibid.*, No. 122.

[72] *Ibid.*, No. 123.

[73] *Ibid.*, No. 126. Cf. Joseph Cuppen, S.M.M., *La consécration à la Très Sainte Vierge selon Saint Louis-Marie de Montfort et les derniers Papes*, in *Alma Socia Christi*, Vol. 8 (Romae, 1953), pp. 173-191; J. McMillan, S.M.M., *Perfect Renewal*, in *Queen of All Hearts*, Vol. 5, July-August, 1954, pp. 3-4; J. Hemery, S.M.M., *Dans le perspective baptismale: consécration totale à Marie*, in *Cahiers Marials*, Vol. 3, 1959, pp. 131-143.

least not in an explicit manner; and we do not give Him the value of our good actions. We remain entirely free after Baptism, either to apply them to whom we please or to keep them for ourselves. But by this devotion we give ourselves to Our Lord explicitly by the hands of Mary and we consecrate to Him the value of all our actions."[74]

However, St. Louis is not content with the mere recital of an act of consecration: "It is not enough to have given ourselves once as slaves to Jesus through Mary, ... it is not very difficult to enroll in a confraternity nor to practise this devotion insofar as it prescribes a few vocal prayers every day; but the great difficulty is to enter into its spirit. Now its spirit consists in this, that we be interiorly dependent upon Mary."[75] This interior spirit of total consecration to Mary, St. Louis sums up in the formula, "to do all our actions through Mary, with Mary, in Mary, and for Mary; so that we may do them all the more perfectly through Jesus, with Jesus, in Jesus, and for Jesus."[76] Although differing somewhat in his explanation of this formula in his *Secret of Mary* and *True Devotion*, these interior practices are paramount in the living of the Montfortian consecration.

To do all our actions "through Mary" implies renouncing our own dispositions and trying to do everything with the intentions of the Mother of God: we must "deliver ourselves to the spirit of Mary to be moved and influenced in the manner she chooses. We must put ourselves in her virginal hands, like a tool in the grasp of a workman, like a lute in the hands of a skillful player. We must lose ourselves and abandon ourselves to her, like a stone one throws into the sea."[77]

"With Mary" means imitation, accomplishing our actions as Mary would, were she in our place: "We must in all our actions regard Mary as

---

[74] *True Devotion*, No. 126.

[75] *Secret of Mary*, No. 44.

[76] *True Devotion*, No. 257. This fourfold formula "through, with, in, and for Mary" was not invented by St. Louis; it is of a much more ancient origin. Nicholas of Clairvaux († after 1176) used somewhat the same expression (cf. *Sermo de Annuntiatione*), as did the Carmelites Arnold Bostius († 1499) and the Venerable Michael of St. Augustine († 1684). However, it does not appear that any of these authors had any influence on St. Louis. Cf. P. Boundonno, S.M.M., *Le pratiche interiori della vera devozione*, in *Alma Socia Christi*, Vol. 8, pp. 205-209. Montfort's source for this expression appears to be the liturgy of the Mass where the formula "per ipsum, cum ipso et in ipso" is used, and the French School of Spirituality, especially John Olier and Saint John Eudes.

[77] *True Devotion*, No. 259.

an accomplished Model of every virtue and perfection which the Holy Ghost has formed in a pure creature for us to imitate according to our little measure."[78]

The practice "in Mary" is founded upon St. Louis' repeated statement that we are in this world "hidden in the womb of Mary." We must, therefore, "become accustomed little by little to recollect ourselves interiorly and thus try to form within us some idea or spiritual image of Mary. She will be, as it were, the oratory of our soul in which we offer up all our prayers to God."[79]

"For Mary" does not mean "that we take her for the last end of our services, for that is Jesus Christ alone; but we take her for our proximate end, our mysterious means, and our easy way to go to Him ... we must work for no recompense ... except the honor of belonging to so sweet a Queen and the happiness of being united through her to Jesus her Son by an indissoluble tie, in time and in eternity."[80]

III. APPROVALS OF ST. LOUIS' DOCTRINE

Hidden in a trunk for many years, as St. Louis himself had prophesied,[81] the *Treatise on True Devotion* was found only in 1842 at the Motherhouse of the Montfort Fathers, Vendée, France. Together with the other writings of Montfort, it was sent to Rome for careful scrutiny in view of his proposed beatification. The first reaction of the Promoter of the Faith was a stinging condemnation: "the devotion which the pious author proposes and upholds ... could never be approved by the Church; ... every sign of approbation or commendation of this writing must be avoided by all means."[82] However, other censors appointed by Rome clearly answered all objections against the *True Devotion,* and in 1853 it was officially declared to be free from all error and in no way an

---

[78] *Ibid.,* No. 260.

[79] *Secret of Mary,* No. 47.

[80] *True Devotion,* No. 265. For a detailed study of these interior practices, cf. J. M. Hupperts, S.M.M., *La vie mariale d'après Saint Louis-Marie de Montfort,* in *Alma Socia Christi,* Vol. 8, pp. 225-254.

[81] *True Devotion,* No. 114. Although the manuscript of *True Devotion* was not found until 1842, the devotion or "Holy Slavery" was continually practiced and preached by the congregations founded by St. Louis. Cf. T. Ronsin, S.M.M., *Historique du "Traité de la Vraie Dévotion,"* in *Marie,* Vol. 6, Sept.-Oct., 1952, pp. 28-31.

[82] *Positio super scriptis beatificationis et canonizationis Ven. Servi Ludovici Mariae Grignon de Montfort* (Romae, 1851), p. 23.

impediment to Montfort's cause for beatification.[83]

This approval of the Congregation of Rites has been re-echoed by bishops and theologians of the Church, as Francis Parisi declared in an address before Pope Pius XII in one of the preliminary steps to the canonization of Louis de Montfort: "There exists an extraordinary witness to his [Montfort's] Marian devotion — his *Treatise on True Devotion to Mary*, written in his own hand. This work has merited for him in the past and continues to merit for him today the praise and admiration of theologians, bishops, cardinals, and of the Sovereign Pontiffs themselves."[84]

Of the many encomiums showered upon St. Louis de Montfort by the Sovereign Pontiffs, none can equal those of St. Pius X. Not only did he declare his dependence on this French missionary in writing his encyclical *Ad diem illum*,[85] but he granted a plenary indulgence "in perpetuum" to those who recite St. Louis' formula of consecration.[86] He also granted special indulgences to the Confraternity of Queen of All Hearts, founded to further total consecration,[87] and in 1913 erected it into an Archconfraternity.[88] He himself joined the Association of the Priests of Mary (composed of the members of the clergy who practice the "Holy Slavery of Love") and granted the apostolic blessing to all those who even merely read the *True Devotion*, declaring in his concession of the blessing, "we eagerly recommend the *Treatise of True Devotion*."[89]

Benedict XV, in a letter to the Superior General of the Montfort Fathers on the occasion of the second centenary of the death of their founder, declared that it was their vocation to spread devotion to Our Lady by explaining the *True Devotion*, which he declared was "of great unction and high authority."[90]

The love of Pope Pius XII for St. Louis de Montfort and his works is

---

[83] Cf. *Ibid.* (Romae, 1853), p. 30.

[84] Cf. *A.A.S.*, Vol. 39, 1947, p. 113; the text of the address is found in *Queen of All Hearts*, Vol. 8, July-August, 1957, pp. 6-9.

[85] Cf. note 50 above.

[86] Cf. *Enchiridion Indulgentiarum, preces et opera* (Civitas Vaticana, 1950), No. 96. Leo XIII had granted the indulgence for seven years.

[87] Cf. *A.A.S.*, Vol. 2, 1910, p. 185.

[88] Cf. *A.A.S.*, Vol. 5, 1913, p. 485.

[89] Autograph copy of the concession is preserved at the Generalate of the Montfort Fathers, Rome.

[90] Cf. *A.A.S.*, Vol. 8, 1916, p. 172.

well known. In the *De tuto* decree for Montfort's canonization, the saint's *True Devotion* is spoken of as a shorter path to perfection,[91] and in the homily delivered on the day of the canonization, the Holy Father declared the saint's devotion to Our Lady to be "flagrans, solida, ac recta."[92] On the following day, addressing the pilgrims who had come to Rome for the canonization, the Holy Father spoke of St. Louis as the guide "who leads you to Mary and from Mary to Jesus; ... he is incontestably one of those who have worked the most ardently and the most efficaciously to make Mary loved and served."[93] And addressing himself especially to the members of the communities Montfort founded, the Pope, alluding to the Marian doctrine of St. Louis, declared: "Remain faithful to the precious heritage which this great saint has left you in legacy! A magnificent heritage, worthy of being continued by you, and of devoting yourselves to it and sacrificing yourselves for it without ever counting your strength or your life."[94]

Bishops and theologians alike have repeated these praises of the Sovereign Pontiffs. The first International Marian Congress, held at Fribourg in 1902, was eloquent in its praise of St. Louis de Montfort: "Considering that the devotion to the Blessed Mother according to Blessed de Montfort is a magnificent synthesis of the most developed Marian theology; that it is the most perfect form of cult to the Blessed Mother; that it harmonizes so well with the actual movement of Catholic piety and that it seconds it powerfully; that it answers the present-day needs and offers in the present strife a special and providential help, the Congress defers to the desires expressed by a great number of cardinals, bishops, and theologians, and formulates the wish that this devotion be propagated among the faithful and principally among the clergy and religious institutes."[95] The Marian Congress of Rome (1904) repeated similar praise for St. Louis,[96] as did the Marian Congresses of Einsiedeln (1906),[97] Trier

---

[91] Cf. *A.A.S.*, Vol. 37, 1945, p. 328.

[92] Cf. *A.A.S.*, Vol. 39, 1947, p. 331.

[93] Cf. *A.A.S.*, Vol. 39, 1947, pp. 410-411.

[94] *Ibid.*; cf. also *Litterae decretales*, in *A.A.S.*, Vol. 41, 1949, p. 267.

[95] *Compte-rendu du Congrès Marial de Fribourg*, Vol. 2 (Blois, 1903), p. 538.

[96] *Atti del Congresso Mariano mondiale tenuto in Roma l'anno 1904* (Roma, 1905), p. 282.

[97] *Compte-rendu du Congrès Marial International tenu à Einsiedeln en Suisse* (Lyon, 1907), pp. 214-352, 599-658, 722-749.

(1912),[98] and the special Marian-Montfortian Congress held at Barcelona in 1918.[99]

Father Faber summed up the praises of the Church for the writings of St. Louis —and in particular for the *True Devotion* — when he wrote: "I would venture to warn the reader that one perusal will be very far from making him the master of it. If I may dare to say so, there is a growing feeling of something inspired and supernatural about it, as we go on studying it; and with that we cannot help experiencing that its novelty never seems to wear off, nor its fulness to be diminished, nor the fresh fragrance and sensible fire of its unction ever to abate."[100]

---

[98] *Compte-rendu du Congrès Marial International tenu à Trèves en Allemagne* (Lyon, 1913), pp. 68-70.

[99] *Crónica del Congreso Mariano-Montfortano, celebrado en Barcelona el año 1918* (Totana, 1919), passim.

[100] F. W. Faber, "Preface to the True Devotion," found in *True Devotion*, p. xiii. Well known theologians like R. Garrigou-Lagrange, C. Dillenschneider, A. H. Lépicier, A. Paquet, and many others have voiced their esteem for the Marian doctrine of St. Louis. Cf. G. Ghidotti, S.M.M., *Influence mariale de Montfort: concert des théologiens*, in *Marie*, Vol. 6, Sept.-Oct., 1952, pp. 62-66.

Filial Piety

by VERY REV. PETER A. RESCH, S.M.

FILIAL PIETY is not a devotion in the sense that it is bound up with special prayer-programs or blessed objects; it is a pattern or way of life.

Etymologically, the term filial piety is a literal rendering of the Latin *pietas filialis,* which signifies the sum-total of dispositions that constitute the attitude of *childlike devotion* and adult reverence which a good son or daughter manifests for his or her parents. Thus we speak properly of filial piety to God, to our parents, to our spiritual fathers, to our heavenly patrons, to our earthly fatherland; thus also, filial piety to Mary our Mother; thus also, the filial piety of Jesus, the divine Model, to Mary His Mother.

The Marian devotion called Filial Piety (capitalized), which it is the object of this Chapter to explain, consists in the reproduction or extension of the filial piety of Jesus to Mary in the life of the Christian.

The principal proponent of this aspect of Marian doctrine and practice was William Joseph Chaminade (1761-1850), founder of the Marianists, who belonged to the "French School" of spirituality. Filial Piety is the proper physiognomy and distinguishing trait of Marianist spirituality and apostolate. The practice of Filial Piety is best expressed in the work of the Marianist Mariologist, the Reverend Emile Neubert, entitled *My Ideal, Jesus, Son of Mary.*

The *foundation* of Filial Piety is Christ, "for other foundation no one can lay, but that which has been laid, which is Christ Jesus" (1 Cor. 3:11). In the French School, "Christianity comprises three points, and all its method is contained therein — namely, to contemplate Jesus, to unite self to Jesus, and to act in Jesus." This is the admirable doctrine of the Mystical Body of Christ: by the fact that we are in the state of grace we live the life of Christ. All our striving should be to live with Christ in the most intimate union possible. Little by little, we take on the spirit of Jesus Christ, "this mind which was also in Christ Jesus" (Phil. 2:5), and we advance toward transformation into, and identification with, the divine Model. "Your life is hidden with Christ in God" (Col. 3:3).

All the perfection of the Christian life consists in conformity with

Jesus Christ. "Jesus Christ," writes Father Chaminade, "practiced all the virtues to the most sublime perfection; some of these virtues have entered more especially into the plan of His admirable mysteries, for example, His love for the Blessed Virgin."[1] Since, then, as followers of Christ, we have the obligation to imitate His virtues, we cannot neglect striving to imitate His example of filial piety to Mary. It is thus through Jesus that we go to Mary and, vice versa, through Mary that we are formed to the likeness of Christ. Such devotion to Jesus Christ is indispensable for the practice of true Filial Piety. The Marian "devotion" taught by Father Chaminade is Christo-centric in the highest degree.

How did the Son of God manifest His filial piety to Mary? From all eternity He predestined her to be His mother. He lavished unique privileges upon her. He exempted her from the laws to which the whole human race is subject. He made her immaculate in her conception, free from all concupiscence, unsullied by any imperfection, more replete with grace than all the angels and saints — the Mother of God and ever a Virgin. He willed that she should have an essential part in the very mission with which the Father has entrusted Him: He, the Redeemer, determined that she should be the Coredemptrix with Him. He willed that she be associated with Him in heaven where He "assumed" her, body and soul, after her sojourn on earth, so that, as He is advocate with the Father, she should be advocate with Him in the distribution of all graces to all men. In His Mystical Body, directed by the Holy Spirit, He lives in the Church. What the Church does is really done by Him — all the veneration and love which the Church has shown her: the defense and proclamation of her privileges, the institution of feasts and devotions in her honor, the approval of sodalities and religious societies destined to serve her. The piety of the children of the Church: the saints, the great servants of Mary, the fervent souls drawn to honor her in a special way, the ordinary faithful, interested, enthusiastic, when there is question of devotion to Mary — what is all this, if not a grand manifestation of the incomparable filial love of Jesus for Mary?

Thus almost imperceptibly we enter into the vital stream of Filial Piety — of Christ's very filial piety toward His mother.

Evidently our Filial Piety toward Mary cannot become *identical* with that of the divine Model. Mary gave Jesus His *natural* life; she is our mother in the *supernatural order*. She could not, of course, give

---

[1] *Spirit of Our Foundation*, Vol. 1 (Dayton, Ohio, 1911), p. 598.

supernatural life to Jesus; on the contrary, it is from Him that she drew hers. Our Filial Piety will, therefore, not be identical with, but *analogous* to that of the divine Model. Our reproduction of the filial piety of Jesus will consist in "taking on" the filial dispositions, both natural and supernatural, of Jesus for Mary in order to reproduce them with all the possible perfection consistent with our condition as members of the Mystical Body.

Our Filial Piety should *complete* that of Jesus. "What is lacking in the sufferings of Christ," says St. Paul with astonishing boldness, "I fill up in my flesh for his body, which is the Church" (Col. 1:24). Nothing assuredly was lacking in the sufferings of Christ as Head of the Mystical Body, but in view of the co-operation needed for their application to the members, the sufferings of the Head needed completion. In this respect, all the dispositions of Christ lack something in His members. That is why we must endeavor to imitate Him "until we all attain to the mature measure of the fullness of Christ" (Eph. 4:13). What is thus true of the virtues of Christ — His humility, His charity, His gentleness — is true also of His filial piety toward Mary, His Mother. In us, His members, there is something lacking in this filial piety; we must endeavor to fill up this lack by reproducing as perfectly as possible in ourselves the filial dispositions of Jesus for Mary so as to attain the mature measure of Christ, Son of Mary.

Our Filial Piety is a *participation* in that of Jesus. In the natural order we may, as we do for a hero or a saint, study his traits and copy them in our conduct. But there is a more profound reproduction, and it is a problem of the interior life. Faith teaches us that by grace we become participants of the divine life (2 Pet. 1:4); that we become members of a body of which Christ is the head. Thus St. Paul could dare to write: "For me to live is Christ" (Phil. 1:21) ... "It is now no longer I that live, but Christ lives in me" (Gal. 2:20). Hence, if I am humble, chaste, patient, it is Christ who is humble, chaste, patient in me. If I love the Blessed Mother, it is no longer I that love her, it is Christ who loves her in me. Thus my filial piety toward Mary is more than a simple extension or imitation of that of Jesus, the result of my efforts to resemble Him; it is a genuine sharing in His filial piety; it is Jesus who, through me, loves and honors Mary and desires to make her loved and honored better.[2]

For whoever would embrace *the practice of Filial Piety* the essential act

---

[2] Cf. E. Neubert, S.M., *Notre don de Dieu* (Tours, 1954), p. 159.

is *total consecration* (belonging) to Mary according to one's state of life. From all eternity the Son of God determined to become the Son of Mary. At the first moment of the Hypostatic Union, He ratified with His human will this disposition of the divine will. Henceforth He will persevere throughout eternity, consciously and fully, in His filial belonging to her. In imitation, then, of the divine Model, the Christian will constitute himself, as totally as possible, in the state of a son of Mary; he will renew, affirm, and strengthen this consecration on every occasion, formally, spontaneously, habitually. (Marianists make this total consecration to Mary the object of a special perpetual religious vow.)

As Jesus on earth grew in the experiential knowledge of Mary, our Marian Filial Piety must prompt us to study ever more and more thoroughly the prerogatives and glories of our heavenly Mother.

As Jesus honored, and still honors, His Mother on earth and in heaven, we too must honor her by participating in the approved veneration of her, celebrating her feasts, reciting her office and rosary, wearing her scapular and miraculous medal, etc.

Jesus resembled Mary, in a human way, as any good son resembles his mother. "If you are children of Mary," said Father Chaminade, "imitate Mary ... The greatest obligation contracted by this wonderful filiation is to imitate the virtues of which Mary has given the example to the whole world."[3] We must allow ourselves to be formed, as other Christs, "as members of Christ, in the bosom of the august Mary, where Jesus Christ, conceived by the operation of the Holy Ghost, was formed, through her maternal care, to our resemblance."[4]

Jesus taught us to come to Him through Mary: "Behold thy mother!" We must teach and preach Mary to the world by word and example.

In a human way, Jesus confided in Mary during His mortal life; so also will the imitator of Christ daily confide to Mary both his temporal and his spiritual problems.

Among all the manifestations of the filial piety of Jesus for Mary which the Gospel allows us to discern, none is so plain as His life of union with her: a physical union first, then a union of thought, of sentiment, of will, and of action. It would be outside the scope of this chapter even to begin to enumerate ways and means for the child of Mary to imitate his divine Model on this point.

---

[3] *Manuel du serviteur de Marie* (Bordeaux, 1804), p. 13.

[4] *L'Esprit de notre fondation,* Vol. 1 (Nivelles, 1910), p. 142.

Jesus associated Mary in the work of the Redemption. The *apostolic mission of Mary* is an integral and essential part of Marianist Filial Piety. If we mention it only in conclusion, we do so to give it a position of emphasis to bridge the idea of Marian *apostolate* over with that of *consecration* mentioned in the beginning. From Mary's function as *spiritual Mother* and from her mission in the *apostolate* Father Chaminade drew the conclusion that the essential act of Filial Piety is a *special consecration* to Mary in order (1) to recognize her *maternity* and freely to accept it, as Jesus freely became her child, and (2) to assist her in her *apostolate* and raise up others to do so. Father Chaminade was a precursor in expounding this doctrine; no theologian, before the 1950 Marian Congress of Rome, had treated it. Here we can merely point out that the practice of total Filial Piety implies that we aid and assist the Blessed Virgin in her apostolic mission of saving the world.[5]

The prayer of St. Anselm, indulgenced for Marianists, expresses succinctly the mystique of Filial Piety: "O good Jesus, by the love with which thou didst love thy Mother, grant me, I beseech thee, that I also may truly love her as thou lovest her and desirest her to be loved."[6]

---

[5] Cf. E. Neubert, S.M., *Queen of Militants* (St. Meinrad, Ind., 1947).

[6] St. Anselm, *Orat. 52; PL* 158, 959. Cf. J. S. Bruder, S.M., *The Mariology of St. Anselm, of Canterbury* (Dayton, Ohio, 1939), pp. 139-140. Further literature on Chaminade and Filial Piety: J. Artadi, S.M., *Naturaleza de la piedad filial,* in *Memoria del Congreso Mariano Nacional de Zaragoza* (Zaragoza, 1956), pp. 875-896; E. Baumeister, S.M., *The Soul of Marian Devotion,* Marian Reprint No. 12 (Dayton, Ohio, 1953); W. J. Cole, S.M., *The Spiritual Maternity of Mary according to the Writings of Father William Joseph Chaminade. A Study of His Spiritual Doctrine* (Dayton, Ohio, 1958); J. A. Elbert, S.M., *Filial Piety, The Ideal Devotion to Mary* (Dayton, Ohio, 1952); Id., The Perfect Devotion, in *The Marianist,* Vol. 46, March, 1955, pp. 14-15; F. Fernández, S.M., *De la esclavitud a la Piedad Filial,* in *Estudios Marianos,* Vol. 10, 1950, pp. 33-60; William J. Chaminade, *Petit traité de la connaissance de Marie* (Paris, 1927); the same translated: *Our Knowledge of Mary* (Milwaukee, 1930); F. J. Friedel, S.M., *Mother of Jesus, My Mother, Meditations on Filial Piety to Mary* (Dayton, 1958); E. Neubert, S.M., *My Ideal, Jesus, Son of Mary* (Kirkwood, Mo., 1952); Id., *La doctrine mariale de M. Chaminade* (Juvisy, 1937); J. J. Panzer, S.M., *Christ's Devotion to Mary,* Marian Reprint No. 43 (Dayton, Ohio, 1956); P. A. Resch, S.M., *The Marianist Consecration,* in *Queen of All Hearts,* July-August, 1951, pp. 10-11; G. J. Schnepp, S.M., *Filial Piety — Marian and Family,* Marian Reprint No. 47 (Dayton, Ohio, 1956); T. A. Stanley, S.M., *The Mystical Body of Christ according to the Writings of Father William Joseph Chaminade* (Fribourg, 1952); Id., *Mary and the Mystical Body* (Dayton, Ohio, 1953).

THE IMMACULATE HEART

by REV. JOHN F. MURPHY, S.T.D.

N 1944 when the Holy Father extended the Feast of the Immaculate Heart of Mary to the universal Church as a principal Marian observance, he indicated that beyond serving as a memorial and reminder of his earlier solemn consecration of the world to the Immaculate Heart (December 8, 1942), the Feast would be instrumental also in preserving peace among nations, ensuring liberty for the Church of Christ, and effecting a strengthening of the faithful in the love of purity and the practice of virtue.[1]

With these statements the Holy Father gave a final sanction to a devotion which, in the designs of God, had in recent times become widely appreciated,[2] and yet which, in his own words, could actually be traced back in vestige to the commentaries of the Fathers on the *Sponsa* of the Canticle of Canticles.[3]

I. HISTORY OF THE DEVOTION

In his Gospel, St. Luke himself twice mentions the Heart of our Blessed Mother; first on the occasion of the arrival of the shepherds at Bethlehem (Lk. 2:18-19), and again upon finding our Blessed Lord in the temple (Lk. 2:51). It is because of these two references that St. John Eudes claimed, in a sense, a scriptural foundation for the devotion.[4]

Actually, in the early centuries of the Church we have no indication of any notable devotion to the Immaculate Heart, yet Christian literature through the years transmitted the seeds of the devotion which eventually, through the instrumentality of St. Bernard and later, through St. Bernardine of Siena and others, became determined as a special Marian veneration.

From the sixteenth century especially, there is evidence of specific references and devotional practices to Mary's Immaculate Heart. As an

---

[1] Pius XII, *A.A.S.*, Vol. 37, 1945, p. 51.
[2] Pius XII, *A.A.S.*, Vol. 39, 1947, p. 543.
[3] Pius XII, *A.A.S.*, Vol. 37, 1945, p. 50.
[4] St. John Eudes, *Le Coeur admirable de la très Sacrée Mère de Dieu*, in *Oeuvres Completes*, Vol. 7 (Paris, 1908), p. 234.

instance, Julius II († 1513), the great Renaissance Pope, promulgated certain invocations to the Immaculate Heart to be recited at the sound of the Angelus. Prior to St. John Eudes, and as a link between the sixteenth and seventeenth centuries, St. Francis de Sales († 1622) formulated something of a synthesis of what had developed up to his day. He spoke of the perfections of the Heart of Mary, the model of love for God, and dedicated to her most chaste Heart his *Theotimus*.[5]

However, barring a number of private revelations, prior to the writings of St. John Eudes there is not to be found any theological treatise dealing directly and expressly with the devotion to the Immaculate Heart.[6] Certainly there is a constant growth of associated references, and an awareness of the distinctive role which the virginal Heart of Mary had been predestined to play in the salvation of souls and in the whole divine economy, but the fixed terms describing the devotion were yet to be determined, and the devotion was still private in nature.

With St. John Eudes (1601-1680) the devotion to Mary's Heart was made public and received ecclesiastical approbation, but was limited to certain locales and religious communities. Through St. John's efforts also, there arose liturgical veneration of the Most Pure Heart of Mary, and since his day the science of the liturgy has played an influential role in clarifying the exact nature of the devotion. In the course of the process of beatification and canonization of St. John Eudes the Church emphasized his role in establishing this liturgical devotion, and the brief of beatification notes that, not without divine guidance, he rendered Mary's Heart liturgical veneration, and should be regarded as the Father, Doctor, and Apostle of this devotion.[7]

Early in his influential years St. John had a feast established for his own Congregations and with episcopal approval in certain French dioceses. In 1641 he composed its special Office and Mass. In the year 1680

---

[5] Cf. G. Geenen, O.P., *Maria Koningin der Wereld* (Antwerp, 1944), pp. 32-33; C. Olmi, S.M., *La dévotion au Coeur Immaculé de Marie* (Paris, 1945), p. 28.

[6] A number of private revelations were instrumental in furthering the devotion. Most notable were those described by SS. Mechtilde, Gertrude the Great, and Brigid of Sweden. The *A.A.S.*, Vol. 37, 1945, p. 50, itself mentions the "mulieres" who were instrumental in the spread of the devotion. Cf. St. Mechtilde, *Revelationes; Liber specialis gratiae*, Part 1 (Parisiis, 1877), c. 2 and 39; St. Gertrude, *Revelationes; Legatus divinae pietatis* (Parisiis, 1875); St. Brigid, *Revelationes* (Romae, 1606), Lib. 1, c. 35, p. 56.

[7] Leo XIII, *Pulchrum sane*, in *A.S.S.*, Vol. 35, 1903, p. 380; Pius X, *Divinus Magister*, in *A.A.S.*, Vol. 1, 1909, p. 480; Pius XI, *A.A.S.*, Vol. 17, 1925, pp. 222, 482.

he completed his famous work, *Le Coeur Admirable,* consisting of 12 books, characterized by sound theology and deep piety, the first complete work to be published on the subject.

As early as 1644 St. John had wished to observe the Feast of the Most Pure Heart of Mary as the patronal feast of his Congregations of priests and nuns; he celebrated it on October 20. The first public feast in honor of the Heart of Mary was celebrated in Autun in 1648, the result of the Saint's efforts and with episcopal approval. The Holy See, when petitioned in 1669, refused approbation of this Office and Mass. However, by this time many French Bishops, according to accepted custom, were allowing the feast to be celebrated in their dioceses on February 8.

By 1672 the feast was celebrated more or less throughout all France. In 1729 the Holy See, when petitioned again, refused official approbation of the proposed Office and Mass, although the Papal Legate to France had approved an office as early as 1668. Somewhat later, in 1773, a proper office received papal approval for the first time; this by Pope Clement XIV († 1774). Shortly thereafter, in 1787, the feast received further papal endorsement from Pope Pius VI († 1799).

It was not until 1805 that a general papal approbation was granted. Pope Pius VII († 1823) gave the faculty for the celebration of the Feast of the Most Pure Heart of Mary on the Sunday after the Octave of the Assumption to all dioceses and religious institutes which asked for it. In 1855 under Pope Pius IX († 1878), a complete proper Office and Mass for this feast was approved by the Sacred Congregation of Rites. The Office composed by St. John Eudes, universally used in France for over a hundred years, was finally approved for the Eudists in 1861. The Office found in the Appendix of the old Roman Breviary was granted in the year 1857.[8]

In the ensuing years liturgical cult and nonliturgical practices continued to gain popularity. This was due partially to the success of the cause with which it was associated in earlier decades — that of the Sacred Heart.[9] But it was not until many years later and due to various influences that the Office and Feast of the Immaculate Heart received final acknowledgment.

---

[8] Cf. G. Postius, C.M.F., Il *culto del Cuore Immacolato di Maria attraverso i* secoli, in *Il Cuore Immacolato di Maria* (Roma, 1946), p. 31 ff.; H. Pujolrás, C.M.F., *La festa liturgica del Cuore Immacolato di Maria,* in *Il Cuore Immacolato di Maria* (Roma, 1946), p. 107 ff.; Geenen, O.P., *op. cit.,* pp. 55-60.

[9] In seeking papal approval the causes were separated in 1765 to insure the approbation of the Feast of the Sacred Heart.

In recent decades, although there have been instances of local and limited consecration of individuals, families, and dioceses to the Immaculate Heart of Mary,[10] these consecrations were in no way universal. Hence in 1942 the devotion received a great impetus in the action of the Holy Father, Pius XII, when in St. Peter's Basilica on the Feast of the Immaculate Conception, not as a merely spontaneous act, but as the consequence of historical developments of high moral significance, he solemnly consecrated the entire world to the Immaculate Heart of Mary.[11]

In 1944, to commemorate this special solemn consecration, he extended the Feast to the whole world, to be celebrated with a special Office and Mass on the twenty-second day of August, the octave-day of the Assumption, as a double of the second class.[12]

The Holy Father's action was the crowning of a vast movement springing from a heritage of many years, and embodying the highest of tributes to Our Lady on the part of the Church.

II. THE OBJECT OF THE DEVOTION

Not only because of her fullness of grace and her preeminence among men, but especially because she is really and truly the Mother of God, Mary deserves a special and unique veneration. The Divine Motherhood, the basic motive for the cult of hyperdulia, is the basis also for our devotion to Mary's Immaculate Heart.

When we honor Mary's Immaculate Heart, we honor her entire person.[13] All special venerations, whether of a mystery of Mary's life, or of a special virtue, or of something pertaining to her body or soul, have in common the same object: the person of Mary.

A special devotion to Mary's Heart is most reasonable, however, because such a veneration, directed to a more noble part of the Blessed

---

[10] Geenen, O.P., op. cit., pp. 61-78; Id., Les antécédents doctrinaux et historiques de la consécration du monde au Coeur Immaculé de Marie, in Maria. Études sur la Sainte Vierge, ed. H. du Manoir, Vol. 1 (Paris, 1949), p. 825 ff.; G. Roschini, O.S.M., La consacrazione al Cuore Immacolato di Maria, in Il Cuore Immacolato di Maria (Roma, 1946), pp. 55-59.

[11] Cf. Pius XII, A.A.S., Vol. 37, 1945, p. 51. The solemn consecration of December 8, 1942, was preceded by an earlier consecration on October 31 of the same year, but this consecration is not mentioned in the decree of 1944 establishing the universal feast. Cf. Pius XII, A.A.S., Vol. 34, 1942, p. 317 ff.

[12] Cf. Pius XII, A.A.S., Vol. 37, 1945, pp. 50-51.

[13] Cf. III, q. 25, a. 1; II-II, q. 82, a. 2, ad 3um.

Mother's body, includes also and especially all that the Heart of Mary itself represents, symbolizes, or implies.[14]

In all languages the word *heart* is rich in connotation and deep in symbolism. Primarily, of course, the heart is a natural symbol of love and of internal affections, but it is a symbol which is commonly greatly extended. In fact, because men use the word *heart* in a proper, symbolical, and metaphorical sense, we understand the Immaculate Heart of Mary to represent Mary's entire sanctity, with all her virtues, gifts, and perfections, and all especially as consummated in her love.[15]

To understand thoroughly the meaning of the devotion to the Immaculate Heart it is necessary to describe accurately the *object* of the devotion, for cult, being a relative thing, is determined by the object with which it has relationship. In regard to objects in the concept of cult in general, we distinguish two things — the *material* object, or that which we venerate, and the *formal* object, or the precise reason why we offer this worship or veneration.[16]

In the case of the Blessed Mother, all cult rendered to Mary, all types of devotion shown her, are directed ultimately to her person as such. Thus in the devotion to the Immaculate Heart we realize as the material object of our veneration the person of Mary in her physical and moral integrity, to which, of course, her Heart pertains.[17] It is evident from the title of the devotion that we venerate in a special way the Heart of the Mother of God, and the reasons why Mary's Heart is chosen as a special object of veneration are multiple.

As a noble physical organ, the heart of Mary played an important role in her physical maternity, and is intimately connected with the affections

---

[14] Cf. II-II, q. 162, a. 3 ad 4um.

[15] Gregorio de Jesús Crucificado, O.C.D., *Objeto del culto al Corazón de María*, in *Estudios Marianos*, Vol. 4 (Madrid, 1945), pp. 288-291; H. Pujolrás, C.M.F., *Cultus purissimi Cordis B. Mariae Virginis* (Mediolani, 1943), p. 15 ff.; H. Nix, S.J., *Cultus SS. Cordis Jesu cum additamento de cultu purissimi Cordis B. V. Mariae* (Friburgi, 1889), p. 54.

[16] John of St. Thomas, *Cursus philosophicus thomisticus; Phil. nat.*, IV P, q. 2, a. 3, ed. Reiser, Vol. 3, p. 76; *Ars logica*, II P, q. 21, a. 4, ed. Reiser, Vol. 1, p. 670 ff.

[17] Cf. P. Parente, *Oggeto e legittimità del culto del Cuore Immacolato di Maria*, in Il Cuore Immacolato di Maria (Roma, 1946), p. 17; G. Puerto, C.M.F., *Objeto del culto al Corazón de María*, in *Estudios Marianos*, Vol. 3 (Madrid, 1944), p. 325 ff.; K. J. Healy, O.Carm., *Theology of the Doctrine of the Immaculate Heart of Mary*, in *Proceedings of the Fourth Annual Meeting of the Catholic Theological Society of America* (Cincinnati, 1949), p. 102 ff.

of Mary's maternal soul. The splendor of Mary's sanctity and the mysteries of her life, especially her maternity, are concentrated in the love reflected in her Heart. "The synthesis of the life of the Mother of God is love, which makes her heart, after the heart of Christ, a most worthy object of religious devotion."[18]

Moreover, Mary's Heart is reasonably an object of veneration inasmuch as the Church ordinarily approves for veneration only objects in some way concretized and possessing a material element. Such objects fulfill man's spiritual needs more adequately and correspond to man's own make-up of both body and soul. In her wisdom the Church desires to impress men sensibly as well as spiritually; hence the appropriateness of a physical element in this devotion to Mary's great charity.

For men to honor the love of Mary without reference to her physical heart, or the heart of Mary entirely divorced from the idea of love is a practice of salutary piety, but not the devotion to Mary's Immaculate Heart as approved by the Church.[19] Thus we say that Mary's physical heart, together with her love, enters into the particular devotion to the Immaculate Heart of the Mother of God.[20]

As indicated above, the formal object of our veneration is always the excellence found in the material object which merits our veneration. Thus in the case of the devotion to the Immaculate Heart of Mary, we note the august excellence of Mary's entire person, body and soul. However, the precise aspect of her excellence, and the particular quality of Mary upon which we focus our attention in this devotion, following the indications of the Holy Father, is Mary's extraordinary holiness, and especially her love for God and man. And this excellence of Mary's love, the primary reason for our devotion, is understood in its normal full extension, thus

---

[18] Parente, *art. cit.*, p. 27; cf. T. M. Sparks, O.P., *The Immaculate Heart of Mary*, in *Cross and Crown*, Vol. 1, 1949, p. 375 ff.

[19] Special consideration is due the words *Immaculate Heart*. They designate the heart of Mary as it actually exists now along with its particular symbolism. Cf. T. M. Sparks, O.P., *The Immaculate Conception and the Immaculate Heart of Mary*, in *The Thomist*, Vol. 19, 1956, p. 240 ff.

[20] N. Nilles, S.J., *De rationibus festorum SS. Cordium*, Vol. 1 (Oeniponte, 1885), p. 340; G. Puerto, C.M.F., *art. cit.*, p. 340: "In the devotion to the Immaculate Heart these notions are as two intimate realities, compenetrated, offering a notable advantage to our spiritual life." To be accurate, according to the mind of the Church, the complete symbol in the devotion is the *Immaculate Heart*, for the Church says (cf. *A.A.S.*, Vol. 37, 1945, p. 50): "Sub *huius* Cordis symbolo. ..." *Immaculate* here undoubtedly stresses the sanctity of the Blessed Virgin.

including her extraordinary and singular sanctity, her virtues and gifts, and her entire interior life.[21]

In Marian cult generally we venerate Mary for three reasons — her eminent sanctity, her Maternity, and her share in the redemptive work of Christ. But all these are intimately connected with her love.

In the case of her sanctity, it is seen as the fruit of sanctifying grace which culminates in charity. The quintessence of Mary's sanctity is her supernatural love, which St. Thomas calls the form, root, and motive of all the other virtues, and hence the source of all supernatural activity.[22]

Mary's Maternity is also profoundly related to love, and therefore to her heart. Love preceded it, entered the act, and marked the existing relationship thereafter.

In the role of Coredemptrix, Mary's participation in the redemption of men was the fruit of her love. It was because of her love that she consented to share in this redemptive work, and because of the strength of her love that she carried out her role perfectly.

Therefore, the splendor of Mary's sanctity, the entire grand mystery of her Maternity, and the fullness of her mission as Coredemptrix of mankind are inseparable from her love, and therefore truly reflected in her Heart.

Because of the connection between Mary's sanctity and her Maternity, and between her role as Coredemptrix and her Maternity, the devotion to the Immaculate Heart in its final analysis resolves itself in an exaltation of Mary's love in the function of her Maternity.[23]

In the devotion to Mary's Immaculate Heart, it is from the material object, Mary's heart, that we draw the title for the devotion; and it is from the formal object, Mary's love, that we derive the meaning of the devotion. Both the material and formal objects are distinguishing marks differentiating the devotion to the Immaculate Heart from all other Marian venerations.[24]

---

[21] Cf. *A.A.S.*, Vol. 37, 1945, p. 50; J. Lintello, S.J., *Le Saint Coeur de Marie* (Paris, 1922), p. 34; M. Llamera, O.P., *La devoción al Corazón de María y el santísimo Rosario*, in *Estudios Marianos*, Vol. 4 (Madrid, 1945), pp. 374-375.

[22] II-II, q. 23, a. 8.

[23] Parente, *art. cit.*, p. 27; G. Sinibaldi, *Il Cuore della Madre di amore* (Roma, 1925), p. 84 ff.; E. Pichéry, *Le Coeur de Marie Mère du Dieu Sauveur* (Paris, 1947), pp. 235-236.

[24] E. Dublanchy, *Coeur de Marie*, in *D.T.C.*, Vol. 3, cols. 351-354; J. Calveras, *Objeto del culto al Corazón de Maria*, in *Estudios Marianos*, Vol. 7 (Madrid, 1948), p. 373; T. M. Sparks, O.P., *Summarium de cultu Cordis Immaculati B.V.M.* (Taurini, 1951), p. 30.

We can define it, then, paraphrasing official ecclesiastical documents, as the veneration of the physical Heart of Mary, considered as the symbol of her eximious and unique holiness, and reflecting especially her most ardent love for God and Jesus Christ her Son, and her motherly affection for men redeemed by the divine blood.[25]

III. THE PURPOSE OF THE DEVOTION

An understanding of the end and purpose of the devotion to the Immaculate Heart of Mary is indispensable for a full appreciation of this special Marian veneration.

The very nature of the devotion indicates clearly that its purpose is to unite men to God through Mary's Heart, and this union is accomplished primarily by two acts which are themselves part of the devotion — the acts of consecration and reparation.

A. Consecration

In an act of consecration to the Immaculate Heart, our act is ultimately referred to God Himself, for one is consecrated to Mary only because she is God's Mother, and by her offices, especially that of Queenship, is closely associated with Him, becoming for us a link or steppingstone to God Himself.[26]

Moreover, since consecration amounts to a total gift of self, an offering and pledging of complete and exclusive service and devotion, a handing over of not only what we have but of what we are, not for a time but perpetually, such an act can be referred ultimately to God only, for He alone has the right of complete ownership over our body and soul. Consecration to Mary remains valid and salutary, however, because of her peculiar relationship with Him.

An act of consecration as such is an act of religion, or more specifically an act of devotion, embodying within itself also acts of faith and love.[27] In every act of consecration we can distinguish three basic elements: a transition from the profane or secular to the domain of the

---

[25] A.A.S., Vol. 37, 1945, p. 50.

[26] Cf. J. Lebon, *Les fondements dogmatiques de la consécration au Coeur Immaculé de Marie* (Liège, 1946), p. 12 ff.

[27] Although it participates in the virtue of religion, consecration to Mary is elicited by the virtue of *hyperdulia,* and at least when the devotion is more perfectly practised, pertains also to the Holy Spirit's gift of piety.

sacred, a constancy and stability in the new pledge or bond, and the existence of some kind of rite.[28]

An act of consecration to the Immaculate Heart of Mary has as its theological foundation Mary's universal sovereignty or dominion. In view of this fact, a consecration implies two things: the recognition of our dependence on Mary, and the regality and dominion which demand this submission. The act itself, though often repeated, implies an habitual attitude of dependence on Mary as our Queen.

The dogmatic foundation of consecration, then, is the dominion and universal sovereignty of Mary. Beyond her Queenship, some would regard her Maternity as also a foundation in view of the association and dependence of Mother on Son and Son on Mother. Certainly the divine Maternity is the foundation of Mary's Queenship, and in this sense is also the foundation of consecration. Commonly, however, we refer to her Queenship and dominion as the adequate foundation of our act.[29]

Thus it is fitting, and not a mere coincidence, that the opening words of the formula of consecration employed by His Holiness Pope Pius XII in the solemn consecration of the world referred to earlier, concern directly Mary's sovereignty ... "Queen of the Most Holy Rosary, Help of Christians ..."

The more directly and profoundly the nature of Mary's Queenship is understood, the more clearly we see the nature of our dependence on her in the order of grace, and understand our consecration. Our Lord possesses dominion over us by a double right: by nature, as the Son of God and King of Kings, and by an acquired title, as our Redeemer. With Mary, we see an analogy — as Christ is our King, she is our Queen. As Christ has a natural right to sovereignty by reason of the Hypostatic Union, Mary has a right by reason of the divine Maternity. Christ has an acquired right by the Redemption of men; Mary has an acquired right by reason of her Coredemption.[30] There can also be added to this double title

---

[28] Cf. J. Bittremieux, *Consecratio mundi Immaculato Cordi B. Mariae Virginis*, in *Ephemerides Theologicae Lovanienses*, Vol. 20, 1943, p. 100 ff.; G. Roschini, O.S.M., *La consacrazione al Cuore Immacolate di Maria*, in *Il Cuore Immacolato di Maria* (Roma, 1946), pp. 59-64.

[29] Lebon, *op. cit.*, p. 9; Bittremieux, *art. cit.*, p. 100; Roschini, O.S.M., *La consacrazione della Chiesa e del genere umano all'Immacolato Cuore di Maria*, in *Marianum*, Vol. 5, 1943, p. 6.

[30] Cf. Leo XIII, *Annum sacrum*, in *A.S.S.*, Vol. 31, 1899, p. 648; Pius XI, *Quas primas*, in *A.A.S.*, Vol. 17, 1925, p. 599; A. Musters, O.E.S.A., *La Souverainté de la Vierge* (Paris,

a third, namely, dominion through divine choice, or as the Holy Father expressed it, "by singular [divine] election."[31]

Fittingly, the Holy Father ordained that on the Feast of Mary's Queenship, May 31, the act of consecration of the human race to the Immaculate Heart of Mary is to be renewed with the hope that through our consecration an era of Christian peace and triumph of religion may begin.[32]

Because of the value of a consecration made freely and willingly, an act of consecration to the Immaculate Heart is a marvelous tribute to Mary's Queenship and the most genuine manifestation of devotion to her Heart. It is more than an ordinary prayer and more than a promise, for a true and complete act of consecration is a *state* whereby we habitually realize the import of our belonging to Mary.

Consecration as an habitual state, moreover, is more salutary than a single act or even a series of acts. In consecration to the Immaculate Heart, the whole world and all in it is separated from the profane and given over totally and perpetually to Mary's Heart. In this way Mary is shown a complete veneration, and nothing of greater significance can be offered her. The solemn act of consecration in this sense synthesizes all other elements and acts which constitute Marian devotion.[33]

B. REPARATION

According to the Holy Father, in honoring God it is not sufficient that our worship and prayer be that of adoration and gratitude alone; we must also, through the act of reparation, "satisfy the just anger of God," and

---

1946), p. 98; J. B. Carol, O.F.M., *Mary's Co-Redemption in the Teaching of Pope Pius XII*, in *The American Ecclesiastical Review*, Vol. 121, 1949, p. 359; E. Carroll, O.Carm., *Our Lady's Queenship in the Magisterium of the Church*, in *Marian Studies*, Vol. 4, 1953, p. 66 ff.; F. M. Schmidt, O.F.M., Cap., *The Universal Queenship of Mary*, in *Mariology*, ed. J. B. Carol, O.F.M., Vol. 2 (Mediatrix Press, 2019), p. 529.

[31] Pius XII, A.A.S., Vol. 38, 1946, p. 266: "Mary is Queen by grace, by divine relationship, by right of conquest, and by singular election." Cf. W. Most, *Mary in Our Life* (New York, 1954), p. 49 ff.

[32] Cf. *L'Osservatore Romano*, 24-10-54; A.A.S., Vol. 46, 1954, p. 638. The booklet *Pius XII on Consecration to Mary*, ed. H. M. Pocock, S.M.M. (New York, 1955), contains 139 papal texts on the importance of consecration to the Immaculate Heart.

[33] According to some, an act of consecration to Mary exceeds in excellence all other acts of veneration even regarded collectively. Cf. J. Bittremieux, *art. cit.*, p. 102; Roschini, O.S.M., *Mariologia*, Vol. 2, part 3, p. 227; L. Barbé, *La consécration au Coeur de Marie*, in *Le Sainte Coeur de Marie* (Paris, 1948), p. 105.

begin the union with God which an act of consecration confirms.[34]

In the devotion to the Immaculate Heart, Mary's love for God and Jesus her Son as well as her love for man redeemed by the blood of Christ, calls forth in like fashion our reparation for the sinful ingratitude and forgetfulness of men. Reparation to Mary is rooted in her union with Christ. Jesus and Mary, inseparable in life and action, are likewise inseparable in cult and in our acts of reparation. Every outrage committed against our Blessed Lord is necessarily an outrage to His Mother and causes her more displeasure than offenses committed directly against her own person.

Since Jesus and Mary, in virtue of *one,* not two distinct decrees, are united inseparably in the work of Redemption, in a parallel way the practice of reparation is integrated in the devotion to the Immaculate Heart.[35]

In the case of Mary, then, as in the case of the Sacred Heart, our act of reparation prepares us for the union which the act of consecration effects, and along with our acts of veneration and imitation is actually embodied in our consecration to the Immaculate Heart.[36]

In all our acts of reparation in atonement for our sins we are mindful that Mary herself is the model and "Mother of Reparation."[37] It is she who, principally through her sufferings at the foot of the cross, merited the title of Coredemptrix and universal Mediatrix. Through her example of love for God we are led to a closer union with our divine Saviour, and through our acts of reparation and through our consecration to Mary there is effected the purpose of our devotion to her Immaculate Heart, the uniting of ourselves to God through the Heart of His Blessed Mother.

---

[34] Pius XI, *Miserentissimus Redemptor,* in *A.A.S.,* Vol. 20, 1928, p. 169.

[35] Cf. W. Most, *Reparation to the Immaculate Heart, in* Cross and Crown, Vol. 8, 1956, p. 139 ff.

[36] Cf. T. M. Sparks, O.P., *Reparation to the Immaculate Heart of Mary,* in *From an Abundant Spring* (New York, 1952), p. 39 ff; Roschini, O.S.M., *La Riparazione Mariana* (Rovigno, 1942), p. 13.

[37] Pius XI, *A.A.S.,* Vol. 20, 1928, p. 180.

THE PIOUS PRACTICE OF EXPIATION TO MARY

BY LEONARD PEROTTI, O.F.M.

F THE *Pious Practice of Expiation to Mary* (*Pia Praxis Expiatoria Mariana*) is rather new in the United States as a manner of honoring the Mother of God, this is not true of Europe. There it has flourished for the past twenty-five years, especially in Italy where it originated and where it has been introduced into almost every diocese. In addition, eighty religious Orders have adopted it, as have also many Vicariates and Prefectures Apostolic all over the world. A brief sketch of the history of this practice is in order before we explain its nature and the place it has in the field of Marian devotion.

The *Pious Practice* owes its origin to Dr. Luigi Picchini, a fervent Franciscan Tertiary. Dr. Picchini was present at the closing May devotion in the church of Santa Maria Formosa, Venice, in 1932. This was a solemn function in honor of Our Lady, taking the form of expiation for all the blasphemy and scurrilous speech by which her Immaculate Heart is so offended. Very much inspired by this practice, Dr. Picchini pondered the question, Why not propagate over the whole world the reservation of a day during May to express to Mary our deep grief at what she suffers from so many of her children — from their unbelief and denial of her privileges, from their distrust of her intercessory power, and above all, from the blasphemies leveled at her?

Cardinal La Fontaine, Patriarch of Venice, encouraged Professor Picchini to pursue this objective; and so, in June of 1933, he approached the bishops of Italy as well as the heads of religious Orders. His plea was that by the following May this Marian devotion of expiation would be practised in every diocese and in all the churches of religious institutes. The response was most heartening. The month of May, 1934, witnessed a marvelous propagation of this form of love for the Mother of God. Prior to this, in September of 1933, the founder of the *Pious Practice* enjoyed the favor of a private audience with Pope Pius XI. The Holy Father warmly encouraged Dr. Picchini in this spiritual enterprise, and a few months later spoke publicly in approbation of the practice. Then, at the request of Cardinal La Fontaine, the Holy Father, through his Secretary of State, Cardinal Eugenio Pacelli, issued a document which was to become the Magna Carta of the *Pious Practice*. The same warm approval was later given by Pope Pius XII to Cardinal Piazza, Patriarch of Venice, and to Father Matteo Micheluzzi, Director of the *Pious Practice*, in 1941 and 1952 respectively. In letters to the above-mentioned, the Holy Father showed great delight at knowing how far this devotion had spread, and encouraged a special day of Marian expiation during the month of May.

World War II had the sad effect of interrupting and retarding the growth of Dr. Picchini's spiritual enterprise. Still, at war's end, he very patiently brought together the loose ends once more. But now his advanced age and failing health were against much activity — he was 91 years old when he began searching for someone to carry on his work! His one great desire was that after his death the success of the *Pious Practice* would be assured. With this in mind, he considered entrusting it to the Order of Friars Minor. He approached the Minister General of the Franciscans, not only because he was a Tertiary, but also because the Seraphic Order had been among the first to receive the *Pious Practice* with enthusiasm, as far back as 1933. On February 2, 1947, the Most Reverend Pacificus M. Perantoni, General of the Order, wholeheartedly accepted the direction and propagation of the *Pious Practice* and officially aggregated it to the Seraphic Order. Headquarters were set up at San Francesco della Vigna, Venice, in the Seraphic Province of St. Anthony.

The *Pious Practice* has been called "the most beautiful flower of the month of May that can be offered to the Virgin most holy." The well-known mariologist, Father Gabriel M. Roschini, O.S.M., has written that this practice of Marian expiation is a flower far surpassing all others in the luxuriant field of Catholic piety by the delicacy of its perfume.[1] The attractiveness of this devotion is explained by Pius XI as due to its being inspired with the purpose and the spirit of Fatima's message — reparation to the Immaculate Heart of Mary. The *Pious Practice* has no other program or scope than this: to atone for the injuries and the offenses which sadden the Heart of our heavenly Mother.

The filial duty of reparation to our Mother's Immaculate Heart springs from faith and love. The fervent child of Mary believes that the sins which repeat the Passion of Jesus also renew the painful sword which pierced the Heart of Mary. These sins present a frightful picture: a steadily advancing materialism, lapses from the Faith, profanation of the sacraments, the impiety of the baptized, the desecration of marriage by

---

[1] G. M. Roschini, O.S.M., *La Madonna secondo la fede e la teologia*, Vol. 4 (Roma, 1954), pp. 403-404.

sins preceding and following it, and others. The affectionate child of Mary desires to make reparation as much as possible for the offense which these sins cause the Hearts of Jesus and Mary, and particularly to console the Sorrowful Heart of God's Mother for the blasphemies hurled against her, and for the scornful denial of her sublime prerogatives, especially her Immaculate Conception.

In holding a Marian day of expiation during the month of May, the greatest liberty is allowed pastors and superiors of religious groups. The faithful also are completely free in doing what their piety suggests. There are no prescribed prayers or set functions. It is suggested, however, that this day of expiation be held on the last Sunday of May, or on the last day of that month. This can be announced in the parish bulletin on the preceding Sunday. In many dioceses this day assumes a definite solemnity: in the morning, Holy Mass and a general Communion of the people in a spirit of reparation; in the afternoon, a Holy Hour of reparation with an appropriate sermon and prayers. Chaplains of hospitals and similar institutions would ask the patients to offer their sufferings and prayers for the intentions of the *Pious Practice.*

In promoting this day of reparation in May, the *Pious Practice* is by no means content to rest there, as though the goal had been reached. This is a beginning; this is the least that Mary may ask of those who love her. The spirit of this holy enterprise goes far beyond any passing act of one day; it instills into loving souls an attitude, a need, a desire of frequent, even daily reparation as something demanded in return for Mary's sacrificial love of us. The Marian day of expiation in the fairest of months will serve as a rallying point for many deeds of reparation to Mary during the entire year. Opportunities for this are innumerable: frequent acts of sincere sorrow for one's sins; willing acceptance of the hardships and inconveniences which life brings; the observance of the Five First Saturdays; and, above all, fidelity to the daily Rosary. Sincere and persevering reparation to Mary's Immaculate Heart is the best means of insuring genuine expiation to the Sacred Heart of Jesus. In this, as in all, we go most safely to Jesus when we go through Mary.[2]

---

[2] For further information cf. B. Barban, O.F.M., *Consoliamo il Cuore Immacolato di Maria* (Venezia, 1953).

MARIAN ORDERS AND CONGREGATIONS

by MARION A. HABIG, O.F.M.

THROUGH the centuries the veneration of the Blessed Virgin Mary, the Mother of God, has flourished increasingly in the Catholic Church. Since this is true of the ordinary faithful, the so-called laity, one should not be surprised to find that it is even more strikingly true of the religious orders and congregations in the Church. In a certain sense, all of them may be called "Marian"; some of them, however, have a special claim. The most evident is the fact that the name of Mary, in some form or other, appears in the official name of the order or congregation.

But there are other reasons which are no less valid. A religious order or congregation may rightly be called "Marian," for instance: (1) because it honors Mary as its special patroness or Queen; (2) because its Rule and Constitutions prescribe special community exercises of devotion to Our Lady; (3) because its members have championed the great prerogatives of the Blessed Virgin or made important contributions to Mariology; (4) because its members have introduced various forms of devotion, such as rosaries, crowns, scapulars, medals, prayers, hymns, etc., among the faithful; (5) because they have founded and directed confraternities, sodalities, societies of Our Lady; (6) because they have written and distributed devotional literature concerning Our Lady; (7) because they have built churches and shrines in honor of Our Lady and encouraged pilgrimages to such shrines or ministered to the spiritual needs of the pilgrims; (8) because they have commenced the celebration of new feasts of the Blessed Virgin; (9) because they have promoted devotion to Our Lady by preaching sermons or conducting novenas in her honor; etc.

In one short chapter it will not be possible to treat this vast subject adequately. We can only present a selection of the principal facts, and indicate where more information can be found. We shall endeavor to adhere strictly to proved historical facts and the most recent findings and data available.[1] First we shall discuss the orders and congregations of men

---

[1] Editor's note: During the following essay, any place where the author gives the "present" status or number of members, it should be borne in mind that this was published in 1961 and does not reflect the current numbers or whether the order still

with papal approval which have a Marian name; then add some remarks on the larger and older orders of men whcih have a special claim to being styled "Marian," even though their name is not such; and finally offer a list of Marian orders and congregations of women in the United States, arranged according to various titles of Our Lady.

I. ORDERS AND CONGREGATIONS OF MEN WITH A MARIAN NAME

The religious orders and congregations of men, approved by the Holy See, whose official name contains the name of Mary in some form or other are 38 number. Of these 20 are represented in the United States. The latter we shall treat more at length; and the remaining 18 we shall merely list with date and place of founding, place of headquarters, and total membership.

Both groups will be enumerated in the order in which they appear in *Annuario Pontificio* 1959. The *Annuario*, which is the official directory fo the Holy See, divides all religious orders and congregations of men with papal approval into the following groups: (1) Canons Regular; (2) Monks; (3) Mendicant Friars; (4) Clerics Regular; (5) Ecclesiastical Congregations, including clerical religious congregations whose members take vows but no solemn vows, and societies of secular priests who do not take vows; (6) Religious Institutes or Brotherhoods. To these are now added the Secular Institutes with papal approval, whose members, however, are not regarded as "Religious." None of these Secular Institutes thus far has a Marian name.

1. THE CARMELITES (O.CARM.)

Carmelite writers have described their order as being "wholly marian" in character. They have also claimed its members to be "first-born spiritual sons of the Blessed Virgin Mary." To the Carmelites themselves it was long an accepted tradition that the order was founded some nine centuries before Christ by the Prophet Elijah and that his disciples on Mt. Carmel in Palestine were the first members of the order: likewise, that the order continued to exist through the centuries in the Holy Land until it was transplanted to Europe in the fourth decade of the thirteenth century. However, Father Élisée de la Nativité, himself a Discalced Carmelite, in

---

exists.

1952 wrote a scholarly study in which he declares that the Old Testament origin of the order must be classified as a legend, although this legend contributed not a little to the evolution of the order's Marian character.[2] The gradual development and growth of devotion to Our Lady in the Carmelite order is an important historical fact which is often overlooked. This is true also of other religious orders which date back to the Middle Ages.

The first historical documents concerning the Carmelite Order go back only to the twelfth century. About 1155, a Crusader from Calabria, Berthold of Malifaye, son of the Count of Limoges, with ten companions retired to Mt. Carmel and began living there as a hermit. In 1210 Albert, Patriarch of Jerusalem, gave the hermits of Mt. Carmel a rule, based on that of St. Basil. The hermits built a chapel in honor of Our Lady in 1220 — and this is the first time the name of Mary appears in the documents. Pope Honorious III gave the Hermits of Mt. Carmel his approval in 1226, 1227, and 1228. In the bull of 1227 they are called, for the first time, the Hermits of St. Mary of Mt. Carmel.

About 1235, the victories of the Saracens made it more and more difficult to live the religious life on Mt. Carmel, and hence the Hermits migrated to Europe and established themselves in a short time on Cyprus and Sicily and in France, Flanders, and England. As the Carmelite chronicler, Friar William, put it, the Hermits moved from Mt. Carmel to Europe that they might be able "to devote themselves for all times to the service of the Lord God and His Mother the Virgin Mary."

The Rule of the Hermits of Mt. Carmel was adapted to the life in Europe, and in 1247 the Order of the Blessed Virgin Mary of Mt. Carmel, as it was now called, received renewed papal approval. At that time St. Simon Stock was the superior general of the order. He it was who introduced the Brown Scapular of Our Lady[3] as a means of promoting devotion to Our Lady among the faithful, and thus emphasized the Marian character of the Carmelite Order. The Carmelites became one of the orders of mendicant friars in 1253 by a decree of Pope Innocent IV.

Among the aims of the Carmelite Friars are mentioned: special

---

[2] Élisée de la Nativité, O.C.D., *La vie mariale au Carmel*, in *Maria. Etudes sur la Sainte Vierge*, ed. H. Du Manoir, S.J., Vol. 2 (Paris, 1952), pp. 833-861 (subsequently abbreviated as: *Maria*).

[3] On the history of the Brown Scapular, cf. Chapter VI of this same volume, *The Scapular Devotion*.

MARIAN ORDERS AND CONGREGATIONS 189

devotion to the Mother of God, and promotion of devotion to the Blessed Virgin under the title of Our Lady of Mt. Carmel particularly by means of the Brown Scapular. At the present time the order has 2187 professed members. The prior general and his assistants reside in Rome.[4]

The Second Order of Carmelites, a contemplative order of nuns, was founded in 1452 by the Prior General John Soreth. Blessed Jane of Toulouse (about 1400) is regarded as the first member of the Third Order of Our Lady of Mt. Carmel. It was certainly in existence by 1452, as is evident from a pronouncement of Pope Nicholas V. Carmelite Tertiaries of Avranches in Normandy in 1702 formed the first community of the Carmelite Third Order Regular.

In the United States the Carmelite Fathers have two provinces: the Province of the Most Pure Heart of Mary with headquarters in Chicago, established in 1864; and the Province of St. Elias with headquarters in New York, erected in 1922.[5]

2. THE DISCALCED CARMELITES (O.C.D.)

A stricter autonomous branch of the Carmelite Order was founded in 1562 by the two well-known saints, St. Teresa of Jesus of Avila and St. John of the Cross. The Order of Discalced Carmelite Friars, *Ordo Fratrum Carmelitarum Discalceatorum*, is now more numerous than the original order, having 3433 professed members. Headquarters are also in Rome. Its aims are: the contemplative and apostolic life, missions among the infidels, and the cult of Our Lady of Mt. Carmel. In the United States this order has the following units: the Province of St. Therese with headquarters in Oklahoma City, and the Province of the Immaculate Heart of Mary with headquarters at Holy Hill, Hubertus, Wis., both erected in 1947; also foundations of four European provinces, with headquarters at Sonora, Arizona; Alhambra, Calif.; Murdo, S. Dak.; and Munster, Ind.

In India there is a Carmelite Order of men, of the Third Order Regular, with 463 professed members: the Third Order of Discalced Carmelites of

---

[4] Information concerning the location of mother houses and present membership of religious orders and congregations has been gathered from *Annuario Pontifico per l'anno 1959* (Città del Vaticano, 1959), pp. 878-946. Other sources consulted are: E. Gambari, *Ordini e congregazioni religiose di nome e di orientamento mariani*, in *Encyclopedia mariana*, ed. R. Spiazzi, O.P. (Milano, 1954), pp. 599-615; M. Heimbucher, *Die Orden und Kongregationen der katholischen Kirche*, 3rd ed. 2 vols. (Paderborn, 1934).

[5] Brief information concerning religious orders and congregations represented in the United States may be found in *The Catholic Directory* (New York, 1959), pp. 824-839.

Malabar, *Tertius Ordo Carmelitarum Discalceatorum Malabarensium* (T.O.C.D.). They were founded in 1855, and approved in 1906. Their purpose is similar to that of the Discalced Carmelites. There are also some sisterhoods of the Third Order Regular of the Discalced Carmelites. Most of the monasteries of contemplative Carmelite nuns in the United States belong to the Second Order of Discalced Carmelites.[6]

3. THE MERCEDARIANS (O. DE M. OR O.D.M.)

The Order of Our Lady of Mercy, *Ordo Beatae Mariae de Mercede redemptionis captivorum,* was founded in 1218 as a military order for the purpose of liberating Christian captives from the hands of the Saracens. The founders were St. Peter Nolasco (Nolasque), King James I of Aragon, and the Dominican St. Raymond of Peñaforte. Peter Nolasque was born about 1189 at Carcassone in southern France. According to a tradition of later date, he took part as a young man in the crusade of Simon IV of Montfort against the Albigensians. Jayme or James, son of Peter II of Aragon, who was an ally of the Albigensians, was taken as a hostage, and Peter Nolasque became his tutor. Subsequently Peter followed his pupil to Barcelona. There he conceived the idea of founding a special order for ransoming Christians who had been enslaved by the Mohammedans — an order similar to the then recently established Trinitarian Order.

According to a tradition of the Mercedarians, which however is found recorded for the first time only in 1445, Peter Nolasque was deliberating whether to found this order or to devote himself to an eremitical life in a cave near the famous shrine of Our Lady of Montserrat, near Barcelona, when, in 1218, Our Lady of Montserrat appeared to him as well as to King James I of Aragon and Raymond of Peñaforte and urged them to found the Order of Our Lady of Mercy.

In 1223 Peter Nolasque pronounced the usual three religious vows and added a fourth binding him to offer himself as a substitute, if this should be necessary, to free a Christian captive of the Mohammedans who was in danger of apostatizing. Soon afterwards he was joined by thirteen

---

[6] On the Carmelites, besides the article by Fr. Élisée, already referred to, cf. *De vita mariologico-mariana apud Ordinem Carmelitarum, in Ephemerides Mariologicae,* Vol. 5, 1955, pp. 111-114; Alberto de la Virgen del Carmen, O.C.D., *La Virgen María en la espiritualidad carmelitana,* in *Revista de Espiritualidad,* Vol. 13, 1954, pp. 239-270; E. R. Carroll, O.Carm., *Legendes mariales au Carmel,* in *Marie* [Nicolet], Vol. 6, No. 4, 1952, pp. 13-16; *Id., The Immaculate Conception and Carmelite Theologians,* in *The Sword,* Vol. 17, 1954, pp. 120-141.

MARIAN ORDERS AND CONGREGATIONS

noblemen, of whom six were priests. Raymond of Peñaforte undertook the direction of the new order, which observed the Rule of St. Augustine; and he wrote special constitutions which exhorted the members to cherish a special devotion to Our Lady. Pope Gregory IX gave his approval in 1235.

The new order consisted of knights and brothers, some of the latter being priests. During the lifetime of St. Peter Nolasque, 2718 Christian prisoners were freed by the Mercedarians from Mohammedan servitude, 890 of these by St. Peter himself. In the course of its history, the order liberated a total of about 70,000 prisoners from the hands of the Moslem. In 1318 Pope John XXII ordered that henceforth the superior general be a priest. The knights then separated from the order and joined the military order of Our Lady of Montesa, founded in 1319 by King James II of Aragon for the purpose of battling against the Moors in Spain. Thus the Mercedarians ceased to be a military order. The privileges of religious orders in the strict sense were granted to them in 1690; and in 1725 they were placed among the mendicant orders.

The Discalced Mercedarians were founded in 1602 by Father John Baptist González, O.D.M., and approved in 1606. This stricter branch lasted in Spain till 1835, and in Italy till 1866.

As early as 1265 several women of Barcelona banded together to form the Third Order Secular of Our Lady of Mercy. The first superior of a religious community of the Mercedarian Third Order Regular was St. Mary of Cervello, who died in 1281. This sisterhood continued in existence till 1835, and was reestablished in 1860. In 1933 it had a membership of over 700.

The Second Order of Mercedarian nuns was founded by Father Anthony Velasco, O.D.M., in Seville, and approved by Pius V in 1568.

The Discalced Mercedarians also had their Second Order and Third Order. The latter was founded by St. Mary Anne of Jesus in 1624.

A special feast of Our Lady of Mercy was observed on September 24. Pope St. Pius X in 1904 granted a *toties quoties* plenary indulgence to all the faithful visiting a church of the Mercedarian First Order or of the Mercedarian Sisters of the Third Order on this feast.

The Mercedarian First Order has its headquarters in Rome. At the present time it has 810 members. In the United States a monastery of the Mercedarians was founded in 1921 at Middleburg Heights, Ohio.[7]

---

[7] For further information, cf. D. Vásquez, O. de M., and J. M. Delgado Varela, O. de M., *Le culte marial dans l'Ordre de Notre Dame de la Merci*, in *Maria*, Vol. 2, pp. 721-735. As

4. THE SERVITES (O.S.M.)

Seven prominent citizens of Florence, who had long been members of the *Laudesi* confraternity, having for its main purpose the veneration of Our Lady, were assembled in the confraternity church on the feast of the Assumption in 1233. Suddenly all of them felt inspired to give up their earthly possessions and to enter upon a religious life. With the permission of Bishop Ardinghus of Florence they carried out this desire on the feast of the Nativity of Our Lady by retiring to the secluded Villa Camaria outside the city walls and putting on a rough penitential garment of gray color. Bonfiglio Monaldi, one of the seven, served as the superior of the group.

On the feast of the Epiphany, 1234, as two of them went on a begging tour through the streets of Florence, little children cried out: *"Ecco i servi della Madonna* — Behold the servants of Our Lady!" From that time on they were called "the Servants of Mary."

According to a tradition of the order, Our Lady appeared in 1240 to the seven founders, as the Mother of Sorrows, holding in her hands a black habit, a palm branch, and the Augustinian Rule upon which were inscribed the words: *"Servi Mariae."* That same year they pronounced the three religious vows and put on a black habit as a symbol of the Sorrows of Our Lady. The Order of the Servants of Mary, *Ordo Servorum Mariae*, received papal approval in 1249 and 1304. Pope Martin V placed it among the mendicant orders.

From the beginning, the Servants of Mary or Servites have distinguished themselves by practicing and promoting devotion to Our Lady, particularly to Our Lady of Sorrows. The first chapter of their constitutions, edited about 1280 by St. Philip Benitius, fifth superior general, is entitled: *"De reverentiis Beatae Mariae Virginis* — Concerning reverences to be shown to the Blessed Virgin Mary." Later the following practice was introduced: before beginning the Mass prayers at the foot of the altar, a Servite priest says: *Ave Maria, gratia plena, Dominus tecum!* — and the server answers: *Benedicta tu in mulieribus et benedictus fructus ventris tui, Jesus!* Every church of the Servites is dedicated to Our Lady.

Devotion to Our Lady of Sorrows has been promoted by the Servites particularly through the Black Scapular,[8] the Crown of the Seven Sorrows

---

of January, 1961, the feast of Our Lady of Mercy (or Ransom) is reduced to a mere commemoration in the Roman calendar.

[8] Cf. G. M. Roschini, O.S.M., *Mariologia*, 2nd ed., Vol. 4 (Romae, 1948), p. 184.

of Our Lady,[9] and, since the beginning of the eighteenth century, the *Via Matris Dolorosae* — the Way of the Sorrowful Mother.[10] The latter is a devotion resembling the Way of the Cross and consists of seven stations recalling the Seven Sorrows of Our Lady. Since 1937 the Servites of Chicago have fostered this devotion in the United States with phenomenal success.

There are two Servite Provinces in the United States, both of them having headquarters in Chicago: the American Province, established in 1870, and the Italian Province of St. Joseph, erected in 1927. Headquarters of the order are in Rome; and the total number of professed members is 1700.

Stricter branches of the Servites have existed in the past: the Servites of the Observance, begun in 1411; the Servite Observants of Corvara, founded in 1491; and the Hermit or Discalced Servites, established in 1593.

The Second Order of Servite Nuns was founded by St. Philip Benitius in the thirteenth century; and hence they are also called Philippine Nuns. The Servite Third Order Secular, which had its beginnings in Perugia already in 1255, received the approval of Pope Martin V in 1424. The Sisters of the Servite Third Order Regular, also known as *Mantellate*, were founded 1306 in Florence by St. Juliana Falconieri.[11]

5. THE PIARISTS (SCH.P.)

The Piarists, known in Italy as "Scolopi" (from *scuole pie*) and in Spain as "Escolapios," have the following official name: *Ordo Clericorum Regularium Pauperum Matris Dei scholarum piarum* (the last word being the source of the name Piarists); in English, Order of Poor Clerics Regular of the Mother of God of Pious Schools. Their headquarters are in Rome; and they have a total of 2300 professed members. In the United States they have two foundations: one, the "American Branch," at Derby, Buffalo, N. Y.; and the other, the "Catalan-Spanish Branch," in Los Angeles, Calif.

The founder of the Piarists was St. Joseph of Calasanz, born in 1556 in

---

[9] Roschini, *op. cit.*, pp. 183-184.

[10] Roschini, *op. cit.*, p. 219.

[11] On the Servites, cf. G. M. Besutti, O.S.M., *I Servi di Maria ed il movimento mariano contemporaneo*, in *Alma Socia Christi*, Vol. 11, 1953, pp. 182-206; Roschini, *L'Ordre des Servites de Marie*, in *Maria*, Vol. 2, pp. 885-907; P. M. Soulier, O.S.M., *Les traditions mariales des Servites*, in *Congrès Marial tenu à Lyon* [1900], Vol. 2 (Lyon, 1901), pp. 455-462.

the castle of that name at Petralta de la Sal in Aragón, Spain, and died in 1648 at the age of 92 in Rome. In 1597 he opened the first free school in Rome. By 1604 he had twelve associates, and they began to live in a community. Ten years later they were placed under the jurisdiction of the Congregation of Clerics Regular of the Mother of God which had been founded in 1574 at Lucca by St. John Leonardi and had charge of the Church of Santa Maria in Portico.[12] However, in 1617 St. Joseph and his companions were organized into a separate congregation, the founder taking the name of Father Joseph of the Mother of God. Besides the usual three vows, they took a fourth vow binding themselves to the Christian education of youth without remuneration. They observed the Rule of St. Augustine. St. Joseph wrote special Constitutions, which were approved in 1621; and in the same year, the new congregation was raised to the rank of a religious order and was granted the privileges of the mendicant orders. Subsequently, difficulties arose, and for a time the order was reduced to a congregation; but in 1769 it became an order once more and all privileges were restored.

The Congregation of the Daughters of Mary, a branch of this Order for women, was founded in Spain in 1832.

St. Joseph of Calasanz distinguished himself by a special devotion to the Mother of God; he taught his pupils to recite, before going to sleep, the *Hail Mary* five times in honor of the five letters of the name *Maria;* and when he was at the point of death, Our Lady, as the *Madonna dei Monti,* appeared to him. The Constitutions which he wrote prescribe special devotions to Mary; and the members of the Piarist Order take special pains to foster devotion to Our Lady among the boys whom they teach.[13]

---

[12] This congregation became the Order of Clerics Regular of the Mother of God in 1619. Cf. F. Farraironi, *Le culte marial dans l'Ordre des Clercs Réguliers de la Mère de Dieu,* in *Maria,* Vol. 2, pp. 917-924. It is No. 2 in the list of Marian congregations which have no establishment in the United States (cf. below).

[13] On the Piarists, cf. L. Picanyol, Sch. P., *Le culte marial dans l'Ordre des Clercs Réguliers Pauvres de la Mère de Dieu,* in *Maria,* Vol. 2, pp. 925-934. There is also a Congregation of St. Joseph of Calasanz for Christian Workers (C.Op.), founded in 1889 by Fr. Anthony M. Schwartz in Vienna, who observe the rule of the Piarists in an adapted form. Cf. Heimbucher, *op. cit.,* Vol. 2, pp. 431-432.

6. THE PICPUS FATHERS (SS.CC.)

The Picpus Fathers are so named because of Picpus Street in Paris, where their mother house was established in 1805. They are called also the Fathers of the Sacred Hearts. Their full name is: *Congregatio Sacrorum Cordium Jesu et Mariae necnon adorationis perpetuae Ss. Sacramenti Altaris*, Congregation of the Sacred Hearts of Jesus and Mary and of Perpetual Adoration of the Most Blessed Sacrament of the Altar.

They were founded by Father Joseph Peter Coudrin († 1837) at Poitiers, France, in 1797 (1800); and they were approved as a religious congregation by Pius VII in 1817. In 1826 they began to do missionary work in Oceania, where one of their best known missionaries was Father Damian de Veuster († 1889), the Apostle of the Lepers at Kalawao on Molokai.

The purpose of the congregation is "the devotion to the Sacred Hearts of Jesus and Mary, practised and propagated by a contemplative-active life." Its headquarters are at Grottaferrata near Rome; and its professed members are 1700 in number. A North-American Province was established in 1946, with headquarters at Fairhaven, Mass. There is also a Hawaiian Province.

The Sisters of the Sacred Hearts and of Perpetual Adoration were also founded at Poitiers in 1797. They are called "Zelatrices" by the people.[14]

7. THE HOLY GHOST FATHERS (C.S.SP.)

Near the Sorbonne in Paris, Father Claude Francis Poullart de Places in 1703 founded the Seminary of the Holy Spirit under the protection of the Immaculate Conception. This marked the beginning of the Congregation of the Holy Spirit, whose Constitutions were approved by the Holy See in 1824. Since it encountered great difficulties in recruiting new members, this Congregation was united in 1848 with the Congregation of the Immaculate Heart of Mary, which had been founded in 1841 by the Ven. Francis Mary Paul Libermann for the purpose of supplying missionaries to the colored of Africa and America. Father Libermann, a saintly convert from Judaism, became the first superior general after this union. The official name of the new congregation is:

---

[14] Cf. F. Wandrille, SS.CC., *Les traditions mariales de la Congrégation de Picpus*, in *Congrès Marial tenu à Lyon* [1900], Vol. 2 (Lyon, 1901), pp. 522-524; Ignatius a Cruce Baños, SS.CC., *Devotio Immaculati Cordis Mariae in Congregatione Sacrorum Cordium*, in *Virgo Immaculata*, Vol. 12, 1956, pp. 186-195.

Congregatio Sancti Spiritus sub tutela Immaculati Cordis Beatissimae Virginis Mariae, the Congregation of the Holy Ghost under the patronage of the Immaculate Heart of the Most Blessed Virgin Mary. Its headquarters are in Paris; and it has a total of 4500 professed members. A Province of the United States was established in 1873, with headquarters in Washington, D. C. The society conducts Duquesne University in Pittsburgh.[15]

8. THE MONTFORT FATHERS (S.M.M.)

The Montfort Society of Mary or Company of Mary was founded in 1705 by St. Louis Mary Grignon [or Grignion] de Montfort (1673-1716), the author of *The True Devotion to Mary.* After he had labored zealously as a parish missionary in many dioceses of France, and had thought for five years of founding a special society of priests for this purpose, he established his congregation at St. Laurent-sur-Sèvre in the Vendé, France. He wrote a Rule which received preliminary approbation in 1825 and final approbation in 1872. The society spread to other parts of the world, including the foreign missions. Its headquarters are in Rome; and its professed members are 1563 in number. A United States Province was established in 1948, and has its headquarters at Ozone Park, N. Y.[16]

9. OBLATE FATHERS (O.M.I.)

The Oblates of Mary Immaculate were founded at Aix in the Provence, France, in 1816, by Father Charles Joseph Eugene de Mazenod, subsequently Bishop of Marseilles (1837-1861). Originally the members of the new society were called Missionaries of Provence, then Oblates of St. Charles; but since there was a society in Milan which had the latter name, the French society's name, at the suggestion of the founder, was changed to the Oblates of the Immaculate Virgin Mary, *Congregatio Oblatorum Beatae Mariae Virginis Immaculatae.* This was done in the papal brief of 1826 which approved the society. In 1841 its first missionaries departed for overseas missions. Then its membership began to grow quite rapidly. The

---

[15] Cf. J. A. Lauritis, C.S.Sp., *The Congregation of the Holy Ghost and the Immaculate Heart of Mary,* in *The Age of Mary,* Vol. 4, Aug.-Sept., 1957, pp. 79-84; H. Barré, C.S.Sp., *Spiritualité mariale du Venerable Père Libermann,* in *Maria,* Vol. 5 (Paris, 1954), pp. 381-401.

[16] Cf. D. M. Huot, S.M.M., *De vita mariologico-mariana apud religiosos S.M.M.,* in *Ephemerides Mariologicae,* Vol. 4, 1954, pp. 469-479.

MARIAN ORDERS AND CONGREGATIONS 197

founder added special regulations to the Rule for missionaries. As aims of the society are mentioned: parish missions, direction of seminaries, and missions among the infidels. The headquarters are in Rome. Its total membership is 6833. In the United States four provinces have been established: the Eastern Province, in 1883, with headquarters in Washington, D. C.; the Southern Province, in 1904, with headquarters in San Antonio, Tex.; the Province of St. John the Baptist, in 1921, with headquarters at Lowell, Mass.; and the Central Province, in 1924, with headquarters at Belleville, Ill.[17]

10. THE FATHERS OF MERCY (S.P.M.)

In 1808, at Lyons, France, a society of secular priests, called the Missionaries of France, was founded by Father Jean Baptiste Rauzan, in order to repair the harm done to the Church by the French Revolution. Several times their houses were confiscated and the members were dispersed; but they always reestablished themselves. In 1834 the Society was formally approved by Pope Gregory XVI. They came to the diocese of New Orleans, La., in 1839, and two years later to New York City. From 1814 to 1903 their motherhouse was in Paris; but now it is in Brooklyn, N. Y., and there is a Procure in Rome. The name Missionaries of France has been changed to the Fathers of Mercy or the Society of the Priests of Mercy of the Immaculate Conception. Its members take the vows of obedience, chastity, and stability, and make the promise to observe the spirit of poverty. The congregation now has fourteen establishments in the United States and Canada, and a total membership of 163, of whom 95 are priests and the rest seminarians and novices.[18]

11. THE MARIST FATHERS (S.M.)

The Society of Mary, *Societas Mariae*, was founded in 1822, and approved in 1836. In the pilgrimage church of Our Lady near Lyons, France, known as Notre Dame de Fourvière, a group of priests in 1816 dedicated themselves to the service of Mary by missionary work. Encouraged in 1822 by Pope Pius VIII, they began to live in a community

---

[17] Cf. G. Cosentino, O.M.I., *De vita mariologico-mariana apud religiosos O.M.I.*, in *Ephemerides Mariologicae*, Vol. 4, 1954, pp. 375-381; Père Praet, *La Vierge et les Oblats de Marie Immaculée*, in *Mémoires et Rapports du Congrès Marial tenu à Bruxelles* [1921], Vol. 2 (Bruxelles, 1922), pp. 333-342.

[18] Cf. Heimbucher, *op. cit.*, Vol. 2, p. 634.

at Belley. The purpose of the society includes the self-sanctification of its members by special devotion to Mary, the education of boys in higher schools and seminaries, the preaching of parish missions, and missionary work abroad. The first superior general of the society was Jean Claude Marie Colin, one of the founders. Headquarters are in Rome; and the members are 1898 in number. In the United States, the Washington Province was begun in 1863, and the Boston Province was established in 1924.

Father Champagnat, one of the first Marists, in 1817 founded the Marist Brothers, who will be mentioned later. And in 1816, Father Colin founded the Marist Sisters, or Sisters of the Most Holy Name of Mary, for the education of girls. Their motherhouse is now at Martelange in Belgium. These must be distinguished from the Marist Missionary Sisters (of the Third Order Regular of Mary) who were founded in 1880 at Saint-Foy-les-Lyon, and have an American motherhouse at Framingham Centre, Mass., since 1922. A separate German branch of the latter, the Missionary Sisters of the Most Holy Name of Mary, were founded at Meppen in 1920. In the Fiji Islands, the Marists founded the native religious congregations of the Little Brothers and the Little Sisters of Mary, in 1882. The Third Order of the Society of Mary was established in 1850, and has its main centre in Rome.[19]

12. THE MARIANISTS (S.M.)

Another Society of Mary, known also as the Marianists or the Brothers of Mary, came into being about the same time as the Marists. Their founder was Father William Joseph Chaminade (1761-1850). During the French Revolution (1789-1796), he secretly exercised the sacred ministry in Bordeaux with constant danger to his life. Finally he was banished to Spain (1797-1800), and there, at the shrine of Our Lady del Pilar in Saragossa, he received his mission to restore Christian life in France as an apostle of Our Lady. In 1801 he began to establish Marian confraternities for all classes of society. From his young men's confraternity at Bordeaux developed, in 1817, the Society of Mary; and from his young ladies' confraternity arose, in 1816, the Daughters of Mary.

The Society of Mary consists of priests and brothers; and although the brothers constitute the greater portion of the membership, the superior

---

[19] Cf. *De vita mariologico-mariana apud Societatem Mariae*, in *Ephemerides Mariologicae*, Vol. 6, 1956, pp. 230-233.

general is always a priest. The members seek to sanctify themselves through the education of boys and the direction of Marian societies. Besides the usual three vows, at their solemn profession they take a fourth vow of stability; that is, they dedicate themselves by a special vow to Mary and receive a golden ring which they wear on the right hand as a sign of their dedication to Our Lady. After receiving preliminary approbation in 1839, the Congregagation was approved in 1865, and their Rule in 1891. Their mother house is now in Rome; and they have 2600 members. In the United States and possessions, the Society has three provinces: the Cincinnati Province, established 1849, with headquarters at Dayton, Ohio; the St. Louis Province, established 1908, with headquarters at Kirkwood, Mo.; and the Province of the Pacific, established 1948, with headquarters at Honolulu, T. H.[20]

13. THE EUDIST FATHERS (C.J.M.)

The Congregation of Jesus and Mary was founded at Caen, France, in 1643, by St. John Eudes (1601-1680). The founder's name explains their popular title of "Eudist Fathers." The purpose of the society is the preaching of parish missions and the direction of seminaries for the secular clergy. Following the example of their founder, the members also seek to promote devotion to the Sacred Heart of Jesus and the Immaculate Heart of Mary. Born at Mezerai in 1601, Father Eudes joined the Oratorians in 1623 and was made superior of the Oratory at Caen in 1639. In 1632 he began to devote himself to the preaching of parish missions. Realizing the need of seminaries conducted in accordance with the decrees of the Council of Trent, he and several other secular priests of Normandy founded a secular congregation for the purpose of directing such seminaries. They began to live in a community at Caen in 1643; and although they took no vows, they promised obedience to a superior who was elected for life. Father Eudes, the first superior, wrote a twofold Rule, consisting of a Rule of Our Lord Jesus Christ which outlined the duties of members, and a Rule of the Blessed Virgin which described the virtues they were to practice. Both consisted to a great extent of passages from Holy Scripture. The Rule was approved by the Holy See in 1674.

---

[20] Cf. E. Neubert, S.M., *Raisons de la dévotion speciale envers le mystère de l'Immaculée Conception dans la Société de Marie*, in *Virgo Immaculata*, Vol. 8[3], 1956, pp. 216-228; also *De vita mariologico-mariana apud Societatem Mariae*, in *Ephemerides Mariologicae*, Vol. 5, 1955, pp. 457-465.

By 1792 the society was conducting twelve major and five minor seminaries in France. In the French Revolution the congregation became extinct; but in 1826 it was founded anew, and in 1874 it was approved once more by the Holy See. In 1934, the society had about 625 members. The headquarters are now in Rome. A Province has been established in Canada, and the Society is represented in the United States with headquarters at Washington, D. C.[21]

14. THE ASSUMPTIONISTS (A.A.)

After he had founded a teaching sisterhood, called Ladies of the Assumption, in 1839, Father Emmanuel Joseph Maria Maurice d'Alzon, Vicar General of Nîmes, France, with four companions founded the Augustinians of the Assumption in 1845. Officially they are also called Pious Society of Priests of the Assumption, *Pia Societas Presbyterorum ab Assumptione*. Pope Pius IX gave his approval to the new society in 1864. Devoting themselves especially to educational and missionary work, the Assumptionists spread rapidly, especially in France and the Near East. With the aid of a ship of their own, named *Notre Dame de Salut* and later *Étoile*, they organized pilgrimages to Lourdes, Rome, and Jerusalem. In Jerusalem they built a hospice for pilgrims and called it "Notre Dame de France." In the Near East they sought to promote the reunion of Bulgarian and Greek schismatics with the Holy See. They founded the parish of the Assumption in Belgrade in 1928, and another of the same name in the Kum-Kapu district of Istanbul (Constantinople). They are the directors of the Archconfraternity of the Assumption of Our Lady for the conversion of the Orient, which was erected in the Greek Catholic Church of Anastasis in Istanbul on May 25, 1898. When the congregation was suppressed by the French government, it spread to other parts of the world. It is back in France again at the present day, but headquarters are in Rome. A United States-Canada Province was established in 1946, with headquarters in New York City. The total number of members in the world is now 1900.

For missionary work in the Balkan countries and the Near East, Father d'Alzon in 1864 founded a second sisterhood, the Oblate Sisters of the Assumption; and in the same year Father Pernet, one of the first

---

[21] Concerning the Eudists, cf. L. Barbé, C.J.M., *La Congrégation de Jesus et Marie*, in *Maria*, Vol. 3, pp. 165-179; also, *De vita mariologico-mariana apud Congregationem Jesu et Mariae, seu Eudistas*, in *Ephemerides Mariologicae*, Vol. 6, 1956, pp. 481-487.

companions of Father d'Alzon, founded a nursing sisterhood called the Little Sisters of the Assumption. Father Picard, the second superior general of the Assumptionists, in 1896, founded the "Orantes" or Praying Sisters of the Assumption.[22]

15. CLARETIAN FATHERS (C.M.F.)

The Claretian Fathers were founded 1849 at Vich in Spain by St. Anthony Maria Claret for missionary work at home and abroad. Their official name is Congregation of the Missionary Sons of the Immaculate Heart of the Blessed Virgin Mary, *Congregatio Missionariorum filiorum Immaculati Cordis Beatae Mariae Virginis*. At their religious profession the members make a solemn promise to propagate the devotion to the Immaculate Heart of Mary. Preliminary approval was granted in 1860 and final approval in 1924. Headquarters are in Rome; and the Congregation now has 2800 professed members. In the United States it has a Western Province with headquarters in Los Angeles, and a Vice-Province of the East with headquarters in Chicago. During the Spanish Revolution which preceded World War II, 286 Claretians won the martyr's crown at the hands of the Communists in Spain.[23]

16. LA SALETTE FATHERS (M.S.)

The Missionaries of Our Lady of La Salette, *Missionarii Beatae Mariae Virginis a La Salette*, were founded 1852 by Bishop Philibert de Brouillard of Grenoble, France, to provide priests for the shrine of Our Lady of La Salette. However, the society grew beyond the limits of La Salette, and now also counts among its purposes the conducting of missions and retreats, parochial and social work, and missionary work among infidels. The Holy See approved of the society in 1879, 1890, and 1929. Headquarters are now in Rome. The professed members are 937 in number. In the United States three provinces have been established. The

---

[22] On the Assumptionists cf. A. Sage, A.A., *La doctrine et le culte de Marie dans la famille augustinienne*, in *Maria*, Vol. 2, pp. 707-712. On pp. 681-707 of this article the author discusses the Canons Regular of St. Augustine, and the Augustinians or Hermits of St. Augustine.

[23] Cf. J. M. Canal, C.M.F., *Praecipua opera et ephemerides marialia a PP. Claretianis (C.M.F.) edita*, in *Marianum*, Vol. 12, 1950, pp. 476-478; N. García Garcés, C.M.F., *La dévotion a la Très-Sainte Vierge dans la Congrégation des Missionnaires Fils du Coeur Immaculé de Marie*, in *Maria*, Vol. 3, pp. 405-428.

so-called American Province, begun in 1892, was canonically erected in 1933 and has its headquarters at Bloomfield, Conn.; the Province of the Immaculate Heart of Mary, with headquarters at East Brewster, Mass., was established in 1945; and the Province of Our Lady Queen of Poland has headquarters at Olivet, Ill. Since 1958 there is also the Vice-Province of Mary Queen, with headquarters in St. Louis, Mo.[24]

In 1895 the La Salette missionary, Father John Baptist Berthier founded at Grave in Holland a special religious congregation to care for belated vocations, the Congregation of the Missionaries of the Holy Family (M.S.F.), which is also represented in the United States.[25]

17. THE SCHEUT FATHERS (C.I.C.M.)

At the ruins of a chapel of Our Lady in the field of Scheut (Scheutveld), near Brussels, Belgium, Father Theophilus Verbist in 1863 laid the cornerstone for a foreign mission seminary. That marked the beginning of the Missionaries of Scheut, or the Congregation of the Immaculate Heart of Mary, *Congregatio Immaculati Cordis Mariae,* which was approved by Pope Leo XIII in 1900. When China was reopened to missionaries in 1861, Father Verbist and some other priests of Belgium wanted to go to that country as missionaries; but Cardinal Barbaro, prefect of the Sacred Congregation of Propaganda, urged them to found a mission seminary in Belgium before departing for the missions, and so this Belgian foreign mission society was established. Its first missionaries, Father Verbist one of them, went to Mongolia in 1865; and in 1888 the society commenced missionary work also in the Congo. Headquarters are at Scheut-lez-Bruxelles, Belgium, although there is a procure in Rome. The society has 1765 members. A United States Province with headquarters at Arlington, Va., was established in 1949.[26]

---

[24] On the La Salette Fathers, cf. Père Liaud, M.S., *Les traditions mariales des Missionnaires de la Salette,* in *Congrès Marial tenu à Lyon* [1900], Vol. 2 (Lyon, 1901), pp. 558-561; B. M. Morineau, S.M.M., *Les congrégations religieuses d'hommes du XVII° siècle à nos jours,* in *Maria,* Vol. 3, pp. 360-361. The entire article, from p. 339 to p. 378, is very rich in bibliographical references concerning the various orders and congregations.

[25] Cf. Heimbucher, *op. cit.,* Vol. 2, p. 432.

[26] Cf. A. Van Hoeydonck, C.I.C.M., *La dévotion au Coeur Immaculé de Marie dans la Congrégation du Coeur Immaculé de Marie,* in *Virgo Immaculata,* Vol. 12, 1956, pp. 196-220; Anon., *Immaculate Heart of Mary Mission Society, C.I.C.M.,* in *The Age of Mary,* Vol. 4, Aug.-Sept., 1957, p. 93.

18. THE CONSOLATA FATHERS (I.M.C.)

Another missionary society named for Our Lady is the Missionary Institute of La Consolata, *Institutum Missionum a Consolata,* which was founded 1901 at Turin, Italy, by two priests, Fathers Allamano and Camisassa. The Holy See gave the society preliminary approval, in 1909, and final approval in 1923. It is engaged in missionary work in Africa. Headquarters are in Turin, but there is a procure in Rome. At the present day it has 750 professed members. The society is aided in its missionary work by the Consolata Sisters. In the United States the Consolata Fathers have a foundation at Batavia, N. Y.[27]

19. THE MARIAN FATHERS (M.I.C.)

The Marian Fathers' full name is the Congregation of the Marian Clerics Regular under the title of the Immaculate Conception of the Most Blessed Virgin Mary, *Congregatio Clericorum Regularium Marianorum sub titulo Immaculatae Conceptionis Beatissimae Virginis Mariae.* This congregation was founded 1673 at Corabiev, Poland, by the Piarist Father Stanislaus Papczynski. It devoted itself to the sacred ministry and to educational and missionary work. By 1909 the congregation had become all but extinct, only one member being left at the time. Archbishop George Matulewicz then began its restoration and thus became its second founder. It obtained renewed papal approval in 1910; and today it has 435 professed members. Headquarters are in Rome. In the United States two provinces have been established: the Province of St. Casimir, begun in 1913 and erected in 1930, which has headquarters in Chicago; and the Province of St. Stanislaus Kostka, begun in 1931 and erected in 1948, which has headquarters at Stockbridge, Mass.[28]

20. THE MARIST BROTHERS (P.F.M. OR F.M.S.)

The Marist Brothers of the Schools, *Institutum Fratrum Maristarum Scholarum,* also called Little Brothers of Mary, *Institutum Parvulorum Fratrum Mariae,* were founded 1817 at La Valla, near Lyons, France, by one of the first Marist Fathers, Blessed Marcellin Joseph Benedict Champagnat. They devote themselves to educational work in Christian and pagan countries. The brotherhood was approved by the Holy See in

---

[27] Cf. Heimbucher, *op. cit.,* Vol. 2, p. 609.
[28] Cf. Heimbucher, *op. cit.,* Vol. 2, p. 129.

1859, 1863, and 1903. At the present day they have 8646 members; and hence, after the Christian Brothers, they are the largest religious brotherhood in the Catholic Church. Their generalate is at Saint-Genis-Laval, Rhône, France; and there is a procure in Rome. A United States Province, with headquarters at Esopus, N. Y., was established in 1912.[29]

* * *

The orders and congregations of men with papal approval which have no establishment in the United States are the following:[30]

Teutonic Order of St. Mary in Jerusalem, founded at Acre or Akko, then in Syria, in 1190. Headquarters in Vienna. Professed members, 88.

Order of the Clerics Regular of the Mother of God (O.M.D.), founded at Lucca, Italy, in 1574. Headquarters in Rome. Members (R), 84.[31]

Congregation of the Oratory of Jesus and Mary Immaculate, founded 1611 in Paris. Headquarters in Paris.

Congregation of the Oblates of the Blessed Virgin Mary (O.M.V.), founded at Pinerolo, Italy, in 1815. Headquarters in Rome. Members (R), 160.

Congregation of the Sons of Mary Immaculate, founded 1821-1847 in Italy. Headquarters in Brescia. Professed members, 250.

Congregation of the Sons of the Blessed Virgin Mary Immaculate (of Luçon) (F.M.I.), founded at Chavagnes-en-Paillers, France, in 1828. Headquarters at Ste. Marie, France, Members (R), 166.

Pious Society of Priests of the Immaculate Conception of the Virgin Mary (of Lourdes), founded 1848 in France. Headquarters at Garaison, France. Professed members, 86.

Congregation of the Canons Regular of the Immaculate Conception

---

[29] On the Marist Brothers, cf. Frère Théophane, *Les traditions mariales des Petits Frères de Marie*, in *Congrès Marial tenu à Lyon [1900]*, Vol. 2 (Lyon, 1901), pp. 582-584. There is another Marian Congregation in the United States which is still in its initial stage and hence has not as yet received papal approval. They are the "Sons of Mary, Health of the Sick" (*Filii Mariae Salutis Infirmorum*), founded in 1952 by Fr. Edward Garesche, S.J. Their mother house is in Framingham, Mass. In Europe, too, there are some Marian congregations of men which have only episcopal approval.

[30] Wherever in our list the membership is given as "professed members," the figures are taken from the *Annuario Pontificio, 1959;* when the membership is indicated merely by the word "Members (R)," the total is taken from Roschini, *Mariologia*, Vol. 4, pp. 194-196.

[31] Cf. M. Feroci, O.M.D., *Scritti e opere mariane nell'Ordine della Madre di Dio*, in *Alma Socia Christi*, Vol. 11, 1953, pp. 207-218.

(C.R.I.C.), founded in Genoa, Italy, in 1866. Headquarters in Rome.

Congregation of the Priests of St. Mary of Tinchebray, founded 1851 in France. Procure in Rome.

Capuchin Brothers of the Third Order of St. Francis of the Blessed Virgin Mary of Sorrows, founded 1889 in Spain. Headquarters in Madrid. Professed members, 330.

Congregation of the Sons of St. Mary Immaculate, founded 1904 in Italy. Headquarters in Rome. Professed members, 102.

Congregation of the Missionaries of the Sacred Hearts of Jesus and Mary (of Mallorca), founded 1890 in Spain. Headquarters at Paz. Professed members, 134.

Institute of St. Mary of Guadalupe for Foreign Missions (M. de G.), founded 1949 in Mexico. Headquarters in Mexico City.

Institute of the Brothers of the Blessed Virgin Mary of Mercy (F.D.M.), founded 1839 in Belgium. Headquarters at Starrenhof, Belgium. Professed members, 400.

Hospital Brothers, Sons of the Immaculate Conception (Conceptionists), founded 1857 in Italy. Headquarters in Rome.

Brothers of the Pious Congregation of the Presentation, founded 1802 in Ireland. Headquarters at Mt. St. Joseph, Ireland. Professed members, 315.

Brothers of Mercy of St. Mary Auxiliatrix or Our Lady of Help, founded 1850 in Germany. Headquarters at Trier, Germany. Professed members, 390.

Brothers of Our Lady of Lourdes, founded 1830 in Belgium. Headquarters at Oostakker, Ghent, Belgium. Professed members, 924.

It may be well to point out that the membership of these 18 Marian orders and congregations, with the exception perhaps of the Brothers of Our Lady of Lourdes, is comparatively small; hence, all of the larger orders and congregations of men which have a Marian name are represented in the United States.

Noteworthy too is the fact that of the 38[32] such orders and congregations (6 orders and 32 congregations), which we have discussed

---

[32] Roschini, *op. cit.*, pp. 189-196, lists only 34 orders and congregations of men which have a Marian name, and gives details about four of them only (i.e., Servites, Carmelites, Mercedarians, and Montfort Fathers). Our enumeration has a total of 38. The difference is due to the fact that Roschini does not discuss the Discalced Carmelites as a separate order, and does not mention the Fathers of Mercy (No. 10 of those having houses in the United States), nor Nos. 13 and 17 in the above list.

or enumerated, 2 were founded in the twelfth century, 2 in the thirteenth, none in the fourteenth and fifteenth centuries, 2 in the sixteenth, 4 in the seventeenth, 3 in the eighteenth, 22 in the nineteenth, and 3 in the twentieth century. And of the four founded in the seventeenth century, one was re-established in the nineteenth and another in the twentieth. Thus the nineteenth century, with all its revolutions and persecutions of the Catholic Church in Europe, stands out as the one in which the most Marian congregations of men by far were established.

It is of interest to note also that in France more such congregations were established than in any other country. Of the 38 Marian orders and congregations of men with papal approval, 15 were founded in France, 9 in Italy, 5 in Spain, 3 in Belgium, and one in each of the six countries of Palestine, Syria, Germany, Ireland, Poland, and Mexico.

II. NOTABLE MARIAN ORDERS AND CONGREGATIONS OF MEN WITHOUT A MARIAN NAME

After enumerating 34 papal orders and congregations of men which have a Marian name, Father Roschini reminds us that all religious families without exception honor the Blessed Virgin as their Patroness, Queen, and Mother, and with great zeal promote devotion to her. In this respect, however, he adds, the Cistercians, Franciscans, Dominicans, Jesuits, Salesians, and others are worthy of special mention.[33]

We shall discuss briefly the following older and larger orders and congregations: Benedictines, Cistercians, Carthusians, Dominicans, Franciscans, Augustinians, Jesuits, Vincentians, Redemptorists, and Salesians.

1. THE BENEDICTINES (O.S.B.)

The Order of St. Benedict, named for its founder, was established in the sixth century. Not counting four smaller, separate communities like the Camaldolese Benedictines, but only those belonging to a confederation which was formed in 1893, the Benedictines now have a total membership of 11,500.

The first indications of devotion to Our Lady among the Benedictines are found in the eighth century. In the ninth century, the Benedictines played an important role in the development of Marian theology; and in

---

[33] Roschini, *op. cit.*, p. 196.

the eleventh century, they contributed much to the growth of devotion to Our Lady among the faithful, particularly in Normandy and England.

Abbot Ambrose Autpert of St. Vincent-au-Vulturne († 784) is regarded by Dom Morin as the first great Mariologist of the Latin rite before St. Bernard. His sermons on the Nativity and the Assumption of the Blessed Virgin are the first Latin sermons which treat exclusively of Our Lady. Herman Contractus, a monk of the abbey of Reichenau († 1054), wrote sequences in honor of Mary and is the author of the *Alma Redemptoris Mater*, and probably also of the *Salve Regina*.[34] St. Anselm of Canterbury († 1109) wrote eloquently of the prerogatives of Mary and fostered a tender, childlike devotion to her. "Nothing except God," wrote St. Anselm, "is greater than Mary." Eadmer († 1124), a monk of St. Saviour in England and secretary of St. Anselm, in his *De conceptione Sanctae Mariae,* clearly affirms the Immaculate Conception, deducing this prerogative from the principles set down by St. Anselm; and he contributed much to the devotion to Mary Immaculate. Another English monk, Nicholas of St. Albans, writing to Peter of Celle who opposed the celebration of a feast of the Immaculate Conception because of St. Bernard's opinion on the matter, replied that we should rather seek to promote the glory of Mary than that of St. Bernard. The first to apply to Mary the words of the Canticle of Canticles was Abbot Rupert of Deutz († c. 1130). At the end of the fourteenth century, Abbot Hugh I of Cluny ordered that the *Salve Regina* be chanted daily after Compline in all the monasteries of the Cluny Congregation of Benedictines.[35] This, of course, is not the whole story. We have merely selected a few examples which will have to suffice in this brief survey. The same will be true of the other orders and congregations which we shall discuss in the following paragraphs.

2. THE CISTERCIANS (S.ORD.CIST. AND O.C.R.)

The Holy Order of Cistercians, which also observes the Rule of St. Benedict, was founded by St. Bernard in 1098. According to Heimbucher,

---

[34] Roschini, *op. cit.,* p. 91. M. Britt, *Hymns of the Missal and Breviary* (New York, 1924), p. 68, is of the opinion that the *Salve Regina* was probably composed by Bishop Adhémar of Le Puy in the eleventh century. Cf. Chapter IV on *Marian Prayers,* in this volume.

[35] Cf. J. Leclercq, O.S.B., *Dévotion et théologie mariales dans le monachisme bénédictin,* in *Maria,* Vol. 2, pp. 547-578; F. Curiel, O.S.B., *Influencia de los Benedictinos en la propagación del culto de María en España,* in *Actas del Cuarto Congreso Mariano Internacional celebrado en Zaragoza* 1908 (Madrid, 1909), pp. 725-728.

the Cistercians, in 1933, had over 1000 members; while the Reformed Cistercians or Trappists (O.C.R.), in 1955, had 3612 members.

Among Mariologists as well as clients of Mary, St. Bernard stands out as one of the greatest. Even though he held the opinion that Mary was not immaculately conceived, his sermons contain an almost complete synthesis of Marian doctrine; and in those sermons he, more than anyone else of his time, fostered a genuine devotion to Our Lady. He and St. Anselm were the two great Marian writers of western monasticism. Rightly, therefore, has he been called *Citharista Mariae,* Mary's Harpist. The Cistercians and Trappists of subsequent centuries down to the present day have followed St. Bernard's example. The general chapter of the Cistercians in 1134, for instance, made the ruling that all monasteries of the order should henceforth be dedicated to St. Mary, giving as a reason the fact that the founders of Cîteaux came from Molesme where the church was dedicated to the Virgin Mary.[36]

3. The Carthusians

The Order of Carthusians was founded by St. Bruno in 1084. At the present time it has a membership of 679. The Carthusian monks have manifested their devotion to Our Lady from early times by their liturgical and private prayers, by votive Masses in her honor, by the practice of repeating the Angelic Salutation, by the quadruple Angelus, etc.

Especially noteworthy is the role that they played during the fourteenth and fifteenth centuries in the development of the Rosary. In the Middle Ages the 150 Psalms, divided into fifties or one third part, was a favorite form of devotion for religious and learned persons; and the common people imitated them by repeating the same number of *Paters.* In the eleventh century, for instance, the monks of Cluny who were not priests recited either fifty Psalms or fifty *Paters* for a deceased confrere. Strings of beads used for the purpose of counting the number of *Paters* recited, were called "paternosters" throughout Europe in the Middle Ages; and in the thirteenth century at least the manufacturers of such strings of beads, called "paternosterers," formed an important craft guild. The English "paternosterers" were wont to congregate in what is still known as Paternoster Row. In the twelfth century, when the Angelic Salutation,

---

[36] Cf. J. B. Auniord and R. Thomas, *Citeaux et Notre Dame,* in *Maria,* Vol. 2, pp. 581-624; S. Lenssen, O.C.S.O., *L'âme mariale des cisterciens contemporains,* in *Marie* [Nicolet], Vol. 7, No. 6, 1954, pp. 104-105.

that is the first part of the *Hail Mary*, came into general use as a formula of devotion, it became customary also to repeat 50 or 100 or 150 *Aves* in place of the same number of Psalms. The practice was a familiar one by the middle of that century; and the 50 *Aves* were even divided into sets of ten. Since it was a Salutation of Our Lady, the repetition of the *Ave* was accompanied by genuflexions and other marks of reverence. The recitation of 150 *Aves* was called the Psalter of Our Lady. It was only toward the end of the fifteenth century that the complete *Hail Mary*, with the *Holy Mary* added, came into use.[37]

Now, the contributions made by the Carthusians to the development of the Rosary are the following. It was Dom Henry Egher of Kalcar, a monk of the Carthusian monastery at Cologne († 1408), who introduced the practice of separating the 15 decades of the Psalter of Our Lady by inserting a *Pater noster* before each decade. And the two monks of the Carthusian monastery of St. Alhan near Trier, Dom Adolph of Essen († 1439) and especially Dom Dominic Helion of Prussia († c. 1450), introduced the practice of meditating on certain definite mysteries of the life of Our Lord and Our Lady during the recitation of a Rosary of 50 *Aves*. In fact, the legend that St. Dominic, the founder of the Dominicans, was the author of the Rosary, which dates back only to about 1470, may well have had its origin in the erroneous identification of the fifteenth-century Carthusian Dominic as the St. Dominic of the thirteenth century.[38]

4. THE DOMINICANS (O.P.)

The Order of Preachers or the Dominican Friars were founded at the beginning of the thirteenth century by St. Dominic. At the present day they have a total membership of 8500.

There is no longer any doubt, as Dominican scholars themselves admit, that St. Dominic was not the author of the Rosary and that the Rosary as we have it now dates back only to the latter part of the fifteenth century. However, St. Dominic and his first companions did have a great devotion to Our Lady. The first chapter of the old chronicle *Vitae fratrum*, the Fioretti of the Dominicans, is entitled: "That Our Lady by her intercession obtained from her Divine Son the institution of the Friars

---

[37] Roschini, *op. cit.*, p. 195. H. Thurston, S.J., The Rosary, in *The Catholic Encyclopedia*, Vol. 13, pp. 184-187.

[38] Cf. Y. Gourdel, *Le culte de la Très-Sainte Vierge dans l'Ordre des Chartreux*, in *Maria*, Vol. 2, pp. 627-678. See also Chapter V of this book.

Preachers."[39] Friar Romeo de Livia, one of the Companions of St. Dominic, was wont to recite the *Ave* a thousand times a day; and he died holding in his hands a knotted cord which he had used to count his *Aves*. On his apostolic journeys St. Dominic loved to sing the *Ave maris stella;* and Friar Jordan of Saxony used to chant the *Salve Regina*. The latter had the conviction that Our Lady was particularly solicitous in guarding and promoting the Order of Preachers. Though he was not the author of the practice, it was his custom to recite after the *Ave maris stella,* the *Magnificat* and four Psalms the initial letters of which formed the word *MARIA*.[40] Already in 1266 Dominican lay brothers began to add the *Ave* to the *Paters* of their Office.

As far as the Rosary is concerned, it is due to the zealous efforts of the Dominicans, who began to establish confraternities of the Rosary in the latter part of the fifteenth century, that the Rosary has been universally adopted in a fixed and definite form — the form in which we have it now — as a favorite form of devotion to Our Lady. The Dominican Alan de Rupe (de la Roche) and his confreres established the first confraternities of the Rosary in 1470-1475. One of the first confraternities of the Rosary is known to have been established at Cologne in 1474 by the Dominican Father Jacob Sprenger. In 1569 Pope St. Pius V, himself a Dominican, placed the Confraternity of the Rosary in the exclusive care of the Dominicans.[41]

5. THE FRANCISCANS (O.F.M., O.F.M.CONV., O.F.M.CAP.)

The First Order of St. Francis of Assisi, founded in 1209, comprises the three autonomous branches: Friars Minor (*Ordo Fratrum Minorum*), with 25,848 members; Friars Minor Conventual (*Ordo Fratrum Minorum Conventualium*), with 3650 members; and, since 1525, Friars Minor Capuchin (*Ordo Fratrum Minorum Capuccinorum*), with 14,225 members.

Regina Ordinis Minorum, ora pro nobis — Queen of the Franciscan Order, pray for us! The privilege of adding this invocation to the Litany

---

[39] *Quod Domina nostra ordinem fratrum praedicatorum impetravit a Filio.* Cf. A. Duval, O.P., *La dévotion mariale dans l'Ordre des Frères Prêcheurs,* in *Maria,* Vol. 2, p. 739, note 1.

[40] These four psalms were: Ps. 119, *Ad Dominum cum tribularer;* Ps. 118, section 17, *Retribue;* Ps. 125, *In convertendo;* Ps. 24, *Ad te levavi.* Cf. Roschini, *op. cit.,* pp. 114-115.

[41] Cf. I. Body, O.P., *Les traditions mariales de l'Ordre de Saint-Dominique,* in *Congrès Marial tenu à Lyon* [1900], Vol. 2 (Lyon, 1901), pp. 446-454; also Chapter V of this book.

of Loreto was granted to all the Franciscan orders by St. Pius X in 1910. The Pope expressly declared at the time that the permission was given, not only to the three branches of the First Order (43,723 members), but also to the Poor Clares or Second Order (*ca.* 17,000 members), to the priests, brothers, and sisters of the Third Order Regular[42] (more than 30,000 Franciscan Sisters in the United States alone), and to the Third Order Secular (*ca.* 2,000,000).

In 1950 Pope Pius XII instituted a special feast of the Blessed Virgin Mary Queen of the Franciscan Order (*Regina Ordinis Minorum*), to be celebrated annually by the Franciscan orders as a double of the second class on December 15. That day is the octave day of the feast of the Immaculate Conception, who was chosen as the *Patrona principalissima* by the Friars Minor in their general chapter at Toledo, Spain, in 1645, by the Friars Minor Capuchin in 1714, and by the Friars Minor Conventual in 1719.

Actually it was St. Francis himself who chose Our Lady as the special Patroness of his orders. His first biographer, Thomas of Celano, writes: "What is a very special source of joy, is the fact that he (Francis) chose her (Mary) as the Advocate of his order; and he entrusted to her shielding mantle his children whom he was to leave that she might guard and protect them to the end."[43]

St. Francis of Assisi was not only the Herald of the Great King but also the Knight of Our Lady. With knightly love and filial devotion he venerated Our Lady especially as the Queen of Heaven, who like our Blessed Redeemer embraced holy poverty as her lot on this earth. His

---

[42] The Franciscan Third Order Regular includes the Third Order Regular of St. Francis (T.O.R.), established as a regular order in 1447, with 736 members, priests and brothers; the Franciscan Friars of the Atonement (Graymoor), founded in 1898, with 173 members, priests and brothers; the Franciscan Tertiary Brothers of the Holy Cross of Waldbreitbach, Germany, founded in 1862, with 225 members; the Missionary Brothers of St. Francis of Assisi of Bombay, India, founded in 1896, with 102 members; the Poor Brothers of the Seraphic St. Francis of Aachen, Germany, founded in 1857, with 195 members; and the Brothers of the Third Order Regular of St. Francis of Assisi of Mt. Bellew, Ireland, founded in 1818, with 110 members — all having papal approval; also other Franciscan brotherhoods having only episcopal approval, e.g., those of Brooklyn, N. Y., and Eureka, Mo.; lastly, numerous sisterhoods, with papal or episcopal approval, of which there are seventy-six autonomous communities in the United States alone, several of them having more than one province.

[43] Cf. Thomas of Celano, O.F.M., *Vita II*, cap. 150, in *Analecta Franciscana*, Vol. 10 (Quaracchi, 1904), p. 243.

ardent devotion to Our Lady is indicated by the fact that he made the beloved chapel of Our Lady of the Angels (which he had received from the Benedictines) the mother church of his order, and there obtained from Our Lord, through Mary's intercession, the unusual Portiuncula Indulgence.

St. Francis wrote a paraphrase, not only of the Our Father, but also of the Angelic Salutation, commencing with the words: *Ave Domina sancta, Regina sanctissima* ("Hail holy Lady, most holy Queen"). This beautiful and poetic prayer he recited daily before beginning the Divine Office, and he often exhorted his brethren to do the same. It is found in the breviary of the Friars Minor (Rome, 1951) before the *Ordinarium Divini Officii*. It is significant, too, that all four of the final antiphons in honor of the Blessed Virgin are found for the first time in the Franciscan breviary of 1249; and the *Regina coeli* appears here for the first time anywhere.

Following the example of their founder, the sons of St. Francis through the centuries have distinguished themselves as devoted clients of Our Lady, as champions of her great prerogatives, and as promoters of childlike devotion to her among the faithful. Some of those eminent in this regard, especially by their writings and sermons, have been: St. Anthony of Padua († 1231), whose authentic sermons contain a complete exposition of the Mariology of his times; St. Bonaventure († 1274), who by his decree of 1263 greatly promoted the custom of saying the *Angelus,* if he did not actually introduce it; Friar Conrad of Saxony († 1279), whose commentary on the Angelic Salutation was one of the popular books of the later Middle Ages; Ven. John Duns Scotus († 1308), the Subtle and Marian Doctor, who is justly regarded as the champion of the Immaculate Conception inasmuch as he satisfactorily answered the objections which were raised against this prerogative of Mary; St. Bernardine of Siena († 1444), the great Marian preacher, who, as Card. Dominic Ferrata has said, "has few equals in writing and singing the praises of Mary, and is excelled by none"; Friar Bernardin de Bustis († 1515), who was the author of a *Mariale,* which was held in high esteem until the eighteenth century, and also of the Little Office of the Immaculate Conception, which was formerly attributed to St. Alphonse Rodríguez, S.J.; St. Leonard of Port Maurice († 1751), who zealously promoted the devotion of the Three *Aves* and the proclamation of the dogma of the Immaculate Conception; and lastly, the modern Franciscan missionary bishop, the Most Rev. Ange-Marie Hiral, Vicar Apostolic of the Suez Canal, who labored indefatigably to bring about the institution of the new feast of Our Lady Queen of the Universe.[44]

Of Franciscan devotions to Our Lady, space will permit us to mention only one, the Franciscan Crown of Seven decades, which had its origin in the middle of the fifteenth century and was promoted by St. Bernardine of Siena. At first the 72 *Aves* of which it consists recalled the traditional 72 years of Our Lady's life on earth; subsequently its seven decades also commemorated the seven joys of Our Lady, a devotion which dates back to the beginning of the thirteenth century.[45] And of Franciscan Marian associations, we can allude only to a few: the Pious Union of the Militia of Mary Immaculate, founded 1917 in Rome mainly through the efforts of the Servant of God, Fr. Maximilian Kolbe, a Conventual Franciscan (and promoted in the United States by the Friars Minor Conventual);[46] the Great Marian Union of Masses of Ingolstadt, Bavaria, with over a million living members (and United States headquarters at St. Anthony Friary in St. Louis); and the Guard of Honor of the Immaculate Heart of Mary (with United States headquarters at St. Francis Church in New York City).

6. THE AUGUSTINIANS (O.S.A.)

Besides the Canons Regular of St. Augustine, who were established in the eleventh and twelfth centuries and earlier and now have 910 members, there are the Hermit Friars of St. Augustine (O.E.S.A. or O.S.A.), organized in 1256 and now having a membership of 3755; the Recollects of St. Augustine (O.R.S.A.), founded in 1588 and having 1009 members; the Discalced Hermit Friars of St. Augustine, a stricter branch begun in 1592-1599, which according to Heimbucher had 982 members in 1925; and the

---

[44] Cf. Jean de Dieu, O.F.M.Cap., *La Vierge et l'Ordre des Frères Mineurs Conventuels, Franciscains, Capucins,* in Maria, Vol. 2, pp. 785-831 (with copious bibliography); Anon., *De vita mariologico-mariana apud O.F.M.Cap.,* in *Ephemerides Mariologicae,* Vol. 6, 1956, pp. 478-480; C. Balić, O.F.M., *Il contributo dei Frati Minori al movimento mariologico moderno,* in *Marianum,* Vol. 11, 1949, pp. 440-460; L. Craddock, O.F.M., *The Blessed Virgin in the Writings of Franciscans,* in *Mary in the Franciscan Order* (St. Bonaventure, N. Y., 1955), pp. 117-127; L. Di Fonzo, O.F.M.Conv., *De vita mariologico-mariana apud religiosos O.F.M.Conv.,* in *Ephemerides Mariologicae,* Vol. 4, 1954, pp. 480-487; A. Emmen, O.F.M., *Die Bedeutung der Franziskanerschule für Mariologie,* in *Franziskanische Studien,* Vol. 36, 1954, pp. 385-419; R. Lawler, O.F.M.Cap., *Feasts of Mary in the Franciscan Order,* in *Mary in the Seraphic Order. Franciscan Educational Conference* [1954], Vol. 35 (Washington, D. C., 1956), pp. 323-347.

[45] Cf. L. Bracaloni, O.F.M., *Origine, evoluzione ed affermazione della Corona francescana mariana,* in *Studi Francescani,* Vol. 29, 1932, pp. 257-295.

[46] Cf. Chapter XIII on *Marian Associations* in this volume.

Assumptionist Augustinians, who have already been mentioned and have 1900 members — a total, therefore, of 8556 Augustinians. All of these, observing the Rule of St. Augustine and heirs of this great doctor's learning and spirit, have always manifested a great devotion to Our Lady and zealously fostered it among the faithful.

The writings of St. Augustine, although they do not discuss the Immaculate Conception, contain numerous references to Mary and expound Catholic doctrine concerning the Mother of God in a brilliant manner; and the spiritual children of St. Augustine in later centuries have contributed much to the development and better understanding of Mariology.

Worthy of special mention is the Congregation of St. Victor of the Canons Regular of St. Augustine, established in Paris about 1110. Deservedly renowned for their mystical writings on Mary, are the famous teachers of this congregation's theological school: Hugh of St. Victor († 1141), called the second Augustine; Achard of St. Victor († 1171); Richard of St. Victor († 1173); Gauthier of St. Victor († 1180); and Adam of St. Victor († 1192).

Among the Hermit Friars of St. Augustine, the two outstanding Mariologists were St. Thomas of Villanova († 1576) and Bartholomew de los Rios († 1652).

Devotion to Our Lady among the faithful has been promoted by the Augustinians especially in the form of devotion to Our Lady of Consolation (although the shrine of Our Lady of Consolation at Carey, Ohio, is in the care of the Friars Minor Conventual), and devotion to Our Lady of Good Counsel.[47]

7. THE JESUITS (S.J.)

The Society of Jesus may rightly be called also the Society of Mary. Not only the Jesuits themselves but others, too, have made that assertion, for instance, the Dominican Van Ketwigh in his *Panoplia Mariana*. And the glorious history of the Jesuits bears out that statement.

Founded by St. Ignatius of Loyola in 1540, the Society now has 30,958 members, the largest number of religious in the Church under one superior general.

Our Lady played an important part in the conversion of St. Ignatius.

---

[47] Cf. A. Sage, A.A., *La doctrine et le culte de Marie dans la famille Augustinienne*, in *Maria*, Vol. 2, pp. 677-712.

He began his conversion by lying prostrate one night before an image of the Blessed Virgin and consecrating himself irrevocably to the service of God under Mary's patronage. Another night soon afterward, his biographers tell us, he had a vision of the Mother of God, surrounded by a bright light and holding the Infant Jesus in her arms; and this vision filled his soul with such spiritual delight that ever after all sensual pleasures were insipid to him.

St. Ignatius then made a pilgrimage during which he visited three shrines of Our Lady: first to Aránzazu, where probably he took the vow of chastity; then to Navarra, where he restored an image of Our Lady; and then to Montserrat, near Barcelona, where he made a general confession of his past life to a saintly Benedictine priest. Later, when he founded the Society of Jesus in Rome, he wished to establish the first house at the shrine of Our Lady de la Strada. These are merely some instances indicating St. Ignatius' devotion to Our Lady, a devotion which he bequeathed to his spiritual sons.

One of the first companions of St. Ignatius, St. Francis Borgia, had a certain number of copies made of the ancient painting of Our Lady in St. Mary Major's Basilica in Rome, a picture which is attributed to St. Luke; and he gave these to the first missionaries of the Society to carry along to pagan lands. St. Francis Xavier always concluded his catechism instructions in the mission countries of the East with the prayer, *Salve Regina*. The Little Office of the Immaculate Conception, written by the Franciscan Friar Bernardin de Bustis, owes its widespread diffusion especially to the efforts of the two Jesuit saints, Alphonse Rodríguez and Peter Claver. The famous Jesuit theologian, Francisco Suárez, who received his extraordinary mental endowments in a miraculous manner through Mary's intercession, has been called the Father of Mariology, not as a separate study, but as a part of theology.

However, it is the Sodality of Our Lady above all, which in the hands of the Jesuits has served as an effective means of promoting genuine devotion to Our Lady among the faithful throughout the world. The Sodality has sought to imbue its members "not with a vaguely enthusiastic piety and asceticism, but a sober genuinely Catholic devotion and a joyous, zealous effectiveness for good in the sphere in which each member moves."[48]

---

[48] Cf. J. Hilgers, S.J., art. *Sodality,* in *The Catholic Encyclopedia,* Vol. 14, p. 128. See also Chapter XIV on *The Sodalities of Our Lady* in this volume.

Shortly before his death in 1942, the Jesuit superior general, Father Ledochowski obtained for the Jesuit Order the Holy See's permission to celebrate the feast of the Blessed Virgin Mary Queen of the Society of Jesus, as a double of the first class. Under that title the Jesuits had been invoking Our Lady for a long time past. The feast is observed on April 22, the anniversary of the solemn profession of St. Ignatius and his first companions.[49]

8. THE VINCENTIANS (C.M.)

The Vincentians or Lazarists, founded by St. Vincent de Paul in 1625, at the present day have 5200 members. The spiritual sons of St. Vincent are especially known as promoters of the devotion to Our Lady of the Miraculous Medal. After Mary Immaculate had appeared in 1830 to St. Catherine Labouré, a member of the Sisters of Charity, who were also founded by St. Vincent, M. Aladel, assistant of the Vincentians, had struck the "miraculous medal" of Mary conceived without sin; and within four years more than 4,000,000 of these medals were distributed throughout the world. In 1838 the Association in honor of the Holy and Immaculate Heart of Mary, whose members wear the miraculous medal as a badge, was founded at the church of Notre Dame-des-Victoires in Paris. In the same year it was raised to the rank of a confraternity. Pope Leo XIII, in 1894, granted the Vincentians the privilege of celebrating, on November 26, a special feast commemorating the manifestation of Mary Immaculate through the miraculous medal.[50]

9. THE REDEMPTORISTS (C.SS.R.)

St. Alphonse Maria Liguori, who is counted among the greatest clients of Mary, founded the Redemptorists in 1732. Today they have 8138 members. Of the writings of St. Alphonse, his work on *The Glories of Mary* is probably the best known. When St. Alphonse was appointed a bishop, he kept an image of Our Lady of Good Counsel in his rooms, which were the poorest in the episcopal residence. During his last illness, which lasted fourteen days, he prayed almost constantly, keeping his eyes fixed on the

---

[49] For further references on the Jesuits, cf. A. Drive, S.J., *Marie et la Compagnie de Jésus* (Paris, 1913); E. Villaret, S.J., *Marie et la Compagnie de Jésus*, in *Maria*, Vol. 2, pp. 937-973.

[50] Cf. E. Crapez, C.M., *La dévotion mariale chez Saint Vincent de Paul et les Lazaristes ou Prêtres de la Mission*, in *Maria*, Vol. 3, pp. 79-118.

crucifix and a picture of Our Lady. And during the night before his holy death, when an image of the Blessed Mother was carried to his bed, he immediately opened his eyes and, as he gazed upon the image, his whole countenance became radiant with delight.

Although the Redemptorists have always imitated their founder in his devotion to Our Lady, it was in the course of the past century that they became in a particular manner the apostles of devotion to Our Lady of Perpetual Help. In 1866 the ancient picture of Our Lady of Perpetual Help was solemnly enthroned on the high altar of the Church of St. Alphonse in Rome (in Via Merulana, not far from St. Mary Major); and the next year this picture was solemnly crowned. From that time on, the Redemptorists began to acknowledge and to venerate Our Lady of Perpetual Help as their own Patroness and to promote devotion to her all over the world. A special Confraternity of Our Lady of Perpetual Help and St. Alphonse was founded in 1871; and in 1876 it was raised to the rank of an archconfraternity. Pope Pius IX became its first member; and today it has about 2,700,000 members. A special feast of Our Lady of Perpetual Help was also instituted in 1876 for April 26. At Santiago, Chile, the Redemptorists began what is called the perpetual veneration of Our Lady of Perpetual Help, which means that a series of "choirs" spend ten continuous hours daily in devotions to Our Lady of Perpetual Help.[51]

10. THE SALESIANS (S.D.B.)

Little more than a century ago, 1841, the Salesians were founded by St. John Bosco; but today they are the largest congregation in the Church, having a membership of 17,356. Even among the orders, only the Jesuits and the Franciscans have a larger membership.

St. John Bosco is rightly called the apostle of devotion to Our Lady Help of Christians. It was not only a personal devotion of his, but he wished his followers also to cherish a special devotion to Our Lady under this title. The sisterhood which he founded is called the Daughters of Our Lady Help of Christians. In 1869 he founded an association of clients of Our Lady Auxiliatrix or Our Lady Help of Christians, which has been raised to the rank of an archconfraternity and now has some 25,000,000

---

[51] Cf. P. E. Vadeboncoeur, C.Ss.R., *Le Redemptoriste et la Vierge Marie*, in *Marie* [Nicolet], Vol. 3, No. 2, 1949, pp. 51-53; M. de Meulemeester, C.Ss.R., *La littérature mariale de la Congrégation des Redemptoristes*, in *Alma Socia Christi*, Vol. 11, 1953, pp. 171-181; P. Hitz, C.Ss.R., *La culte marial chez les Redemptoristes*, in *Maria*, Vol. 3, pp. 277-305.

members.[52]

III. MARIAN SISTERHOODS IN THE UNITED STATES

Religious orders and congregations of women, having papal approval, are about 300 in number, according to Father Roschini.[53] In *Annuario Pontifico 1959* there are 38 pages of fine print, listing the religious sisterhoods of the world which have received papal approval. Very many of these are Marian sisterhoods in the sense that the holy name of Mary, in some form or other, is contained in their official name. All of them are Marian sisterhoods in the sense that their members excel in devotion to Our Lady. This is true also of the sisterhoods which have only diocesan approval.

In this survey we can present only a list of the 123 sisterhoods in the United States, including both papal and diocesan communities, which are named for Our Lady. But even this list may perhaps be regarded as a contribution to Mariology, especially since the various sisterhoods are classified according to the several titles of Our Lady.

In the list that follows, the date following the name of the sisterhood indicates the year in which it was established in the United States. (U.S.) after the date means that the sisterhood had its origin in the United States. The place name which follows shows where the headquarters (provincial or general mother house, or independent convent) are located.[54]

I. Assumption of Our Lady:

1. Congregation of the Assumption, 1919, Germantown, Philadelphia, Pa.
2. Little Sisters of the Assumption, 1891, New York, N. Y.

---

[52] Cf. P. Brocardo, S.D.B., *Culte marial dans la famille salesienne,* in *Maria,* Vol. 3, pp. 449-463; R. Tiggiotti, S.D.B., *De vita mariologico-mariana apud Congregationem Salesianam,* in *Ephemerides Mariologicae,* Vol. 6, 1959, pp. 227-229.

[53] Roschini, *op. cit.,* p. 196.

[54] Cf. *The Catholic Directory* (New York, 1959), pp. 843-872. For further details concerning these sisterhoods, besides Heimbucher's two-volume work, consult E. Tong Dehey, Religious Orders of Women in the United States, Catholic, Accounts of their Origin, Works, and Most Important Institutions, Interwoven with Histories of Many Foundresses, rev. ed. (Cleveland, 1930), xxxi-980 pp.; Ch. W. Currier, *History of Religious Orders: A Compendious and Popular Sketch of the Rise and Progress of the Principal ... Orders and Congregations...* (New York, 1896), x-684 pp. On religious communities in the Anglican Church, cf. P. F. Anson, *The Call of the Cloister* (New York, 1955), 655 pp.

3. Sisters of the Assumption B.V.M., 1891, Nicolet, P. Q., Canada (with houses in the United States).

II. Heart of Mary:
4. California Institute of the Sisters of the Most Holy and Immaculate Heart of the Blessed Virgin Mary, Los Angeles, Calif.
5. Daughters of the Heart of Mary, 1851, New York, N. Y.
6. Dominican Sisters of the Congregation of the Immaculate Heart of Mary, 1929, Akron, Ohio.
7. Franciscan Handmaids of the Most Pure Heart of Mary (Colored), 1917 (U.S.), New York, N. Y.
8. Franciscan Sisters, Daughters of the Sacred Hearts of Jesus and Mary, 1872, Wheaton, Ill.
9. Religious of the Holy Union of the Sacred Hearts, 1886, Fall River and Groton, Mass.
10. Sisters, Daughters of the Immaculate Heart of Mary, 1878, Tucson, Ariz.
11. Sisters of St. Francis of the Immaculate Heart of Mary, 1913, Hankinson, N. Dak.
12. Sisters, Servants of the Immaculate Heart of Mary, 1882, Bay View, Saco, Me.
13. Sisters, Servants of the Holy Heart of Mary, 1889, Beaverville, Ill.
14. Sisters, Servants of the Immaculate Heart of Mary, 1845 (U.S.), Monroe, Mich.; West Chester, Pa.; Scranton, Pa.

III. Immaculate Conception:
15. Dominican Sisters of the Congregation of the Immaculate Conception (also called: Dominican Sisters of the Sick Poor), 1879, New York, N. Y.
16. Dominican Sisters of the Congregation of the Immaculate Conception, 1902, Great Bend, Kans.
17. Dominican Sisters of the Congregation of the Immaculate Conception, 1929, Justice, Oak Lawn, Ill.
18. Congregation of the Third Order of St. Francis of Mary Immaculate, 1865 (U.S.), Joliet, Ill.
19. Daughters of Mary of the Immaculate Conception, 1904 (U.S.), New Britain, Conn.
20. Franciscan Missionary Sisters of the Immaculate Conception, 1927,

San Fernando, Calif.
21. Franciscan Missionary Sisters of the Immaculate Conception of the Mother of God, 1922, Paterson, N. J.
22. Franciscan Sisters of the Immaculate Conception, 1891 (U.S.), Little Falls, Minn.
23. Franciscan Sisters of the Immaculate Conception, 1936, Buffalo, N. Y.
24. Franciscan Sisters of the Immaculate Conception of the Order of St. Francis, 1901 (U.S.), Rock Island, Ill.
25. Franciscan Sisters of Mary Immaculate of the Third Order of St. Francis in Pasto, 1932, Amarillo, Texas.
26. Franciscan Sisters of the Immaculate Conception and St. Joseph for the Dying, 1919 (U.S.), Monterey, Calif.
27. Little Servant Sisters of the Immaculate Conception, 1926, Woodbridge, N. J.
28. Minim Sisters of Mary Immaculate, 1926, León, Guanajuato, Mexico (with houses in the United States).
29. Missionary Franciscan Sisters of the Immaculate Conception, 1873 (U.S.), Newton, Mass.
30. Missionary Sisters of the Immaculate Conception, 1946, Marlboro, Mass.
31. Parish Visitors of Mary Immaculate, 1920 (U.S.), Monroe, N. Y.
32. Sisters of the Immaculate Conception, 1874, (U.S.), New Orleans, La.
33. Sisters of the Immaculate Conception of the Blessed Virgin Mary (Lithuanian), 1936, Putnam, Conn.
34. Sisters of St. Francis of the Immaculate Conception, 1891 (U.S.), Peoria, Ill.
35. Sisters of St. Francis of the Mission of the Immaculate Virgin, Conventuals of the Third Order, 1892 (U.S.), Hastings-on-Hudson, N. Y.
36. Sisters, Servants of Mary Immaculate, 1935, Toronto, Ont., Canada (with houses in the United States).
37. Sister-Servants of the Holy Ghost and Mary Immaculate, 1888 (U.S.), San Antonio, Tex.
38. Sisters of the Third Order of St. Francis of the Immaculate Virgin Mary, Mother of God, 1868 (U.S.), Millvale, Pittsburgh, Pa.
39. Sisters of the Third Order of St. Francis of the Immaculate

MARIAN ORDERS AND CONGREGATIONS

Conception of the Blessed Virgin Mary, 1868 (U.S.), Clinton, Iowa.

IV. Mary:
40. Company of Mary, 1926, Douglas, Ariz.
41. Congregation of the Sisters Marianites of Holy Cross, 1843, New Orleans, La.; Princeton, N. J.
42. Cordi-Marian Missionary Sisters, 1926, San Antonio, Tex.
43. Daughters of Mary, Health of the Sick, 1935 (U.S.), Vista Maria, Cragsmoor, N. Y.
44. Daughters of Mary, Help of Christians (also called: Salesian Sisters of St. John Bosco), 1908, Paterson, N. J.
45. Daughters of Mary and Joseph (also called: Dames de Marie), 1926, Los Angeles, Calif.
46. Daughters of St. Mary of Providence, 1913, Chicago, Ill.
47. Dominican Sisters of the Congregation of St. Mary, 1860, New Orleans, La.
48. Dominican Sisters of the Congregation of St. Mary of the Springs, 1830, Columbus, Ohio.
49. Franciscan Missionaries of Mary, 1903, New York, N. Y.
50. Little Company of Mary Nursing Sisters, 1893, Evergreen Park, Ill.
51. Little Franciscan Sisters of Mary, 1889 (U.S.), Baie St. Paul, P.Q., Canada (with houses in the United States).
52. Mantellate Sisters, Servants of Mary, 1916, Blue Island, Ill.
53. Marist Missionary Sisters (also called: Missionary Sisters of the Society of Mary), 1922, Framingham Centre, Mass.
54. Medical Missionaries of Mary, 1950, Winchester, Mass.
55. Religious of Jesus-Mary, 1877, Highland Mills, N. Y.; El Paso, Tex.
56. Servants of Mary, 1893, Omaha, Nebr.; Ladysmith, Wis.
57. Servants of Mary (also called: Servite Sisters), Portland, Ore.
58. Sisters of Charity of the Blessed Virgin Mary, 1833 (U.S.), Dubuque, Iowa.
59. Sisters of the Holy Names of Jesus and Mary, 1859, Marylhurst, Oregon; Los Gatos, Calif.; Albany, N. Y.
60. Sisters of Mary of the Catholic Apostolate, 1949, Corpus Christi, Tex.
61. Sisters of Providence of St. Mary-of-the-Woods, 1840, St. Mary of the Woods, Ind.
62. Sisters of Reparation of the Congregation of Mary, 1890 (U.S.),

New York, N. Y.
63. Sisters of St. Mary, 1886 (U.S.), Beaverton, Ore.
64. Sisters of St. Mary of Namur, 1863, Kenmore, N. Y.; Fort Worth, Tex.
65. Sisters of St. Mary of the Third Order of St. Francis, 1872 (U.S.), St. Louis, Mo.
66. Sisters Servants of Mary (Trained Nurses), 1914, Kansas City, Kans.
67. Sisters of the Holy Humility of Mary, 1864, Villa Maria, Pa.; Ottumwa, Iowa.
68. Sisters of the Purity of Mary, 1916, Aguascalientes, Mexico (with houses in the United States).
69. Society of Mary Reparatrix, 1908, Cincinnati, Ohio.
70. Society of the Sisters of St. Ursula of the Blessed Virgin, 1902, Kingston, N. Y.

V. Mother of God:
71. Sisters of Mary Mother of God, 1952 (U.S.), Long Beach, Calif.
72. Sisters Poor Servants of the Mother of God, 1947, Norton, Va.; High Point, N. C.

VI. Notre Dame:
73. School Sisters de Notre Dame, 1910, Omaha, Neb.
74. School Sisters of Notre Dame, 1847, Milwaukee, Wis.; Baltimore, Md.; St. Louis, Mo.; Mankato, Minn.
75. Sisters of the Congregation de Notre Dame, 1860, Grymes Hill, S. I., N. Y.
76. Sisters of Notre Dame, 1874, Cleveland, Ohio; Covington, Ky.; Toledo, Ohio.
77. Sisters of Notre Dame de Namur, 1840, Waltham, Mass.; Ilchester, Md.; Reading, Pa.; Cincinnati, Ohio; Saratoga, Calif.
78. Congregation of Notre Dame de Sion, 1912, Kansas City, Mo.

VII. Our Lady of Africa:
79. Missionary Sisters of Our Lady of Africa (also called: White Sisters), 1929, Belleville, Ill.

MARIAN ORDERS AND CONGREGATIONS

VIII. Our Lady of the Angels:
  80. Franciscan Sisters of Our Lady of the Holy Angels, 1923, St. Paul, Minn.

IX. Our Lady of Charity:
  81. Sisters of Our Lady of Charity of the Good Shepherd, 1843, 7 Provinces in the U.S.
  82. Sisters of Our Lady of Charity of Refuge, 1855, 12 independent convents in the United States.

X. Our Lady of Christian Doctrine:
  83. Sisters of Our Lady of Christian Doctrine, 1910 (U.S.), Nyack, N. Y.

XI. Our Lady of Guadalupe:
  84. Sisters of Perpetual Adoration of the Blessed Sacrament of Guadalupe, 1925, Mexico City, Mexico (with houses in the United States).

XII. Our Lady of Loretto:
  85. Institute of the Blessed Virgin Mary (also called: Ladies of Loretto), 1892, Toronto, Canada (with houses in the United States).
  86. Sisters of Loretto at the Foot of the Cross (also called: Loretto Literary and Benevolent Institution), 1812 (U.S.), Loretto, Nerinx, Ky.; Webster Groves, Mo.; Kansas City, Mo.; Denver, Colo.

XIII. Our Lady of Lourdes:
  87. Sisters of St. Francis of the Congregation of Our Lady of Lourdes, 1916 (U.S.), Sylvania, Ohio.
  88. Sisters of the Third Order Regular of St. Francis of the Congregation of Our Lady of Lourdes, 1877 (U.S.), Rochester, Minn.

XIV. Our Lady of Mercy:
  89. Daughters of Our Lady of Mercy, 1919, Newfield, N. J.
  90. Missionaries of Our Lady of Mercy, 1946, Kansas City, Mo.
  91. Sisters of Charity of Our Lady of Mercy, 1829 (U.S.), Charleston, S. C.

224 MARIOLOGY

    92. Sisters of Charity of Our Lady, Mother of Mercy, 1874, Baltic, Conn.

XV. Our Lady of Mt. Carmel:
    93. Carmelite Sisters of the Aged and Infirm, 1929 (U.S.), Germantown, N. Y.
    94. Carmelite Sisters of the Divine Heart of Jesus, 1912, Wauwatosa, Wis.
    95. Carmelite Sisters of the Third Order, Alhambra, Calif.
    96. Carmelite Sisters of St. Therese of the Infant Jesus, 1917 (U.S.), Oklahoma City, Okla.
    97. Congregation of Our Lady of Mount Carmel, 1833, New Orleans, La.
    98. Corpus Christi Carmelite Sisters, Middletown, N. Y.
    99. Discalced Carmelite Nuns (also called: Second Order of Carmel), 1790, 45 convents in the U.S.
    100. Institute of the Sisters of Our Lady of Mt. Carmel, 1947, Hamilton, Mass.

XVI. Our Lady of Perpetual Help:
    101. Franciscan Sisters of Our Lady of Perpetual Help, 1901 (U.S.), Ferguson, Mo.

XVII. Our Lady of the Cenacle:
    102. Congregation of Our Lady of the Retreat in the Cenacle, 1892, New York, N. Y.; Milwaukee, Wis.

XVIII. Our Lady of the Rosary:
    103. Congregation of Our Lady of the Rosary, 1899, Rimouski, Canada (with houses in the United States).
    104. Dominican Sisters of the Congregation of the Most Holy Rosary, 1849, Sinsinawa, Wis.
    105. Dominican Sisters of the Congregation of the Most Holy Rosary, 1859, Newburgh, N. Y.
    106. Dominican Sisters of the Congregation of the Most Holy Rosary, 1877, Adrian, Mich.
    107. Dominican Sisters of the Congregation of Our Lady of the Rosary, 1876, Sparkill, N. Y.

MARIAN ORDERS AND CONGREGATIONS

108. Dominican Sisters of the Congregation of the Queen of the Rosary, 1876, Mission San José, Calif.

XIX. Our Lady of the Sacred Heart:
109. Dominican Sisters of the Congregation of Our Lady of the Sacred Heart, 1873, Springfield, Ill.
110. 110. Dominican Sisters of the Congregation of Our Lady of the Sacred Heart, 1877, Grand Rapids, Mich.

XX. Our Lady of Sorrows:
111. Franciscan Missionary Sisters of Our Lady of Sorrows, 1949 (U.S.), Beaverton, Ore.
112. Poor Sisters of Jesus Crucified and the Sorrowful Mother, 1924 (U.S.), Brockton, Mass.
113. Sisters of the Holy Cross and of the Seven Dolors, 1881, Manchester, N. H.
114. Sisters of the Sorrowful Mother of the Third Order of St. Francis, 1889, Milwaukee, Wis.

XXI. Our Lady, Queen of the Clergy:
115. Congregation of Antonian Sisters of Mary, Queen of the Clergy, 1932, Chicoutimi, Canada (with houses in the United States).
116. Servants of Our Lady, Queen of the Clergy, 1936, Lac-au-Saumon, Canada (with houses in the United States).

XXII. Our Lady of Victory:
117. Our Lady of Victory Missionary Sisters, 1918 (U.S.), Huntington, Ind.

XXIII. Presentation of Our Lady:
118. Dominican Sisters of Charity of the Presentation of the Blessed Virgin Mary, 1906, Fall River, Mass.
119. Sisters of the Presentation of the Blessed Virgin Mary, 1854, 10 mother houses in the U.S.
120. Sisters of the Presentation of Mary, 1873, Hudson, N. H.: Biddeford Pool, Me.
121. Sisters of St. Mary of the Presentation, 1903, Spring Valley,

Ill.; Valley City, N. Dak.

XXIV. Visitation of Our Lady:
- 122. Sisters of the Visitation of the Congregation of the Immaculate Heart of Mary, Dubuque, Iowa.
- 123. Visitation Nuns, 1799, 19 independent convents in the United States.

MARIAN CONFRATERNITIES

by CHARLES J. CORCORAN, C.S.C.

CONFRATERNITY is a voluntary association of the faithful, established and guided by competent ecclesiastical authority, for the furtherance of public worship through the promotion and exercise of special works of Christian charity or piety. It is distinct from the sodality and the pious union. Unlike the sodality, its essential function is works of devotion; nor does it demand its members to fulfill the obligations normally imposed upon sodality members. It differs from the pious union in so far as it is always canonically erected and stresses the personal sanctification of its members rather than the good of the neighbor. A confraternity which has received the authority to aggregate to itself other associations and to communicate its advantages to them is called an archconfraternity.[1]

The confraternity appears to have been the peculiar prerogative of the cult of the Blessed Virgin. Whenever and wherever the faithful have united to promote the Christian life, they have invariably tended to form a Marian confraternity. And among these associations is found such stimulating diversity that we cannot but recognize that each has its own genuine contribution to make to Marian devotion. It is not sheer coincidence that confraternities first appeared in the East, for devotion to Mary began and developed in the Orient far earlier than in the West. The great Marian feast days were adopted by the Latin liturgy from the Greek-speaking part of the Empire where they had already been celebrated for several centuries. The first recorded apparition of Mary occurred in the East when she appeared to St. Gregory of Nazianzen. The first literary documents of Marian devotion issued from the Fathers of the Greek Church. Images of Mary were originally venerated in the Orient, and the first Marian shrines were to be found in Caesarea, Edessa, Lydda, and on

---

[1] Cf. *Codex Juris Canonici*, Can. 707; W. H. W. Fanning, art. *Confraternity*, in *The Catholic Encyclopedia*, Vol. 4 (New York, 1908), p. 223; L. Di Fonzo, O.F.M.Conv., *Associazioni, organizzazioni, opere mariane*, in *Enciclopedia Mariana*, ed. R. Spiazzi (Milano, 1954), pp. 615-628.

Mount Athos.[2]

We have meager information about the Oriental prototype of the Marian confraternity. We do know that confraternities existed in very ancient times at Constantinople and Alexandria, and among these were several expressing some Marian virtue or trait. We are told that members of such associations invoked the aid of Mary in some private and public difficulty. Possibly the Oriental version of the confraternity does not antedate the fourth century, for it is recorded in the sixth century that the Abbot Leontius, a famed theologian of the era, belonged to a confraternity in Jerusalem founded by the Patriarch St. Elias in A.D. 494.[3] No consequent history of a Marian confraternity is recorded until nearly nine hundred years later.

The later centuries of the Middle Ages, characteristically described as the "Age of Mary," provided fertile soil for the re-flowering of the confraternity. It might not be far amiss to suggest that the Marian confraternity of the Middle Ages epitomized the extent and variety of the spiritual life of the faithful, that interior life which provided the inspiration and aspiration for the still unrivaled creations of medieval art. H. Durand asserts that the first Marian confraternity in the West of which there is record was founded in Greece sometime prior to the thirteenth century. But since its devotions were more of a private or domestic nature — an icon was carried from house to house and private devotions were held before it — it could hardly qualify as a confraternity in the technical sense.[4] The first such confraternity is thought to have been the association founded at Paris by Bishop Odo around 1208. Among its members were men and women of the highest social rank. We have records of at least seven others established before the end of the century. From this time on, Marian confraternities rapidly multiplied throughout Europe. A few of these primitive associations are still extant and thriving today, but most of the current confraternities are of later origin. In the following paragraphs, brief notices will be given of only the larger and better known among the confraternities.

---

[2] W. Juhasz, *Mother of the Church of Silence*, in Th. J. M. Burke, S.J. (Ed.), *Mary and Modern Man* (New York, 1954), p. 221.

[3] Joannes Moschus, *Pratum spirituale*, in *PG* 87, 2913; G. M. Roschini, O.S.M., *La Madonna secondo la fede e la teologia*, Vol. 4 (Roma, 1954), p. 465.

[4] Cf. H. Durand, art. *Confrérie*, in *Dictionnaire de Droit Canonique*, fasc. 19, col. 140.

1. ARCHCONFRATERAITY OF THE ROSARY

This confraternity is one of the more popular and prevalent of all the Marian associations. Though figures are not available, it probably enjoys the largest membership of all by far. The reason is quite obvious. For centuries the rosary has been proclaimed, and has been in fact, the most common and popular form of devotion to Our Lady; little wonder, then, that the faithful should so readily enroll in an association which, while it commits them to the recitation of the rosary, also assures them substantial additional benefits.[5] These include, besides the special protection of Our Lady of the Rosary, affiliation with the Dominican Order and a share in the merits of all its members throughout the world. Obligations incumbent upon members of the confraternity are: recitation of the fifteen decades of the rosary within each week, on beads blessed for Dominican indulgences, and reflection on the mystery of each decade. The fifteen decades may be recited all at once or at separate times or in part, provided only the total obligation is discharged within the week. Failure to recite the rosary entails no sin but the omission entails the loss of membership benefits. An indispensable condition for affiliation is the inscription of one's name on the register of the Dominican Church or house where the confraternity has been canonically erected.

We have no clear-cut evidence of the existence of the Rosary Confraternity prior to the latter part of the fifteenth century. Certainly there were some Dominican guilds and associations before that time, but the available data does not warrant their identification with the Rosary Confraternity. In 1470 Blessed Alan de Rupe founded at Douai (France) the first rosary association, and four years later a successful confraternity was launched in Cologne by the Dominican James Sprenger.[6] Through the efforts and zeal of the Dominican Fathers membership in the new association quickly increased, and new affiliates multiplied rapidly throughout the universe.[7] Organization of these confraternities has always remained the exclusive prerogative of the Dominicans, and no new association anywhere may be founded without the consent of the Dominican General. On October 2, 1898, Pope Leo XIII issued the

---

[5] Cf. M. Llamera, O.P., *Efficacia attuale della confraternità del santissimo Rosario*, in *Alma Socia Christi*, Vol. 9 (Romae, 1953), pp. 204-223.

[6] Cf. J. G. Shaw, *The Story of the Rosary* (Milwaukee, Wis., 1954), pp. 80-92, 163-164.

[7] H. Thurston, S.J., art. *Confraternity of the Holy Rosary*, in *The Catholic Encyclopedia*, Vol. 13 (New York, 1912), p. 188.

Apostolic Constitution *Ubi primum* which proved equivalent to a new charter for the Rosary Archconfraternity insofar as it specified its rights, privileges, and indulgences. The confraternity is the largest organization of its kind within the Church and today may be found erected in virtually every parish.

2. The Confraternity of Our Lady of Mount Carmel

Ever since the coming of the Carmelite Friars to Europe about 1280 certain benefactors were granted a participation in the prayers and good works of the Order and admitted to certain suffrages after death. These were known as *Confratres*. From this practice there developed in the sixteenth century, according to all probability, the Confraternity of Our Lady of Mount Carmel, or, as it is more popularly known, the Confraternity of the Scapular.[8] From the date of its formal establishment the growth of the association bordered on the miraculous. At the outset of the seventeenth century it existed in over a thousand Carmelite houses, and numbered among its members practically every pope, bishop, and prince of the era. The confraternity has continued to prosper in contemporary times and enjoys the reputation of being one of the oldest as well as one of the more prominently known devotions to Mary.

Affiliation with the confraternity is automatic upon enrollment in the Brown Scapular; in other words, the association comprises all those who have been so enrolled. Sole condition for membership is the wearing of the scapular of Our Lady of Mount Carmel. Members, if they wish, may gain the Sabbatine Privilege which is associated with, but independent of, the confraternity. This requires the observance of two simple conditions: recitation of the Little Office and the observance of chastity according to one's state of life. Since virtually every other Catholic is enrolled in the scapular, current membership in the confraternity is roughly estimated to be in excess of 200,000,000 persons.

3. Confraternity of Our Lady of Perpetual Help

No Marian cult boasts the colorful and tumultuous history associated with the founding of this confraternity. Since the fifteenth century the devotions of the confraternity have been related to the veneration of the

---

[8] B. Zimmerman, O.C.D., art. *Carmelite*, in *The Catholic Encyclopedia*, Vol. 3 (New York, 1908), p. 369.

image of Our Lady of Perpetual Help now actually in the Church of St. Alphonsus in Rome. Originally venerated in Crete (this oriental origin explains its icon form), the image was stolen by a merchant of the island and placed in the Church of St. Matthew in Rome on March 27, 1449. In the Revolution of 1798 the Church was plundered and the image removed from public cult and secreted. Sixty-five years later, through a series of providential circumstances, it was located in an oratory at Santa Maria in Posterula. Meanwhile, the Redemptorists had erected a house on the ruins of old St. Matthew's dedicated to their holy Founder. On December 11, 1865, Pope Pius IX ordered the picture transferred to this Redemptorist house, thus returning the image to the site which the Blessed Mother herself was said to have chosen for its veneration by the faithful. From that time on, the Redemptorists have assumed the propagation of the devotion to Our Lady of Perpetual Help.[9]

Restoration of the image to the Church of St. Alphonsus precipitated fresh devotion to Mary through the image. At the request of Father Mauron, Superior General of the Redemptorists, Pius IX granted permission for the canonical erection of the confraternity in Rome.[10] This was effected on the feast of the Holy Trinity, June 4, 1871. So popular did the devotion become, and so rapid the growth of similar associations, that on March 31, 1876, Pope Pius IX raised it to the dignity of an archconfraternity and himself enrolled as its first member.[11]

The archconfraternity proposes to honor Mary as Our Lady of Perpetual Help, and to have particular recourse to her in spiritual and temporal necessities. Members must be enrolled in the confraternity catalogue of a Church where the association has been canonically erected; practically every Redemptorist Church enjoys this right. The Act of Consecration to Our Lady of Perpetual Help with renewals on stipulated occasions is required of all members. In return, members share in the public works and devotions of the confraternity and of the Congregation, and enjoy the advantages of many plenary and partial indulgences. World-wide in scope, the confraternity numbers units throughout Europe

---

[9] Cf. *Manual of the Archconfraternity of Our Lady of Perpetual Help* (New York, 1926), pp. 16-28.

[10] The first nucleus of this confraternity had already been formed three years earlier in Limerick, Ireland. Cf. C. M. Henze, C.Ss.R., *Mater de Perpetuo Succursu* (Bonnae, 1926), p. 83.

[11] Cf. *Manual of the Archconfraternity ...* , pp. 6-9.

and the Americas. Each year new associations have been aggregated to the archconfraternity so that the latest estimate (May, 1948) recorded 2713 confraternities, numbering 2,700,600 members dispersed throughout the world.

4. Confraternity of Our Lady Help of Christians

This association is the third living monument founded by St. John Bosco to the honor and glory of Mary. The erection of the confraternity in the Sanctuary of Baldocco in Turin on April 18, 1869, was the Saint's reply to the insistent plea of the faithful who desired to unite in a mutual spirit of prayer and devotion to Mary under the title *Help of Christians*. Canonical erection of the confraternity occasioned world-wide requests for membership.[12]

Devotion to Mary under the aegis *Help of Christians* is very ancient and replete with historical significance. The appellation is anterior to the pontificate of Pius V, and in origin it antidates that of the Litany of Loretto.[13] Even the new confraternity was not the first to honor Mary under that title but was, in part, a revival of the original association founded in Bavaria in 1684 in thanksgiving to Mary for the signal graces with which she favored the Christian warriors in the delivery of Vienna from the siege of the Turks in 1683.

Revival of the confraternity culminated Don Bosco's ambition, inspired by a prophetic dream, to devote himself with Mary's help to mission work, most especially among boys. A papal brief of March 16, 1869, established the association; on April 5, 1870, Pope Pius IX favored it with the status of an archconfraternity. Later, Pope Leo XIII granted it two other privileged concessions.[14] Membership is effected through registry with a Salesian institution where the confraternity has been canonically erected. The sole obligation binding upon members, though not under pain of sin, is the observance of seven simple rules. More than one hundred branches with a total membership of 25,000,000 persons are currently affiliated with the archconfraternity.[15]

---

[12] P. Ricaldone, S.B.D., *Our Devotion to Mary Help of Christians* [Turin, 1948], in *Acts of the Superior Chapter of the Salesian Society*, year 27, No. 149 (London, 1948), pp. 36-39.

[13] Cf. Roschini, *Mariologia*, Vol. 2, part 3 (Romae, 1948), pp. 207-208.

[14] Cf. P. Brocardo, S.B.D., *San Giovanni Bosco, apostolo del titolo "Auxilium Christianorum,"* in *L'Ausiliatrice nel domma e nel culto* (Torino, 1950), p. 87.

[15] Cf. *Help of Christians Novena* brochure (Boston, Mass., 1951), pp. 2-3, 16-18.

5. Confraternity of Mary Queen of All Hearts

This confraternity was founded by Father Lavallée in Ottawa, Canada, on March 25, 1899, and approved by Leo XIII on June 22 of the same year.[16] Numerous branches took root from the Ottawa foundation and soon spread through all North America. In the United States the first canonical erection of this confraternity took place on December 8, 1928 in the Church of St. Francis of Assisi, New York City, through the efforts of Brother Cajetan Baumann, O.F.M. In 1906 it was established in Rome, and seven years later it was raised to the dignity of an archconfraternity by Pope St. Pius X. A clerical branch of the confraternity was founded in 1906. Both lay and clerical groups are administered by the Company of Mary (the Montfort Fathers) founded by St. Louis M. Grignion de Montfort.[17]

The purpose of the confraternity is to establish within men the reign of Mary as a means of facilitating the reign of Jesus in souls — the holy slavery of Jesus through Mary which St. Louis de Montfort formulated into a definite method of the spiritual life. Obligatory conditions for membership are enrollment in the official register of the association, recital of the Act of Consecration, and some accompanying good works. Currently, the confraternity numbers 89 branches throughout the world. No membership figures of the worldwide association are available, but the Ottawa branch exceeds 100,000 members while the Bay Shore unit in the United States approximates 40,000 persons.[18]

6. Confraternity of the Seven Sorrows of Our Lady

The founding of this confraternity anticipated the establishment of the religious order which was to direct its destiny. In the early years of the thirteenth century seven youths from as many prominent patrician families formed a community of laymen known as *Laudesi*, or *Praisers of Mary*. While engaged in the exercises of the association on the feast of the Assumption (1233), the Blessed Virgin appeared to them and recommended the foundation of a religious order. On April 15, 1240,

---

[16] Cf. H. Richard, C.M. [= Compagnie de Marie = S.M.M.], *La confrérie de Marie Reine des Coeurs*, in *Compte rendu du Congrès Marial tenu à Fribourg, 1902*, Vol. 1 (Blois, 1903), pp. 598-604.

[17] Cf. E. Campana, *Maria nel culto cattolico*, Vol. 2 (Torino-Roma, 1933), pp. 276-278.

[18] St. Louis M. Grignion De Montfort, *The Secret of Mary* (Bay Shore, N. Y., 1950), pp. 85-89.

following another apparition of the Blessed Virgin, the Order of the Servants of Mary was established. Thus, from humble beginnings as an association of pious laymen, was born one of the most remarkable and zealous Orders in the Church.[19]

The history of the confraternity was either terminated or obscured with the founding of the Order, for it does not appear again until 1645. The immediate predecessor of the confraternity appears to have been the Third Order, or the Association of the Habit, as it was known prior to 1645. Somewhat earlier than this, about the turn of the sixteenth century, several associations dedicated to Our Lady of Sorrow had been established in the city of Bruges through the efforts of John Van Coudenberghe. Eventually, certain of these groupings were aggregated to the Servite Order which has since propagated the devotion of the Seven Sorrows of Our Lady. Branches of the Confraternity exist throughout the world.[20]

7. Confraternity of the Immaculate Heart of Mary

The first canonically erected confraternity to the Immaculate Heart of Mary was founded in Naples in 1640 by Father Vincent Guinigi, Cler. Reg. Much better known, however, are those associations dedicated to the Heart of Mary founded by St. John Eudes beginning in 1648. Most famous of these foundations is that of Morlaix, established in 1666. In 1806 the Archconfraternity of the Sacred Heart was founded in the parish church of St. Eustace in Rome and approved two years later. Perhaps the most patronized confraternity dedicated to the Immaculate Heart of Mary is that founded in Paris in 1836 by Father Degennetes. This association enjoyed the status of an archconfraternity and was especially devoted to Mary as the patroness for the conversion of sinners. The over-all purpose of the Immaculate Heart confraternities is the more perfect living of the Christian life and the adoption of the spirit of the Immaculate Heart of Mary as a preparation for union with Jesus. Current membership is in

---

[19] P. J. Griffin, O.S.M., art. *Servites*, in *The Catholic Encyclopedia*, Vol. 13 (New York, 1912), pp. 736-737.

[20] Cf. Aug.-M. Lépicier, O.S.M., *Mater Dolorosa; notes d'histoire, de liturgie et d'iconographie sur le culte de Notre-Dame des Douleurs* (Spa, 1948), pp. 48-52, 236-239; P. Soulier, O.S.M., *La confrérie de N.-D. des Sept Douleurs dans les Flandres* (Bruxelles, 1913), p. 66, where a description is given of the now rare work by John Van Coudenberghe, *Ortus, progressus et impedimenta fraternitatis B. V. Mariae de Passione, quae dicitur de Septem Doloribus* (Antverpiae, 1519). Cf. also J. A. F. Kronenburg, C.Ss.R., *Maria's heerlijkheid in Nederland*, Vol. 2 (Amsterdam, 1904), p. 259 ff.

excess of 50,000,000 persons.[21]

8. THE CONFRATERNITY OF THE THREE HAIL MARYS

In the year 1261 Our Lady appeared to St. Mechtilde and assured her that the daily recitation of three Hail Marys in thanksgiving to each of the Three Divine Persons of the Holy Trinity would obtain for her the Blessed Virgin's assistance in the hour of death. The Saint immediately propagated the devotion which soon gained great renown. Much of the subsequent history of the association has been lost, and it appears to have gone into temporary eclipse. Within comparatively recent years it was revived in France by Father John Baptist of Blois, O.F.M.Cap. From this time on, it began to prosper again and was elevated to the rank of an archconfraternity in 1921 by Pope Benedict XV.[22] Members of the group are obligated to recite daily the three Hail Marys with the ejaculation: "My Mother, deliver me this day from mortal sin." The association is credited with the conversion of innumerable sinners.[23]

9. THE CONFRATERNITY OF THE BLUE SCAPULAR

Origins of this association are traceable to a vision of the Blessed Virgin granted to Venerable Ursula Benincasa on the feast of the Purification in 1617. The Blessed Virgin bade the nun to found a hermitage in which consecrated women would lead solitary and penitential lives. Eager for the sanctification of all men, the holy woman begged the Blessed Virgin for a similar devotion for the laity. Mary consented, stipulating that the laity wear a small blue habit and faithfully discharge the duties proper to their state of life. The Scapular, as it came to be known, was received with incredible favor, and eventually led to the founding of the confraternity. The association was established in 1894 in the Theatine Church of St. Andrea della Valle in Rome and was raised to the dignity of a confraternity within a year. Admission to the confraternity requires investiture with the Blue Scapular and inscription in the register of the Association. Those who received the Scapular prior to September 18, 1894, are not obliged to enroll in the confraternity. The

---

[21] H. Pujolrás, C.M.F., *Sodalitates Cordi B. Virginis Mariae dicatae*, in *Commentarium pro Religiosis et Missionariis*, Vol. 24, 1943, pp. 75-79; Roschini, *La Madonna secondo la fede e la teologia*, Vol. 4, pp. 466-467.

[22] *A.A.S.*, Vol. 14, 1922, p. 419. Cf. Roschini, *op. cit.*, pp. 472-473.

[23] Cf. Roschini, *Mariologia*, Vol. 2, part 3 (Romae, 1948), pp. 208-209.

association is administered and propagated by the Theatine Fathers.[24]

10. THE CONFRATERNITY OF THE IMMACULATE CONCEPTION

This Marian association stems from the eighteen apparitions of the Blessed Mother to St. Bernadette Soubirous at Lourdes, in Southern France, in 1858. The confraternity was established shortly after the apparitions. The American unit of the association was founded at Notre Dame, Indiana, December 8, 1874, as part of the University's total consecration of its life and activity to the glory of Mary. This foundation is now affiliated with the archconfraternity since established at Lourdes. Membership in the association is free and every name inscribed on its register is in perpetuity. Members are obligated to a few simple devotions which do not bind under pain of sin. The society enjoys many plenary and partial indulgences.[25]

11. THE CONFRATERNITY OF OUR LADY OF THE BLESSED SACRAMENT

Early in January of the year 1851 Blessed Pierre Eymard, a Marist priest renowned for his devotion to the Blessed Sacrament, made a pilgrimage to the shrine of Our Lady of Fourvière in France. Shortly after, the Blessed Virgin appeared to him and proposed the establishment of the Congregation of the Blessed Sacrament. In Paris, on January 6, 1857, the new congregation was duly approved and constituted, and became the champion of the devotion to Our Lady of the Blessed Sacrament.[26] The confraternity itself was established in Lyons, France, in 1870, and was disseminated throughout Europe and the Americas where it has been held in high repute.[27] It should be noted that the confraternity aroused much theological speculation and contention as to the nature of Mary's

---

[24] Cf. Campana, *op. cit.*, Vol. 2, pp. 428-431.

[25] Cf. *The Confraternity of The Immaculate Conception* (Notre Dame, Ind., 1950); a 4-page leaflet without pagination. Further information may be obtained by addressing the Director, Confraternity of the Immaculate Conception, Notre Dame, Ind.

[26] Actually, the first to use and promote the title of *Our Lady of the Blessed Sacrament* was Father Michael of Cosenza, O.F.M.Cap., in his work *Tractatus de gloriosa Virgine Deigenitrice Sanctissimi Sacramenti nuncupata*, written between 1638 and 1678, but never published. The manuscript is preserved in the Municipal Library of Assisi. Its contents are described at length by J. Knox in his book *De necessitudine Deiparam inter et Eucharistiam* (Romae, 1949), pp. 221-254.

[27] Cf. H. Evers, S.S.S., *La diffusion de la dévotion à Notre-Dame du Très Saint Sacrement*, in the symposium *Marie et l'Eucharistie* (Montreal, 1954), pp. 225-228.

relationship with the Eucharistic Christ.[28]

12. THE CONFRATERNITY OF THE GUARD OF HONOR

Chronologically, the latest Marian association to be raised to the rank of an archconfraternity is the one popularly known as *The Guard of Honor of The Immaculate Heart of Mary*. It was founded by the zealous German Franciscan, Father Bonaventure Blattmann († 1942), at St. Anne's monastery in Munich, and canonically established by an Apostolic Brief of Pius XI in 1932. By 1951 *The Guard* had attained to such prominence in the field of Marian apostolate that Pius XII elevated it to the dignity of an archconfraternity on December 17 of that year.

The aim of *The Guard* members is to give a practical answer to the message of Fatima: to pray, to do penance, to promote devotion to Our Lady and consecration to her Immaculate Heart, and to accept willingly the trials that God sends them for the conversion of sinners. The guards are also exhorted to engage in catechetical instruction, to visit the dying and prepare them to receive the sacraments, and to work actively for the conversion of pagans.[29]

Ever since its foundation *The Guard of Honor* has spread all over the world, particularly in the United States, with amazing speed. Its present membership is estimated to be well over three million.[30]

Conclusion. These brief notices by no means exhaust the number of Marian confraternities.[31] However, they are representative of the nature,

---

[28] The most recent papal approval of this devotion may be gathered from the Mass and Office granted by the Holy See to the Blessed Sacrament Fathers on April 25, 1955. Cf. T. Urquiri, C.M.F., *Festum Beatae Mariae Virginis sub titulo Dominae Nostrae a SSmo. Sacramento*, in *Ephemerides Mariologicae*, Vol. 5, 1955, pp. 449-454.

[29] Cf. G. M. Allegra, O.F.M., *Little Manual for the Members of the Association of the Guard of Honor of the Immaculate Heart of Mary* (Hong Kong, 1958), pp. 3-13.

[30] Figures of present enrollment were graciously furnished by Father Irenaeus Schönherr, O.F.M., National Director of *The Guard* in the United States, and editor of *Messenger of The Guard of Honor of The Immaculate Heart of Mary*, published twice a year in New York City.

[31] Cf., for example, C. Berthet, C.R.S.P., *Archiconfrérie de Notre-Dame de la Divine Providence*, in *Compte rendu du Congrès Marial tenu à Fribourg, 1902*, Vol. 1 (Blois, 1903), pp. 582-588; A. S. Montferrier, *L'archiconfrérie de Notre-Dame Consolatrice des Affligés*, ibid., pp. 589-595; G. Breffy, *L'archiconfrérie de Notre-Dame de Victoires*, in *Actas del Cuarto Congreso Mariano Internacional celebrado en Zaragoza, 1908* (Madrid, 1909), pp. 461-468.

scope, purpose, and function of the confraternity in the prayer and devotional life of the Church. In summation, we may say that virtually all these associations originated with one or another of the various religious orders and congregations. The name "confraternity" itself probably comes from the Latin "confratres," the appellation given to members of the laity who allied themselves with the various religious houses and participated in the spiritual goods of the community without being actual members. A final distinguishing mark of the confraternity is that its members are not bound in conscience to observe its rules and obligations.

Marian confraternities suggest a simple but effective way to honor Our Blessed Lady in her various titles and privileges. In addition, they help us to realize and understand the fundamental truth expressed by Pope Pius XII in 1947 at the time of the canonization of St. Louis Grignion de Montfort: "True devotion, that of Tradition, that of the Church, that, We say, of Christian and Catholic good sense, tends essentially toward *union with Jesus under the guidance of Mary.*"[32]

Finally, the Marian confraternity assists in bringing to fruition Mary's own prophecy in her sublime *Magnificat:* "All generations shall call me blessed."[33]

---

[32] A.A.S., Vol. 34, 1947, p. 412.
[33] Luke 1:48.

Marian Associations

by WILLIAM F. KEEGAN, C.S.C.

SSOCIATIONS of the faithful erected for the exercise of some work of piety or religion are called "pious unions." When constituted as organic bodies, they are known as "sodalities"; when erected for the embellishment of public worship, they are termed "confraternities." The basic concept — pious unions — while distinct from the third order, confraternity, and sodality, is, nevertheless, an alliance with an explicit religious purpose. It possesses spiritual benefits, enjoys ecclesiastical approbation, and has the privilege of aggregating to itself similar groups under the aegis of a "primary" pious union.[1] These concepts and distinctions are applicable to the organizations to be considered in the following pages.

Marian associations have existed and flourished in the Church since the middle of the sixteenth century. Originally, they were classified into three distinct groups: associations for young men, associations for girls, and associations for the faithful of both sexes. This division has more or less continued down to the present, although different ages have witnessed the predominance of one or another of these categories in the spiritual life and devotion of the faithful. In contemporary times emphasis is placed upon associations for the faithful of both sexes. This tendency has been accompanied by a deeper stress upon personal sanctification rather than upon the exercise of public cult.

In this chapter we shall give a brief account of: (1) The Children of Mary; (2) The Pious Union of Our Lady of Good Counsel; (3) The Court of Mary; (4) The Militia of Mary Immaculate; (5) The Reparation Society of the Immaculate Heart of Mary; and (6) The Blue Army.[2]

I. THE CHILDREN OF MARY

The oldest known *Children of Mary* sodality was founded by Bl. Peter

---

[1] Cf. Bouscaren-Ellis, *Canon Law. A Text and Commentary* (Milwaukee, 1951), pp. 360, 367, 373.

[2] Elsewhere in this volume the reader will find two separate chapters on other Marian associations: Chapter XIV on *Our Lady's Sodality,* and Chapter XV on The Legion of Mary.

de Honestis (degli Onesti) in Ravenna (Italy) in the thirteenth century. However, no further traces of it have been discovered after the founder's death.³ Similar groups were started by St. Peter Canisius († 1597) in Freiburg in 1581;⁴ by provost Jost Knab († 1658) in Luzern, approved by Alexander VII in 1650;⁵ by Father Lucchetti of Bergamo, in Lugano, 1817;⁶ and by Father X. de Ravignan, S.J. († 1858), in Paris.⁷

Historically more important than the above is the Children of Mary sodality originating from the apparitions of Our Blessed Lady to St. Catherine Labouré in 1830. It was formally organized through the zeal of the Superior General of the Vincentians in 1847, and approved by Pius IX that same year. There are about 5000 sodalities attached to this group, and their total membership is now in the millions. It is from this pious union that the most famous Children of Mary sodality actually derives, namely, the one established in the parish of St. Agnes in Rome in the year 1862 by the Lateran Canon Orestes Passeri. It was approved by Pius IX and later raised to the rank of "primary."⁸

The Children of Mary sodality is perhaps the most highly organized of all the various Marian associations. Minimum age for membership is fifteen years, and applicants remain in the category of postulants for a period of from three months to a year before being formally enrolled as members. Characteristic of this sodality is the wearing of the Miraculous Medal. By authorization of the Sacred Congregation of the Council in 1931, the pious union may be erected in all the parishes and institutions whose pastors or chaplains request it. The Paris motherhouse of the Sisters of Charity is the nerve-center of the association, but for all practical purposes each group retains its independence. The primary aim of the sodality is the veneration of Our Blessed Lady in her Immaculate Conception, and the personal sanctification of its members coupled with

---

³ Cf. G. M. Roschini, O.S.M., *La Madonna secondo la fede e la teologia*, Vol. 4 (Roma, 1954), p. 477.

⁴ Cf. G. Boero, *Vita del B. Pietro Canisio* (Roma, 1864), p. 379.

⁵ Cf. *Die grosse lateinische Kongregation unter dem Titel von Unser Lieben Frauen Unbfleckter Empfängniss in Luzern* (Luzern, 1885), p. 23. Ref. from E. Campana, *Maria nel culto cattolico*, Vol. 2 (Torino-Roma, 1933), p. 540.

⁶ Cf. Campana, *op. cit.*, Vol. 2, pp. 541-543.

⁷ *Ibid.*, pp. 543-544.

⁸ Cf. Roschini, *op. cit.*, Vol. 4, p. 478.

a true social apostolate.⁹

II. THE PIOUS UNION OF OUR LADY OF GOOD COUNSEL

The pilot model for Marian associations of the faithful of both sexes is the one known as *The Pious Union of Our Lady of Good Counsel*. It was founded in the second half of the eighteenth century in Genazzano (Italy) for the purpose of honoring Mary under the title of Our Lady of Good Counsel, whose miraculous icon is said to have appeared in the Augustinian church of that town in 1467. The association, formally approved by Benedict XIV in 1759, has since enjoyed wide popularity, not only in Italy, but also in the United States where it claims over one million members. In 1903 Leo XIII added to the Litany the invocation: "Mother of Good Counsel, pray for us."[10]

III. THE COURT OF MARY

This pious union was founded by Father Raymond Leal, S.J., in Madrid in the year 1839. It is made up of "choirs" of 31 persons, each of whom undertakes to visit a church on a different day of the month, particularly during May, and recite the Litany and the *Hail, Holy Queen* before an image of Our Lady in order to obtain the grace of a happy death.

This association, which was approved by Pius IX in 1847, and enriched with many indulgences by Gregory XVI, has witnessed an amazing growth within recent decades, not only in Spain, but in other countries as well. At present it boasts of some 20,000 "choirs."[11]

IV. THE MILITIA OF THE IMMACULATE CONCEPTION

Of more recent origin is the association known as *The Militia of Mary Immaculate*. It drew its inspiration from the celebrated story of Alphonsus Ratisbon's conversion in 1842 through the mediation of Mary Immaculate. Learning of this spiritual saga while a student in Rome (1917), a Polish Conventual, Friar Maximilian Kolbe, was inspired to invoke Mary's intercession anew for the conversion of contemporary anti-Christians.

---

[9] Cf. *Manual of The Children of Mary* (Emmitsburg, 1946), pp. 1-5; *Manuel de la Congrégation des Enfants de Marie* (Quebec, 1917); N. Lardi, *Association des Filles de Marie*, in *Congrès Marial tenu à Fribourg* [1902], Vol. 1 (Blois, 1903), pp. 500-507.

[10] Cf. T. C. Middleton, art. *Our Lady of Good Counsel*, in *The Catholic Encyclopedia*, Vol. 11 (New York, 1911), p. 361.

[11] Cf. Roschini, *op. cit.*, Vol. 4, pp. 478-479.

Accordingly, together with six other Franciscan friars, he founded the *Militia* in Rome on October 17, 1917. The express purpose of the organization is to conquer souls for Christ through absolute self-dedication to Mary Immaculate.

Under the auspices of the Friars Minor Conventual, the *Militia* received the formal approval of Benedict XV on April 4, 1918. On January 2, 1922, it was canonically established as a pious union by Cardinal Pompilj. Pius XI later elevated it to the dignity of a primary union with affiliates in Europe, Asia, and the Americas. The ranks of the organization grew from 450 members in 1920 to a current enrollment of two million. Membership is open to any Catholic of either sex, and members are free to choose their own appropriate means of promoting the specific aims of the organization. No member of the *Militia* contracts any obligation binding under pain of sin. After many years of apostolic labors, Father Kolbe met a holy and heroic death in the Nazi concentration camp at Oswiecim, Poland, on the Vigil of the Assumption, August 14, 1941. His cause for beatification has been officially initiated.[12]

V. THE REPARATION SOCIETY OF THE IMMACULATE HEART OF MARY

The Fatima apparitions of Our Lady in 1917 provided the incentive for the creation of two recent and popular Marian associations, both of which are dedicated to implement the desires expressed by Our Lady to the three Portuguese children. The first of these associations is *The Reparation Society of the Immaculate Heart of Mary,* founded in Baltimore, Maryland, in 1946 by Father John Ryan, S.J. As its name implies, its members endeavor to offer public reparation to the Immaculate Heart of Mary and thereby obtain the conversion of sinners. The principal means for achieving this purpose: daily recitation of the Rosary, daily sacrifices, the First Saturday communion and meditation.[13]

The organization of the group was made purposely flexible so that the members could adapt the movement to local needs and circumstances, while, of course, adhering to the primary goal of the association, namely,

---

[12] Cf. B. Hess, O.F.M.Conv., *La Milizia di Maria Immacolata nel suo XXV anniversario di fondazione, 1917-1942* (Roma, 1942), pp. 42-46; *Manual of The Militia of Mary Immaculate* (Carey, Ohio, 1948), pp. 2-5; A. Blasucci, O.F.M. Conv., *La Milizia di Maria Immacolata,* in *Virgo Immaculata,* Vol. 17, 1957, pp. 244-260.

[13] Cf. *Manual of The Reparation Society of Mary Immaculate* (Baltimore, 1947), pp. 5-21.

the rebuilding of human society through the sanctification of its members. The association may be organized anywhere by anyone. A monthly publication, *Fatima Findings,* supplies a meditation for the First Saturday of each month, adapted to the liturgical season. As of 1954, membership in the society was estimated to be 62,679 in 54 countries. It is particularly strong along the eastern seaboard of the United States.

VI. THE BLUE ARMY

Another important and rapidly developing association which draws its inspiration from the Fatima apparitions is *The Blue Army,* founded in 1947 by the Rt. Rev. Msgr. Harold V. Colgan, pastor of St. Mary's church in Plainsfield, N. J. Headquarters are now located in the newly constructed East-West Shrine near the site of the Fatima basilica. An information center has also been established in Paris to co-ordinate the activities of the association throughout the network of its member nations which now encircle the Iron Curtain. Monsignor Colgan is the international director of the movement, while the American national commander is Mr. John M. Haffert.[14]

Members of *The Blue Army* pledge themselves to carry out Our Lady's requests at Fatima for the conversion of Russia and for world peace through the practice of prayer and self-denial. They likewise bind themselves (although not under pain of sin) to recite the Rosary. The Rosary, the Scapular, self-sacrifice and reparation are the weapons with which *The Blue Army* endeavors to achieve its goal. The association publishes a bi-monthly organ entitled *Soul.* It also gives an annual award for outstanding service in counteracting the evil of Communism and promoting world peace. In 1954 *The Blue Army* numbered five million members in 33 countries; of these, two million and a half were in the United States.[15]

The above selective sampling will afford some understanding of the scope and variety of the ubiquitous Marian associations. While regarded,

---

[14] Cf. J. Mowatt, *God's Blue Answer to the Reds,* in *Pastoral Life,* Vol. 2, March-April, 1954, pp. 27-32.

[15] Anon., *Blue Against Red,* in *Our Lady's Digest,* Vol. 10, Aug.-Sept., 1955, p. 119; A. Rivera, C.M.F., *El Ejército Azul de Nuestra Señora (The Blue Army),* in *Ephemerides Mariologicae,* Vol. 7, 1957, p. 368. Further references to Marian associations may be found in L. Di Fonzo, O.F.M.Conv., *Associazioni, organizzazioni, opere mariane,* in *Enciclopedia Mariana,* ed. R. Spiazzi, O.P. (Milano, 1954), pp. 615-628; Roschini, *I sodalizi mariani e Maria,* in *Maria nell'economia della salute ...* (Milano, 1953), pp. 261-274.

in a sense, as the nadir in the firmament of religious organizations dedicated to the honor of Our Lady, these and other pious unions do shed together an effulgence which they may lack individually. Their very informality, their flexibility of rules and organization, admirably lend themselves to the varying temperaments and inclinations of the faithful; thus they provide ready and facile means for the veneration of Mary under her numerous titles and prerogatives. In addition to providing excellent means for the cultivation of Marian virtues, they also furnish a suitable outlet for that spontaneous devotion which has so often contributed to the promulgation of Marian doctrines.

THE SODALITIES OF OUR LADY

by RICHARD L. ROONEY, S.J.

EPTEMBER 27, 1948, is a date that will long be remembered. It was on that day that Pius XII, on the occasion of the second centenary of the publication of the Golden Bull, *Gloriosae Dominae* of Benedict XIV on the Sodalities of Our Lady, gave to the Universal Church his Apostolic Constitution, *Bis saeculari*, on the same subject.[1] Unquestionably this great document, which the Pope himself called their *Magna Charta*,[2] marks the opening of a new epoch in the life of these Marian organizations. To understand the full significance that this constitution has for them and for the Church in this Age of Mary and Age of the Laity, it must be seen against the background of the previous four hundred years of the Sodalities' existence.

Even a cursory review of those four centuries will show anyone the clear fact that, since their inception in 1563, the Sodalities of Our Lady have written more than one page ablaze with light and life in the history of mankind and of the Mystical Body of Mary's Son. To relate their achievements in full would require a volume. What follows in these pages is but a thumbnail sketch of the breadth and depth of the influence these organizations have exerted — and are still exerting — in the Church of Christ.

Just one of their accomplishments, however, can be seen from the following statistics. Sixteen sodalists have risen to the Chair of Peter, Pope Pius XII being the most outstanding sodalist of our own age. Forty-three sodalists have been canonized. More than sixty of them have been beatified. Thirty-eight sodalists, twenty-seven of them men, have founded forty-three religious communities. Many other sodalists have governed nations; not a few of them have had supreme command of armies.[3]

---

[1] *A.A.S.*, Vol. 40, 1948, pp. 393-402. English translation in *Acies Ordinata* (Supplementum ad No. 8) (Rome, 1948).

[2] Cf. *Action Now!*, Vol. 8, No. 3, 1954, p. 12, No. 9.

[3] Cf. *Acies Ordinata*, April, 1954, p. 93. The forty-third community, not mentioned there, is the one founded in Detroit, Mich., for work among Negroes. Cf. *The Queen's Work*, Vol. 47, No. 2, 1954, p. 28.

Even if the Sodalities had nothing else to show for their existence than these great souls, they would be well worthy of consideration in any volume that deals with what men have done and are still doing today for Jesus through Mary.

I. BIRTH AND CRADLE DAYS

The year 1563 came in the midst of a critical period of the Church's life, a period not unlike today's in fact.

Within the Church itself the dark night of ignorance of religious truth reigned in the souls of many. Men's minds were plunged into a whirlpool of revolutionary ideas and false theories. The lower classes were forsaking the bosom of Mother Church. In many places, too many of the clergy lacked both the knowledge and the conduct that their station called for.

The Moslem hordes had risen again out of the East and were battering at the gates of Christian Europe. It was only in 1571 that their assault was finally repulsed by the famous victory at Lepanto.

In Northern Europe the Protestant revolt was in full swing. The Eucharistic Christ and His Mother were being exiled from the Scandinavian peninsula, from England, parts of the Netherlands, Germany, and France.

It was with this frightening and challenging world-picture before his eyes that a young priest, John Leunis by name, a teacher at the Roman College of the Society of Jesus, called together a few of his most promising students one afternoon in the fall of 1563. This was the first of what grew into a series of meetings held daily throughout the remainder of that school year. It was out of these mustard-seed beginnings that the nearly 80,000 Sodalities spread across the world today took their start.[4]

On a table, arranged like an altar, around which these meetings centered, there was a statue of Our Lady. Devotion in the sense of complete devotedness to her was to characterize everything that this original band and their successors did. They have always, right from the beginning, looked to her as Queen of Apostles, for it was not Fr. Leunis' intention that these original sodalists should meet, say a few prayers, go through some devotional exercises in Mary's honor, listen to a talk, and then let it go at that.

Such piety as this was hardly sufficient to meet the terrible dangers

---

[4] Cf. E. Villaret, S.J., *Les congrégations mariales. Petit abrégé d'histoire* (Montreal, 1953), p. 34 ff.

and exciting challenge of those times any more than it would be equal to those of our own century. After the mind of the founder of his Order, St. Ignatius, it was the young Jesuit's intention to make real, active apostles of these young men.[5] They were to be apostles, first of all, to their fellow students, then to their families and their environment. He wanted these young men to develop such an intensely vigorous apostolic Christ-life within themselves that after college they would go forth to cast the fire of their zeal on all those with whom they came in contact wherever they might go in the world.

Father Leunis' ambition and plan were not entirely original. Twenty years before, St. Ignatius and his first companions had formed lay men and boys into apostolic groups which were to give a lasting quality to their own priestly ministries.[6] Similar organizations had also been instituted for the students of the infant colleges of the newly founded Society of Jesus. The original group that surrounded Fr. Leunis was apparently at first only another one of these earlier groups. They little knew, unpretentious as their meeting and their actions were, that they were actually the seedlings of organizations that would spread over the whole globe and be characterized some four hundred years later by Pope Pius XII as being "among the most powerful spiritual forces" in the Church.[7]

All the students of the Roman College in those days talked Latin. Hence they called this group of theirs by the names of *congregatio, sodalitium, sodalitas*. These are the names that have been retained and have been used interchangeably in all official documents and in the papal bulls, apostolic letters, and constitutions ever since. Today, while those in other countries adhere to the word "congregation," the word "sodality" is the common usage among those who speak English.

As Fr. Leunis' group met day after day during the scholastic year of 1563-1564 and as it grew from the first mere handful to some seventy-odd members from among all the classes in the College a definite plan formed in the young Jesuit's mind. By the end of that year it had crystallized as follows.[8]

---

[5] Cf. Villaret, *Les congrégations mariales, I: Des origines à la supression de la Compagnie de Jésus* [1540-1773] (Rome, 1947), p. 43.

[6] Cf. Villaret, *op. cit.*, p. 23 ff.

[7] Const. *Bis saeculari*, English trans., p. 2.

[8] Cf. J. Wicki, S.J., *Le Père Jean Leunis, S.J.* (Rome, 1950), p. 39.

Although no formal patron had been chosen in their earliest days, by the spring of 1564 the group dedicated itself to the Blessed Virgin Mary as its heavenly patroness under the title of her Annunciation, the title of the Roman College Church that was then abuilding. This original Marian character has remained ever since as an outstanding mark of all the Sodalities that have grown out of that original one.

The organizational structure of this first Sodality was simple enough. The seventy or so sodalists were divided into a number of small groups, twelve in all. At the head of each of these was a sodalist whose office it was to see to the conduct and studies of the other sodalists under his care. These twelve division heads were appointed to their positions by a Prefect, a man elected from among the older and more mature Sodality members. At the peak of this organizational pyramid was Fr. Leunis himself as Priest Director.

In order to achieve the twofold purpose of this Sodality, namely, continual advance in apostolic holiness and progressive proficiency in studies, Fr. Leunis drew up a set of rules (*leges*).[9] Subsequent editions, those, for example, of 1587, 1855, and 1910, have not changed these substantially but have only given them greater detail and applied them to the needs of the times.[10] These rules saw to it that the sodalists went through certain daily and weekly spiritual exercises and engaged in the labors of the apostolate.

Each day they assisted at Mass and recited the Rosary or some other prayer in honor of Our Lady. Further, as part of their daily after-class meetings, they made a mental prayer for a quarter of an hour, discussed what they had done or were planning to do, and made an examination of conscience. Every week the sodalists received the Sacrament of Penance and went to Holy Communion. Though these latter seem quite ordinary at present, they were very revolutionary actions in those days. On Sunday the Priest Director gave a short, informal, inspirational instruction. On feast days, after Vespers, some sodalists went to visit the sick in hospitals, others made pilgrimages to the tombs of the saints, and still others devoted themselves to various works of mercy and of the apostolate.[11]

So much space has been devoted to this original Sodality simply because it set the essential pattern from which all subsequent Sodalities

---

[9] Cf. Villaret, *Congrégations de la Sainte Vierge; esquisse général* (Rome, 1950), p. 11.

[10] Villaret, *loc. cit.*

[11] *Ibid.*

have deviated but little. The four essential characteristics of today's Sodalities noted by Pius XII in the *Bis saeculari* are easily discernible in their original prototype: a consecrated devotion to Mary, a deep and intense interior life flowing over into a dynamic apostolate, and all of these being worked at under the leadership of Christ in His Church.[12]

II. THE SODALITIES GROW

It was not long before this first Sodality of the Roman College showed that sign characteristic of all living bodies: the power of reproduction.

The original sodalists almost to a man, after they had finished their studies, initiated Sodalities for the faithful in every state of life and every class of society where they went.

Both by reason of their activities, and because Fr. Leunis himself was sent by his superiors to Perugia, Paris, and other cities and towns in Europe where he repeated what he had done in Rome,[13] by 1573 or in the space of ten short years, there were Sodalities in twenty-two important cities of Italy, France, Spain, and Portugal. Not long after, they sprang up also in Belgium, the Netherlands, the Rhineland, Bavaria, Bohemia, Austria, Poland, Switzerland, and Mexico.[14] They constituted a very militant section of the laity's spearhead of Counter Reformation in those countries where Protestantism had made its inroads. God alone knows how many sections of those countries and how many thousands of souls these early Sodalities brought back to the true faith.[15]

III. THE PRIMA PRIMARIA

Twenty years after the foundation of his first Sodality, Fr. John Leunis died at Turin on November 19, 1584.

Only sixteen days later Pope Gregory XIII issued his bull *Omnipotentis Dei* by which he gave the original Sodality at the Roman College full canonical status and enriched it with many and valuable indulgences and privileges. In this same bull the Pope designated it as the *Primary* Sodality and declared that all other Sodalities that existed in the colleges of the Society of Jesus for students and for all classes of the faithful would

---

[12] Const. *Bis saeculari*, English trans., p. 10 ff., IV-XII.
[13] Cf. Wicki, *op. cit.*, p. 44 ff.
[14] Cf. J. Sommer, S.J., *Marian Catholic Action* (St. Louis, Mo., 1953), p. 7.
[15] Cf. J. Stierli, S.J., *Devotion to Mary in the Sodality* (St. Louis, Mo., 1953), p. 8.

henceforth depend on the Roman College Sodality "as members on their head." Finally, this Pope also gave the General of the Society of Jesus the authority to aggregate other Sodalities to the First Primary Sodality, thus enabling them to share in the indulgences and privileges he had bestowed upon it.[16]

It is easy enough to see why this first Sodality should be called Primary. The term *First* Primary or *Prima Primaria,* however, can be confusing. Its meaning becomes clear when one remembers that the Sodality at the Roman College had expanded greatly in the twenty years of its existence. By 1569 it had been broken down into two main divisions: one for high school students, the other for collegians and students of theology. By 1590 it had grown yet more, so that further division was necessary. While these divisional groups together made up but one Sodality (the Primary [*Primaria*] Sodality mentioned by Pope Gregory), they were named individually First Primary, Second Primary, Third and Fourth Primary. With the passage of time the Primary Sodality was reduced again in numbers to such an extent that only the First Primary, the *Prima Primaria* remained. It is this *Prima Primaria* or First Primary Sodality that is in existence today. It is to this same *Prima Primaria* also that all those who wish to share in its spiritual riches are aggregated even at the present time.[17]

As the Sodalities increased in popularity and spread, they encountered certain difficulties. To clear these up, further papal documents and grants were issued. For example, Pope Sixtus V in his bull *Superna dispositione,* of January 5, 1587, authorized the General of the Jesuits to erect more than one Sodality in a single college or religious house of the Order, and to affiliate them to the *Prima Primaria*.[18] Again, the same Pope on September 29 of that same year by another bull, *Romanum decet,* extended this power of affiliation so that Sodalities in religious houses that did not belong to the Society of Jesus as such but that were under Jesuit care could erect Sodalities and affiliate them also.

By the year 1658 the Sodality of the Roman College had some 1459 other Sodalities affiliated with it. In those days membership in these organizations was restricted to men only. It was not until September 8, 1751, that Pope Benedict XIV granted the General of the Society of Jesus

---

[16] Cf. Villaret, *op. cit.,* p. 13.

[17] *Op. cit.,* p. 14.

[18] *Op. cit.,* p. 16.

the right to affiliate Sodalities of women to the *Prima Primaria*. Actually, many vigorous Sodalities of women and girls were functioning prior to this grant, one of them being that founded in 1705 at Marseilles, France, by Fr. Joseph Croiset, S.J.[19]

It is interesting to note that the Sodalities in those days were to be found in every walk of life and on every social level of the faithful. There was a Sodality of sailors and fishermen of the Port of Naples. There were Sodalities for priests, seminarians, artisans, civic officials, merchants, students, folk of the middle class, nobles, apprentices, domestics, yes, even one for beggars![20]

Two other facts are also noteworthy. First, all these early Sodalities were formed along functional or vocational lines. Until 1825 there were no Parish Sodalities. The reason for this is obvious. The Jesuits did not have parish churches as we know them today, but only what are called "collegiate" churches. Hence their Sodalities were not parochial but city-wide in membership. Second, even a very brief run-through of the work done by those same earlier-day Sodalities shows that they were deeply engaged in what we call today the Social Apostolate. Cardinal Bausset of France, speaking of them in 1808, summed up their labors in these words:

> Men still remember that in the principal commercial towns there never was more order and peace, more honesty in business, less bankruptcy and less depravity, than when the Sodalities existed. The Jesuits knew how to link the Sodalities with all professions and with all social institutions. These Sodalities helped maintain among all classes and conditions that public morality, that spirit of order, and that prudent economy which keeps peace and harmony in families and makes for the prosperity of empires.[21]

When the Society of Jesus was suppressed in 1773, the Sodalities ceased to be mere lay prolongations of a religious Order and became the direct possession of the Church as such. At that time, there were about 2500 of them throughout the then-known world. This is a small number, of course, in comparison with their present count of nearly 80,000. Nevertheless, we gather from history and from the *Bis saeculari* of Pope Pius XII that these two centuries were actually the Golden Age of the Sodalities' existence.

---

[19] *Ibid.*

[20] Cf. A. Drive, S.J., *The Sodality of Our Lady. Historical Sketches* (New York, 1916), pp. 26-37, 85-86.

[21] Cf. Drive, *op. cit.*, pp. 62-63.

IV. DEATH AND RESURRECTION

In their earliest years the Sodalities of Our Lady fought valiantly against the horrendous evil of the Protestant Deformation.

In the midst of the seventeenth century, however, they joined battle with another even more insidious enemy, one that was spawned within the household of the Church itself: Jansenism.

One instance will suffice to show how bitterly the Jansenists opposed the Sodalities. During the reign of Louis XIV, the marshals of the French armies actively recruited officers for the Sodalities of the military. Immediately on the death of the King, however, the Jansenists obtained from the French Regent an order banning all Sodalities in the armed forces.[22]

To protect and strengthen the position of the Sodalities which they admired so thoroughly, the Popes who reigned during these troublous times praised them highly and poured fuller favors on them. On September 27, 1748, for example, in the Golden Bull mentioned before, Pope Benedict XIV extolled them and granted them tremendous new privileges and indulgences. Despite the fact that all the Sodalities of France had been suppressed by then as a result of Jansenist pressure — those in Spain and Portugal and Naples soon underwent the same fate — Pope Clement XIII in his bull *Apostolicum,* which was a vigorous rebuke to the Sodalities' enemies, solemnly praised them and confirmed and renewed all the grants made in their favor by the bulls and apostolic constitutions of his predecessors.

By 1773, however, the political pressure brought to bear on the Papacy by the anticlerical and Jansenistic rulers and statesmen of France, Spain, Portugal, and Italy became insufferable. On July 21 of that year, in a brief entitled *Dominus ac Redemptor,* Clement XIV yielded and suppressed the Society of Jesus and all its works and ministries. He withdrew all jurisdiction from the General of the same Society and all the faculties and powers he had enjoyed up to that time. Among these latter, of course, was that of aggregating Sodalities to the *Prima Primaria.* With this power gone, fresh erections and affiliations of Sodalities became impossible. To all appearances the Sodalities were crushed. It looked as though they had been crucified and buried in the tomb of complete and final extinction.

However, like the Son of her to whom the Sodalities had dedicated themselves, they were to rise again. As a matter of fact, only four months

---

[22] Cf. Villaret, *op. cit.,* p. 17.

after the suppression of the Society of Jesus, Clement XIV himself provided expressly for their survival by his brief *Commendatissimam*, by which he set up a special commission of three cardinals to whom he entrusted the Roman College and the power to aggregate Sodalities to its *Prima Primaria*. For the time being and in principle at least, the Sodalities were saved from oblivion.

Nevertheless, certain distressing questions began to arise. Where, how, by whom could Sodalities be erected? And affiliations, what of them? On May 2, 1775 Pope Pius VI, successor to Clement XIV, gave the answer to these perplexities. In his letters patent of that date he turned over to his own Cardinal Vicar and his successors whatever powers were needed to erect and affiliate Sodalities of Our Lady in the future. These powers were later extended and given over to the Director of the *Prima Primaria*. Finally, Pope Leo XII in 1824, some ten years after the restoration of the Society of Jesus, returned fully and definitively to the General all of the powers he had once enjoyed. At last, on March 7, 1825, this same Pope granted the Father General of the Jesuits the new power to affiliate to the *Prima Primaria*, with the consent of the local Ordinary, even those Sodalities erected in his diocese that are completely independent of all direction by the Society of Jesus itself.[23]

V. THE SODALITIES IN MODERN TIMES

The resurgence of the Sodalities was rather slow at first. Two old enemies account for that: the anticlericals and the Jansenists. This pair were bitterly disappointed at seeing the Sodalities rise out of the grave to which they had consigned them, stand on their feet again and deploy themselves as of old against atheism, irreligion, secularism, and the avoidance of frequent Communion.

The anticlericals followed the tactic of ridiculing the Sodalities, labeling them as associations exclusively for overly pious women and children.

The more the sodalists tried to promote closeness to Christ in the Eucharist by frequent reception of Holy Communion, the more the Jansenists raged against them. Pope St. Pius X, of course, at once gave the accolade to the Sodalities and sealed the doom of Jansenism with his decree of December 20, 1905.

Almost as an echo of this decree, a clarion call came from the General

---

[23] *Op. cit.*, p. 20.

of the Society of Jesus to the sodalists of the world challenging them to return to a full living-out of the Sodality way of serving Jesus through His Blessed Mother. To help them answer this call, the General began about 1910 to establish National Sodality Secretariates or Service Centers in all the countries of the globe. The Jesuits assigned to these offices are to devote themselves totally to serving all kinds and types of Sodalities in every way possible, to help them develop practical and effective programs of action and thus fulfill their purpose of producing Catholics marked by the outstanding depth and fervor of their interior lives and the zeal and vigor of their apostolic labors.

VI. SIGNS OF DECADENCE

At the time this challenge was issued it was much needed. During the years that had elapsed between the suppression of the Society of Jesus and the present, three major crippling defects had crept into too many Sodalities.

First, they became largely mass organizations. The careful selectivity that had marked the earlier days was put aside. Quantity, not quality, became the watchword.

Second, the distinction between the Sodalities of Our Lady and those groups of later origin stemming from the Rue du Bac in Paris and called "The Children of Mary" was lost sight of. These latter are restricted in membership to women and girls. Many men and even priests thought that the Sodalities, too, were for women only.

Finally, the vitally apostolic nature of the Sodalities of Our Lady that is of their very essence was neglected. Too many of them became little more than societies for the pietistic, for the recreation-minded, for raising funds.[24]

Both experience and the following figures show that the first two of those impressions were not unfounded. A percentage breakdown of the number of affiliations from 1585 to the present indicates that 30 per cent of the total number were Sodalities of men, 60 per cent of women, and 10 per cent of those which enroll both men and women.

Incidentally, one of the surest ways to lay the all-too-common bogey that all of these Sodalities are Jesuit-dominated is the presentation of the stark and conclusive fact that only from 3 to 5 per cent of the Sodalities

---

[24] Cf. E. Besuttil, S.J., *Commentarium in Constitutionem Apostolicam "Bis saeculari"* (Romae, 1949), p. 88, No. 166.

throughout the world are under Jesuit direction.[25]

VII. SODALITIES IN THE UNITED STATES

The immediate successors of the North American Martyrs established Sodalities here on the North American continent among the Hurons as early as 1647.[26]

The first Sodality in what is now the United States, however, was one for workingmen established in New Orleans in 1738.[27] The first one to come into existence after the Revolutionary War was that at Georgetown University, Washington, D. C. The initial reception of new members took place on December 9, 1783, but the Sodality itself was not affiliated officially with the *Prima Primaria* until February 5, 1833.[28]

The number of Sodalities in the United States has grown from about 50 in 1850 to 18,761 in 1959.

The greatest impetus to the Sodality movement in our country should be attributed chiefly to two men: Fr. Edward Garesche, S.J., who was appointed National Promoter of Sodalities for the United States in the Autumn of 1913, and Fr. Daniel A. Lord, S.J., who, though still a scholastic in that year, aided Fr. Garesche and then succeeded him in his national post in 1925.

Fr. Garesche stated that the initial investigation he made on setting up the first National Secretariate here to ascertain the actual condition of our American Sodalities disclosed "an extremely discouraging condition in the Sodalities themselves. ... All the activities of the Sodalities were confined, in most places, to attendance at meetings where some prayers and the Office of the Blessed Virgin were recited, and to monthly Communion."

Beyond the field work that he did to remedy this, Fr. Garesche, with the then Mr. Lord's assistance, initiated *The Queen's Work* magazine, as "the Official Organ of the Sodalities in America." The first issue appeared appropriately enough in May of 1914. At present, its field of appeal has been restricted to teen-age sodalists. This was supplemented by *Action Now!*, a magazine for interested adult sodalists, *Direction*, published first in 1954, for Sodality Directors, Moderators, and Officers, and *The Junior*

---

[25] Sommer, *op. cit.*, p. 22.

[26] Sr. Mary Horence, S.L., *The Sodality Movement in the United States [1926-1936]* (St. Louis, Mo., 1939), p. 17.

[27] *Op. cit.*, p. 19.

[28] *Op. cit.*, p. 21.

Sodalist and *The Children's Moderator,* publications for those working on the elementary school level.

Continuing Fr. Garesche's apostolate in 1925, Fr. Lord traveled back and forth across the country for the next thirty years igniting the light of faith and the fire of enthusiasm for Christ and His Mother and their common cause in the minds and hearts of thousands of young people. By his genius, personality, prodigious writing and talking, by means of his plays, music, and pageants, he brought newness of life to countless old and dying Sodalities. During more than a quarter of a century Fr. Lord wrote numberless books and pamphlets, gave many, many retreats and lectures, conducted hundreds of Sodality rallies and conventions, instituted the Annual Meeting of Diocesan, Deanery, and Union Directors, initiated the now nationally famous Summer Schools of Catholic Action, wrote the official Motion Picture Production Code (1930) for decent movies, and promoted the "Knights and Handmaids of the Blessed Sacrament."

By the time of his death in 1955, Fr. Lord had also built up the national office from a staff of four priests with whom he started out, to the institution that was then housed in a six-story office building in St. Louis with a staff of eight priests and some seventy lay people.

The ensuing figures give some idea of what these two main leaders of the Sodality movement along with their fellow workers accomplished over the years in the United States.

Over half of the parishes listed in the *Official Catholic Directory* have Sodalities. Sodalities of Our Lady are to be found also in nearly 2500 high schools and academies, in 250 Catholic colleges and universities, and in some two thirds of the approximately 400 Catholic nursing schools in our country. Junior Sodalities, corresponding to the Junior Holy Name Societies here and the Blau-ring and Maria-garde in Europe, are active in about 40 per cent of our Catholic grade schools.[29]

On May 31, 1948, the first of several now active Sodalities for priests, instituted and directed by Fr. Joseph Hughes of the Diocese of Duluth, was affiliated with the *Prima Primaria.*[30]

In 1950 Fr. Gerald Seguin, at that time an assistant at Notre Dame Parish, Malone, New York, Diocese of Ogdensburg, selected seven married couples from the roster of 1200 families in that parish and formed them

---

[29] Cf. Sommer, *op. cit.,* p. 22.
[30] *Op. cit.,* p. 41.

into a Cana Sodality which has been copied elsewhere since.

Two outstanding Sodalities are to be found in Cleveland, Ohio. One of them is the undergraduate students' Sodality at John Carroll University. The other is the Cleveland Alumni Sodality, directed by Msgr. Joseph Spitzig, Archdiocesan Director of Sodalities.

There are numerous Faculty Sodalities in various colleges, v.g. at Xavier University in Cincinnati, Ohio, and Fairfield University, Fairfield, Connecticut.

In 1954, under the inspiration of Fr. Francis K. Drolet, S.J., Promoter of the Sodalities for that region, a Sodality was instituted for professional people, both men and women, from all over New York City. Philadelphia, too, has its excellent Xavier-Damian professional Sodality, now under the direction of Fr. Lewis Delmage, S.J.

Sodalities in schools of nursing throughout the United States and Canada owe a deep debt of gratitude for their success to the tireless labors in their behalf of Fr. J. Roger Lyons, S.J., Fr. Lord's first successor as National Promoter.

Over the years the high school Sodalities, on whom Fr. Lord concentrated especially, have been undoubtedly the most active and enthusiastic.

After the sudden demise of Father Lyons, on September 22, 1949, the International Sodality Secretariate appointed Fr. Aloysius J. Heeg, S.J., internationally known as a teacher of catechetics and outstanding leader in work with Junior Sodalities, as National Promoter. He was followed in this office in October of 1953 by the present writer. During the summer of 1956 Fr. James J. McQuade, S.J., succeeded to the appointment as Director of the National Sodality Service Center.

In November, 1956, Pope Pius XII wrote to the Rev. Irwin Juraschek, President of the National Diocesan Sodality Directors Conference, encouraging the directors to form a National Federation of Sodalities here in the United States. The first meeting of this Federation took place in St. Louis, January 19-20, 1957. Today 36 diocesan federations of Sodalities are members of the Federation, an affiliate of the National Council of Catholic Men, Women, and Youth and of the World Federation of Sodalities. It was this group that carried off the Second World Congress of Sodalities in Newark, N. J., August 20-23, 1959.

Besides the Sodalities already mentioned, there have been others erected both on military installations and in the armed forces themselves.

Fr. Joseph T. O'Callahan, S.J., for example, the only chaplain ever to receive the Congressional Medal of Honor, established a Sodality on the *Ranger*, one of our Navy's airplane carriers in World War II.

Finally, in 1945 a young arthritic invalid, Mary Ellen Kelly of Marcus, Iowa, conceived the idea of a Sodality of Shut-Ins. At first, because of technical difficulties, she was allowed to have only a League of Shut-Ins who were already sodalists. By November 1, 1950, however, her prayers and sufferings were rewarded with the establishment and affiliation of a real Sodality of Shut-Ins erected at St. John's McNamara Hospital, Rapid City, South Dakota, which now takes in Shut-Ins from all over the country.

VIII. A LOOK AT THE SODALITIES' FUTURE

With the publication of his Apostolic Constitution, *Bis saeculari*, Pope Pius XII threw open the gates to a newer, fresher era in the life and history of the Sodalities of Our Lady. In that all-important document he called for the following: a full living of the Sodalities' Rules of 1910, a modification of those of the famous Sodality of Barcelona directed by Fr. Aloysius Fitter, S.J.;[31] a renewal of spirit to be effected primarily and essentially by the observance of Rule 24, which calls for greater selectivity in the admission of new members, a fuller and closer co-operation with the Hierarchy and with other Catholic Action organizations. He also made it very clear in that constitution that Catholic Action, while one in spirit, should be multiple in form. He further declared that the Sodalities of Our Lady, when they followed his directives, are Catholic Action strictly so-called "under the auspices and inspiration of the Blessed Virgin Mary."[32]

Pius XII was rightly called "The Pope of Mary." He may well be called "The Pope of the Sodalities" as well. His great faith in their possibilities is evident not merely from the *Bis saeculari*, not only from the eight official statements he made about them while he was still a cardinal, and from the thirty-six other statements he issued in the form of apostolic letters, exhortations, telegrams, discourses, and radio messages as Pope,[33] but especially from his erection of the World Federation of Sodalities[34] and his presence and Allocution at the opening at St. Peter's on September 8, 1954,

---

[31] Cf. Drive, *op. cit.*, p. 99.

[32] Bis saeculari, English trans., p. 7.

[33] Cf. G. Caprile, S.J., *Al servizio della Chiesa* (Roma, 1954), pp. 245-247.

[34] Cf. *Acies Ordinata*, A. 22, No. 217, 1953, p. 226 ff.

of the First International Sodality World Congress.[35]

It was this great Pope's will and hope that the Sodalities of Our Lady throughout the world follow out the leads he had given them in so many ways and on so many occasions, and that they become more selective, more deeply imbued with the interior life and hence more vigorous and effective in all forms of the apostolate, "especially the social apostolate" — all, of course, *duce Ecclesia.*

A statement issued by the headquarters of the Sodality World Federation in the summer of 1955 regarding the first year's life of the Sodalities that followed upon the World Congress indicates that Pius XII's desires and hopes are being realized. All over the world now, a new, more vigorous life is stirring. The dead and dying bones are rising from the plain again. All signs point to the fact that the Sodalities of tomorrow, fired again with the same spirit of fervent love of God and souls and with the same dynamic apostolic zeal of the early days may, in fact, eclipse their progenitors' achievements and establish an even more splendid record of deeds done for Jesus through Mary.

---

[35] Cf. *Action Now!*, Vol. 8, No. 3, 1954, p. 11 ff. For further literature on the Sodality see L. Brien, S.J., *Valeur et sens de la Constitution Apostolique sur les Congrégations Mariales,* in *Marie* [Nicolet], Vol. 3, No. 1, 1949, pp. 22-24; A. Cantens, *La congregación mariana, impugnadora de las teorías del modernismo social,* in *Actas del Cuarto Congreso Mariano Internacional celebrado en Zaragoza,* 1908 (Madrid, 1909), pp. 496-501; C. Gómez Robeles, S.J., *Acción social de las congregaciones marianas del siglo XVI al XVIII, ibid.,* pp. 770-774; J. Pascual Dodero, *La vida interna de las congregaciones marianas,* in *Compte-rendu du premier Congrès de la Fédération Mondial des Congrégations Mariales* (Rome, 1955), pp. 55-50; A. González del Valle, *El apostolado social y las congregaciones marianas, ibid.,* pp. 105-110; P. Lefebvre, S.J., *Les congrégations de la T.S.Vierge dans les collèges,* in *Mémoires et Rapports du Congrès Marial tenu à Bruxelles,* 1921 (Bruxelles, 1922), pp. 642-645; L. Paulussen, S.J., *Religious Formation in the Sodality of Our Lady,* in *Lumen Vitae,* Vol. 8, 1953, pp. 257-270; Id., *Situation des congrégations mariales,* in *Christus,* July, 1954, pp. 124-129; Id., *Quelques réflexions sur la fédération mondiale, sa nature et sa tache,* in *Compte-rendu du premier Congrès de la Fédération Mondiale des Congrégations Mariales* (Rome, 1955), pp. 77-80; R. Plus, S.J., *Les congrégations mariales* (Nicolet, 1950), 26 pp.; P. Sträter, S.J., *Die Marianische Kongregation,* in *Katholische Marienkunde,* ed. P. Sträter, S.J., Vol. 3 (Paderborn, 1951), pp. 247-293; J. Dehergne, S.J., *Les congrégations dans l'empire de Chine aux XVIIe et XVIIIe siècles,* in *Maria. Études sur la Sainte Vierge,* ed. H. du Manoir, S.J., Vol. 4 (Paris, 1956), pp. 967-980.

THE LEGION OF MARY

by ROGER M. CHAREST, S.M.M.

N SEPTEMBER 7, 1921, in a modest "upper room" of Myra House, Francis St., Dublin, Ireland, was born a Marian Catholic Action organization that was soon to encircle the globe and merit to be called "a miracle of these modern times."[1] We refer, of course, to the Legion of Mary.

"The Legion of Mary is an Association of Catholics, who, with the sanction of the Church and under the powerful leadership of Mary Immaculate, Mediatrix of all Graces ... have formed themselves into a Legion for service in the warfare which is perpetually waged by the Church against the world and its evil powers."[2] This broad definition, taken from the *Official Handbook of the Legion of Mary*, will be brought into focus, we believe, once we have taken a closer look at the Legion in its origin, its organizational framework, its methods and techniques, its doctrinal and spiritual outlook and, finally, its prodigious growth and world-wide apostolic accomplishments.[3] Such a study should amply justify these words of its founder, Mr. Frank Duff: "The Legion is Our Lady's spirit come to life in people."[4]

I. MARIAN ORIGIN

Tracing the origins of the Legion of Mary, John Murray, former president of the Concilium, writes: "The nucleus of the Legion in its personnel was that little group attending the monthly Pioneer Council meeting in Myra House. It was in these informal 'talks' after the gathering that the spirit which characterized the Legion from its first meeting was formed. In a consecutive number of these talks, Mr. Frank Duff had outlined to his listeners the True Devotion to Our Lady, as taught by Saint

---

[1] H. E. Riberi, as quoted in *Official Handbook of The Legion of Mary*, 6th. American ed. (Louisville, Ky., 1953), p. 20. Hereafter abbreviated: Handbook.

[2] *Handbook*, pp. 1-2.

[3] For an excellent study of the Legion system, cf. L. J. Suenens, *Spiritualité et rayonnement de la Légion de Marie*, in *Maria. Études sur la Sainte Vierge*, ed. H. du Manoir, Vol. 3 (Paris, 1954), pp. 637-658.

[4] F. Duff, *Address to the New York Senatus*, Dec., 1956, p. 2 (mimeo).

Louis Marie de Montfort in his *Treatise*. Those who established the Legion and guided the new movement from the first moment were those who had heard those spiritual talks each month at Myra House."[5]

Then came that historic first meeting — the evening of September 7, 1921, First Vespers of the feast of Our Lady's Nativity. The scene: a modest "upper-room" of an apartment on Francis St., in an old and poor quarter of the city of Dublin. In the center of the room, on a table covered with a white cloth, flanked by two lighted candles and two vases of flowers is enthroned a statue of the Immaculate Conception, Miraculous Medal type. This simple setting, rich in Marian piety — the inspired idea of one of the early arrivals — admirably expresses the spirit of the organization which is about to be born.[6]

At the hour agreed upon, this little group of inconspicuous persons — fifteen girls, most of them in their late teens or early twenties; one layman, Mr. Frank Duff; and one priest, the late Michael Toher — kneel on the floor around the improvised altar. They recite an invocation and prayer to the Holy Spirit; then their work-hardened hands finger their rosaries. Their prayers ended, they take their seats, we are told, and under the maternal watchfulness of Mary they consider "how they could best please God and make Him loved in His world."[7]

The program of work they propose to accomplish is a precise one. They will visit an almshouse of the city to console the forgotten poor and to bring them spiritual solace and relief. On one point they are unanimous: if this is the work they are to undertake, then they will organize it in a way that will insure regularity of visitation. In other words, it will be done seriously, methodically, or not at all. They will follow the rules of the St. Vincent de Paul Society to a certain extent — weekly meeting, prayer, spiritual talk, reports of each member on the previous week's work; and then concentrate upon an apostolate with Mary, a service for Mary, a life with Mary, in accordance with the teachings of St. Louis de Montfort.

As much as that first meeting had been characterized by the unforeseen, by simplicity, by faith and limitless confidence, the succeeding one was to abound in promise and hope beyond all expectations. Witness

---

[5] J. Murray, *A Journey of a Thousand Leagues Begins*, in *Symposium on The Legion of Mary* (Dublin, 1957), p. 11.

[6] *Handbook*, p. 2.

[7] *Ibid.*, p. 3.

the account of the very first visit made to the woman in the first bed. Let's call her Mrs. Smith. Now Mrs. Smith had been away from the Sacraments for many years. She immediately confided her wish to "get right" again. Then there was Mrs. Little, bedridden for five years, who wrote on a scrap of paper a little note addressed to her daughter: "If I can see you once before death, then I shall die in peace." There followed the case of Mary Browne, a profligate, who confided her uneasiness at being obliged, because she had nowhere else to go on her dismissal from the hospital the following week, to return to the man to whom she was not married. "If I could only find a job," she pleaded with the Legionary, "then I could make him return to his own wife." Would the kind visitor perhaps help her in this difficult situation?

One report followed another as a living proof that the hand of the Virgin Mary was in the work; that the visitation was indeed hers and not theirs. These first Legionaries understood their role in this soul-to-soul apostolate; they were to be mere docile instruments in the hands of the Virgin Mary. Their intention was clear-cut: self-sanctification through the sanctification of others. Their message was a precise one: to bring Christ into the world of souls through Mary's all-powerful Mediation.

A new organization had been born — a spiritual army that was soon to encircle the globe: *The Legion of Mary*.

II. ORGANIZATIONAL FRAMEWORK

During the first four years of its existence the organization was known as the *Association of Our Lady of Mercy*. Later, in November, 1925, it adopted the name: *Legion of Mary*.[8]

The Legion Handbook tells us that "The Legion is an army — the army of the Virgin most humble."[9] Like any army, it is built on discipline, "unrelaxed discipline," a discipline which is based on true humility and which must "bear on all the affairs of daily life and be ever on the alert for opportunities to promote the general object of the Legion, namely, to destroy the empire of sin, uproot its foundations and plant on its ruins the standard of Christ the king."[10]

Since the Legion "places before its members a mode of life rather than the doing of a work," it provides "an intensely ordered system, in which

---

[8] Cf. Murray, *art. cit.*, p. 10.
[9] *Handbook*, p. 98.
[10] *Ibid.*, p. 160.

much is given the force of rule that in other systems is merely exhorted or left to be understood, and in regard to every detail of which it enjoins a spirit of scrupulous observance."[11] This point of faithful adherence to the Legion system in all its details is so important that the Legion "deems a member to be a member to the degree to which he submits himself to the Legion system, and no more."[12]

Like any army, the Legion is composed of members who are in active service (active members), and those who support the troops by their work and their prayers (auxiliary members). Modeled on the armies of this world, the Legion takes its nomenclature from the old Roman Legion. The use of such Latin terms as *Praesidium, Curia, Senatus,* etc., gives the Legion a note of universality and unity.

The basic unit of the Legion is the *Praesidium*. This is the parish or institutional unit and it ranges from approximately four to twenty active members, to which may be affiliated an indefinite number of auxiliary members whose obligation it is to sustain the work of the active members by their prayers and sacrifices. The prayers which the Legionaries, both active and auxiliary, must say every day are to be found in the official prayer leaflet of the Legion, called the *Tessera*.

Each *Praesidium* — headed by four officers: president, vice-president, secretary, and treasurer — holds its meetings once a week. Since the Legion "took root from the St. Vincent de Paul Society," it is to be expected that its method of procedure is much the same. It is invariable and consists of: (1) Prayer to the Holy Spirit; (2) Recitation of the Rosary; (3) Spiritual Reading; (4) Reading of the minutes of the previous meeting; (5) Verbal account of preceding week's work given by each member; (6) Recitation of the *Magnificat;* (7) Assignment of work for the coming week; (8) Discussion based on the Handbook; (9) Concluding prayers; (10) Blessing by the Spiritual Director.[13]

Let it be noted here that "No *Praesidium* shall be established in any parish without the consent of the parish priest or of the Ordinary."[14] Note also that no *Praesidium* can be organized in a locality without the express permission of the governing body immediately above it, called the *Curia;* and this permission can be given only if the new group pledges itself to

---

[11] *Ibid.,* p. 37.

[12] *Ibid.,* p. 38.

[13] For the role of the Spiritual Director, cf. *Handbook,* pp. 186-189.

[14] *Ibid.,* p. 73.

adhere faithfully to the rules and regulations as set down in the Legion Handbook.

When two or more *Praesidia* are established in a certain area, a higher body called a *Curia* is formed. This group is made up of all the officers of the *Praesidia* in the locality, and chooses its own officers from among them. When one *Curia* is placed in charge of several *Curiae* it becomes a *Comitium*. This body does not generally exceed the boundaries of a diocese. Above the *Comitium* is the *Senatus*, which is the governing body for an entire area. Finally, there is the *Concilium*, which is the central governing body of the Legion throughout the world, with its headquarters in Dublin, Ireland.[15]

III. METHODS AND TECHNIQUES

At this point it may be well to ask ourselves two questions: First, what is the objective of the Legion of Mary? Second, how does it achieve this objective?

"The object of the Legion of Mary is the sanctification of its members by prayer and active co-operation, under ecclesiastical guidance, in Mary's and the Church's work of crushing the head of the serpent and advancing the reign of Christ."[16] It is interesting to note how the Legion Handbook identifies Mary's work with that of the Church, in what concerns "advancing the reign of Christ." It is also well to point out that the above-mentioned Legion objective gives it full right to be called "Catholic Action," in the truest sense of the word.

Pope Pius XI once defined Catholic Action as, "The participation and collaboration of the laity in the apostolate of the hierarchy."[17] The Legion of Mary is Catholic Action founded on Mary.[18]

To recognize from the very outset the role and influence of Mary in

---

[15] It may be well to note here that in order to foster a higher spiritual level among its members, the Legion has established the *Praetorians*. This is not a distinct group, but simply a higher degree of active service in the Legion. It comprises the following obligations: (1) The daily recitation of all the prayers contained in the *Tessera* of the Legion; (2) Daily Mass and daily Communion; (3) The daily recitation of some form of Office approved by the Church, such as the Little Office of the Blessed Virgin (cf. *Handbook*, p. 210).

[16] *Handbook*, p. 4.

[17] Pius XI, *Non abbiamo bisogno*, in A.A.S., Vol. 23, 1931, p. 287; cf. also *Cum ex epistola*, in A.A.S., Vol. 20, 1928, p. 296.

[18] *Handbook*, p. 20.

THE LEGION OF MARY 265

the dual work of personal sanctification and the apostolate, then to submit oneself fully to this maternal influence through intimate union with the Mediatrix of all graces in order to become an instrument of conquest in her virginal hands, such is the secret of the Legionary apostolate, such is the method proper to the Legion of Mary.

To be sure, there are many approved forms of Catholic Action. As Pope Pius XII pointed out: " 'Catholic Action is not confined within a closed circle' ... nor is it such that 'it pursues its object according to a special method and system,' so as to abolish or absorb the other active Catholic organizations."[19] The fact is, some organizations will stress the study and the application of the laws of psychology; others will concentrate their efforts on studying the social and intellectual milieu, etc., all methods which, it will be readily conceded, merit our admiration and support. In the Legion of Mary, however, the method is entirely different. Placing itself from the very outset above all human strategy, it establishes a soul firmly in the realm of faith. And here is how.

Since the Legionary's principal task is "to bring Mary to the world as the infallible means of winning the world to Jesus," it is obvious that "the Legionary without Mary in his heart can play no part in this."[20] Hence the necessity for each Legionary to seek union with Mary through imitation of her virtues and complete dependence upon her. "Its members ... thus grown into living copies of Mary, the Legion sees itself in truth a Legion of Mary, united to her mission and guaranteed her victory."[21]

This union with Mary and imitation of her virtues will inevitably lead to an apostolate which is essentially Marian, i.e., an apostolate through which Christ will not only be seen in every person but will be tended to and cared for with the love of Mary herself. To quote the words of the Handbook: "... in and through her Legionary, Mary participates in every Legionary duty, and mothers souls so that in each of those worked for ... not only is the person of Our Lord seen and served, but seen and served by Mary, with the same exquisite love and nurturing care which she gave to the actual body of her divine Son."[22]

For the Legionary, as for Mary herself, a crowd is never just a crowd. It is an assemblage of individual souls, each meriting particular attention,

---

[19] Const. *Bis saeculari*, in *A.A.S.*, Vol. 40, 1948, p. 393.
[20] *Handbook*, p. 128.
[21] *Ibid.*, p. 130.
[22] *Loc. cit.*

infinite love. Hence the Legionary instruction: "The Legion must direct itself to the individual soul."[23] This is the way the Legion faces the problem of people in the aggregate. It does not presume to belittle or ignore crowd psychology, rather it seeks to transform that crowd by approaching and transforming the individuals in it.

Thus the Legion method and technique may be said to be both spiritual and psychological. It is spiritual in the sense that it is based on union with Mary; it is psychological because it is grounded on sound elementary psychology.

IV. SPIRITUAL OUTLOOK

This brings us to our fourth consideration: the Legion Spirituality. Does the Legion of Mary have a spirituality of its own ... a spirituality that can be universally adopted and which rests on good solid theological grounds? If so, where is this spiritual doctrine to be found?

Let us begin by answering the last question first. The spiritual doctrine of the Legion of Mary is to be found principally in the Legion Handbook. A storehouse of doctrine and action in which theory and practice intermingle freely — lest one should dominate to the detriment of the other — the Legion Handbook holds the key to a spirituality which has already reaped its fruits of holiness and even martyrdom!

The Legion's spirituality, symbolized in the Legion of Mary Standard, is centered on the Holy Spirit, the Sanctifier, the One who not only overshadowed Mary in the work of the Incarnation but who also came down upon the Apostles on the day of Pentecost. And the reason for this is obvious: the Legion is essentially Marian and apostolic. It must, therefore, be animated by the Holy Spirit both for the sanctification of its members and for their apostolic action.

That is why every Legion meeting is opened with a prayer to the Holy Spirit. The "Legionary Promise" which marks the formal entry into Mary's Legion is made directly to the Holy Spirit. It is not our purpose here to elaborate on the Legion Promise which, to our way of thinking, embodies the very spirit of the Legion of Mary. Suffice it to refer the reader to the masterful commentary of the Legion Promise, by Bishop Suenens, in his book *The Theology of the Apostolate*.[24]

It may be well to point out here, with Bishop Suenens, that the Legion

---

[23] *Ibid.*, p. 293.

[24] L. J. Suenens, *The Theology of the Apostolate* (Chicago, 1955), pp. 1-12.

Promise, though directed to the Holy Spirit, is essentially Christo-centric because, in this Promise, "neither the Holy Spirit nor the Blessed Virgin have any meaning for us without reference to the mystery of the Incarnation."[25] Christianity, says the author, has been defined as an exchange of two loves in Jesus Christ. First, the Love that descends from heaven to seal the sacred alliance is called the Holy Spirit. And second, the love which ascends to meet that Infinite Love is called Mary. The secret meeting place of these two loves: in Christ Jesus.

The work of the Holy Spirit in the Church, therefore, is to bring to realization the work of Christ in the world, just as it is the work of Mary to lead us to Christ. Briefly, the Legionary is asked to lend himself to the action of the Holy Spirit in and through Mary to serve Christ and to continue His mission on earth.

And this brings us to the Marian outlook of the Legion. "Under God," says the Legion Handbook, "the Legion is built upon devotion to Mary."[26] Not any kind of devotion, but an adequate devotion which can only be acquired "by union with her."[27]

We have already indicated that the Legion seeks union with Mary through imitation of her virtues. Here we would like to show how the Legion seeks to identify itself with Mary, particularly in her motherhood of souls. Mary's whole life and destiny, says the Handbook, have been a motherhood, first of Christ, then of men. "On the day of the Annunciation she entered on her wondrous work, and ever since she has been the busy mother attending to her household duties. For a while these were contained in Nazareth, but soon the little house became the whole wide world, and her Son expanded into mankind. And so it has continued: all the time her domestic work goes on and nothing in that Nazareth-grown-big can be performed without her. Any caring of the Lord's body is only supplemental to her care; the apostle only adds himself to her maternal occupations; and in that sense," concludes the Handbook, "Our Lady might declare: 'I am Apostleship,' almost as she said: 'I am the Immaculate Conception.'"[28]

If Mary's motherhood of souls is her essential function in the Church today, then the Handbook rightly concludes: "Without participation in it

---

[25] Suenens, *art. cit.*, in *Maria*, Vol. 3, p. 649.
[26] *Handbook*, p. 10.
[27] *Ibid..*, p. 136.
[28] *Ibid.*, p. 137.

[her motherhood of souls] there can be no real union with her."[29] In other words, "true devotion to Mary must comprise the service of souls. Mary without motherhood and the Christian without apostleship would be analogous ideas. Both the one and the other would be incomplete, unreal, unsubstantial, false to the divine intention."[30]

In order to obviate the danger of dissociating devotion to Mary from apostleship in the Legion system, let us look a little further into the doctrinal sources of the Legion's Marian spirituality.

"To understand the spirituality of the Legion of Mary," writes Bishop Suenens, "one must know its history and especially one must grasp the spiritual bond that links the Legion to the doctor of Marian Mediation, St. Louis Marie de Montfort."[31] And Bishop Patrick Flynn, of Nevers, once wrote: "The Legion spirituality is but the applying to the modern apostolate of the admirable doctrine of Blessed Grignion de Montfort. The Handbook explains and comments upon, in its sometimes diffuse but always orthodox way, the classical *Treatise on True Devotion to Mary*."[32]

That the Legion spirituality owes much to St. Louis De Montfort's writings is attested to by Frank Duff himself. The founder of the Legion says: "The Legion of Mary owes, you might say, everything to the Montfort devotion."[33] And the Legion Handbook states: "It can be safely asserted that no Saint has played a greater part in the development of the Legion than he. The Handbook is full of his spirit. The prayers re-echo his very words. He is really the tutor of the Legion: thus invocation is due to him by the Legion almost as a matter of moral obligation."[34]

If the Legion Handbook is full of De Montfort's spirit, and if the Legion prayers re-echo his very words, it may be well for us to dwell briefly on the intimate relationship between the Handbook and the True Devotion. "It cannot be denied that the Handbook of the Legion of Mary is a striking follow-up of the *Treatise on True Devotion*. It takes up the same doctrine and carries it over into the field of effective and concrete

---

[29] *Loc. cit.*

[30] *Loc. cit.*

[31] *Art. cit.*, in *Maria*, Vol. 3, p. 637.

[32] Bishop P. Flynn, *La Légion de Marie*, offprint from *Lumen Vitae*, Vol. 8, 1953, p. 4.

[33] F. Duff, in his talk to the Montfort Fathers in Bay Shore, N. Y., on December 6, 1956. Cf. *Queen of All Hearts*, Vol. 7, March-April, 1957, p. 3.

[34] *Handbook*, p. 56.

action, within the reach of all men of good will."[35]

After pointing out that union with Mary entails sharing in her motherhood of souls, the Handbook invites each and every Legionary to read and study the writings of its "tutor," St. Louis De Montfort. In Chapter twenty-seven, entitled: "The duty of Legionaries towards Mary," we read that "Legionaries should undertake De Montfort's True Devotion to Mary." A few gleanings from this chapter will suffice to illustrate how the Legion of Mary strives to identify itself, so to speak, with the De Montfort way of spiritual life.

"It is desirable that the practice of the Legionary devotion to Mary should be rounded off and given the distinctive character which has been taught by St. Louis De Montfort under the titles of 'The True Devotion' or the 'Slavery of Mary' and which is enshrined in his two books, the *True Devotion to the Blessed Virgin* and the *Secret of Mary*."[36]

Describing the nature of this "Holy Slavery," the Handbook continues: "That devotion requires the formal entry into a compact with Mary, whereby one gives to her one's whole self, with all its thoughts, and deeds and possessions, both spiritual and temporal, past, present and future, without the reservation of the smallest part or slightest little thing. In a word, the giver places himself in a condition equivalent to that of a slave possessing nothing of his own, and wholly dependent on, and utterly at the disposal of Mary."[37]

Lest this total consecration to Mary be mistaken for a mere passing act of devotion toward the Mother of God, the Legionary is immediately reminded that although the True Devotion is inaugurated by a formal act of consecration, "... it consists principally in the subsequent living of that consecration. The True Devotion must represent not an act but a state."[38]

This state or attitude of soul of the individual Legionary will blossom forth, as we have already shown, into a Marian apostolate. "The work of the Legion," says the Handbook, "is essentially a hidden one. It commences in the heart of the individual Legionary, developing therein a spirit of zeal and charity."[39] Through the Legion system, this zeal and

---

[35] Suenens, *Saint Louis-Marie de Montfort et la Légion de Marie*, in *Marie*, Vol. 6, No. 3, 1952, p. 86.
[36] *Handbook*, p. 142.
[37] *Ibid.*, p. 142.
[38] *Loc. cit.*
[39] *Ibid.*, p. 282.

charity will ever become manifest by direct personal contact, in a soul-to-soul apostolate that will gradually raise the spiritual level of the entire community.

If we inquire now into the nature of this Legion approach to souls, again we will find that it is not only distinctly Marian but also, one might add, Montfortian. We quote from the Handbook: "Souls are not approached except with Mary."[40] Legionaries are asked to bring Mary to the world by leading souls to a "calm examination of the role of Mary" in God's plan of our redemption.[41] This will prompt them to give to others a full explanation of Mary's part in our lives and of the consequent "rich and full devotion" we owe her in return. Indeed, the Handbook asks: "How can Legionaries talk in any other terms of her?"[42]

Adopting De Montfort's method of interior life with Mary, the Handbook takes up the formula of "Through, With, In and For Mary," and transposes it into the apostolic life of the individual Legionary. Here are a few of its slogans, so to speak, culled at random from the Handbook: "Souls are not approached except *with* Mary."[43] "To tell Legionaries to immerse themselves in their work is but the same thing as to urge them to bury themselves *in* Mary."[44] "The Legion operates *through* Mary."[45] And, finally, "The Legionaries work *for* Mary, quite irrespective of the simplicity or the difficulty of the task."[46]

Such is the Marian spirituality of the Legion of Mary — a spirituality that is totally Marian, totally Montfortian. It might be noted here that although the actual making of the act of consecration known as *Holy Slavery* is not enjoined as an obligation or condition of membership in the Legion but rather left to the discretion and free choice of each Legionary, nevertheless, all Legionaries are reminded that the Legion "... declares itself to be built on a fulness of devotion to Mary which approximates, or is equivalent to, De Montfort's own special form."[47]

We can think of no better way of closing these considerations than by

---

[40] *Ibid.,* p. p. 308.
[41] *Ibid.,* p. 317.
[42] *Ibid.,* p. 316.
[43] *Ibid.,* p. 308.
[44] *Ibid.,* p. 179.
[45] *Ibid.,* p. 133.
[46] *Ibid.,* p. 140.
[47] Frank Duff, *The De Montfort Way* (Bay Shore, N. Y., 1947), p. 35.

quoting once again from the writings of the Legion's founder, Frank Duff. "It is desirable that every Legionary — not alone its Active Members, but likewise each one of its great host of Auxiliary Members — should possess a copy of De Montfort's monumental exposition of the *True Devotion*. They should read it again and again, and fully comprehend it and bring it into wholehearted play in their spiritual life. Only then will they enter into the spirit of the Legion of Mary, to which, as the Legion itself declares, Grignion de Montfort is veritably tutor."[48]

Such is, in broad outline, the basis for the Marian spirituality and apostolate of the Legion of Mary, an organization that seeks to identify itself with Mary in her essential function of mothering souls.

V. GROWTH AND CONQUESTS

Since the Legion is Our Lady working in and through her Legionaries, a study of this kind would be incomplete without at least a few statistics indicating the ever growing influence of this Catholic Action organization upon our modern world. Speaking of the growth of the Legion, Frank Duff once compared it to the growth of a tree. The process, he said, operates along the lines of a geometrical progression, that is, as the number of producing points grow, the rate of acceleration becomes prodigious.

For example, here is a listing of the Legion foundations in chronological order. 1921, Ireland; 1928, Scotland; 1929, England and Wales; 1931, United States and India; 1932, Canada and Australia; 1933, South Africa, British West Indies, New Zealand, Nigeria; 1936, Kenya; 1937, China, Burma, Tanganyika; 1938, Ceylon, Central America (Panama), Uganda; 1939, Southern Rhodesia; 1940, Philippines, France, Mauritius, Malta, Gold Coast, Nyasaland, Sierra Leone; 1941, Egypt; 1942, Netherlands, Gibraltar, Israel; 1943, Belgian Congo; 1944, Germany, Liberia; 1945, Reunion, Belgium, Luxembourg, Seyschelles (Indian Ocean), Mexico; 1946, Madagascar, Italy, Switzerland, Dominican Republic, Gambia; 1947, Colombia, Denmark, Sudan, Malaya, Martinique, Br. Cameroons, Northern Rhodesia; 1948, Japan, Vietnam, Algiers, Fr. Equatorial Africa, Fr. Cameroons; 1949, Austria, Lebanon, Portugal, Borneo, Hong Kong, Bahamas, Pakistan; 1950, Spain, Venezuela, Argentine, Paraguay, Puerto Rico, Haiti, Fiji Islands, Fr. Togoland; 1951, Chile, Indonesia, Cyprus, Peru, Angola; 1952, Macao, Taiwan, Thailand; 1953, Brazil, New Guinea, Cuba; 1954, Ecuador, Korea; 1955, Bolivia,

---

[48] *Loc. cit.*

Greece, Turkey, Norway, Nicaragua, Dutch Guiana, French Guiana; 1956, Costa Rica, Guatemala, El Salvador, Honduras, Dutch West Indies, Iceland; 1957, Arabia, Ethiopia, Kingdom of Jordan; 1958, Iraq, Sweden.

At this writing the Legion of Mary exists in approximately eleven hundred dioceses and vicariates, and we are told that each week two new dioceses are being added to the growing list. The greatest point of growth right now is in the Philippines. There are approximately five thousand five hundred *Praesidia* at work there at this time, and this number is increasing presently at the rate of not less than one new *Praesidium* every day. Another rapidly growing area is the Belgian Congo where there are over two thousand five hundred *Praesidia* at this writing.

The Legion of Mary Handbook has already been published in nineteen languages: English, Spanish, French, Dutch, Italian, Chinese, German, Japanese, Arabic, Lungunda (E. Africa), Swahili (E. Africa), Singhalese, Tamil (India), Telegu (India), Malayan, Portuguese, Korean, Maltese, and Sesuthol (Basutoland, So. Africa). Translations are in preparation in: Polish, Irish, Burmese, Russian and Indonesian. The Legion prayers have been published in approximately one hundred languages and dialects.

In a letter to this author, dated August 9, 1958, Frank Duff writes: "The Legion is in point of majority of members a coloured organization. It is working among all classes of people from the lettered to the most primitive. It has shown its power to get a *real* membership out of the latter. Also, a remarkable aspect of things has been the capacity of the Legion to convert. This has applied to all the separated sections, i.e., Protestants, Buddhists, Hindus, Mohammedans. Mohammedans have hitherto been considered as unconvertible, but the Legion in Africa has been getting plenty of successes among them, especially in the Belgian Congo."

To our request for statistics on validation of marriages, return to the Sacraments, etc., through the Legion apostolate, Brother Duff answers: "It would be absolutely impossible to give you any idea of those figures, because they are too immense. We had the Bishop of Cebu City, in the Philippines, here with us recently and he told us that in a single day, two thousand five hundred marriages were validated in that City, in the Stadium. It was all due to Legionary activity...

"In Chicago, in 1956, a visit to every home in one parish brought three hundred and sixty persons into Instruction Classes, of whom two hundred and thirty were received into the Church on the following 8th of

December. In the following year, another parish attempted the same visitation and succeeded in gathering together four hundred and eighty five. It will be realized," Mr. Duff concludes, "that there is nothing special about those particular parishes, and that the same sort of results could be gained elsewhere with the same sort of effort."

We could not conclude this brief study without mentioning the Legion in chains — we refer to the Legion behind the "Iron" and the "Bamboo" curtains. Yes, we refer to the glorious and immortal pages written in the blood of its martyrs in China, where four thousand Legionaries have already been put to death for their faith and for their membership in the Legion of Mary, and where some twenty thousand are still in prison and yet a vast unknown number retained in forced labor camps.

If a tree is judged by its fruits, and if the blood of martyrs is the seed of Christians, then the Legion of Mary has every reason to hope for a glorious future in the battle front of Mary's and the Church's warfare against the forces of evil. And if Edel Quinn (whose cause for heroic virtue has already been introduced) is any indication as to what heights of holiness the Legion's Marian spirituality and apostolate can lead a soul, then we believe with the Legion and with St. Louis De Montfort that "Mary has produced, together with the Holy Ghost, the greatest thing that has been or ever will be — a God-Man; and she will consequently produce the greatest of the saints that there will be in the end of time. The formation and the education of the great saints who shall come at the end of the world are reserved for her. For it is only that singular and miraculous Virgin who can produce, in union with the Holy Ghost, singular and extraordinary things."[49]

To anyone who wants to see the Holy Spirit working through Mary in an organization of Catholic Action, we say: look at the Legion of Mary.

BIBLIOGRAPHY

Anonymous, *La Légion de Maria,* in *Ephemerides Mariologicae,* Vol. 3, 1953, pp. 130-132; P. Flynn, Bp. of Nevers, *The Legion of Mary and Religious Formation,* in *Lumen Vitae,* Vol. 8, 1953, pp. 271-282; Ch. H. Helmsing, Bp. of Springfield-Cape Girardeau, Mo., *Priests Who Have Made the Legion of Mary,* in *Queen of All Hearts,* Vol. 4, Nov.-Dec., 1953, pp. 12-13; M. Lefevre, *La Légion de Marie,* in *Evangéliser,* Vol. 7, 1953, pp. 441-466; Fr. Leonard, C.P., *The Legion of Mary,* in *The Clergy Review,* Vol. 4, 1932, pp. 380-388;

---

[49] *True Devotion to the Blessed Virgin Mary* (Bay Shore, N. Y., 1946), p. 23, No. 35.

M. O'Carroll, C.S.Sp., *The Legion of Mary*, in *The Irish Ecclesiastical Record*, Vol. 66, 1945, pp. 353-359; L. J. Suenens, *The Theology of the Apostolate of the Legion of Mary* (Westminster, Md., 1954), 159 pp.; *Id., Saint Louis-Marie de Montfort et la Légion de Marie*, in *Marie*, Vol. 6, n. 3, 1952, pp. 85-87; *Id., Spiritualité et rayonnement de la Légion de Marie*, in *Maria. Études sur la Sainte Vierge*, ed. H. du Manoir, Vol. 3 (Paris, 1954), pp. 637-658; I. Omaechevarría, O.F.M., *La Legión de María en el mundo*, in *Semanario Católico*, mayo 9-15, 1954, pp. 48-59; Frank Duff, *The De Montfort Way* (Bay Shore, N. Y., 1947), 38 pp.; *Id., The Spirit of the Legion of Mary* (Glasgow, 1956), 241 pp.; *Official Handbook of the Legion of Mary*, 6th American edition (Louisville, Ky., 1953), 348 pp.; *Maria Legionis*, Official quarterly publication, Dublin.; L. J. Suenens, *Edel Quinn* (Dublin, 1954), 272 pp.; *The Marianist*, Dayton, Ohio, Vol. 46, No. 9; Vol. 48, No. 9; R. M. Charest, S.M.M., *Are You Acquainted With the Legion of Mary?* (Bay Shore, N. Y., 1955), 63 pp.; N. Tchistiakoff, *Des sans-Dieu à la Légion de Marie*, in *Marie, salut du monde* (Paris, 1954), pp. 178-186; *Symposium on the Legion of Mary*, reproduced from the *Capuchin Annual* (Dublin, 1957), 96 pp.; Cecily Hallack, *The Legion of Mary* (London, 1940), 192 pp.; F. J. Ripley, *Holiness Through Mary. A Companion to the Handbook of the Legion of Mary* (Glasgow, 1950), 63 pp.

MARIOLOGICAL SOCIETIES

by ERIC MAY, O.F.M.Cap.

A VERY strong indication that ours is a Marian century lies in the recent great advancement of Mariology as a science. One factor which made this possible was the establishment over the past thirty years of several national Mariological Societies in different parts of the world. The very number of such specialized groups and the outstanding quality of the work they have produced within so short a time is a phenomenon perhaps unparalleled in the history of the Church.

In this brief, factual treatise we propose to discuss in outline form the history and work of all known national Mariological Societies throughout the world. It should be kept in mind that we are not speaking here of Marian centers, academies, congresses, and similar activities. We limit our discussion to those groups of priests and theologians, united on a national level, who convene at least annually to discuss Mariological questions. So far as data are available, we intend also to mention the topics treated by these learned societies and to note the papers they have published.

I. BELGIUM (Flemish Society)

First in point of time was the *Flemish Mariological Society*.[1] Under the guidance of the noted Marian scholar, Canon Joseph Bittremieux, a group of interested theologians met in 1931 at the Norbertine Abbey of Tongerloo, Belgium. Various aspects of Mariology were discussed, and those present agreed to continue meeting at Tongerloo annually, as a society. When Canon Bittremieux died in 1950, Prof. Al Van Hove succeeded him as president, and the scholarly work continued. The valuable annual proceedings have been published under the general title,

---

[1] Cf. M. Bélanger, O.M.I., *Sociétés d'Études Mariales*, in *Ère mariale*, Vol. 1, March, 1956, p. 2 ff.; A. Van Hove, *25 Jaar "Mariale Dagen,"* in *Mariale Dagen*, Vol. 14, 1956, pp. 113-127; R. Spiazzi (ed.), *Enciclopedia Mariana "Theotocos"* (Milano, 1954), pp. 630-631; J. B. Carol, O.F.M., *The Mariological Movement in the World Today*, in *Marian Studies*, Vol. 1, 1950, p. 27.

Mariale Dagen.[2] Even a bare listing of the topics discussed year by year gives a sure indication of the Flemish society's vitality and thoroughness. The following schema indicates the main topics discussed annually. All meetings took place at Tongerloo.

1. 1931 — Various Aspects of Mariology.
2. 1932 — Mary as the New Eve.
3. 1933 — Mary's Perpetual Virginity.
4. 1934 — Mary's Assumption.
5. 1935 — Mary's Queenship.
6. 1936 — Mary's Divine Maternity.
7. 1937 — Mary's Immaculate Conception.
8. 1938 — Mary's Fullness of Grace.[3]
9. 1946 — Mary's Coredemption.[4]
10. 1948 — Mary as Dispensatrix of All Grace.
11. 1951 — Mary's Assumption and Her Other Prerogatives.
12. 1953 — Mary's Spiritual Maternity.[5]
13. 1955 — Mary's Queenship in the Light of the Encyclical *Ad Caeli Reginam.*
14. 1956 — Devotion to Mary in the modern Era.
15. 1957 — The Fundamental Principle of Mariology.
16. 1958 — Our Lady in the Liturgy.
17. 1959 — Mary in the Annunciation Narrative.

II. FRANCE

Next, chronologically, came the French society of Mariologists,

---

[2] The volumes of *Mariale Dagen* are published at Norbertijner Abdij, Tongerloo, Belgium.

[3] After the year 1938, war and the preparation for war took their toll. It is worthy of note that in 1943 — shortly before a French-Belgian session at Namur — the *Mariale Dagen* group met once more to discuss Consecration to Mary. These proceedings, however, were published apart from the regular *Mariale Dagen* series, under the title *De Toewijding aan O.L. Vrouw* (Tongerloo, 1944). Cf. the Editorial in *Consécration Mariale* (Louvain, 1948), p. 5.

[4] In the year 1947, a National Marian Congress was held at Maastricht. This replaced the meeting of the Belgian Flemish society for that year.

[5] In the year 1954, a National Marian Congress again replaced the *Mariale Dagen*. These proceedings, dealing with the Immaculate Conception, were published at Tongerloo in 1955 under the title *Verslagboek der Priester-Vergaderingen.*

officially known as *La Société Française d'Études Mariales*. This group of twenty-four scholars with a common interest in Marian theology met for the first time in 1935, at Paray-le-Monial. First president of the society was Fr. B.-M. Morineau, who guided the destiny of the group well until his death in 1949. He was succeeded by the well-known patrologist, Msgr. G. Jouassard. With the exception of the war years, 1939-1946, the members of this society have met faithfully every year to discuss problems of Mariological interest. And each year the annual proceedings have been published under the title *Bulletin de la Société Français d'Études Mariales.*[6] Unlike the Flemish group, the French society convenes in a different city of France each year. And unlike most other Mariological groups, the French scholars have frequently devoted as many as three meetings to various aspects of a single topic. The work accomplished in their yearly conventions is truly impressive.

1. 1935 — Paray-le-Monial — the Mariology of Various Doctors of the Church, and Mary's Spiritual Maternity.
2. 1936 — Mours — Various Mariological Problems, Especially Mary's Merit.
3. 1937 — La Pierre-qui-Vire — Mary's Queenship, Mary and the Hypostatic Order, Mary and the Mystical Body.
4. 1938 — Saulchoir — Mary's Primacy, and the Role of Analogy in Mariology.
5. 1947 — Chartres — Mary's Sanctity.
6. 1948 — Lyons — Mary's Assumption (session 1).
7. 1949 — N.-D. du Chêne and Solesmes — Mary's Assumption (session 2).
8. 1950 — St.-Laurent-sur-Sèvre — Mary's Assumption (session 3).
9. 1951 — Allier — Mary and the Church (session 1).
10. 1952 — Le Puy — Mary and the Church (session 2).
11. 1953 — Lille — Mary and the Church (session 3).
12. 1954 — Lyons — Mary as the New Eve (session 1).
13. 1955 — Angers — Mary as the New Eve (session 2).
14. 1956 — Besançon — Mary as the New Eve (session 3).
15. 1957 — Chevilly — Mary as the New Eve (session 4).
16. 1958 — Lourdes — Mary's Queenship.
17. 1959 — Blois — Mary's Spiritual Motherhood (session 1).

---

[6] Issues of the *Bulletin* are obtainable through P. Lethielleux, 10 rue Cassette, Paris.

According to the latest *Bulletin* available, the French Mariological Society numbered one hundred and nine members in 1959 and is growing rapidly.

III. SPAIN

The Marian authors and theologians of Spain entered the picture as a society in 1941. Their founder was the renowned theologian Fr. Narciso García Garcés, C.M.F. The decision to found the *Sociedad Mariológica Española,* as it is officially called, took form at a national Marian Congress in the city of Saragossa the previous year and was put into effect with an initial meeting at Madrid.[7] A point of particular interest to the Spanish theologians was the desire to bring to the fore the excellent Mariological studies of Spanish scholars from the sixteenth to the eighteenth centuries. The society began with forty-eight charter members. After the first three meetings in Madrid, the group began meeting annually in various cities throughout Spain. All the painstaking work done by the members has been published in the society's organ, *Estudios Marianos.*[8] One gets a good idea of what has been done by considering the topics of the annual conventions.

1. 1941 — Madrid — Various Mariological Problems.
2. 1942 — Madrid — Mary's Coredemption.
3. 1943 — Madrid — the Principles of Mariology.
4. 1944 — Fátima — Mary's Immaculate Heart.
5. 1945 — Saragossa — the Nature of Mary's Grace.
6. 1946 — Montserrat — Mary's Assumption.
7. 1947 — Valencia — Mary's Spiritual Maternity.
8. 1948 — Madrid — Mary's Divine Maternity.
9. 1949 — Salamanca — Mary's Death.[9]
10. 1950 — Rome — Current Mariological Problems.
11. 1951 — Madrid — the Encyclical *Munificentissimus Deus.*

---

[7] Cf. Bélanger, in *Ère mariale,* Vol. 1, March, 1956, p. 4; Spiazzi, *op. cit.,* p. 631; and the introduction to the first volume of *Estudios Marianos,* 1942.

[8] Issues of *Estudios Marianos* are obtainable from Edit. Coculsa, Victor Pradera, 65, Madrid, Spain. The first three volumes are now out of print.

[9] A second volume covering the proceedings of this 1949 meeting, contains papers contributed by visiting Mariologists from other lands.

12. 1952 — Barcelona — Mary and the Eucharist.
13. 1953 — Santander — the Mariology of St. Bernard.
14. 1954 — Saragossa — the Immaculate Conception.
15. 1955 — Valencia — Mary's Queenship.
16. 1956 — Aránzazu — Mary and the Church.
17. 1957 — Madrid — Mary's Coredemption.
18. 1958 — Lourdes — Mary's Motherhood of the Church.
19. 1959 — Madrid — Mary's Virginity.

In 1959 the members of this Spanish society numbered forty-two, the membership being distinguished more for its quality than for its quantity.

IV. PORTUGAL

Portugal followed the lead of her next-door neighbor, Spain, by attempting to establish a similar Mariological Society under the name of *Academia Marial Portuguesa*. In 1944, Portuguese scholars had joined their Spanish colleagues in a Marian Congress at Fátima to discuss the Immaculate Heart of Mary. As a result of that congress, theologians in Portugal were encouraged to found their own Mariological society. The work of organization was entrusted to Canon Manuel Mendes de Carmo and Fr. Aníbal Coelho.[10] A first meeting in 1945 found His Excellency, Bishop José Alves Correia da Silva presiding. Unfortunately, the nascent society appears to have died at birth; there has been no further evidence up to now of work done by its members as a group.[11]

V. CANADA

Once the disastrous war years were over, interest in Mariology spanned the ocean and found ready roots in Canada and the United States. In Canada, this interest was fanned to flame by the great fervor attendant upon the Marian Congress held at Ottawa, June 22, 1947. A few months later, December 16th, a dream of many years began to materialize with an official notice from His Excellency, the Most Reverend Alexandre Vachon, Archbishop of Ottawa, of the existence of *La Société Canadienne d'Etudes*

---

[10] Cf. the prologue of the volume *Estudos Marianos* (Congresso Mariologico Luso-Espanhol na Fátima), Fátima, 1945. The constitution of the proposed society is found on pp. 197-199. This single volume represents the work done by the Portuguese at the Fátima meeting, and was intended to be the first of a series of annual volumes.

[11] Cf. J. B. Carol, *art. cit.*, p. 28.

Mariales. Then in 1948, a meeting was organized at Montreal by the *Comité Marial Franciscain du Canada,* forerunner as it were of the national organization. The first theological convention of the new Canadian Mariological Society was held at Ottawa in February, 1949, under the presidency of the well-known scholar, Dr. Augustus Ferland, P.S.S.[12] The meetings held and the topics discussed so far, are as follows:

1. 1949 — Ottawa — Mary's Assumption and Coredemption.
2. 1950 — Ottawa — Mary's Assumption and Coredemption.
3. 1951 — Cap-de-la-Madeleine — Mary's Assumption and Coredemption.
4. 1952 — Nicolet — Mary's Assumption and Coredemption.
5. 1953 — Montreal — Mary's Assumption and Coredemption.
6. 1954 — Cap-de-la-Madeleine — Immaculate Conception.
7. 1955 — Quebec — Mary's Queenship.
8. 1956 — Sherbrooke — Mary's Spiritual Maternity.
9. 1957 — Ottawa — Mary's Spiritual Maternity.
10. 1958 — Lourdes — Mary's Coredemption.

Some of the valuable dissertations read at the above meetings have already been published.[13] The society publishes also a modest bulletin of information on the current Mariological movement, called *Ère mariale.* In 1950 and 1954 the Canadian Mariological Society participated actively in the International Mariological Congresses held in Rome.

At first, the number of active members was limited to twenty, then thirty — as a means of preserving intact the scientific aims of the group. This measure was dropped as unnecessary at the 1954 meeting. In 1956, forty-five active members were listed, including eleven diocesan priests, two members of the laity, and thirty-two religious. There are numerous other members spiritually affiliated to the society.

---

[12] Cf. M. Bélanger, *Sociétés d'Études Mariales,* in *Ère mariale,* Vol. 1, April, 1956, pp. 2-4.

[13] For example, in the proceedings of the 1954 meeting, under the title *L'Immaculée Conception de la Bienheureuse Vierge Marie* (Editions de l'Université d'Ottawa, 1955); the proceedings of the 1955 meeting, under the title *La Royauté de l'Immaculée* (Editions de l'Université d'Ottawa, 1957); and the proceedings of the 1957 and 1958 meetings, two volumes under the title *La Maternité spirituelle de la Bienheureuse Vierge Marie* (Editions de l'Université d'Ottawa, 1958). We note that some of the papers read at the 1952 meeting appeared in the periodical *Marie* (Nicolet), Vol. 6, No. 5, 1953.

VI. UNITED STATES

In the United States of America, a country consecrated to the Blessed Mother of God, it was only a matter of time before her scholars pooled their talents and efforts toward the establishment of a Mariological Society.[14] The spadework of this movement was done at a preparatory meeting held in Holy Name College, Washington, D. C., the evening of October 11, 1949. At the invitation of Fr. Juniper B. Carol, O.F.M., the founder and constant guiding spirit behind this society, thirty-nine theologians met and agreed to establish *The Mariological Society of America*.[15] This decision was remarkable in that only several years previous, a very vigorous and flourishing sister society had been founded: *The Theological Society of America*. The Most Rev. Patrick A. O'Boyle, Archbishop of Washington, gave his blessing to the Marian project, and the society struck root at a second preliminary meeting one month later, November 8. The fruit was not long in coming. Early in January, 1950, the first annual national convention of the Mariological Society was held at the Catholic University of America, in Washington, D. C. One hundred and thirty-one charter members were listed. The constitution of the society was approved and the purpose of the group affirmed: "to promote an exchange of views on Marian doctrines and to further research in Mariology." Each succeeding convention of these American theologians has proved the wisdom of establishing such a society, and the results in terms of learned Mariological papers and fruitful discussion have been outstanding.[16] Even a bare listing of the topics discussed at the annual meetings is most imposing.

1. 1950 — Washington, D. C. — Various Marian Topics, Especially the Mariological Movement in the World Today, and the Use of Sacred Scripture in Mariology.
2. 1951 — Worcester, Mass. — Mary's Coredemption.
3. 1952 — New York City —Mary's Spiritual Maternity.

---

[14] For a fuller account, cf. *The Foundation of the Society*, in *Marian Studies*, Vol. 1, 1950, pp. 11-16.

[15] Cf. J. C. Fenton, *America's Two Theological Associations*, in *The American Ecclesiastical Review*, Vol. 125, 1951, pp. 449-458.

[16] The proceedings of the annual meetings have been published faithfully in a series called *Marian Studies*. With the exception of the first three volumes, the series is still obtainable from the editor, Fr. Juniper B. Carol, O.F.M., Franciscan Monastery, 174 Ramsey Street, Paterson 1, N. J.

4. 1953 — Cleveland, Ohio — Mary's Universal Queenship.
5. 1954 — Washington, D. C. — Mary's Immaculate Conception.
6. 1955 — St. Louis, Mo.— Mary's Divine Maternity.
7. 1956 — New York City — Mary's Virginity.
8. 1957 — Chicago, Ill. — Mary's Death.
9. 1958 — Dayton, Ohio — Mary and the Church.
10. 1959 — Paterson, N. J. — The Fundamental Principle of Mariology.
11. 1960 — Detroit, Mich. — Our Lady in the Gospels.
12. 1961 — Pittsburgh, Pa. — Mary in the Old Testament.

An indication of the vitality of this American group is the constant increase in membership. As of January, 1961, three hundred and thirty-three active members and sixty-five associate members were listed. An average of one hundred members attend each meeting.

VII. BELGIUM (French Society)

The Belgian Mariological Society for French-speaking priests had its inception in a noteworthy day of "Marian Sacerdotal Studies" in 1943. Led by His Excellency, Bishop Charue of Namur, almost three-hundred participants, mostly parish priests, took an active and interested part in the studies, and were encouraged to think in terms of founding their own counterpart of the Flemish *Mariale Dagen*. World conditions being what they were at the time, realization of these high hopes had to be deferred until 1951. In that year, through the initiative of the Bishop of Namur, the hierarchy of Malines, Liège, and Tournai selected a committee to found this Mariological society for French-speaking Belgians. The first president, Msgr. J. Lebon, was assisted by four professors and doctors of theology. Yearly meetings were planned under the official title *Journées Sacerdotales d'Études Mariales*. One year the tone of the meeting was to be scientific and doctrinal; the next year the presentation was to be practical and popular. Thirty-nine scholars were present for the first annual convention in 1951.[17] To the best of our knowledge, the following schema represents the fruitful work done by this society.

---

[17] The above information was gathered from the introductions to the first two volumes published by the society, as indicated in footnotes 18 and 19. Cf. also the article *Le mouvement marial en Belgique*, in *Ephemerides Mariologicae*, Vol. 2, 1952, pp. 449-450.

1. 1943 — Namur — Consecration to Mary.[18]
2. 1951 — Dinant — (doctrinal) the Scientific Structure of Mariology.[19]
3. 1952 — Basse-Wavre — (practical) Means Toward an Easier Understanding of Marian Doctrine, and Giving It Its Proper Place in the Faith of the People.[20]
4. 1953 — Dinant — (doctrinal).[21]

VIII. GERMANY

In the closing days of December, 1951, Dr. Carl Feckes, professor of Mariology at the Seminary of Cologne, gathered together a group of twenty-three interested German theologians and Marian authors at Königstein, to discuss the feasibility of a Mariological society for Germany. With their enthusiastic support, and more from scholars unable to attend the meeting, plans were laid to found the *Mariologische Arbeitsgemeinschaft Deutscher Theologen.* Those present decided to treat relevant Marian topics scientifically, in their relationship to ecclesiology, anthropology, mysticism, the doctrine on grace, and the like. Yearly meetings were agreed on, to be held during the Christmas holidays, and at Frankfurt if possible. Though in existence only a half-dozen years, the German Society has already made its mark in the field of Mariology, as is evident from the work done at its annual conventions.

1. 1952 — Frankfurt-Main — Pope Leo XIII's Marian Phrase: "[B.V.] ipsius generis humani personam quodammodo agebat."
2. 1953 — Königstein — Mary as Representative of the Church.[22]
3. 1955 — Würzburg — the Importance and Significance of the

---

[18] These proceedings were published in 1948 by the Secrétariat de Marie Médiatrice, Boulevard de Diest, 121, Louvain.

[19] These doctrinal proceedings were published in 1952 by the Abbayé Notre Dame de Leffe, Dinant.

[20] The papers delivered at the Journées Sacerdotales Mariales (session pratique) were published in the periodical *Évangéliser,* Vol. 7, No. 40 (Bruxelles), 1953.

[21] This latest available information is supplied by M. Bélanger, in *Ère mariale,* Vol. 1, April, 1956, p. 2.

[22] The German society has published the 1952 and 1953 proceedings in one volume, edited by C. Feckes, and entitled *Die Heilsgeschichtliche Stellvertretung der Menschheit durch Maria,* Paderborn, 1954.

Franciscan School With Regard to Mariology.[23]
4. 1956 — Frankfurt-Main — the Dogmatico-Scriptural Proof in Mariology.
5. 1958 — Lourdes — Parallelism Between Mary and the Church.

The presence of fifty-five members at the 1957 meeting is an indication of the increasing prestige of the German society.

IX. ITALY

Many important Marian Congresses and Academies have been held over the years in Rome and other Italian cities. As yet, however, nothing corresponding to the specialized Mariological societies of other nations has materialized in Italy. That attempts to found such a society may well be realized soon seems evident from a number of resolutions passed at recent Marian gatherings.[24]

X. MEXICO

The *Mexican Mariological Society* had its origin in a Marian meeting held in the city of Guadalajara (Jalisco) in 1954, the Marian Year. It was promoted principally by His Excellency, The Most Rev. Alfonso Toriz, Bishop of Chilapa (now Bishop of Querétaro), the Rt. Rev. Msgr. José Ruiz

---

[23] No local meeting of the society took place in 1954, since some of its members participated in the International Mariological Congress in Rome that year. The proceedings of the 1955 meeting were published in the periodical *Franziskanische Studien*, Vol. 39, 1957, fasc. 2-4. Cf. also R. Graber, *Arbeitsgemeinschaft deutscher Theologen*, in *Lexikon der Marienkunde* (Regensburg, 1958), fasc. 2, coll. 338-339.

[24] In 1954, the *Centro di Orientamento Pastorale* held a Mariological week in conjunction with several Marian Academies and Centers, under the presidency of Prof. D. G. Ceriani. At its close, the following resolutions were passed: "Che anche in Italia, come già in altre Nazioni, si constituisca una Società Mariana allo scopo di coordinare gli studi e i movimenti mariani italiani." And again, "Promuoviamo la fondazione di una 'Società Mariologica Italiana' che ha come scopo l'incremento degli studi mariologici in Italia e l'orientamento della vita pastorale nella luce di Maria." Cf. *La Società Mariologica Italiana*, in *L'Osservatore Romano*, 7 Nov., 1954, p. 4. Later on, a Sacerdotal Marian Congress on Mary's Queenship was held in Bologna in September, 1956, organized by the *Centro Mariano Montfortano di Roma*, under the presidency of His Eminence, Cardinal G. Lercaro, Archbishop of Bologna. At its end His Eminence made another impassioned plea for the foundation of an Italian Mariological Society like those of other nations. Cf. G. M. Barbera, S.M.M., in *Marianum*, Vol. 18, 1956, pp. 420-422.

Medrano, and Fr. Prudencio Lerena, C.M.F. The date October 16, 1957, marked the formal foundation of the society, in the Basilica of Our Lady of Guadalupe. The following three days were devoted to the first theological meeting, the subject of discussion being Mary's Spiritual Maternity in the Fourth Gospel. Four papers were read. M. Peinador, C.M.F., gave an introduction to biblical sources and theological method of investigation. He followed this with an exegetical paper on John 19:25-27 in which the words of Christ are seen to proclaim Mary's universal motherhood. Fr. Joseph G. Vergara, S.J., gave an exposition of John 19:25-27 according to the magisterium of recent popes, and Fr. A. Mercado, O.F.M., explained the same text according to some Franciscan theologians of the Middle Ages, especially St. Bernardine of Siena. It is expected that all of these studies will be published soon as the first volume of the society's proceedings.[25]

XI. POLAND

The latest addition to the growing list of national societies devoted to the study of Mariology is that of Poland. Already since 1953 Polish Mariologists of various religious orders had gathered annually to discuss Marian topics, particularly Our Lady's Mediation; but the Society, as such, was not formally organized until it held its first meeting at the national shrine of Jasna Góra on October 14 and 15, 1958. First president of the Society is the well-known theologian, Father Bernard M. Przybylski, O.P.[26]

From the foregoing survey, brief but factual, it is readily apparent why the twentieth century is indeed the "Age of Mary," and that Mary's loyal sons and scholars in virtually every nation under heaven are probing deeper and deeper into her mysteries and prerogatives.[27]

---

[25] For this information on the Mexican Mariological Society, the author is indebted to Fr. Máximo Peinador, C.M.F., and to Fr. Juniper B. Carol, O.F.M. Cf. likewise M. de L., C.M.F., *Sociedad Mariológica Mexicana*, in *Ephemerides Mariologicae*, Vol. 8, 1958, pp. 353-354.

[26] Cf. Anon., *Jasnogórskie Studium Mariologieczne*, in *Ephemerides Mariologicae*, Vol. 9, 1959, pp. 345-346.

[27] As this chapter is submitted to the Editor, we learn of activities leading to the formation of a Mariological Society in Colombia, South America. Headquarters of the organization will be the newly erected "Marian Centre" attached to the famed national shrine of *Nuestra Señora de la Peña*, in Bogotá. For further information, cf. R. Tisnés, C.M.F., *Sociedad Mariológica Colombiana*, in *Virtud y Letras*, Vol. 17, 1957, pp. 259-264.

MARIAN CENTERS, LIBRARIES, AND PUBLICATIONS

by REV. WILLIAM G. MOST, Ph.D.

NOT the least among the many evidences of growth in interest in Mariology during the past few decades is the development of many Marian centers of study, libraries, and publications. It is primarily through these media that our students and scholars are ever enriching their fund of knowledge concerning Our Blessed Lady's unique prerogatives. Hence it is felt that the present chapter will be of some profit to readers seeking further information on things Mariological.

While all Marian libraries may, of course, be regarded as Marian centers, there are many Marian centers which do not possess a library. We shall endeavor to be complete only in our mention of the former; space limitations allow us to give only a few examples of the latter.

I. MARIAN LIBRARIES AND MARIAN CENTERS

1. *Rome.* Probably the oldest and most important of all Marian libraries in the world is that under the direction of the Servite Fathers at the International Marian Center of the College of St. Alexius Falconieri in Rome. The idea of a specialized Marian library, to serve as a memorial of the 50th anniversary celebration of the definition of the Immaculate Conception, was proposed at the Marian Congress of 1904 in Rome. An appeal made at that time resulted in the gathering of some 2250 Marian volumes by September, 1905, not counting 213 special albums commemorating the anniversary in a special way. In accordance with the wish of Pope St. Pius X, the library was housed at first in the Pontifical Leonine College. Later (the date and reason are uncertain) it was moved to the Pontifical Apollinaris Seminary. In 1945, realizing that the library was not developing and was used relatively little, Father Gabriel M. Roschini, O.S.M., in a private audience with Pope Pius XII, suggested that the collection be moved to the College of St. Alexius. His Holiness was pleased, and accordingly, after a formal request was made and granted in 1946, the library was transferred to the Servite college in November of the same year. Since then it has grown into an important and much frequented center of Marian research. On January 1, 1956, the library

possessed 7851 volumes, not counting some 24 manuscripts, 44 microfilms, many reviews (both scientific and popular), and a special collection of Marian works written by members of the Servite Order since 1940. In addition, on January 13, 1956, Pope Pius XII entrusted to the library also the albums and special volumes sent to the Holy See from all over the world during the Marian Year of 1954. Those who use the facilities of this library also have the important advantage of being able to consult the numerous theological works in the general library of the college, which contains some forty-five thousand volumes, a facility which is essential if one wishes to study the development of theological thought on various Marian theses as presented *passim* in the more general theological writings of past centuries.

Actually, the Marian library is but one of many Marian activities of the *Centro Mariano Internazionale* (founded in 1945) at the College of St. Alexius. The center publishes many Marian works, including the *Ragguaglio Mariano* (beginning in 1948), the *Rassegna Bibliografica Mariana*, the *Bibliografia Mariana*, and the important quarterly, *Marianum* (founded by Father Roschini in 1939), the oldest scientific journal of Mariology. The center also maintains an agency for the sale of Marian books. This service began with expositions of Marian books, and grew to such an extent that in April, 1951, it was moved to a separate location, at Via SS. Apostoli 14.[1]

2. The International Franciscan Marian Commission, established in 1946 at the Pontifical Roman University of St. Anthony, developed, in 1950, into the *Accademia Mariana Internazionale.* The Academy is not a Mariological society in the usual sense. Its chief activity is the promotion of Marian congresses and scholarly publications, under the direction of Father Charles Balić, O.F.M. The publications fall chiefly into seven important collections: The *Bibliotheca Assumptionis,* the *Bibliotheca Immaculatae Conceptionis,* the *Bibliotheca Mediationis,* the *Bibliotheca Mariana Medii Aevi,* the *Studia Mariana* (8 volumes containing more than 100 conferences given at six congresses organized by the Friars Minor

---

[1] Cf. G. M. Besutti, O.S.M., *La Biblioteca Mariana*, and *Movimento Mariano O.S.M.* in *Studi Storici dell'Ordine dei Servi di Maria*, Vol. 5, 1953, pp. 120-126, 127-130; L. W. Monheim, S.M., *Some Marian Collections in the World*, in *Marian Studies*, Vol. 1, 1950, pp. 46-47; L. Di Fonzo, O.F.M.Conv., *Istituti, manifestazioni e centri mariani di studio e di cultura*, in R. Spiazzi, O.P. (Ed.). *Enciclopedia Mariana "Theotocos"* (Genova, 1954), pp. 631, 633; G. M. Roschini, O.S.M., *La Biblioteca Mariana Pio XII* (Roma, 1956); N. García Garcés, *Instituto Mariológico*, in *Ephemerides Mariologicae*, Vol. 9, 1959, pp. 344-345.

before the definition of the Assumption). *Alma Socia Christi* (12 volumes with the papers given at the Mariological Congress of 1950 in Rome) and, more recently, the *Bibliotheca Mariana Moderni Aevi, Virgo Immaculata* (18 volumes containing the papers read at the Mariological Congress of Rome in 1954), and *Maria et Ecclesia*, a set of several volumes now in course of publication, which gathers the dissertations read at the 1958 International Mariological Congress of Lourdes.[2]

3. *Lérida*. Leaving the Eternal City, we travel westward to Spain, where, in 1862, the Rev. D. José María Escolá Cugat, an apostolic missionary, founded the Pontifical and Royal Marian-Bibliographical Academy of Lérida, as a permanent memorial of the definition of the Immaculate Conception. The founder wished to proclaim in his native land that, as the motto of the Academy says: "Spain is the Patrimony of Mary," and to urge Catholics everywhere to do "All for and through Mary." The Academy, as its title indicates, strives to publish and circulate, at a very low price, both ancient and modern writings in praise of Mary. Annual contests for Marian works are held. Pope Pius IX and every subsequent Pope have shown special marks of favor to the Academy. The Pontifical title was granted by Pope Pius XI, the Royal title by Alfonso XII. The Academy has members even outside of Spain, especially in Venezuela and the Philippines. It possesses a special shrine, having an image of the Immaculate Conception distinguished by a silver heart adorned with jewels, made in 1866.[3]

4. *Pontmain*. To the north, at Pontmain, France, at the site of an apparition of Our Lady in 1871, we find a Marian library and museum, founded in 1928 by Mlle. de Crozé as the first Marian museum in France. It holds a wide variety of documents, engravings, images, photographs, medals, relics. It is especially rich in literature relative to Marian apparitions and Marian shrines in France and elsewhere. In January, 1956, the library had about 1600 books, brochures, and notices on Mariology and Marian pilgrimages, Orders, art, and literature.[4] A special feature is a room having the *Hail Mary* in 600 languages and dialects. The museum also has

---

[2] Cf. Di Fonzo, *art. cit.*, p. 631, and A. A. Maguire, O.F.M., *The International Marian Academy*, in *The American Ecclesiastical Review*, Vol. 131, 1954, pp. 178-179. Since this chapter went to press, Pope John XXIII has raised this Academy to the rank of "Pontifical." Cf. *Maiora in dies*, of Dec. 8, 1959, in *A.A.S.*, Vol. 52, 1960, pp. 24-26.

[3] Cf. Luis Borrás, *La Pontificia y Real Academia Bibliográfico-Mariana de Lérida*, in *Ephemerides Mariologicae*, Vol. 4, 1954, pp. 499-503; and Di Fonzo, *art. cit.*, p. 630.

[4] Cf. *La Croix*, July 4, 1950, p. 3 (figures based on a personal letter from Pontmain).

wax images of many persons to whom Our Lady has appeared.

5. *Vauban.* At the Abbey of Our Lady of the Turning Stone, at St. Leger, Vauban, France, we meet with another Marian museum and library, established by Dom Marie Dannay, O.S.B., in 1939. The museum houses a permanent Marian exposition of objects of art, tokens of pilgrimages, pictures, statues, medals, etc. The Marian library, which is especially rich in monographs on French Marian sanctuaries, contained, on January 1, 1956, about 1200 Marian books and pamphlets.

6. *Dreux.* There is also a Marian library at the Redemptorist seminary in Dreux (Eure-et-Loire) in France. It was founded in 1900 by the Rev. John Herrmann, C.Ss.R., along with the general theological library of the seminary conducted by the Redemptorist Fathers. It is especially rich in older works, having forty-five books of the sixteenth century, three hundred and fifty of the seventeenth century, twenty of the eighteenth century, one thousand of the nineteenth century, and five hundred of the twentieth century.

7. *Banneux.* A specially fine Marian library is located at Banneux in Belgium, where Our Lady appeared in 1933. Abbé L. Arendt, a priest of the diocese of Liège, began his library in July, 1942. By the end of 1957, it possessed well over 13,000 volumes, not counting several hundred Marian magazines.[5] The Banneux library has become an important center of information to hundreds of students of Mariology throughout the world.

8. *Benburb.* The Servite Priory of Our Lady of Benburb, in Benburb, North Ireland, has a Marian Library which was founded in 1948 by the Very Rev. James M. Keane, O.S.M. By the end of 1955 it had approximately 700 Marian books.

9. *Nicolet.* The zeal of a distinguished Canadian layman, Commander Roger Brien, S.G.G., is chiefly responsible for the splendid growth of the *Centre Marial Canadien,* at Nicolet, P.Q., founded in 1946 with M. Brien as its director. It has become an international center of information and promotion of Marian interests. The first project of the center was the outstanding popular magazine *Marie,* begun in 1947, which *L'Osservatore Romano* justly appraised as "the most beautiful Marian review in the world." Its regular circulation is about 30,000 copies, but special numbers may run to more than 60,000 copies. The center also publishes *Marian Tracts,* which appear monthly from September to June (begun in 1949). It

---

[5] Cf. L. Arendt, *La bibliothèque de Banneux, Notre-Dame,* in *Evangéliser,* Vol. 7, 1953, pp. 509-511; and Monheim, *art. cit.,* p. 47.

now has a museum, with an unique collection of Marian iconography (over 350 artistic Madonnas, in addition to 3000 photographs of Marian masterpieces from all over the world), and also a Marian library (begun in 1949) as well as a sanctuary with a statue of Our Lady of the Interior Life.[6] In addition, the Centre maintains a press service to more than 100 journals in Canada. Its releases are often read over Canadian radio stations.

10. *Iberville, Valcartier.* Two smaller Marian libraries in Canada have been opened by the Marist Brothers. The one, at Iberville, Quebec, had about 500 volumes on January 1, 1956; the other, at the *Ecole Normale* of the Marists at Valcartier, Quebec, although it was founded only in 1954 (by Brother Eudore-Joseph), by the end of 1955 boasted of about 420 Marian volumes.

11. *Dayton.* The first large active library in the United States devoted exclusively to Marian works is located at the University of Dayton, Dayton, Ohio. It was founded in 1943 by Father Lawrence Monheim, S.M., as a project for the 1950 centennial of the Society of Mary in America. On January 1, 1956, the library contained about 9100 books and 4050 pamphlets; in addition, 85 Marian periodicals are received regularly. The library also has a fine collection of other Marian materials: films, recordings, statues, medals, stamps. A very important feature is the union catalog, listing the whereabouts of Marian books in over 1000 general libraries. The library has several publications of its own: a *Marian Booklist* (based on the union catalog — first published in 1949); the monthly *Marianist* magazine; the scholarly *Marian Library Studies* (three studies had appeared by the end of 1955) and *Marian Reprints* (mostly popular, and some scientific articles on Mary; begun in 1952, seventy-six numbers had appeared by October, 1960). Two annual prizes are awarded by the library: the Marianist Award, for outstanding service to the Mother of God (since 1950) and the Marian Library Medal (since 1953) for the best book on Our Lady, written in English during the previous year.[7]

12. *Paterson.* Father Juniper B. Carol, O.F.M., founder of the

---

[6] Cf. R. Brien, *Autour du Centre Marial Canadien*, in *Marie*, Vol. 7, 1953, pp. 96-97; Monheim, *art. cit.,* p. 48; Di Fonzo, *art. cit.,* p. 631; and *La Patrie,* May 16, 1954, p. 69 ff. Cf. also M. Bélanger, O.M.I., *Le centre marial canadien,* in *Ère mariale,* Vol. 1. September, 1956, pp. 1-4.

[7] Cf. Monheim, *art. cit.,* pp. 50-55; G. Besutti, *Un'utile iniziativa della Marian Library di Dayton,* in *Marianum,* Vol. 12, 1950, pp. 472-476; and S. Mathews, S.M., *La bibliothèque mariale de l'Université de Dayton, U. S. A.,* in *Marie,* Vol. 8, 1954, pp. 114-121. Since October, 1960, the series *Marian Reprints* appears under the title Marian Library Studies.

Mariological Society of America, an internationally known authority on the Co-redemption, has gathered, over the past twenty-five years, an especially fine theological Marian collection, now at the Franciscan Monastery in Paterson, N. J. The library contains over 10,000 items (books, pamphlets, articles) including photostatic copies and microfilms of hundreds of out-of-print pieces. It is estimated that Father Carol has virtually everything written on the Co-redemption in any language.[8]

13. *Washington.* About 1922, Msgr. Bernard McKenna began a Marian library at the National Shrine of the Immaculate Conception on the grounds of the Catholic University of America, in Washington, D. C. That collection has now been added to the Marian works in the Mullen Library of the University, where its usefulness is enhanced by the presence of a large general theological collection. The total of Marian books at present (January, 1956) is about one thousand.

14. *Poughkeepsie.* Our Lady's Library at Marian College, Poughkeepsie, N. Y., has had a remarkably rapid growth. Founded in 1950 by Brother Cyril Robert, F.M.S., it had on hand, by the end of 1955, a total of 9268 books, not counting magazines. The library also houses a large collection of Marian art and Marian stamps.

15. *New York.* Another Marian center and library was established in New York City in 1954 by Father Donald Maria O'Callaghan, O.Carm. By January 1, 1956, the library held about 1200 volumes, as well as a collection of Marian art. Marian forums are held annually for sisters and lay persons. The center is also the headquarters for the work of the Scapular Apostolate and Militia, which distributed three million scapulars to the armed services during World War II. Since the close of the war, another million scapulars have been distributed to the armed services, and almost another million to foreign missions. The *Scapular* magazine, now published at the center, appears every two months.

16. *Bay Shore, N. Y.* As we have said, the number of Marian centers not having Marian libraries is so great that we could not hope to treat all of them. We select, therefore, as especially interesting examples, three outstanding centers in the United States.

Father Roger Mary Charest, S.M.M., of the Montfort Fathers, Bay Shore, N. Y., founded a Consecration Center in that city on December 8, 1953. An annual prize, the Pius XII Marian Award, is conferred yearly (the first was on December 8, 1955) on an individual or group that has done

---

[8] Cf. *The Catholic News*, August 7, 1954, p. 28; Monheim, *art. cit.*, pp. 48-50.

outstanding work in promoting consecration to the Immaculate Heart as requested by Pope Pius XII. The center also conducts a direct mail campaign yearly for consecration to the Immaculate Heart. *Queen of All Hearts*, a bimonthly magazine (founded in 1950) is also edited at Bay Shore, and specializes in the form of consecration to Our Lady taught by St. Louis de Montfort. In connection with the center, Montfort Publications (founded about 15 years ago) publishes or serves as an agency for a considerable number of Marian books and pamphlets. In addition, the major seminarians of the Montfort seminary in Litchfield, Conn., began to offer by correspondence a Marian Home Study Course (in nine lessons) at the close of the Marian Year, 1954. By February 12, 1956, two thousand three hundred and forty-seven persons had taken the course.

17. *St. Louis, Mo.* The General Office of the Sodalities of Our Lady now located in St. Louis, Mo., was first opened in 1913. It is the headquarters of the great Sodality movement in the United States, which, in April, 1956, included 18,247 units. It publishes two periodicals, the *Queen's Work* and *Direction*, as well as a large number of pamphlets (not all on Marian topics, however). The center also furnishes various supplies to Sodalities throughout the nation. In 1931, it inaugurated the Summer Schools of Catholic Action, which, between 1931 and 1956, had enrolled 170,000 students. Six day sessions are held each year in various cities throughout the United States and Canada.

18. *Chicago, Ill.* The Immaculate Heart Center was opened in Chicago, Ill., in December, 1955, by Very Rev. James Mary Keane, O.S.M. It grew out of the Ambassadors of Mary, a lay organization founded by Father Keane in 1946. For a long period, a weekly television program, *Behold Thy Mother*, was given over Station WBKB-TV in Chicago. It also published, until 1959, an exclusively Marian magazine, *The Age of Mary*, and maintains a Marian Information Bureau and a Marian Bookshop. In addition, the Ambassadors keep eighteen Pilgrim Virgin statues in circulation in the Chicago area, and have for some years provided First Saturday Retreats. The center promotes especially the consecration taught by St. Louis de Montfort. All work is done by volunteers.

19. *Windsor, Ont.* Chronologically the latest Marian Center to be erected is that in Windsor, Ontario, for English-speaking Canada. Definitive plans were approved in October, 1955, and the headquarters are at Assumption University, in charge of the Basilian Fathers. The

announced purpose of the Center is, among other things, to build up a Marian library eventually, to disseminate Marian information, to publish Marian booklets, pamphlets and reprints, and to conduct courses in Mariology.[9]

II. MARIAN PUBLICATIONS

We have already mentioned a considerable number of Marian publications which emanate from the above-mentioned Marian centers. A few other sets and periodicals may be recalled here.

In the entire world there are only two strictly scientific journals devoted exclusively to Mariology: *Marianum*, of which we have already spoken, and *Ephemerides Mariologicae*, begun in 1951 by the Claretian Fathers of Madrid, Spain. Both of these journals appear quarterly, and each issue normally contains articles in several languages (most commonly: Italian, Spanish, French, Latin, English, Portuguese).

Besides these scientific periodicals, there is a very large number of magazines having a Marian title, and devoted partially or entirely to Marian subject matter. Although these are, as a whole, on the popular level, some of them do publish occasional theological articles. We could not hope even to list all of these from all parts of the world, and so must be content with a partial list of those published in the United States. We have already spoken of *Direction*, the *Marianist*, *Queen of All Hearts*, the *Queen's Work*, *The Age of Mary*, and the *Scapular*, in connection with the centers from which each is published. Besides these, probably the best known are: *Ave Maria, Fatima Findings, Immaculata, Mary, Miraculous Medal, Perpetual Help,* and *Soul. Our Lady's Digest* is especially notable for the relatively high number of theological articles it publishes.[10]

---

[9] After finishing our chapter we learn of a new Marian Center now being erected in Bogotá (Colombia) for the same purpose as those previously mentioned. Cf. R. Tisnés, C.M.F., *Sociedad Mariológica Colombiana*, in *Virtud y Letras*, Vol. 17, 1957, pp. 259-264. Cf. also E. Valentini, S.D.B., *L'Accademia Mariana Salesiana*, in *Salesianum*, Vol. 20, 1958, pp. 492-507.

[10] *The Ave Maria is* published by the Holy Cross Fathers at Notre Dame, Indiana; *Fatima Findings* by the Reparation Society of the Immaculate Heart of Mary, Baltimore, Md.; *Immaculata,* by the Conventual Franciscan Fathers at Marytown, Kenosha, Wis.; *Mary,* by the Carmelite Fathers, Chicago, Ill.; *Miraculous Medal* by the Association of the Miraculous Medal in Philadelphia; *Perpetual Help,* by the Redemptorist Fathers in Esopus, N. Y. (There is another *Perpetual Help* published by the Redemptorists in Liguori, Mo.); *Soul,* by the Ave Maria Institute, Asbury, Warren Co., N. Y.; and *Our Lady's Digest,* by the Missionary Fathers of La Salette, Olivet, Ill.

The Mariological Societies described in Chapter 16 have many Marian publications, commonly in the form of annual volumes containing the proceedings of the yearly meetings.[11] The oldest group of such volumes is *Mariale Dagen*, which began to appear at Tongerloo in 1931, as the journal of the Flemish Mariological Society (17 volumes had appeared by the end of 1959). In France, the *Bulletin de la Société Française d'Études Mariales* began publication in 1936 (17 volumes so far). Some of the most detailed studies are those of the Spanish Mariological Society, the *Estudios Marianos* (now in its 21st volume). In the United States, the proceedings of the Mariological Society of America have appeared annually as *Marian Studies*, since 1950.

Finally, we may mention some of the principal encyclopedic works in the field. One of the oldest is the *Summa Aurea de laudibus Beatissimae Virginis Mariae*, edited by Joannes J. Bourassé.[12] It has the general character of a source collection, gathering up "all the more important things that are found written about the most glorious Mary, Mother of God, in the Sacred Scriptures, the works of the holy Fathers, the decrees of the Councils, the constitutions of the Roman Pontiffs, and the books of celebrated Doctors." There are eleven extensive indices.

Z. C. Jourdain has gathered together in his *Somme des grandeurs de Marie*[13] the preaching on Our Lady from the first centuries to our day. It falls into five parts, treating of Mary in the thought of God and in the Old Testament, during her mortal life, in the glory of Heaven, in the Church, and in the Christian pulpit (this last section occupies volumes 5-11, and is a collection of instructions and sermons from the Fathers, Doctors, theologians, ascetics, and orators of all centuries).

The five volumes of the German *Summa Mariana*[14] of Jacob H. Schütz are divided into four parts. The first volume contains the dogmatic and exegetical matter, together with a life of Mary. The second and third volumes present the history of Marian devotion, especially such topics as devotion to Mary in the oriental rites, in various nations, and in poetry

---

[11] Not all publish a volume every year.

[12] J. J. Bourassé, *Summa Aurea de laudibus Beatissimae Virginis Mariae* (J. P. Migne, Parisiis, 1862), 12 volumes.

[13] Z. C. Jourdain (Ed.), *Somme des grandeurs de Marie; ses mystères, ses excellences, son culte* (H. Walzer, Paris, 1900-1903, Nouvelle édition), 11 vols.

[14] J. H. Schütz, *Summa Mariana. Allgemeines Handbuch des Marienverehrung für Priester, Theologie-Studierende und gebildete Laien* (Junfermannsche Buchhandlung, Paderborn, 1908-1921), 5 volumes and supplement to Vol. 2.

and the arts, as well as Marian apparitions, shrines, orders, and congresses. Marian feasts, litanies, hymns, scapulars, confraternities, and related topics are treated in the fourth volume. The final volume is a large collection of Marian sermons. In addition, there is a supplement to the second volume, discussing the Marian poetry of Poland.

Some source collections of recent papal utterances on Mary have already been mentioned in the first volume of this set.[15] We might add here a more recent, very important collection: *Doctrina Pontificia IV, Documentos Marianos,* edited by Hilario Marín, S.I., in the *Biblioteca de Autores Cristianos.*[16] It is the closest approach we have to a complete collection of the statements of Popes and Councils on Mary. It takes in all the more important pronouncements from the beginning to November 1, 1954 (inclusive). A Spanish translation is given at the top of each page, with the original language at the bottom. There is an extensive, though not exhaustive index.[17]

The *Enciclopedia Mariana, "Theotokos,"* recently appeared in Italy.[18] It is edited by R. Spiazzi, O.P. The various articles were contributed by thirty-six theologians of various religious orders and dioceses in Italy. It is in the form of essays, rather than in short alphabetic entries. It is truly encyclopedic in scope, endeavoring to cover, at least briefly, every Marian topic.

France is fortunate in having the several splendid large volumes of the collection *Maria, Etudes sur la sainte Vierge,* edited by H. du Manoir, S.J.[19] The first volume, the most important of the set, treats of Mary in Scripture, in the Fathers, in liturgy, in dogma, in spirituality, and in the apostolate. The other volumes deal with the history of Marian cult in the

---

[15] *Mariology,* Volume I, p. 2, note 2, and p. 433, note 244. The most important are: A. Tondidi (Ed.), *Le Encicliche Mariane* (Roma, 1950); R. Graber, *Die marianischen Weltrundschreiben der Päpste in den letzten hundert Jahren* (Würzburg, 1950); W. Doheny and J. Kelly, *Papal Documents on Mary* (Milwaukee, 1954); and Paul Palmer, S.J., *Mary in the Documents of the Church* (Westminster, Md., 1952).

[16] H. Marín, S.J., (Ed.), *Doctrina Pontificia IV, Documentos Marianos,* in *Biblioteca de Autores Cristianos* (Madrid, 1954).

[17] Unfortunately, there are a few occasional small inaccuracies in the transcription of documents in the original language.

[18] R. Spiazzi, O.P. (Ed.), *Enciclopedia Mariana, "Theotokos"* (Bevilacqua & Solari, Genova: Massimo, Milano, 1954). A second edition appeared in 1958.

[19] H. du Manoir, S.J. (Ed.), *Maria, Etudes sur la Sainte Vierge* (Paris, 1949, 1952, 1954, 1956, 1958), 5 vols. (another is yet to appear.) Cf. also note 13 above.

religious orders, congregations, the diocesan clergy, and in the various countries of the world.

Germany is favored with two recent encyclopedic Marian works. The *Katholische Marienkunde*,[20] edited by P. Sträter, S.J., is in three volumes. Its general scope resembles that of the Du Manoir collection, though it is on a considerably smaller scale. More recent is the *Lexikon der Marienkunde*,[21] edited by K. Algermissen, L. Böer, C. Feckes, and J. Tyciak. It promises to be, when completed, the most comprehensive Marian encyclopedia. Thus far, only five fascicles have appeared.

In Italy, Father Gabriel M. Roschini, O.S.M., has written two works which are virtually encyclopedic. The earlier is his Latin *Mariologia*, in four large volumes.[22] It is practically indispensable to Mariologists. More recently, his *La Madonna secondo la fede e la teologia* appeared.[23] It is not a mere Italian translation of the previous work, though it could be considered an adaptation of it. It is by far the best, most up-to-date, and most complete systematic treatise on Mariology written by a single author. In it the author modifies a few of the opinions previously held in his Latin *Mariologia*.

We have not, of course, done more than to mention some of the countless Marian publications, and have confined ourselves to a few special classes.[24] The actual total of Marian works issued since the invention of printing is estimated by Father G. M. Besutti, O.S.M., an

---

[20] P. Sträter, S.J. (Ed.), *Katholische Marienkunde* (Paderborn, 1947-1951) 3 vols. Cf. also note 14 above. This set has been translated into Italian under the direction of Joseph Filograssi, S.J. It is entitled simply *Mariologia*, 3 vols. (Roma, 1952, 1955, 1958).

[21] K. Algermissen, L. Böer, C. Feckes, J. Tyciak, *Lexikon der Marienkunde*, published by F. Pustet, in Regensburg, Germany.

[22] G. M. Roschini, O.S.M., *Mariologia* (Belardetti, Romae, 2nd ed. 1947-1948), 4 vols.

[23] Idem, *La Madonna secondo la fede e la teologia* (Ferrari, Roma, 1953-1954), 4 vols.

[24] For a select list of modern general treatises on Mariology, see Volume I, note 233 on pp. 320-321, of this set. We might add that the treatise of Merkelbach, long out of print, has now appeared in a revised edition in Spanish, entitled *Mariología* (revision and translation by P. Arenillas, O.P., Desclée, Bilbao, 1954); and the *Volledige Marialeer* of C. X. J. M. Friethoff, O.P., has appeared in an English translation as *A Complete Mariology* (Blackfriars, 1958). Likewise, E. Neubert's *Marie dans le dogme* has been translated as *Mary in Doctrine* (Milwaukee: Bruce, 1954). The distinguished editor of this set, Father Juniper B. Carol. O.F.M., has written also *Fundamentals of Mariology* (New York: Benziger, 1956), an excellent general treatise.

authority on Marian bibliography, as about 100,000 volumes.[25] So great a total is not surprising. For the Holy Spirit of truth brings to the Church an ever deepening realization of the great things which He that is Mighty has done for her. And so it is likely that the literary production centering on our Blessed Lady will continue to increase in quantity, and we hope, in quality, to the praise and honor of her whose dignity and holiness "no one except God can comprehend."[26]

---

[25] G. M. Besutti, O.S.M., *La Biblioteca Mariana,* in *Studi storici dell'Ordine dei Servi di Maria,* Vol. 5, 1953, p. 126.

[26] Pius IX, *Ineffabilis Deus,* Dec. 8, 1954, in *Acta et decreta sacrorum Conciliorum recentiorum. Collectio Lacensis,* Vol. 6, p. 536.

Marian Congresses

by EAMON R. CARROLL, O.Carm.

ARIAN congresses are a distinctively twentieth-century contribution to the cult and study of the Mother of God. The first international Marian congress was held in 1900. Along with the international movement similar series of congresses on national and regional levels or in terms of particular topics have taken place. And there have been almost countless individual congresses, some small, others immense, some exclusively devotional in character, others both popular and scientific, still others entirely theological. Such gatherings multiplied almost beyond enumeration during the Marian Year, 1954, and were echoed in the Lourdes centenary observances in 1958.

The Marian and Mariological congresses of the past sixty years have played a role not only in spreading devotion to our Blessed Lady, but also in deepening Marian theology. Many of the conventions have featured study sessions as well as public manifestations in Mary's honor. Theologians have come together at Marian congresses to discuss Our Lady's place in God's plan, and the results of their researches have sometimes been significant explanations of Marian doctrines.

Many of the Mariological lectures held at congresses have been published in the printed proceedings. Studied in order, such articles present a picture of the development of theological thought about Our Lady in recent decades. The consideration has not been limited to the few truths about the Mother of God that have been dogmatically defined. Under the guidance of the teaching authority of the Church, theologians have attempted to see ever more clearly the marvelous harmony that exists among all of Mary's privileges, and in so doing they have pushed forward the frontiers of Mariology.

The Holy See has repeatedly blessed the work of the congresses, and on occasion singled out the study sessions. Speaking of the effects of the definition of the Immaculate Conception, the late Pope Pius XII wrote in the bull of the Assumption:

> Crusades of prayer were set on foot for this purpose; the study of the question was actively and zealously encouraged by many eminent

theologians either privately or publicly in ecclesiastical universities and in other schools of theology. In many parts of the Catholic world national or international Marian congresses were held. These studies and researches made it clearer that the dogma of the Assumption of the Virgin Mary into heaven was also contained in the deposit of faith entrusted to the Church; and usually there followed many petitions beseeching the Apostolic See for the solemn definition of this truth.[1]

An important example of direct advice to the members of a congress was the radio message of Pope Pius XII for the international Mariological congress held in Rome, 1954: *Inter complures*, October 24, 1954, setting forth directives for the study of the sacred science of Mariology.[2] One of the last messages of Pope Pius XII was his radio address for the solemn closing of the Lourdes international congress, September 18, 1958, *Vénérables Frères et bien-aimés fils, pèlerins de Lourdes*.[3]

The present Chapter is a survey of the principal Marian congresses in the period 1900-1958.[4] The field of investigation is too vast to attempt complete coverage; for example, the congresses of the Marian Year alone, held in almost every country of the free world, would require a full-length book even to list and to summarize. The survey begins with the international congresses, of which there have been ten to date. Next will be treated the major national congresses, namely, the group of five held in Brittany, and the French National series, held at four-year intervals since 1927. Finally, a selection of principal single congresses will be given, e.g., the Brussels 1921 congress on Mary Mediatrix of all graces. The

---

[1] *Munificentissimus Deus,* in *A.A.S.,* Vol. 42, 1950, p. 755.

[2] *A.A.S.,* Vol. 46, 1954, pp. 677-680; English translation, *Mariology and the Standards Which Govern Its Study,* in *The Pope Speaks,* Vol. 1, 1954, pp. 343-346.

[3] *L'Osservatore Romano,* September 19, 1958.

[4] The author acknowledges a debt of gratitude for the use of indispensable materials to Father Juniper B. Carol, O.F.M., to the Fathers and Brothers of the Marian Library at the University of Dayton, to Abbé L. Arendt of the Bibliothèque Mariale, Banneux, Belgium. Thanks to their generosity it was possible to consult firsthand printed proceedings, some of them extremely rare, from practically all the congresses here surveyed. Secondary sources were: E. Campana, *Maria nel culto cattolico,* 2nd ed. by G. Roschini, O.S.M., Vol. 2 (Torino, 1944), pp. 485-652; G. Roschini, *Mariologia,* 2nd ed., Vol. 4 (Romae, 1948), pp. 185- 189; J. Bittremieux, *Marialia* (Nijmegen, 1936), pp. 334-340; G. M. Besutti, O.S.M., *I congressi mariani internazionali,* in *Un Secolo di Storia Mariana,* 1854-1945 (Napoli, 1953), pp. 51-60; Besutti, *Bibliografia Mariana,* 3 vols. (Roma, 1950, 1952, 1958); also chronicles and reviews in the Mariological quarterlies *Marianum,* Rome, since 1939, and *Ephemerides Mariologicae,* Madrid, since 1951.

meetings of the Mariological societies of various countries are not the proper concern of this Chapter, and these will be mentioned only in so far as their foundation or some of their gatherings were in common with a Marian congress. Among the myriad materials and events of which the congresses have been composed, emphasis has been placed in this report on Mariological features, i.e., those elements which have advanced the study of Our Lady. Particular note has been taken of relevant documents of the Holy See.

I. INTERNATIONAL CONGRESSES

First mention belongs to the international Marian congresses, which began in 1900. A proximate preparation for them was a number of national congresses held in the last decade of the nineteenth century. A Eucharistic congress at Turin in 1895 passed a resolution to hold Marian congresses, and there were Marian congresses at Florence in 1897 and at Turin in 1898. At the same time similar interest was expressed in France. The project was proposed at the twelfth international Eucharistic congress at Lourdes in 1898. These hopes were realized in the Marian congress held at Lyons in September, 1900. There is some difference of opinion as to whether the Lyons meeting deserves to be called the first truly international Marian congress, or whether it was a national congress. Without intending to settle the dispute, the listing used by the *Academia Mariana Internationalis* is here followed, and Lyons named as the first. The complete list follows:

1. Lyons-Fourvière, September 5-8, 1900
2. Fribourg, Switzerland, August 18-21, 1902
3. Rome, November 30-December 4, 1904
4. Einsiedeln, Switzerland, August 17-21, 1906
5. Saragossa, Spain, September 26-30, 1908
6. Salzburg, Austria, July 18-27, 1910
7. Trier, Germany, August 3-6, 1912
8. Rome, October 23-November 1, 1950
9. Rome, October 24-November 1, 1954
10. Lourdes, September 10-17, 1958

The Roman congress of 1950 was clearly divided, for the first time, into a scientific (Mariological) part, and a popular (Marian) part. This useful arrangement was carried through at Rome in 1954 and at Lourdes in 1958, so that the last three international assemblies have been at the same time the eighth, ninth, and tenth Marian congresses, and the first, second, and third Mariological congresses.

(1) Lyons, often referred to also as Fourvière, the name of the nearby shrine of Our Lady: the majority of the many papers in the two volumes of proceedings deal with historical, or devotional topics; e.g., a series of thirty sanctuaries, mostly in France, are treated in volume 2.[5] Fifty-six separate essays deal with the Marian cult of various religious orders. Among the fifteen resolutions of the congress, the first requests a feast of Our Lady's universal queenship, that the world be consecrated to the Blessed Virgin under her title of queen, and that "Queen of the universe, pray for us" be added to the litany. The final resolution asks that a permanent commission be nominated by the bishops to continue the Marian congresses. At the head of the proceedings is printed Pope Leo XIII's letter to Cardinal Coullié of Lyons, *Multis praeclarisque nominibus*, September 12, 1899.[6]

(2) Fribourg, Switzerland, was the site of the 1902 congress. A Marian exposition was held, and the city was consecrated to Mary, queen of the universe. At the same time four study sessions were held under the leadership of Msgr. Kleiser. Part of Pope Leo XIII's letter of June 10, 1902, to Msgr. Kleiser, *Cum Nobis nihil antiquius*, is reproduced in the acts.[7] There is little unity of theme; the topics range over dogma, cult, history, art, and social matters. Yet in comparison to the Lyons emphasis on history, Fribourg may be said to have had a doctrinal direction, especially regarding the spiritual maternity.

The published French acts have a long dogmatic section, including studies on Pope Leo XIII's Marian encyclicals. Dom Paul Renaudin and Canon Pieraccini both discussed the definability of the Assumption. J.-V. Bainvel is represented by an article on "Mary, Mother of Grace." At the German sessions similar topics were discussed: the encyclicals of Pope Leo

---

[5] *Compte rendu du Congrès Marial tenu à Lyon les 5, 6, 7 et 8 septembre 1900* (Lyon, 1900-1901), Vol. 1, 662 pp., Vol. 2, 780 pp.

[6] *Op. cit.*, Vol. 1, pp. 8-9.

[7] *Du 18 au 21 Août 1902 à Fribourg en Suisse. Congrès Marial. Compte rendu* (Blois, 1903), Vol. 1, 612 pp., Vol. 2, 550 pp. Campana, *op. cit.*, pp. 547-565, refers to a volume of German proceedings that the present author was unable to examine personally: *Vom 18 bis 22 August 1902, zu Freiburg in der Schweiz International Marian Kongress.* Pope Leo's letter, here given only in part, is to be found in full in the Saragossa acts, pp. 22-25, see note 14.

XIII; Aug. Lehmkuhl, S.J., and J. Groellner on the definability of the Assumption; Our Lady and the Eucharist; Mary's mediation of grace. Papers were given in French (A. Lhoumeau) and in German (L. M. Obermeier) on Marian devotion according to B. Grignion de Montfort, and a resolution to spread this devotion was passed.

(3) The Roman congress of 1904 commemorated the fiftieth anniversary of the definition of the Immaculate Conception. Pope Leo XIII established the first commission to prepare for the congress, and Pope St. Pius X confirmed it. Study sessions, though many in number, took second place to popular manifestations. The printed acts are mostly a descriptive record of the many events; few of the papers were ever published.[8]

At the direction of the Holy Father, the congress took an eminently practical line. The pontiff's brief to the commission urged the development of practical means to increase genuine devotion to Mary.[9] Among those presenting papers were Father (later Cardinal) A. H. Lépicier, O.S.M.: "The Immaculate Mother of God and Co-redemptrix of the Human Race," and Father B. Vaughan, S.J., in English: "The Social Mission of the Virgin as the Second Eve."[10] Among the results of the congress was the creation of a Marian library, which has in recent years passed into the care of the Servites in Rome.

(4) Originally planned for Cologne, the fourth international meeting was actually held at Einsiedeln, Switzerland.[11] Pope St. Pius X sent a letter

---

[8] *Atti del Congresso Mariano Mondiale tenuto in Roma l'anno 1904* (Roma, 1905). In addition, the Order of Friars Minor published its own congress brochure: *L'Ordine dei Frati Minori al Congresso Mariano internazionale tenuto in Roma dal 30 nov. al 4 dec. 1904 per celebrare il cinquantenario del dogma dell'Immacolata* (Roma, 1905), 91 pp., containing, inter alia, D. Fleming, *The dogma of the Immaculate Conception and the Franciscan Order*, pp. 15-21; see also the entries in the extensive Bibliography (1830-1957), in *The Dogma of the Immaculate Conception*, ed. E. D. O'Connor, C.S.C. (Notre Dame, Ind., 1958), pp. 532-561.

[9] *Se è Nostro dovere*, September 8, 1903, in *A.S.S.*, Vol. 36, 1903-1904, pp. 65-66.

[10] See B. Vaughan, S.J., *Sinless Mary and Sinful Mary* (London, 1905), pp. 7-42, for the text of this Roman address.

[11] *Compte rendu du Congrès Marial International tenu à Einsiedeln en Suisse du 17 au 21 Août 1906* (Lyons, 1907), 844 pp. The writer has seen only references to the German acts: Internationalischer Marianischer Kongress in Einsiedeln (Freiburg-i/B). The Spanish-American section of Einsiedeln published its own proceedings, *Actas de la Sección Hispano-Americana del Congreso Mariano Internacional de Einsiedeln*, 290 pp., which could not be found in preparing this chapter, but which are referred to by J. Postíus in the Saragossa acts, see note 14.

of encouragement, *Honori magnae Parentis*, in which he reaffirmed the ideals proposed to the Roman congress two years before: the increase of devotion to Mary most holy, and the improvement of the spiritual life of the faithful. "If we are truly convinced — as your program so well states — that Mary is the most perfect example of the Christian life, your congress must set out to arouse in the faithful of the whole world a new fervor, and to lead them to imitate the Mother of God with a firmer will than they had before."[12] Another directive of the pope retains its value still for Marian congresses: "In consideration of the many good results which can come from your meeting, We urge all the faithful who are devoted to the Virgin to come in great numbers to the congress and urge all to prove themselves both prudent in making decisions and prompt in putting their resolves into practice."[13]

The group of twenty papers on De Montfort's teaching well illustrates the "practical" character of Einsiedeln. The congress had sections not only in French and German, but also in such languages as Spanish, Portuguese, Netherlandish; and Canada, England and the United States were among the many nations taking part. Among the resolutions, a greater recognition of Our Lady's queenship was urged, e.g., by a proper Mass and Office. One organizational result of this meeting was the formation of an international committee to plan future congresses. Msgr. Bauron of Lyons and Msgr. Kleiser of Fribourg were named officers of the new committee.

(5) With the Saragossa gathering, 1908, the international movement took on a more theological character, without prejudice to the popular and public honor to the Mother of God. The published acts serve as a good chronicle not only of Saragossa, but of the whole background to the international congresses. Fairly complete reports are given on Lyons, Fribourg, Rome, and Einsiedeln, along with transcripts of documents from the Holy See. There is also a review of contemporary regional congresses.[14]

The menace of Modernism was the principal theme of the study sessions, based on St. Pius X's encyclical *Pascendi*. Mary, queen of the universe, destroyer of heresy, was invoked to crush the head of the

---

[12] *Compte rendu* ... , pp. 9-11; the date of the letter was April 23, 1906, and it was sent to J. Kleiser and J. Guyot who were in charge or the congress.

[13] *Ibid.*

[14] *Actas del Cuarto Congresso Mariano Internacional celebrado en Zaragoza de España en los dias 26, 27, 28, 29 & 30 de Septiembre de 1908* (Madrid, 1909), 984 pp.

serpent of Modernism. The Assumption was also among the study subjects. Canon Pieraccini's paper on the opportuneness of a definition of the Assumption is reduced to a one-page summary; C. Crosta's report on the actual state of belief in the Assumption receives more space. Among the resolutions were requests for the Assumption definition and for the consecration of the whole world to the Immaculate Heart of Mary. The resolutions run to twenty pages, drawing from Campana the just complaint that this was done in spite of secretary-general Bauron's request that they be limited to gain greater effectiveness.[15]

(6) Salzburg, Austria, was the city of the sixth congress.[16] There were seven national sections: German, Spanish, Franco-Belgian, Italian, Hungarian, Slovenian, and Polish. Each group issued its own set of resolutions, in some cases suggesting that the next international congress be held in its own country. It was decided to grant the French request for the next meeting at Rheims. Among the final *vota,* the German section, seconded by the Hungarians, petitioned for the dogmatic definition of the Assumption.

A number of papers dealt with the threat of Modernism; one bore this descriptive title: "The faith in authority shown by Mary at the Annunciation is a condemnation of the Modernist concept of faith." Several conferences considered the bond between devotion to Mary and loyalty to the Holy Father. This was in response to the pope's words about the congress: "Under the protection of her who has destroyed all heresies, let the Marian congress of Salzburg strengthen the unity of Catholics among themselves, and with the head of the Church."[17] A Spanish resolution urged that the connection between Mary and the Roman pontiff be further studied in future meetings, and hoped for future "papal" congresses, like the Eucharistic and Marian ones.

(7) Trier, August 3-6, 1912: the well-ordered acts with their abundant material reflect the congress itself, and show what advances had been

---

[15] *Op. cit.,* p. 249; Campana, *op. cit.,* p. 600.

[16] *Bericht über den fünften Marianischen Welt-Kongress, abgehalten zu Salzburg vom 18 bis 21 Juli 1910* (Salzburg, 1911). In the enumeration of congresses we are following in this article, Salzburg is sixth in the international list, not fifth, despite the title of its acts. The reference to the proceedings is from Campana, *op. cit.,* pp. 601-613; no copy of them could be obtained even for consultation.

[17] As quoted by Campana, *op. cit.,* pp. 609-610; the pontifical brief is apparently in the proceedings. The present writer has been unable to find this document otherwise listed.

made in the twelve years since Lyons.[18] The seventh meeting was transferred to Trier in Germany because Rheims was controlled by a Socialist city government. A five-point program was followed in the study sessions:

a) Pope Pius X's "restore all things in Christ" is realized in De Montfort's "Let the kingdom of Mary come, that the kingdom of Christ may come."
b) the universal queenship of Mary, achieving its final expression in the Assumption and coronation.
c) the universal mercy of Mary, dispenser of all graces.
d) the miracles worked at Mary's shrines, especially Lourdes, confirm her royal and maternal mercy.
e) the papacy is the Marian kingdom par excellence. Devotion to Mary and loyalty to the pope are counterparts.

These five major themes were all developed from theological, historical, and moral points of view. German papers are the largest group in the acts, but there are also many French contributions, and to a lesser extent Flemish, Polish, Italian, and Spanish (simply a list of topics). The French studies include one by Dom Paul Renaudin on the Assumption, "The Triumph of the Co-redemptrix." His sage opening words are still applicable:

> There is no doubt that the Marian congresses are not councils; they do not pretend to publish dogmatic decisions, or to put themselves in the place of the teaching authority, or even to dictate to the teaching authority a line of conduct. They wish only to place in relief more and more the person of Mary, her virtues, her dignity, and the glory she enjoys in her eternal happiness.[19]

In the German section such names appear as A. Miller, O.S.B. (Mary in the Old Testament); Dr. J. Pohle (Mary's Place in God's Plan of Salvation); Dr. B. Bartmann (on the Immaculate Conception); Fr. A. Lehmkuhl, S.J. (Mary, Mother of Mercy.) Over and over again the rapport between the Blessed Virgin and the Holy See is stressed. Our Lady is "queen of the Holy See" — she reigns through the actions of the supreme

---

[18] *Sechster Internationaler Marianischer Kongress in Trier vom 3. bis 6. August 1912* (Trier, 1912), Vol. 1, 216 pp., Vol. 2, 327 pp., Vol. 3, 349 pp. Again, despite the title of the acts, this congress is seventh of our international list, not sixth.

[19] *Op. cit.*, Vol. 3, pp. 337-338.

pontiffs.[20] A sign of the times was the Spanish resolution, "that all who are devoted to Mary pray for Portugal, a land of the Immaculate, now victim of Masonry."

The outbreak of World War I prevented a congress in 1914, and it was not until after still another World War that the interrupted series was resumed with the Roman congress of 1950. For the first time there were clearly distinguished Mariological (October 23-28) and Marian (October 29-November 1) divisions. The congress was called "Mariological-Marian," or in the line of the international series, the eighth Marian and the first Mariological. The proceedings have been published in twelve volumes under the title *Alma Socia Christi,* a phrase similar to several in *Munificentissimus Deus,* and expressive of the association of the Mother of God with her Son the Redeemer. Many of the papers dealt with phases of our Lady's association in the redemptive work of Christ. A student of years to come, comparing *Alma Socia Christi* with the acts of the congresses between 1900 and 1912, will see for himself the strides made in Marian studies through the half-century.

In 1950 whole national Mariological societies collaborated, faculties of pontifical universities, theologians from religious orders. There were plenary sessions held for the most part in Latin; and then the individual sessions of the different groups, in various languages, including a United States section, which studied the queenship. The more popular aspect, the "Marian" portion of the congress, was not passed over. Indeed this was the occasion in the Holy Year when the world gathered to pay tribute to the Mother of God. No Marian congress in history ever ended on so glorious a note as the event that marked the closing of the 1950 congress. For on November 1, 1950, the Vicar of Christ infallibly proclaimed that the doctrine of our Blessed Lady's corporeal Assumption into heaven was a divinely-revealed truth. No attempt will be made here to survey the studies given in 1950. The printed volumes are available and have been outlined and reviewed in modern periodicals that are at the disposal of all.[21]

---

[20] *Catholicis hominibus,* brief of St. Pius X, July 12, 1912, in *A.A.S.,* Vol. 4, 1912, p. 578.

[21] *Alma Socia Christi,* in 12 vols., 1951-1953, plus an index volume, 1958, Roma, Academia Mariana Internationalis, Via Merulana 124; most are still in print as of January, 1959. The United States papers are in Vol. 3, 1952, *De praedestinatione et regalitate B. Virginis Mariae.* For reviews, summaries, and further information on the congress see particularly *Marianum,* the Roman quarterly published by the Servites, and other theological journals. Some of the papers were separately published and do

(9) The ninth Marian and second Mariological congress was a feature of the Marian Year, 1954, and again held at Rome, from October 24 to October 28 for the scientific part, and from October 29 to November 1 for the popular part. And again it was under the auspices of the International Marian Academy, presided over by Charles Balić, O.F.M. Many of the papers in the eighteen volumes of the acts, *Virgo Immaculata,* deal with the Immaculate Conception, but there is hardly a significant matter in Mariology that is not treated by a capable author. The so-called *debitum peccati* in Our Lady was a vividly debated topic in the congress. Members of the meeting were the recipients of an important message from His Holiness, October 24, 1954, the eve of their opening deliberations.[22]

The organization of the program was similar to 1950, but there were many more participating groups. General sessions were usually held in the mornings, and in the afternoons the specialized groups held their meetings. Even the most skeletal survey of the vast amount of material that resulted from these sessions, plenary and particular, would take pages. The reader is referred to readily available sources.[23] The United States provided sections from the Catholic University of America, Washington, D. C., and from the Franciscan National Marian Commission.

As in 1950, the Marian part followed the Mariological meetings, and the scholars left their lecture halls to join the Christian people in parading through the Roman streets to honor Our Blessed Lady and to see the Holy Father solemnly crown the ancient picture, *Salus populi Romani.* On November 1, 1954, the supreme pontiff proclaimed the new feast of Mary's queenship.[24]

(10) In the Lourdes centenary year, 1958, Our Lady's shrine city in the

---

not appear in *Alma Socia Christi;* e.g., the Redemptorist section is printed as *Pietas Alfonsiana erga Matrem Gloriosam Mariam* (Lovanii, 1951), 189 pp.

[22] *Inter complures,* in *A.A.S.,* Vol. 46, 1954, pp. 677-680; see note 2, above.

[23] *Virgo Immaculata,* in 18 volumes, 1955-1958, Roma, Academia Mariana Internationalis — all are in print at this writing (January, 1959). See also the reports in *Marianum, Ephemerides Mariologicae,* and the complete listing of the contents of the entire set of *Virgo Immaculata* in *The Dogma of the Immaculate Conception,* ed. E. D. O'Connor, C.S.C. (Notre Dame, Ind.: 1958), pp. 611-621. Still other papers from the 1954 congress have been published apart from *Virgo Immaculata,* e.g., the section of the Discalced Carmelites, which makes up a special number of *Ephemerides Carmeliticae,* Vol. 7, 1956, fasc. 1, pp. 1-228.

[24] *Le testimonianze,* the pope's homily of November 1, 1954, in *A.A.S.,* Vol. 46, 1954, pp. 662-666, and *Ad Caeli Reginam,* encyclical on the queenship, in *A.A.S.,* Vol. 46, 1954, pp. 625-640.

Pyrenees was the site for the third Mariological congress (September 10-14) and the tenth Marian one (September 15-17). Profiting by the experience of the Roman meetings of 1950 and 1954, the central committee, which was again the Academia Mariana Internationalis, had drawn up the program well in advance.[25] The number of special sections was limited mainly to the national Mariological societies. "The triumph of the Church through Mary" was the central theme; this was considered both in the general sessions with Latin as the common tongue, and in the various vernaculars of the particular sections. The division of material was as follows:

a) The parallelism between Mary and the Church — German Mariological Society.
b) The share of Mary and the Church in the redemption of Christ — Canadian Mariological Society.
c) Mary's queenly power in the Church — Committee for the French National Marian Congresses in association with the French Mariological Society.
d) Mary, Mother of the Church, and her influence on the mystical body of Christ, which is the Church — Spanish Mariological Society.
e) The relationship of Mary to the priesthood, both hierarchical and spiritual — Latin American committee.
f) Mary and the Eucharistic life of the Church — Central Committee for International Eucharistic Congresses.
g) Mary and the spread and consolidation of the Church — committee of the "Church suffering"
h) Mary and the unity of the Church — international association "Unitas"
i) Mary and the apostolate of the Church — the Catholic University of America, in association with the Mariological Society of America and the Franciscan National Marian Commission of the United States.
j) Appearances of Our Lady and their meaning in the Church — Portuguese Mariological Society.

---

[25] An information bulletin, *Nuntia Periodica,* five numbers, 1957-1958, was sent periodically to those interested in the congress; numbers 4 and 5 give the full program of the Mariological and Marian parts of the meeting. This bulletin is being continued after Lourdes as the permanent organ of the International Marian Congress Committee.

k) The miraculous cures of Lourdes and miracles — International Medical Bureau of Lourdes.
l) Marian cult in the liturgy of the Church — Flemish-speaking Mariological Society ("Mariale Dagen")
m) Mary and religious art, with particular reference to the parallelism between Mary and the Church — Pontifical Academy of the Immaculate Conception.

The Marian portion of the congress began with the arrival of the papal legate, Cardinal Tisserant. The public events — open-air masses, sermons by cardinals and bishops, processions, vigils, etc. — offered the crowds of pilgrims many opportunities to take part in the festivities. At length on September 17 Pope Pius XII delivered what was to prove the last major Marian message of his life, the radioaddress, *Vénérables Frères et bien-aimés fils, pèlerins de Lourdes.*[26]

The International Marian Academy is preparing the proceedings of the Lourdes congress for publication; they will no doubt run to many volumes.[27]

II. NATIONAL AND PARTICULAR CONGRESSES

In addition to the international series, our century has seen innumerable other Marian congresses. Certain groups of these have played a noteworthy role in the development of Marian studies. Attention will be devoted to the following; (A) the Breton series; (B) the French national meetings; (C) the Franciscan Assumptionist set; and, finally, (D) some single congresses of more than ordinary importance.

(A) The Breton Series, 1904-1924

Probably the most significant series of regional congresses, in some respects surpassing even the international movement, e.g., in the quality of the proceedings, was the set of five held in Brittany, from 1904 through

---

[26] *L'Osservatore Romano*, September 19, 1958; the addresses of the papal legate to the general public on his arrival, September 13, and to the final meeting of the Mariological congress, September 14, are in *L'Osservatore Romano*, September 15-16, 1959.

[27] These proceedings are entitled *Maria et Ecclesia*. Eleven volumes have been published so far. Since this chapter went to press, Pope John XXIII has raised the International Marian Academy to pontifical rank; cf. *Maiora in dies*, Dec. 8, 1959, in *A.A.S.*, Vol. 52, 1960, pp. 24-26. The Academy has announced Canada as the site of the fourth Mariological (Ottawa, Aug. 21-28, 1962) and eleventh Marian (Cap-de-la-Madeleine, Aug. 29 to Sept. 2, 1962) international congresses.

1924. The sites were pilgrimage places of Our Lady, and the meetings were gatherings of priests to study Marian doctrines.[28]

(1) Josselin, November 21-24, 1904, on the Immaculate Conception: the acts contain a letter of Cardinal Merry del Val, voicing the Holy Father's interest.[29] The greater part of the meeting was devoted to dogma, although there were also sections on devotion, art, and cult. The first dogmatic paper was J.-V. Bainvel's "The History of a Dogma," on the Immaculate Conception.

(2) Rennes, March 22-24, 1908, in honor of the divine maternity and the Annunciation.[30] Seven papers were devoted to the divine maternity, six to the Annunciation, and a set of nine papers was on the cult of Our Lady in the diocese of Rennes. J.-V. Bainvel, S.J., contributed an article on the maternal heart of Mary.[31] The Rennes meeting had the character of reparation for the harm done to Mary's honor, especially her divine motherhood, by a renegade son of Brittany; this was the unfortunate Ernest Renan, although his name is not mentioned.

(3) Guingamp, sanctuary of Notre Dame de Bon-Secours, September 6-8, 1910, "in honor of the Marian co-redemption and the Visitation."[32] The first section of the congress considered the coredemption, with papers by Hervé, Belon, Burlot, and DuBois. Belon's paper was "Mary-Priest — the Marian Coredemption Realised."[33] Belon had good reason to discuss this subject, because Bishop Morelle of Saint-Brieuc in convoking the congress had come out for a Marian priesthood "strictly so-called."

Belon shows the magnitude of the problem by his own indecision

---

[28] Campana, *op. cit.*, pp. 632-642, gives the story and summaries of the Breton series. It might be noted in passing that these volumes are, unfortunately, very rare.

[29] *Premier Congrès Marial Breton tenu à Josselin en l'honneur de l'Immaculée Conception, 21-24* Novembre 1904 (Paris, 1905), 600 pp. The cardinal's letter of October 31, 1904, is on page 31.

[30] *Deuxième Congrès Marial Breton tenu à Rennes en l'honneur de la Maternité Divine et de l'Annonciation les 22, 23, et 24 Mars 1908* (Rennes, 1908), liii & 613 pp.

[31] J. V. Bainvel, S.J., is well known to English readers on this subject from his *Catholic Encyclopedia* article, *Heart of Mary, Devotion to*, Vol. 7, pp. 168-169, and from his book *And the Light Shines in Darkness* (New York, 1953).

[32] *Troisième Congrès Marial Breton tenu au sanctuaire de Notre-Dame de Bon-Secours de Guingamp en l'honneur de la Corédemption mariale et de la Visitation* (Saint-Brieuc, 1912), lviii & 484 pp.

[33] *Marie-Prêtre — La Corédemption Mariale realisée*, in *op. cit.*, pp. 61-132; R. Laurentin discussed this paper of Belon at length in *Marie, l'Église et le Sacerdoce*, Vol. 1 (Paris, 1952), pp. 493 ff.

about the nature of the Blessed Virgin's priesthood. He grants her this title, yet says clearly at one point: "The Virgin Mary is not a priest in the sense of that priesthood which is true of Christ and of his priest ministers. But theology recognizes another priesthood: this, it is true, is simply analogous, of an order which is purely spiritual and private. It is this which belongs to the baptized" (p. 104). Yet this general priesthood, he continues, "stamped as it is by the divine motherhood, takes on such proportions that it seems to pass to another order." Laurentin relates that Belon had had an audience with Pope St. Pius X not long before the 1910 congress, and told one of his students that the pope had said in regard to the title "Virgin-Priest" (*Virgo sacerdos*), "one must proceed slowly" (*bisogna andare piano*). As is well known, a decree of the Holy Office, dated 1913, but not published until 1916, forbade images showing the Blessed Virgin in priestly vestments. Subsequent documents have reinforced the disapproval, at least in the sense that the Holy See wishes silence to be maintained lest poorly-instructed people misunderstand it.

A second main division of the congress took up Our Lady's Visitation, the only such extended treatment of this mystery known to the present writer. The papers considered the Visitation from various standpoints — theological, topographical, artistic; and, of course, included studies on the Magnificat, one of them by the Marist Père Georgelin, then of the *Institut Sainte-Marie de Washington*. In addition to some essays on devotion to Our Lady in the diocese of St. Brieuc, there was an article on the cult of Mary in Brittany across the sea, that is, in Wales. The Welsh language and Breton belong to the same Celtic family.

(4) Folgoät (also spelled Folgoet), September 4-6, 1913.[34] The theme was Mary's spiritual maternity, and a resolution was passed that it be declared a dogma. In orderly fashion the speakers developed the foundations of the doctrine, and the scriptural facts: the *fiat* at the Incarnation, then individual lectures on John's sanctification at the Visitation, on Cana (two papers), on Calvary, and on Pentecost. J. de Tonquedec, Jesuit editor of *Etudes,* a native of the Quimper diocese, spoke on the prayer of the holy Virgin. J. Le Rohellec, C.S.Sp., presented a long paper, "Mary, Dispensatrix of Divine Graces," which later appeared as a book.[35]

---

[34] *Quatrième Congrès Marial Breton tenu en Folgoät en l'honneur de Marie, Mère de Grace, 4, 5 & 6 Septembre 1913* (Quimper, 1915), xviii & 484 pp.

[35] J. Le Rohellec, C.S.Sp., *Mary, Mother of Divine Grace,* trans. S. Rigby and D. Fahey (London, 1937).

(5) After the interruption of World War I the Breton series did not take up again until 1924, when a final meeting was held at Nantes, October 14-16, on the subject of the Assumption.[36] The printed proceedings open with a survey of the work of the Breton congresses by Canon E. Le Garrec, associated with them from the start.

The assigned theme of the Assumption was studied in four sections. First was a discussion of Our Lady's death — its reason and manner, the possible place of her burial (Ephesus or Jerusalem), the apocryphal *transitus* accounts, and an appraisal of them. Section two concerned the resurrection of the Blessed Virgin; a preamble presented the contrasting opinions of J. Ernst and Bainvel, while subsequent papers examined Scripture texts cited in favor of the Assumption, and the theological reasons, especially the connection with Mary's other privileges. The third part consists of Bainvel's article on the definability of the Assumption. The fourth division contains various articles on the art and feast of the Assumption in France, as well as an essay on the woman of the twelfth chapter of the Apocalypse.

(B) French National Congresses, 1927-

The celebrations at Chartres in 1927 provided the opportunity to begin French national Marian congresses, similar to the national Eucharistic congresses. The cardinals and archbishops ratified this plan in March, 1928, and set up a "National French Committee of Marian Congresses," with headquarters at Chartres.[37] To date, seven congresses have been held. They are intended to be, and have been in fact, country-wide manifestations of devotion toward Mary, but at the same time have contained a strong doctrinal element, with leading theologians of France on their speakers' rosters.

(1) Chartres, May 31-June 6, 1927, was occasioned by the ninth centenary of the founding of the crypt of the *Virgo paritura* by St. Fulbert and the tenth centenary of the giving of the veil of the Virgin.[38] The doctrinal themes were the divine maternity and the spiritual maternity.

---

[36] *Congrès Marial Breton. Cinquième Session tenue à Nantes en 1924*: L'Assomption de la B. Vierge Marie (Nantes, Paris, Vannes, 1925), xvi & 175 pp.

[37] A survey article by A. Boucher, secretary-general of the committee in charge, *L'Oeuvre du comité national français des congrès marials*, appears in *Maria. Études sur la Ste. Vierge*, ed. H. du Manoir, S.J., Vol. 3 (Paris, 1954), pp. 615-625.

[38] *Fêtes Mariales. Chartres, 31 mai-6 juin, 1927* (Chartres, 1927), 426 pp.

Practical aspects were the promotion of the cult of Our Lady in the home and in the parish. Cardinal Dubois was the papal legate; the acts contain the apostolic letter appointing him.[39]

The congress days followed this order: a doctrinal point developed in a theological paper, then a practical point of application to life, and finally in the evening a literary or artistic offering. On the first day, for example, P.-M. Verrier, S.M., spoke of the virginity of Our Lady, two conferences were given on the role of Our Lady of Chartres in individual and family life, and in the evening papers on the Christian art associated with Chartres were given by G. Goyau and M. Denis.

(2) Lourdes, July 23-27, 1930, was the scene of the second national congress.[40] The doctrinal papers dealt with the Immaculate Conception — the dogma, the history of its definition, and a study of its place in theology, by E. Longpré, O.F.M., M. P. Pourrat, S.J., and J. Auriault, S.J., respectively. The sermons were on the Lourdes message relative to the Eucharist, prayer, and penance. Three petitions were put in the form of resolutions: (*a*) consecration of the human race to the Immaculate Heart of Mary by the pope; (*b*) extension of the feast of Mary Mediatrix to the whole Church; (*c*) canonization of Blessed Bernadette.

(3) Liesse-Laon, July 18-22, 1934. There were meetings both at the Liesse shrine and at Laon. Notre Dame of Liesse is devoted to Our Lady's joy and this determined the direction of the papers.[41] The doctrinal studies covered such topics as: Mary, cause and model of our joy; Mary, cause of our joy by her mediation; Mary and the joy of a good death. The sermons carried on the same theme, gathering a brilliant group of preachers: Pinard de la Boullaye, S.J., M. Gillet, O.P., Louis of the Trinity, O.C.D. Among the resolutions was a request "that the Holy Father deign to make an official consecration of the human race to the Immaculate Heart of Mary, according to the resolutions of the congresses of Chartres and Lourdes." The acts include two documents from the Holy See, directed to the legate, Cardinal Binet.[42]

---

[39] *Cum feliciter*, May 18, 1927; see also *A.A.S.*, Vol. 19, 1927, p. 410.

[40] *2ᵉ Congrès Marial National de Lourdes, 23-27 juillet 1930. Compte rendu officiel* (Lourdes, 1931), 316 pp.

[41] *Notre Dame de Liesse. 8ⁱᵉᵐᵉ Centenaire 1134-1934. IIIᵉ Congrès Marial National* (Liesse, 1935), 272 pp.

[42] *Toutes les manifestations*, May 3, 1934, appointing the legate, signed by Cardinal Pacelli; and *Laetitia singulari*, July 2, 1934; the latter is also in *A.A.S.*, Vol. 27, 1935, p. 73.

(4) The congress at Boulogne, July 20-24, 1938, was in honor of Our Lady's queenship.[43] Cardinal Liénart was the papal legate. Again a double anniversary was saluted: the thirteenth centenary of Marian cult at Boulogne, and the third centenary of the consecration of France to Our Lady by Louis XIII, an event enthusiastically described by Duc de la Force of the French Academy.[44]

In the doctrinal reports P. Aubron, S.J., discussed Our Lady's queenship from the historical standpoint of positive theology, presenting the evidence of the liturgy, the catechesis, and the magisterium. C. Dillenschneider's approach was dogmatic — the theological foundations for the queenship. He stressed that Mary's royal power must be considered according to her feminine character, hence especially in terms of her unique intercessory power. H. Barré, C.S.Sp., treated the practical consequences of Mary's sovereignty — our duties as her servants. An interesting and acute study by Canon L. Détrez, "Pilgrimages — Their Spirituality," answered objections against pilgrimages in the light of recent directives of the Holy See. Among the resolutions was a renewed request for the consecration of the entire world to the Immaculate Heart of Mary, and for the addition to the litany of "Queen of the world, pray for us."

(5) La Salette — Grenoble, September 2-8, 1946.[45] A congress had been scheduled for Notre Dame du Puy in 1942, but was impeded by World War II. As early as 1943 the national committee decided to go ahead with the meeting planned for the La Salette centenary in 1946. The La Salette congress had few public manifestations, but it was the quiet of intensity, in a land still aching from the war, and in a Christian people mindful of the penitential message of Our Lady of La Salette. Mary as coredemptrix was the main motif. An autograph letter of Pope Pius XII to S. Cruveiller, superior general of the Missionaries of Our Lady of La Salette, appears at the head of the acts.[46]

Distinguished theologians presented reports on Mary's coredemption:

---

[43] *Souveraineté de Marie. Congrès Marial de Boulogne s/Mer (Juillet, 1938)* (Paris, 1938), 572 pp. The papal brief appointing the legate, *Tertio decimo exeunte saeculo,* July 2, 1938, is on pp. 38-40.

[44] Le Voeu de Louis XIII, *op. cit.*, pp. 9-25.

[45] *Marie Coredemptrice. Ve Congrès Marial National. Grenoble-La Salette* (Lyon, 1948), xxxvii & 409 pp.

[46] *Notre dévotion vers la très sainte Verge Marie,* October 8, 1945, *op. cit.,* pp. xii-xiii, also in *A.A.S.,* Vol. 38, 1946, p. 155.

C. Dillenschneider, C.SS.R., M.J. Nicholas, O.P., and Canon Joussard. H. Rondet, S.J., spoke on the "Mother of mercy," and A.-M. Lépicier, O.S.M., on "The Sorrowful Mother." Another set of scholarly studies dealt with the appearances and advice of Our Lady of La Salette. Sermons given at the congress related both the coredemption and the events of La Salette to daily Christian life.

(6) The next congress was devoted to the Assumption, and was held at Rennes, July 4-9, 1950. The Holy Father's letter to Cardinal Roques of Rennes is at the beginning of the publihsed acts.[47] The names of those who gave papers indicate the caliber of the congress: F. Cayré A.A., on the germination and development of actual belief in the Assumption; B. Capelle, O.S.B., on the Assumption in the liturgy; M.-J. Nicolas on the theology of the Assumption; H. Du Manoir on the spiritual meaning of the doctrine; H. Barré on the possibility of hte definition; Msgr. L. Soubigou on the benefits deriving from a definition. In the general conferences two De Montfort Fathers spoke on the Marian doctrine and apostolate of their founder, who had passed his student years in Rennes. Jean Guitton addressed the general assembly on "The Virgin Mary and the Mystery of Human Existence."

(7) The Marian Year supplied the theme at Lyons, June 29—July 4, 1954. The papal letter naming Cardinal Gerlier legate recalls the glories of Lyons' past, and the fact that this city was the cradle of the work for the propagation of the faith.[48] The doctrinal reports presented a number of French Mariologists, all treating different phases of the Immaculate Conception. Some of these papers were: F.M. Braun, O.P., "Progress of the scriptural proof apropos of the Immaculate Conception since the bull *Ineffabilis*;" B. Capelle, "The feast of the Conception in the West;" and a particularly noteworthy paper by Msgr. Joussard, "The Marian theology of St. Irenaeus." The general conferences and the address to specialized groups were of the same high standard, e.g., H. Du Monoir's talk to religious women, "The Spiritual meaning of virginity."

---

[47] *Compte Rendu du VIe Congrès Marial National (Assomption de Notre Dame)*, (Rennes, 1951), 326 pp.; *Multiples et fécondes*, June 30, 1950, the papal letter is on pp. 7-9.

[48] *Congrès Marials Nationaux. VIIIe Congrès, Lyons 1954. L'Immaculée Conception. Compte-Rendu in Extenso* (Lyon, 1954), 442 pp.; the pope's letter, *Auspicato sane*, June 13, 1954, *op. cit.*, pp. 26-27, also in *A.A.S.*, Vol. 46, 1954, pp. 366-367.

(C) Franciscan Assumptionist Congress

The subject of the Assumption entered many of the congresses already reviewed, e.g., the Rennes national congress of 1950 was entirely on this theme. The place of honor, however, belongs to the series of Assumptionist congresses held in various countries under the sponsorship of the Franciscan Fathers. The proceedings have been published in the series *Studia Mariana* by the Academia Mariana Internationalis. In 1946 the superior general of the Order of Friars Minor set up a central committee to promote the study of the Assumption. The committee decreed that study congresses be held as soon as possible, first at Rome, and then throughout all the provinces of the Franciscan world.[49]

(1) The Roman congress, April 29—May 3, 1947, set the pattern for the subsequent ones.[50] The material was divided into *(a)* historical-positive studies, covering the Fathers, the apocrypha,, the tradition of the dormition at Jerusalem, the feast in eastern and western liturgy, the Assumption in medieval literature, etc., and *(b)* exegetical-speculative studies — on the Scriptures, the dogmatic value of the liturgy, the doctrine in the faith of the Church, and such favorite Franciscan themes as the Assumption in the light of the absolute primacy of Christ, and the Assumption according to the Scotist Marian principles. C. Balić gave a final paper on the definability of the belief.

(2) The Lisbon meeting, October 9-13, 1947, considered scriptural, patristic, and ancient apocryphal references to the Assumption.[51] Several papers concerned Portugal and the Assumption, as J. Montalverne's

---

[49] Surveys of the Franciscan Assumptionist congresses are to be found in: C. Balić, O.F.M., *Il contributo dei Frati Minori al movimento mariologico moderno*, in *Marianum*, Vol. 11, 1949, pp. 440-460; R. Ohlmann, O.F.M., *The Assumptionist Movement and the Franciscan Marian Congresses, A Survey*, in the acts of the Washington congress (see below), *Studia Mariana*, Vol. 7, pp. 19-30; Melchior a Pobladura, O.F.M.Cap., *Recent literature on Mary's Assumption*, in *The American Ecclesiastical Review*, Vol. 120, 1949, pp. 376-387.

[50] *Atti del Congresso Nazionale Mariano dei Frati Minori d'Italia; Studia Mariana*, Vol. 1 (Roma 1948), vii & 732 pp. The congress held at Cracow, August, 1937, is sometimes listed among the Assumptionist congresses, although its Latin and Polish papers ranged over many topics; one in Polish by B. Domagala, O.F.M., was on the historical evolution of the Assumption: see *Acta secundi Congressus Cracoviae, 25-29 augusti, 1937* in *Collectanea Franciscana Slavica*, Vol. 2 (Sibenici, 1940), xix-339 pp.

[51] *Actas do Congresso Mariano dos Franciscanos de Portugal, Lisboa, 9 a 13 outubro de 1947; Studia Mariana*, Vol. 2 (Lisbon, 1948), 212 pp.; also under the title *Colectânea de Estudos*, Numero 3, 1947, suplementos do *Boletin Mensal*, Braga.

MARIAN CONGRESSES 317

exhaustive report on the ancient manuscripts in the monastery of Alcobaza.

(3) Madrid, Spain, October 21-26, 1947.[52] The Spanish studies considered (*a*) general themes relative to the Assumption, e.g., a study by A. Eguiluz on prayer formulas as indicative of doctrinal belief — the old axiom *"lex orandi, lex credendi";* (*b*) special subjects, as Father Montalverne's on the silence of the first centuries concerning the Assumption. The indefatigable Father Balić reported his researches on manuscript codices in Spanish libraries, and then provided a summing-up paper on the significance of the Assumptionist movement in the world.

(4) The Canadian meeting, Montreal, August 15-18, 1948, was bilingual, and other theologians, Redemptorist, Jesuit, Dominican, Sulpician, etc., joined efforts with the Franciscans.[53] In the larger French section, the topics ranged from the problem of the Assumption through the reply of tradition, to the teaching of theology. Among the studies, we find one on the Apocalypse by L. Poirier, O.F.M.; on the first four centuries, by Cayré; on the Franciscan school, by Longpré; and on the definability, by A. Ferland. The five papers of the English section included C. Morin, P.S.S., "The Assumption and Liturgy," and B. Lonergan, S.J., "The Teaching of Theology."

(5) Buenos Aires, Argentina, September 28-October 4, 1948, closely followed the Roman division of material: an historical-positive section, then an exegetical-speculative section.[54] The first section included reports on the doctrine of the dissident Churches of the East, on the queenship of Mary in the liturgy, and studies on the cult of the Assumption in Ecuador, Peru, Bolivia, Chile. The second section contained a conference on the queenship of Mary in the Scriptures, and a theological explanation of the

---

[52] *Actas del Congreso Mariano Franciscano-Español, Madrid, 21-26 octubre, 1947; Studia Mariana,* Vol. 3 (Madrid, 1948), 396 pp. This appeared also as a special number of *Verdad y Vida,* Vol. 6, enero-septiembre, 1948.

[53] *Vers le Dogme de l'Assomption. Journées d'études mariales; Studia Mariana,* Vol. 4 (Montreal, 1948), xi & 445 pp. See J. B. Carol, O.F.M., *Verso la definizione dommatica dell'Assunta,* in *Marianum,* Vol. 11, 1949, pp. 88-94.

[54] *Actas del Congreso Asuncionista Franciscano de América Latina; Studia Mariana,* Vol. 5 (Buenos Aires, 1949), xxiv & 401 pp. Another South American congress concerned with the Assumption was the first Brazilian theological congress held at São Paulo, January 23-29, 1950; the proceedings are to be found as a special number of the *Revista Eclesiástica Brasileira,* Vol. 10, Margo, 1950, pp. 296; see the report in *Marianum,* Vol. 10, 1950, pp. 250-259.

queenship, as well as studies more immediately concerned with the Assumption. Among the better-known speakers who took part were J. M. de Goicoechea, O.F.M., of Peru, and C. Koser, O.F.M., of Brazil.

At Puy-en-Velay, August 11-16, 1949, the talents of scholars of five nations were enlisted, e.g., the Jesuits Rondet and Boyer along with Franciscans Piana, Emmen, Bonnefoy, and Longpré.[55] Among the eleven dissertations are Piana's on the Assumption according to the fifteenth century Franciscan school. C. Boyer, S.J., of the Gregorian University, discussed the question of Our Lady's immortality *de iure* and *de facto*, in a paper titled "The Reasons for the Death of the Blessed Virgin." Longpré studied the relationship between the Immaculate Conception and the Assumption from a Scotistic viewpoint. The divergent views of the various contributors provide a good index to the healthy freedom of theological thought.

The United States congress was held at Washington, D. C., October 8-11, 1950, shortly before the dogmatic definition.[56] Archbishop O'Boyle of Washington preached at the opening Mass. In the academic sessions ten papers were presented by members of the three Franciscan branches of the First Order. R. Ohlmann surveyed the Assumptionist movement, especially the Franciscan congresses. A. de Guglielmo, O.F.M., discussed "The Immortality of Mary in the Light of Sacred Scripture." I. Brady, O.F.M., spoke on "The Relation between Sin and Death according to Medieval Theologians." M. Habig, O.F.M., reported on the cult of the Assumption in the United States, 1598-1888. M. Grajewski, O.F.M., took up the Marian cult of American Franciscans in terms of modern Mariological studies.

N. Moholy, O.F.M., read a well-documented paper, "St. Irenaeus, The Father of Mariology." R. Huber, O.F.M.Conv., of the Catholic University of America, offered a similar study on the Mariology of St. Anthony of Padua. N. Sonntag, O.F.M.Cap., discussed the Assumption according to St. Lawrence of Brindisi. E. May, O.F.M.Cap., spoke of the Assumption in Franciscan exegetical works. T. Plassmann, O.F.M., closed the collection with "The Papal Definition of the Dogma of the Assumption," written in

---

[55] *Congrès Marial du Puy-en-Velay. L'Assomption de la très sainte Vierge; Studia Mariana*, Vol. 6 (Paris, 1950), 291 pp. See J. B. Carol, O.F.M., *The Recent Marian Congress at Le Puy-en-Velay*, in *The American Ecclesiastical Review*, Vol. 123, 1950, pp. 273-283.

[56] *First Franciscan National Marian Congress in Acclamation of the Dogma of the Assumption, October 8-11, 1950; Studia Mariana*, Vol. 7 (Burlington, Wisconsin, 1952), 315 pp.

anticipation of the event.

Although not customarily enumerated in this Franciscan Assumptionist series, the Jerusalem congress, December 8-11, 1950, can be conveniently listed with them, for it concerns the Assumption and was under the aegis of the Franciscan custodians of the Holy Places. Other scholars collaborated with the Friars Minor.[57] Among the subjects were the Assumption in the liturgy and theology of the Armenian, Chaldean, Maronite, Melkite, and Syrian (Antioch) Churches. There is a carefully documented study by G. Giamberardini, O.F.M., "The Theology of the Assumption in the Egyptian Church." Another paper concerns the Islamic cult at the tomb of the Virgin.

(D) Other Congresses

The international, Breton, French national, and Franciscan Assumptionist congresses have all been discussed. To attempt to review the other smaller series and the almost countless individual congresses, even those which were held during the Marian Year alone, would require a full-length book. Moreover, many of the local congresses were almost exclusively popular in character, and if proceedings have been published, these acts are often no more than extended chronicles of the public displays of honor toward the Mother of God. In the present chapter the main emphasis has been on meetings that have made a contribution to Mariology. Adhering to this criterion, a choice will be made of the more important among individual congresses.

(1) At the initiative of the Capuchins, a "First De Montfort Marian Congress" was held at Barcelona, Spain, September 18-21, 1918.[58] The bishop of Barcelona was the papal legate to this meeting entirely devoted to the theme of true devotion to Mary. Father Arintero, O.P., was among those who presented papers on Mary and the mystical body; his topic was the mission of Mary in sanctification as the spouse of the Holy Spirit.

(2) Both in its study aspects and as a tribute of the trust of Christian peoples in the Queen of peace, the Brussels congress, September 8-11, 1921, is a modern landmark regarding the mediation of Mary. The

---

[57] *Atti del Congresso Assunzionistico Orientale organizzato dalla Custodia di Terra Santa* (Gerusalemme, 1951), xiii & 267 pp.

[58] *Crónica del Primer Congresso Mariano Montfortiano* (Totana, 1920), 479 pp. J. Bittremieux, *Marialia* (Nijmegen, 1936), p. 336, gives credit to the Capuchins; see also Campana, *op. cit.*, pp. 648-649.

congress was bilingual, French and Flemish.[59] Cardinal Mercier had sounded the keynote in a pastoral letter:

> ... a more profound theological study of the place Mary, the Immaculate Virgin, occupies in the plan of the redemption. There are corollaries still to be deduced from the divine maternity of Mary, from her Immaculate Conception, from the fullness of her holiness, and above all from the share of her sorrowing and immaculate heart in the redemptive sacrifice accomplished on Calvary. She is divinely associated in a special degree in the mediation of Jesus, in His redemption; with Him she is His co-mediatrix, His co-redemptrix, as no one else is.[60]

The Holy See authorized a proper Office and Mass on May 31, feast of Mary Mediatrix of all graces, for Belgium and any other dioceses in the world that requested it. The Office and Mass were originally composed by J. Lebon, but altered by other hands before they were finally submitted for approval in Rome; hence the present propers, especially the collect, do not represent fully the thought of Msgr. Lebon and the other associates of Cardinal Mercier.[61]

The first part of the French study-reports was divided into (*a*) sources of Mariology — Scripture and tradition; (*b*) Marian theology; (*c*) special questions. A second part dealt with history and liturgy. L. Cerfaux showed the mediatory character of Mary's grace, as expressed by Gabriel's greeting. P. Galtier, S.J., spoke on the maternity of grace in St. Irenaeus; Dom Capelle on the Augustinian texts relative to the Immaculate Conception; B. Merkelbach, O.P., on the eminent dignity of the Mother of God; and F. X. Godts, C.Ss.R., on the co-redemptrix. A. Vermeersch, S.J., spoke of "Mary, Queen of Peace," and extended the significance of this title so meaningful in 1921 to the reconciliation effected in the redemption. Another volume of the French acts examined Marian cult. M. Nepper, S.J., spoke on Russian cult of our Lady; Dom del Marmol, O.S.B., of twelfth-century devotion to Mary; members of various orders on their

---

[59] *Mémoires & Rapports du Congrès Marial (Sections d'expression française) tenu à Bruxelles, 8-11 Septembre 1921* (Bruxelles, 1922), Vol. 1, lxxv & 252 pp., Vol. 2, pp. 253-682; *Handelingen van het Vlaamsch Maria-Congres te Brussel, 8-11 September 1921* (Brussel, 1922), Vol. 1, 367 pp., Vol. 2, 375 pp.

[60] Pastoral letter of Pentecost, 1921, as reported in *Mémoires & Rapports...*, Vol. 1, p. lxx.

[61] J. Lebon, À *propos des textes liturgiques de la fête de Marie Médiatrice*, in *Marianum*, Vol. 14, 1952, pp. 122-128, and also the obituary by G. Geenen, O.P., Monseigneur J. Lebon (1879-1957), in *Marianum*, Vol. 20, 1958, pp. 120-126.

respective approaches to the Blessed Virgin — Benedictines, Dominicans, Carmelites, Jesuits, Redemptorists, Oblates of Mary Immaculate, etc.

The Flemish had similar subjects. Doctrinal lectures were given by B. Merkelbach, J. Bittremieux, L. J. Kerkhofs, J. Coppens — members of the distinguished company of theologians Cardinal Mercier gathered around him, and whose studies contributed greatly to the present-day appreciation of Mary's mediation. An appendix to volume 2 of the French proceedings lists some of the answers received from members of the hierarchy of various countries in reply to Cardinal Mercier's question about celebrating a feast of Mary Mediatrix of all graces.[62]

(3) The Hispano-American congress of Seville, May 15-21, 1929, spanned the Old World and the New.[63] Preparations for it began in 1927, under the leadership of J. Postíus, C.M.F., anxious to provide a substitute for the interrupted series of international congresses. Besides Spain, and, to an extent, Portugal, many Central and South American countries took part. Pius XI named Cardinal Ilundain his legate.[64]

The topics covered a wide range: doctrine, cult, spirituality, iconography, colonial history. The selection of seventeen papers printed in full in the Acts are taken mainly from the section on Marian theology and exegesis. D. Luis Rubio Moreno presented a lengthy report on Marian traces in the Indies, documented from the general archive of the Indies located at Seville. During the congress a solemn Mass was sung for the repose of the souls of the discoverers and colonizers of America, with an absolution by the nuncio, Archbishop F. Tedeschini.

The major theological conferences were held on successive days. On May 15 the bishop of Madrid preached on behalf of the definition of the Assumption and the Mediation of Mary. On the next day Bishop Gomá y Tomás spoke on "the mediation of the Virgin and the mission of the Catholic priesthood in the Church of Christ." On May 17 Canon A. F. Nistal spoke on the Assumption. Finally, on May 18 J. M. Bover, S.J., lectured on the "organic synthesis of Mariology from the standpoint of the association of Mary in the redemptive work of Christ."

(4) The United States joined the movement with the congress held at

---

[62] *Mémoires & Rapports*, Vol. 2, pp. 653-679.

[63] *Crónica Oficial del Congreso Mariano Hispano-americano de Sevilla y de los actos complementarios del mismo celebrado del 15 al 21 de mayo de 1929* (Madrid, 1930), 1062 pp.

[64] By the letter, *Cum valde equidem*, February 20, 1929, in the *Crónica Oficial*, p. 144.

the Sanctuary of the Sorrowful Mother, Portland, Oregon, August 13-15, 1934, seventh centenary year of the founding of the Order of the Servants of Mary.[65] Cardinal A. Lépicier, O.S.M., presided, and gave several addresses. He also presented the series of themes which were studied at the congress, e.g., "Mary the holy Virgin, the new Eve, is justly and rightly called the coredemptrix of the human race because of her real and efficacious cooperation in the work of human redemption." Among the speakers who took part were T. Burke, C.S.P., P. K. Meagher, O.P., J. Zeller, C.Ss.R., S. Juergens, S.M., and A. Mayer, O.S.M. The attendance was in the tens of thousands.

(5) During the Marian Year the Catholics of the United States expressed their devotion to the Mother of God in many ways. Universities held special lectures and convocations, e.g., the Marian convocation, November 15-16, 1954, at the Catholic University of America in Washington, D. C. Religious orders arranged special gatherings, dioceses celebrated Marian hours in huge stadiums. The most impressive of these efforts, both doctrinally and devotionally, was the national Marian congress organized by the Franciscan National Marian Commission, and held in San Francisco, Los Angeles, Santa Barbara, and Sacramento, May 4-9, 1954.[66]

There was a tremendous variety of public expressions of devotion — Pontifical Masses, pageants, plays, concerts, pilgrimages, exhibits, even a pyrotechnical display over Monterey Bay. Several days were set aside for theological sessions. Among the papers presented were: "The Cult of the Immaculate Conception in the United States before 1854," by M. Habig, O.F.M.; "Doctrine of the Immaculate Conception in the Early Franciscan School," by A. Wolter, O.F.M.; "The Fathers of the Church and the Dogma of the Immaculate Conception," by N. De Amato, O.F.M.; and "Our Lady

---

[65] No printed proceedings for the Portland congress could be found, nor a reference to any. It is chronicled briefly in Campana, *op. cit.*, p. 651; Roschini, *Mariologia*, Vol. 4, p. 187; and more fully in B. M. Morineau, S.M.M., *L'Année Mariale; Les Cahiers de la Vierge*, No. 6 (Juvisy, 1934), pp. 34-40. Two books inspired by the congress were: A. Lépicier, *Behold Thy Mother* (Rome, 1934), 68 pp., and A. M. Mayer, *Advanced Mariology* (Portland, Oregon, 1934), xii & 168 pp.

[66] The proceedings are in two volumes: one is an illustrated chronicle —*Franciscan National Marian Congress. The Story of an American Tribute to Our Lady Immaculate in California of the Padres* (San Francisco, 1957), 197 pp. The other volume is scientific: *Second Franciscan National Marian Congress in Celebration of the Marian Year in Honor of the Centenary of the Definition of the Dogma of the Immaculate Conception, May 4-9, 1954* (San Francisco, 1957), 197 pp. Alfred Boeddeker, O.F.M., edited both volumes.

of Guadalupe, Bishop Zumárraga and the Immaculate Conception," by F. de J. Chauvet, O.F.M.

(6) Saragossa, Spain, October 8-12, 1940, held a congress which led to the foundation of the Spanish Mariological Society, which met for the first time in 1941, and which is justly known for its proceedings, *Estudios Marianos*. In Saragossa's printed acts, which are otherwise mainly a chronicle of events, there is the book-length study on the queenship by Angel Luis, C.Ss.R., a significant contribution concerning this Marian truth.[67] At the actual congress there were many other subjects, doctrinal, ascetical, etc. Dogmatic topics included the mediation, the Assumption, the coredemption, and the relationship between the Blessed Virgin and the Eucharist. One of the resolutions seconded the requests made at Lyons, Fribourg, and Einsiedeln for a consecration of the universe to Mary Queen, and the granting of a liturgical feast.

Congresses, both national and international, of the various Marian congregations, the Children of Mary, the sodalists, etc., might well receive a treatment all their own. Two will be considered here:

(a) The Sodality world assembly at Barcelona, November 29-December 10, 1947, had as its principal purpose to petition the Holy See to define the Assumption. The Holy Father addressed the members by radio, December 7, 1947.[68] Recalling his own membership in the Marian Sodality, the pontiff urged his hearers to avoid both the heresy of action and that timorous piety which neglects the apostolate. Recalling how the Marian sodalities of a century before had petitioned Pius IX to define the Immaculate Conception, and then awaited the great event, saying in the silence of their hearts, "and now, Peter, instruct us," Pope Pius XII made the same application to the Assumption.

A first world-congress of the federated Marian sodalities gathered at

---

[67] *Crónica Oficial del Congreso Mariano Nacional, Zaragoza, Octubre, 1940* (Zaragoza, 1942), 358 pp.; Luis' study also appeared separately, *La Realeza de María* (Madrid, 1942), 144 pp. A report on the meeting in the form of a letter from N. García Garcés, C.M.F., to G. Roschini, O.S.M., is found in *Marianum*, Vol. 3, 1941, pp. 73-79.

[68] The papal discourse was *Nos sentimos*, in *A.A.S.*, Vol. 39, 1947, pp. 632- 634. There is a brief report on the congress by A. Luis, C.Ss.R., in *Marianum*, Vol. 10, 1948, p. 298. In some listings, Barcelona, which had representatives from twenty-seven nations, is placed among the international congresses, next after Trier, 1912, e.g., by Roschini, *Mariologia*, Vol. 4, pp. 188-189.

Rome, September 8-12, 1954.[69] Ten thousand members gathered in St. Peter's heard the Holy Father speak (September 8) on the congress themes: (1) the selection of candidates; (2) union with the hierarchy; (3) co-operation with other apostolic associations.[70]

Canadian congresses: (*a*) In 1929, June 13-16, a Marian congress was held at Quebec. In addition to the enthusiastic and crowded popular manifestations, there were six sessions at the University of Laval, on the subject of Mary's mediation.[71] And in recent years in Canada there has been a series of congresses, some national and bilingual, some local and mainly French. On several of these occasions the Canadian Mariological Society has held its meeting at the same time as a popular congress, and presented one or more of its papers to the general public. In fact, the plans for the *Société Canadienne d'Études Mariales* were first drawn up at the important national congress of Ottawa, 1947.[72]

(*b*) Ottawa, June 18-22, 1947.[73] The pope named Cardinal McGuigan his legate by *Ab Octaviensi Archidioecesi,* March 25, 1947, a letter containing counsels on the true concept of liberty in the light of Our Lady's life.[74] On June 19, 1947, the Holy Father delivered a bilingual radio message to the congress, recalling Mary's role in the history of Canada, and speaking of the spiritual motherhood.[75]

---

[69] The proceedings are bi-lingual, French and English on facing pages: *Compte-rendu du premier Congrès de la Fédération Mondials des Congrégations Mariales. Report of the First Congress of the Sodalities World Federation* (Rome, 1955), 175 pp. The purpose was "not a congress of studies but a world family gathering and to apply the directives of the Church which we already possess in abundance. Everything must tend towards a renewal of the spirit," *op. cit.,* p. 71. The first of the ten resolutions was a request for the definition of the "dogma of Mary, Mediatrix of graces."

[70] *C'est avec une grande joie,* in A.A.S., Vol. 46, 1954, pp. 529-534.

[71] *Le premier Congrès Marial de Québec, du 12 au 16 juin, 1929. Compte rendu, discours, sermons et rapports* (Québec, 1931), 413 pp.

[72] *Ère mariale,* Vol. 1, Avril, 1956, p. 3; this is the bulletin of the Canadian Mariological Society.

[73] *Le Congrès Marial d'Ottawa* (Gardenvale, 1948), viii & 346, and the identical acts in English, same publisher, date and number of pages: *The Marian Congress of Ottawa,* trans. Emmet O'Grady. These are no more than extended chronicles; no summaries are given of the papers.

[74] A.A.S., Vol. 39, 1947, pp. 254-256.

[75] *C'est avec une douce,* in A.A.S., Vol. 39, 1947, pp. 268-272.

Marian Year congress at Cap-de-la-Madeleine, August 5-15, 1954.[76] The Canadian Society of Marian Studies held its reunion August 12-13, so that the larger public was able to profit from some of its sessions on the Immaculate Conception. A. Ferland, P.S.S., spoke on "The Immaculate, Rule of Life for Christians."[77] Papal interest was shown by the letter naming Cardinal Valeri legate, *Permagnus profecto,* July 2, 1954, and by the Holy Father's bi-lingual radio address of August 15, 1954, on Canada's ancient love of Our Lady and her influence on Christian life in the present day.[78] On August 15 Cardinals McGuigan and Léger read the act of consecration of the nation in English and French, and then Cardinal Valeri solemnly crowned the statue of Notre Dame du Cap.

Three Marian Year congresses: Philippines, India, Brussels. There were very many congresses held all over the world in 1954. For the most part these have been well chronicled in the standard magazines, *Marianum, Ephemerides Mariologicae,* the French-Canadian *Marie,* etc. Periodicals specializing in papal pronouncements, as *The Pope Speaks,* devoted considerable space to the many letters, radio messages, and other documents of Pope Pius XII directed to the Marian Year congresses.[79] The majority of these gatherings were popular in character, and often exclusively so; but a good number also contained doctrinal sessions and lectures. Short summaries will here be given of congresses held in the Philippines and India, and mention also made of Brussels.

The meeting in the Philippines, December 1-5, 1954, is known as the second national, for there had been an earlier one in 1926. Different days were assigned to the three themes — divine maternity, Immaculate

---

[76] *Le Congrès Marial National,* 5-15 *Août* 1954. The National Marian Congress, August 5 to 15, 1954 (Trois-Rivières, 1954), 157 pp. in French, 151 pp. in English.

[77] *L'Immaculée, règle de vie des chrétiens,* in *L'Immaculée Conception de la Bienheureuse Vierge Marie. Journées d'Études, Cap-de-la-Madeleine, 12-13 Août, 1954* (Ottawa, 1955), 197 pp., Ferland's talk, pp. 165-172; this was the first year the Canadian Mariological Society published its proceedings in book form.

[78] *Permagnus profecto,* in *A.A.S.,* Vol. 46, 1954, pp. 481-482; radio address, *Le Seigneur a rendu,* in *A.A.S.,* Vol. 46, 1954, pp. 498-500, English translation, *Mary Help of Christians: This World and the Next,* in *The Pope Speaks,* Vol. 1, 1954, pp. 277-279.

[79] *The Pope Speaks, for example, in addition to a number of full-length* discourses, *printed a series of selections from ten messages to national Marian congresses all in the latter part of 1954: The World Pays Its Honor to Mary,* Vol. 2, 1955, pp. 53-64, representing the Philippines, Montevideo, Sicily, Mexico, Spain, Nigeria, Lebanon, India, Peru, and Colombia.

Conception, and Assumption.[80] The attendance of the people shattered records in Philippine Church history. Special conferences were held for men, for women, for youth, for religious, for priests. Three languages were used: Spanish, English, Tagalog. The University of Santo Tomás was the meeting place for the priests' section, which heard such speakers as Archbishop Vagnozzi, the Papal Nuncio, and F. Vacas, O.P. A special theological session was held at Santo Tomás, December 7. Cardinal Quiroga was the papal legate, and the Holy Father addressed the congress by radio, December 5, 1954.[81]

Valerian Cardinal Gracias was the papal legate to the Bombay, India, congress, December 4-8, 1954, a demonstration of faith unparalleled in Indian history.[82] The acts tell of all the details — civic events, ordinations to the priesthood, a feeding of the poor. Cultural sessions were conducted in various native tongues. There were also special meetings of priests and sessions for nuns. The pope's address given in English explained how genuine devotion to Mary is rooted in devotion to Christ her Son.[83]

Another bilingual national congress was held at Brussels, September 2-5, 1954. The pope's address was on consecration to Mary, its benefits and obligations.[84] Printed proceedings of both French and Flemish sections apply Marian doctrine and example to all states of life. The Flemish-speaking Mariological Society (Mariale Dagen of Tongerloo) met at the same time. One day of the congress featured lectures in German for people from eastern Belgium, with Carl Feckes as the speaker.[85]

---

[80] IInd *Marian Congress of the Philippines. Manila, December 1-5, 1954, Souvenir Program.* No publisher or page markings or date are indicated; only titles of the talks are given. See the report by F. Vacas, O.P., in *Marianum*, Vol. 17, 1955, pp. 397-399.

[81] *Philippinae insulae*, November 4, 1954, appointing the legate, is in *A.A.S.*, Vol. 46, 1954, pp. 700-701, and the pope's address, *Como el ágil viandante, ibid.*, pp. 718-721.

[82] *Bombay: National Marian Congress, Bombay, India, December 1954. Souvenir* (Bombay, 1955), viii & 232 pp., an indexed report on devotional and doctrinal events with some of the talks given in full.

[83] *It would indeed*, December 8, 1954, in *A.A.S.*, Vol. 46, 1954, pp. 725-728; the letter naming the legate, *In latissimis*, was in *A.A.S.*, Vol. 46, 1954, pp. 706-707.

[84] *Dépuis le 8 décembre*, in *A.A.S.*, Vol. 46, 1954, pp. 540-543, English translation in *The Pope Speaks*, Vol. 1, 1954, pp. 281-284.

[85] *Actes du Congrès Marial, Septembre 1954* (Bruxelles, 1955), 157 pp., *Nationaal Marial Congres, Brussel, 2-3-4-5 September 1954* (Brussels, 1955), 161 pp., *Verslagboek der Priester-Vergaderingen* (Tongerlo, 1955), 85 pp.

Conclusion

Historically, the movement of Marian congresses dates only from the end of the nineteenth century. The first international congress was held at Lyons, 1900, and Lourdes in 1958 was the tenth. The congress movement has reflected and encouraged the growing interest in the study of Our Lady as well as devotion to her; the last three world assemblies, Rome in 1950 and 1954, and Lourdes in 1958, are good evidence of this with their specifically Mariological sections.

The Breton meetings, although limited in attendance, form a distinguished series of five from 1904 through 1924. After them may be mentioned the seven French national congresses, since 1927, both popular and theological, and the Assumptionist congresses organized in various countries by the Franciscan International Marian Academy — scientific in character. The Marian Year congresses, almost beyond accurate enumeration, ranged from the exclusively popular to the very scientific.

What is the over-all balance from the doctrinal standpoint? One answer to this question is that the congresses not only show the centers of Marian interest of the last sixty years, but also indicate the development of doctrine, in so far as one can justly speak of development of doctrine in so relatively short a period.

The Assumptionist movement is reflected in this period, perhaps less strongly, however, than might have been expected, except in the years immediately preceding the definition. There is evident a great interest in Our Lady's queenship, in terms of doctrinal studies and resolutions as well. Many petitions express the desire that the Holy Father consecrate the world to the Immaculate Heart of Mary, although few papers treat this as a doctrinal theme.

In his address at the closing session of the Mariological congress at Lourdes, 1958, the legate Cardinal Tisserant alluded to the role the century's congresses had played in the development of devotion to Mary, and reviewed in particular their influence on consecration to the Immaculate Heart of Mary, Mother and Queen. He proposed this consecration to the Lourdes congress as a goal: "The tenth international Marian congress should encourage the development of consecration to the Immaculate Heart of Mary on the part of individuals, of families, of societies."[86]

---

[86] *L'Osservatore Romano*, September 15-16, 1958. The part played by the congresses in preparation for the consecration of the world to the Immaculate Heart is also brought

The mediation of Mary was studied particularly at the 1921 Brussels congress under Cardinal Mercier's leadership. Essays on this and associated truths, e.g., the spiritual maternity, the coredemption, etc., occur throughout the sixty-year period.[87]

Not all is gold in the final balance; much is alloy, and as one should expect of human effort, there is a great deal of gilt. In some of the many published proceedings virtually the only parts of lasting value are the documents from the Holy See. R. Laurentin tells how a distinguished Mariologist by whose side he was standing at the closing session of a recent study congress on our Lady —a congress productive of excellent work — remarked as the "resolutions" were being read: "What a pity that all this dross is here too!"[88] But despite such human failings, the over-all reckoning of the congress movement is an encouraging one. And the counsels of the Holy See sent to the members of congresses have emphasized the lasting values of deeper understanding of the mystery of Mary and the sound devotion founded on true doctrine.

---

out by G. Geenen, O.P., *Les antécédents doctrinaux et historiques de la Consécration du Monde au Coeur Immaculé de Marie*, in *Maria. Études sur la Sainte Vierge*, ed. H. du Manoir, S.J., Vol. 1 (Paris, 1949), pp. 825-873. Cf. J. M. Canal, C.M.F., *La consagración a la Virgen y a su Corazón Inmaculado*, in *Virgo Immaculata*, Vol. 12, 1956, pp. 293-297.

[87] I. Valle, S.J., gave a report at the 1954 world congress of Marian Congregations in Rome on the movement for the dogmatic definition of the mediation as initiated by Cardinal Mercier: *Mouvement mondial pour la définition dogmatique de la médiation universelle de Marie. Le Cardinal Mercier initiateur du mouvement, op. cit.*, (see note 69); the same report appeared in *Marie*, Vol. 9, Jan.-Fev., 1956, pp. 389-392.

[88] R. Laurentin, *Conclusion, in* Maria. Études sur la Sainte Vierge, ed. H. du Manoir, S.J., Vol. 3 (Paris, 1954), p. 735.

MARIAN SHRINES AND APPARITIONS

by SALVATORE J. BONANO, C.M.F.

IN ORDER to keep this chapter within the boundaries of manageable exposition, the history of the Marian shrines around the world will be confined to a mere condensation of available material to the essential facts. It has not always been an easy task to determine which are to be considered the main shrines of a given country, but the reader may rest assured that the great majority of those dealt with here are certainly the principal national shrines, while the remaining few may be ranked as at least important. Footnotes will enumerate other possibly noteworthy shrines in the same country.

The liturgical coronation ceremony of Marian statues and paintings is intended to be a tribute of honor paid by the faithful to their heavenly Queen, and a symbol of gratitude for countless favors received. This ceremony, however, is reserved only for the more ancient and outstanding shrines of Our Lady. The custom was established since at least the seventeenth century, when the Chapter of the Vatican Basilica became heir to the legacy of Count Sforza Pallavicini that provided gold crowns for celebrated images in the City.[1] The Canons of the Chapter determine which paintings or statues shall be so honored.

I. THE HOLY LAND

Shrine of the Immaculate Conception

A wide-spread tradition of the ninth century points to the ancient town of Nazareth as the birthplace of Our Lady, but a more solidly established second-century tradition favors the Holy City of Jerusalem.

---

[1] G. Montague, *Ceremony of Crowning an Image of the Blessed Virgin*, in *The Irish Ecclesiastical Record*, Vol. 82, 1954, pp. 430-431; Alessio M. Rossi, O.S.M., *Reine et souveraine*, in *Marie*, Vol. 8, 1955, p. 521; Edward Keating, *How the Queen is Crowned*, in *Mary*, Vol. 15, 1954, pp. 86-88. Since so many of the shrines owe their origin to an apparition of Our Lady, the following articles may prove helpful: M. Castellano, *La prassi canonica circa le apparizioni mariane*, in *Enciclopedia Mariana*, ed. R. Spiazzi, O.P. (Milano, 1954), pp. 465-486; C. Staehlin, *Apariciones*, in *Razón y Fe*, Vol. 49, 1949, pp. 445-464 (I); 546-562 (II); C. Truhlar, S.J., *Principia theologica de habitudine christiani erga apparitiones*, in *Virgo Immaculata*, Vol. 16 (Romae, 1956), pp. 1-17.

After the year 400, numerous writers testify to the existence of a Marian basilica, located in the northeastern sector of the Old City of Jerusalem, not far from the Temple, near the Pool of Bethsaida. At the beginning of the seventh century, the Patriarch Sophronius refers to this church as the place of Mary's birth, and the recent findings of archaeology have brought out the truth of his statement. Built in the first half of the fifth century over a small oratory that had been in existence a hundred years previous, this church was destroyed by the Persians in 614 and rebuilt between the eighth and ninth centuries.[2] In 1856 it came under the jurisdiction of the French Government and was entrusted to the White Fathers of Cardinal Lavigerie.

Church of the Annunciation

As early as A.D. 326, Constantine the Great had built a church in Nazareth above the grotto where the Blessed Virgin heard the angel's message that she was to be the Mother of God. After its destruction by the Saracens, the Crusaders under Tancred erected a new church in 1100, smashed, in turn, by the Moslems under Sultan Bibars in 1263.[3] Four hundred years later, a small church was built on the ruins of the ancient basilica, and was replaced by the actual provisional shrine erected by the Franciscans in 1730 to meet a deadline set by Turkish authorities. "In process of construction at the present time and to be complete in 1957, is a new $2,000,000 Church of the Annunciation. Only the foundations of the existing church, built in 1730, will be saved. Excavations of the Franciscans and other archaeologists, preparatory to building the new Basilica, have uncovered evidence, not only of the Crusader church, but of an earlier primitive and much attended shrine at the very site of the Annunciation."[4]

---

[2] General bibliography on shrines throughout the world: Zsolt Aradi, *Shrines to Our Lady Around the World* (New York, 1954); H. M. Gillet, *Famous Shrines of Our Lady*, 2 vols. (Westminster, Md., 1952); W. Gumppenberg, S.J.,

[3] E. Levesque, *Annonciation*, in *Dictionnaire de la Bible*, Vol. 1, cols. 650-654; F. Cabrol, *Fête de l'Annonciation*, in *Dictionnaire d'Archéologie et de Liturgie*, Vol. 1, cols. 2241-2255; Paschal Kinsel, O.F.M., *The Catholic Shrines of the Holy Land* (New York, 1951), pp. 58-60.

[4] Anthony Bruya, O.F.M., Basilica to Mark Spot Where Mary Conceived Jesus, *in* The Denver Register, *October 3, 1954. Cf.* De Vogüe, Les églises de la Terre Sainte *(Paris, 1860). Mauro Laconi*, Luoghi e itinerari mariani della Palestina, *in* Enciclopedia Mariana, ed. cit., pp. 138-150.

Church of the Visitation

South from Haifa, about five miles west of Jerusalem, among the hills of Judaea, Mary hastened to visit her cousin Elizabeth in the town of Ein Karin, today a picturesque village of 3200 inhabitants. In the year 700, the rather vague reference of the pilgrim Theodosius indicates Ein Karin as the place of the Visitation, explicit mention appearing for the first time in a document of the twelfth century. There are two venerable sanctuaries here, one at the east end of the village at the site, according to a twelfth-century tradition, of the home of Zachary and Elizabeth, where now stands the church of St. John the Baptist; the other, known as the Church of the Visitation, which indicates the summer house to which Elizabeth retired and where she was visited by Our Lady. The Church of St. John is said to date from the eleventh century and was built on an earlier Byzantine church that had been destroyed by Arabs. Literary evidence seems to bear out that the second shrine of the Visitation is based on an apocryphal legend that Elizabeth fled with her child during Herod's persecution into the mountain country.[5] There was a church on the site from the fourth century to the end of the Crusades, but recent excavations have still failed to throw light on how this shrine was given the title of the Visitation. The Franciscans have been custodians of the post-Crusade church since 1679.

II. EUROPEAN SHRINES
ITALY

Our Lady of Loreto

On the Italian Adriatic shore, some 16 miles south of Ancona, lies the

---

[5] Sylvester J. Saller, O.F.M., Discoveries at St. John's, Ain Karim, 1941-1942 *(Jerusalem, 1946)*; B. Bagatti, O.F.M., Il santuario della visitazione ad Ain Karim (Montana Judaeae), esplorazione archeologica e ripristino *(Gerusalemme, 1948)*; J. McDwyer, Our Lady's Shrines in the Holy Land, in The Sign, *Vol. 33, 1954, pp. 55-56;* Libro d'oltramare. Part I. Text by A. Bacchi Lega, annotations by B. Bagatti, O.F.M. (Gerusalemme, 1955). General titles: Donatus Baldi, O.F.M., *Enchiridion locorum sanctorum*, 2nd ed. (Jerusalem, 1955). An appendix is dedicated exclusively to Marian shrines. Fr. Termes Ros, *Santuarios marianos en Palestina*, in Cultura Bíblica, Vol. 11, 1954, pp. 412-421. On the Church of the Virgin at Gethsemane: P. Luis Suárez, *Sepulcro de María en Getsemaní*, in Cultura Bíblica, Vol. 8, 1951, pp. 48-50. On the Church of the Dormition: P. Barnabé, *Le tombeau de la Sainte Vierge à Jérusalem* (Jerusalem, 1903). For other Marian shrines in the Middle East, cf. J. Goudard, S.J., *La Sainte Vierge au Liban*, 2nd ed. (Beyrouth [Liban], 1955).

little town of Loreto, the scene of a monumental shrine, enclosing and protecting the Holy House of Nazareth. According to a tradition prevalent from the fifteenth century, this is the original house used by the Holy Family at Nazareth and transported by angels in 1291 to Italy's Loreto. A few arguments usually alleged in favor of its authenticity are: (1) A document given by Pope Clement V, authorizing the General of the Carmelites to build a church in Germany with donations offered by the Schevenden family in fulfillment of a vow made before the miraculous image of Loreto. (2) The fact that the House does not rest and has never rested upon foundations sunk into the earth where it now stands. (3) The stone of the original walls and the mortar used are unknown in the neighborhood of Loreto, but are chemically identical with materials most commonly found in Nazareth.[6]

Over the House of the Holy Family, Constantine built a church which was destroyed by the Arab invaders (cf. Church of the Annunciation, *supra*) and rebuilt by the Crusaders. The history of the House between 1263 and 1291 is wrapped in mystery. The present Gothic basilica at Loreto was built in the second half of the fifteenth century and was under the care of the Franciscans. The Carmelites followed in 1489 and inaugurated the Litany which is now world-famous. In 1801, Pope Pius VII crowned the original cedar-wood statue found in the House, but after the fire which destroyed both altar and statue, Pope Pius XI crowned a replica of Our Lady of Loreto in 1924. The Capuchin Fathers now care for the Shrine.

Saint Mary Major

Of first rank in the city of Rome is the Basilica of St. Mary Major, erected about the year 352, during the reign of Pope Liberius. Legend has

---

[6] Howard Rafferty, O.Carm., *Loreto and the Holy House*, in *Mary*, Vol. 15, 1954, pp. 64-69. The entire May-June issue of *Miriam* (Seville) deals with this shrine: Vol. 7, 1955. M. Battigelli, *Il volo della Santa Casa di Nazareth* (Firenze, 1948); R. Riccardi, *Loreto*, in *Enciclopedia Italiana*, Vol. 21, cols. 504-506. In defense of the shrine's historicity: C. M. Henze, C.Ss.R., *Andiamo a Loreto* (Roma, 1954); Cassiano da Langasco, *Santuari e luoghi sacri mariani*, in *Enciclopedia Mariana, ed. cit.* (Milano, 1954), pp. 593-595; A. Caillau, *Histoire critique de Notre-Dame-de-Lorete* (Paris, 1843). I. Rinieri, *La Santa Casa di Loreto*, 3 vols. (Torino, 1910-1911). This is a refutation of Chevalier's work (see below). Against the historicity: H. Leclercq, *Lorette*, in *Dictionnaire d'Archéologie Chrétienne et de Liturgie*, Vol. 9, cols. 2473-2511; Canon Ulysse Chevalier, *Notre-Dame de Lorette. Étude historique sur l'authenticité de la Santa Casa* (Paris, 1906).

it that a wealthy patrician and his wife were favored, in a dream, by an apparition of Our Lady on the night of August 4-5, and were requested to build a church in her honor on the Esquiline Hill, at a spot that would be marked out by snow. During that hot August night, while a miraculous snowfall traced the form and shape of the basilica. Our Lady appeared to the Pope and informed him of the same event. A century later, when the Council of Ephesus defined Mary's divine Maternity, Pope Sixtus III rebuilt the present basilica. From the seventh century on, it became known as St. Mary Major, because it was then, and is to this day, the most important church in Rome dedicated to Mary.[7] It is flanked by the Papal Palaces of Sixtus V on the right, and of Benedict XIV on the left. The imposing facade was built by Pope Eugene III (1145-1153). Its greatest treasures are a painting of the Madonna and Child known as the *Salus Populi Romani,* attributed to St. Luke and canonically crowned in 1838 by Pope Gregory XVI, and the manger from the stable at Bethlehem.

Our Lady of Pompei

In the year 1872, Bartolo Longo, an Italian lawyer of Pompei in southern Italy, who had heard a voice urging him to promulgate
the Rosary, journeyed to Naples in search of an image of Our Lady for the Rosary Confraternity. There, at the cost of less than a dollar, he bought a poor old painting, depicting Our Lady with the Holy Child, and giving a Rosary to St. Dominic and St. Catherine of Siena. It was first enshrined in a small chapel at Pompei in 1876 and later in a new church that was consecrated by Cardinal La Valetta in 1891. By command of Pius XI, the splendid structure we see today was erected in 1939.[8]

---

[7] John C. Glennon, *St. Mary Major,* in *Mary,* Vol. 15, 1954, pp. 16-23. Msgr. John K. Cartwright, *The Catholic Shrines of Europe* (New York, 1954), pp. 39-42. M. Armellini, *Le chiese di Roma,* 2nd ed. (Roma, 1891), pp. 224-226.

[8] Bartolo Longo, *Storia del santuario di Pompei dalle origini al 1878* (Pompei, 1949); Idem, *Histoire de sanctuaire de Pompei* (Valle di Pompei, 1900); Don Sharkey, *The Woman Shall Conquer* (Milwaukee, 1952), pp. 86-91. On other famous Italian shrines cf.: A. R. Bandini, *The Miracle at Syracuse* [Sicily] (Fresno, Calif., 1955); G. Badame, *Madonna delle lacrime in Siracusa* (Siracusa, 1953). An exhaustive account is given by the director of *El Iris de Paz:* Cf. Thomas Pujadas, C.M.F., in all issues of Vol. 1 from January to June, 1955. F. Gosso, *La "Consolata" de Turin,* in *Marie,* Vol. 9, 1955, pp. 18-19. Other articles on this shrine in the same issue. P. J. Pascucci, *Don Bosco's Shrine to Mary,* in *Our Lady's Digest,* Vol. 9, 1955, pp. 285-287; A. Addeo, *Le sanctuaire de Notre-Dame du Bon Conseil a Genazzano,* in *Marie,* Vol. 2, 1948, pp. 6-9; H. Hussu, C.M.F., *Il tempio votivo internazionale dell'Immacolato Cuore di Maria,* in *Alma Socia Christi,* Vol. 6, fasc. 2

FRANCE

Our Lady of Chartres

Famed throughout the world for the perfection of its Gothic architecture is the Cathedral of Notre-Dame de Chartres, seventy miles southeast of Paris. Here existed, if we are to believe tradition, the first Marian shrine in the western world. On the spot where the Cathedral crypt now stands, the first Christian missionaries of apostolic times found a grotto or vault where the Druids had erected an altar "to the virgin about to conceive," and a statue of a woman holding a child, known since the founding of the Cathedral as *Notre-Dame-sousterre*. The oldest document relating to the Druidic cult at Chartres is dated 1389, but it is considered by some historians as a fabled account. However, the tradition reappears extensively in literature of the sixteenth century.[9]

The first church, built probably in the fourth century, was destroyed by the Normans. Work on a new church was begun in 1020 by St. Fulbert, but it was leveled by fire in 1194. The present Gothic Cathedral, begun in 1260, was consecrated by Bishop Pierre de Mincy in the presence of King St. Louis. In the Cathedral's upper part, the objects of veneration are a fifteenth-century Black-Virgin statue of Our Lady, known as *Notre-Dame du Pilier*, and the veil of the Blessed Virgin.

Our Lady of Lourdes

In 1858, at the time of the apparitions, the town of Lourdes numbered some 4000 inhabitants. It was here, in the extreme southwest of France, in the foothills of the Pyrenees, that Our Lady appeared 18 times to 14-year-old Bernadette Soubirous, called herself the Immaculate Conception, asked that a chapel be built on the spot where people might come in procession, and requested penance in a spirit of prayer.

On May 19, 1866, the Bishop of Tarbes, François Laurence (1845-1870), blessed the crypt and said the first Mass in it in the presence of

---

(Romae, 1952), pp. 203-216; C. Testore, S.J., *I santuari mariani d'Italia*, in *Mariologia*, ed. P. Sträter, Vol. 3 (Torino, 1958), pp. 80-92.

[9] G. Duhamelet, *L'enchantement de Chartres*, in *Marie*. Vol. 8, 1955, pp. 428-433; K. Dugan, *The Cathedral Built by Love. The Story of Chartres*, in *Our Lady's Digest*, Vol. 8, 1953, pp. 206-210. Favoring the Druid tradition: A. Clerval, *Guide chartrain, Chartres, sa cathédrale, ses monuments* (Chartres, 1896); R. Merlet, *Les puits des saints-forts dans la crypte de Chartres* (Caen, 1902); Idem, *La cathédrale de Chartres et ses origines*, in *Revue Archéologique*, Vol. 41, 1902, pp. 236 sq. Against the tradition: H. Leclercq, art. *Chartres*, in *Dictionnaire d'Archéologie Chrétienne et Liturgie*, Vol. 3, cols. 1019-1045.

Bernadette. Five years later on the feast of the Assumption, Bishop Pichenot dedicated the magnificent Basilica of the Immaculate Conception. Next, in 1883, construction was begun on the Byzantine-Romanesque style Basilica of the Rosary. Six years later Bishop Dilleres of Tarbes consecrated it and in 1885 built the Charity Hospital nearby.[10] Three Little Sisters of the Poor founded the Hospital of Our Lady of Health for the disabled in 1876, and in 1912 the Sisters of Charity of Nevers established a second Municipal Hospital. Since 1885 an International Medical Bureau has been set up at Lourdes, whose purpose is to determine the validity of the cures and witness their extraordinary character.

Pope Leo XIII authorized a special Office and Mass for Our Lady of Lourdes and extended the feast to the Universal Church.

Our Lady of Salette

Though it occurred eight years before the apparitions of Mary at Lourdes, the story of La Salette is little known. The weeping Mother of God appeared on September 19, 1846, to two untutored children, 15-year-old Melanie Calvat and 11-year-old Maximin Giraud, on Mount Gargas, above the village of La Salette Fallavaux, in the Diocese of Grenoble, southeastern France. Our Lady's message forewarned of dire punishment that would come upon the people if God's law continued to be broken and

---

[10] G. M. Besutti, O.S.M., *Alcune recenti publicazioni su Lourdes,* in *Marianum,* Vol. 10, 1948, pp. 382-385; Gustave Combes, *Lourdes. Sanctuaire mondial de la prière* (Albi, 1947); J. Curtain, *Lourdes. Le domaine de Notre-Dame de 1858 a 1947* (Rennes, 1947). An entire issue of *Marie* is on the shrine: Vol. 7, No. 5, 1954. For a lively exchange of views: J. B. Haldane and convert-writer Arnold Lunn discuss the Lourdes' miracles very thoroughly through the medium of a series of letters in *Science and the Supernatural* (New York, 1935). J. Belleney, *Les apparitions de Lourdes* (Paris, 1950); Michel de Saint-Pierre, *Bernadette and Lourdes,* transl. from the French by E. Fitzgerald (New York, 1954); Henri Lasêrre, *Les apparitions de Notre-Dame de Lourdes* (Paris, 1952); M. Gasnier, O.P., *Le message de Lourdes* (Paris, 1951); Dr. Bissarie, *Heaven's Recent Wonders, or the Work of Lourdes,* translated from the French by C. Van der Donckt, 3rd ed. (New York, 1915); Anon., *Orientación bibliográfica sobre Lourdes,* in *Revista de Espiritualidad,* Vol. 17, 1958, pp. 423-453; L. Cros, S.J., *Lourdes 1858. Témoins de l'événement. Documents présentés par M. Olphe-Galliard, S.J.* (Paris, 1957); R. Laurentin, *Lourdes. Dossiers des documents authentiques,* 4 vols. (Paris, 1957-1958). The last two volumes are in collaboration with B. Billet. Other papers on the same subject may be found in *Virgo Immaculata,* Vol. 16 (Romae, 1956).

penance ignored.[11] The apparitions were canonically approved by Pius IX in 1851. Four years previously a small chapel had been erected, and on May 25, 1872, the foundation stone of the Sanctuary of Our Lady of La Salette was blessed. With a capacity for 2500 people the basilica was consecrated in 1879, and the statue of Our Lady of La Salette solemnly crowned. The Missionaries of La Salette were approved in 1890 to care for the sanctuary and the needs of the pilgrims.

SPAIN

Our Lady of the Pillar

Devotion to Mary under the title of Our Lady of the Pillar goes back to the time of the Apostles, when St. James was preaching on the banks of the Ebro River in Zaragoza (Roman Caesar-Augusta), in what is now the Province of Aragón, Spain. Our Lady, while still living, appeared to him, holding the Divine Child in her arms, and surrounded by a choir of angels carrying a pillar. She asked that a church be built on the spot in her honor and that the pillar be placed therein as a symbol of the faith which

---

[11] John S. Kennedy, *Light on the Mountain* (New York, 1953); E. Ladoucer, M.S., *Saga of La Salette*, in *Our Lady's Digest*, Vol. 7, 1952, pp. 173-185; M. Massard, *Pilgrimage to La Salette*, in *Our Lady's Digest*, Vol. 7, 1952, pp. 98-100; Estienne Yvonne, *La Vierge sur l'Alpe* (Paris, 1946); J. Jaouen, M.S., *La grace de La Salette* (Paris, 1946); Msgr. J. Giray, *Les miracles de La Salette* (Grenoble, 1946); René Duvillard, *La grand nouvelle de La Salette* (Grenoble, 1946); Adrien Gamier, *L'Expansion de La Salette dans le monde (1846-1946)* (Grenoble, 1946); E. Picard, *L'apparition de La Salette. Glanes historiques* (Lyons, 1946); G. Bernoville, *La Salette* (Paris, 1946); V. Hostachy, *Commentaire du message de La Salette pour le temps présent* (Grenoble, 1947). On other French shrines, cf.: M. Aubert, *La cathédrale de Notre-Dame de Paris* (Paris, 1950); P. M. Auzas, *Notre-Dame de Paris* (Grenoble, 1949); L. Lejeune, *Notre-Dame de Boulogne* (Paris, 1925); A. Chatelle, *Les grands heures de Notre-Dame de Boulogne* (Boulogne-sur-mer, 1938); Marie André, *La magnifique histoire de Notre-Dame du Puy* (Nicolet, Canada, 1951); Georges Paul, *Notre-Dame du Puy. Essai historique et archéologique* (Le Puy, 1950); Marie Simone, *Notre-Dame de Pontmain et son message à la France* (Paris, 1950); Bro. Ernest, *Our Lady Comes to Pontmain* (Notre Dame, Ind., 1954); Marcel Cardineau, *La Vierge vous parle* [Pellevoisin] (Paris, 1946); Fr. Hubert, O.C.D., *Our Lady at Pellevoisin*, in *Our Lady's Digest*, Vol. 4, 1950, pp. 517-518. Of a more general character: Isabelle Couturier de Chefdubois, *Mille pèlerinages de Notre-Dame*, 3 vols. (Paris, 1953-1954); Idem, *Du Sud au Nord de la France: Douze pèlerinages mariales historiques* (Nicolet, Can., 1951); *Petit lexique des pèlerinages de Notre-Dame en France* (Nicolet, Can., 1954); Sr. M. Dorcy, *Lady Shrines of France*, in *Our Lady's Digest*, Vol. 8, 1953, pp. 161-165; O. Engelbert, *Les apparitions de la Vierge au XIXe et XXe siècles* (Mulhouse, Haut-Rhin, 1948); Jean Helle, *Miracles*, transl. by L. Sheppard (New York, 1952).

the people would retain to the end of time. According to tradition, St. James built the first chapel there, which later gave way to a more splendid church, destroyed by fire in the fifteenth century. The present Gothic basilica was built at the beginning of the sixteenth century by Don Hernando de Aragón under Bishop Castrillo (1681-1715).[12] The Spanish baroque or Churriguerresque chapel housing the miniature statue of Our Lady and Child and the six-foot-high jasper pillar on which it rests were designed by Ventura Rodríguez and completed in 1765. The statue was canonically crowned in 1905, and Pius XII granted the shrine the title and dignity of a Minor Basilica.

Our Lady of Covadonga

The battle of Guadalete and the defeat of King Don Rodrigo by the Moors in 711 marked the end of Spanish independence under the Visigothic dynasty. But high up in the Pyrenees mountains of Asturias, a small group of Spaniards under their leader Don Pelayo kept a guerilla warfare against the Moors. A formidable army of Moslems, captained by Alcamor, resolved in 718 to wipe out Don Pelayo's soldiers. The latter, shortly before battle, retired into a cave in the mountain fastnesses where they pledged themselves to fight for God and country under the protection of Our Lady. In the ensuing battle, a thousand Christians routed a Moslem army of approximately 80,000 through Mary's favor.

In the middle of the eighth century, King Alfonso I built a chapel in the cave (Covadonga means: deep cave) and a Benedictine Monastery nearby to commemorate the event, dedicating both to Our Lady.[13] The present church, in Greco-Roman style, was built in 1874 to replace the first destroyed by fire in 1777. The statue was canonically crowned in 1918. The Augustinians succeeded the Benedictines in the guardianship of the shrine in 1635.

---

[12] Ricardo del Arco, *El templo de Nuestra Señora del Pilar en la Edad Media* (Zaragoza, 1945). Extraordinary number of *El Pilar* (Zaragoza), Vol. 70, 1954. Ribera-Floret, O.Carm., *The Story of Zaragoza,* in *Mary,* Vol. 16, 1955, pp. 38-41. *Nuestra Señora del Pilar,* in *Miriam,* Vol. 7, 1955, p. 234; C. McDonald, *Our Lady of the Pillar,* in *Our Lady's Digest,* Vol. 7, 1952, pp. 162-166; F. Gutiérrez, *La Virgen del Pilar* (Zaragoza, 1954); Aina Naval, *El Pilar de Zaragoza* (Zaragoza, 1939).

[13] Luciano López, *Covadonga* (Oviedo, 1945); Felix de Aramburu, *Asturias* (Gijón, 1894); Zsolt Aradi, *Shrines to Our Lady Around the World* (New York, 1954), pp. 43-45. Article, *Covadonga,* in *Enciclopedia Universal Ilustrada,* ed. Espasa, Vol. 15, cols. 1406-1409.

Our Lady of Guadalupe

High up in the mountains of Extremadura, in the extreme western part of New Castille, stands the historic shrine of Our Lady of Guadalupe. According to legend, the statue of Our Lady venerated here belonged originally to the oratory of Pope St. Gregory the Great in Rome. When St. Leander, Archbishop of Seville, visited the Pope, the latter donated the statue for Seville's Cathedral church. During the Moorish occupation it was hidden and, at the end of the thirteenth century, miraculously discovered near the Guadalupe River, by a shepherd named Gil Cordero. In gratitude to Our Lady of Guadalupe for a victory over the Moors at the battle of Salado (1340), King Alfonso XI erected the present shrine over the ruins of an early chapel. It has been under the care successively of the Mercedarians, Jeronymites, and Franciscans. On March 20, 1907, Our Lady of Guadalupe was proclaimed Patroness of Extremadura, and in 1928 crowned Queen of all Spain and Spanish America by Cardinal Segura.[14]

PORTUGAL

Our Lady of Fatima

Between April and November of 1917, Our Lady appeared six times to three Portuguese children in a field called Cova da Iria near Fátima, a village about 70 miles north of Lisbon. In her apparitions she made an appeal for devotion to her Immaculate Heart, for prayer and penance, for the consecration of Russia to her Immaculate Heart and first Saturday Communions of reparation; she spoke of wars and persecution. On

---

[14] M. S. Byne, *Forgotten Shrines of Spain* (Philadelphia, 1926); Carlos Villacampa, O.F.M., *La Virgen de la Hispanidad* (Sevilla, 1942); Germán Rubio, O.F.M., *Historia de Nuestra Señora de Guadalupe* (Barcelona, 1926); Diego de Ecija, *Libro de la invención de Santa María de Guadalupe* (Cáceres, 1953). Cf. also entire May-June issue of *Miriam*, Vol. 6, 1954. On other Spanish shrines, cf. A. de Maricuña, *Santa Maria de Begoña en la historia espiritual de Vizcaya* (Bilbao, 1950); S. Echevarría, Historia del santuario e imagen de *Nuestra Señora de Begoña* (Tolosa, 1892); Angel Frau, *Santuarios marianos de Barcelona* (extensive on Our Lady of Montserrat) (Barcelona, 1954). On Marian shrines of Navarre cf. Jacinto Arangua, C.M.F., *Iconografía y santuarios de la Virgen en Navarra* (Madrid, 1941). Of a more general nature: I. Allardyce, *Historic Shrines of Spain* (New York, 1912); Nazario Pérez, S.J., *Historia mariana de España*, (Valladolid, 1948), 4 vols. so far, and two more announced. P. Sanjulián, *Historia de la Santísima Virgen y del desarrollo de su culto y de sus principales advocaciones en España y en América* (Madrid, 1902); Sánchez Pérez, *El culto mariano en España* (Madrid, 1943); María de Echarri, *Madones espagnoles. Sanctuaires de l'Espagne*, in *Marie*, Vol. 8, 1953, pp. 88-94; V. de la Fuente, *Vida de la Virgen María con la historia de su culto en España* (Barcelona, 1877).

October 13, the day of the final apparition, the dramatic episode of the dance of the sun took place, witnessed by a crowd of 70,000. A declaration of the Bishop of Leiria, in whose diocese the apparitions occurred, approved the cult of Our Lady of Fátima in 1930.[15]

The first structure to be erected was a kind of an archway, replaced soon by a tiny chapel over the spot of the apparitions. A second but still diminutive chapel was built in 1922 after the dynamite outrage, and next to it, the Chapel of the Confessions, also known as the "Pavilion of the Sick." On May 13, 1928, the foundation stone of the Basilica of Our Lady of the Rosary was laid, and the finished structure consecrated on October 6, 1953, by Cardinal Cerejeira, Patriarch of Lisbon. There are fifteen altars in honor of the fifteen mysteries of the rosary, and on either side of the basilica stands a hospital with various offices including a Medical Bureau. The Papal Legate of Pius XII, Cardinal Masella, crowned Our Lady's statue on May 13, 1946, the 300th anniversary of Portugal's consecration to Mary Immaculate.

SWITZERLAND

Our Lady of Einsiedeln

The history of this shrine begins with the hermit St. Meinrad, who in the ninth century chose this spot in the village of Einsiedeln (meaning hermitage) just a few miles from the Swiss city of Zurich as a place to build a cell. After his death a chapel was built over the place of his oratory and cell and the present Madonna chapel or Chapel of Grace within the shrine indicates the original site. An ancient wooden wonder-working statue of the Madonna and Child, known as the Black-Virgin, and enshrined in the primitive chapel, was destroyed in the fire of 1465, but

---

[15] C. Barthas and G. da Fonseca, S.J., *Our Lady of Light* (Milwaukee, 1947); Thomas McGlynn, O.P., *Vision of Fátima* (New York, 1948); W. T. Walsh, *Our Lady of Fátima* (New York, 1947); J. de Marchi, I.M.C., *The Crusade of Fátima* (New York, 1948); C. C. Martindale, S.J., *The Message of Fátima* (London, 1950); C. Brochado, *Fátima in the Light of History* (Milwaukee, 1955); Montes de Oca, C.S.Sp., *More About Fátima* (Westminster, Md., 1950); F. Ryan, O.P., *Our Lady of Fátima* (Westminster, Md., 1944); J. Pelletier, A.A., *The Sun Danced at Fátima* (Worcester, Mass., 1951); Idem, *Fátima, Hope of the World* (Worcester, Mass., 1954); April and Martin Armstrong, *Fátima, Pilgrimage to Peace* (New York, 1954); L. G. da Fonseca, S.J., *Fátima e a crítica* (Lisboa, 1951); Idem, *Le meraviglie di Fátima* (Rome, 1950); C. Barthas, *Fátima, merveille du XXe siècle* (Toulouse, 1952); Idem: *Autour de Fátima. Quelque documents* (Toulouse, 1949); J. Rambaud, O.P., *La Dame toute belle. Études objective et psychologique des événements de Fátima* (Paris: Lyons, 1949).

was reproduced shortly afterward. In the middle of the tenth century a huge Basilica and an adjacent Benedictine Monastery were built during the abbacy of St. Eberhard of Strasbourg, but the present abbey is the sixth that has been built on the site.[16]

GERMANY

Our Lady of Altötting

In upper Bavaria, about 60 miles east of Munich, stands the early Romanesque "Holy Chapel" of Altötting. Built in the eighth century, it enshrines the miraculous age-blackened thirteenth-century statue of the Madonna. The heathen temple, where about the year 700, St. Rupert baptized Otto the Bavarian, was turned into a Christian chapel, and is basically the same structure as the Holy Chapel today. Here a Benedictine Monastery was founded in 876 and the shrine entrusted to the care of the monks for over four hundred years.[17] After a short tenure by the Jesuits, the Capuchins took up residence at the shrine.

Our Lady of Kevelaer

Perhaps the most famous of all shrines in Germany, Our Lady of Kevelaer, is located in the far north of the Rhineland near the Dutch border and dates back to the seventeenth century. Its origin was due to a paper picture of Our Lady, Comforter of the Afflicted, in the possession of a soldier from Luxemburg, where devotion to Mary under that title had been flourishing. The Busmann couple, living near the city of Kevelaer, had been requested by Our Lady to build a church there in her honor.

---

[16] Ludwig Raeber, O.S.B., *Images d'Einsiedeln* (Einsiedeln, 1949); Idem: *Einsiedeln im Bild* (Einsiedeln, 1949); Rudolph Henggeler, O.S.B., *Das Gnadenbild Unsere liebe Frau von Einsiedeln* (Einsiedeln, 1935); M. Jungo, O.S.B., *Notre-Dame d'Einsiedeln. Son monastère et son pèlerinage*, in *Marie*, Vol. 8, 1954, pp. 190-192 (The entire issue is on Swiss shrines); Ethel Huegli, *The Black Madonna of Einsiedeln*, in *Our Lady's Digest*, Vol. 4, 1949, pp. 183-184; J. Landolt, *Ursprung und erste Gestaltung des Stiftes Maria-Einsiedeln* (Einsiedeln, 1845). For other shrines cf. Ferdinand Andina, *Santuari mariani nella Svizzera* (Lugano, 1954).

[17] Hans Geiselberger, *Der Gnadenort Altötting*, 5th ed. (Altötting, 1950); Msgr. John K. Cartwright, *The Catholic Shrines of Europe* (New York, 1954), pp. 157-158; H. Gillet, *Famous Shrines of Our Lady*, Vol. 2 (Westminster, Md., 1952), pp. 131-146. J. Mehler, *Unsere liebe Frau von Altötting* (Altötting, 1902); A. Landgraf, *Geschicte Unserer liebe Frau in Altötting* (Altötting, 1899); S. Beissel, S.J., *Die Verehrung Marias in Deutschland* (Freiburg-im-Breisgau, 1909), pp. 25-27.

MARIAN SHRINES AND APPARITIONS 341

They bought the soldier's picture and set it up in a small shrine, over which, in 1650, was built the Chapel of Mercy (Gnadenkapelle). Papally crowned in 1892, the miraculous picture is here venerated by thousands of pilgrims.[18]

HOLLAND

Our Lady of 'sHertogenbosch

Christianity in Holland has always been characterized by an ardent devotion to Our Lady. Perhaps the most magnificent shrine in the Netherlands is the Marian Gothic Cathedral of 'sHertogenbosch, in Northern Brabant. The Lady Chapel that houses the thirteenth-century statue of the "Sweet Mother" was built in 1268, while the Cathedral itself dates in large part from the fifteenth century. The statue was canonically crowned by authorization of Pope Leo XIII in 1878, and St. Pius X granted the feast a Proper Office.[19]

BELGIUM

Our Lady of Beauraing

Between November 29, 1932, and January 3, 1933, Our Lady appeared to five children of the Voisin and Deggeimbre families in the small town of Beauraing, Province of Namur, south Belgium. The message of Our Lady was an appeal for sacrifice, prayer, and devotion to her Immaculate Heart.[20] In 1943, Bishop Andrew Charue of Namur expressed official,

---

[18] Fritz Dyckmans, *Kevelaer. Das Marienheiligtum am Niederrhein* (Kevelaer, 1951); Theodor Bergmann, *Der Wallfahrtsort Kevelaer* (Kevelaer, 1949); H. Wester, *Kevelaer, Wallfahrt und Pfarrei* (Kevelaer, 1936).

[19] Jan Mosmans, *De St. Janskerk te 'sHertogenbosch* ('sHertogenbosch, 1931). General titles: H. Minderop, S.J., *La Hollande catholique et mariale*, in *Marie*, Vol. 7, 1953, pp. 55-62; H. M. Polman, *Nederland — Marialand*, in *De Standaard van Maria*, Vol. 24, 1948, pp. 355-365; O. Förster, *Niederländische Madonnen* (Berlin, 1938).

[20] Arthur Monin, *Notre-Dame de Beauraing. Origines et dévelopements de son culte* (Bruges, 1949); J. Debergh, *Virgin of the Golden Heart*, in *Our Lady's Digest*, Vol. 7, 1952, p. 288; Canon Massart, *La belle histoire de Beauraing*, (Bruxelles, 1948); G. Maes, *Beauraing, le Coeur Immaculé de Marie* (Louvain, 1946); Paul Piron, *Le message de Notre-Dame de Beauraing* (Liège, 1946); D. Sharkey, *I Will Convert Sinners. Our Lady's Apparitions at Beauraing*, 1932-1933 (Techny, Ill., 1955); C. Lambot, O.S.B., *Le "message" de Beauraing*, in *Virgo Immaculata*, Vol. 16 (Romae, 1956), pp. 152-163; F. Toussaint, *Enquête canonique sur les faits de Beauraing*, *ibid.*, pp. 164-181; E. Ranwez, *Nos raisons de croire aux apparitions de Beauraing*, *ibid.*, pp. 182-196; D. Sharkey and J. Debergh,

though reserved, approbation of cult to Our Lady of Beauraing, but in 1949 he declared: "We are able in all serenity and prudence to affirm that the Queen of heaven appeared to the children of Beauraing during the winter of 1932-1933. ..." On the feast of the Immaculate Heart of Mary in 1946, the statue of Our Lady was blessed and the following year the cornerstone laid for the chapel of the apparitions.

Our Lady of Banneux

Just twelve days after the last apparition at Beauraing, Our Lady revealed herself to an 11-year-old girl, Mariette Beco, in the village of Banneux, a hundred miles distant from Beauraing, just ten miles east of Liège, in eastern Belgium. In her apparitions Mary called herself the Virgin of the Poor, and asked that a spring not far from the site be dedicated to her for the sick of all nations.[21] Official recognition of the eight apparitions was given by Bishop L. Kerkhofs in 1949. The chapel requested by Our Lady was built in 1933, and in 1948 the cornerstone was laid for a new basilica to be dedicated to Our Lady, Queen of Nations.

ENGLAND

Our Lady of Walsingham

Excluding Wales and Scotland, England has 250 Marian shrines, of which none ever rivaled that of Walsingham, situated in the east coast County of Norfolk. In 1061, when St. Edward the Confessor was on the throne, Our Lady appeared to a widow named Richeldis Faverches, of Walsingham, and bid her to build in England a replica of the Holy House of Nazareth in honor of the Annunciation. This she did, and in the thirteenth century, a Gothic church and Priory of Augustinian Canons was established next to the Lady Chapel enshrining the Holy House. Henry VIII destroyed the Priory and shrine in 1538, and the statue of Our Lady was brought to London and burned publicly at Chelsea. At the end

---

O.M.I., *Our Lady of Beauraing* (New York, 1958).

[21] L. Kerkhofs, *Notre-Dame de Banneux. Etudes et documents* (Louvain, 1950); Ludo Bastijns, *Aux pieds de la Vierge de Banneux* (Liège, 1943); J. Speltz, *The Virgin of the Poor* (Middlesex, 1955); A. Geradin, *Les apparitions à Banneux* (Louvain, 1933). On other Belgian shrines cf. Ademar Gits, *La dévotion à Notre-Dame de Basse-Wavre* (Basse-Wavre, 1951); *Précis historique de Notre-Dame de Basse-Wavre*, in *Revue de Basse-Wavre*, Vol. 10, 1947 (the entire August issue); Aug.-M. Lépicier, O.S.M., *Montaigu, palladium Marial de la Belgique*, in *Marie*, Vol. 7, 1953, pp. 51-58.

of the nineteenth century, English Catholics again erected a shrine near the original site, and in 1922 the first pilgrimage since the Reformation made its way to Walsingham.[22] A new shrine was built in 1938 on property belonging to the Anglicans. A new statue, designed after the original burned in 1538, was enshrined in 1934 in the restored "Slipper Chapel" near the original Walsingham shrine. Canonically crowned in 1954, Our Lady of Walsingham is the Patroness of England.

IRELAND

Our Lady of Knock

Nearly three quarters of a century ago, Our Lady revealed herself to a group of villagers in the chapel yard of a little parish church in the town of Knock (Cnoc) Mhuire, in the southeast end of County Mayo, western Ireland. It was the evening of August 21, 1879, that she appeared, with St. Joseph on her right and the Apostle St. John on her left. In the center of the wall of the church was an altar and a cross in brilliant light, and at the foot of the cross a lamb.[23] Archbishop McHale of Tuam declared the testimony of all witnesses, taken as a whole, trustworthy and satisfactory. In 1936 a Medical Bureau was established where hundreds of cures have been scientifically validated. Knock (official name: Mary's Knoll or Hill) is now a National Shrine where Our Lady, in the words of Pius XI, reigns as the Queen of Ireland.

AUSTRIA

---

[22] Cf. J. J. Coyne, *Our Precious Lady St. Mary*, in *The Clergy Review*, Vol. 39, 1954, pp. 257-266; G. M. Corr, *Ritorno a Walsingham*, in *Ragguaglio Mariano* (Roma, 1949), pp. 69-71; W. Reany, *The Shrine of Our Lady of Walsingham* (London, 1939); M. Gillet, *The History of a Famous Shrine* (London, 1950); Olivier Marault, P.S.S., *Les "Lady Chapels" d'Angleterre et Walsingham*, in *Marie*, Vol. 8, 1954, pp. 100-103. On the shrine of Our Lady of the Assumption at Aylesford, cf. Winifrede Kingston, *The Story of a Vow*, in *Mary*, Vol. 15, 1954, pp. 76-84; Fabian Cunliffe, O.Carm., *Simon's Home in England*, in *Mary*, Vol. 16, 1955, pp. 81-90.

[23] Daniel O'Keefe, *The Story of Knock* (Cork, 1959); Liam Cavan, *Cnoc Muire in Picture and Story* (Galway, 1945). Mrs. Thomas Concannon, *The Queen of Ireland. An Historical Account of Ireland's Devotion to the Blessed Virgin* (Dublin, 1938); W. J. Smith, *The Mystery of Knock. Our Lady of Ireland* (New York, 1954); F. Carey, *Knock and its Shrine* (Dublin, 1937); W. Coyne, *Our Lady of Knock* (New York, 1948); *Idem*, *Cnoc Mhuire or the Irish Shrine of the Holy Rosary* (Dublin, 1937); Fr. James, O.F.M.Cap., *The Story of Knock* (New York, 1950); A. J. Reilly, *Mary's Hill in Ireland*, in *Our Lady's Digest*, Vol. 7, 1953, pp. 377-380.

Our Lady at Mariazell

Mariazell is the West's nearest shrine to the Iron Curtain, located in the Styrian Alps, at the head of the Salza Valley, near the town of Enns, 50 miles southwest of Vienna. Though basically Austrian, the shrine is the mecca for pilgrims from all of Central Europe. It owes its origin to the Benedictine monk, Magnus, who in 1157 had set up a miniature statue of Our Lady and Child for veneration on the spot that is marked by today's three-towered basilica.[24] The first Romanesque chapel gave way to a more splendid church, erected by King Louis the Great of Hungary in 1340, and transformed in the seventeenth century into a Baroque basilica. On August 21, 1955, the Carmelite Order laid the foundation stone of a new monastery dedicated to the Immaculate Heart of Mary, adjacent to the shrine of the *Magna Mater Austriae* at Mariazell. The project was completed in 1957, the shrine's eighth centenary.

POLAND

Our Lady of Czestochowa

Of some 600 Marian shrines in Poland which possess miraculous statues and paintings, that of Our Lady of Jasna Góra at Czestochowa holds first rank. According to legend, Our Lady's painting here is the work of St. Luke and was brought from Jerusalem to Constantinople by St. Helena. Thence it passed into possession of various Russian princes until, in 1382, Duke Ladislas of Opole sent it from the Castle of Belz in Ruthenia to Czestochowa. The Pauline Fathers are the custodians of the painting.[25]

In 1665, Charles Gustave and his Swedish army of 2000 invaded Poland, but met defeat at the hands of a small military force led by the Prior of Czestochowa's monastery. In gratitude, King Casimir proclaimed

---

[24] Franz Jantsch, *Mariazell. Das Heiligtum der Gnadenmutter Österreichs* (Graz-Vienna-Altötting, 1952); F. Hattler, *Pilgerreise nach Maria-Zell* (Düsseldorf, 1898); J. P. Kaltenbäck, *Die Mariensagen in Österreich* (Wien, 1845), pp. 24-28.

[25] Robert McBride, *Towns and People of Modern Poland* (New York, 1938), pp. 215-235; M. André, *Le Sainte Vierge, Reine de la Pologne*, in *Marie*, Vol. 7, 1955, pp. 442-443; *Le culte de la Sainte Vierge en Pologne*, in *Marie*, Vol. 8, 1955, pp. 510-511; A. J. Rozewicz, C.S.C., *Czestochowa and Fátima*, in *Our Lady's Digest*, Vol. 7, 1952, pp. 125-127; A priest of the Congregation of the Holy Cross: *Our Lady of Czestochowa* (Chicago, 1953). Cf. also Roman Witoski, *Our Lady of Wilno*, in *Mary*, Vol. 16, 1955, pp. 38-42. R. de Journel, S.J., *Marie et l'iconographie Russe*, in *Maria. Études sur la sainte Vierge*, ed. H. du Manoir, S.J., Vol. 2 (Paris, 1952), pp. 472-473.

Our Lady "Queen of the Crown of Poland." Pope Clement IX authorized the solemn coronation which took place on September 8, 1717.

III. AFRICA

Our Lady of Africa

On a hill overlooking the Mediterranean near Algiers stands the majestic Basilica of Our Lady, Queen of Africa. Through the initiative of Bishop Pavy of Algiers and two pious women, M. Berger and A. Cinquan, sufficient funds were gathered to erect a provisional chapel in 1857, on the spot where thousands of pilgrims had come to venerate a small bronze statue of Our Lady, not far from the site of the present basilica.[26] A year later, Bishop Pavy laid the cornerstone of the present Byzantine-style church, completed in 1866. Pius IX decreed the coronation of the statue and the elevation of the church to the rank of a basilica in 1876. The Trappists, White Fathers, and White Sisters carry on their missionary work under the shadow of Our Lady of Africa.

IV. NORTH AMERICAN SHRINES
CANADA

Our Lady of the Cape

It was on a little cape that juts out into the St. Lawrence east of Three Rivers in the Diocese of the same name, midway between Montreal and Quebec, that the Jesuits built a small chapel and dedicated it to St. Mary Magdalene. Eventually, the neighboring settlement took the title of the Saint and it is now known as Cap-de-la-Madeleine. In 1715 Father Paul Vachon built the present chapel. The miracle-working statue, known as Our Lady of the Cape, was a parishioner's donation to the Confraternity of the Rosary in 1845 during the pastorate of Father Tourigny. In the spring of 1879, during a novena to Mary, an ice bridge formed across the

---

[26] J. B. Cazaunau, *La basilique de Notre-Dame d'Afrique*, in *Marie*, Vol. 8, 1954, pp. 105-107; *La Vierge Marie dans l'Église d'Afrique*, by a missionary of Oran (Oran, 1904), pp. 164-210; L. Pavy, *Histoire critique du culte de la Sainte Vierge en Afrique* (Algiers, 1858). General titles: A. L. Delattre, W. F., *Le culte de la Sainte Vierge en Afrique d'après les monuments archéologiques* (Paris, 1907); Sr. M. St. Eucher, W. S., *Our Lady in Central Africa*, in *Our Lady's Digest*, Vol. 4, 1949, pp. 225-227; Jean Perraudin, *Marie, reine d'Afrique*, in *Marie*, Vol. 8, 1955, p. 514. On Our Lady of Egypt cf. S. Guisasola, O.F.M., *La Virgen de la Encrucijada*, in *Catolicismo*, No. 120, 1951, pp. 22-23; F. Anderson, *The Shrine in Port Saïd*, in *Our Lady's Digest*, Vol. 8, 1953, p. 198.

river under extraordinary circumstances, and served for the transportation of stones for the erection of a new church to supplement the old chapel.[27] This church was dedicated June 22, 1888, as a shrine to the Queen of the Most Holy Rosary. St. Pius X authorized the coronation of the statue in 1904. Five years later the First Plenary Council of Quebec declared the Church a shrine of national pilgrimage.

UNITED STATES

Our Lady of "La Leche"

At the beginning of the seventeenth century, on the grounds of the ancient mission of *Nombre de Dios* in St. Augustine, Florida, early Spanish settlers erected the oldest shrine on United States territory, under the title of *Nuestra Señora de la Leche y Buen Parto* (Our Nursing Mother of Happy Delivery). Though devotion to Our Lady as Nursing Mother dates back to the first centuries, its origin in Florida is traced to Madrid, where in 1602 a statue representing Mary nursing her Child saved a mother threatened with death at childbirth. King Philip III of Spain personally undertook the erection of a shrine in Madrid to honor Mary's motherhood, and pioneer Spanish mothers spread the same devotion when they came to Florida.[28]

---

[27] J. Mole, O.M.I., *The Story of the Cape* (Cap-de-la-Madeleine, 1950); J. Shaw, *Canada's Shrine to Mary* (Cap-de-la-Madeleine, 1952); Idem: *Canada's Shrine to Our Lady*, in *The Sign*, Vol. 34, 1954, pp. 28-29; G. Morin, O.M.I., *La Madonne des Canadiens* (Cap-de-la-Madeleine, 1952); R. Lawrence, *Canada's Shrine to Mary*, in *Mary*, Vol. 15, 1954, pp. 39-43; J. de Orleans, *Notre-Dame du Cap* (Montréal, 1949); P. Brenton, *Cap-de-la-Madeleine. Cité mystique de Marie* (Trois Rivières, 1937).

[28] M. Kenny, S.J., *The Romance of the Floridas* (New York, 1934), pp. 102-105; S. Bonano, C.M.F., *Our Lady's Influence in the Discovery of America*, in *Ephemerides Mariologicae*, Vol. 5, 1955, pp. 47-86; J. Ebel, *America's First Shrine to the Blessed Mother*, in *The Denver Register*, October 31, 1954, p. 7; A. Burbank, *Our Lady's First Shrine in America*, in *Queen of All Hearts*, Vol. 4, 1953, pp. 20-23; C. Smith, *Hallowed Acre*, in *Our Lady's Digest*, Vol. 4, 1949, pp. 26-29. On the first chapel dedicated to Mary in United States territory, built by the Jesuits in 1570 in what is now the State of Virginia, cf. F. Zubillaga, S.J., *Monumenta historica Societatis Jesu. Monumenta antiquae Floridae (1566-1572)*, Vol. 3 (Romae, 1946), pp. 351 sqq. The first mission church in honor of the Immaculate Conception was established at Hawikuh, New Mexico. Cf. Marion Habig, O.F.M., *The First Immaculate Conception Mission*, in *The American Ecclesiastical Review*, Vol. 131, 1954, pp. 73-80. The first church dedicated to the Immaculate Conception was that of the Franciscan Friary in St. Augustine, Florida. Cf. M. Habig, O.F.M., *Our First Church of Mary Immaculate*, in *The American Ecclesiastical Review*, Vol. 131, 1954, pp. 313-319. Cf. also Wilfrid Parsons, S.J., *Marian Devotion in the Early United States*, in *Marian Studies*, Vol. 3, 1952, pp. 236-250; V. A. Yzermans, *Churches of Mary in the United States*,

The present little chapel, enshrining a replica of the ancient statue, was begun in 1915 on the site of the original Spanish church where Our Lady was venerated as the Nursing Mother.

National Shrine of the Immaculate Conception

The largest church in the United States dedicated to Mary is *The National Shrine of the Immaculate Conception,* in Washington, D. C. The project, sponsored by Cardinal Gibbons, was presented to Pius X for approval in 1914, and then placed for execution in the capable hands of Bishop T. Shahan and his secretary, Father B. McKenna. Cardinal Gibbons laid the cornerstone of the shrine's crypt in 1920.[29] The style of the National Basilica is Byzantine-Romanesque and cruciform in shape, surmounted by a great dome and a 317-foot-high bell-tower dominating the façade. This magnificent multi-million dollar structure was solemnly dedicated on November 20, 1959.

Our Lady of Victory

The last great work of Msgr. Nelson H. Baker was the National Shrine and Basilica of Our Lady of Victory which he started building in Lackawanna (Buffalo, N. Y.) at the age of eighty. Completed at the cost of over three million and a half dollars, it was opened, dedicated, and consecrated by Patrick Cardinal Hayes in May of 1926, and raised to the honors of a basilica by Pius XI a year later.[30] Built of white marble in Renaissance style, it has two large towers and a great dome, depicting

---

in *The American Ecclesiastical Review,* Vol. 132, March, 1955, pp. 169-180.

[29] W. Kennedy, *The National Shrine of the Immaculate Conception* (Washington, D. C., 1927); J. Reilly, *Mary's National Shrine; a Statement of Progress,* in *The American Ecclesiastical Review,* Vol. 120, 1949, pp. 458-462; V. Dore, *Our National Marian Shrine,* in *The American Ecclesiastical Review,* Vol. 131, 1954, pp. 289-292; B. McKenna, *National Shrine of the Immaculate Conception,* 2 vols. (Washington, D. C., 1925, 1928); A. McCarthy, O.Carm., *Finish Her Shrine,* in *Mary,* Vol. 15, 1954, pp. 69-71; J. Burke, *A Nation's Prayer to Our Lady,* in *Columbia,* Vol. 33, 1953, pp. 5 and 18; E. N. Grainer, C.M.F., *The National Shrine of the Immaculate Conception in the United States,* in *Ephemerides Mariologicae,* Vol. 10, 1960, pp. 295-302.

[30] F. Van Eich, *National Shrine of Our Lady of Victory* (Lackawanna, 1955); Msgr. J. Maguire, *Shrine Notes,* in *Victorian,* Vol. 61, 1955, pp. 55-56. The *Victorian* is published by the Shrine. Cf. also F. B. Thornton, *Catholic Shrines in the United States and Canada* (New York, 1954), pp. 58-59; F. Anderson, *Father Baker* (Milwaukee, 1960).

within the Assumption of Our Lady and surmounted by a large bronze cross. Attached to the shrine are several homes of charity.

Our Lady of Perpetual Help

The shrine of Our Lady of Perpetual Help, popularly known as *The Mission Church*, was built by the Redemptorists in 1871 in the Roxbury district of Boston.[31] The image venerated in the church is an exact copy of the original in the Church of St. Alphonsus on the Via Merulana in Rome. Well known to Catholics the world over, it portrays the Blessed Virgin holding the Child Jesus on her left arm, with the Archangels Gabriel and Michael presenting the instruments of the Passion to the Child. The original mission church was replaced by a more stately temple in April of 1878.

The Sanctuary of Our Sorrowful Mother

This shrine was founded in Portland, Oregon, by the Servite Fathers in 1924. A truly unique shrine, covering 60 acres on two levels or terraces, it is the goal for nearly a half million pilgrims and visitors annually. Dominating the entrance is a crucifixion group in Carrara marble, leading, on the lower level, to the heart of the Sanctuary, which is the grotto of Our Sorrowful Mother, hollowed out of the granite walls of a cliff. On the Sanctuary's upper level, directly above the grotto, rises an imposing monument depicting the Seven Sorrows of Mary, and crowning it, a bronze statue of "Mary Our Mother." Structural work on a new Grotto Chapel of stone and marble in contemporary classical vein is now more than half complete.[32]

MEXICO

Our Lady of Guadalupe

It was on December 9, 1531, ten years after the Spanish conquest of

---

[31] John Byrne, C.Ss.R., *The Glories of Mary in Boston* (Boston, 1921). (The entire work is on this shrine); James Sullivan, *The Catholic Church of New England, Archdiocese of Boston* (Boston, 1895); W. Leucking, C.Ss.R., *Reminiscences of Four Redemptorist Fathers* (Ilchester, Md., 1891).

[32] *The Sanctuary of Our Sorrowful Mother*, published by the Servite Fathers (Portland, Ore., 1952); F. Thornton, *op. cit.*, pp. 138-142. General titles: D. MacLeod, *Devotion to the Blessed Virgin in North America* (New York, 1866. 1888); Daniel Sargent, *Our Land and Our Lady* (New York, 1939). A second edition of this work was published by The University of Notre Dame Press in 1955.

Mexico, that Our Lady appeared on five occasions to a poor Indian convert, Juan Diego, on Tepeyac Hill, not far from Mexico City, and told him to convey to Bishop Juan de Zumárraga her wish that a shrine be built on the spot where she stood. The sign given was the miracle of the roses and the life-size portrait of Our Lady miraculously etched on the Indian's cloak. To this day the picture may be seen above the main altar of the Basilica of Our Lady of Guadalupe.[33]

A small adobe chapel was erected at the site of the apparitions probably in 1531, and later three others nearby. The largest church was begun in 1695, completed in 1709, and raised to the rank of a basilica in 1904. The image was canonically crowned in 1895.

V. CENTRAL AMERICAN SHRINES
DOMINICAN REPUBLIC

Our Lady of Altagracia

The ancient basilica of *La Altagracia* at Higuey in the easternmost part of the Dominican Republic is Mary's first shrine in the New World. The painting of Our Lady under this title was brought to the parish church of Higuey by two colonists, 14 years after the discovery of America.[34] The present stone church, completed in 1569 by Alonso de Peña, is now too small for the number of pilgrims flocking to it, so in 1952 the cornerstone was laid for a much larger and more magnificent shrine. The image was

---

[33] Mariano Cuevas, S.J., *Documentos inéditos del siglo XVI para la historia de México* (México, D. F., 1914); G. Lee, C.S.Sp., Our Lady of Guadalupe *(New York, 1947)*; F. P. Keyes, The Grace of Guadalupe *(New York, 1953)*; J. Romero, S.J., Breve historia de las apariciones y del culto de Nuestra Señora de Guadalupe *(México, D.F., 1945)*. Cf. the entire Nov.-Dec. issue of Miriam, Vol. 6, 1954; K. Campbell, *María de Guadalupe* (New York, 1954); the entire May-June issue of Marie, Vol. 7, 1954; M. Cuevas, S.J., *La Santa Sede y Nuestra Señora de Guadalupe* (México, D. F., 1945); Thomas Kaiser, *From Tepeyac Hill,* in Mary, Vol. 15, 1954, pp. 96-107; J. L. Cassidy, *Mexico, Land of Mary's Wonders* (Paterson, N. J., 1958); Demarest-Taylor, *The Dark Virgin. The Book of Our Lady of Guadalupe* (Freeport, Me., 1956). On other Mexican shrines cf. Albert Santoscoy, *Historia de Nuestra Señora de San Juan de los Lagos* (Guadalajara, 1904); N. Quirós y Gutiérrez, *Breve historia de Nuestra Señora de Ocotlán* (Ocotlán, Tlaxcala, Mex., 1953); S. Monroy, *Rosary Chapel in Puebla* (Puebla, Mex., 1947).

[34] Addison Burbank, *The First Marian Shrine in America,* in The [Brooklyn] *Tablet,* May 13, 1955, p. 17. Cf. also the article *Altagracia,* in Enciclopedia Universal Ilustrada, Vol. 4 (Barcelona, 1929), col. 949. For other Marian shrines and apparitions in the West Indies, cf. R. Vargas Ugarte, S.J., *Historia del culto de María en Iberoamérica y de sus imágenes y santuarios más celebrados,* 2 vols., 3rd ed. (Madrid, 1956).

solemnly crowned in 1922.

COSTA RICA
Our Lady Queen of the Angels

Situated a few miles east of San José, the capital of Costa Rica, is the town of Cartago, numbering 10,000 inhabitants. Here a miracle took place on the feast of the Queen of the Angels, August 2, 1635, when a small Madonna and Child statue was discovered in a forest by a mulatto girl named Juana Pereira.[35] The statue mysteriously returned to its original place after having been twice taken to the girl's home and once locked in the tabernacle of the parish church. The present shrine is the fourth and was consecrated by Bishop Llorente in 1852. Declared Patroness of Costa Rica in 1824, Our Lady Queen of the Angels was crowned in 1926 in virtue of a papal rescript.

VI. SOUTH AMERICAN SHRINES
ARGENTINA
Our Lady of Luján

Said to be the most magnificent in the entire western hemisphere, the shrine of Our Lady of Luján owes its origin to a Portuguese landowner of Córdoba, Argentina, who in 1629 wrote to a friend in Brazil for a statue of Mary Immaculate. When Our Lady had manifested her wish that a chapel be built for the statue near the Luján River in the Córdoba region, the natives set to work and built the first shrine in 1677.[36] A second more beautiful church was erected in 1763; this, in turn, was replaced by today's grand basilica, consecrated in 1910. The solemn coronation took place in 1886 in the name of Pope Leo XIII.

BOLIVIA
Our Lady of Copacabana

This renowned Bolivian shrine is dedicated to Our Lady of the

---

[35] Victor Ortíz, *La aparición de la imagen de Nuestra Señora de los Ángeles* (Cartago, Costa Rica, 1905); Carlos Lewis, S.V.D., *The Black Virgin of Costa Rica*, in *Our Lady's Digest*, Vol. 4, 1949, pp. 136-137.

[36] George M. Salvaire, *Historia de Nuestra Señora de Luján*, 2 vols. (Buenos Aires, 1882-1883); A. Tansey, *Our Lady of Luján*, in *Mary*, Vol. 16, 1955, pp. 87-92; Paul Hallett, *Our Lady of Luján vs. Perón*, in *Mary*, Vol. 16, 1955, pp. 68-73.

Purification, and is situated on the banks of Lake Titicaca, near the borderline of Peru and Bolivia, in the ancient town of Copacabana. Shortly after the Spanish conquest, an Indian convert claimed to have had a vision of Our Lady and reproduced that vision in the form of a statue which he carved in 1582.[37] It was the source of mass conversions of the natives, and soon a small shrine was built to house it. Today's Baroque basilica dates back to 1640, the work of the Augustinian Fathers. The statue of Our Lady was crowned on the feast of the Assumption in 1925.

BRAZIL

Our Lady of Aparecida

While Brazil was still a colony of Portugal (1717), a certain Domingo García and his sons set out to fish on the River Parahybam near Cabo Frio. They had had little success and were about to return home when a last throw drew up from the rough waters a small wooden statue of Our Lady.[38] Miracles were later attributed to it and the first chapel to enshrine it was built by Father Villela in 1745. The Bishop of São Paulo crowned the statue in 1904. Under construction at present is a huge basilica in the form of a Greek Cross which will supplement the church built in 1888.

COLOMBIA

Our Lady of Chiquinquirá

The city of Chiquinquirá nestles high up on the Andean plateau to the north of Bogotá, Colombia. Its origin was occasioned by the working of a miracle at the country house of the Spaniard Don Santana in the year 1586. While María Ramos, a cousin of Santana, was in prayer before a shred-torn painting of the Madonna of the Rosary, Our Lady appeared and left her beautiful image on the canvas.[39] The Capuchins built the present

---

[37] F. Cepeda, C.M.F., *Miscelanea Mariana. Coronación de Nuestra Señora de Copacabana*, in *El Iris de Paz*, Vol. 42, 1925, pp. 844-846; F. Sanguines, O.F.M., *Historia de Copacabana* (La Paz, Bolivia, 1919); Alonso Ramos, *Historia de Copacabana*, 3rd ed. (La Paz, Bolivia, 1886).

[38] Maurice Bruni, O.Cann., *Brazil's National Temple*, in *Mary*, Vol. 15, 1954, pp. 114-118; Felix Cepeda, C.M.F., *América Mariana*, Vol. 2 (Madrid, 1925), pp. 483-492.

[39] Vicente Cornejo, O.P., and Andrés Mesanza, O.P., *Historia de Nuestra Señora de Chiquinquirá, de su ciudad y su convento* (Bogotá, 1919); idem, *Historia de la milagrosa imagen de Nuestra Señora de Chiquinquirá* (Bogotá, 1942); Alberto Ariza, O.P., *Hagiografía de la milagrosa imagen de Nuestra Señora del Rosario de Chiquinquirá*

basilica in 1824 over the ruins of an early stone church. Our Lady of Chiquinquirá was solemnly crowned in Bogotá in July of 1919 during Colombia's first Marian Congress.

VENEZUELA

Our Lady of Coromoto

The village of Guanare (originally, *Espíritu Santo*) in the State of Zamora, Venezuela, was founded by Fernández de León in the year 1593. What has made it famous throughout South America is a diminutive, oval-shaped painting of Our Lady Queen and the Infant King, known to the Cospe Indians as Our Lady of Coromoto. In 1651 the Chief of the Cospes and his wife were on their way to fetch water in the Coromoto region when Our Lady appeared to them with the Child in her arms. In a second and third apparition she asked them to receive Baptism, and in a fourth, gave them a painting of herself.[40] After having been venerated in Guanare's parish church for over 200 years, the image was finally transferred to a new Spanish-Baroque shrine, which today enjoys the rank of a minor basilica. Our Lady of Coromoto was declared Patroness of the Republic in 1942, and crowned on September 11, 1952.

(Bogotá, 1950); *idem, The Rosary Virgin of Chiquinquirá*, in *Our Lady's Digest*, Vol. 6, 1952, pp. 491-492. On Our Lady of Lajas: An article by the Marian Center of the Claretian Theologate in Manizales; cf. *Notre-Dame de Lajas*, in *Marie*, Vol. 7, 1953, pp. 46-50; A. Mesanza, O.P., *Célebres imágenes y santuarios de Nuestra Señora en Colombia* (Chiquinquirá, 1950).

[40] P. Barola, S.J., *La Santísima Virgen y Venezuela*, in *Revista de Orientación Católica* (Caracas), Vol. 12, 1949, pp. 45-57, 89-94. *A.A.S.*, Vol. 41, 1949, p. 318 (declared Patroness); Vol. 44, 1952, p. 739 (on coronation); Vol. 42, 1950, p. 328 (raised to basilica). Other important South American shrines: In Chile: M. Munizaga, *El santuario y la fiesta de Nuestra Señora del Rosario de Andacollo* (Barcelona, 1900). In Ecuador: C. Sono, *Nuestra Señora del Quinche* (Quito, Ecuador, 1903). In Paraguay: Anonymous, *La Virgen de los milagros de Caacupé* (Asunción, Paraguay, 1898). General titles: Felix Cepeda, C.M.F., *América Mariana*, 2 vols. (Madrid, 1925); M. Cidad, *Monumentos, santuarios, imágenes, y principales advocaciones con que se ha honrado a la Virgen en los paises americanos, especialmente en Chile*, in *Primer Congreso Pan-Americano de las Congregaciones Marianas* (Santiago de Chile, 1922), pp. 503-508. A list of all the paintings and statues of Our Lady in South America and Mexico which have been canonically crowned, has been drawn up by Guillermo Rozo, C.M.F., *La royauté de Marie dans l'Amerique Latine*, in *Marie*, Vol. 8, 1955, pp. 512-513. For further information, cf. R. Vargas Ugarte, *op. cit.*

VII. ASIATIC SHRINES
PHILIPPINE ISLANDS

Our Lady of Antipolo

The original title of this national shrine at Antipolo near Manila in the Philippines was Our Lady of Peace and Happy Traveling (*Nuestra Señora de la Paz y del Buen Viaje*), a popular Sevillian invocation. Governor Juan Niño de Tavora brought the statue from Acapulco, Mexico, to the Philippines in 1626, and donated it to the Jesuits at the mission center of Antipolo.[41] Here in 1632 construction on a shrine for the miracle-working statue was near completion, when Chinese revolutionaries sacked the city and burned the shrine. Twenty years later, faithful Philippines saw their dream fulfilled in the splendid church one can see today and where Our Lady reigns as Patroness of the Philippine Archipelago.

CHINA

Our Lady of Zo-Se

The shrine of Our Lady of Zo-se, the center of Marian devotion for Chinese Catholics, does not owe its origin to the working of a miracle or an apparition. It grew out of the zeal of a Jesuit missionary, Father Della Corte, who in 1868 dedicated a little chapel to Mary and placed in it a picture of Our Lady Help of Christians. It is on a hill called Zo-se, near the ruins of a former Buddhist monastery, in the Province of Son-Kiang, about 25 miles southeast of Shang-hai.[42] Later Bishop Languillat, S.J., laid the cornerstone of a beautiful basilica that was completed in 1873. Our Lady of Zo-se was crowned and proclaimed Patroness of China in 1947.

JAPAN

Our Lady of Oura

In 1576, twenty-four years after the death of St. Francis Xavier, the first church dedicated to Mary in Japan was erected in the town of Kyoto with the title of Our Lady of the Assumption. The church of Our Lady of

---

[41] Constantino Bayle, S.J., *Santa María de Indias* (Madrid, 1928), pp. 67-69; C. C. Martindale, S.J., *Our Blessed Lady* (New York, 1940), pp. 180-185; M. Romero, *Historia de Nuestra Señora la Virgen de Antipolo* (Manila, 1886).

[42] Wu Ching Hsiung, *Il culto della Madonna in Cina*, in *Marianum*, Vol. 9, 1947, pp. 143-147; idem, *Le culte Mariale en Chine*, in *Marie*, Vol. 8, 1955, p. 501; Stanislaus Lokuang, *Il culto della Madonna in Cina*, in *Vita e Pensiero*, Vol. 31, 1948, pp. 326-331.

the Rosary was built in Edo in 1599, and a third shrine in Saga seven years later. But the outstanding Japanese shrine is that of Our Lady of Oura, the little Gothic church built in 1865 by Father Petitjean, Chaplain of the French Consulate on Oura Hill in the city of Nagasaki.[43] Damaged by the atomic bomb in 1945, it was restored by the Japanese government and has been declared a national monument.

RUSSIA

Our Lady of Vladimir

Our Lady of Vladimir (the *Vladimirskaia*) is the most famous Russian icon belonging to the class known as Eleousa or tenderness images. It was brought to Kiev from Constantinople between 1125 and 1130, and subsequently transferred by Prince Andrew Bogolioubski to the cathedral of the city of Vladimir. All the czars were crowned and all Patriarchs consecrated in the presence of this miraculous image. Tradition attributes the icon to St. Luke, and historical sources inform us that Chrysoberg, Patriarch of Constantinople, made a gift of it to George Dolgorouki who brought it to Kiev.[44]

When Moscow was threatened with invasion by the Tartar leader, Tamerlane, in 1395, Our Lady's image was taken there and placed in the Cathedral of the Assumption as a pledge of protection. The liberation of the city from the invader is commemorated on Mary's feast day, August 26. The icon remained in Moscow's cathedral until 1919 when it was moved to the Tretyakov Art Gallery.

---

[43] E. F. Hammo, *Dévotion mariale au Japon*, in *Marie*, Vol. 8, 1955, p. 38; Daniel Ehman, C.Ss.R., *The Nagasaki Story*, in *Our Lady's Digest*, Vol. 8, 1953, pp. 136-139.

[44] Maurice Vloberg, *Les types iconographiques de la Mère de Dieu dans l'art byzantin*, in *Maria*, ed. H. du Manoir, S.J., Vol. 2 (Paris, 1952), pp. 403-443; Rouët de Journel, S.J., *Marie et l'iconographie russe*, ibid., pp. 444-481; A. Anisimov, *Our Lady of Vladimir* (Prague, Seminarium Kordakovianum, 1928).

DEVOTION TO OUR LADY IN THE UNITED STATES

by EDWARD A. RYAN, S.J.

AITH in the divinity of Jesus is central in Marian devotion. Those who reject the Incarnation can neither worship God in His human nature nor admit that He really assumed flesh from the flesh of Mary.[1] Where faith in the Incarnation of the Eternal God in time and place is affirmed, there of necessity veneration of the Mother of the Incarnate God flourishes. The Catholic Church has remained true to this faith through the centuries, and consequently has taught and promoted devotion to Mary. The Catholic Church in the United States follows the Catholic pattern in this respect. The truth of the Incarnation and its consequences have been cherished by American Catholics throughout their history. Indeed some fifty years ago when, in Europe, faith in the divinity of Christ weakened and some Catholics succumbed to disbelief, the faith of American Catholics remained on the whole unshaken. The Modernist crisis was scarcely felt in this country. Even the errors ascribed to certain Americans at the time under the title of "Americanism" contain nothing on this score. It can, then, be said with truth that the Church in America has been constantly faithful to devotion to Mary.[2]

---

[1] For a classic exposition of the foundations of devotion to Mary see Orestes Brownson's *The Worship of Mary*, in *Brownson's Review*, Vol. 10 (Boston, 1853), pp. 1-25. The use of "worship" for "veneration" was common at the time. Even certain magistrates were worshipful. Francis Patrick Kenrick, Archbishop of Baltimore (1851-1893) and a leading American theologian of the nineteenth century, writes in his *Dogmatica Theologia,* Vol. 4 (Philadelphia, 1840), p. 221 f., "Id quidem exploratum est, quo altior est de mysterio incarnationis sensus, eo teneriorem plerumque et ardentiorem erga Deiparam esse devotionem." R. Schimmelpfennig, *Die Geschichte der Marienverehrung im deutschen Protestantismus* (Paderborn, 1951), makes the same remark, p. 146.

[2] W. L. Sullivan, one of the few American priests to apostatize during the Modernist crisis, has some criticism of Catholic teaching on Mary's privileges and sanctity in his posthumous *Under Orders* (New York, 1944), pp. 73 ff. *Testem Benevolentiae,* the letter on Americanism, is translated in *The Great Encyclical Letters of Pope Leo XIII* (New York, 1903), pp. 441-453. The brief First Rule of the Paulists prescribes the daily recitation of the Rosary and of the Litany of the Blessed Virgin as well as a visit to the Blessed Sacrament and to the Blessed Virgin. Cf. J. McSorley, *Father Hecker and His Friends* (St. Louis, 1952), p. 191.

The principle upon which veneration of Mary rests is that of honoring God in His works, especially in His works of grace. He who loves and honors God's creatures because they are the works of God, honors their Creator, God Himself. We do not honor Mary as God; we know she is a creature, and that it is only as a creature that we can honor her. We honor her as a saint and the greatest of the saints.

On this score there is little with which to reproach American Catholicism in its devotion to Mary. Living as a minority among Protestants, many of whom look askance at manifestations of Marian piety, American Catholics have constantly been obliged to square their devotion with theological science. The result is that there have been few excesses in devotion to Mary. A recent critic of American Catholicism has apparently found very little on this point. True, he goes to Quebec to show us nuns kneeling as floats carry statues of Mary through the streets. He crosses the ocean to Portugal and Poland in order to sharpen his barbs. He even launches an attack on the definition of the Assumption by Pope Pius XII — an attack, incidentally, in which he betrays his ignorance of the point at issue, the Catholic doctrine of tradition. But the only specifically American fact he produces is an *Imprimatur* given to a circular on the Brown Scapular.[3]

If we ask, on the contrary, whether American devotion to Mary has not been blanched by the chilling atmosphere in which American Catholics live, and by the fear of the assaults of carping critics, the answer is not difficult. Veneration of Our Lady in the United States, as this Chapter will show, has taken on countless forms with none of the time-honored practices of the Catholic past omitted. While it is possible that isolated ecclesiastics may have avoided certain popular manifestations of Marian piety so that our Protestant friends might feel at ease about her, it must be affirmed that no Catholics anywhere have surpassed American Catholics in the frankness of their devotion to Mary. Moreover, the atmosphere has not been too chilly since not a few Protestants in all the denominations have a deep regard for the Mother of Jesus.

I. MARY'S PRIVILEGES

Because of the divine maternity, Mary has numerous privileges. She

---

[3] P. Blanshard, *American Freedom and Catholic Power* (Boston, 1949), pp. 13, 76, 110, 187, 211, 216, and 223; *Communism, Democracy and Catholic Power* (Boston, 1951), pp. 164, 235, 238 ff.

was prepared in body and soul for a mystery which affected not only herself but the whole Church. This preparation is expressed principally in the dogma of the Immaculate Conception, viz., that from the first moment of her existence she was free from all taint of original sin. Her freedom from any venial sin is also a teaching of faith. Sinful concupiscence never stirred in her.[4]

The fact that the dogma of the Immaculate Conception was proclaimed during the nineteenth century when the American Church was developing was not without its effect on American veneration of Mary. A century ago Orestes Brownson spoke of the marked growth of devotion to her among Catholics in Great Britain and in the United States, and of the general desire for the definition of the Immaculate Conception as a dogma of faith. In his eyes this was a response to the action of the Holy Spirit in the hearts of the faithful. At a time when the Incarnation was widely rejected, the Spirit of God inspired special devotion to the Blessed Virgin.

Brownson drew another lesson from the sinlessness of Mary which illustrates the power of the Marian ideal and still has force. For him this devotion was the best preservative against the moral dangers of the times. Mary, as the Mother of chaste love, has a lesson for epochs in which true love is rather rare. "The predominate sin of our times," Brownson wrote in 1853, "is that of impurity, at once the cause and effect of modern sentimental philosophy. All the popular literature of the day is unchaste and impure, and it boldly denounces marriage as slavery, and demands that loose reins be given to the passions. Catholic morality is scouted as impracticable and absurd; law is regarded as fallen into desuetude; intellect is derided; reason is looked upon as superfluous, if not tyrannical; and the heart is extolled as the representative of God on earth. Feeling is honored as the voice of the Most High, and whatever tends to restrain or control it is held to be a direct violation of the will of the Creator. Hence passion is deified, and nothing is held sacred but transitory feelings. In the non-Catholic world, and even in nominally Catholic countries, impurity has gained a powerful ascendancy, and seeks to proclaim itself as law, and to denounce whatever is hostile to it as repugnant to the rights both of

---

[4] B. J. Otten, S.J., *Manual of the History of Dogmas*, Vol. 2 (St. Louis, 1918), pp. 397 ff. Cf. S. Bonano, C.M.F., *Mary's Immunity from Actual Sin*, in *Mariology*, ed. J. B. Carol, O.F.M., Vol. 2, pp. 179-195; Carr-Williams, O.F.M.Conv., *Mary's Immaculate Conception*, ibid., 109-178.

God and man."[5]

Brownson thought that the love of Mary would save the world from moral corruption by sustaining the Catholic family and securing the fruits of sacramental marriage. Imitation of Mary would influence the hearts of those devoted to her and tend to unite them to her by a virtue kindred to her own. "We cannot love her, dwell constantly on her merits, on her excellencies, her glories, without being constantly led to imitate her virtues, to love and strive after her perfect purity, her deep humility, her profound submission and her unreserved obedience. Her love checks all lawlessness of the affections, all turbulence of the passions, all perturbation of the senses, fills the heart with sweet peace and serene joy, restores to the soul its self-command and maintains perfect order and tranquillity within."[6]

Brownson's words, which describe what some might term the process of sex sublimation, are as true today as they were a century ago, but with this difference. Devotion to Mary has not been able to halt the flood of vice and impurity, but it has kept the spirit of resistance alive in Catholic hearts in this country where the struggle has been intense. A great deal has been salvaged and resistance continues and is on the increase. Even before Brownson wrote, Archbishop Kenrick had pointed out how profitable it would be for Catholic young people, and especially for girls, to take Mary as an exemplar and patroness to be imitated, as well as venerated and invoked. He also stressed the power of Mary's intercession to inspire sinners to turn their backs on their vices.[7]

The late Father Daniel A. Lord, S.J., an outstanding promoter of Marian devotion among the young, wrote of the Catholic high regard for purity and the American attitude which Europeans at times regard as prudery. "In Catholic education it is insisted that the young men hold the same high standards of purity that are expected of women. The system of the double standard is regarded as traitorous to Mary." We also hear of a countermove against the low type of pin-up girl by the introduction of the

---

[5] O. Brownson, *op. cit.*, "The Love of Mary," p. 230.

[6] *Ibid.*, p. 232.

[7] *Loc. cit.:* "Qui juventutem, praesertim puellas, voluerit a labe saeculi servare immunem, et omni informare genere virtutum, oportet ut Mariam proponat exemplar, et patronam, quam a tenerioribus annis venerari et invocare discant, eam pari studio imitari haud praetermittentes. Peccatoribus etiam in vitiorum barathrum demersis magno cum emendationis fructu Maria exhibetur advocata, quae Filii deprecetur iram, eaque obtineat gratiae subsidia, quibus infirmae voluntati subveniatur."

picture of the Madonna into barracks and between decks, and of drives for modesty in dress, inspired by Marian piety. Father Lord in his apostolate did not hesitate to bring devotion to Our Lady into Junior Proms and other dances sponsored by Catholic schools.[8]

The perpetual virginity of the Blessed Virgin is another of her privileges. In the United States the struggle within Protestantism between the Fundamentalists and the Liberals (1909-1925) centered on the doctrine of the Virgin Birth. The real issue was, of course, the whole supernatural structure of Christianity, but the corollary of the Virgin Birth was the point about which the acrimonious conflict raged, and it soon became clear that those who were not sure about the Virgin Birth were not sure about the Incarnation either. Catholics were not much impressed. They pointed out that the new truths of the Liberals were merely old denials, and that really there was no essential difference between the contending parties as long as both held to the principle of private judgment and free interpretation of the Bible. The fundamentalists would never be able to defend the Virgin Birth by appealing merely to the Bible. No human interpretation of the Gospels would ever be divinely infallible. Recourse must be had to an infallible Church. In refuting the critical animadversions of the Liberals, Catholics stressed the chaotic character and changing principles of their positions.[9]

The Protestant defenders of the dogma, for the most part, thought it necessary to explain their position in such a way as to escape the suspicion of being Romanizers. One of their leaders wrote: "We are, indeed, as far as possible from accepting the Roman Catholic picture of the Queen of Heaven." He then went on to contradict the Catholic teaching on Mary's virginity after the birth of Christ, holding that she bore other children to Joseph.[10]

The controversy on the Virgin Birth bulks larger in the history of Christianity in the United States than it does in that of Catholic devotion

---

[8] D. A. Lord, S.J., *Our Lady in the United States*, in *Lumen Vitae*, Vol. 8 (Brussels, 1953), p. 314. Cf. P. Blanshard in *Communism, Democracy and Catholic Power*, p. 164.

[9] W. Parsons, S.J., in *America*, Vol. 30, 1923-24, pp. 249 f., 273 f., and 297 f.

[10] J. Gresham Machen, *The Virgin Birth of Christ* (New York, 1924), pp. 134, 144 ff. B. L. Conway's, *The Virgin Birth* (New York, 1924), contains a learned exposition of the Catholic position and a brief history of the problem. The author avoids contemporary controversy. Martin J. Scott's *The Virgin Birth* (New York, 1925) is popular and wider in scope. He also avoids the Protestant controversy. Father Parson's articles, already referred to, meet the Protestant positions.

to Mary. It gave Catholic apologists an occasion for reaffirming the traditional positions but, except in isolated instances, led to no rapprochement with the Protestants who came out in defense of supernaturalism in Christianity. Although these latter defended the article of the Apostles' Creed affirming that Jesus was born of the Virgin Mary, their view of Our Lady was so far from Catholic that they received little encouragement from the Catholic camp.

II. MEDIATRIX OF ALL GRACES

Devotion to Mary comprises not only the veneration of her excellence, but also an appeal to her intercession. This supposes that God carries on His works of providence and grace by the agency of ministers. He could, of course, accomplish His ends immediately without the employment of any intermediate agency. But He does not so choose. In His works, especially in the supernatural order, He admits His creatures to a share. He does this, not because He would impose a task on them. Rather, since He delights in honoring them, He permits them to be agents for obtaining and communicating His favors and graces to others. God, obviously, does not need the intercession of anyone to render Him disposed to confer graces on mankind. The charity that leads to intercession comes from Him as its fountain. But God desires it for the honor and reward of the saints.

It is in accord with this plan of His providence that God puts Mary first, and gives her the privilege of interceding in all cases, and of always having her intercession effectual. Her will, always one with God's will because moved by divine charity, is even in heaven regarded by Jesus as the will of His Mother, and has that weight which the right will of a mother must always have with a good son. We see, then, the reasonableness of the teaching that Mary is the channel through which Our Lord dispenses His graces, and that He dispenses none save through her intercession. While not of faith, this is the general belief of the faithful and the common opinion of Catholic theologians; so much so that in the judgment of many it could be defined as an article of faith.[11] Mary, on her part, as the spiritual Mother of the faithful and universal queen, delights, according to Catholic teaching, in using her prerogative of efficacious intercession. As refuge of sinners, she intercedes for her erring children particularly at the hour of death. As cause of Christian joy, she watches

---

[11] Cf. A. J. Robichaud, S.M., *Mary, Dispensatrix of All Graces*, in *Mariology*, ed. J. B. Carol, O.F.M., Vol. 2, pp. 453-488.

over the just with maternal solicitude. Mary loves her children with an invincible and effectual love, desiring, willing, and procuring their greatest spiritual and temporal good.[12]

That American Catholics have not been behind Catholics of other countries in invoking the intercession of Mary is certain and will be clearly demonstrated throughout the rest of this Chapter. While certain democratic and Anglo-Saxon principles concerning the equality of man, rugged individualism, and the advisability of going directly to headquarters might seem to militate against the principle of intercession, in practice things have not worked out that way.

III. MARIOLOGY IN AMERICA

The century and a half which has seen the rise and development of the American Church has been most fruitful in the development of Marian theology. Devotion to Mary had long been at a high level throughout the Church, and the practices of this Marian piety had for centuries been numerous and varied. The American Church naturally entered into this Catholic heritage and borrowed its practices and manifestations of devotion for the most part from other lands and peoples. What is perhaps more surprising is that its theological thought, or the greater part of it, has been borrowed also. The American Church in the nineteenth and early twentieth centuries was not prepared to take any great part in the contemporary development of doctrine concerning Mary. The contributions of American theologians have been noted for fidelity to tradition rather than for originality or profundity.[13]

The solemn definition of the Immaculate Conception by Pius IX in 1854 caused a revival of Marian theology. This was echoed in the United States in a few doctrinal works which served to put at the disposition of American Catholics the results of the advances which had been made in Europe.[14]

---

[12] Brownson, *op. cit.*, p. 225. Cf. R. V. O'Connell, S.J., *Our Lady Mediatrix of All Graces* (Baltimore, 1926).

[13] This is the view of Father Cyril Vollert, S.J., *Le mouvement mariologique aux Etats-Unis*, in *Maria. Études sur la Sainte Vierge*, ed. H. du Manoir, S.J., Vol. 3 (Paris, 1954), pp. 593-614.

[14] Vollert, *art. cit.*, lists a number of these works including J. D. Bryant, *The Immaculate Conception of the Most Blessed Virgin Mary* (Boston, 1855), R. F. Quigley, *Mary the Mother of Christ in Prophecy and Its Fulfillment* (New York, 1892), and the articles of Brownson referred to above.

The preparation for the definition of the dogma of the Assumption saw an increase in American contributions to Marian theology. Much of this appeared in magazines. As a rule the American theologians held that the doctrine of the Assumption is a doctrine of faith and definable, while maintaining that only the Pope could judge of the opportuneness of a dogmatic pronouncement. In one case, at least, attempts to influence the decision of the Sovereign Pontiff were looked upon with disfavor and as manifesting a lack of regard for the prerogatives of the Holy See.[15]

When in 1946 Pius XII in his Encyclical *Deiparae Virginis Mariae* asked the bishops of the Catholic world to inform him about devotion to Our Lady's Assumption among their people, and about their judgment as to the opportuneness of a definition, numerous articles appeared in Catholic reviews in favor of the action. When in 1950 the solemn definition was proclaimed by Pius XII a flood of articles, some of them theological in character appeared in Catholic periodicals.[16]

A subject which has occupied the attention of Marian theologians in recent years is that of Mary's co-operation in the Redemption. As early as 1878 a remarkable book by Father J. de Concilio taught that in consenting to the Incarnation, the Blessed Virgin accepted not only the maternity of the Redeemer, but also a coredemptive share in His sufferings.[17] Since that time, and especially of late, Mary's role in the Redemption has been brought to the fore. Not only has it been the subject of discussion at a meeting of the Mariological Society of America, but it has also been the object of an exhaustive study by the leading American Mariologist. This work is not only an outstanding contribution to Mariology, but has been called "the most important single contribution to the literature of sacred theology ever made by an American writer."[18]

Summing up, we may say that in the domain of theological Mariology, America has only just begun. With few exceptions, the works produced so far have not been distinguished. Weighed down by apostolic labors,

---

[15] Unsigned note in *The American Ecclesiastical Review*, Vol. 53, 1915, p. 347 f.

[16] A.A.S., Vol. 42, 1950, pp. 782 f. Vollert, *art. cit.*, pp. 598 ff.

[17] J. de Concilio, *The Knowledge of Mary* (New York, 1878), a learned work by a Jersey City pastor. Cf. Abram J. Ryan, *A Crown for Our Queen* (Philadelphia, 1882), an important work by the poet-priest.

[18] J. B. Carol, O.F.M., *De Coredemptione Beatae Virginis Mariae disquisitio positiva* (Vatican City, 1950). Cf. Review by Monsignor J. C. Fenton in *The American Ecclesiastical Review*, Vol. 126, 1952, p. 79; and by C. Vollert, S.J., in *Theological Studies*, Vol. 13, 1952, pp. 442-444.

American thinkers have had too little time for theological problems. The future promises better things. The more thorough training which existing faculties have received and the creation of new ones furnishes more workers in the field. In addition, the foundation and success of the Mariological Society and of its organ *Marian Studies* mean that the necessary stimulus and direction are at hand.[19]

IV. OFFICIAL DEVOTION

The official attitude of the American Church is the most authoritative manifestation of Marian piety. From the beginning American bishops and synods have been outspoken on this point and, taken together, their pronouncements are quite impressive.

On November 10, 1791, at the First National Synod, John Carroll, founder of the American hierarchy, recalled that on the feast of the Assumption, August 15, 1790, he had been consecrated first Bishop of Baltimore and that he had chosen the Blessed Virgin Mary as the principal patroness of his diocese, which embraced the original thirteen States and practically all the country east of the Mississippi, except Florida. He did so in order that by her intercession, the faith, piety, and good morals of his flock might flourish and increase. He considered, therefore, that she should be honored in a special way (*singulari cultu*) and he urged his priests to venerate her and frequently and earnestly to recommend the devotion to their people. The feast of the Assumption was made the principal feast of the diocese and all were urged to confess and communicate on that day. Carroll proposed to ask Rome for the grant of special indulgences to encourage these practices.[20]

The Fathers of the Fourth Provincial Council of Baltimore (1840) asked

---

[19] Preliminary steps were taken in 1949 by Father Juniper B. Carol, O.F.M., and the first national meeting of the Mariological Society took place in 1950. *Marian Studies* is published annually. On the activities of the Mariological Society, cf. S. G. Mathews, S.M., *Mary in America,* in *The Ave Maria,* Vol. 89, April 11, 1959, pp. 9-11 and 26. Among religious orders, the Franciscans have been active in studying Marian theology and devotion as well as promoting it. The First Franciscan National Marian Congress was held in Washington, D. C., in 1950 and listened to communications from the members of the principal branches of the Order. The proceedings have been published: *First Franciscan National Marian Congress in Acclamation of the Dogma of the Assumption, October 8-11,* 1950 (Burlington, Wis., 1952). Cf. Fr. Maurice Grajewski, O.F.M., *The Franciscan Marian Cult in the United States in Our Times, ibid.,* pp. 120-125.

[20] Mansi, *Sacrorum Conciliorum nova et amplissima collectio,* Vol. 39 (Paris, 1907), p. 966.

permission to celebrate the feasts of the Espousals of the Blessed Virgin (January 23), of Our Lady, Help of Christians (May 24), and of the Expectation of Our Lady (December 18). These petitions do not appear to have been granted, but the privilege of saying the Office and Mass of the Immaculate Conception on Saturdays throughout the year by priests traveling to care for souls was confirmed. The Fathers of the Council of 1840 recalled that this had been customary in the Diocese of Baltimore, following a grant of Pius VI.[21]

Mary, under the title of the Immaculate Conception, was unanimously chosen by the Sixth Provincial Council of Baltimore (1846) as Patroness of the United States. The Fathers also asked permission to introduce the word "immaculate" before "conception" in the Office and Mass of the feast. Pius IX confirmed the choice and sanctioned the changes.[22]

Replying to an inquiry of Pius IX about the devotion of the American people and clergy to Our Lady under the title of her Immaculate Conception, the Fathers of the Seventh Provincial Council of Baltimore (1849) asserted that it was great and fervent. They went on to request the Pope to define the doctrine, if he thought it opportune, as a dogma of faith. One of the acclamations recited at the end of this Council reads, "To the Most Blessed Virgin Mary, conceived without original sin, patroness of these provinces, eternal honor."[23]

The Fathers of the Second Plenary Council of Baltimore (1866) willingly and reverently accepted the definition of the Immaculate Conception which had been proclaimed by Pius IX in the Constitution *Ineffabilis Deus* of December 8, 1854.[24] Among the six holy days of obligation retained with the sanction of the Holy See by the Third Plenary Council of Baltimore (1884) were those of the Immaculate Conception (December 8) and the Assumption (August 15). The Fathers of this synod also recommended special devotion to the Blessed Virgin to minor seminarians.[25]

The national pastorals of the American hierarchy follow the pattern

---

[21] Mansi, Vol. 39, p. 377 ff.

[22] Mansi, Vol. 43, pp. 7-11. The invocation *Regina sine labe originali concepta* was also to be added to the litanies.

[23] Mansi, Vol. 43, p. 409. Similar acclamations were used in the First and Second Plenary Councils of Baltimore (1852 and 1866). Cf. Mansi, Vol. 44, p. 673, and Vol. 48, p. 830.

[24] Mansi, Vol. 48, p. 901.

[25] *Acta et Decreta* ... (Baltimore, 1886), pp. cv ff., 74.

created by Bishop John Carroll in his letter of May, 1792, six months after the close of the First National Synod. Carroll urged the faithful to cherish "a fervent and well-regulated devotion to the Holy Mother of Our Lord and Saviour Jesus Christ." He expressed the hope that they would "place great confidence in her intercession and have recourse to her in all necessities." He concludes that "having chosen her as the special patroness of this diocese, you are placed, of course, under her powerful protection: and it becomes your duty to be careful to deserve its continuance by a zealous imitation of her virtues, and reliance on her motherly superintendence."[26]

In the pastoral of 1846, the prelates of the Sixth Provincial Council notified the faithful that they had unanimously determined "to place ourselves and all entrusted to our charge throughout the United States under the especial patronage of the Mother of God whose Immaculate Conception is venerated by the faithful throughout the Catholic Church." The Fathers go on to say, "By the aid of her prayers, we entertain the confident hope that we will be strengthened to perform the arduous duties of our ministry, and that you will be enabled to practice the sublime virtues of which her life presents a most perfect example. The Holy Ghost by her own lips has foretold that all generations shall call her blessed; and we cannot doubt that a blessing is attached to those who take care to fulfil this prediction. To her then we commend you, in the confidence that, through the one Mediator of God and men, the man Christ Jesus, who gave himself a redemption for all, she will obtain for us grace and salvation."[27]

The Seventh Provincial Council of Baltimore had, as we have seen, spoken of the fervent belief of Americans in Our Lady's Immaculate Conception, and requested the Pope to define it as of faith. The Fathers of this Council devoted a part of their pastoral to the belief and practice of the Church regarding the Immaculate Conception. Disclaiming any intent to anticipate the solemn judgment of Pius IX, they urged their people "to cherish a tender devotion to the Mother of Our Lord, since the honor given to her is founded on the relation which she bears to Him and is a homage rendered to the mystery of the Incarnation. The more highly you venerate her, as the purest and holiest of creatures, the deeper sense you

---

[26] *The National Pastorals of the American Hierarchy (1792-1919)*, edited by Peter Guilday (Washington, 1923), p. 13 f.

[27] *Ibid.*, p. 168 f.

manifest of His divinity. Wherefore her devout clients in ancient and later times have always been distinguished by zeal to maintain the great mysteries of faith and by the purity of their lives and their zeal for the attainment of Christian perfection. On the contrary, those who have assailed the veneration of the Virgin have easily fallen into the denial of the divinity of her Son. Devotion to her is an outwork of the Church protecting the belief of the divine mystery." The Fathers of the Council also spoke of their confidence in the intercession of Mary, "When we raise our thoughts on high to the kingdom of light and love, where Mary stands near the throne of her divine Son, we are inspired with confidence that she, who, at the foot of the Cross, received us all as her children in the person of the beloved disciple, will effectually plead our cause. Through her we have received all grace, since she brought forth Him who has redeemed us by His blood and through Him she has crushed the head of the infernal serpent. Let us, then, go with confidence to the throne of mercy, relying on the infinite merits of Jesus Christ, our only Saviour, and commending ourselves to the prayers of His holy Mother, who is always heard on account of her intimate relation to Him, and her tender love of Him."[28]

The pastoral letter of 1919 sums up the official exhortations of the hierarchy to the faithful in America in the following words: "What grace can accomplish in His creatures, God has shown in the person of her whom He chose to be his Mother, preserving her from all stain and endowing her with such pureness of heart that she is truly 'full of grace' and 'blessed among women.' The unique privilege of Mary, as cooperating in the Incarnation, entitles her to reverence and honor; but in the Catholic mind it is love that prompts veneration for the Mother of Christ. It is indeed beyond comprehension that any who sincerely love Jesus should be cold or indifferent in regard to His Mother. No honor that we may pay her can ever equal that which God Himself has conferred, and much less can it detract from the honor that is due to Him."[29]

V. MARIAN CHURCHES AND INSTITUTIONS

Another official manifestation of devotion to Mary, and an important one, is the dedication of churches to God under the invocation of the Blessed Virgin, and the bestowal of the name of Mary, or of one of the

---

[28] *Ibid.*, p. 178 ff.
[29] *Ibid.*, p. 279.

events of her life, or of one of her privileges, on a Catholic school, convent, or other institution. The use of Mary's name or titles for such purposes is very ancient, and in America goes back to the days of the explorers. The flagship of Columbus was the *Santa María*. Chesapeake Bay was called St. Mary's Bay by its Spanish discoverers. Father Jacques Marquette named the Mississippi "the River of the Immaculate Conception." Maryland was named for a princess, but the first colonists called their settlement St. Mary's. Los Angeles was originally St. Mary of the Angels.[30] Despite her losses of the Chesapeake, the Mississippi, Los Angeles, and other places, Our Lady still figures prominently among those after whom places are named in the United States. There are over sixty localities called after her. In addition, her name is so widely used by women that it is the most popular given name in our country. A great multitude of American women are called Mary or one of the variants like Marie, Marian, May, Maureen, and Marilyn. All this is the more amazing in view of the fact that so much of America was colonized and settled by groups which disliked Catholic veneration of the Blessed Virgin.

More impressive still is the large number of Catholic churches dedicated to God under the invocation of Our Lady. According to unofficial figures, there were in 1955 some 4379 churches, including more than two score cathedrals, which bear the name of Mary, or one of her titles, in the 50 United States and its possessions, Puerto Rico, Canal Zone, Caroline and Marshall Islands, Guam and the Virgin Islands. Of these, 641 are mission churches and all but 150 of the 4379 are located in the fifty States.[31]

---

[30] Daniel Sargent, *Our Land and Our Lady* (New York, 1939), passim.

[31] The statistics on churches, etc., are the writer's, made on the *Official Catholic Directory, Anno Domini 1955* (New York, 1955). Anyone undertaking the task of ascertaining precise numbers will naturally be faced with problems despite the excellence of this *Directory*. To give one example: mission churches, i.e., churches served by no resident pastor, are not mentioned by title in some dioceses. In others there are no mission churches or practically none. This may be due to the automobile in populous regions where distances are not great. Some dioceses list missions under the parish where the priest in charge lives. In others they are listed with reference to the place of residence. Father Vincent Yzermans (in *Churches of Mary in the United States*, in *The American Ecclesiastical Review*, Vol. 132, 1955, pp. 169-180) finds 3815 Marian churches. Father Daniel A. Lord in a list made some years ago stated that there were 3114 parish churches, dedicated to Mary. Cf. the list of Marian Churches made in 1862 by X. D. MacLeod and given by W. Parsons, S.J., *Marian Devotion in the Early United States* in *Marian Studies*, Vol. 3, 1952, p. 241 f.

Some 2260 convents also bear the name or a title of Mary, as well as 2048 elementary schools, 523 high schools and 77 colleges. In addition, the Catholic dead rest in at least 1203 cemeteries bearing the name, or a title, of Our Lady. There are 283 hospitals, clinics, and convalescent homes under her patronage. One hundred nineteen seminaries for the formation of the diocesan and regular clergy are under the protection of her who bears the title of Seat of Wisdom. This custom began in 1791 with St. Mary's Seminary, Baltimore, which is not only the oldest but also the largest seminary in the country. Miscellaneous institutions such as monasteries, homes, shrines, centers, and nurseries add up to another 313 Marian dedications.[32]

The New York Archdiocese alone has 116 churches bearing our Lady's name in some form; Philadelphia 107; and Boston 85; while the Diocese of Brooklyn has 84, and Buffalo 77. Other archdioceses with large numbers of Marian churches are Chicago with 77, Los Angeles with 69, and Newark with 67. Among the dioceses, Scranton has 66 and Albany 60. These figures are, without exception, paralleled by proportionately large numbers in all American sees. The Church in the United States has literally enveloped the country in a finely meshed network of Marian churches and institutions.

A glance at the titles of these Marian churches will prove of interest. No less than 1226 churches are dedicated to God under the invocation of Our Lady as St. Mary. This is a striking indication of the traditional nature of this devotion in the United States. Practically no one speaks of Mary nowadays as St. Mary. She is popularly either simply Mary, or Our Lady, or the Blessed Virgin, or the Blessed Mother. The use of the title St. Mary, while it is probably due in part to the use of Latin in official documents, recalls an earlier time when she was so styled. By contrast, the popular names are practically nonexistent as the titles of churches — at least without some combining form. Our Lady, even if we count foreign language forms, such as Notre Dame, can muster only twenty-three churches. Of course, there would be many more if we counted all those called Our Lady of Victory, Our Lady of Mercy, etc.

The second largest number of Marian churches in the United States

---

[32] Most doubtful among these statistics are those on convents. It is difficult to determine at times whether the Sisters live where they teach. Still the numbers are probably fairly accurate. In the statistics on elementary schools neither catechetical nor summer schools are included.

are those dedicated to God under the invocation of the Immaculate Conception.[33] There are no less than 588 such churches. If we add to them the 115 churches bearing the title of the Immaculate Heart, and the 149 under the invocation of the Immaculate of Lourdes, we have a grand total of 852 which may be attributed to Our Lady under the title of this mystery. This seems to prove the impact of the definition of the Immaculate Conception in 1854 on the then rapidly expanding American Church. In a few dioceses the churches of the Immaculate Conception are more numerous than those called St. Mary's. The Archdiocese of St. Louis, for example, has 17 Immaculate Conception churches and only nine St. Mary's. In the Diocese of St. Joseph, there are ten Immaculate Conception's and nine St. Mary's.

The events of Mary's life are commemorated in hundreds of churches: her Nativity in 55, her Presentation in 22, the Annunciation in 74, the Visitation in 45, the Divine Maternity in 23, the Purification in nine, the Assumption in 273, the Crowning in Heaven in ten. There are 118 churches under the invocation of Our Lady of Sorrows, 203 with the title of the Rosary. And, of course, in many of these instances, a church means a convent and a school with the same title.

Marian churches point at times to the various nations which have been united in the American Church. There are in the United States 202 churches of Our Lady of Mt. Carmel, many of them dating from the time of the large Italian immigration. The influence of Italy is also discernible in the fifteen churches of Our Lady of Pompeii, as also, undoubtedly, in the seventeen dedicated under the invocation of Our Lady of Loreto. Poland is represented by 26 churches of Our Lady of Czestochowa as well as by scattered churches under the invocation of Our Lady of Ostrabrama and Our Lady of Poland.

Although natives of German-speaking lands and of Ireland have certainly played leading roles in the development of the American Church, there is very little to indicate this in the litany of Marian churches. The great German, Austrian, and Swiss titles — Altötting, Kevelaer, Absam, Mariazell and Einsiedeln — are conspicuous by their absence. There is one instance each of the use of Our Lady of Limerick and Our Lady of Melleray, but Our Lady of Knock is missing. A satisfying explanation is not forthcoming. In the case of the Irish, devotion to St.

---

[33] Cf. M. Habig, O.F.M., *Our Oldest Church of Mary Immaculate*, in *The American Ecclesiastical Review*, Vol. 134, January, 1956, pp. 5-9.

Patrick is not a sufficient reason. The fact that Irish priests had adopted English habits of speech before coming to this country is probably a partial cause, while German love of the Rosary may have something to do with the missing titles from German-speaking lands. Other churches betraying national connections include those dedicated to Our Lady of Mt. Lebanon, to Our Lady of Hungary, Our Lady of Vilna, and Our Lady of the Pillar.[34]

What is probably most significant in this catalogue is the fact that only one of the popular titles is non-European, and even that is Mexican, i.e., Our Lady of Guadalupe with 134 churches.[35] The vast majority of titles are imported. There are, it is true, a number of churches dedicated to Our Lady of the Lake, or Lakes (58 according to this count), but there is scarcely need to say that the lakes indicated are all but as numerous as the churches. There are 59 Star of the Sea churches, some of them located on the Atlantic Ocean, some on the Pacific, others on the Gulf of Mexico, others on the Great Lakes, and a few apparently near no large body of water. There is, however, a small fraction of unmistakably American titles, among them: Our Lady of the Ozarks, Our Lady of Cincinnati, and Our Lady of the Redwoods. Just what we are to say of Notre Dame de Chicago is not clear.

Original titles have been used more frequently for convents and other institutions than for churches. We find the attractive creations: Marygrove, Marylake, Maryfield, Maryvale, Marydale, Maryview, Marywood, Marylawn, Maryridge, Maryvilla, Marycrest, Marydell, Marycliff, and even Marynook. In addition, there are Ladycrest, Ladycliff, Ladywood, Glenmary, and many others. Our Lady's name has been given

---

[34] Our Lady of Fátima already has 60 church-dedications. There are churches of Our Lady of Chartres, Our Lady of Bethlehem, Our Lady of Monserrate (in Puerto Rico), Our Lady of Prouille, of Talpa, of Celle, des Canadiens, etc.
There are also in the United States 281 Holy Family churches and 69 All Saints churches in which dedications Our Lady shares. Indeed all Catholic churches honor Our Lady: the formula of the *Pontificale* reads, "In nomine Patris et Filii et Spiritus Sancti, in honorem Dei, et gloriosae Virginis Mariae atque omnium sanctorum, ad nomen et memoriam sancti N." Cf. J. Catalanus, *Pontificale Romanum prolegomenis et commentariis illustratum*, Vol. 2 (Paris, 1851), p. 170.

[35] Even Guadalupe is only secondarily American. Spain has an ancient and celebrated shrine under that title. Indeed, Guadalupe Hidalgo in Mexico was so named because its Aztec name seemed to the Spanish conquerors to resemble Guadalupe. Still because of the vision to Juan Diego, of December 9, 1531, it seems legitimate to trace American titles directly to Mexico and indirectly to Spain.

to newspapers as well as to places and institutions. There is at least one diocesan paper which is named after her, *El Correo de la Virgen* (Diocese of Corpus Christi); and to mention only one periodical, one of the oldest and most beloved Catholic magazines is the *Ave Maria,* published at Notre Dame University, with contributions by leading Catholic authors.[36]

VI. MARIAN SHRINES

No American shrine, it seems, has as yet attained the fame of the great European pilgrimages like Lourdes, Lisieux, Paray-le-Monial, or of the Canadian sanctuary of Our Lady's mother, St. Anne de Beaupré. Still there are many shrines in the States and some of the best known are Marian. We can mention only a few. Most venerable is that of Our Lady of La Leche in St. Augustine, Florida, the oldest city on the North American continent. In the early years of the seventeenth century the Spanish settlers built a chapel and dedicated it under the title of *Nuestra Señora de La Leche y Buen Parto* (Our Nursing Mother of Happy Delivery). Here they installed the little statue of the Virgin holding the Child and offering Him her breasts. Today thousands of mothers come annually to Our Lady of La Leche and in peaceful, prayerful surroundings ask through her intercession for the blessings of motherhood.[37]

Scarcely less venerable is the shrine of *La Conquistadora* in the Lady Chapel of the Cathedral of Santa Fé with a little statue which Fray Alonso de Benavides brought there in 1625. Every year thousands of clients and tourists visit her. During the Marian Year she left her honored place in the Cathedral to tour the Archdiocese of Santa Fé and bring joy to the villages and cities of the New Mexicans.[38]

Our Lady of Martyrs Shrine at Auriesville, New York, rises on the site of the seventeenth century martyrdom of St. Isaac Jogues, St. René Goupil, and St. John de la Lande. There also the Venerable Kateri Tekakwitha, the "Lily of the Mohawks," was born. Since 1885 Our Lady has been venerated

---

[36] Notre Dame University itself is probably the best known Marian title in the country. Another way in which some American prelates show their devotion to Mary is by the motto of their coat of arms. Among those of living bishops we find: *Maria, Spes Nostra; Ad Nutum Reginae; Maria, Impende Juvamen; Maria Me Custodiat; Auspice Maria; Per Matrem Dei; Ad Jesum Per Mariam; Omnia Per Mariam,* and not a few others.

[37] Z. Aradi, *Shrines of Our Lady Around the World* (New York, 1954), p. 169 ff. Cf. M. Habig, O.F.M., *The First Marian Shrine in the United States,* in *The American Ecclesiastical Review,* Vol. 136, February, 1957, pp. 81-89.

[38] A. Chavez, O.F.M., *La Conquistadora* (Paterson, N. J., 1954).

at the Shrine as Queen of Martyrs and also as Our Lady of Joy. In 1953 Paul Emile Cardinal Léger, Archbishop of Montreal, presided at a large pilgrimage, and the same year other pilgrimages were led by Archbishop Amleto Giovanni Cicognani, Apostolic Delegate to the United States, and by Auxiliary Bishop Henry Klonowski, of Scranton. During the Marian Year (1954) more than 300,000 pilgrims visited Auriesville. The Martyrs Shrine, which is under the care of the Jesuit Fathers, has established itself as one of the leading pilgrimage centers of the New World.[39]

The Sanctuary of Our Sorrowful Mother founded in 1926 by the Servite Fathers in Portland, Oregon, is conceived as a place of spiritual recreation. Vast in every respect, it serves many thousands of people as a place of recollected prayer. The Shrine of Our Lady of Perpetual Help at Roxbury, near Boston, Massachusetts, is noted for instantaneous cures for which no merely natural explanation can be given. The Miraculous Medal Shrine at Germantown in Philadelphia, and the Shrine of Our Lady of Prompt Succor in New Orleans are influential centers of Marian piety. A peculiarly American Shrine is that of Our Lady of the Sioux, where a picture of Our Lady of Lourdes painted by a Sioux Indian is venerated. At Pittsfield, New Hampshire, there is a Shrine of Our Lady of the Smile; at Watertown, New York, the Shrine of Our Lady of the Sacred Heart.[40]

A Shrine which is believed to owe its origin to a vision of Mary is that of Our Lady of Good Help, at Robinsonville, Wisconsin. In 1858, the year of the apparitions at Lourdes, the Blessed Virgin clothed in dazzling white, with long wavy, golden hair, with a yellow sash around her waist and a crown of stars encircling her head, is said to have appeared to Adele Brisse (1831-1896), a recent immigrant from Belgium, and to have instructed her to teach children catechism and to do penance for sinners. Adele's father built a log chapel on the spot shortly after the apparitions. A second chapel, a frame structure, was constructed in 1861 and replaced by a substantial brick chapel in 1880. In 1942 a beautiful Gothic shrine was constructed. Adele Brisse faithfully carried out her mission till her death. Many striking cures have been attributed to the Robinsonville Shrine which is becoming better known. Probably as striking as any Marian Shrine in the world is the Basilica of Our Lady of Victory at Lackawanna, a suburb of Buffalo, New York, erected by the Right Reverend Monsignor

---

[39] *The Catholic Encyclopedia*, Vol. 12, p. 88; also recent issues (1953, 1954) of the Pilgrim, the Shrine bulletin.

[40] Z. Aradi, *op. cit.*, pp. 173 ff., 181 ff.

Nelson Baker († 1936), distinguished apostle of charity. Mary's statue is enthroned in a baroque church made impressive by richness of ornamentation and architectural design. Thousands of Catholics and not a few non-Catholics visit this costly Shrine every year.[41]

The National Shrine of the Immaculate Conception on the campus of Catholic University at Washington, D. C., is also one of the great Marian centers of the world. The crypt has for years been a magnet for tourists and pilgrims, and at present [1959] the superstructure of a great church has been completed. Not far away, in Baltimore, stands the Basilica of the Assumption of the Blessed Virgin Mary, begun by Archbishop John Carroll and now the site of his tomb. For dignity and quiet beauty it takes a leading place among American Marian shrines. Although it will soon be supplanted by another beautiful Marian church as the Cathedral of the Archbishops of Baltimore, it can never be forgotten by American devotees of Mary since it is the symbol alike of the beginnings of Marian devotion after the foundation of the Republic and of hierarchical sanction for manifestations of that devotion.[42]

VII. NOVEL FORMS OF DEVOTION

In giving some account of the manifestations of Marian piety, it must frankly be stated that they are so numerous as to defy listing. Some of the most important are treated on other pages of this volume.

Here we limit ourselves to a few which cast light on American devotion to Mary. Necessarily the selection will be somewhat arbitrary, but incomplete as it is, it should be illuminating.[43]

Most striking are the novel creations which center in the person of Father Patrick Peyton, C.S.C., and his Family Rosary Crusade and Family Theatre. Father Peyton was born (1908) in Ireland in a family whose religious spirit was fostered by the daily recitation of the Rosary. He came to America in 1928 and after a year entered Holy Cross Seminary, Notre Dame, Indiana. Some ten years later he was stricken with tuberculosis. He

---

[41] For the Robinsonville Shrine see *The Chapel: Our Lady of Good Help. A Wisconsin Shrine of Mary* (Green Bay, 1950). Also *The Catholic Encyclopedia*, Vol. 7, p. 418.

[42] A. M. Melville, *John Carroll of Baltimore: Founder of the American Catholic Hierarchy* (New York, 1955), p. 264 ff.

[43] We omit, for example, the notable Marian apostolate centered in St. Meinrad's Monastery at St. Meinrad, Indiana, the annual Marian Week of the Marian Fathers at Stockbridge, Massachusetts, and the work done by the De Montfort Fathers, Bay Shore, New York, in propagating True Devotion.

believes that Our Lady cured him, and since his ordination in 1941 has promoted the Family Rosary Crusade throughout the world. In America he has been able to secure the top talent in radio, movies, television, and advertising for his Crusade. Most Americans, probably, have heard the leading entertainers recite the Rosary under his leadership. Great cities in many parts of the world have seen his devout rallies.

These last are very well organized. When episcopal permission has been obtained, an experienced staff, directed by Father Peyton, visits the diocese for a period of six weeks with the object of promoting the Family Rosary. The clergy and key laymen are moulded into a compact body to educate Catholics on the importance of family prayer. The slogan is, "The Family that Prays Together Stays Together." The campaign includes sermons in all churches, special editions of the diocesan newspapers, articles in the secular press, radio and television programs, and outdoor advertising. Central in the campaign is a general rally which never fails to bring together tens of thousands. In New Orleans the gathering was estimated at 105,000; in Hyde Park, London, at 100,000; in Malaga, Spain, at 150,000, with an equal number in Melbourne, Australia. In Bombay 200,000 turned out; in Rangoon 28,000. As a lasting result of these rallies and crusades, millions of signed pledges bind families to recite the daily Rosary.

Certainly no Marian devotion launched anywhere has had such repercussions as the Family Rosary Crusade. Father Peyton's marshalling of the actors and actresses of Hollywood, and his simple but effective pleas for the introduction of Our Lady into the family circle, have an actual significance which is compelling. Nor can it be doubted that the pledging of so many families "to pray together in order to stay together" will produce decisive and durable results. It is difficult to see in the Crusade something of ephemeral importance. One thing the Family Rosary has already effected. It has turned the current of American Marian piety outward. In the past the flow was from overseas. This in itself gives the Crusade singular importance in the history of Marian piety in the United States.[44]

Another manifestation of American devotion to Our Lady, which has already had international results, is the Blue Army of Our Lady of Fátima,

---

[44] P. J. Peyton, *The Ear of God* (New York, 1951). The statistics are taken from publications of the Family Theatre (7201 Sunset Boulevard, Hollywood, California) and the Family Rosary (432 Western Avenue, Albany, New York).

founded by the Right Reverend Monsignor Harold Colgan, of Plainfield, New Jersey. Less than ten years ago, Father Colgan lay in a hospital, doomed, it was thought, to an early death. After a promise to preach the message of Fátima, he recovered. Leaving the hospital, he preached in fulfillment of his promise on ten successive Sundays, pleading with his people to join in a "mighty army of prayer under the blue banner of Our Lady." The response was immediate. Not only has his Army spread far and wide, but Father Colgan has lived at a killing pace to keep up with it. Since 1947 he is reported to have averaged some 300 lectures yearly in some fifty cities. The Blue Army, which claims millions of members with some thousands behind the Iron Curtain, is building an international headquarters at Fátima in Portugal. The requirements for membership are: (*a*) proper recitation of a part of the Rosary daily; (*b*) wearing of the Brown Scapular of Mt. Carmel as a sign of consecration; and (*c*) the offering up to God of the sacrifices demanded by daily duty. Members are urged, besides, to make the five First Saturdays and wear an outward sign of their consecration in the form of a blue ribbon, string, or pin.[45]

If the claims of the Blue Army are even fifty per cent accurate, and there is no reason to suspect them, it is a movement of considerable and lasting importance. The approbation of the Fátima apparitions not only by the local ecclesiastical leaders but also, to a degree, by the Roman authorities helps to accredit and propagate this form of Marian devotion.

Another form of American devotion to Our Lady is the Block Rosary. The movement started in Detroit in 1945 and has spread to much of the world. Information and materials have gone out from the headquarters to at least forty-five countries and have been translated into dozens of languages. The success of the Block Rosary lends support to the claim that its origin goes back to an apparition of Our Lady, dressed in black, to a Detroit housewife in 1944. It has been greatly helped by a simple formula. The fundamental idea is an effort to meet the problems of the hour by united prayer. Neighbors meet in their homes, progressing from house to house until each home has been made a place of prayer for the group. Then the process begins over again. An act of consecration to the Immaculate Heart and five decades of the Rosary are recited for: (*a*) peace in the world; (*b*) the overthrow of atheism and communism; (*c*) the conversion of Russia; (*d*) renewed fervor among Catholics; and (*e*) that

---

[45] Our information is taken principally from *Soul* (Asbury Park, New Jersey), official organ of the Blue Army.

there may be one flock and one shepherd. After the Rosary, the neighbors immediately disband, emphasizing the nonrecreational character of the gathering. Care is also taken to secure the approbation of the local authorities and to avoid any conflict with parish services. Although the Block Rosary is aimed especially at urban areas, it has been applied in the country and even, by missionaries, in the jungle.[46]

Another devotion associated with the apparitions at Fátima is the National Radio Rosary Organization. In 1947, through the initiative of a layman in New Orleans, the Rosary was broadcast in that city. The response was immediate and enthusiastic. Over 3500 post cards and 400 letters flooded the WJBW offices during the first twenty days of the program. Since that time, with a short interruption, this form of devotion has been put on the air in New Orleans on weekdays and Sundays. From New Orleans the Radio Rosary spread rapidly throughout the country. In San Francisco, a five-station hook-up carries it. In Boston, Richard Cardinal Cushing personally leads the recitation of the beads. The director of the Baltimore Radio Rosary estimates that the broadcast has 100,000 listeners. This peculiarly American form of devotion to Our Lady has already crossed the border into Canada and Cuba. At present (1955) efforts are being made to establish it in Ireland and Belgium.[47]

Still another group connected with Fátima is The Reparation Society of the Immaculate Heart of Mary founded at St. Ignatius Loyola Church in Baltimore. This association grew out of a nocturnal adoration society and has retained the character of a crusade for prayer, reparation, the daily Rosary, and acts of self-denial. A bulletin *Fátima Findings* is published for the members and carries a monthly Rosary meditation for use on the First Saturday. Members live in all the States of the American union as well as in fifty-one foreign countries. One of the distinctive features of this movement has been the use of the pilgrimage, not a prominent feature as yet of American Catholic life. Several were made

---

[46] Our information on the Block Rosary was furnished by Mr. N. J. Schorn, of the Block Rosary Lay Apostolate, 651 Marlborough Avenue, Detroit 15, Michigan, and taken from a pamphlet by A. Gargan, *The Block Rosary* (St. Louis, 1953).

[47] Information on the National Radio Rosary Organization was furnished by A. J. Cummings, founder of the group (4101 State St. Drive, New Orleans 15, Louisiana). An advance in this line has been made by the Servite Fathers of Chicago who produce a weekly television program. The Servites also put out automobile windshield stickers with a picture of Our Lady and the legend: "Ride with Mary. Pray the Rosary. The Soul You Save May Be Your Own."

during the Marian Year to nearby shrines and one to Auriesville, New York. In these pilgrimages the penitential element was stressed.[48]

Among the most assiduous in promoting devotion to Our Lady in this country have been the Congregation of the Mission of St. Vincent de Paul and the Daughters of Charity who look back to Mother Elizabeth Seton as well as to St. Vincent. The Miraculous Medal devotion, given to St. Catherine Labouré in 1830, has been popularized to a degree unknown by other symbols of the Marian cult, with the exception of the Rosary and the Scapular. The Medal has been spread far and wide in many ingenious forms. Tiny blue medals, for example, attract the eye on the wristwatches of fashionably attired ladies. Medals are impressed on plastic Rosary cases. Some Christmas cards carry a Miraculous Medal, while note paper and letter paper are also used as vehicles of propaganda.[49]

Equally phenomenal has been the propaganda in recent years for the Green Scapular, recommended in 1840, it is believed, by Our Lady to Sister Justine Bisqueyburu, who, like St. Catherine Labouré, was a Daughter of Charity. During the Marian Year, the Marian Center at Emmitsburg, Maryland, sent out about three quarters of a million manufactured Green Scapulars with a covering leaflet. About 600,000 were also sent out in materials to be made up by the recipient. Since the close of the Marian Year over 15,000 Green Scapulars have been sent out weekly from this center. We have here an example of American mass production applied to an object of devotion.[50]

In May, 1949 — to give but one example of an occurrence which is by no means uncommon — a Congress of the Children of Mary was held in Emmitsburg, Maryland, to celebrate Our Lady's apparition to St. Catherine Labouré and the foundation of the Children of Mary. Over a thousand delegates from twenty States assembled in this rather remote locality. The proceedings were afterward published in an attractive volume which contains much that has an American flavor. One sermon is entitled, "Be Ladylike," and its theme is the obvious one that to be ladylike means to be like Our Lady. In the various sections, talks given by the young women

---

[48] Information on the Reparation Society of the Immaculate Heart of Mary is taken from a pamphlet available at headquarters (720 N. Calvert St., Baltimore 2, Maryland). Nocturnal adoration societies often sponsor Marian devotions. Outstanding in this respect is the work of Fred Niehaus, of Cincinnati, Ohio.

[49] Cf. *The Catholic Encyclopedia,* Vol. 10, p. 115.

[50] M. E. Mott, *The Green Scapular and Its Favors* (Emmitsburg, 1942). The statistics were kindly furnished by the Marian Center, Emmitsburg, Maryland.

have such titles as, "Does My Mirror Reflect Another Mary?" and "Fátima's Beauty Hints," to give two examples.[51]

An organization of importance is Our Lady of Fátima Rosary Making Club, founded in 1949 by the late Brother Sylvan, C.F.X., at Louisville, Kentucky. The purpose of the club is to furnish handmade Rosaries free to the missions. Units were soon established throughout the United States and during the first three years the annual output of Rosaries reached about 50,000. The Baltimore Unit, organized in 1953, is now producing five to six hundred excellent Rosaries a month. They go to the home and foreign missions.[52]

The United States is what might be called novena-conscious. In some places novenas seem to be replacing the time-honored parish mission. It is significant that two of the most popular novenas are the Novena of the Miraculous Medal and that of the Sorrowful Mother. The former is a part of Vincentian devotion, which we mentioned above; the latter has been developed by the Servite Fathers.

In no country in the world, probably, is a more sincere and spontaneous affection manifested to Our Lady than that which marks the month of May in the United States. Many churches, convents, and seminaries conduct May devotions daily with special prayers to the Queen of the May. Almost every church has its solemn May procession with a formal crowning of the Blessed Mother and a consecration of the parish to her. There are few Catholic high schools or colleges in which the May Day celebration is not one of the events of the scholastic year. May Day, which may be any day of the month, approximates in America the solemnity of a liturgical feast of high rank.

Working among Americans are scores of religious congregations of men and women who are under the direct patronage of the Blessed Virgin and use her name or one of her titles as their own. Some of these congregations were founded in the United States as, for example, the Sisters of Charity of the Blessed Virgin Mary, the Sisters of Loretto at the Foot of the Cross, and the Sisters of the Immaculate Heart of Mary. An American missionary order also bears Our Lady's name. The Fathers, Brothers, and Sisters are known throughout this country, where they were

---

[51] *First National Marian Congress of the Children of Mary* (Emmitsburg, 1949).

[52] Information on the Rosary Making Club is taken from publications of the Club (118 West Broadway, Louisville 2, Kentucky).

founded, and in many foreign lands, by the name of Maryknoll.[53]

Societies for laymen and women dedicated to Our Lady are enormously popular. The Sodality works through some 14,000 units in the parishes, schools, and other Catholic institutions of the country. Its Summer Schools of Catholic Action now train 15,000 Catholics in the Marian apostolate each year. The Legion of Mary has steadily grown in membership. The Altar and Rosary Society for married women has been established in hundreds of parishes. Second only to the practice of the First Fridays in honor of the Sacred Heart are the First Saturdays in honor of Mary.[54]

The amount of Marian devotional literature appearing in the United States is considerable and ever increasing in volume. Its vehicles are periodicals, pamphlets, and books. The periodical output is so extensive that for the last ten years it has had, like other branches of periodical literature, a flourishing digest under the title of *Our Lady's Digest*. Pamphlet literature scarcely less popular pours out from many centers. Books promoting devotion to Mary in some way or other are becoming more numerous. As in the field of Mariology, so in that of devotional literature, in so far, at least, as books are concerned, the past has witnessed much borrowing from abroad; in this instance, particularly in the form of translations from the French and German. Books from other English-speaking lands are also widely circulated here. Of late, however, there has been a marked increase of devotional works by American writers. How many of these are destined to stand the test of time and become Marian classics it is difficult to say. In one instance this seems assured. *A Woman Wrapped In Silence,* a book-length poem in blank verse, by Father John W. Lynch, a priest of the diocese of Syracuse, New York, has been hailed by competent judges as an artistic production of permanent value. It typifies all that is best in American devotion to Mary.[55]

---

[53] In *the Early Days. Pages from the Annals of the Sisters of Charity of the Blessed Virgin Mary* (St. Louis, 1925); A. C. Minogue, *Loretto: Annals of the Century* (New York, 1912); Sister M. Rosalita, *No Greater Service. The History of the Sisters, Servants of the Immaculate Heart of Mary,* 1845-1945 (Detroit, 1948); Sister Maria Alma, *Sisters, Servants of the Immaculate Heart of Mary* (Philadelphia, 1937); *Sisters of the I. H. M.* (New York, 1921); R. A. Lane, *The Early Days of Maryknoll* (New York, 1951).

[54] Cf. Chapters XII, XIII, XIV, XV, and others in this volume.

[55] *Our Lady's Digest* is published at Olivet, Illinois, under the editorship of Rev. Stanley Matuszewski, M.S., J. W. Lynch, *A Woman Wrapped in Silence* (New York, 1941). *I Sing*

Conclusion

In a book published in 1866 an early historian of Marian devotion in America wrote, "that there never has been a country in which reverent love and earnest, heartfelt devotion for the Blessed Mother of God was more deeply rooted, more ardently cherished, or more fervently and fruitfully practised, than in North America."[56] In 1953 another well-informed priest wrote that "Mary is very much at the heart and center of American Catholic devotion."[57] Our study certainly proves the second of these judgments. There is, indeed, a sense in which the American Catholic Church might even say to Our Lady, "What is there which I could have done to honor you which I have not done?"

Nevertheless, a problem remains. Writing in 1949, a leading German Protestant church historian makes much of the *Heiligenpolitik* (saint-policy) of the Catholic Church under the pontiffs of the twentieth century, and he finds that devotion to Our Lady is the center of these celestial politics.[58] Is then all the outpouring of love and devotion of American Catholics for the Virgin Mary merely a result of the clever manipulations of the Vatican? Or worse still, when we speak of it in a post-Freudian world, must the sex drive in human nature be called upon as the hidden reason for its success?

The description of Marian piety as a sublimation of the sex drive has

---

of a Maiden. *The Mary Book of Verse*, edited by Sister M. Thérèse (New York, 1947), contains many American lyrics on Our Lady. Some American devotional works on Mary are: Bishop Fulton Sheen, *The World's First Love* (New York, 1952); D. A. Lord, S.J., *The Song of the Rosary* (St. Louis, 1953) and *Our Lady in the Modern World* (St. Louis, 1940); H. Blunt, *Mary's Garden of Roses* (New York, 1939); W. Most, *Mary in Our Life* (New York, 1954) with a new edition in 1959; *Mary and Modern Man*, edited by T. Burke, S.J. (New York, 1954); and E. F. Garesche, S.J., *The Most Beloved Woman* (New York, 1919). Father Paul Palmer's *Mary in the Documents of the Church*, a help to both devotion and theology, has been reprinted in England. The Gallery of Living Catholic Authors has popularized a new title, *Our Lady of Letters.* The University of Dayton, conducted by the Society of Mary, has assembled a large library of Marian books and manuscripts. Marian College, Poughkeepsie, New York, also has an important Marian Library under the direction of Brother Cyril Robert, F.M.S., and publishes the *Bulletin Board of Our Lady's Library.* Cf. Chapter XVII in this volume.

[56] Father Xavier D. MacLeod, a converted Protestant minister, *Devotion to the Blessed Virgin in North America* (New York, 1866), p. 22.

[57] Cf. *Lumen Vitae*, Vol. 8, 1953, p. 312, article by Father Daniel A. Lord, S.J.

[58] H. Hermelink, *Die katholische Kirche unter den Pius-Päpsten des 20. Jahrhunderts* (Zürich, 1949), p. 126.

already been touched upon in these pages and need not be reconsidered here. We should point out, perhaps, that those who have never practiced devotion to Mary, as it is taught in the Catholic Church, must labor under serious handicaps when they endeavor to apply to it the yet uncertain principles of modern psychology.

The objection that Marian piety is Vatican-inspired reveals a lack of knowledge of the life of devotion in the Catholic Church. It is true that there is an official liturgy emanating from Rome that must be followed, but our study has shown that this is only one element among many in the massive totality of American devotion to Mary. Catholic authorities, far from launching devotional practices, are traditionally unfavorable, or at best indifferent, to them. New devotions have to prove themselves before they are sanctioned. American Marian devotion is, as we have seen, no more tributary to Rome and Italy than to Lourdes and France. It is part of a Catholic tradition whose origins lie in the distant past and whose developments betray the ideas and practices of many peoples. Since American devotion to Mary is traditional, it cannot be said to be entirely spontaneous. Still its manifestations have nothing forced or artificial about them. And in our study we have not come across the slightest indication of Rome-generated enthusiasm.

As we remarked at the beginning of this chapter, those who deny the truth of the Incarnation can never give the credit to Mary which to the Catholic mind she deserves. Those who do not believe that Jesus Christ is true God of true God must always find Marian devotion an empty show masking reality. But to those who believe that the Second Person of the Blessed Trinity became incarnate in the chaste womb of Mary, the exhortation of Orestes Brownson, leading American Catholic layman of the nineteenth century, a thinker and a convert from Protestantism, is the only answer: "We must feel that nothing is more important than the cultivation of the love and worship of Mary. She is our life, our sweetness, our hope, and we must suffer no sneers of those without, no profane babblings about 'Mariolatry' to move us, or in the least to deter us from giving our hearts to Mary. We must fly to her protection as the child flies to its mother, and seek our safety and our consolation in her love, in her maternal embrace."[59] The action of Mary which Brownson describes in such concrete terms is for the most part hidden. It is true, as we have had occasion to note, that miraculous occurrences have taken place in

---

[59] O. Brownson, *op. cit.*, p. 235.

America as they have abroad. But Catholics everywhere look for Mary's help especially in the order of grace. And they are convinced, in the words of a much loved prayer, "that never was it known that any one who sought her intercession was left unaided." The vitality of Marian devotion in this country is, in the eyes of Catholics, an outward response to the inward solicitude of a loving Mother.

This chapter should not be brought to a close without mention of one who was, in some ways, the greatest of Mary's American clients. He fits into none of the categories we have used, for, if a Christian, he was certainly not a Catholic. Henry Adams was the author of perhaps the greatest books any American has written. A genius, he sought to understand the universe and discover, otherwise than on his knees, the secret of peace. But the rise of the machine and the clear vision he had of the coming of thermonuclear power, brought him to the feet of Our Lady as the greatest force the Western world had ever felt. Writing of himself, he confesses, "He never doubted her [the Virgin's] force since he felt it to the last fibre of his being, and could no more dispute its mastery than he could dispute the force of gravitation of which he knew nothing but the formula."[60]

It was impossible for the head of Henry Adams not to make reservations, to turn Our Lady into a symbol or into energy. But he gave his heart to her. Scores of times he visited her shrines scattered over rural France. Despite his insistence that religion had nothing to do with this, he could not exclude from his books hints of his deepest convictions. We have besides the testimony of the niece who knew him best that Our Lady had enthroned herself in his mind not merely as mankind's grandest and loveliest dream but as the most satisfying of realities.

Henry Adams is then the symbol of the effect the spiritual Morning Star has on the hearts of those who love her without knowing her. He was a great American and a great client of Our Lady. In these pages he represents her children whom the mysteries of history have separated from a loving mother but whom she cherishes nonetheless.

---

[60] Cf. *The Education of Henry Adams. An Autobiography* (Boston, 1918), p. 469. Cf. J. Brodrick, *The Quest of Henry Adams*, in *The Month*, Vol. 170, 1937, pp. 301-309, 397-406.

THE BLESSED VIRGIN IN LITERATURE

by HAROLD C. GARDINER, S.J.

N MANY a tome and treatise, the influence of Our Lady on old and modern literature has been traced. To those who believe that she is what she is, and who also realize that literature is, in some way or other, a record of man's quest for a happiness that is ultimate, it is not surprising that her influence is there to reveal itself to the investigator. For if she is the Mediatrix of all graces, surely it is not strange that she should have mediated in the literature of the world, revealing herself — and therefore her Son, to whom she is the way — in the sweet and unobtrusive fashion that is her wont whenever she looks upon our thirst and turns to say to Him: "They have no wine." If literature is one draft that is destined, in its degree, to satisfy that thirst, Our Lady, we instinctively feel, must be at hand somewhere, holding forth our empty cup to be filled by Him, even in the lesser realms of literature.

But most of the treatises that have sought out her influence on our literature have, it seems to me, set their sights too low. They have generally been content to compile the instances in which Our Lady has been written *about*, in which she has been merely the subject matter of poems, of plays. Many of these compilations are impressive, indeed, and the better of them come as a revelation of the extent to which Our Lady's praises have been sung even by those outside the household of the faith and — even more astonishingly — in an age and a civilization in which Mariology is too often looked upon as Mariolatry. In Sister Marie Thérèse's beautifully discriminating yet complete anthology, *I Sing of a Maiden*,[1] one cannot help but note with joy the great number of modern and current poets who have added their contemporary voices to the age-old canticle.

If I seem to suggest that Our Lady's influence on literature goes a little deeper than these anthologies would give us at first glance to suspect, it is not because I feel that these compilations do not frequently add up to more than a mere catalog of names and poems. Such rosters do indeed suggest more than they actually state, though frequently the compilers do

---

[1] New York, 1950.

not lead us on to more than the mere fact of the listings. Is not the further thought inescapable that the fact that poets and artists down the ages have thought of the Mother of God and been impelled to sing her praises — has not this mere fact, I say, been enough to win from her hands graces that have preserved the world from who knows what catastrophe, or at least somehow brought civilizations and cultures that seem almost alienated from God, by God's mysterious grace, closer to Christ? The fact — the "mere" fact — that Our Lady's name shines beautiful and all-glorious on the pages of countless books in myriads of bookshops and libraries over the civilized world is an external grace for men. Must not God's eye lighten with ineffable joy when He sees that lovely name so spread abroad among the sons of man who, all unwittingly perhaps, are fulfilling through their poets and their dramatists her own prophecy that "all generations shall call me blessed"?

But this is a spiritual and devotional suggestion rather than a fact of literary history. Is there a way in which Our Lady's influence on literature can be traced other than by lining up the individual poets and dramatists who have spoken of her? Is there any large way in which her presence in a culture can be shown to have influenced thinking, attitudes, customs, in such a manner that the literature that mirrors these things became quite different from what it would have been, had she not been present, so to speak, at the source? It is indubitable, I take it, that the whole literature of the Western world is now what it is (apart from its excesses and abuses) because of the Incarnation. Jesus Christ, Christianity, have so gotten into the blood-stream of Western man that he cannot write now (though many may try to for a time) as though the Son of God had never become man. Has Our Lady, as well, so got into that bloodstream? Has she co-operated with her Son in this, as in all His other salvific works?

Such thoughts in connection with this chapter were first given an impetus by Daniel Sargent's excellent essay on *Our Lady and Our Civilization* wherein the author states:

> It is always a religious cult that gives pattern to a civilization and it could hardly be expected that the cult of our Lady would not leaven its mark on medieval civilization, and it did.[2]

Mr. Sargent then goes on to discuss how medieval English poetry was influenced by the Blessed Virgin. This began with Latin poetry, which, if

---

[2] In the symposium *Mary and Modern Man,* ed. by Th. J. M. Burke, S.J. (New York, 1954), p. 84.

it did not always sing directly of her, yet found in singing of her "its supreme chiseling. The surprise of its rhythms was developed in expressing an enduring surprise that Our Lady could have been both a Maid and a Mother." This, in turn, influenced vernacular poetry, first when Anglo-Saxon poetry, "time-honored and in its way highly developed, put itself to school in singing to our Lady, and little by little became ... one of the languages that praised her best." Then came the Norman invasion, with its softening influences, so that "by the time that Anglo-Saxon had become so little insular that it was almost modern English, her bards could sing of her as if their skill were made for nothing else." Finally, by 1400, "no English poet could count himself a poet unless he could sing of the Mother of God. Like a medieval craftsman he was no more than an apprentice till he had presented his proper masterpiece, and that had to be in praise of her." Mr. Sargent then goes into a most stimulating discussion why the greatest poem of the Middle Ages, the *Divine Comedy,* "is the poem that was most our Lady's"; but I have quoted enough of his thought already to indicate on what lines I would like to expand this chapter.

It must first of all be said that many scholars do not agree with the specific instance that Mr. Sargent adduces of Our Lady's influence in the sphere of medieval poetry. The pendulum in this matter has gone through many arcs. It had long been thought that the secular love-lyrics in England held the field first, and that the religious love-poem was adapted by the Church as a means of lessening the popularity of the too-frequently suggestive verses of the *jongleurs.* Then came an interpretation that reversed the process. One authority[3] holds explicitly that "divine love, in the medieval sense, became a new theme in English literature, before secular love-poetry ... could take root there." More recently, however, Ten Brink's theory is being adandoned. Such an authority as C. S. Lewis rejects it completely in stating that "there is no evidence that the religious ... tone of medieval love poetry had been transferred from the worship of the Blessed Virgin; it is just as likely — it is even more likely — that the coloring of certain hymns to the Virgin had been borrowed from the love poetry."[4] Lewis makes an even more sweeping denial when he states: "Nor is it true in any unequivocal sense that the medieval Church encouraged

---

[3] B. A. U. Ten Brink, *Early English Literature,* Vol. 1, p. 200; quoted by G. R. Owst, *Literature and Pulpit in Medieval England* (Cambridge, 1933), p. 17.

[4] C. S. Lewis, *The Allegory of Love, a Study in Medieval Tradition* (Oxford, 1936), p. 8.

reverence for women at all."[5]

I do not care to labor this particular point. It must be obvious, however, that there is no clean line of demarcation between the religious and the secular love-poem. There was an overlapping down the decades, and we find both types of love-poems flourishing at the same time, sometimes complementing one another, sometimes in rivalry. But without specific reference to the love-poetry of the Middle Ages, it is possible, I believe, to trace a wider influence of Our Lady on English literature. That will be the burden of the rest of this chapter.

An important fact of cultural and religious history that is not too well known, especially among American Catholics, is the great change that took place in the features of Christianity toward the end of the thirteenth century. I say "in the features," because the essence of the faith, of course, remained unchanged. The historian of religious culture who has delved most originally and deeply into this transformation of the character of Christianity is M. Emile Mâle, to whose monumental three-volume work the following outline is in large part indebted.[6]

Religious art up to the middle, say, of the thirteen century revealed unfailingly the more serene aspects of the faith, one might almost say the more intellectual aspects. The great portals of the French cathedrals, for instance, show forth a spirit of peace, of serenity, of majesty. Even representations of the Passion of Our Lord rarely appealed to any emotions of sorrow; Christ is normally represented as reigning from His Cross or as teaching from it; He is rarely shown as suffering on it. One of the standard depictions of Christ on the Cross during this period shows Him erect and majestic, vested as the High Priest, crowned not with thorns but with the diadem of His Kingship, and the Cross itself is not infrequently adorned with jewels. And, just as Christ's death is portrayed as a triumph, so the death of His members, the saints, is a victory. Much of the statuary and iconography that M. Mâle uses to illustrate this point consists of the decoration of tombs and funerary monuments and it is striking how often the reclining figure reflects serenity, peace, and majesty. But by the fifteenth century much of this had changed. A sudden

---

[5] *Ibid.*

[6] E. Mâle, *L'art religieux du XIIe siècle en France,* 3rd ed. (Paris, 1928); *L'art religieux du XIIIe siècle en France,* 7th ed. (Paris, 1931); *L'art religieux de la fin du Moyen Age en France,* 4th ed. (Paris, 1931). A summary of the three volumes has recently been published in a Harper paperback Torchbook, *The Gothic Image* (1958).

and not too subtle change had come over the external character of Christianity — at least as far as it reveals itself in art. "The greater part of the works we possess from this epoch," says M. Mâle,[7] "are somber and tragic; art offers us little, save the face of grief and of death. Jesus does not now teach any more; He suffers; or rather He seems to show forth to us His wounds and His blood as the supreme teaching."

What has happened to the visage of Christianity? Whence this change? What was its effect on the whole culture (not, mark, on the dogmatic bases) of Christianity?

Many currents, of course, joined to swell the stream of this change, and it would be impossible to trace the runnels of them all in the course of this short chapter. M. Mâle, however, believes — and I believe that he is the first historian of culture to point out his belief in full detail — that the main stream was what he calls the new Franciscan emphasis on human sensibility, on the humanity of Christ, His mother, the saints; on, in a word, the human element implicit in the whole structure of dogma and devotion. "I believe," he states,[8] "that if one wished to mount to the source whence so much pity has flowed out over the world, one must go straight to Assisi. In the presence of a Christ painted on a Cross, Francis received a revelation of the Passion, and he suffered so profoundly from it that he finally bore in his body the marks of that Passion: that was the miracle of love that astonished Europe and gave birth to new forms of sensibility."

Now obviously this arousing of a new spirit through St. Francis was going to be in turn the same thing that would affect the talent of the artists, whose work in those times was so predominantly religious. In his work M. Mâle dwells at length on the Passion and how it was consistently treated in the fourteenth and fifteenth centuries under these new aspects of tenderness, of compassion for the suffering, of sensibility.[9] But there was another element that was working with almost equal vigor — and this will finally bring us to the real point of this chapter. The "Passion of Our Lady" began to be treated almost as frequently as the Passion of her Son. This is the period, for instance, when we begin to get the first representations of Our Lady as the Mother of Sorrows, her heart pierced by the seven swords, whereas "the thirteenth century, always captured by

---

[7] *L'art religieux de la fin du Moyen Age*, p. 86.
[8] *Loc. cit.*
[9] *Op. cit.*, pp. 91-122.

light, had been attracted uniquely to the happy aspects of the life of the Virgin."[10]

The same thing was at the same time happening to the representations of the saints. They are now no longer portrayed primarily as mere victors; now all the aspects of their lives — some authentic, some legendary — begin to attract the talent of the artists. It seems that in these two centuries the whole hierarchy of heaven is being more and more — how shall we put it? — domesticated, more and more closely linked to the hopes and fears, the trials and triumphs, of the ordinary people. This development carried with it, of course, a concomitant danger, for this interest in sensibility can all too easily degenerate into a passion for sentimentality. Perhaps the present state of religious art in the United States, so often lamented for its fatal attraction to the sweet and the feminine, can be traced back precisely to a misinterpretation of this Franciscan tenderness. (It may be of tangent interest to note that the Eastern Church has never been touched with this sensibility in its art: icons are still largely serene and majestic, rarely humanized in aspects of the ordinariness of daily Christian life.)

Whatever be the roots of present-day sentimentality, there is apparently no denying the fact that this new approach of the Middle Ages had vast results, not merely on the art which so early represented it, but on the literature of the times as well. This will be the key to the rest of our consideration.

While the artists were portraying this new aspect of Christian culture in their statues and their stained glass, the Christian *plebs* at large had been touched by it earlier. The great masses of them could not, indeed, read for themselves some of the sources from which the new sensibility sprang, such as the *Meditations* of St. Anselm, but they were hearing the new approach from their preachers and seeing it on the stages of their mystery and miracle plays.

And so it was that Our Lord and Our Lady, presented to the vast body of Christians more and more in art and in the preaching and entertainment of the age under the guise of tenderness, of close human intimacy, acted as a leaven on popular taste. The emotional content of Christianity became more glowing, warmer, more down-to-earth, if we may put it that way; *pari passu,* the emotional content of literature followed suit.

---

[10] *Op. cit.,* p. 123.

This influence of religious instruction and popular devotion on literature is the main thesis of an epoch-making book, *Literature and Pulpit in Medieval England,* by G. R. Owst,[11] and though the author does not devote much space to examining the specific influence of the Blessed Virgin, that influence is nevertheless there. What Mr. Owst is at great pains to prove is that English literary history makes no sense unless one is willing and able to allow for and estimate the influence of the humble preacher, the little devotional book, the popular literature of the Middle Ages in shaping the literature of the Elizabethan period and so of our own age. He asks, for instance:

Where ... in our modern literary historian's digest are the hundreds of religious works in prose and verse fairly represented and discussed, outnumbering, as they do, every other species of contemporary writing? Even if for earlier centuries they receive due recognition, there is little to suggest in his pages that the output multiplies a hundredfold as later generations succeed, much less that their contents have any significance for his theme.[12]

My point here is that the contents of this vast body of literature deal time and time again with Our Lady, and that her presence has, therefore, helped incalculably in shaping our present literature, which, as R. W. Chambers shows conclusively in his *On the Continuity of English Prose from Alfred to More and His School,*[13] did not "develop miraculously" into a new Tudor prose, but grew, mainly through the work of St. Thomas More and his followers, by "means of the living tradition of the English pulpit and a mass of religious and homiletic literature."[14]

Dr. Owst's books abound with examples of how the Blessed Virgin collaborated with her Son in the work of cultural transformation we have been discussing mainly in terms of art. The fourteenth century *Speculum Laicorum* "in setting forth her mercy, speaks of Our Lady as 'Star of the Sea,' she is the 'Lady of Tribulation,' rescuing the sinners and the straitened, and the 'Glorious Lady.' She is to be honored first for her 'admirable beauty,' second for her 'incomparable sweetness,' thirdly for her 'inconsumable plenitude.' " As time goes on, she is referred to more and more as "a lady more lovely and gentle than the loveliest dame in

---

[11] Cf. footnote 3, above.

[12] Owst, *op. cit.,* p. viii.

[13] London, 1932; Introduction to Harpsfield's *Life of More,* pp. cxxi-cxxiv.

[14] *Loc. cit.*

Camelot, a queen more potent alike in her conquests and in her miracles than the wisest of earthly kings and magicians." She is the moon "among the sterres of heaven" and "the sonne, the wiche is chosen the cheff of all the seven planetys," in the words of the famous fourteenth-century preacher, John Bromyard.[15] The tenderness and the intimacy with which she was referred to by the popular preachers of the day comes through well in this brief extract from a sermon on the Assumption by the same preacher:

The goyne of this maide was measured with-oute dissolucion, hur eyen declaryng all chastitie, hur face full of delites and amyabull to angels. The wordes that she spake was full swete and full esye, ever sowndyne to the thankynge of God.

She is compared to the Paradise of Genesis, and "she was wondurly faire, fayer than I may tell, and she was luffing and gracious in every mans sight."[16]

Instances could be multiplied, in which the preachers' or the authors' quaint (to us) words breathe forth the sweet influence of the Maid and Mother. In all the instances, she is seen exercising her power to soften the rude manners of the age, to deepen sensitivity to religious truth, and to broaden refinement in social intercourse, and so to prepare the way for a literature that would mirror some of these characteristics, even if on a plane that is not consciously supernatural and not at all conscious that it owes her a great debt.

But if the pulpit and manuscript bore testimony to the influence of Our Lady, the medieval stage did so even more vividly and in a fashion to impress the people more profoundly. Our Lady trod the boards, as it were, in the England of the thirteenth and fourteenth centuries, and in her various roles carried on her — and her Son's — work of touching and humanizing (and by that I mean making both more human and divine) the hearts of the people. It is needless to mention here in detail many of the mystery and miracle plays that have come down to us. In all the great English cycles, those of York, Coventry, Townley (Wakefield), and Chester, Our Lady is prominently dramatized in all the episodes in which she appears in the Gospel narratives — and in some apocryphal accounts,

---

[15] Owst, *op. cit.*, p. 19.
[16] Owst, *op. cit.*, pp. 19-20.

as well.[17]

In the lovely — and, it must be admitted, the somewhat slapstick (to modern tastes) — Second Shepherd's Play in the Townley cycle, for example, here she is, all gracious and lovable in the scene in which the shepherds offer their gifts to the newborn Infant. She has only a few "lines," to be sure, but her influence is brooding over the scene like a sweet blessing, especially if we compare the rowdiness of the shepherds in the earlier part of the play with their gentleness and "good manners" when they are in her presence:

First Shepherd:

> Hail, pure and sweet one; hail, thou holy Child!
> Maker of all, born of a maiden mild.
> Thou hast o'ercome the Devil, fierce and wild.
> That wily Trickster now has been beguiled.

And so the salutations go on until a more intimate note enters. Face to face with the Child on His mother's lap, the First Shepherd says:

> Look, how he laughs, sweet thing!
> As my poor offering
> A cherry bunch I bring.

The Second Shepherd counters:

> Hail, Saviour King, our ransom Thou has brought!
> Hail, mighty Babe, Thou madest all of nought.
> Hail, God of mercy, Thou the Fiend has fought.
> I kneel and bow before Thee. Look, I've brought
> A bird, my tiny one!
> Other faith I have none,
> Our day star and God's Son.

The Third Shepherd is not to be outdone:

---

[17] Since this chapter is concerned only with Our Lady in English literature, this may be the place to refer to other literatures. The classic work on French miracle and mystery plays is L. Petit de Julleville's *Les Mystères* (Paris, 1880). The same field is covered, with special reference to Germany, in W. Greinzenach's *Geschichte des neueren Dramas* (Halle, 1893-1916). In these and similar works covering the medieval stage in other countries, reference to the name "Maria" or "Virgin" or similar titles will reveal how often Our Lady was presented on the stage to the people of the times. Much research has gone over the dam since the present writer published his *Mysteries' End* (New Haven, 1942), but some indication of the influence of the popular medieval stage on the building Elizabethan drama is given in his pages.

> Hail, pretty darling, Thou art God indeed.
> I pray to Thee, be near when I have need.
> Sweet is Thy look, although my heart does bleed
> To see Thee here, and in such poor weed.
> Hail, Babe, on Thee I call.
> I bring a tennis ball;
> Take it and play withal.

To that, Mary responds:

> The Lord of Heaven, God omnipotent,
> Who made all things aright, His Son has sent.
> My name He named and blessed me ere He went.
> Him I conceived through grace, as God had ment.
> And now I pray Him so
> To keep you from all woe.
> Tell this where'er you go.

The "family note," so to speak, comes through in the final scene. First Shepherd:

> Fair well, Lady, thou fairest to behold,
> With Christ Child on thy knee.
> Second Shepherd:
> He lies full cold,
> But well it is for me
> That Him you hold.

Third Shepherd:

> Already this does seem a thing oft told.

First Shepherd:

> Let's spread the tidings round!

Second Shepherd:

> Come; our salvation's found.

Third Shepherd:

> To sing it we are bound.
>   (Exeunt Shepherds singing)[18]

We find the same tone in the Coventry Plays, in which no less than

---

[18] *Representative Medieval and Tudor Plays,* translated and edited by H. W. Wells and R. S. Loomis (New York, 1942), pp. 93-94.

"thirteen scenes from the life of the Virgin are handled with great tenderness and reverence."[19] A delightful sample might be this farewell of Our Lady to the Angel Gabriel, after the Virgin had said her *fiat:*

> With all meekness I cling to this accord,
> Bowing my face with all benignity,
> See here the handmaiden of the Lord —
> After thy word be it done to me.

And the angel responds:

> Gramercy, my lady ffre (noble),
> Gramercy of your answer on hight
> Gramercy of your great humility,
> Gramercy, thou Lantern of Light,
> Farewell, turtle, God's mother dear,
> Farewell, God's mother, I honor thee,
>   Farewell, God's sister and pleynge frere (playmate),
> Farewell, God's chamber and His bower.

Our Lady, in seemly courtesy, responds:

> Farewell, Gabriel especially,
> Farewell, God's messenger express,
> I thank you for your travel here
> Gramercy of your great goodness.[20]

Now it is worth remembering that the age of the mystery plays' popularity was the age of Chaucer (1340c.-1400). There can be little doubt that young Geoffrey stood with the audience before the pageants in London or other centers, and heard, perhaps from his earliest days, these accents of courtesy, of graciousness, of human kindness — we might say, of domesticity — from the characters who represented Our Lady. The "homely" touch is everywhere in evidence, as when, in the Annunciation scene in the Wakefield cycle, we encounter this dialog between Mary and Joseph after his doubts over her conception have been resolved:

JOSEPH:
Ah, Mary, wife, what cheer?

---

[19] Wells and Loomis, *op. cit.,* p. 23.

[20] *Ludus Coventriae,* or the *Playe Called Corpus Christi,* ed. by K. S. Block (Oxford, 1932), pp. 106-108. The spelling has been modernized, except where the old form is necessary for the rhyme.

MARY:
The better, sir, that ye are here;
How long 'tis since ye went!

JOSEPH:
In truth I've talked here like a fool,
Because I was both wrong and cruel,
I knew not what I meant.
But I know well, dear wife and free,
I've trespassed against God and thee;
Forgive me now, I pray.

MARY:
If ever ye did me belie,
May God forgive you; so do I,
With all the might I may.

JOSEPH:
Gramercy, Mary, thy good will
Sweetly forgives that I said ill,
When I did thee upbraid.
'Tis good for him who has for wife
One meek as thou; for all his life
He may hold him well paid.
Now light as linden leaf am I!
He that both release and tie
And every wrong amend
Give me the grace and power and might
My wife and her sweet child of light
To keep to my life's end.[21]

These few instances are to be taken merely as samples. A thing we find difficult to realize today, especially here in the United States where the center of dramatic activity is focused almost exclusively on New York's Broadway, is that these representations of the Blessed Virgin were seen and savored all over the country.

Our Lady was a popular "star," if we may so say. According to Alfred W. Pollard, "throughout the fourteenth, fifteenth and sixteenth centuries, we have continued evidence of the popularity and frequent production of Miracle Plays in nearly every part of England. During this period we have

---
[21] Wells and Loomis, *op. cit.*, pp. 65-66.

record of the performance of plays in nearly a hundred English towns and villages, some of them quite small places."[22] What has been said of the influence of Our Lady on the mores of the times with respect to France (and especially in so far as her influence was exercised through her presence in the cathedral of Chartres) can certainly be multiplied a hundredfold and brought even closer to the lives of the people when we stop to consider the manifold presence of our Lady in the villages and towns of England through these plays. Here is what Henry Adams says of the nearness of Mary to the people of France in the statuary and glass of the superb cathedral:

> Then the reality was the Queen of Heaven on her throne in the sanctuary, and her court in the glass; not the queens or princes who were prostrating themselves, with the crowd, at her feet. These people knew the Virgin as well as they knew their own mothers; every jewel in her crown, every stitch of gold-embroidery in her many robes; every colour, every fold; every expression of the perfectly familiar features of her grave, imperial face; every care that lurked in the silent sadness of her power; repeated over and over again, in stone, glass, ivory, enamel, wood; in every room, at the head of every bed, hanging on every neck, standing at every street-corner, the Virgin was as familiar to every one of them as the sun or the seasons; far more familiar than their own earthly queen or countess, although these were no strangers in their daily life; familiar from the earliest childhood to the last agony; in every joy and every sorrow and every danger; in every act and almost in every thought of life, the Virgin was present with a reality that never belonged to her Son or to the Trinity, and hardly to any earthly being, prelate, king, or kaiser; her daily life was as real to them as their own loyalty which bound to her the best they had to offer as the return for her boundless sympathy ... they knew the Virgin as though she were one of themselves. ...[23]

Later on, the same author dwells on the same thought:

> The Virgin was a real person [to the people of the Middle Ages] whose tastes, instincts, wishes, passions, were intimately known. Enough of the Virgin's literature survives to show her character, and of course her daily life. We know [and how much more the people of the Middle Ages] more about her habits and thoughts than about those of earthly queens.[24]

---

[22] A. W. Pollard, *English Miracle Plays, Moralities and Interludes* (Oxford, 1927), pp. xxii-xxiii.

[23] H. Adams, *Mont-Saint-Michel and Chartres* (Boston, 1913), p. 183.

[24] *Op. cit.*, p. 258. Those who would like to pursue further the thoughts in this essay would do well to consult *Maria. Études sur la Sainte Vierge*, ed. H. du Manoir, S.J., Vol.

Adams has been criticized as being extremely romantic in his approach to the Middle Ages, and quite obviously, some of his remarks about the worship of the Virgin Mary and her role in displacing her Son and the Trinity in the minds of the faithful must be somewhat discounted (though there is actually evidence enough that the Church had constantly to recall the Christian people to recognize the proper role of Our Lady in the scheme of redemption). Taking account of the reservations that dry-as-dust scholars may lay upon Adams' enthusiasm, we must admit, however, that the spirit of the Middle Ages comes through more unmistakably in a work such as Adams' than in the analytical study of many an historian.

And here we are at the crux of the matter of Our Lady's influence on literature. It is not a matter of defining with precision whether the religious lyric preceded the secular song; it is not a matter of tracing the exact degree to which the Blessed Virgin features in the actual literature of any period. It is a matter of trying to discern how her familiar and frequent presence may have shaped the attitudes, the responses to daily life, the whole framework of thought and impression that in turn shaped the writers who have given us English literature as we now know it. I cannot, obviously, go into this vast field in this small space; but it would be greatly interesting and instructive, I think, if some eager candidate for a doctorate would take up such a theme as, for instance, the lineaments of the Blessed Virgin as mirrored in the women characters in Shakespeare. The Bard must have met Our Lady on the stage of his day — if indeed he did not meet her in the circle of his own family — and it would be a most fruitful study of the influence of popular taste on the stream of literature to try to trace just how Our Lady got into the stream of English literature as we now know it. This chapter can do no more than suggest that such an influence does exist. How else can we account for the presence of Our Lady in modern poetry, to take one instance? These poets are not, as far as we may judge, impelled to speak of her from any sense of personal devotion, from any agreement on doctrinal grounds; but speak of her they feel they must, just as often as they have to speak of womanhood, its

---

2 (Paris, 1952). This is a rich treasure-house, treating (in Book 5) the place of Our Lady in letters and arts in almost all Old World countries. The chapter on Our Lady in English literature, by C. C. Martindale, S.J., is a little sketchy (pp. 97-123), consisting mainly in recalling the many English writers who have referred to her. This, as I have said in the body of this chapter, is one way of tracing Our Lady's influence, but not, I feel, the way to get at any real seminal influence.

destiny, its glory. The same impulse may be seen in modern sociological authors who must inevitably refer to the Virgin Mary when they deal with the problems of womanhood; all too often their references are all askew, are posited on the supposition that Mary was like all other women — but, for all that, it is impossible to talk about womanhood without referring to the paragon of womanhood, Our Lady.

It is time, I suppose, to try to gather together all the loose ends of this rather rambling treatment. It has tried no more than to suggest that Our Lady in English literature means more than the fact that she has been written about. It has tried to suggest that her presence in the hearts and minds of the medieval people spilled over, as it were, into the hearts and minds of the writers, and that, just as Christ, by coming nearer and nearer to the lives of the people, became more and more a focus of realism to the authors, so she, in consort with her Son, made life more real to the medieval world and so to the writers who emerged from that world to shape the literature of our day.

It may sound strange to refer all this to a trend toward "realism" in literature. That horrid word means to our modern ears "suggestive" in the bad sense; it connotes sex and naturalism. But in its primitive sense it means only what it says: that the writer is bent on seeing what he sees in the framework of the real — what actually happened, what the facts were, what real life disclosed. In this sense — and it is the fundamental sense — we may say that Our Lady helped to inject realism into English literature. Her life was, to the people of the Middle Ages, a real life, as Adams was at great pains to point out. The reality of her life and of all the episodes which the medieval world knew so well served to shake literature loose from the romantic world of courtliness, jousts, and knights pursuing dragons that held fair maidens in thrall. Our Lady brought a breath of reality into the world — because she brought the Real Presence into the world — and, in so doing, wakened literature to the fact that it deals with the reality of man and his relations with fellow man and God, her Son.

If we end this chapter with this thought alone, we shall have made a point, we hope. Go through the history of Christian art, whether that art be architecture, painting, sculpture, or letters — and you will find that Our Lady emerges progressively as the Lady of Reality. Legends did and do still cluster about her, but even these legends have a base in the impulses, the needs and aspirations of the common people. And as literature draws away from the pure myth, from the saga and the heroic epic, it draws nearer and nearer to a realism that first appealed to the Christian world through the cathedrals and their windows and statuary and then got caught in the homely tones of the mystery and miracle plays. From them, in turn, rose the secular literature of the late Middle Ages and the Renaissance in "popular" language, and to that development Our Lady contributed. This is a thought that has not thus far engaged the attention of scholars, but it is a thought with which, without being able to defend it in all its ramifications, I would like to conclude this chapter on Our Lady in literature.

OUR LADY IN MUSIC

by JOHN C. SELNER, S.S.

HILE we realize with joy that the Marian year, 1954, successfully called the attention of the world to the glories of Our Blessed Lady, and that, as a result, she has received from men the most concerted and co-ordinated praise that has ever been given her, we cannot forget that the Church is only giving voice to essentially the same sentiments which were expressed toward her almost from the first attempts at organized Christian worship.

I. OUR LADY IN EARLY LITURGY

The era of persecution left little opportunity for the embellishment of ritual; then it was a question of survival and dogged apostolic efforts to make the faith known. The stories of the Annunciation, Birth of our Lord, His public life, the fulfillment of ancient prophecies, the Crucifixion, Resurrection, and the Coming of the Holy Spirit, were used as data to back up the doctrines of the Trinity, the Incarnation, and the Redemption which were the main preoccupations in the instructions given during the apostolic age. But in connection with all these events the place of the Mother of Our Savior was often alluded to, and very early begot a devotion towards her which sprang into metrical poem and song. Our effort therefore, will be to indicate, as specifically as may be, the idealistic expressions of praise which have been offered to Our Lady throughout the centuries by means of texts which were put to music.

Speculations about the music to which these texts or poems may have been set would only lead us off into a rather clumsy repetition of the little that is known about the singing in the early Church. There is only questionable validity in going beyond the commonly accepted belief that divine services in the first two or three centuries of the Christian era were solemnized mainly by psalmodic recitations based on scales and tonalities of Greek and Jewish origin. Modern treatises of music history have given us as scientific a development of this probability as the scarcity of ancient data and the non-existence of a system of musical notation would presently allow.¹ However, it may be legitimate to infer that with the gradual co-ordination of the liturgy some of the music for divine services took on a more ornate form, likely in the manner of embellishments at increasingly frequent junctures in the straight recitatives. Perhaps by the time of St. Ambrose, fourth-century Bishop of Milan, the iambic dimeters which he composed for devotional purposes fell more or less naturally into melodic formulae not unlike the Gregorian hymnody with which we are familiar today. Some efforts, not entirely convincing, have been made to recast such tunes from the substrata of the more ancient Gregorian repertoire.² It was many centuries before metrical hymns found their way into formal Christian worship. The Mass, of itself, was not liturgically organized to admit of the versification of texts; tropes and sequences were gradually added to the discursive texts more or less as medieval amplifications and excrescences, most of which were wisely abolished by St. Pius V in the sixteenth century.³

The Canonical Hours which lend themselves easily to the use of metrical poems did not become a part of the Roman liturgy until probably the twelfth or thirteenth centuries,⁴ so that much of the poetry which accumulated in the early ages was relegated to private use or informal religious gatherings. The solemn liturgical worship in both the East and the West was accompanied mostly by non-metrical texts and passages from Scripture or by a series of invocations and responses. In all of these latter forms there is evidence enough that Our Lady was mentioned and honored from the beginning.

II. DOGMATIC THEMES

Doctrinally, the first of Mary's glories in the early days of Christianity was her virginity coupled with her maternity. The Council of Ephesus (A.D. 431) would have given considerable impetus to devotion for the divine motherhood and, in fact, the suppression of the Nestorian heresy gave

---

¹ Cf. E. Dickerson, *Music in the History of the Western Church* (London, 1902); G. Reese, *Music in the Middle Ages* (New York, 1940); P. H. Lang, *Music in Western Civilization* (New York, 1941).

² Cf. G. M. Dreves, S.J., *Aurelius Ambrosius* (Freiburg, 1893), p. 111.

³ Cf. A. Fortesque, *The Mass. A Study of the Roman Liturgy* (New York, 1937), p. 205 ff.

⁴ Cf. J. Braun, *Liturgisches Handlexikon*, 2nd ed. (Regensberg, 1924), p. 121. It should be recalled that the monasteries were observing the canonical hours centuries before they were made a part of the Roman liturgy. In that respect a good number of Marian hymns were current and regularly used.

occasion to sermons and panegyrics on the Annunciation.[5] Hilary of Poitiers († 367), considered by Gerbert[6] as the first writer of a hymn in the Latin language, tells us of Gabriel's message and reminds us of a "marvel never seen before, a virgin mother."[7] The hymns of St. Ambrose († 397) and those of his era give constant emphasis to the same doctrine and glorify the Virgin who alone was Mother and Maid.[8] Many ascetical sentiments expressed about the Blessed Virgin in the hymns of this time may have had their inspiration from St. Ambrose's treatise *De virginibus*. Sedulius (fifth century) is author of a Christmas hymn, *A solis ortus cardine*, which seems to represent an expansion of the tributes offered to Our Lady. He opens with a greeting to Christ the Lord, born of the Virgin Mary, in whose chaste, maternal bosom a heavenly grace had entered, and whose virginal womb bore secrets undreamed of. The mansion of her modest breast suddenly becomes the temple of God; unsullied and not knowing man, she conceived in her womb a Son as Gabriel had predicted, and the Baptist, still unborn, recognized from the womb of his own mother.

III. FIRST COMPOSITIONS AND FEASTS

Venantius Fortunatus (530-601) seems to have been the first to write a hymn devoted exclusively to the Blessed Virgin, *Quem terra, pontus, sidera*. It is panegyrical in spirit and the author uses expressions which indicate a transition from the more factual, narrative style of hymn to the openly devotional, picturesque, and even emotive manner of expression; the latter spirit seems to have become, from this time on, the accepted purpose for writing in rhyme and meter. We now encounter terms such as *beata, gloriosa, benedicta*, etc. Encomiums such as *regis alti janua, aula lucis fulgida*, are suggestive of the future Litany of Loretto. Fortunatus, whose style seems to have set the standard for devotional poetry in honor of the Blessed Virgin, is the author of the famous Passiontide hymn, *Vexilla Regis prodeunt*. He seems to have composed a great number of

---

[5] Cf. F. Cabrol, art. *Marie, Mère de Dieu*, in Dictionnaire d'Archéologie Chrétienne et Liturgie, Vol. 10[2], Col. 2035.

[6] Cf. M. Gerbert, *De cantu et musica sacra*, Vol. 1 (Typis San-Blasianis, 1774), p. 80.

[7] *Hymnum dicat turba fratrum*, lines 11-13; cf. J. S. Phillimore, *The Hundred Best Latin Hymns* (London, 1926), p. 3.

[8] *Jesu, corona virginum;* cf. M. Britt, O.S.B., *The Hymns of the Breviary and Missal* (New York, 1924), p. 339.

religious verses, most of which have been lost.[9]

Feasts of Our Lady were not numerous in Rome until after the seventh century.[10] At first they were importations from the Eastern Church, which after being established in Rome were finally accepted by the Gallican Church when it adopted the Roman Liturgy. Rome kept the octave day of the Nativity with special attention to the Blessed Virgin; the feast of the Circumcision, as we now know it, was not of Roman origin, but on January 1, the stational church being St. Mary *ad Martyres,* the liturgical texts indicated and emphasized the inevitable connection of Our Blessed Lady with the birth of Christ. The feast of the Purification seems to be the first which was specifically dedicated to the Mother of Our Saviour. One of the texts for that feast may have been an Eastern form of the *Ave Maria* which dates back to A.D. 600. There is a translation of it which reads like this: "Hail Mary, endued with grace, the Lord is with thee; blessed art thou amongst women and blessed is the fruit of thy womb, because thou didst conceive Christ, the Son of God, the Redeemer of our souls."

The Annunciation is also mentioned by the first half of the seventh century as an established feast, and the festival may have been observed in Ephesus as early as the fifth century, and even then it may have come thither from certain monastic churches in Palestine. So that while the Purification is the oldest of the Marian feasts observed at Rome, the Annunciation may have been the earliest of such observances in the Eastern Church.

By the time of the Council of Trullo (692) four festivals are mentioned, namely, the Purification, the Annunciation, and two commemorations which celebrated the Nativity of Our Lady and her Assumption (*Dormitio*).[11] The Mass texts had by this time much the same order we are familiar with today: introit, gradual, offertory, and communion verse. For the original feast of January 1, the Introit was *Vultum tuum deprecabuntur omnes divites plebis,* which is verse 13 of Psalm 44. At a very early date this psalm was used in an accommodated sense for the Blessed Virgin, and while a number of its verses have been shifted to the Common of Virgins, several of them are still reserved for the feasts from the Common of the Blessed Virgin. It is an interesting fact that the inspiration for the use of *Vultum tuum* may have come from a picture in the catacomb of St.

---

[9] Cf. J. Julian, *Dictionary of Hymnology* (London, 1892), p. 383.

[10] Cf. Cabrol, *art. cit.,* Col. 2038.

[11] Cf. L. Duchesne, *Christian Worship* (London, 1923), pp. 269-275.

Callistus which represents Our Lady with the Child Jesus in her arms receiving homage from richly dressed people offering presents.[12]

IV. GREGORIAN MUSIC

A considerable library of Gregorian music has grown up around the Mass and Office texts used in honor of Our Lady. The actual age of the music itself will always be a matter of conjecture, no doubt. But by the time of St. Gregory the Great (590-604) the work of compiling existing chants had so far progressed that the music sung on later Marian feasts was in the general modal character of all the music used in the liturgy. It is quite possible that we still sing excerpts of music which was used on the original festivals in honor of the Blessed Virgin.

Here and there through Advent we come upon texts and music celebrating Our Lady's part in the Nativity. One of the finest pieces of Gregorian repertory is the *Ave Maria* which is used as an offertory verse for the Fourth Sunday of Advent and also for the feast of the Annunciation. The communion verse for the same Sunday reminds us that a Virgin shall conceive and bring forth a Son. These melodies as we now have them are likely twelfth century adaptations of more ancient tunes.[13]

The feasts of Our Lady throughout the year have brought into being many excellent chant melodies which are described in detail by Dom Joseph Gajard, choirmaster of Solesmes.[14] Other melodies fall into the modal channels more or less regularly and are, for the most part, admirably adapted to the Marian texts. As the form of the canonical hours gradually became set, the greater volume of Gregorian music was applied to responsoria in Matins of the Divine Office and, above all, in the

---

[12] Cf. A. Gastoué, *Les origines du chant romain* (Paris, 1907), p. 48.

[13] Cf. J. Gajard, O.S.B., *Notre Dame et l'art grégorien*, in *Maria. Études sur la Sainte Vierge*, ed. H. du Manoir, S.J., Vol. 2 (Paris, 1952), p. 341 ff. It may be well, at this point, to refer the reader to the excellent album of chants released by the monks of Solesmes through *London ffrr*, containing a 36-page descriptive booklet with commentary by Dom Gajard. The set consists of five 12 inch LP recordings offering a great number of Marian chants and hymns sung with admirable artistry by the monks. Among the outlets through which this set may be obtained is the Gregorian Institute of America, 2132 Jefferson Avenue, Toledo 2, Ohio. Many other Marian chants may be found likewise in *Gregorian Chants* by the choir of Our Lady of Consolation Abbey, Stanbrook, Worcester, England. The set has two 10 inch LP records. Address Gregorian Institute, etc., as above.

[14] Cf. Gajard, *loc. cit.*

antiphons for the psalms. The latter serve as elegant little vignettes in praise of Our Lady's many glorious prerogatives and titles. The *Salve, Sancta Parens* which is used as the introit in the seasonal Common of the Blessed Virgin and on certain specific feasts, is a text from the *Carmen Paschale* of Sedulius, fifth century poet,[15] and like many other such texts still in use for festivals of the Blessed Virgin, it represents an ancient cult of which our modern devotion to the Mother of God is the logical development and the faithful reflection.

With the introduction of metrical hymns as part of the Divine Office, the Western Church was given a large store of religious poetry in honor of Our Lady. Among the most popular is the ninth century hymn, *Ave maris stella,* used in the vespers for the Common of the Blessed Virgin. No doubt the sentiments expressed in the hymn are a contonization of similar ideas in previous texts honoring Mary as our patroness and protectress. Some authors attribute it to Fortunatus (sixth century) and all seem to agree that it antedates the tenth century.[16] The Vatican edition of chant assigns five different melodies to it, dating variously from the eleventh to the thirteenth centuries, with most of the manuscripts of those centuries still extant.[17]

V. THE MAJOR ANTIPHONS

Deserving of special attention are the antiphons to the Blessed Virgin which are sung after compline in the Divine Office. These are the *Alma Redemptoris* for the season of Advent until the Feast of the Purification; the *Ave Regina caelorum,* from Purification until Holy Thursday; the *Regina caeli* for Eastertide until Trinity; and the *Salve Regina* for the rest of the year.

Hermanus Contractus, a monk of Reichenau who died in 1054, is beyond doubt the author of the text of the *Alma Redemptoris.* It was very popular in England before and after Chaucer's mention of it in his *Prioress' Tale* of the famed Canterbury pilgrims:

> This little child, his little lesson learning,
> Sat at his primer in the school, and there,
> While boys were taught the antiphons, kept turning,
> And heard the *Alma Redemptoris* fair,

---

[15] *Art. cit.,* p. 370.

[16] Cf. Julian, *op. cit.,* p. 99.

[17] Cf. Gajard, *art. cit.,* p. 372.

And drew as near as ever he did dare,
Making the words, remembering every note
Until the first verse he could sing by rote.[18]

Two melodies are assigned in the Vatican Edition for each of these antiphons, the simple and the solemn tone. Their origins are hard to trace, though it is possible that the solemn tone for the *Alma Redemptoris* goes back to the twelfth century. The simple tones are all clearly a syllabic reduction of the solemn tones, likely having a much later date of composition.

The *Ave Regina caelorum* is surely a twelfth century composition, though its author is unknown.[19] It was introduced into the Divine Office, so we are told, by Pope Clement VI (1342-1352). Its general sentiment reflects expressions of such Eastern Doctors as Athanasius, Ephraem, and Ildephonsus. The antiphon is used during Lent and Passiontide to remind the faithful of Our Lady's part in reopening heaven and reigning gloriously there herself.

The *Regina caeli,* a joyous antiphon for Eastertide, is traced by most to the twelfth century also. It was used by the Franciscans in the thirteenth century and was put into the Divine Office by command of Pope Nicholas III (c. 1280). The solemn melody for it is found in manuscripts of the thirteenth century.[20]

Various authors have been named for the most popular of the four antiphons, the *Salve Regina,* among them Hermanus Contractus, author of the *Alma Redemptoris*. It is generally agreed, however, that the *Salve* is of eleventh century origin and it is most commonly ascribed to Adhémar, Bishop of Le Puy (1087-1098), who is said to have composed it as the official hymn of the crusade under Pope Urban II. The solemn melody for this antiphon is among the choicest in the whole Gregorian repertoire. It is sung in some monasteries, notably the Carthusians and the Carmelites, many times a day. Other religious orders use it each night before retiring. It may actually be the origin of our present service of Benediction of the Blessed Sacrament which grew out of the custom of singing these antiphons, especially the *Salve,* before the Blessed Virgin's statue every evening. At times the Blessed Sacrament was exposed to give the "Salut,"

---

[18] *Chaucer's Tales; Works,* ed. Walter Skeat (Oxford, 1894).

[19] Found in St. Alban's Book (twelfth century); Munich ms. (thirteenth century); Sarum Breviary (fourteenth century); York and Roman Breviaries (fifteenth century).

[20] Cf. Gajard, *art. cit.,* p. 373.

as it was called, greater solemnity. Martin Luther complained that the *Salve* was sung everywhere and great church bells were rung in its honor. It was especially dear to all who went to sea: Christopher Columbus and his men are said to have gathered each evening to entrust their venture to the guidance of the Mother of Mercy. The Dominicans have had the custom of singing it at the deathbed of a confrere when possible. It has been translated into almost every language of the Western Church and sung in various forms at almost any service in which the Blessed Virgin is to be invoked. Wherever Marian music is mentioned, the *Salve Regina*, both in its solemn and its simple melodic form, is entwined in the loftiest sentiments of praise and petition that men have ever expressed to the Virgin Mother in this vale of tears.

Much more could be said about the glories of Mary as expressed in Gregorian chant, but we have reviewed the chief points of history regarding it. We might add that the Gregorian *Kyriale* dedicates two Masses to the honor of the Blessed Virgin, namely Masses IX and X, called *Missa cum jubilo* and *Missa alme Pater* respectively, both of them among the most elegant music of the *ordinarium*.

As devotion to Our Lady of Sorrows began to spread we find an important poem, the *Stabat Mater*, which has been variously ascribed to Jacopone da Todi, O.F.M. († 1306), St. Bonaventure († 1274), and others. Fifteenth century English missals reflect its use, but it was not added to the Roman liturgy until 1727, when it took its place among the five sequences currently used in the Latin Church. The syllabic chant to which it is set cannot be dated with any certainty. It is rather broken melodically and represents little ingenuity from a musical standpoint. A more popular melody in the sixth mode has been set to the twenty stanzas of the poem and it is now better recognized by that melody than by the combination of second mode tunes to which it is set as a sequence on the Feast of Our Lady of Sorrows (September 15).[21]

The first hymnal in honor of Our Lady appeared in the thirteenth century under the title *Les miracles de Notre-Dame*. It contained about thirty pieces in all which were sung and copied for nearly two centuries. The author was a monk of Soissons, Gautier de Coincy.[22] While we are still in the age of chant, so to speak, it may be well to call attention to a

---

[21] Reese, *op. cit., p.* 192. Cf. E. Lapierre, *Comment les musiciens chantent leur psaume à Marie*, in *Marie*, Vol. 1, March-April, 1948, pp. 34-35.

[22] Cf. Reese, *op. cit.*, p. 216.

fairly large collection of Marian hymns by the renowned Dom Joseph Pothier, monk of Solesmes, which is entitled *Cantus mariales*.[23] A rather considerable number of older chants will be found in this collection with references to the sources of the existing manuscripts. There are, however, many chants of recent origin. No doubt the vast labors of the Solesmes monks in the atelier of the monastery have brought to light many corrections for the out-of-print edition of *Cantus mariales,* and one might wish a new edition could be published for both academic and practical purposes.

VI. POLYPHONIC ERA

The history of Marian music changes with the polyphonic era. Guillaume de Machaut, born about 1300, is said to have written the first complete Mass in polyphonic style. It was called the *Messe Notre-Dame*. While its various parts depend for thematic inspiration on chants from the *Kyriale,* the very impressive treatment of the words *ex Maria Virgine* in the *Credo* give clearly the Marian emphasis he wished the Mass to maintain. This work was still being performed in the sixteenth century, and no doubt proved a worthy ancestor to the monumental achievements of the later polyphonists, including Palestrina.[24]

The beginnings of polyphonic efforts in the Netherlands are linked with the names of John Dunstable († 1453) and his younger contemporary William Dufay († 1474). The former, an Englishman, was a typical representative of the growing art of polyphony both in England and on the continent; the latter was a connecting link between the Flemish School and that of the Netherlands. All of the polyphonic composers of this era, as well as those of the second Netherlands School, headed by Joannes Ockeghem,[25] and illuminated by his pupil, Josquin de Prés († 1521), took a great deal of thematic material for their Masses and motets from the chants in honor of the Blessed Virgin, and perhaps it may be safely said that their efforts at composing church music in the new style depended in large measure on liturgical texts from the Masses and Office for feasts of Our Lady. The four great Marian antiphons, sung at the end of the Divine Office, were apparently very popular as a source of inspiration for new compositions.

---

[23] Paris, 1903.

[24] Cf. Reese, *op. cit.,* p. 357.

[25] Cf. E. Krenek, *Joannes Ockeghem* (New York, 1953).

Palestrina († 1594) with his contemporaries, Orlando di Lasso († 1594) and Victoria, the Spaniard († 1613) who had formed an intimate friendship with Palestrina, and was the first musician to set to music all the hymns of the liturgical year[26] — these are the three great names among a host of lesser composers in the golden age of polyphony.

Joannes Petrus Aloysius Praenestinus, *"Musicae Princeps,"* as Palestrina was designated on his epitaph in St. Peter's, composed ninety-three Masses, and one hundred and thirty-nine motets, Lamentations, Offertories, *Magnificats,* and Vesper-psalms. Of this enormous output of masterpieces, there are at least fifteen Masses specifically dedicated to the Blessed Virgin under various titles, probably the finest and the most famous of which was the *Missa Assumpta est Maria* for six voices. About thirty-five of his motets are composed in honor of Our Lady, and he seemed to have a special predilection for the *Salve Regina* for which there are three or four different settings.[27] Besides, there are several hymns, Offertories, Litanies of the Blessed Virgin, and thirty-five *Magnificats,* each based on one of the Gregorian modes.

Orlando di Lasso († 1594) was composer of more than two thousand works, of which about two thirds were sacred music, including about one hundred *Magnificats.* What Orlando was for the Netherlands School, Tomás de Victoria was for the Spaniards. The glorious *Ave Maria,* based on the Gregorian intonation, will carry his name all through time.

VII. THE CHANGE IN MUSICAL ART

Musicians will argue endlessly whether or not compositions for the choral art reached their greatest sublimity during the golden age of polyphony or since. But with Monteverdi († 1643) we witness the most important shift in the art of music that history will ever record: it changed from an ecclesiastical art with imitations in secular uses to a secular art with more and more ecclesiastical uses. One of the reasons was that while the choral concepts of the great polyphonists reached the noblest and most ecstatic heights, they were, nevertheless, cool and emotively unexpressive; they had an oratorical appeal and were perfect from the point of view of sheer vocality, but they made no attempt, nor were the masters quite aware that they could make any attempt, to be representative of feeling, as such. This device Monteverdi discovered; and

---

[26] *Hymni totius anni secundum S. Romanae Ecclesiae consuetudinem* (Romae, 1581).

[27] Cf. H. Coates, *Palestrina* (New York, 1938), appendix B.

it made him father to the opera and the symphony; it brought about a change in the general concept of musical function. Now the interest began to develop in a union between music and words (*stile espressivo*) which was to become in succeeding generations one of the chief preoccupations of musical composers. In the drama, music was brought in to enhance the imitative effort (*stile rappresentativo*), and both of these notions of the function of music mightily affected the music destined for religious use.

At any rate, Claudio Monteverdi, the illustrious Venetian musician, chapel-master of St. Mark's, was also a polyphonist and wrote much of his music for the Church on the basic principles of polyphony, being still aware, perhaps, that the style he espoused for secular music had a character distinct from the music of worship.

Nevertheless, there were vast embellishments even in his music for the Church. His *Vespers of the Blessed Virgin* is written for six voices and six instruments which contribute something of a dramatic, if not profane, character. His *Magnificat* for seven voices and six instruments offers an astounding variety in which solos alternate with the choir. The *Salve Regina* for two voices, admittedly beautiful, gives the effect of a love duet, and another *Salve* for one voice approaches the operatic aria. Here we must begin to recognize the definite break between medieval music and the age of baroque styles which developed in the seventeenth and the eighteenth centuries.[28] Representative names in this transition are those of the Roman masters, Carissimi († 1674) and Rossi († 1653), who brought a great deal of flexibility and tenderness into their music, and hastened, through their oratorios and cantatas, the use of the *stile rappresentativo* in compositions for the Church. As long as the liturgy of the Protestant churches remained in many respects like ours, Marian hymns continued to be in popular use, and music of the contemporary composers was often dedicated to texts in her honor, particularly the *Magnificat*.

VIII. MODERN TIMES

The divided choirs which gave so much delight to the Venetians fostered the acoustical idea of repetition and close musical development. The echo-form came to be known as the *concerto* style, whether it applied

---

[28] Cf. Dufourcq-Spycket, *Esquisse d'une histoire de la musique en l'honneur die la Vierge*, in *Maria. Études sur la Sainte Vierge*, ed. H. du Manoir, S.J., Vol. 2 (Paris, 1951), pp. 385-400.

to instruments or to choral offerings.[29] This greatly involved and brilliantly developed form found its true master in Johannes Sebastian Bach (1685-1750), though he was not recognized as such in his own time.

While he was choirmaster at St. Thomas Church in Leipzig, there came from his pen a *Magnificat* for voices, organ, and instruments, which was destined for Vespers of Christmas in 1723 at St. Thomas. Though unsuited for liturgical use in the Catholic Church, it represents well the seriousness of its composer and the artistic inspiration which could come to him from the contemplation of the Mother of Our Savior. Pergolesi, who died in 1736 at the age of twenty-six, is the composer of a *Stabat Mater* which, for grandeur of style and dramatic power, is typical of the best music of the period.[30]

By the time of Mozart's death in 1791, the secular style had so completely claimed the genius of the great composers that it was rare to find any of them preparing music of an essentially religious character. Though Mozart composed four litanies to the Blessed Virgin, a Mass in her honor, several motets, among them a *Regina caeli* and a *Magnificat,* he seemed far more preoccupied with the effect of the music than with the communication of the text as such. The same tradition was carried on by Joseph Haydn († 1809) whose *Stabat Mater* exhibits a flowery, orchestral concept with only a dramatic relation to the words.[31]

The *Stabat Mater* reached a typical climax in the profane treatment of sacred texts by the time of Gioacchino Rossini, the operatic composer (1792-1868). Produced during a long period of musical inactivity, Rossini's *Stabat Mater* will always serve as paradigm of the elimination of textual latencies in favor of entertainment music of a rather indolent and frivolous pattern.[32]

As a matter of fact, serious church musicians have sometimes questioned whether the musical delineation of the text of the *Stabat Mater* by Rossini should not be classified as "comic opera,"[33] so disparate is the music from the poem it was supposed to serve.

---

[29] Cf. Lang, *op. cit.,* p. 364 ff.

[30] Cf. Dufourcq-Spycket, *art. cit.,* p. 396. For further reference to this type of Marian music, cf. Guido Anichini and Cassiano da Langasco, *La Madonna nella musica,* in *Enciclopedia Mariana,* ed. R. Spiazzi, O.P. (Milano, 1954), pp. 689-699.

[31] *Oxford Dictionary of Music,* Vol. 3 (Oxford, 1902), p. 184. The same should be said for his *Salve Reginas* and Ave Reginas.

[32] *Ibid.*

[33] Cf. *The Catholic Choirmaster,* Vol. 6, October, 1920, pp. 122-123.

Probably the most popular Marian piece among English-speaking people, particularly in this country, is the *Ave Maria* of Charles Gounod (1818-1893). Based on the first prelude of Bach, and not originally conceived as an *Ave Maria* at all, it is a hybrid both as regards music and text. The story persists that it was written as a setting for a Lamartine love poem and dedicated, with that text, to a lady in whom Gounod had at least a passing interest. At any rate, the lady is supposed to have returned the piece to Gounod after substituting the text of the *Ave Maria*, which was in effect a disavowal of his amorous advance. Likewise, the celebrated *Ave Maria* of Franz Schubert (1797-1828) exhibits some disparity between text and music which indicates that it may have been written either for a vernacular paraphrase of the Angelic Salutation, or perhaps with no idea of a Marian hymn at all. The composer's extraordinary talent for song writing makes it very unlikely that he would have approved the present setting of the Latin words to his music. Nevertheless, his melodious style is too fascinating for many church musicians, and they would be strongly tempted to include this piece in their repertoire, no matter what the text might have been originally. Among Schubert's genuinely Marian compositions there are five *Salve Reginas* and two *Stabat Maters* which are seldom heard any more.

Johannes Brahms too (1833-1897) carries something of the same musical tradition into his *Ave Maria* for female voices, orchestra, and organ.[34] But in general, the romantic period offered little from composers in the way of genuine church music in honor of Our Lady or for any other truly devotional purpose. However, a reaction to this type of music began in Germany with the formation of the Cecilian Society under Franz Witt at Bamberg in 1868.

Franz Witt (1834-1888) was an eminent priest-musician, choirmaster of the cathedral of Ratisbon, who became convinced that something had to be done to restore church music to its functional place in the liturgy. The Society he founded for this end was given papal approval in 1870, and as a result, many sincere church musicians devoted themselves to the composition of Masses and motets worthy of divine worship. Their music while it attained a rather conventional style, was nevertheless respectful and, in some instances, reached a laudable standard of artistic achievement. Names such as Ebner, Goller, Griesbacher, Wiltberger, Singenberger, and Stehle are very highly respected still in choirlofts where

---

[34] Cf. H. M. Miller, *An Outline History of Music* (New York, 1947), p. 149.

appropriate church music is the rule. All of these men composed very impressive motets in honor of the Blessed Virgin, chiefly based on the vesper antiphons for the four seasons and the offertories of the Masses in her honor. Gradually, societies comparable to the Cecilian Verein, were founded in Italy, England, Ireland, Holland, and the United States, and musicians of these schools of composition have, for more than fifty years, set the better standards of church music.[35]

IX. CONTEMPORARY COMPOSITIONS

Contemporary musicians in this era of experimentation with the art of sounds have produced nothing noteworthy thus far in Marian music. But English hymnody used commonly in our American churches has been a mixture of good, fair, and very poor material. Regrettably, the better hymns are to a great extent unknown, and the worst achieve amazing popularity. The usual novena hymns currently used in this country are, for the most part, in the latter classification. The texts are generally poetic translations of the *Salve Regina* and the *Ave maris stella*. A few popular hymns come to us from Father Frederick W. Faber († 1863), but perhaps the most frequently sung Marian hymns are very poor from the literary and textual standpoint, most of them being very sentimental or aimlessly repetitious.[36]

However, as the result of ages of inspiration, the Church has an impressive repertoire of songs to Our Lady, and there is little doubt that the ever increasing devotion to the Blessed Mother of God in all her titles will serve as a strong incentive to the best musicians and poets to produce a music in our modern times which will not be too unworthy of her glorious dignity and of the love she deserves from us.

---

[35] Cf. K. Weinmann, *History of Church Music*, trans. from the German (Ratisbon, 1906), p. 169 ff.

[36] Further references to recordings of Marian music: RCA VICTOR, LM-6015 *History of Music in Sound*, Vol. 2 (Pre-Gregorian chant to early Renaissance). Available in set of two 12 inch records with Oxford University book of music. — CONCERT HALL SOCIETY, CHS 47, Josquin de Prés, *Ave Maria*, etc., one 12 inch record; CHS 1107, Machaut, *Mass of Notre Dame*, one 12 inch record. — PERIOD MUSIC COMPANY, P 513, Palestrina, *Magnificat*, one 12 inch record. See also record list given by Reese, *op. cit.*, p. 465 ff.

OUR LADY IN ART

by LAWRENCE A. BURKE, O.F.M.

 UR LADY is represented so often in the art of the past twenty centuries that her image alone would comprise almost a complete history of art. She is depicted in every age; on the walls of the Catacombs, in the mosaics of the Byzantine basilicas, in the sculptured portals of Romanesque and Gothic churches, on Renaissance and Baroque canvases, and in the painting and sculpture of the Moderns. It is not at all remarkable to a Catholic that Mary's influence was so profound and far-reaching. Concerning the Middle Ages when her influence reached its peak, Emile Mâle says: "Of all holy men and women the Virgin was the most honored and the most loved. Art exalted her above all creatures, and conceived her as an eternal thought of God. And the men of the Middle Ages loved the Virgin with a disinterested love — they did not beseech her incessantly for miracles. They conceived of her as a sublime idea, in which the soul and the heart may forever discover new wonders. Her purity in particular was the eternal subject of the solitary's conversation with himself. Womankind, fallen, fragile, and dangerous, stood forth perfect and spotless in the celestial essence of womanhood, worthy of infinite love."[1] The artist, in marble or mosaic, in pigment or in stained glass, always sought new ways to express that love.

Space permits only a general presentation of the principal images to indicate the influence that devotion to Mary had in each period.

I. CATACOMBS

The Catacomb of Priscilla, the oldest Christian cemetery of Rome, contains what is probably the earliest picture of Mary. The painting, an adoration of the Magi, dates to about the first half of the second century. This subject is represented no less than eighty-five times in early Christian paintings and sculptures; it is one of the most important scenes of the art of Christian antiquity. In the same place is another picture of Our Lady which is considered to be artistically one of the best pictures found in the catacombs. Before Mary seated with the Christ Child at her

---

[1] E. Mâle, *Religious Art from the Twelfth to the Eighteenth Century* (New York, 1949), p. 132.

breast stands a man dressed as a philosopher who points to a star above her head. The man probably represents the prophet Balaam. In other representations Mary is pictured as an Orant with her hands lifted in the ancient attitude of prayer and is sometimes found with the Good Shepherd or saints. These old and sometimes crude images began the iconography of the Virgin Mary.[2]

II. BYZANTINE

After the persecutions and when official recognition of the new religion was given by Emperor Constantine, Christian art came out of the catacombs. The invading barbarians threatened the Western Empire, and the emperor transferred his capital from Rome to the shores of the Bosphorus and renamed it Constantinople. The Byzantine Empire endured for a thousand years, and succeeding emperors built their great basilicas and adorned them with the mosaics that became the glory of Christian art.

Reaction to the heretic Nestorius, Archbishop of Constantinople, who denied the Divine Maternity, was evident in the art of the period. The Third Ecumenical Council at Ephesus (431) condemned the heresy. Following this, a multitude of icons or holy images were produced under the title *Theotokos,* Mother of God.

The Golden Age of Byzantine art began in the fifth century and lasted for three-hundred years. One of its greatest achievements was the church of *Haghia Sophia* or Divine Wisdom, begun by Constantine and rebuilt by Justinian. The great dome was described by a contemporary historian as "at once marvelous and terrifying. ... It is as if hung by a golden chain from heaven."[3] Working with tiny stones of marble, porphyry, and glass, the Byzantine artists adorned the walls with mosaics, so characteristic of Eastern art, on a gigantic scale. These mosaics, among the finest works of art ever produced, show Mary in a prominent place in many scenes from

---

[2] Cf. Anichini-Belvederi, *Maria "Mater Dei" nelle catacombe e nella basilica liberiana* (Roma, 1931); G. Belvederi, *La "Mater Dei" nelle catacombe di Priscilla* (Roma, 1954); M. Belvianes, *La Vergine nella pittura* (Novara, 1951); P. Buondonno, S.M.M., *La mariologie des catacombes romaines* (Nicolet, 1954); C. Cecchelli, *art. cit.,* pp. 67-75; J. Ferretto, *Vestiges du culte de la Sainte Vierge dans certaines fresques des catacombes,* in *Marie,* Vol. 3, No. 5, 1950, pp. 10-20; Hertling-Kirchbaum, *The Roman Catacombs and Their Martyrs* (Milwaukee, 1956); V. M. O'Shea, O.S.M., *The Most Ancient Picture of the Blessed Virgin Mary,* in *The Age of Mary,* Vol. 3, May, 1956, pp. 5-7; G. Sartoris, O.S.M., *La più antica pittura di Maria SS. La Madonna di Priscilla,* in *Marianum,* Vol. 2, 1940, pp. 109-113.

[3] Cf. *Proud Byzantium's Christian Treasure,* in *Life,* Vol. 29, No. 26, 1950, p. 57.

the New Testament.

Precedent determined the procedure followed in the decoration of Byzantine churches. Treatises on art specified not only the manner in which biblical scenes were to be depicted but also their location in the church. In the apse the most important figure was Christ represented as the *Pantocrator,* the All Powerful One. Sometimes the image of the Virgin seated upon a throne holding her Divine Child occupied this place in the apse. Scenes from the Old and New Testaments were set in chronological order in the church. The life of the Virgin was frequently portrayed. To the New Testament scenes of the Annunciation, Visitation, etc., the mosaic artists added many from the apocryphal gospels which allowed a more imaginative treatment. Frequently found in Eastern iconography is the "Dormition" or death of the Virgin, one of the twelve great Byzantine feastdays.

The Golden Age of Byzantine art ended in the year 726 when Leo the Isaurian ordered the destruction of all icons to discourage idolatry. In 787, however, the Second Council of Nicea formally decreed that images of God, His Blessed Mother, and the saints were to be venerated. This impetus resulted in a new flowering of Byzantine art, less formal and more naturalistic in treatment. Eastern Christendom remained the creator and custodian of great religious art until the capture of Constantinople by the Moslems in 1453.[4]

III. GOTHIC

In the West, the centuries that followed the destruction of the Roman Empire were not without high artistic achievement. The monasteries preserved the treasures of Western learning. Patient monks copied by hand the Bible and liturgical books, and decorated them with exquisite miniature paintings. These books gave the artists of the Middle Ages the models for the decoration of their great cathedrals.

The age of the cathedrals represents the triumph of the Christian faith in the West. Their soaring towers rose first in France, the center of

---

[4] Cf. S. Bettini, *Mosaici antichi di San Marco a Venezia* (Bergamo, 1944); E. M. Jones, O.S.B., *The Iconography of the Falling Asleep of the Mother of God in Byzantine Tradition,* in *The Eastern Churches Quarterly,* Vol. 9, 1951, pp. 101-112; G. P., *The Hodegetria Eikon, ibid.,* Vol. 5, 1944, pp. 277-284; V. Lasareff, *Studies in the Iconography of the Virgin,* in *The Art Bulletin,* Vol. 20, No. 7, 1938, pp. 26-65; M. Vloberg, *Les types iconographiques de la Mère de Dieu dans l'art byzantin,* in *Maria. Études sur la Sainte Vierge,* ed. H. du Manoir, S.J., Vol. 2 (Paris, 1952), pp. 405-443.

medieval culture, and later in all of Western Europe. The entire populace took part in their construction. Robert de Mont-Saint-Michel tells us, "Men and women were seen carrying heavy loads through bogs, singing and praising the wonders of God which were happening before their very eyes."[5] France had its masterpieces in Chartres, Rheims, Amiens, and Paris.

The high degree of perfection which sculpture in France achieved is seen in the portals of the cathedrals where the story of Mary's life is told with scenes of the Annunciation, Visitation, Nativity, the Adoration of the Magi, and the Passion. Traditional scenes such as the death of the Virgin in the midst of the Apostles and her triumphal ascent into Heaven were added to the scenes from the Gospels. The frequency of the images of the Virgin attests to the high place she had in that culture.

All the medieval cathedrals honor Mary, but Notre Dame of Paris in particular is her church. Four of the six portals are dedicated to her. In the two great rose windows she occupies the center. "In one the holy men of the Old Testament, in the other, the labors of the months are given their order in relation to her. She is the center towards which all things turn. Nowhere was the Virgin more devoutly loved; the twelfth century in the Saint Anne portal, the thirteenth in the Virgin portal, the fourteenth in the bas reliefs of the north side, glorify her unceasingly from age to age."[6]

What the cathedral with its sculpture and stained glass was to France, painting in the thirteenth century was to Italy. The genesis sprang from two great figures, St. Francis of Assisi and Giotto. The gentle Poverello, inflamed with the love of Christ and all His creation, prompted a new warmth and feeling in painting. The Florentine master, Giotto, who painted in Assisi the famous murals of the life of St. Francis, reflected the spirit of the saint in all his work. Paul Gay says, "Giotto discovered the life-value of a smile, the eloquence of a look, the weight of a tear."[7] The best preserved of his frescoes are in the Arena Chapel in Padua, where he painted many tender scenes from the childhood and betrothal of the Virgin, subjects so popular with Byzantine artists.

A great influence on the artists of the day was a popular book, the *Meditations on the Life of Jesus Christ,* attributed to St. Bonaventure but actually written by an unknown Franciscan of the thirteenth century. The

---

[5] *The Praeger Picture Encyclopedia of Art* (New York, 1959), p. 199.

[6] Mâle, *op. cit.,* p. 94.

[7] P. Gay, *Giotto* (Paris, 1949), p. 5.

imaginative scenes are designed to touch the heart rather than the intellect. It gave artists new material for the familiar scenes of the Annunciation, the Nativity, the Adoration of the Magi and the Passion. For the first time the Nativity is depicted with Mary kneeling before her Son.

The Virgin predominated in the thought of the sculptors of the French cathedrals and she occupied no less an honored place in Italian painting. Reverent and skilled portrayals of her are to be found in abundance. One painter in particular who expressed the praise of Mary with exceptional feeling is the Dominican friar, Giovanni di Fiesole, better known as Fra Angelico. Looking on the radiant and mystical world he painted, one may agree with Vasari that Fra Angelico "never took up his brush without first making a prayer."[8] With tenderness and majesty he tells again the glories of the life of the Virgin Mother. His fame spread beyond the walls of the monastery and he was eventually called to Rome by the Pope to decorate the Vatican. But it was for his brother friars in the convents of Fiesole and Florence and in the church of Cortona that he did his greatest works. Fra Angelico is of the full flowering of the Middle Ages, but he anticipates the glory of the Renaissance.

Contemporaneously with Fra Angelico and the Italian artists, a remarkable group of painters headed by the Van Eyck brothers flourished in the Netherlands. They painted on wooden panels in glowing colors and with great precision. The charming Madonnas by these Nordic masters, seated on a Gothic throne in a great cathedral or praying in the stillness of an immaculate room, are among the most exquisite of any age. They clearly resemble the miniatures of the illuminated manuscripts which inspired them. The fame of the Van Eyck brothers and their contemporaries Robert Campin and Roger van der Weyden reached Italy, where they were greatly admired. Two centuries later the styles of the Nordic and Italian schools were wonderfully fused in the Madonnas of the Flemish master, Peter Paul Rubens.[9]

---

[8] G. Vasari, *Lives of the Artists* (New York, 1946), p. 101.

[9] Cf. H. de Cardonne, *L'art marial du XIIe au XVIe siècle*, in *Compte rendu du Congrès Marial tenu à Fribourg*, 1902, Vol. 2 (Blois, 1903), pp. 479-484; Canon Van den Gheyn, *La Vierge de Van Eyck*, in *Mémoires et rapports du Congrès Marial tenu à Bruxelles*, 1921, Vol. 2 (Bruxelles, 1922), pp. 504-508. Specifically on the cathedrals, cf. R. G. Anderson, *The Biography of a Cathedral* (New York-Toronto, 1946); idem, *The City and the Cathedral* (New York-Toronto, 1948); A. Temko, *Notre-Dame of Paris* (New York, 1955); Henry Adams, *Mont-Saint-Michel and Chartres* (Boston-New York, 1933).

IV. THE RENAISSANCE

The Renaissance began in Italy in the fifteenth century with the great revival of interest in the learning of ancient Greece and Rome. Man began to displace God as the center of the intellectual and artistic universe. The new spirit was reflected in the arts by an increasing emphasis on secular and pagan themes, a trend perhaps best exemplified in the work of Botticelli. But even though the fervor of the Middle Ages was beginning to ebb, Mary still claimed the foremost attention of the artists. Everyone is familiar with the frequently reproduced Madonnas of the period, and the names of three of their great creators, Leonardo da Vinci, Raphael, and Michelangelo, are known to every schoolboy.

Michelangelo was the master of the High Renaissance and one of the greatest artists of all time. Painter of the magnificent frescoes in the Sistine Chapel and designer of the dome of St. Peter's Basilica, he nevertheless claimed to be primarily a sculptor and made several superb images of the Madonna and Child. His famous "Pietà" was so novel in its day that many of his contemporaries considered it heretical. He carved it when he was only twenty-three years old.

Raphael, probably the best known of all painters of the Madonna, was the creator of the "Sistine Madonna" and the "Madonna of the Chair." Of him it has been said: "Hardly any other artist has been so loved and cherished over the centuries. In him the connoisseur has found a degree of artistic perfection such as has seldom been attained; while the pious have found in his work an expression of divine gentleness and beauty."[10]

Only half a dozen paintings by Leonardo da Vinci have come down to us. Besides the well-known "Last Supper," he painted the "Madonna of the Rocks" and the even more beautiful "St. Anne, Virgin and Child."

In the sixteenth century, Venice, the romantic and wealthy city that linked the East and West, became as important as Rome as a center of painters. Its art, productive of sacred and profane works in equal abundance, is one of opulence and splendid color. Its greatest painters, Giorgione, Titian, and later Tintoretto, executed several masterful works that honor the Mother of God.

When the Reformation erupted in Germany and began to spread through the Continent, the forces of iconoclasm were brought to bear on sacred art. Luther and Calvin opposed the veneration of religious pictures. The Council of Trent declared in 1564, however, that "the images of the

---

[10] *The Praeger Picture Encyclopedia of Art*, p. 310.

Virgin Mother are to be kept, especially in churches, and due honor and veneration are to be given them."[11] The Reformers retaliated violently. Thomas Bodkin relates: "In 1566, the memorable revolt of the Image Breakers devastated the Netherlands. On the day following the great feast of the Assumption the mob invaded the cathedral of Antwerp and began an orgy of desecration by smashing to atoms the statue of the Blessed Virgin which a few hours earlier had been carried in solemn procession through the streets of the city. Before they left they had destroyed every one of the hundreds of pictures and statues in the building, with the single exception of the statue of the Impenitent Thief. Within six weeks they had swept like a tornado through every church in the country, burning, breaking and tearing up those works of art that had constituted their country's greatest claim to glory.

"The English Iconoclasts proceeded in more orderly, but even more efficient fashion. Under Edward VI, Elizabeth and Cromwell, official commissions sought out and systematically destroyed every object of religious veneration in ecclesiastical or private possession upon which they could lay hands. In our own days, a few things that they failed to discover, usually because they had been hidden away under coats of whitewash, have reappeared to testify to the wealth and wonderful quality of the religious art which embellished England during the centuries in which the nation took pride in England's title 'The Dowry of Mary.' "[12]

V. BAROQUE

It was inevitable that the Reformation should leave its mark upon religious art. But the Counter-Reformation, led chiefly by the Society of Jesus, resulted in a revival. Art, reflecting the feelings of the times, was no longer serene and unperturbed as it was in the Middle Ages but became ecstatic and charged with emotion.

Catholic Spain met the challenge with the towering genius of Domingo Theotocopulos, better known as El Greco. In 1577 he painted his famous "Assumption of the Virgin," one of many works in which he paid homage to the Mother of God. He was so generally admired in Spain that almost every church sought and obtained his work. His flame-like figures

---

[11] Council of Trent, sessio 25; *D.B.*, 986.

[12] T. Bodkin, *The Virgin and Child* (New York, 1959), p. 5. Cf. likewise A. Weis, *La Madonna nell'arte occidentale*, in *Mater Christi*, ed. G. Filograssi, S.J. (Roma, 1958), pp. 486-504; Vloberg, *art. cit.*, pp. 511-519.

glowing in phosphorescent colors have a strange and mysterious quality that belongs to another world.

This was the golden age for the art of Spain. Francisco Pacheco summed up its spirit with the statement: "Art has no other task than that of showing mankind the way to faith and to God."[13] It produced a Ribera and a Zurbarán, a Velázquez and a Murillo. The latter is well known as the painter of several notable versions of Our Lady's Immaculate Conception.[14] More and more this doctrine was occupying the mind of the Church, and Spain more than any other country defended this singular privilege of Mary which was declared a dogma of the Church two centuries later.

After the golden age of Spanish painting, the Virgin became less and less the favorite subject of the great artists. This was due to the increasing secularization of society as well as to the effects of the Reformation. Aristocratic society rather than the Church assumed the role of patron of the arts. Even that patronage died with the French Revolution.[15]

VI. MODERN PERIOD

Modern art began as a revolt against the Classicism and Romanticism of the nineteenth century. Its direction was determined mainly by Vincent van Gogh, Paul Gauguin, and especially Paul Cezanne, whose work opened up a whole new world of seeing and eventually led to the emergence of Expressionism, Surrealism, Abstractionism, etc. Although these three painters rarely turned to religious subjects, Paul Gauguin created a notable Madonna and Child entitled "Ia Orana Maria" in a South Seas setting.

Among the moderns of the twentieth century the exceptional Georges Rouault developed a highly personal religious art. Outstanding contemporary artists who have attempted the ancient theme of the Madonna in modern form are Henry Moore, Jacob Epstein, and Jacques Lipchitz. Ivan Mestrovic, more of a traditionalist, has created several notable religious works.

Regarding the expectation of future religious art, Jacques Maritain has written: "If amid the indescribable catastrophies which the modern world

---

[13] *The Praeger Picture Encyclopedia of Art*, p. 334.

[14] Cf. F. Rios, *Las Inmaculadas de Murillo. Estudio crítico* (Barcelona, 1948); I. Elizalde, *En torno a las Inmaculadas de Murillo* (Madrid, 1955).

[15] Cf. Vloberg, *art. cit.,* pp. 521-527; Weis, *art. cit.,* pp. 504-510.

invites there should occur a moment, however brief, of pure Christian springtime ... the reflowering of a truly Christian art, the resurrection to active life of mind and spirit may then be reasonably expected for the joy of angels and men. There is already some indication of such an art in the individual efforts of a few artists during the last fifty years, some of whom are to be reckoned among the greatest. But we must above all be careful not to elicit or isolate it prematurely, by an academic effort, from the main movement of contemporary art. It will emerge and impose itself only if it springs spontaneously from a common renewal of art and sanctity in the world."[16]

---

[16] J. Maritain, *Art and Scholasticism* (New York, 1949), p. 56. Cf. also G. Perocco, *La Madonna nell'arte moderna*, in *Enciclopedia Mariana*, ed. R. Spiazzi, O.P., 2nd ed. (Milano, 1958), pp. 743-751; M. A. D'Arcy, S.J., *L'art religieux en Angleterre*, in *L'art de l'Eglise*, Vol. 23, No. 1, 1955, pp. 5-10. Further literature: On the IMMACULATE CONCEPTION: V. Alce, O.P., *L'Immacolata nell'arte della fine del sec. XV al sec. XX*, in *Virgo Immaculata*, Vol. 15 (Romae, 1957), pp. 107-135; Anon., *La Inmaculada Concepción y la pintura española*, in *Estudios*, Vol. 10, 1954, pp. 217-222; P. Cancani, *La più antica icone dell'Immacolata in Roma*, in *L'Osservatore Romano*, Dec. 4, 1954; C. Cecchelli, *Note sulla più antica iconografia della Immacolata*, in *Virgo Immaculata*, Vol. 15 (Romae, 1957), pp. 199-203; M. Gómez Moreno, *La Inmaculada en la escultura española* (Comillas, 1955); F. de Hornedo, S.J., *La pintura de la Inmaculada en Sevilla (primera mitad del s. XVII)*, in *Miscelanea Comillas*, Vol. 20, 1953, pp. 169-198; Aug.-M. Lépicier, O.S.M., *L'Immaculée Conception dans l'art et l'iconographie* (Spa, 1956); M. Vloberg, *The Iconography of the Immaculate Conception*, in *The Dogma of the Immaculate Conception*, ed. E. D. O'Connor, C.S.C. (Notre Dame, 1958), pp. 463-506. On the ASSUMPTION: T. Bodkin, The *Assumption in Art*, in *The Furrow*, Vol. 1, 1950, pp. 517-522; L. Di Stolfi, O.F.M., *La morte e l'Assunzione di Maria SS. nell'arte*, in *Atti del Congresso Nazionale Mariano dei Frati Minori d'Italia* (Roma, 1948), pp. 163-193; M. Gavriloff, *The Dormition and Assumption of the Blessed Virgin in Slav Iconography*, in *The Eastern Churches Quarterly*, Vol. 9, 1951, pp. 113-119; N. Pérez, S.J., *La Asunción de Nuestra Señora en el arte*, in *Estudios Marianos*, Vol. 5, 1947, pp. 457-466. On the QUEENSHIP: E. Amadei, *La royauté de Marie dans la peinture*, in *Marie*, Vol. 8, 1955, pp. 531-532; G. Geppetti, O.S.M., *La royauté de Marie dans l'archeologie*, ibid., p. 530; P. Indekeu, *Maria-Koningin in de kunst*, in *Mariale Dagen*, Vol. 5, 1935, pp. 187-196; M. Lawrence, *Maria Regina*, in *Art Bulletin*, Vol. 7, 1924-1925, pp. 150-161; M. Lefrançois-Pillion, *La souveraineté de Marie dans l'art*, in *Souveraineté de Marie. Congrès Marial de Boulogne s/M* (Paris, 1938), pp. 436-440. On the NEW EVE: J. De Mahuet, S.M., *Le thême de Marie Nouvelle Eve dans l'iconographie chrétienne*, in *Bulletin de la Société Française d'Études Mariales*, Vol. 14, 1956, pp. 27-48. On these and various other Marian prerogatives cf. G. Fallani, *Interpretazioni artistiche del dogma mariano*, in *Enciclopedia Mariana*, ed. R. Spiazzi, O.P., 2nd ed. (Milano, 1958), pp. 751-758.

SELECT BIBLIOGRAPHY

A. Basquin, O.S.B., *Les peintres de Marie. Essai sur l'art marial (Bruxelles,* 1912); Birchler-Karrer, *Maria. Die Madonna in der Kunst (Zürich, 1941);* T. Bodkin, *The Virgin and Child (New York,* 1949); P. de Bouchaud, *Mosaiques de Notre-Dame (Paris,* 1954); J. Bruyère, S.J., *Marie dans la peinture chinoise,* in *Marie,* Vol. 6, No. 2, 1952, pp. 52-55; D. S. Cary, *Our Lady in Art,* in *The Marianist,* Vol. 49, November, 1958, pp. 26-31; Cassiano da Langasco, O.F.M.Cap., *La Madonna nell'arte,* in *Enciclopedia Mariana,* ed. R. Spiazzi, O.P., 2nd ed. (Milano, 1958), pp. 731-743; C. Cecchelli, *Archeologia e iconografia mariana primitiva, ibid.,* pp. 67-75; Card. C. Costantini, *Marie, la sainte muse de l'art chrétien,* in *Marie,* Vol. 3, No. 4, 1949, pp. 16-24; A. M. Dal Pino, *La Vergine nell'arte francese,* in *Marianum,* Vol. 14, 1952, pp. 276-282; R. de Fleury, *La Sainte Vierge. Etudes archéologiques et iconographiques,* 2 vols. (Paris, 1878); A. L. Delattre, *Le culte de la Sainte Vierge en Afrique d'après les monuments archéologiques* (Paris, 1907); G. Fallani, *Le interpretazioni artistiche del dogma mariano,* in *Enciclopedia Mariana,* ed. R. Spiazzi (Milano, 1958), pp. 751-758; J. Gajard, O.S.B., *Notre Dame et l'art grégorien,* in *Maria. Études sur la Sainte Vierge,* ed. H. du Manoir, S.J., Vol. 2 (Paris, 1952), pp. 343-382; R. Garrucci, *Storia dell'arte cristiana nei primi otto secoli della Chiesa,* 6 vols. (Prato, 1872- 1881); Ghéon-Zeller, *Mary the Mother of God* (Chicago, n.d.); B. Guegan, *Le livre de la Vierge* (Paris, 1943); E. M. Hurll, *The Madonna in Art* (Boston, 1898); *La Madonna e la donna nell'arte orientale* (Venezia, 1954); E. Mâle, *Religious Art from the Twelfth to the Eighteenth Century* (New York, 1949); C. P. Maus, *The World's Greatest Madonnas* (New York, 1947); D. T. O'Dwyer, *Our Lady in Art* (Washington, D. C., 1934); P. Pérez-Dolz, *Las Madonas de la pintura alemana* (Barcelona, 1940); L. Schreyer, *Bildnis der Mutter Gottes* (Freiburg, 1951); E. Tea, *La Vergine nell'arte* (Brescia, 1953); M. Vloberg, *Les types iconographiques de la Vierge dans l'art occidental,* in *Maria. Études sur la Sainte Vierge,* ed. H. du Manoir, S.J., Vol. 2 *(Paris,* 1952), pp. 485-540; E. Vogt, S.J., *O nome de Maria a luz de recentes descobertas arquelógicas,* in *Revista Eclesiástica Brasileira,* Vol. 1, 1941, pp. 473-481. Cf. also *Maria et Ecclesia,* Vol. 15 (Romae, 1960), entirely devoted to Mary and art.

OUR LADY AND THE PROTESTANTS

by KENNETH F. DOUGHERTY, S.A.

N RECENT years a great deal of ecumenical communication has taken place between European Catholics and Protestants on the subject of Our Lady, her mission, her privileges and titles. Among non-Catholics who have been sympathetic toward the Marian cult we may mention particularly the Anglican theologians E. L. Mascall and T. M. Parker, the German Lutheran H. Asmussen, and the French Reformed M. Thurian.[1] The work of these revivalists has been the object of serious study on the part of several Catholic theologians within the past decade.[2]

The preparations in connection with the forthcoming Ecumenical Council on the subject of Christian Unity promise to enrich our Marian literature in the field of ecumenism, for Mariology occupies an important place in contemporary ecumenical dialogue. This was evidenced especially on the occasion of the solemn definition of the Assumption, and also during the Lourdes centennial.

---

[1] E. L. Mascall, *The Dogmatic Theology of the Mother of God*, in *The Mother of God. A Symposium by Members of the Fellowship of St. Alban and St. Sergius*, ed. by E. L. Mascall (Westminster, 1949), pp. 37-50; T. M. Parker, *Devotion to the Mother of God, ibid.*, pp. 64-75; H. Asmussen, *Maria, die Mutter Gottes*, 2nd ed. (Stuttgart, 1951); id., *Maria, die Mutter Gottes, und die Lehre der evangelischen Kirche*, in *Liturgie und Lehrwort*, ed. by Th. Bolger, O.S.B. (Maria Laach, 1954), pp. 80-93; M. Thurian, *Ways of Worship. A Report of a Theological Commission of Faith and Order* (London, 1951); id. *Marie dans la Bible et dans l'Eglise*, in *Dialogue sur la Vierge*, ed. by P. Couturier (Paris, 1951), pp. 107-130; id. *Das Assumptio-Dogma*, in *Oekumenische Einheit*, Vol. 2 [3], 1951, pp. 240-255.

[2] Cf. e.g., C. Crivelli, S.J., *Notre Dame et les protestants*, in *Maria. Études sur la Sainte Vierge*, ed. H. du Manoir, S.J., Vol. 1 (Paris, 1949), pp. 677-693; J. Hamer, O.P., *Marie et le protestantisme à partir du dialogue oecuménique, ibid.*, Vol. 5 (Paris, 1958), pp. 985-1006; idem *Protestants and the Marian Doctrine*, in *The Thomist*, Vol. 18, 1955, pp. 480-502; S. Bonano, C.M.F., *Mary and United States Protestantism*, in *Ephemerides Mariologicae*, Vol. 6, 1956, pp. 369- 424; *idem Protestant Reaction to the Definition of the Assumption, ibid.*, Vol. 1, 1951, pp. 282-284; Y. M. J. Congar, O.P., *Marie et l'Eglise chez les protestants*, in *Bulletin de la Société Française d'Études Mariales*, Vol. 10, 1952, pp. 87-106; A. Bea, S.J., *Maria e i protestanti*, in *Enciclopedia Mariana*, ed. R. Spiazzi, O.P., (Milano, 1954), pp. 367-373; Th. Sartory, O.S.B., *Maria und die getrennten Brüder*, in *Gloria Dei*, Vol. 9, 1954, pp. 210-225; P. Palmer, S.J., *Mary in Protestant Theology and Worship*, in *Theological Studies*, Vol. 15, 1954, pp. 519-540.

In 1951 the report of the Theological Commission on Faith and Order discussed devotion to Mary in preparation for the World Conference at Lund. Representatives of Orthodox Christians, Anglo-Catholics, and Reformed Christians presented papers on *Ways of Worship*.[3] The Reverend T. M. Parker of University College, Oxford, England, regretted the Anglican break from the popular Marian tradition of the West. Echoing Newman, Parker observed that "... absence of devotion to Mary commonly goes with lukewarmness to her son."[4] Brother Max Thurian of the Reformed Church of France spoke of Catholic Mariology as "the most agonizing problem for ecumenical thought."[5] He criticized Catholic Mariology for putting Mary above the Church. He affirmed that "Reformed Theology wishes to keep Mary in the Church ..."[6] Thurian desires to introduce Mary into Protestant worship. He asks Protestants to honor the Mother of the Lord and invoke her aid in the communion of the saints.[7]

The pro-Marian character of these papers is indeed an exception to the general trend of Protestant doctrine and worship. The great majority of Protestants possess no interest in Mary; they are adverse to any veneration of Our Lady which they often regard as "mariolatry." Although many twentieth century Protestants no longer profess the confessional beliefs of the Reformers, they have retained certain protests against Catholicism, such as the refusal to invoke Mary's aid and to attribute any mission to her in the divine economy of salvation.

I. OUR LADY AND THE REFORMATION

Unlike the heresies of the East which were basically Trinitarian or Christological, the errors of the reformers center on grace and the Church. It is from these cardinal errors that the reformation assumed its anti-Marian character. Previous to the reformation the West had experienced the denial of Mary as the Mother of Jesus.

Gnostics in the second century, Manichaeans in the third century, and Albigensians in the Middle Ages contended that Jesus could not have

---

[3] Ways of Worship. A Report of a Theological Commission on Faith and Order (London, 1951), p. 531 ff.
[4] *Op. cit.,* p. 282.
[5] *Op. cit.,* p. 289.
[6] *Op. cit.,* p. 312 ff.
[7] *Op. cit.,* p. 317.

Mary as His mother because Jesus could not have real flesh. The flesh is evil.[8] The Gnostic, Marcion of Pontus, quotes the Scripture in proof of this fantastic thesis: that Jesus had no real mother because he said: "Who is my mother and who are my brethren?"[9]

Protestant reformers never denied that Mary was the mother of Jesus. Although they denied the role of Mary as a subsidiary mediator, they never held the Gnostic principle that Christ had no real body and consequently no real mother. This docetism was to rise in some of the sects allied to the Protestant heritage such as Christian Science, which affirms the Virgin birth but regards all matter as illusory and associated with evil. This would logically imply a denial of Mary, the mother of Jesus. The Mennonites also deny that Mary is Jesus' mother.

On the contrary, the sixteenth century reformers speak of Our Lady as the mother of Our Lord, truly Theotokos, Mother of God. Luther, Calvin, Zwingli, and Cranmer did not hesitate to give her special praise as the Mother of God. The Protestant Dr. Reintraud Schimmelpfennig has shown that there is Marian doctrine in Luther's Works. There is not the complete Mariology held by the once Catholic Luther, but certain elements of it remain after his separation from the Church. It is important, in evaluating Luther, to observe that he is not a systematic thinker.[10]

It is sometimes argued that the Protestant Luther had no devotion to Mary because the sovereignty of God so dominated his thinking that he had no room for Mary and the saints. An objective evaluation of Luther, however, demands that his positive as well as negative judgments about Mary be assembled from his writings.

Luther denied the title "Himmelskönigin" ("Queen of Heaven") to Mary because he thought that it derogated from Christ as our only mediator between God and men. Yet he never denied to Mary the title "Mother of God" which has for the most part disappeared from Protestant belief and worship in our times. At Wartburg the Protestant Luther eloquently proclaimed in his interpretation of the *Magnificat*:

> ... her dignity is summed up in one phrase when we call her the Mother of God; no one can say greater things of her or to her, even if he had as many tongues as leaves and blades of grass, as stars in heaven and sands on the

---

[8] Cf. G. Bareille, art. *Gnosticisme,* in *D.T.C.,* Vol. 6, Cols. 1434-1467.

[9] Mt. 12:47 ff.

[10] Cf. R. Schimmelpfennig, *Die Geschichte der Marienverehrung im deutschen Protestantismus* (Paderborn, 1952), p. 9.

seashore. It should also be meditated in the heart what that means: to be the Mother of God.[11]

Luther's reformed prayer book which appeared in 1522 retained the *Hail Mary* side by side with the *Our Father*. In the same year, however, in his sermon on the Nativity of the Blessed Virgin Luther admitted that Mary prays for him, but he said that she is not his consolation and life.[12] In 1527 he preached that no one should put all trust in Mary and give all service to her since this belongs to God alone. Mary, he said, belongs to the rank of the saints. The distinction between hyperdulia and dulia was for him a matter of words.[13] He claimed that it is not to be found in the Sacred Scriptures.

With great anger Luther rejected the role of Mary as mediator. At Cana, he said, it is shown that not Mary but Christ is the mediator.[14] He harshly observed that Peter is no better than the bad thief and that the Mother of God is no more than the sinner Magdalen.[15] Luther wrongly feared that the veneration of Our Lady would lead one away from devotion to God. He conceded that the Christian must honor the Mother of God, but in the right way.

Schimmelpfennig observes that Luther did pay honor to Mary until his death. He always preached on the Feast of Our Lady's Nativity.[16] He condemned those who would not call her the Mother of God. He always defended Our Lady's virginity before, during, and after the birth of Our Lord. He denied that she had other children, and condemned Helvidius who taught otherwise.[17] He affirmed the Immaculate Conception and in this he showed the influence of the Franciscan School.[18] It is not clear whether he held the bodily assumption of Our Lady, but he did not reject it in his works.[19]

---

[11] *Luther Werke*, Vol. 7 (Weimarer Ausgabe, 1883), p. 544 ff.

[12] Luther, *Evangelium von der Geburt Mariä 1522*, in *Luther Werke*, Vol. 10, p. 321.

[13] Luther, *Evangelium am Tage der heiligen drei Könige 1527, ibid.*, p. 368.

[14] Luther, *Evangelium am anderen Sonntag nach der Erscheinung Christi, Winterpostille 1528, op. cit.,* Vol. 21, p. 65.

[15] Luther, *Evangelium am 24. Sonntag nach Trin. 1526, op. cit.,* Vol. 10, p. 429.

[16] Cf. Schimmelpfennig, *op. cit.*, p. 18.

[17] Luther, *Vom Shem Hemphoras und vom Geschlecht Christi, 1543*, in *Luthers Werke,* Vol. 53, p. 640.

[18] *Ibid.*

[19] *Am Tage der Himmelfahrt Mariä, 1522, op. cit.,* Vol. 10, p. 268.

The first of the Lutheran confessional writings, the Augsburg Confession (1530), professed the teachings of the Council of Ephesus:

> ... the Word, that is, the Son of God assumed a human nature in the womb of the Virgin Mary, with the result that there are two natures, the human and the divine, inseparably united in the unity of the person, one Christ, truly God and truly man, born of the Virgin Mary.[20]

The Formula of Concord (1579), the last of the Lutheran confessional writings, gave the accurate profession of faith in Mary: "Hence she is truly *Theotokos,* Mother of God, and yet remaining a virgin."[21] Luther, the Protestant, thus retained certain Catholic beliefs concerning Our Lady: that she was the Mother of God, Ever-Virgin, that she was immaculately conceived, and he may have held the bodily assumption of Our Lady into heaven. However, he rejected any mediation on the part of Mary along with his denial of the Catholic doctrine of the communion of saints in heaven. He honored Mary but not in the sense of hyperdulia.

Calvin spoke of the Blessed Virgin as "the Mother of God."[22] Zwingli also spoke in this way. He explained that "it was necessary that Christ be born of a virgin, chaste, most pure. ..."[23] The English reformers, who were greatly influenced by Luther and Calvin, continued in the reformation tradition. In Article II of the Thirty-Nine Articles we read: "The Son ... took man's nature in the womb of the Blessed Virgin, of her substance."[24] Mary was still given the titles "Mother of God" and "Blessed Virgin" but the land once called "the Dowry of Mary" despoiled the Marian shrines in the time of Henry VIII, Edward VI, Elizabeth, and afterward in the iconoclasm of the Puritans.

The theology of the principal reformers, i.e., Luther, Calvin, Zwingli, Cranmer, retained the traditional teaching concerning Our Lady in her divine maternity and virginity. All the reformers were against ascribing any mediatorial role to Mary in the divine economy of salvation. They claim that they recaptured the scriptural meaning of the sovereignty of God and brought back the Church to the purity of the worship of the first

---

[20] Cf. *Die Bekenntnisschriften der evangelisch-lutherischen Kirche,* 2nd ed. (Göttingen, 1952), p. 54.

[21] *Ibid.,* p. 1024.

[22] Cf. *Corpus Reformatorum,* Vol. 45 (Breaunschweig, 1827), p. 35; cf. also Vol. 46, pp. 106-107.

[23] H. Zwingli, *Sämtliche Werke,* Vol. 6, Part 1 (Berlin, 1905), p. 205.

[24] E. Bicknell, *The Thirty-Nine Articles of the Church of England* (London, 1955), p. 74.

Christians.[25] They all regarded hyperdulia, the cult of the Blessed Virgin, as unscriptural.

II. CONTEMPORARY PROTESTANTS AND OUR LADY

The reformers established the foundations of the Protestant tradition which continued more or less in their denominations and in post-reformation denominations such as the Baptists, Methodists, Congregationalists, Adventists, and many others. Many Protestant denominations still retain the Apostles' Creed, but it cannot be judged from this fact that they believe that Jesus was "born of the Virgin Mary." There is an alleged democratic spirit in present day Protestantism, which in most of the denominations allows liberal interpretations of the Creed.

Some sects, such as the Unitarians, explicitly deny the divinity of Our Lord and the whole supernatural order. The divine maternity, the perpetual virginity of Our Lady, and all her supernatural titles and privileges are denied by Liberal Protestants, who are found in most of the denominations. In many of the contemporary denominations there are some conservative Protestants who, although they have no cult to Our Lady, affirm that she was the Mother of God and Ever-Virgin. For the most part, however, present-day Protestants (both Conservative and Liberal) deny that Mary is the Mother of God and that she was Ever-Virgin. They have wandered far from the teaching of the reformers on these truths.

Our study of *Contemporary American Protestant Attitudes toward the Divine Maternity* shows that out of one hundred ministers of seventeen denominations responding to the survey, sixty-three ministers denied the divine maternity of Our Lady.[26] Fifteen ministers did not make their replies clear. Twenty-two professed belief in Mary as the Mother of God. More than half of these ministers affirming belief in the divine maternity were Episcopalians.

The present day denial of the divine maternity arises from a denial of the divinity of Our Lord. Frequently it is difficult to obtain from ministers a clear reply to the question: "Is Christ divine in the same sense as the Father is divine?" Our survey showed a neo-Nestorianism current among

---

[25] Cf. L. Bouyer, *The Spirit and Forms of Protestantism*, tr. A. Littledale (Westminster, Md., 1956), p. 59 ff.

[26] K. F. Dougherty, S.A., *Contemporary American Protestant Attitudes Toward the Divine Maternity,* in Marian Studies, Vol. 6, 1955, pp. 137-163.

many of the ministers contacted.[27] Luther, on the contrary, was bitterly anti-Nestorian.

Protestant difficulties arise either from a rejection of tradition or at least from a misunderstanding of the meaning of tradition and the development of dogma in the Church. If a truth is not found explicitly in the Scripture, there is skepticism as to its religious value. This attitude is sometimes called "Fundamentalist."[28] Many Protestants still use the sixteenth century term "mariolatry" in describing the Protestant attitude to Catholic Marian cult.

A recent book by a professor of the Waldensian Seminary at Rome reflects these attitudes.[29] The English translation of this Italian work received wide coverage in the popular press as well as comments by scholars in America and England. It is a direct attack on Catholic Mariology viewed by a twentieth century Protestant scholar. Miegge is a Waldensian, which sect is nowadays largely imbued with Calvinism. He may be classified as an Orthodox Protestant with some Barthian sympathies. It is from this background that Miegge launches his attack on Catholic Mariology as Pelagian: the belief that man can save himself.

> What is important — and it is impossible to exaggerate the importance — is that the heart of the Catholic masses is orientated not toward an authentic manifestation of the divine but toward the "pure humanity" of the Virgin Mary. It must be said that by all the traditional religious canons this is the essence of idolatry. The worship of Mary is a comprehensive transfer in the psychological sense from the person of Jesus to that of his mother, taking over to her the sentiments of affection, trust and dependence.[30]

Miegge then addresses himself to the Catholic explanation that veneration of Mary redounds to the glory of her Son. He observes: "A burning devotion like the Marian has all the characteristics of a cult that is exclusive and jealous."[31] There are, of course, instances of excessive devotion to Our Lady among Catholics, but the Church condemns such exaggerations. The total rejection by Miegge of Mary's secondary role as a mediatress interceding with God for men, because she is a creature, is

---

[27] *Ibid.*, p. 144.

[28] This term originated in America in 1909 to describe a Protestant reaction to Liberal religious thought.

[29] G. Miegge, *The Virgin Mary*, tr. W. Smith (Philadelphia, 1956).

[30] Miegge, *op. cit.*, p. 183.

[31] *Op. cit.*, p. 184.

inconsistent with the truth that Our Lord *in* His sacred *human nature* is the Redeemer, the Word Incarnate, who saved us by His passion and death.

Miegge's attempt to explain the rise of Marian beliefs and practices from a Mediterranean cult, which remained foreign to the Northern countries, evoked the disagreement of an Episcopalian reviewer:

> I suspect the wistfulness of an Italian Protestant in the observation that "the Mediterranean cult of Mary remained foreign" to the northern countries which followed slowly and without enthusiasm and were decidedly freed from it at the Reformation (Miegge, p. 82). Whatever may be true of the last clause the rest of the statement is very doubtful. One thinks of northern France, which is not a Mediterranean country, covered with churches of Notre Dame, or the Feast of the Conception, which though of Eastern origin owed its popularity in the Western Church to the piety of Anglo-Saxon monks. ...[32]

There was much disagreement among Protestant scholars as to the validity of some of Miegge's criticisms. The Abbot of Downside, England, in an article in *The Tablet* records a Protestant scholar's reaction to Miegge's evaluation of St. Irenaeus' famous parallel between Mary and Eve. Miegge called the parallel an ingenious literary construction rather than a considered theological doctrine. The English Methodist scholar, John Lawson, the Abbot relates, says that we find in Irenaeus the idea of atonement as a victory achieved by Christ through obedience. Mary, he says, in her obedience makes a subsidiary recapitulating action analogous to Christ's obedience. Lawson calls St. Irenaeus, "the first theologian of the Virgin Mary."[33] There are many mistranslations in the English edition of Miegge's *Virgin Mary* which show further misunderstandings of Catholic doctrine and cult of Our Lady. Monsignor George W. Shea has presented a detailed study of these errors.[34] The foreword to *The Virgin Mary* was written by the former moderator of the Presbyterian Church in the U. S. A. and president of Princeton Theological Seminary, John A. Mackay. His charges that Our Lady, according to the Catholic Church, is

---

[32] Rev. E. R. Hardy, *The Chosen Instrument*, in *The Living Church* [Milwaukee], June 3, 1956, p. 9.

[33] The Abbot of Downside, *The Church and Our Lady*, in *The Tablet* [London], Vol. 207, April 28, 1956, p. 397.

[34] G. W. Shea, *Triple Anti-Marian Fiasco*, in *The Marianist*, Vol. 47, June, 1956, pp. 3-6, 31; cf. also E. R. Carroll, O.Carm,, *A Waldensian View of the Virgin Mary*, in *The American Ecclesiastical Review*, Vol. 135, December, 1956, pp. 380-397.

"the fulfillment of the Trinity" and that she is "Christ's substitute in the world"[35] are figments of a most imaginative antagonist.

These misstatements of the Church's position on true devotion to Mary are reminders to the Catholic apologist of the immense misunderstanding still current among many Protestants in America and Europe. There is a need for communication between Catholics and Protestants that Protestants may be informed of the true role of Mary in the Church. Many Anglicans, who have made such contact, disdain the imaginative attacks made on Our Blessed Mother by present day antagonists. There is a great deal of ecumenical work required in this area. The opportunities for such a confrontation are perhaps better now than at any time in the past.

Many contemporary Protestants are far removed from the Catholic tradition. They have departed from the vestiges of Catholic thought retained by the reformers. Paul Tillich of Harvard, for example, denies not only that Mary is the Mother of God but also that she is the Mother of Christ. In his system Jesus is only a man, who reveals God to man. In his opinion, Mary has no place in Protestantism. She is for him a symbol which has lost meaning in the concrete circumstances of Protestantism generally taken.[36]

III. THE CONTEMPORARY PROTESTANT MARIAN REVIVAL

It is possible to speak of a Marian "revival" in the beliefs of some Protestants of our times. This is especially true of Anglo-Catholics. Ever since the Oxford Movement there has been a growing interest in the Mother of God and her role in the divine economy of salvation among many prominent Anglican divines who have influenced ways of worship in some Anglican congregations. This trend was championed by the contemporary of Newman, Edward Pusey (1800-1882), who was well read in the Fathers of the Church. He accepted the Catholic doctrine on the divine maternity, Mary's perpetual virginity and sanctity, and found no difficulty in the Immaculate Conception. Pusey, however, believed that Rome put Mary on a level with Our Lord and made her office of intercession co-extensive with her Son's. In his *Letter to Pusey*, Newman shows that devotion to Mary is a consequence of her dignity, her

---

[35] Miegge, *op. cit.*, p. 8.

[36] P. Tillich, *Systematic Theology*, Vol. 1 (Chicago, 1951), p. 128.

grandeurs, her sanctity.[37] Gradually Anglo-Catholics have come to a devotion to Our Lady, which is still developing in their congregations.

Mascall, of Christ Church, Oxford, observes that devotion to Mary was not always characteristic of Anglicans and that today it only occurs in a small portion of the Anglican Church.

> In actual fact, such references [to Marian devotion], while they exist, are lamentably rare, and are in quantity overbalanced by polemics which denounce devotion to Mary as popish, superstitious and even idolatrous. Only since the Oxford Movement have we realized that Christianity without Mary is a monstrosity and even so this recovery has as yet affected only a tiny portion of the Anglican Church and has received neither encouragement nor understanding from the ecclesiastical authorities in these islands. ...[38]

Mascall then relates some of the devotions to Mary that are practiced by some Anglicans:

> ... we have now in an increasing number of churches our Aves and Salves, our statues and candles, and our May processions in honor of the Lord's mother. The ringing of the Angelus has become a widespread custom and has even penetrated to some of our cathedrals, though it may be doubted that the authorities in question always encourage or indeed themselves know the forms of prayer which traditionally accompany it. The use of the rosary has become a normal part of the devotional life of countless Anglicans, and pilgrims flock in their thousands to our Lady's shrine at Walsingham as they did in the days before the Reformation. And what is most significant is that all of this has taken place ... simply because ordinary parish priests and their people have discovered in their own religious experience that devotion to Mary is the natural outcome and accompaniment of adoration of her Son.[39]

In a study conducted at Oxford, England, in 1957, the author surveyed the principal superiors of fifty-two Anglican communities.[40] These are part of the center of Marian devotion in the Anglican Church. Twenty-five replies were received. All the questions were not answered by every

---

[37] Card. J. H. Newman, *Mary, the Mother of Jesus* (New York, n.d.), Chapters 8 and 9, especially p. 80. Cf. also F. J. Friedel, S.M., *The Mariology of Cardinal Newman* (New York, 1928), pp. 345-384.

[38] Cf. E. L. Mascall, *art. cit.*, in the symposium *The Mother of God*, p. 48.

[39] Mascall, *art. cit.*, pp. 48-49.

[40] Cf. K. F. Dougherty, *Our Lady and Christian Unity*, a paper read at the International Mariological Congress in Lourdes, September, 1958.

respondent. There were no denials that Mary is the Mother of God. Twenty-two explicit affirmations were received. Sixteen affirmed that Mary was immaculately conceived. Fifteen affirmed that Mary was ever Virgin. Fourteen believed in the assumption. Eight held that Mary is coredemptrix and dispenser of all graces. Seven affirmed that Mary is Queen of Heaven. The survey observed a widespread devotion to Our Lady among the Anglican Religious. This devotion is in a state of development. The American Protestant Episcopal Church, although it is for the most part Low Church, also has an Anglo-Catholic trend, which is sponsoring a Marian revival in its congregations.

In Germany a Marian cult raised its voice in the Hoch-Kirche. Within the Evangelical Churches there is a High Church movement. In 1917, the Jubilee year of the Reformation, Pastor Löwentraut of Lausitz published an irenicon "One, Holy, Catholic (*allgemeine*) Church" in which he minimized the difference between classic Lutheran doctrine and Catholic dogma. The Protestant authorities at Berlin ordered it suppressed. In the same year Pastor Hansen of Schleswig drew up a new version of Luther's ninety-five theses setting forth conservative Lutheran views. Hansen's manifesto called for a return to the Catholic Church. He distinguished between "Catholic" and "Roman Catholic," and launched a "High Church Union," which published a periodical, *Die Hochkirche*, edited by Heiler. The restoration of the episcopacy was demanded on the basis of the apostolic succession. There was a plea for the elevation of the Eucharist in Lutheran celebrations of the Lord's Supper and the establishment of religious brotherhoods. In 1924 the movement divided. One wing professed an orthodox Lutheran position. The other sought contact with the Anglicans, Greek Orthodox, and Roman Catholics. This latter group issued *Una Sancta* which took the name *Religiöse Besinnung*. The High Church movement did not make great headway in the Evangelical Churches of Germany.[41]

Friedrich Heiler, who left the Catholic Church because of modernism at the turn of the century, is a leading figure in the High Church movement. Heiler observes: "One cannot stand in adoration before the Son of God without looking up in honor to His earthly mother."[42] Another High Churchman, G. Glinz writes: "Is Jesus the man who is God? If you take His divinity earnestly, then likewise His Mother in all her humanity

---

[41] Cf. A. Drummond, *German Protestantism Since Luther* (London, 1951), pp. 260-261.

[42] F. Heiler, *Jungfrau Mutter*, in *Hochkirche*, Vol. 12, 1930, p. 352.

is the Mother of God, as Ephesus calls her."⁴³ However, Glinz objects to Mary represented with a golden crown as Queen of Heaven. He says she should be praised as a humble maiden. For him dogma is unimportant. He holds for what he calls religious-biblical truth.

A far more important trend (*Die Sammlung*) in the Evangelical Churches is represented by Hans Asmussen, who endeavors to revive an Orthodox Protestantism against the spirit of the Liberal theologians. Asmussen is widely known for his celebrated little book entitled *The Mother of God*.⁴⁴ The publication of this work was undoubtedly responsible for his loss of the office of Executive President of the Evangelical Church in Germany. Asmussen has done much to make his Lutheran brethren think about Our Lady. Against the charge that Catholics pay too much homage to her, he has asked whether this is worse than paying her too little. He has pointed out that too often his fellow Evangelicals became aroused against the pope and yet remained silent when Harnack's works were recently reedited. Harnack does not believe in the divinity of Our Lord. Asmussen's wife, his son and daughter have become Catholics. He is still an Evangelical.

Asmussen labors to make Mary better known among German Protestants. He asserts that she must be given a greater role in Evangelical thought. He says: "One does not have Jesus Christ without Mary."⁴⁵ He admits that Mary is the Mother of God, and that in the world God and the saints form a certain unity. We see this unity in the Church. He accepts the mediatorial role of Mary, but rejects what he considers to be the Catholic doctrine of Mary's mediation, which he believes compromises the mediation of Christ. Mary is the first among the witnesses of grace. As Mother of God, she takes part in the divine economy of salvation. But she does not stand between Christ and us, as Asmussen believes the Catholic Church teaches. All Christian life, he says, has a sacerdotal element which includes the idea of mediation.

Asmussen points out that, although Mary is no longer among the living on earth, she lives in heaven and can intercede for us. It is not "human idolatry" to honor Our Lady. Elizabeth honors her in the Scripture.⁴⁶ What is more, the name of Luther occurs in the Feast of the

---

⁴³ G. Glinz, *Marientag*, in *Una Sancta*, Vol. 1, 1925, p. 150.

⁴⁴ H. Asmussen, *Maria, die Mutter Gottes*, 2nd ed. (Stuttgart, 1951).

⁴⁵ *Op. cit.*, p. 13.

⁴⁶ *Op. cit.*, p. 31.

Reformation, while greater saints of the early Church are passed over. Asmussen says that it would appear that between Christ and Luther nothing happened. This is indeed an unchristian attitude.[47]

In general, Evangelical devotees of Mary are not so advanced in Marian belief and practices as the Anglo-Catholic groups, particularly the Anglo-Catholic religious. There is a development of Marian devotion taking place in the new religious communities of the Lutherans: the Ecumenical Sisterhood of Mary in Darmstadt, Germany; the Sisterhood of Mary, the Mother of Jesus, in Sweden; the Little Ecumenical Sisters, and the Daughters of Mary, in Denmark; and the Congregation of the Servants of Christ at Oxford, Michigan.

In the Reformed (Calvinistic) Churches the name of Karl Barth ranks among their important international leaders. The Swiss theologian defends the Incarnation of the Son of God and the virgin birth against Liberal Protestant thought.[48] Barth has what he terms only a "Christological interest" in Mary and not what he labels "a mariological interest."[49] He writes: "The expression 'mother of God' applied to Mary is good, just, legitimate, and necessary in christology, on the condition that one reserves for it an auxiliary role."[50]

Yet Barth rigorously condemns any ministerial role of Mary in our salvation.

> Precisely in the doctrine and cult of Mary there resides par excellence the heresy of the Roman Catholic Church ... the human creature collaborates (ministerialiter) in his salvation, on the basis of a prevenient grace, consequently she [Mary] constitutes also very exactly the principle, the prototype and the sum of the Church Itself.[51]

Although one can find certain positive Marian beliefs in Barth, he himself disdains Mariology as "a diseased construct of theological thought."[52] A Mariological dogma in the Barthian point of view distracts from Christ. Mary is to be considered only from the Christological aspect, as pertaining to Christ. Barth falsely believes that Catholics have developed Mariology as an independent system. He would especially

---

[47] *Op. cit.,* p. 59.
[48] K. Barth, *Dogmatics,* tr. O. Wyon, Vol. 2 (Philadelphia, 1952), pp. 200, 185, 197.
[49] Barth, *op. cit.,* Vol. 2, pp. 153-154.
[50] Barth, *Esquisse d'une dogmatique* (Paris, 1950), p. 127.
[51] *Op. cit.,* pp. 132-133.
[52] Barth, *Dogmatics,* Vol. 2, p. 139.

object to the Marian title "Mediatrix of all graces" as if it were a challenge to the one mediator between God and man, the Lord. Barth shows a remarkable knowledge of Catholic Mariology.[53] He rejects the Liberal Protestant interpretation that Mariology developed from pagan sources.

> It is not to be recommended that we should base our repudiation on the assertion that there has taken place here an irruption from the heathen sphere, an adoption of the idea, current in many non-Christian religions, of a more or less central and original female or mother deity. In dogmatics you can establish everything and nothing from parallels from the history of religions.[54]

Barth rejects Mariology "... because it is an arbitrary innovation in the face of Scripture and the early church."[55] He contends that orthodox Protestantism will not allow creaturely co-operation in God's revelation and reconciliation; they are exclusively God's work.[56] Yet he believes in the Incarnation in which *the created humanity* of Our Lord shares in His revelation and reconciliation.

Among the Reformed Christians (Calvinists) the name of Max Thurian, founder of a religious community at Taizé lès Cluny in France, is important. Although critical of the extent of Roman Mariology, Thurian, unlike Barth, strongly favors the introduction of Mary into Protestant worship. He affirms that Christian theology is a theology of mediation. The Church is the minister of the Word and of the sacraments, the witness and intercession of the faithful. There is not an authentic mediation without the prolongation of Christ and His work in space and time. "The mediation of Mary and the saints is in Christ."[57]

It is important to recall the distinction between the Catholic and Protestant doctrines on grace. For the Catholic, grace transforms the interior man. For the Protestant, grace coexists with sin. Justification is a merciful decision of God to man the sinner. For the Protestant Mary was not immaculately conceived. Thurian says that Mary is "... a personage unique in history but she remains a sinful woman who has need of the

---

[53] *Op. cit.*, p. 141 ff.
[54] *Op. cit.* p. 143.
[55] *Ibid.*
[56] *Op. cit.*, p. 146.
[57] M. Thurian, *Le dogme de l'Assomption,* in *Verbum Caro* [Taizé lès Cluny], Vol. 5, 1951, p. 36.

pardon of her son."[58]

Thurian rejects what he believes to be the Catholic doctrine of Mary's mediation.

> Mary has taken the place of the humanity of Christ, she enjoys the role that the humanity of Christ ought to enjoy for our salvation.[59]

He speaks of Catholic teaching as "mario-christologie."

Thurian opposes the opinion of Barth and so many of his Protestant brethren that devotion to Mary derogates from the adoration of the Lord.

> Recourse to the intercession of Mary by no means takes away from the unique intercession of Christ. All true intercession is made in Christ Jesus.[60]

In a reformed prayer book, *The Divine Office for Each Day,* used at the Taizé Community of Thurian, the Feast of the Purification receives the name of "The Presentation of Our Lord Jesus Christ in the Temple"; the fifteenth of August is the Feast of Mary, Mother of the Lord; and the Annunciation is kept on the Tuesday of the third week of Advent.[61] Thurian is most careful to maintain the dependency of Mary on Our Lord. This is a sound principle of Catholic Mariology, which the Reformed churchman has yet to discover in the Catholic Church.

Especially critical of the dogma of the Assumption, he writes:

> The new dogma of the Assumption, now promulgated as being *de fide*, completes the removal of Mary from the conditions of the Church. There, indeed, Mary passes from the conditions of the Church and enters the level of eschatology. Her body has undergone glorification, has not known corruption, and has nothing more to wait for. She has passed through all the stages of the transformation "from glory to glory."[62]

One wonders whether Thurian realized that this line of reasoning might very well question also the bodily resurrection of Our Lord as

the removal of His sacred humanity from the Church. If no creature can stand between the Church which awaits the end and the Blessed Trinity, why should the created human nature of Our Lord be excepted? This is a difficulty in Thurian's reasoning. It is more or less characteristic

---

[58] Thurian, in *Ways of Worship* ... , p. 311.

[59] Thurian, *Le dogme de l'Assomption*, p. 30.

[60] *Ways of Worship* ... , pp. 318-319.

[61] Cf. Thurian, *Marie dans la Bible et dans l'Eglise*, in Dialogue sur la Vierge, ed. Couturier (Paris, 1951), p. 122.

[62] *Ways of Worship* ... , p. 312 f.

of all reasoning about Mary by Protestant theologians. For a Catholic there is no problem because Christ and Mary are glorified and are members of the Church, Christ the Head and Mary the most eminent member of the Church after Our Lord.

Conclusion

This introductory study of Mary and the Protestant indicates three trends among contemporary Protestants in respect to Our Lady: Marian Revivalists, Anti-Marian Protestant Conservatives, and Liberals. They may be classified in a descending order as they depart from the Catholic tradition.

The first is the Marian Revivalists of the High Church movements of Orthodox Protestantism. They are represented by E. Mascall, T. M. Parker of Anglo-Catholicism, F. Heiler, R. Schimmelpfennig of the Evangelical High Church, H. Asmussen, the Evangelical, and M. Thurian, the Reformed, of the Orthodox Protestants. Karl Barth, inasmuch as he defends the Incarnation of Our Lord, the divine maternity, and virginal conception against the Liberal Protestants, has a place among the Protestant defenders of Our Saviour and Our Lady. He departs from them in his denial that Mary plays any mediatorial role in our salvation.

The second trend is the Low Church, or Protestant Conservatives, to which the great majority of American Protestants belong. The advocates of this position affirm the Incarnation but they are not clear as to what they mean by the divinity of Our Lord. They deny Mary the title of Mother of God and mediatress of all graces because they reject any creature sharing in the divine work of revelation and reconciliation.

The third trend is Broad Church or Liberal. These neo-Gnostics deny the supernatural and, therefore, reject Mary's titles and privileges in the order of supernatural grace. The Unitarians as a sect represent this trend and it is also present in most of the Protestant denominations.

Protestant defenders of Our Lady very often use the same arguments as Catholic Mariologists: from the scripture, tradition, and sometimes the magisterium, which is especially quoted by Anglican papalists. The Council of Ephesus is often cited. These sources are sometimes possessed as vestiges of the Church that have remained in a denomination from reformation times or they are discovered anew by the Marian revivalist. Asmussen and Thurian are aware that they are going beyond the reformation tradition in their particular concern for liturgical progress in their denominations. Theological arguments which reflect a philosophical background appear to be generally lacking except in Mascall, who is an excellent Thomist philosopher.

The antagonists in contemporary Protestantism cannot be united by a common principle in their rejection of Our Lady. This is apparent from the inner contradiction of Conservative Protestantism as opposed to Liberal Protestantism. Conservative Protestants have certain common principles in their antitheses. They reject Our Lady in her titles and privileges because they say that worship is due only to the Sovereign Lord. In this respect they have an exaggerated Christocentric profession of faith, which allows for no subsidiary mediators. They claim to base their position on the Scriptures and the tradition of the early Church.

The Liberals commonly reject Our Lady because they reject Christ, the God-Man. He is for them the model man *par excellence,* but no more. Consequently, they must reject Mary, the Mother of God, and her other subsidiary titles and privileges, which are in subordination to the divine maternity in the order of grace. The belief that the Marian cult evolved in Mediterranean lands from earlier worship of goddesses is largely due to the Liberal interpretation of the evolution of cults in comparative religion.

Catholic apologists of Our Lady can learn much from the Marian Revivalists in their defense of Our Lady against the attacks of Conservative Protestants and Liberals. Very often the Catholic apologist finds himself *in terra aliena* with people who speak with strange tongues, when he enters the lists with Protestant critics of Our Lady. Our dogma texts equip us with ready answers for the *novatores,* Lutherans of Martin Luther's age, and Calvinists of Calvin's times, or the Anglicanism of the Elizabethan period. These *novatores* are about as novel today as the crossbow.

Protestantism has come a long way since the time of the reformers. Luther, who defended the Mother of God, Mary Ever-Virgin, would find himself in strange company among many contemporary Lutherans. The twentieth century denominations must be studied as living phenomena in our age.[63] The Marian revivalists, who are themselves Protestants, are

---

[63] Cf. K. F. Dougherty, S.A., *Seminary Study of American Protestantism,* in *The American Ecclesiastical Review,* Vol. 135, 1956, pp. 313-322. Further references: J. Amstutz, *Die Verehrung Marias vom freien Protestantismus gesehen,* in *Eine Heilige Kirche,* 1955/56, fasc. 1, pp. 37-42; P. Schäfer, *Marienverehrung in der anglikanischen Kirche,* ibid., pp. 16-20; O. Schröder, *Die Diskussion über die wahre Marienverehrung in der römisch-katholischen Kirche von heute,* ibid., pp. 42-60; H. D. Béchaux, O.P., *La Mère entre les frères séparés,* in *La Vie Spirituelle,* Vol. 84, January, 1951, pp. 17-21; G. M. Besutti,

valuable sources of study in the approach to present-day Protestant criticisms of Our Lady. They are not, of course, to be imitated in their shortcomings as regards Catholic doctrine, but their ability to understand their fellow Protestant objectors is well worth studying, for it helps us to formulate adequate Catholic answers to them.

The XXIst Ecumenical Council called by Pope John XXIII will undoubtedly arouse many of the Protestant Marian revivalists to re-examine their positions. It is our hope that this will mean more than an increase in the Marian revival in Protestant ways of worship. A true, complete, genuine Marian revival is only possible in the revival of the faith of their forefathers.

O.S.M., *Segnalazione di alcune pubblicazioni assunzionistiche dei Fratelli Separati*, in *Marianum*, Vol. 13, 1951, pp. 187-190; V. M. Buffon, O.S.M., *La Vergine Maria nel protestantesimo. Rassegna ai alcune recenti pubblicazioni della Chiesa Riformata*, ibid., Vol. 19, 1957, pp. 523-567; G. Philips, *L'opposition protestante à la Mariologie*, ibid., Vol. 11, 1949, pp. 469-488; P. Van Essen, O.F.M.Cap., *Protestantism and the Virginity of Mary*, ibid., Vol. 19, 1957, pp. 79-89; Boscu-Bourguet-Maury-Roux, *Le protestantisme et la Vierge Marie* (Paris, 1950); F. Cavalli, S.J., *Echi del dogma dell'Assunzione tra i protestanti*, in *La Civiltà Cattolica*, a. 102, Vol. 1, 1951, pp. 31-46; G. M. Corr, O.S.M., *La doctrine mariale et la pensée anglicane contemporaine*, in *Maria. Études sur la Sainte Vierge*, ed. H. du Manoir, S.J., Vol. 3 (Paris, 1954), pp. 713-731; N. García Garcés, C.F.M., *Puntos sobre las íes, en que se comentan algunos juicios sobre "La Vergine Maria" del protestante Miegge*, in *Ephemerides Mariologicae*, Vol. 3, 1953, pp. 103-116; L. Giussani, *Atteggiamenti protestanti ed ortodossi davanti al dogma dell'Assunta*, in *La Scuola Cattolica*, Vol. 79, 1951, pp. 106-113; K. Goldammer, *Reaktionen der öffentlischen Meinung in den USA auf das neue Mariendogma*, in *Oekumenische Einheit*, Vol. 2 (3), 1951, pp. 174-193; J. Gonsette, S.J., *L'attitude des anglicans devant la doctrine mariale*, in *Journées Sacerdotales Mariales*, 1951 (Dinant, 1952), pp. 149-157; J. Granero, S.J., *El nuevo dogma frente al irenismo*, in *Razón y Fe*, Vol. 144, 1951, pp. 100-110; B. Grimley, *Protestantism and Our Lady*, in *Our Blessed Lady. Cambridge Summer School Lectures for 1933* (London, 1934), pp. 251-260; S. Pauleser, O.F.M., *Maria und die Reformation* (Würzburg, 1951); H. D. Preuss, *Maria bei Luther* (Gütersloh, 1954); B. D. Dupuy, O.P., *La Mariologie de Calvin*, in *Istina*, Vol. 5, 1958, pp. 479-490; K. Algermissen, *Mariologie und Marienverehrung der Reformatoren*, in *Theologie und Glaube*, Vol. 49, 1959, pp. 1-24; S. Cwiertniak, S.M., *La Vierge Marie dans la tradition anglicane* (Paris, 1958).

www.ingramcontent.com/pod-product-compliance
Lightning Source LLC
Chambersburg PA
CBHW020754230426

43673CB00022B/440/J